Fifth Edition

W9-BSO-815

Reading and Writing in Elementary Classrooms

Research Based K–4 Instruction

Patricia M. Cunningham
Wake Forest University

Sharon Arthur Moore
Peoria Unified School District, Arizona

James W. Cunningham
University of North Carolina, Chapel Hill

David W. Moore
Arizona State University West

PEARSON

Boston   New York   San Francisco
Mexico City   Montreal   Toronto   London   Madrid   Munich   Paris
Hong Kong   Singapore   Tokyo   Cape Town   Sydney

Senior Editor: Aurora Martínez Ramos
Editorial Assistant: Katie Freddoso
Senior Marketing Manager: Elizabeth Fogarty
Editorial-Production Services: Omegatype Typography, Inc.
Manufacturing Buyer: Andrew Turso
Composition and Prepress Buyer: Linda Cox
Cover Administrator: Kristina Mose-Libon
Interior Design: Denise Hoffman
Electronic Composition: Omegatype Typography, Inc.

For related titles and support materials, visit our online catalog at www.ablongman.com.

Between the time website information is gathered and then published, it is not unusual for some sites to have closed. Also, the transcription of URLs can result in typographical errors. The publisher would appreciate notification where these errors occur so that they may be corrected in subsequent editions.

Library of Congress Cataloging-in-Publication Data

Reading and writing in elementary classrooms : research based K-4 instruction / Patricia
    M. Cunningham . . . [et al.].—5th ed.
        p.   cm.
    Includes bibliographical references and index.
    ISBN 0-205-38640-7 (alk. paper)
    1. Language arts (Primary)   2. Reading (Primary)   3. English language—Composition and
exercises—Study and teaching (Primary)   I. Cunningham, Patricia Marr.

LB1528.R43 2004
372.4—dc21

                                                                                                   2003044421

Printed in the United States of America

10   9   8   7   09

Credits: Excerpt on pages 32 and 35 reprinted with the permission of Simon & Schuster Books for Young Readers, an imprint of Simon & Schuster Children's Publishing Division, from *Hattie and the Fox* by Mem Fox. Text copyright © 1986 Mem Fox. Poem on page 155 from *The Collected Poems of Langston Hughes* by Langston Hughes, copyright © 1994 by the Estate of Langston Hughes. Used by permission of Alfred A. Knopf, a division of Random House, Inc.

* *

For all the determined, hardworking, caring, smart, real teachers
after whom we fashioned the fictional
Helen Launch, Rita Wright, Norma Nouveau, Vera Wise, and Yetta Maverick
and for supportive, engaged, underappreciated real administrators and supervisors
after whom we fashioned the fictional
Tip Topps and Sue Port

6 *Reading and Responding to Literature for Children*   **151**

7 *Comprehension*   *184*

10 *Planning and Organizing*   289

Part Two

• •

. . . In Elementary Classrooms   305

In Part Two we transport our readers to a fictional school, Merritt Elementary School, where we follow an imaginary class of children from kindergarten to fourth grade. The various teachers use a variety of approaches to make literacy a reality for all their students.

$\mathcal{T}$eaching children to read and write at high levels of literacy is a complex, long-term commitment that our society and our schools must make if we are going to remain competitive in the twenty-first century. In this fifth edition of *Reading and Writing in Elementary Classrooms*, we have taken into consideration the latest research and best thinking from literacy and language studies, curriculum and instructional practices, and psychology. Culling the best of what we have traditionally done and pulling together the best current practices, we present a balanced, long-term view of literacy development and approaches.

Shared Features of the Fourth and Fifth Editions

The fifth edition of *Reading and Writing in Elementary Classrooms* retains those features of the previous editions that our students and colleagues found especially noteworthy. These include:

- *Focus on Thinking Processes.* Chapter 1 describes eight thinking processes that are critical to reading and writing. These thinking processes—*connect, organize, predict, image, monitor, generalize, evaluate,* and *apply*—underlie the activities and strategies presented in later chapters and help to provide a coherent framework for the development of high-level literacy.

- *Focus on Reading and Writing as Language.* One of the key ideas in Chapter 1 is that *language is the foundation of reading and writing*. Reading and writing build on the oral language foundation the child brings to school and support each other as well as the overall linguistic ability of the child. Throughout the book we suggest activities and strategies that promote the total development of all the language abilities of children.

- *Focus on Affective Domain.* Children are both thinking and feeling people. Their likes and dislikes, attitudes, and interests must be developed and given attention. Applications for the key idea *that feeling is the energizer of reading and writing* established in Chapter 1 are found in all the other chapters in the book.

- *Focus on Reading and Writing across the Curriculum.* Because we believe that reading and writing are best developed across the entire school day and throughout the curriculum, each chapter contains a major section on using reading and writing strategies for teaching in all subject areas.

- *Focus on Balanced Literacy Instruction.* The field of reading appears to be continually under siege by various factions arguing for one approach over another. The fact that children learn in different ways and that acquiring high levels of literacy is a complex long-term process mitigates against any single, narrow approach. This edition, like the earlier editions, promotes a balanced diet of authentic reading and writing activities along with instruction in appropriate strategies as indicated by careful observation of the learners. The best literacy instruction blends features from a variety of approaches to reading and writing.

- *Accommodations and Adaptations for Inclusion and Children Acquiring English.* All the chapters in Part I contain accommodations and adaptations that have been found to be successful for helping all children acquire high levels of literacy.
- *Technology Tips.* Technology is playing an increasingly important role in most elementary classrooms. Many teachers are trying to determine the best uses for the technology they have. The Technology Tips feature presents ways in which successful teachers use technology in their literacy programs and describes some of the newest and most versatile software.
- *Narrative Chapters.* Teachers often bemoan the fact that children have many more skills and strategies than they actually use. The same can be said of teachers. To use knowledge, one must know not only what to do but when and why, for how long, with which children, and in connection with what! The narrative chapters in Part II were created to give teachers concrete examples of how the various ideas and activities presented in Part I might be implemented in different classrooms at different grade levels with a variety of children by teachers with a range of teaching styles.

In Part II we transport our readers to a fictional school, Merritt Elementary School, where we follow an imaginary class of children from kindergarten to fourth grade. With help and support from the principal, Mr. Topps, and the central office facilitator, Sue Port, the various teachers use a variety of approaches to make literacy a reality for all their children. The children emerge into literacy under the enthusiastic tutelage of their kindergarten teacher, Miss Launch. Mrs. Wright provides a balanced approach in her first-grade classroom. She emphasizes shared and guided reading, words, writing, and self-selected reading, and demonstrates how the instruction changes as the children's literacy develops. Miss Nouveau, a first-year teacher, takes the class through second grade. She gets off to a somewhat rocky start, but with help from Mr. Topps, Sue Port, and other teachers, she makes great strides by the end of the year. Mrs. Wise, the third-grade teacher, has acquired huge stores of knowledge and books through all her years of teaching, and she carries out an integrated language arts program with literature as the centerpiece. The fourth-grade teacher, Ms. Maverick, also integrates, but her focus is on integrating across the curriculum. The teachers in this edition are familiar to users of the earlier editions, but they too have been updated and have some new "tricks up their sleeves."

- *Organizing Features.* To increase the comprehensibility of our text, we have included Looking Ahead and Looking Back sections, which preview and then summarize each chapter's major concepts. We have also identified four to six key ideas for each chapter and organized the information under these key ideas. The narrative chapters all have locators in the margin that connect the instruction in the narratives with the key ideas in the first eight chapters.

- ***Theory and Research behind Strategies.*** Each instructional chapter ends with a section that succinctly summarizes the major research and theoretical base for the ideas and strategies presented in the chapter.

- ***Additional Readings.*** Each chapter ends with an expanded and updated annotated bibliography of additional readings.

- ***Application Activities.*** Believing that we learn best when we evaluate and apply what we are learning, we have included activities in each chapter that promote application. Many of these activities can be incorporated easily into a field experience, which is often part of the reading methods course. Listen, Look, and Learn applications contain suggestions for visiting classrooms, viewing videotapes of classrooms, and interviewing teachers and students to check out the ideas presented and learn more about actual classroom practice. Try It Out applications describe lessons and activities students might use and often suggest trying out some of these with a child or small group of children. Do It Together applications suggest cooperative activities in which readers pool their knowledge and experiences with particular concepts and compare their collective experiences with what they are learning in the text. Add to Your Resource File applications suggest books and other resources students might accumulate and add to their "bag of tricks." Add to Your Journal applications end each chapter and suggest ways in which the reader might use writing to reflect on the ideas in the chapter.

New to the Fifth Edition

Content revisions new to this edition include:

- ***A New Chapter on Assessment.*** Assessment is a major focus in all elementary schools today. This chapter contains practical suggestions, checklists, and portfolio ideas teachers can use to assess, monitor, and document growth in reading and writing.

- ***A New Chapter on Fluency.*** Fluency is the ability to read text accurately at a good pace with good expression. Fluency is a bridge between word identification and comprehension. All good readers must develop fluency. This chapter describes classroom-tested strategies for developing fluent readers and writers.

- ***Major Revisions of the Original Chapters.*** All chapters have been updated to reflect the latest research and best practice. The comprehension chapter has been completely rewritten and reflects the current understandings about the importance of strategy instruction and ways to organize for guided-reading lessons.

Acknowledgments

We gratefully acknowledge the following reviewers of this edition for their helpful comments: June Brown, Southwest Missouri State University; Deanne Camp, Southwest Missouri State University; Lee T. Peterson, Ottawa University; and James Rooks, Calvin College.

Part **One**

Reading and Writing . . .

About Reading and Writing

L o o k i n g   A h e a d

The next nine chapters of Reading and Writing in Elementary Classrooms *will describe the major components of effective reading and writing instruction, the theoretical framework for each, and specific teaching activities that you can use to foster the development of high-level literacy for all children. Each chapter has key ideas that summarize the most important information in that chapter. The key ideas in this chapter relate to the nature of reading and writing and to the individual nature of the children we are teaching. The key ideas in this chapter are the basis for the key ideas in all the other chapters.*

As you read this book, you will find a variety of effective ways to teach children to read and write. But you already have a lifetime of experiences with reading and writing yourself. To begin, then, we suggest that you recall what you have personally experienced over the years so that you can relate, or connect, your own experiences with learning to read and write to teaching others to read and write.

*H*ere is an anecdote of one child's reading and writing history.

A tiny baby, David, sits on his grandmother's lap. He can't yet talk, but Grandma holds up objects and makes sounds. "Hey diddle diddle, the cat and the fiddle," she says with a smile. She points to blobs of black and color on a page. "See the funny cat?" she asks. "See the fiddle?" The baby doesn't know what's going on, but he feels good sitting with Grandma, who rocks him and makes nice sounds. A year or so later, David looks forward each evening to being put to bed by Daddy, who stays with him and shows him pictures in books. Frequently, Daddy reads the same book over and over, and

David begins to recognize the rhythms and patterns of the words—even, perhaps, the way they look on the page.

One day David, now three, surprises his parents by pointing to an ad in the evening paper and shouting, "Pizza Hut!" Mommy and Daddy are amazed, but Daddy points out that, after all, it is David's favorite restaurant, and he sees the Pizza Hut sign an average of once every ten days. When he's four or five, David enjoys going with Mommy to the grocery store. He writes his own "list," a page of scribbles, and delights Mommy by telling her what each "word" means—fruit, cookies, cereal—and crossing each one off as Mommy picks it off the shelf. At about the same age, David begins to write "real" words—*David, Mommy, Daddy, love*—when a grown-up spells them out for him. He pretends to read favorite books to his stuffed bear and insists indignantly that he is not pretending at all.

When David starts kindergarten, he learns about libraries; he even has his own library card. Mommy takes him to storytime at the public library on Saturdays, and he can now read signs along the road as they drive: *Stop, Exit, No Parking.* Often he listens to tapes of stories and enjoys the activity because he can rewind and listen to his favorite parts again and again. But he also likes to have Mommy and Daddy read to him because he can ask questions. In kindergarten, the children make "chart stories"—a series of sentences that describe a field trip or special event. In first grade, David is put into the "foxes" reading group; his group, to his surprise, finishes four books before the "bunnies" group is even through with their second. He spends time at the reading center, picking out books that interest him or that his friends recommend and listening to tapes. He enjoys that much more than the worksheets. Sometimes he forgets what a picture is supposed to be and puts *p* for *puppy* next to a picture that is supposed to be a *dog.* He can write words and sometimes sentences of his own, but his teacher is concerned about his occasional inability to do his phonics worksheets correctly.

David does a lot of acting and art activities with his reading in the third grade. "Close your eyes," his teacher says. "Can you hear the waves? Can you smell the salt air?" His third-grade teacher has each child keep a journal and has her students write in it every day. Fourth grade, however, is a disaster. The teacher has everyone take turns reading, and David frequently stops paying attention once he has figured out when his turn will come. In science and social studies, David and his classmates do nothing but read the book and answer the questions at the end of each chapter. He can't wait to move on. Fortunately, fifth grade is better. When the children read, the teacher asks them to look at headings and illustrations first and to predict what might happen in the story. The teacher is supportive even when the predictions are wrong: "Your way might have made a better story!" he says. What David dislikes most in fifth grade is The Kit. Each student is assigned a set of colored cards with a paragraph to be read and questions to be answered on each card. The topics are often boring, and the questions are similar from one color to the next; sometimes David answers the questions without doing the reading.

In the eighth grade, David's teacher presents Preview, Question, Read, Recite, Review (PQ3R). To David, it seems only common sense, but the process seems to remind some of the other students of what they should be doing when they read, and many are especially helped by the reminder to review what they've read. In ninth-grade science, David learns about outlining and "webbing"—ways to organize information. His tenth-grade English teacher actually reads aloud to the class—a technique that brings snickers from the class the first few times but that students eventually look forward to. The books the teacher chooses are exciting and intriguing, and some students who have never liked reading are excited about it for the first time.

Did the preceding story bring back some memories of your own years of learning to read and write? Do you remember having some of the same experiences? Did you respond to them as David did, or were your responses different? We shared this imaginary reading and writing history with you for two reasons: First, it may help you to recall and evaluate your own experiences in learning to read and write, to recognize how many varied approaches are used in learning to read and write, and to connect what you are about to read with your own experiences. Second, we wanted to set the stage for the key ideas in this chapter:

1. Thinking is the essence of reading and writing.
2. Feeling is the energizer of reading and writing.
3. Language is the foundation of reading and writing.
4. The children we teach have individual, cultural, and language differences.
5. Reading and writing are learned in a variety of ways.
6. Children need a balanced literacy program.

Thinking Is the Essence of Reading and Writing

Imagine that you come upon someone who is sitting, pen in hand or fingertips poised over the keyboard, and staring at the blank page or the blank screen and you ask, "What are you doing?" The person will often respond, "I'm thinking!" Continue to observe and you will see the person eventually move into the writing phase, but the writing is not nonstop. There are constant pauses, and if you are rude enough to interrupt during one of these pauses and ask, "What are you doing?" the writer will again probably respond, "I'm thinking!!!"

Eventually, the writer finishes the writing or, more accurately, finishes the first draft of the writing. The writer may put the writing away for a while or may ask someone, "Will you take a look at this and tell me what you think?" Later the writer will return to the writing to revise and edit it. Words will be changed, paragraphs added, moved, or deleted. Again, the writer will pause from time to time during this after-writing phase, and if you ask what the writer is doing, you will get the familiar response, "I'M THINKING!"

We offer this common scenario as proof that writing is at its essence thinking and that even the most naive writer knows this basic truth. Because writing is thinking and because learning requires thinking, students who write as they are learning think more and thus learn more.

When asked what *reading* is, many people would reply, "It's saying words written down." According to that definition, you would be reading if you said the words in the following sentence:

Serny wugs dree biffles.

Although most good readers can say these made-up words, doing so is not really reading because reading implies not only the ability to say the words but also the ability to understand what the words taken together mean. Either saying the words aloud or thinking their pronunciations in your mind is the word identification part of reading. Understanding the meaning the words together convey is the comprehension part. You could not comprehend the meaning of the sentence above because the made-up words had no meaning. Word identification is necessary for comprehension to occur, but clearly word identification does not guarantee comprehension. How do you comprehend the meanings of the many and varied sentences in which you identify the words every day? Comprehension—figuring out the meaning of what you read—is accomplished in your brain as your brain processes the meanings of the words and language structures. In simplest terms, your brain thinks about what you read. But what is *thinking*, and how does it occur? What do you mean when you say, "I'm thinking"?

For more than a century, psychologists have tried to determine the exact nature of thinking, and there are many lists of the possible components of thinking. But because thinking is a complex process, it is difficult to describe. Nevertheless, because thinking is how your brain allows you to comprehend what you are reading and compose what you are writing, it is important for people who teach reading and writing to have some understanding of what some of those components might be. Although reading theorists and writing theorists disagree about which thinking processes are used in reading comprehension and writing, eight processes seem to play a large part in both. These processes are not clearly distinguished from one another, and reading and writing often involve several of them. The eight thinking processes are as follows:

1. *Connect.* Imagine that you are planning a trip to Hawaii and buy a Hawaii travel guide to help you plan your trip. As soon as you begin to read the book, you will connect some of the things you read to things you already know about Hawaii, you will connect some of the other things to questions you have had about Hawaii, and you will probably connect some of the other things to what you thought you knew but which, if the book is right, are mistaken ideas. Perhaps our reading and writing history that began this chapter helped you to connect some of our experiences to your

own literacy memories, either to identify with them or to disagree that you had similar experiences.

2. *Organize.* Organizing the information you gain from reading is a way of making connections. As you are reading about Hawaii, you will read about its history, beaches, climate, hotels, and so on. You will indeed connect this information to what you already knew before reading. But if we could look inside your brain when you finished, the new and old information would probably not look like a list. What we would probably see might look more like an outline with major headings and information under each. We might also see a part that looks like a time line with a listing of dates and important events in Hawaiian history. One part might look like a chart with the various beaches listed across the top and different features listed under each one. Organizing information helps us to remember and use what we've read and to sequence what we write.

3. *Image.* As you are reading about Hawaii, you will probably be imagining what it would be like to be there. You might close your eyes and picture the beaches. You might feel the heat of the tropical sun on your back. You might hear the waves crashing when the surf is up. You might smell the pig roasting for the luau, and your mouth might water as you think about eating it. As we read, we use our senses to imagine what is happening. Based on our past experiences, we create sights, sounds, smells, tastes, and feelings that make the book come alive. We call this thinking process of using some or all of our senses to relate to what we are reading *imaging.*

4. *Predict.* Another way we use our brain to think as we are reading is to predict. A *prediction* is an educated guess about what is coming next. As you are reading about the Japanese bombing of Pearl Harbor, you realize that this probably bodes ill for the many people of Japanese descent living on the islands. Your further reading confirms this prediction that the Japanese Hawaiians are in for a hard time. Sometimes your predictions are not confirmed. As you are reading about how to get to Kauai, you discover that you can fly directly to the small island without changing planes in Honolulu. Your surprise indicates that you had made a prediction. Predictions are important to reading comprehension because they are one of our brain's ways of actively involving us with our reading. In writing, we predict how a story or event could end or how our readers may react to what we are saying. Any inference we make during reading or writing is a prediction of what we will find out when more information is available to us.

5. *Self-monitor.* You will know that your brain is constantly self-monitoring the incoming information when you recall those times in your reading when you have stopped and thought, "That can't be right!" Imagine that you were reading about hotels in Hawaii and saw that one that sounded just right charged $1,000 for a double room. "That can't be right!" you would think. "It must be a misprint of an extra zero." You would check further and might conclude that (1) it was indeed a misprint, (2) the $1,000 was a weekly rate, or (3) you have very expensive taste in hotels! Self-monitoring is our brain's way of double-checking information. When we read and write, we self-monitor constantly. We are usually aware of the self-monitoring only when we realize that something has gone wrong.

6. *Generalize.* Generalizing is another thinking process that is closely linked to reading and writing. It is the process by which the brain takes several small pieces of information and from these small pieces comes to some larger conclusion. As you study the charts giving the average rainfall and average high and low temperatures for each month, you might realize that there is not much variation. It's a little warmer in the summer months and a little cooler in the winter months, but the climate is pretty moderate and they have lots of sunny days year-round. Drawing conclusions and forming generalizations based on facts are of critical importance because these "big ideas" are more easily remembered than the facts on which they were based. Months after reading about Hawaii, you probably cannot remember the average rainfall and temperatures for each month, but you probably do remember your generalization that the weather is pretty moderate with lots of sunny days year-round.

7. *Apply.* To apply something is to use it. When you call your travel agent and make your Hawaii trip plans, you are probably basing some of your decisions about when to go, which islands to go to, and where to stay on what you read in the travel guide. When you apply knowledge to a new situation, you are demonstrating a practical use for what you know.

8. *Evaluate.* To evaluate is to make judgments about things. The root word of *evaluate* is *value.* When you evaluate, you compare something to a criterion and see how it measures up. You evaluate when you decide that the treatment of the Japanese Hawaiians was "not right." You evaluate when you decide you probably won't like poi, a native Hawaiian dish. Applying often includes evaluation. You probably decided which islands to go to based on your judgments about which islands had more things you would like. You evaluated and then applied that knowledge to planning your trip. Had you been reading the Hawaii travel book with no prospects of ever going to Hawaii, you still would have made evaluations, but you would, unfortunately, not have used these judgments to plan your trip.

Thinking is something we do all the time. We daydream, plan, worry, scheme, and ponder. As we think, we use a variety of thinking processes. To comprehend what we read, we think as we are reading. To communicate ideas to a real or hypothetical audience, we think as we are writing. The eight processes we have described here are some of the components of thinking that seem to be the most useful while reading or writing. To help you think about "thinking," we have described each one separately, but in reality several processes are almost always going on simultaneously. In the remaining chapters of this book, you will find many activities designed to help students become better readers and writers. Because reading and writing are so intimately bound up with thinking, you will find that many of these activities help students become better at using the eight thinking processes as they read and write.

When reading and writing, we use some or all of the eight thinking processes.

Feeling Is the Energizer of Reading and Writing

People are both thinking and feeling creatures. When we talk about thinking, we are referring to the cognitive part of us. The feeling part of us is referred to as the affective domain. We have feelings or emotional responses to all of the important parts of our lives. We like certain foods and hate others; we fear certain social situations and eagerly anticipate others. Our feelings are important because, to a large extent, they determine how we will respond in various situations.

Thinking is the essence of what we do when we read or write, but feeling determines how much and how often we choose to read or write, and whether we will persist in reading or writing when we have difficulty. When teachers talk about students' motivation or interest in reading, they are not talking about whether the students can identify words or comprehend, but how the students feel about reading and learning to read better. Likewise, when teachers comment on a student's motivation or interest in writing, they are not talking about whether the student can spell well or express ideas clearly, but how that student feels about writing and learning to write better. In a sense, reading and writing are thinking, but it is feeling that energizes the thinking.

In the past decade or so, literacy theory and research has caught up with teachers' long-standing view that children must be motivated to learn to read and write well. Much of this work has been concerned with what is called "literacy engagement." *Engagement* is probably the most common term used today to talk about the relationship between motivation and the rest of what constitutes literacy and literacy learning. Engaged readers and writers read and write in a motivated way—that is, they employ whatever literacy skills and strategies they have with effort, persistence, and expectation of success. Other students may have equal or even superior skills and strategies, yet they do not engage in reading and writing simply because they do not feel like it. What kinds of feelings energize students' reading and writing? Children need to have at least three main feelings to be successful literacy learners.

Children Must Feel Capable of Learning to Read and Write Better

One of the most important aspects of motivation in literacy-learning is self-efficacy. *"Self-efficacy* refers to beliefs a person has about his or her capabilities to learn or perform behaviors at designated levels" (Schunk & Zimmerman, 1997, p. 34). The research on self-efficacy and learning suggests that students who have doubts about their ability to learn something are less likely to try to learn it in the first place, and more likely—when they do try—to give up when they encounter difficulty. Students who have confidence in their own ability to learn something put forth more effort to learn it and tend to persist even in the face of challenges.

The feeling of being capable of learning is not an all-or-nothing attitude. All of us have self-confidence about learning in some areas yet lack it in others. A person, for example, may have high self-efficacy when learning to play a new musical instrument but lack confidence that he or she can learn to play a new sport. Persons with self-efficacy in learning mathematics do not always have self-efficacy in learning literacy. It is self-efficacy in literacy that literacy learning requires.

Student self-confidence to learn something is not impervious to change. A period of time without success or being repeatedly told that one lacks ability in an area can significantly reduce one's self-efficacy to learn. A string of successes with challenging but not defeating tasks combined with being repeatedly told that one is capable of learning something can substantially increase one's self-confidence as a learner.

The research on literacy engagement supports the value of self-efficacy for students' learning to read and write better (Schunk & Zimmerman, 1997). Many children come to school already knowing a lot about literacy and having confidence that they can and will learn to read and write well. Unfortunately, not all children's early interactions with reading and writing are so positive. Many children are not read to very much or given opportunities and encouragement to write before coming to school. These children start out behind. They don't really understand what reading or writing are. They lack meanings for many words commonly used in picture books. They can't read or write their own name and may not even realize that their name can be written. Kindergarten and first-grade teachers must immerse these children in a variety of positive early literacy activities so that they can acquire those concepts, including self-confidence, that many others gain before coming to school.

Throughout the rest of this book, you will encounter many instances in which instruction is provided in a certain way and situated in a certain social context in order to protect or enhance the self-confidence of children that they are capable of learning to read and write better.

Children Must Feel That Their Strategies Determine Their Success

An important aspect of students' self-confidence to learn literacy is their beliefs about why they have difficulty when they do. If they feel that they are having trouble because they aren't good at learning literacy, their difficulty will undermine their self-confidence. However,

> Negative self-evaluations will not diminish self-efficacy and motivation if students believe they are capable of succeeding but that their present approach is ineffective. (Schunk & Zimmerman, 1997, p. 40)

Students must learn to self-monitor their success when reading or writing and must learn that it is not their ability but "their present approach" that is the cause of their success or failure.

Young children especially are dependent on their teachers and fellow students to acquire the insight that our strategies are different from ourselves. Only by watching teachers and peers actively applying strategies, self-monitoring success, and—if necessary—changing strategies do young children learn that success does not result from some fixed ability one is stuck with, but from knowledgeable and flexible efforts.

In the remaining chapters of this book, you will find an emphasis on strategy instruction through modeling (minilessons and collaborative learning) and on helping students learn to self-monitor as they apply the strategies they are learning. These approaches are designed to teach effective reading and writing strategies, but they are also designed to provide students with the understanding that gets and keeps them motivated to learn literacy.

Children Must Feel Pleasure during Reading and Writing

The imaginary child in the scene that opened this chapter had mostly positive feeling about reading and writing. Even before David knew what the words meant, he liked the feeling of being rocked and read to. Later, he enjoyed being read to and writing messages on his chalkboard. When he went to school, he had success and positive feedback from his teachers, family, and peers. He continued to have good feelings about literacy and about himself as a reader and writer. With the exception of some seatwork activities—workbooks and The Kit—David liked most literacy-related experiences.

As important as self-confidence to learn is, we may have no desire to learn some of the things we have confidence we can learn. Children who dislike reading and writing may avoid them or give only half-hearted attention to learning them even though they have self-confidence to learn them. These are students who have not yet experienced reading and writing as pleasurable activities.

Like learning to play a musical instrument well, learning literacy requires both good lessons and much intense practice. At first, we expect to have to insist that students pay attention to our lessons and that they practice for so long without interruption or distraction. Before long, however, if students still only pay attention during lessons or practice when we insist or reward them for doing so, we know their chances of ever being good readers and writers are low. After a while, reading and writing must become activities that children choose to do because they like doing them. Only then will they stay focused enough on our lessons and engage in enough practice to become truly literate.

Did You Know That?

The National Assessment of Educational Progress in 1986 surveyed a sample of America's third-graders about their pleasure reading. Fourteen percent said they never read for fun on their own time. An additional 11 percent said they read for fun less often than once per week. Less than half reported that most days they read something for fun on their own (Applebee, Langer, & Mullis, 1988). Sadly, this number may be inflated, since some children no doubt reported more pleasurable reading than they actually had done because they thought that is what the researchers wanted to hear.

Language Is the Foundation of Reading and Writing

We would like to take an imaginary trip now. We will go to the Class 3 planet of Norite.

> The planet of Norite is a tropical paradise of white sandy beaches and constant sun. The people who live there are intelligent people who have a variety of occupations. People work in restaurants, hotels, schools, and factories. Here, as in all places, each person is different from the others. Some are short and others are tall; some are fat and others are skinny; some are smart and others are not so smart. They even have television and telephones. The

people of Norite have a rich and wonderful language, with even nineteen words for types of waves.

Imagine that you somehow get stranded on this planet. The people are gracious and treat you like an honored guest, and you are given everything you need to survive. However, you don't speak their language and they don't speak English; you communicate with gestures and motions and by pointing to objects. Quickly, you begin to learn some basic words in their language, and after several weeks there, you want to write down some notes about this strange planet. You look around for pens and paper but don't see any. You approach your host and make writing gestures to show you want writing implements, but your host shows no understanding at all. You look around your hotel and then walk through the shops, and as you do this, you suddenly realize that you have not seen a single written thing or anything to write with. "It can't be!" is your first response, but even as you think this, you realize that you have become stranded on a planet with no written language.

You walk to the local school and talk to the principal—the smartest person in the area. You make writing gestures, and when you see by the blank expression on her face that even she has no conception of reading and writing, you grab her hand and take her to the beach. You say "sand" and use a stick to write the English word *sand* in the sand. She must think you want to know her word for sand because she picks some up and says something that sounds like "jid." Unsure about how to spell it but desperately wanting to communicate what writing is, you use your stick to write *jid* in the sand. You say her name, "Raheeta," and write it, too, and then say your name and write it. You repeat these three words several times and trace the word written in the sand each time. Just when you think you will not be able to make her understand, her eyes get wide and she points to the word *Raheeta* and to herself and asks, "Raheeta?" "Yes, yes!" you shout. The two of you stay on the beach scratching words in the sand until it is too dark to see.

Working with Raheeta, you write down the language of the planet. It is easy to write the words that stand for concrete things such as sand, water, swim, and Raheeta. It is harder to write the words used to connect these concrete words. These words are never said by themselves, and even Raheeta does not know them as separate words. When she says "Jidabhuss" as she touches the sand, you know that *jid* means *sand* and *huss* means *hot,* and you figure out that the sound "ab" between them must be a linking word like *is.* These abstract connecting words are the hardest for you to hear and for Raheeta to learn to read and write.

As you teach Raheeta literacy for her spoken language, you realize how many things all literate persons take for granted that must be taught to someone who is ignorant of reading and writing. When Raheeta begins writing words, she just puts the words where they fit rather than going from left to right. She has to learn that you leave a space after words and what punctuation marks like periods, commas, and question marks signal. Written language has all of these conventions or arbitrary rules that you don't need to know to carry on a conversation but that are essential to written language. She also doesn't understand the meanings of words we commonly use to talk about reading and writing. Terms such as *letter, word,* and *sentence* all have to be explained and are quite confusing to her in the beginning.

After many months of constant writing in the sand, however, Raheeta knows the written words for most of the common spoken words in her language. By then, everyone on Norite has learned about this strange new way to communicate, and Raheeta and you take on the job of making the whole planet—young and old alike—literate. You are very old by the time you are rescued by a spaceship from earth, but you have accomplished something wonderful. You have helped people with a rich spoken language learn to read and write that language.

We can learn something from this imaginary adventure on Norite that we all take for granted. While this story is science fantasy, there have always been and still are peoples on earth whose spoken language has no written form. Considering Norite shows us that language is the foundation of reading and writing. Language is primarily oral, social, and cultural. People first learn to talk and to listen in their social and cultural settings and only later learn that what they say can be written down and read back. Because reading and writing are integrally bound to listening and speaking abilities, reading instruction must build on students' oral language and the cultural background in which it developed and is commonly used. Simultaneously, we must provide social situations that increase children's facility with oral language so that we have more to build on. Because they are closely related language modes, reading and writing abilities develop together for most children. Children who write become better readers, and children who read become better writers.

Throughout this book, you will find suggestions for involving children in discussion, dramatic, and other oral language activities that increase the number of words in their speaking vocabularies and the ways in which they can combine these words to express themselves clearly and cleverly. These activities are invariably social, because oral language facility is socially constructed. You will also find listening comprehension strategies that increase children's ability to listen to a story or piece of informational text that is read to them, as well as increase their ability to understand and respond in speaking or writing to what they have listened to. You will find writing activities that help children learn to express their ideas using written language. As children write their own ideas, they become more aware of how authors communicate ideas, and they use this knowledge to understand better what they read. You will find numerous activities that help children link the phonology of their oral language to the letters they read and write. Language is the foundation of reading and writing. Children become better readers and writers when teachers develop all of the language arts—speaking, listening, reading, and writing—and use each one to support the others.

In thinking about the next key idea, it is important for you to keep in mind the critical dependence of reading and writing on oral language, because many children come to school speaking a language other than English. These children must learn to speak and listen in the language they are also learning to read and write.

The Children We Teach Have Individual, Cultural, and Language Differences

Think about your own family, or a family you know well, with two or more children. Have you noticed and heard others remark on "how different the children are"? One child must have a clearly defined routine and set of rules while the other child does better if allowed more flexibility and self-determination. One child is neat; the other a slob. (Let's hope they don't have to share the same bedroom!) One child has a restless, creative, problem-solving mind and personality. The other child is as smart (perhaps smarter on standardized tests) but less imaginative.

Anyone who has ever observed how children from the same family differ knows that all children do not learn/respond/think in the same manner. Successful parents recognize the differences in their children and adjust their rules, routines, interactions, and so forth to maximize the possibilities for each of their different children.

Not only do children bring to school huge differences in the amount and kind of reading/writing experiences they have had, but they also come with their own personalities. Different personalities seem to prefer or require different kinds of literacy instruction. Some children need and like the structure of a reading series. They know exactly what they are going to read and what to do after they read. Skills are introduced and reviewed in a predictable, logical order. Some children even take pleasure in completing each story and noting the visible signs that they are progressing.

This same order and predictability that allow some children to thrive in reading series approaches can be a total turnoff to children with other personalities. "Reading is always the same," they say. "You talk about what you are going to read, learn some new words, read the story, and do two pages in your workbook! Boring!" These adventuresome types like variety—in what they read, when they read it, and what they do before and after reading. Put these children in a literature approach based on self-selection and a variety of ways of sharing, and they are more apt to become readers.

To some children, their own ideas and imaginations are much more interesting than anything some faraway author might have written. These children love to "express themselves." They love to talk and tell stories and be the center of attention. These expressive children also love to write, and as they write, they use and learn words that they then read. The writing personalities will read—but for them reading is a means, not an end. Reading is one of their sources for ideas about which they can write.

Likewise, some children are better at learning and using letter–sound relationships. They have an ear for sounds—much like the ear of some who become musicians. Other children labor over the letters and sounds and aren't able to blend the sounds they know into words they know.

In addition to these individual differences among children, there are some important cultural and linguistic differences we must think about. Our nation has always had a diverse population coming from many different countries and bringing a variety of languages and customs. Demographic data suggest that we are becoming an increasingly multicultural society. In 2000, more than 40 percent of the school-age population of New York state belonged to ethnic minority groups. In California, the minority has become the majority, with over 50 percent of the school-age population identifying themselves as nonwhite or Hispanic. In addition to cultural differences, many school-age children speak a language other than English. Estimates are that nationwide more than 10 million schoolchildren live in homes where English is not spoken. Many teachers currently teach in classrooms in which more than half of their students are non-native English-speakers, and most teachers will teach in classrooms in which at least one student speaks a language other than English at home. The classrooms in which we help children become literate will increasingly contain larger numbers of children whose cultural and linguistic heritage is quite different from the heritage of the teacher.

Describing all the cultural and linguistic differences that exist among children is impossible and beyond the scope of this book, but since we believe that learning is best accomplished through real, concrete experiences, here are a few examples. Children from some ethnic groups live in large, cooperative family groups in which hugs and other displays of affection, social interaction, and sharing are an integral part of their daily lives. Children take responsibility for each other, and cooperation is highly valued. Other children are used to more formal interactions and are taught "not to speak unless spoken to" and always to wait for and follow adult directions. These children would expect some social distance to be kept between children and adults—particularly adult authority figures such as teachers. Some Native American children live in a culture in which cooperation rather than competition is valued and often don't understand why they can't help each other on a test. Many Native American children are taught in their homes to be keen observers, and a greater priority is placed on doing than on talking. A variety of cultural differences relate to eye contact and the amount of physical distance normally kept between two people who are conversing with one another.

Many children who have recently immigrated from Russia cannot speak, read, or write English but can speak, read, and write two other languages—Russian and Hebrew. Hmong children from the mountains of Laos often come speaking a little English but are unable to read or write in any language. Some Korean children have difficulty learning to use articles and verbs in speaking and writing English because the Korean language contains no articles, and verbs are not inflected for tense or number.

These few examples of cultural and linguistic differences are not intended to be inclusive and certainly aren't meant to stereotype any group. They are included only to try to make real for you the idea that children bring with them expectations, behavior patterns, and varying knowledge based on what they have experienced in their homes and communities. In order to achieve the goal of high levels of literacy for all the diverse children we teach, teachers must know that differences exist and that these differences affect how children learn. The most successful teachers are keen observers. When they have a child in their classroom who comes from a cultural or linguistic environment different from theirs, they watch and think about the child's reaction to the classroom routines and seek information about parents, other members of that cultural/linguistic group, and other sources and make whatever accommodations they can in the classroom routine.

Reading and Writing Are Learned in a Variety of Ways

Children learn a great many things about reading and writing before coming to school. The base for reading and writing is being socially constructed when they are too young even to know what reading and writing are and what books are for. When children are read to, they begin to get a sense of how written language sounds. They learn many concepts from someone reading and talking about the pictures in the books. They also come to realize that it is the "funny little black marks" that people are looking at as they read. Young children who are read to regularly go through a "pretend reading" stage. Although they don't yet recognize most of the words in the book, they can pretend to read a favorite book because they have heard it read many times and they know which things to say for which pictures. Books that children can pretend-read after a few hearings are called predictable books because the pictures, rhyme, and sentence patterns let you predict what the words will say, especially if you have some help from your memory. Perhaps you remember some predictable books such as *Are You My Mother?* (Eastman, 1960), *One Fish, Two Fish, Red Fish, Blue Fish* (Seuss, 1960), and *Brown Bear, Brown Bear* (Martin, 1970).

In addition to learning about reading by being read to, many children have books that are recorded on tape. As they relisten to favorite books, they learn meanings for words, increase their oral language facility, and often learn to read some of the books.

Young children learn to read the signs and labels that are such a big part of their world. Through their excursions to stores and restaurants, they learn to read words such as *Pizza Hut, McDonald's,* and *Stop.* At first, they can recognize these words only when they see them on the sign. But later, they begin to identify the words regardless of whether the pictures, shapes, or other cues are there.

At the same time that these young children are engaging in all these reading activities, most children are also trying to write. Their first writing attempts are usually scribbles and then become collections of circles and lines that resemble letters. The first "real" words most children write are their own names, along with the names of pets and family members. They often copy words to make signs ("Keep Out" is commonly found on young children's bedroom doors). Most children write before they can spell. They ask others to spell words for them, copy favorite words from books, signs, and greeting cards, and invent the spelling of words by putting down some letters they hear in the words they want to write.

For many children, these fledgling reading and writing attempts happen in the preschool years. Print-rich kindergartens promote continued literacy development by providing lots of reading to children, shared reading of predictable Big Books, and many opportunities for children to write. Children who have not had these literacy experiences at home need to be placed in these print-rich kindergarten environments. Children who have had these literacy experiences at home continue to benefit from more of these experiences in kindergarten and first grade.

As children move into the primary grades, the reading to children, shared reading, and opportunities for writing should continue to be a large part of their literacy experience. In addition, children need to begin reading books on their own. Literacy-rich classrooms place a high priority on good literature, on self-selected reading and writing, and on children sharing their reading and writing with one another.

In many classrooms, some of the reading instruction is carried out with an adopted reading series. These series have books for each grade level (sometimes called literature anthologies) that contain a variety of literature, including contemporary fiction, historical fiction, science fiction, fantasy, biography, and nonfiction informational selections. Often, in addition to the reader or literature anthology, children do some work in an accompanying workbook or respond to literature in an accompanying journal. Most series contain periodic tests and other instruments teachers use to assess how children are progressing in their reading. In some classrooms, this reading instruction is carried out in ability groups. In other classrooms, the teacher uses a variety of whole-class instruction, flexible groups, and pairing arrangements instead of fixed reading groups.

Writing is also learned through a variety of activities. In most primary classrooms, teachers record children's ideas and display these on a chart. These activities, sometimes called language-experience activities (LEA) or shared writing, are opportunities for children to watch the teacher write. Through participation in language-experience or shared-writing activities, children learn that what you say can be written down and then read back. They also learn how we write. They begin to understand the left-right conventions of writing as well as develop some sense of punctuation and sentence/paragraph formation.

In addition to participating in activities where the teacher writes down the ideas, children learn to write by writing. Writers' Workshop is the popular term for a process approach to writing in which children choose a topic, write, share, edit, revise, and publish. Teachers teach minilessons in which they demonstrate how to write in various forms, the mechanics of writing and editing, and revision strategies. In many classrooms, children write in a journal, which may include personal writing as well as responses to literature and to what is being learned in the content areas of science and social studies. In many classrooms, children use computers to write, edit, and publish their pieces.

Phonics and spelling instruction play crucial roles in moving all children toward literacy. Children need to learn to read and spell high-frequency words such as *was, have,* and *they,* which are sometimes referred to as sight words. Children also need to develop strategies for figuring out the probable pronunciation of a word they have never seen before. This figuring out of unfamiliar words is what is usually referred to as phonics or decoding. Children also need to learn the most common English spelling patterns so that they can move through the stages of invented spelling toward conventional spelling.

Most of the reading and writing activities just described would take place during the language arts/reading part of the day. In many classrooms, teachers integrate the reading, writing, and other language activities and carry out an integrated language arts program. But children are reading and writing throughout the school day, and these literacy experiences they have while learning in the content areas of science, social studies, math, and health also contribute to their achievement of high literacy levels. These content-area subjects are the place where much new vocabulary is encountered, and teachers use this opportunity to help children build new concepts and learn new words. Children need to learn how to read textbooks as well as other informational sources. Many teachers include study strategies such as PQ3R, organizing strategies such as webbing and data charts, and research strategies such as locating information and note taking in their content-area instruction. In these classrooms, integration occurs not just within the integrated language arts block but across the various content subjects as well.

Children Need a Balanced Literacy Program

The first three key ideas in this chapter refer to the nature of reading and writing—that they have thinking as their essence, feeling as their energizer, and language as their foundation. The next two key ideas refer to the distinctive nature of the children we teach to read and write—that they are individually, culturally, and linguistically different from each other, and that they learn reading and writing in different ways. Together, these first five key ideas support the importance of a balanced literacy program if we are to succeed in teaching reading and writing to all children.

Single-minded or doctrinaire literacy programs always underemphasize at least one of these five key ideas. Some of these programs seem to assume that thinking, feeling, and language are genetic, learned at home, or learned from just reading and writing. Others seem to assume that thinking and language can be taught as isolated skills by completing workbook pages, worksheets, or computerized skill activities and games. All such programs assume that, for the purposes of teaching literacy, children are not distinctive and do not learn differently—they use one method with all the children, and the ones who fail get more of what they failed at.

The remaining chapters of this book make use of insights and discoveries from all camps and traditions in teaching literacy. Only by drawing on the wealth of knowledge and wisdom available to us from all these sources do we stand a chance of teaching today's diverse children the high literacy abilities the future will require them to have.

L o o k i n g   B a c k

In this chapter, we have begun to think about reading and writing by introducing six key ideas. These ideas are key to understanding not only this chapter but the entire book.

1. Because *thinking is the essence of reading and writing,* as you teach them, you both call upon and develop children's thinking processes.

2. Because *feeling is the energizer of reading and writing,* you must constantly consider student attitudes and interests as you plan reading and writing activities.

3. Because *language is the foundation of reading and writing,* reading and writing are supported by and connected to the other language functions of speaking and listening. Reading and writing are best developed in integrated language arts classrooms in which reading and writing are connected to each other and to speaking and listening.

4. The *individual, cultural, and language differences among the children we teach* lead us to consider the nature of the children we teach when we decide how to teach them.

5. To enable you to begin with a broad rather than a narrow understanding, we have stressed that *reading and writing are learned in a variety of ways.* Because of this, teachers need to have in their repertoires a wide variety of different teaching strategies and approaches.

6. *Children need a balanced literacy program.* This last key idea inevitably follows from the first five. Balance is the characteristic of a program that includes multiple methods and is sensitive to the fact that children are at different levels in each area of literacy. Only such a multifaceted program taught well can come close to teaching reading and writing well to all of today's children.

Add to Your Journal

One of the big ideas in this chapter was that both reading and writing are essentially thinking. That idea is the major reason you find this journal-writing prompt at the end of each chapter. This journal is a place for you to think about what you are reading. As you write in this journal, try to use the eight thinking processes described in this chapter. *Connect* your past experiences to what you are reading. *Organize* the new information in a way that will help you to remember it. Try to *image* your classroom and *predict* how the different students in your class might respond to various approaches. *Self-monitor* your reading for what makes sense and what is confusing. Think about what big *generalizations* or conclusions you can make based on your experience and your reading. *Apply* as much as you can to whatever experiences you currently have working with children. *Evaluate* the big ideas and decide what is most important to you. Use your journal to think about each of the key ideas and to record your own personal responses to what you are learning.

Application Activities

Listen, Look, and Learn

Interview a teacher you respect at a grade level you would like to teach. Find out how that teacher teaches reading and writing. Create some questions and ask the teacher to describe a typical daily/weekly schedule. Try to determine if the teacher reads to the students daily and provides time for the children to read materials of their own choosing. What part does writing play in the curriculum? Is a reading series used, and if so, what part does it play in the total language arts program? How much time is devoted to phonics and spelling activities, and are these integrated with the reading and writing that occur? How much is language integrated into the content areas of science, social studies, and math? Summarize what you found in your interview by relating it to the information in the *reading and writing are learned in a variety of ways* key idea.

Try It Out

Find a short magazine article on a topic of interest to you. Read the magazine article and try to be aware of where you use the thinking processes. What connections do you make between the magazine information and your own background knowledge, and what connections do you make between various pieces of information in the magazine article? Do you organize any of the information by mentally categorizing it or seeing time or other relationships? At what point do you image? Predict? Is there a point at which you become aware of the omnipresent self-monitoring function of your brain because something seems not to click? Could you use or apply anything you have learned in your own life? What generalizations and evaluations did you make about what you read? For each of the thinking processes, explain how you used it to comprehend this article or why you think you did not use it.

Try It Out

Our extended example to help you understand each of the eight thinking processes asked you to pretend you were reading a travel book on Hawaii. Create a similar extended example for the eight thinking processes that asks your reader to pretend to be writing something.

Do It Together

Form groups of four or five and pool your knowledge of individual differences among children. Think back to your own experiences in school and in any classrooms you have observed or taught in. Think about yourself as a learner. How were you different from the crowd? Then think of other children you know well—family members, friends, neighbors. What differences do you have personal experience with, and how did teachers respond to those differences? Try to think of instances in which the teacher adapted to the learner and instances in which the learner had to do the adapting. Summarize your findings and make a list of ways you think teachers can adapt to the differences children bring with them.

R e f e r e n c e s

Applebee, A. N., Langer, J. A., & Mullis, I. V. S. (1988). *Who reads best? Factors related to reading achievement in grades 3, 7, and 11.* Princeton, NJ: Educational Testing Service.
Schunk, D. H., & Zimmerman, B. J. (1997). Developing self-efficacious readers and writers: The role of social and self-regulatory processes. In J. T. Guthrie & A. Wigfield (Eds.), *Reading engagement: Motivating readers through integrated instruction* (pp. 34–50). Newark, DE: International Reading Association.

Children's Books/Materials Cited

Are You My Mother? by P. D. Eastman, Random House, 1960.
Brown Bear, Brown Bear, What Do You See? by B. Martin, Jr., Holt, Rinehart, & Winston, 1970.
One Fish, Two Fish, Red Fish, Blue Fish, by Dr. Seuss, Random House, 1960.

A d d i t i o n a l   R e a d i n g s

- How the brain functions and how thinking occurs are explored in terms that are relatively easy to understand in these two books.
  Caine, R. N., & Caine, G. (1991). *Teaching and the human brain.* Alexandria, VA: Association for Supervision and Curriculum Development.
  Vygotsky, L. S. (1978). *Mind in society.* Cambridge, MA: Harvard University Press.

- Because feeling is the energizer of reading and writing, motivating students to enjoy reading and writing is essential. The research on motivation is summarized in the following article and book.
  Brophy, J. (1987). Synthesis of research on strategies for motivating students to learn. *Educational Leadership, 45,* 40–48.
  Guthrie, J. T., & Wigfield, A. (Eds.). (1997). *Reading engagement: Motivating readers through integrated instruction.* Newark, DE: International Reading Association.

- Because language is the foundation of reading and writing, classrooms that integrate the language arts provide children with a variety of ways to learn to read and write. These books and articles explore the interconnections between listening, speaking, reading, and writing and suggest a variety of ways classrooms can provide integrated language and content-area instruction.

Britton, J. (1994). *Language and learning.* Portsmouth, NH: Heinemann.

Hart-Hewins, L., & Wells, J. (1990). *Real books for reading: Learning to read with children's literature.* Portsmouth, NH: Heinemann.

Heller, M. F. (1991). *Reading-writing connections: From theory to practice.* New York: Longman.

Irwin, J. W., & Doyle, M. A. (Eds.). (1992). *Reading/writing connections: Learning from research.* Newark, DE: International Reading Association.

Pappas, C. C., Kiefer, B. Z., & Levstik, L. S. (1990). *An integrated language perspective in the elementary school,* 2nd ed. White Plains, NY: Longman.

Pigdon, K., & Wooley, M. (Eds.). (1993). *The big picture: Integrating children's learning.* Portsmouth, NH: Heinemann.

Stevenson, C., & Carr, J. F. (Eds.). (1992). *Integrated studies in the middle grades.* New York: Teachers College Press.

Tierney, R. J., & Shanahan, T. (1991). Research on the reading–writing relationship: Interactions, transactions, and outcomes. In R. Barr, M. D. Kamil, P. B. Mosenthal, & P. D. Pearson (Eds.), *Handbook of reading research* (vol. 2, pp. 246–280). White Plains, NY: Longman.

Young, K. (1994). *Constructing buildings, bridges and minds: Building an integrated curriculum through social studies.* Portsmouth, NH: Heinemann.

- These books and articles reflect the latest research and best practice about teaching multicultural, multilingual children.

Au, K. H. (1993). *Literacy instruction in multicultural settings.* San Diego, CA: Harcourt Brace College Publishers.

Diamond, B. J., & Moore, M. A. (1995). *Multicultural literacy: Mirroring the reality of the classroom.* New York: Longman.

Faltis, C. J. (1993). *Joinfostering: Adapting teaching strategies for the multilingual classroom.* New York: Merrill.

Fitzgerald, J. (1993). Literacy and students who are learning English as a second language. *The Reading Teacher, 46,* 638–647.

Gibbons, P. (1993). *Learning to learn in a second language.* Portsmouth, NH: Heinemann.

Hernandez, H. (1997). *Teaching in multilingual classrooms.* Columbus: Merrill.

Lessow-Hurley, J. (1996). *The foundations of dual language instruction,* 2nd ed. New York: Longman.

Nurss, J. R., & Hough, R. A. (1992). Reading and the ESL student. In S. J. Samuels & A. E. Farstrup (Eds.), *What research has to say about reading instruction* (2nd ed., pp. 277–313). Newark, DE: International Reading Association.

Weber, R. (1991). Linguistic diversity and reading in American society. In R. Barr, M. L. Kamil, P. B. Mosenthal, & P. D. Pearson (Eds.), *Handbook of reading research* (vol. 2, pp. 97–119). White Plains, NY: Longman.

- A summary of important research that supports the development of balanced literacy programs can be found in the following two books.

Anderson, R. C., Hiebert, E., Scott, J. A., & Wilkinson, I. A. G. (1985). *Becoming a nation of readers.* Washington, DC: National Institute of Education.

Samuels, S. J., & Farstrup, A. E. (Eds.). (2002). *What research has to say about reading instruction,* 3rd ed. Newark, DE: International Reading Association.

Emergent Literacy

Looking Ahead

Like most other complex behaviors, literacy develops gradually and through a variety of experiences with reading and writing. The stage of development, between birth and use of conventional reading and writing, during which children are making their fledgling attempts at reading and writing is called emergent literacy. When children enter school, they have very different levels of literacy development. Some precocious children are already reading and writing fluently. Children who have had many informal reading and writing encounters move more easily into independent reading and writing. Children who have had few experiences with print need a print-saturated environment in which to begin their explorations of reading and writing.

A tremendous amount of research, usually included under the term *emergent literacy*, has shown us what happens in the homes of children where literacy is a priority. We now know that children born into homes where someone spends time with them in reading and writing activities walk into our schools with an incredible foundation upon which our instruction can easily build. These children experience an average of over 1,000 hours of quality one-on-one reading and writing activities (Adams, 1990).

Parents (or parent substitutes including grandmothers, cousins, uncles, and big sisters) read to children and talk with them about what they are reading. This reading is usually done "lap style," where the child can see the pictures as well as the words used to tell about the pictures. Favorite books are read again and again, and eventually most children have a book that they "pretend read"—usually to a younger friend or a stuffed animal.

In addition to reading, these children are writing at an early age. They scribble and make up ways to spell words as they write to grandma or help with the grocery list. They ask (and are told) how to spell favorite words. They make words from magnetic letters and copy favorite words from books. From these over 1,000 hours of reading and writing experiences, children learn some incredibly important concepts and attitudes. This chapter will describe these concepts and attitudes and the activities that foster them. This chapter discusses five key ideas:

1. Emerging readers and writers develop seven crucial understandings about print.
2. Reading to children supports emergent literacy.
3. Shared reading with predictable Big Books supports emergent literacy.
4. Shared-writing and language-experience activities support emergent literacy.
5. Helping children write supports emergent literacy.

Emerging Readers and Writers Develop Seven Crucial Understandings about Print

A great many important concepts and attitudes are developed as children encounter print in various forms. Seven of these stand out and differentiate children who have had many print experiences from those who have not. Children who have had many print experiences know why we read and write, have greater knowledge stores to make sense of the information they read, understand the conventions and jargon of print, have higher levels of phonemic awareness, can read some "important to them" words, know some letter names and sounds, and are eager and confident in their fledgling reading and writing attempts.

Emerging Readers and Writers Know Why We Read and Write

This is one of those "so obvious it is overlooked" variables. Ask five-year-olds from strong literacy backgrounds why people need to read and write, and they reel off a string of answers:

> Well, you have to be able to read. You read books and signs and cereal boxes and birthday cards that come in the mail and recipes and . . . you write notes and stories and signs and lists and you write on the computer and you send postcards when you are on a trip and you write to your aunt and. . . ."

You can tell from their answers that these children who come to school with clear ideas about the functions of reading and writing have had lots of real-world experiences with reading and writing. Reading and writing are things all the bigger people they know do, and they intend to do them too!

Did You Know That?

Learning to read early and easily is associated with four home factors: the home includes a range of print materials, adults and older children are readers, children have easy access to writing materials, and people in the home respond to the child's reading and writing efforts.

Emerging Readers and Writers Build Background Knowledge and Concepts

A lot of what we know about the world we learn from reading. This is also true of young children. Imagine a child who has just had read as bedtime stories *The Ocean Alphabet Book* by Jerry Pallotta and *The Bear Scouts* by Stan and Jan Berenstain and pores over Richard Scarry's *Best Word Book Ever* before turning out the light. Think about all the concepts and words about the ocean developed from the informational alphabet book. Even though *The Bear Scouts* is fiction, the information about scouting, camping, and the outdoors is true. The Richard Scarry book, of course, builds concepts with clear pictures arranged around different categories.

As you will learn in Chapter 7, comprehension is directly tied to prior knowledge. The more you know about any topic, the greater will be your understanding of what you read related to that topic. Word identification is also closely related to topic knowledge. Children who know a lot about oceans can figure out a word like *jellyfish* from the context, pictures, and beginning sounds, but children who don't have the word or concept for jellyfish stored in their brain's "ocean knowledge folder" can't. Your store of background knowledge and concepts directly affects how well you read, and children who have had many books read to them know more than children who haven't.

Emerging Readers and Writers Develop Concepts about Print

Print is what you read and write. Print includes all the funny little marks—letters, punctuation, space between words and paragraphs—that translate into familiar spoken language. In English, we read across the page in a left-to-right fashion. Because our eyes can see only a few words during each stop (called a fixation), we must actually move our eyes several times to read one line of print. When we finish that line, we make a return sweep and start all over again, left to right. If there are sentences at the top of a page and a picture in the middle and more sentences at the bottom, we read the top first and then the bottom. We start at the front of a book and go toward the back. These arbitrary rules about how we proceed through print are called *conventions.* Other languages have other conventions for getting through print. Hebrew, for example, is read from back to front, and Chinese is read from top to bottom in columns. Successful readers understand the conventions of print of their language.

Jargon refers to all the words we use to talk about reading and writing. Jargon includes such terms as *word, letter, sentence,* and *sound.* We use this jargon constantly as we try to teach children how to read: "Look at the first word in the second sentence. How does that word begin? What letter has that sound?"

Using some jargon is essential to talking with children about reading and writing, but children who don't come from rich literacy backgrounds are often very confused by this jargon. Although all children speak in words, they don't know words exist as separate entities until they are put in the presence of reading and writing. To many children, letters are what you get in the mailbox, sounds are horns and bells and doors slamming, and sentences are what you have to serve if you get caught committing a crime. These children are unable to follow our "simple" instructions because we are using words for which they have no meaning or an entirely different meaning.

Many children come to school knowing these print concepts. From being read to in the lap position, they have noticed how the eyes "jump" across the lines of print as someone is reading. They have watched people write grocery lists and thank-you letters to Grandma and have observed the top-bottom, left-right movement. Often, they have typed on the computer and observed these print conventions. Because they have had someone to talk with them about reading and writing, they have learned much of the jargon.

While writing down a dictated thank-you note to Grandma, Dad may say, "Say your sentence one word at a time if you want me to write it. I can't write as fast as you can talk."

When the child asks how to spell *birthday,* he may be told, "It starts with the letter *b,* just like your dog Buddy's name. *Birthday* and *Buddy* start with the same sound and the same letter."

These children know how to look at print and what teachers are talking about as they give them information about print. All children need to develop these critical understandings in order to learn to read and write.

Emerging Readers and Writers Develop Phonemic Awareness

The ability to recognize that words are made up of a discrete set of sounds and to manipulate sounds is called phonemic awareness. Children's level of phonemic awareness is very highly correlated with their success in beginning reading. Phonemic awareness develops through a series of stages during which children first become aware that language is made up of individual words, that words are made up of syllables, and that syllables are made up of phonemes. It is important to note here that the "jargon" is not what children learn. Five-year-olds cannot tell you there are three syllables in *dinosaur* and one syllable in *Rex.* What they can do is clap out the beats in *dinosaur* and the one beat in *Rex.* Likewise, they cannot tell you that the first phoneme in *mice* is *m,* but they can tell you what you would have if you took the *mmm* off *mice—ice.* Children develop this phonemic awareness as a result of the oral and written language they are exposed to. Nursery rhymes, chants, and Dr. Seuss books usually play a large role in this development.

Phonemic awareness is an oral ability. You hear the words that rhyme. You hear that *baby* and *book* begin the same. You hear the three sounds in *bat* and can say these sounds separately. Only when children realize that words can be changed and how changing a sound changes the word are they able to profit from instruction in phonics.

Children also develop a sense of sounds and words as they try to write. In the beginning, many children let a single letter stand for an entire word. Later, they put more letters and often say the word they want to write, stretching out its sounds to hear what letters they might use. Children who are allowed and encouraged to "invent spell" develop an early and strong sense of phonemic awareness.

Emerging Readers and Writers
Learn Some Concrete Words

Another area that demonstrates that emerging readers know things about how words work is concrete words. If you sit down with first-graders on the first day of school and try to determine if they can read by giving them a simple book to read or testing them on some common words such as *the, and, of,* or *with,* you would probably conclude that most first-graders can't read yet. But many first-graders can read and write some words. Here are some words a boy named David knew when he began first grade:

David

Mama

Daddy

Bear Bear (his favorite stuffed animal)

Carolina (his favorite basketball team)

Pizza Hut

I love you (written on notes on good days)

I hate you (written on notes on bad days)

Most children who have had reading and writing experiences have learned some words. The words they learn are usually "important to them" concrete words. It is important to note here that parents rarely teach these concrete words to their children. Children just learn them because they want to know them. Knowing ten to fifteen words is important not because they can read much with these few words, but because in learning these first words, they have accomplished a critical task. Children who come to school already able to read or write some concrete words have accomplished an important and difficult task. They have learned how to learn words.

Emerging Readers and Writers Know Some Letter Names and Sounds

Many children have learned some letter names and sounds. They can't always recognize all twenty-six letters in both upper- and lowercase, and they often don't know the sound of *w* or *c,* but they have learned the names and sounds for the most common letters. Usually, the letter names and sounds children know have come from those concrete words they can read and write. Many children also learned some letter names and sounds through repeated readings of alphabet books and through making words with magnetic letters on the refrigerator. Children learned some letter names and sounds as adults spelled out words they were trying to write. This immersion in print allowed them to make connections among the letters they saw in many places.

Emerging Readers and Writers Want to Learn to Read and Write

The final distinguishing characteristic of children who have had lots of early literacy encounters is that they can't wait to do it! All the big people can do it and they can't and they want to. They pretend-read books and scribble-write and then "read" their scribbling because they want to be able to do it. We all know of children who come home disappointed after the first day of first grade because "We were there all day and we didn't learn to read!" This "can't wait" attitude is a legacy of their literate environments, and the motivation sustains them through some of the work and effort required to become an independent reader and writer.

As you can tell, a lot is happening in the minds and hearts of young children during their early literacy encounters. Many children have these experiences at home. School just helps them continue their process toward literacy. Other children, unfortunately, have few reading and writing experiences before coming to school. For them, we must simulate as closely as possible the experiences they missed. In the remainder of this chapter, we will describe activities for the remaining four key ideas that form the cornerstone of an emergent literacy program through which all children can develop the critical understandings. None of these activities by itself is broad enough to develop all seven understandings, but each activity develops several. With all four activities occurring regularly, children have multiple opportunities to realize why people read and write, expand their knowledge stores, learn print conventions and jargon, develop phonemic awareness, learn to read and write some words, learn some letter names and sounds, and develop an "I can't wait" attitude.

All children can develop these crucial understandings when immersed in appropriate reading and writing activities.

Reading to Children Supports Emergent Literacy

Children are question machines. They come to school asking lots of questions, although the numbers of questions children ask seem to decrease with each year of schooling. One reason early and easy readers do so well in school is that they have had their questions answered as they asked them, and they continue to ask questions and expect responses. As teachers read to young children, they ought to be modeling how they think as they encounter print, just as some parents do when they read aloud to their children (Heath, 1982; Taylor, 1983; Roser & Martinez, 1985).

Did You Know That?

Researchers tell us that parental reading to children consists of specific and routinized activities that help explain how children develop an early story sense and book language.

The world of literature for young children is incredibly rich and varied. Chapter 6 describes some of the wonderful categories of books available. Because there are so many different kinds of books and because different understandings are increased by different kinds of books, teachers should read a great variety of books to children. In addition to storybooks and informational books, teachers should read poetry and nursery rhymes.

One of the best indicators of how well children will learn to read is their ability to recite nursery rhymes when they walk into kindergarten. Teachers should include nursery rhymes as one type of text they read to children. Children should learn to recite these rhymes, should sing the rhymes, should clap to the rhymes, act out the rhymes, and pantomime the rhymes. In some kindergarten classrooms, they develop "raps" for the rhymes. Nursery and other rhymes have been a part of our oral heritage for generations. Now we know that the rhythm and rhyme inherent in nursery rhymes are important vehicles for the beginning development of phonemic awareness. They should play a large role in any preschool, kindergarten, or first-grade read-aloud program.

While on the subject of things that have stood the test of time, do you remember being read *Hop on Pop? One Fish, Two Fish, Red Fish, Blue Fish? There's a Wocket in My Pocket?* These books hold universal appeal for young children, and from them children develop important understandings. You can nudge those understandings on a bit if you help the children notice that many of the words that rhyme are also spelled alike at the end. As you reread one of these favorite books, let the children point out the rhyming words and make lists of these on the board. Read the words together. Add other words that are spelled like that and rhyme, and make rhymes with those. Make up "silly words" and make them rhyme too, and decide what they might be and illustrate them. If you can have a "wocket in your pocket," you can have a "hocket in your pocket." What would a hocket be? What could you do with it?

How Reading to Children Develops Crucial Understandings

The most important reasons for reading to young children relate to the powerful role of read-alouds in concept development, the understanding of what reading is for, and the development of the desire to learn to read. Including lots of rhyming books in the read-aloud program has the added benefit of promoting phonemic awareness and helping children develop some early understandings of letter–sound relationships.

Shared Reading with Predictable Big Books Supports Emergent Literacy

Preschool, kindergarten, and first-grade teachers have always recognized the importance of reading a variety of books to children. One particular kind of book and one particular kind of reading, however, has special benefits for building reading and writing foundations—shared reading with predictable Big Books.

Shared reading is a term used to describe the process in which the teacher and the children read a book together. The book is read and reread many times. On the first several readings, the teacher usually does all of the reading. As the children become more familiar with the book, they join in and "share" the reading.

Predictable books are the best kind of books to use with shared reading. Predictable books are books in which repeated patterns, refrains, pictures, and rhyme allow children to "pretend read" a book that has been read to them several times. Pretend reading is a stage most children go through with a favorite book that some patient adult has read and reread to them. Perhaps you remember pretend-reading such popular predictable books as *Goodnight Moon, Are You My Mother?* or *Brown Bear, Brown Bear.* Shared reading of predictable books allows all children to experience this pretend reading. From this pretend reading, they learn what reading is, and they develop the confidence that they will be able to do it.

When children are read to "lap style," they have the opportunity to observe the print and the eyes of the person reading. They notice that the reader always reads the top print first, then the bottom print. They notice the eyes moving from left to right and then making the return sweep at the end of the line. Children who can see the words of a favorite book as that book is being read notice that some words occur again and again and eventually come to recognize some of these words. As they learn words, they notice recurring letter–sound relationships.

To simulate lap reading, many teachers use Big Books, in which the pictures and the print are enlarged. Not all Big Books are predictable, however. Not all Big Books have good story lines and wonderful artwork. If you want to get the maximum benefits from shared reading with Big Books, you should select carefully.

In choosing a book for shared readings in a preschool, kindergarten, or first-grade class, consider three criteria. First, the book must be very predictable. The most important goal for shared reading is that even children with little experience with books and stories will be able to pretend-read the book after several readings and develop the confidence that goes along with that accomplishment. Thus, you want a book without too much print and one in which the sentence patterns are very repetitive and the pictures support those sentence patterns.

Second, you want a book that will be very appealing to the children. Because the whole class of children will work with the same Big Book, and because the book will be read and reread, you should try to choose a book that many children will fall in love with.

Finally, the book should take you someplace conceptually. Many teachers choose Big Books to fit their units, build units around the books, or share Big Books by the same author or illustrator to study style.

When engaging in shared reading with predictable Big Books, we try to simulate what would happen in the home as a child insists upon having a favorite book read again and again. First, we focus on the book itself, on enjoying it, rereading it, talking about it, and acting it out. As we do this, we develop concepts and oral language. When most of the children can pretend-read the book, we focus their attention on the print. We do writing activities related to the book and help children learn print conventions, jargon, and concrete words. When children know some concrete words, we use these words to begin to build phonemic awareness and letter–sound knowledge.

Here is an example of shared reading using the ever popular *Hattie and the Fox* by Mem Fox. In this book, Hattie, a big black hen, notices something in the bushes:

"Goodness gracious me!
I can see a nose in the bushes!"

The other animals respond:

"Good grief," said the goose.
"Well, well," said the pig.
"Who cares?" said the sheep.
"So what?" said the horse.
"What next?" said the cow.

As the story continues, Hattie sees a nose and two eyes in the bushes, then a nose, two eyes, and two ears. Next two legs appear, followed by a body and two more legs. As Hattie announces each new sighting, the other animals respond with the same lack of concern. But when Hattie announces it is a fox, the other animals respond:

"Oh, no!" said the goose.
"Dear me!" said the pig.
"Oh, dear!" said the sheep.
"Oh, help!" said the horse.
But the cow said "MOO!"

This frightens the fox away, and the animals go on about their business.

Read and Talk about the Book

Observational research of children being read to shows that parents not only read to children but engage the children in conversation about the book and reread favorite books. We try to promote this kind of conversation and interaction as each book is read. After reading the first two pages, the teacher would encourage predictions by asking,

"What do you think Hattie sees?"

Children would be encouraged to infer character feelings by responding to questions such as,

> "Why do the other animals say things like, 'Who cares?' and 'So what?'?"

As the book continues and more body parts are revealed, children express their annoyance with the unconcerned animals:

> "They should figure out it is a fox!"

and their fear that

> "They'd better watch out. That fox could eat them!"

The first reading of any book should engage the children through talking and thinking about what is happening in the book. All the thinking processes can be engaged. Children can connect their experiences and emotions with those portrayed in the book. They can make predictions, form images, and make generalizations. As they predict what will happen next, evaluate the story and the characters, and apply what they learn to their own lives, they are interacting with the book in a very child-centered way.

As with any book, the first and second reading of a Big Book should be strictly focused on the meaning and enjoyment of the book. This book has delightful illustrations, and children will enjoy the suspense of watching the fox emerge.

Encourage the Children to Join in the Reading

There are a variety of ways to encourage children to join in. For this book, children will almost naturally want to say the repeated responses of the animals and join Hattie in adding the body parts as she sees them. You might also want to "echo read" the book, with you reading each line and then the children being your echo and reading it again. Some teachers like to practice and then make a tape recording in which the teacher reads some parts and the whole class or groups of children read the words of the various animals. Children delight in going to the listening center and listening to themselves reading the book.

Act It Out

Young children are natural actors. They pretend and act out all kinds of things. They don't need props or costumes, but you may want to make some simple line drawings of the animals (with several showing the parts of the fox as it emerges). If you punch two holes and put yarn through and laminate these, children can wear the cards around their necks and everyone will know who they are. Act it out several times, letting everyone have a chance to be one of the animals or a part of the fox. Read the part that is not repetitive, and let children in the audience read the repetitive parts with you.

Let the Children Match Sentence Strips and Words to the Book

Write some of the sentences—probably the repeated responses of the animals—on sentence strips. Let children put them in the right order by matching them to the same sentences in the book and arranging them in a pocket chart. Have children read from the sentence strips. Next, let the children watch you cut some sentences into words. Mix up the words and have them recreate the book page from the words. Children enjoy manipulating the words, and it is excellent practice for left-to-right, top-to-bottom print tracking.

Decide What You Notice about the Letters and Words

Choose some sentences from the book, perhaps these:

> "Good grief," said the goose.
>   "Well, well," said the pig.
>   "Who cares?" said the sheep.
>   "So what?" said the horse.
>   "What next?" said the cow.

Ask the children to look at these sentences and come up and point out what they notice. Children will notice a variety of things, depending on their level. These will probably include the following:

> "*Good, grief,* and *goose* begin with a *g.*"
> "*Pig* has a *g* too but it is at the end."
> "*Said* is in every sentence—five times!"
> "*The* is also there five times!"
> "*What* is there two times."
> "The *What* in the last sentence has a capital *W.*"
> "All the sentences have these (pointing to quotation marks) things."
> "These three sentences have question marks."
> "The first two sentences have these (pointing to exclamation marks)."

Whatever the children notice is accepted and praised by the teacher. The teacher also asks more questions:

> "Does anyone know what these marks are called? Why are they there?"

and offers explanations:

> "That is called a question mark, and those animals are all asking questions."
> "Good noticing—*What* has a capital *W* because it is the first word in the sentence."

Make the Big-Book or Little-Book Versions Available for Children to Read

Once the book has been read, enjoyed, reread, acted out, and had some attention focused on the sentences, words, and letters, most children will be able to read (or pretend-read) most of the book. This early "I Can Read" confidence is critical to emerging readers, and the shared book experience as described is a wonderful way to foster this.

Develop Print Concepts by Pointing Out Features of the Book

Make sure children can find the front and back of the book as well as the title and author's name. Have individual children come and point to words as everyone reads to make sure that they know that the words are what you read and that you move in a left-to-right fashion across each line of print. Have children use their hands to show you just one word, the first word in a sentence, the last word, the longest word, and so forth.

Develop Background Knowledge and Concepts

Connect *Hattie and the Fox* to a unit on farm animals and compare real and fictional animals. Reread the book and ask the children questions that will help them understand the differences between real animals and storybook animals: "Do real animals talk? How do real animals communicate?" Read them some informational books about real farm animals and help them understand the difference between fantasy and informational text.

Develop Phonemic Awareness and Letter–Sound Connections

One critical component of phonemic awareness is the ability to hear when words start with the same sound. Once children can distinguish when words begin alike, they can begin to learn which letters make which sounds. Letter sounds, like other learnings, can be learned by rote or by association. Learning the common sound for *h* by trying to remember it or by trying to remember that it begins the words *hen* and *horse* when you can't read the words *hen* and *horse* requires rote learning. Once you can read the words *hen* and *horse* and realize that the common sound for *h* is heard at the beginning of *hen* and *horse*, you no longer just have to remember the sound. You can now associate the sound of *h* with something already known, the words *hen* and *horse*. Associative learning is the easiest, quickest, and longest lasting.

Children from print-rich environments know some concrete words when they come to school. As they are taught letter sounds, they probably associate these with the words they know, thus making the learning of these sounds easier and longer lasting. We can provide this opportunity for associative learning for children who did not know words when they came to school by capitalizing on the words they have learned from *Hattie and the Fox.*

The number of letter sounds you wish to focus on from one book will depend on what your children already know and on what words are available in the book. Choose words that have clear initial sounds and that most of the children have learned through the multiple activities you have done with the book. The words *Hattie, hen,* and *horse* are all important words, and they give children three connections for the sound of *h. Goose, cow,* and *fox* are clear examples for *g, c,* and *f.*

Regardless of how many letter sounds you teach using the key words, the procedure should be the same. Begin with two letters that are very different in look and sound and that are made in different places in the mouth—*h* and *c,* for example. Show the children the words—*Hattie, hen, horse,* and *cow*—that will serve as key words for these letters. Tell the children to pronounce the key words and to notice the position of their tongues and teeth as they do. Say several concrete words (*car, hat, hop, cat, hug, cup, corn*) that begin like *Hattie, hen, horse,* and *cow,* and have the children say them after you. Have them notice where their tongues and teeth are as they say the words. Let the children point to and say the key words to indicate how the word begins.

Begin a key word bulletin board on which you put the letters *h* and *c* and the key words *Hattie, hen, horse,* and *cow.* Repeat the activity just described using other *h* and *c* words until most of the children begin to understand the difference in the letter sound. Then add a third letter and key word—perhaps *f* and *fox.* Have them listen for and repeat words beginning with all three letters—*h, c,* and *f.* Be sure to point out that the words they already know will help them remember the sounds. You could then add in a fourth letter and key word—*g* and *goose.*

This activity just described is a multilevel activity. Multilevel means that there are multiple things to be learned through the same activity—depending on what you are ready to learn. By having children listen to words and decide if they begin like *Hattie, fox, cow,* or *goose,* you are helping those who still need to develop the phonemic awareness sense of which words sound alike at the beginning. When you help them notice that these letters are *h, f, c,* and *g,* you are helping them establish letter–sound connections we call phonics. Children must develop phonemic awareness in order to learn phonics. This multilevel activity has "something for everyone."

Develop Concepts of Rhyme and Phonemic Awareness

Another component of phonemic awareness is the ability to hear when words rhyme. Once children can hear rhymes, they can read rhyming words by changing the beginning sound and making the word rhymes. Three of the concrete words in *Hattie and the Fox*—*hen, pig,* and *sheep*—have lots of words that rhyme and are spelled with the same pattern. Here is an activity you can use to help develop both the ability to hear rhyme—phonemic awareness—and the ability to read new rhyming words by changing the initial letter—phonics.

Show the children the words *hen, pig,* and *sheep,* which most of the children should recognize by now. Tell them that you are going to say words that rhyme with one of the animals. Their job is to repeat the word you say and then say the animal names to decide which one rhymes. Say some common words that rhyme, such as *big, ten, jeep, beep, men, dig, wig, pen, keep.* Have the children decide which word these new words rhyme with. Once they have decided, write the new word under the rhyming word, stretching out the word and letting the children help you decide what letter they hear at the beginning. Your list should look like this:

hen	pig	sheep
ten	big	jeep
men	dig	beep
pen	wig	keep

When you have this list completed, have the children read each group of rhyming words and help them notice that the beginning letter is different but the rest of the word has the same pattern.

This activity, like the preceding one with beginning sounds, is multilevel. Children who still need to develop the oral concept of rhyme have a wonderful opportunity to do so. Other children can begin to see how you read words by blending a beginning sound you know with a pattern you recognize from other rhyming words.

Shared Reading with Poems, Songs, and Chants

In addition to books, many teachers write favorite poems, chants, songs, and finger plays on long sheets of paper, and these become some of the first things children can actually read. Most teachers teach the poem, chant, song, or finger play to the children first. Once the children have learned to say, chant, or sing it, they are then shown what the words look like. The progression to reading is a natural one, and children soon develop the critical "Of course I can read" self-confidence. Once children can read the piece, many teachers copy it and send it home for the child to read to parents and other family members.

How Shared Reading Develops the Seven Crucial Understandings

We hope you can see that shared reading can be used to develop all seven crucial understandings. Even though *Hattie and the Fox* is a fictional book, there are concepts to be learned when you expand the book to study farm animals. Children develop left-right, top-bottom print conventions as they read with you and when they reassemble words to make sentences. They also understand that words make up sentences. When they compare the sounds of different parts of different words, they begin to understand that letters represent sounds. Through all these activities, they firm up their understanding of critical jargon—words, sentences, letters, sounds. When reading a predictable Big Book is extended by word and letter–sound activities, children learn some concrete words, letter names, and sounds and increase phonemic awareness. Of course, children learn that one of the reasons we read is to enjoy wonderful books such as *Hattie and the Fox.* Shared reading also promotes "I can't wait" and "I can do it" attitudes.

Accommodations and Adaptations for Phonemic Awareness

FOR INCLUSION

In addition to rhyme, and blending and segmenting words, phonemic awareness also includes the concepts of how speech is made up of words and how words are made up of syllables. These concepts are easily understood by young children, but some children need extra practice to grasp those concepts. Here are two strategies you might try if some children have difficulty dividing the language stream into words or the words into syllables.

Counting Words

To do this activity, all children should have ten counters in a paper cup. (Anything manipulable is fine. Some teachers use edibles such as cereal or bite-size crackers and let the children eat their counters at the end of the lesson. This makes cleanup quick and easy.) Begin by counting some familiar objects in the room, having all children place one of their counters on their desks as each object is pointed to. Have children return counters to the cup before beginning to count each object.

Tell children that you can also count words by putting down a counter for each word you say. Explain that you will say a sentence in the normal way and then repeat the sentence, pausing after each word. The children should put down counters as you say the words in the sentence slowly, then count the counters and decide how many words you said. Children generally attend better if the sentences are about them. (*Carlos has a new lunch box. Miguel is a good listener.*) Once the children catch on to the activity, let them say some sentences—first in the normal way, then one word at a time. Listen carefully as they say their sentences the first time because they will often need help saying them one word at a time. Not only do children enjoy this activity and learn to separate out words in speech, but they are also practicing critical counting skills.

(continued)

Clapping Syllables

Once children get fairly automatic at separating the speech stream into words, they are ready to begin thinking about separating words into some components. The first division most children make is syllables. Clapping seems to be the easiest way to get every child involved, and the children's names are the naturally appealing words to clap. Say the first name of one child. Say the name again, and this time, clap the syllables. Continue saying first names and then clapping the syllables as you say them the second time, and invite the children to join in clapping with you. As children catch on, say some middle or last names. The term *syllables* is a little jargony and foreign to most young children, so you may want to refer to the syllables as beats. Children should realize by clapping that *John* is a one-beat word, *Kevin* a two-beat word, and *Patricia* a three-beat word.

Once children can clap syllables and decide how many beats a given word has, help them to see that one-beat words are usually shorter than three-beat words—that is, they take fewer letters to write. To do this, write some words children cannot read on sentence strips and cut the strips into words so that short words have short strips and long words have long strips. Have some of the words begin with the same letters but be different lengths so that children will need to think about word length to decide which word is which.

For the category "foods," you might write *ham* and *hamburgers; milk* and *muffin;* and *soup, sausage,* and *strawberries.* Tell the children that you are going to say the names of foods and they should clap to show how many beats the word has. (Do not show them the words yet!) Say the first pair, one at a time (*ham/hamburgers*). Help children to decide that *ham* is a one-beat word and *hamburgers* takes a lot more claps and is a three-beat word. Now, show them the two words and say, "One of these words is *ham* and the other is *hamburgers.* Who thinks they can figure out which one is *ham* and which one is *hamburgers?*" Help the children to explain that because *hamburgers* takes so many beats to say, it probably takes more letters to write.

* *

Shared-Writing and Language-Experience Activities Support Emergent Literacy

Shared writing is a process in which the teacher and children write together. Generally, the teacher leads the children to share ideas and then records the ideas as the children watch. Shared writing, like individual writing, can be used to write a wide variety of things. Regie Routman (1991), in her wonderfully practical book *Invitations,* includes this list of some of the possibilities (p. 60):

Wall stories and Big Books

Stories, essays, and poems

Original story endings

Retellings of stories

Class journal entries

Class observations of pets, plants, and science experiments

Shared experiences such as field trips and special visitors

Class rules and charts

Weekly newsletter to parents

News of the day

Curriculum-related writing

Reports

Informational books

Evaluations of books and activities

Language Experience

Shared writing is similar to the Language-Experience Approach (LEA) in that the teacher writes as the children watch, but it is different in one important feature. One of the cardinal principles of LEA has always been that the teacher should write down exactly what the child says. Allen and Allen (1966), Stauffer (1980), and others who promoted language experience as an approach to beginning reading and writing argued that children must learn that what they say can be written down and then read back.

This important learning can occur only if the child's exact words are recorded. The problem for teachers arises when a child's spoken dialect differs from standard written English. Teachers find it difficult to record sentences such as these:

"She ain't got no money."

"I done hit my head."

Most teachers, when working with individual children, however, will write down the sentences just as they are spoken because they realize that the child will read the sentence the way it was spoken. If the sentence,

"She ain't got no money."

is written down in the standard English form,

She doesn't have any money

the child, remembering what was said, will read the word *doesn't* as "ain't," *have* as "got," and *any* as "no."

Likewise, if the child's spoken,

"I done hit my head."

is changed to the standard,

I hit my head.

the child, remembering what was said, will say "done" while looking at *hit,* "hit" while looking at *my,* "my" while looking at *head,* and run out of written words before finishing the spoken sentence.

When teachers are using language experience with an individual child to help the child understand what reading and writing are and that you can write and read what you can say, then the child's exact words should be written down. To do anything else will hopelessly confuse the child about the very things you are using individual language experience to try to clarify.

The situation changes, however, when you are working with a class or small group of children. The group invariably includes children who use a variety of different language structures. Recording sentences such as the above when you are working with children whose language usage varies will lead to confusion, and sometimes ridicule, on the part of children whose spoken language is closer to standard written English. In addition, the charts, letters, books, and so on that you create during shared writing are apt to be displayed in the classroom or sent home to parents. It is difficult to explain to parents why nonstandard usage should be written down, and there are even examples of teachers being accused of "not knowing how to write good English."

Did You Know That?

LEA, taking down children's dictation as a way to produce material for teaching beginning reading, first appeared in the professional literature in the late 1800s.

Shared Writing

Shared writing differs from **LEA** in that the teacher and the children all "share" the construction of the writing. In creating a daily entry in the class journal, the teacher asks the children what important things they think should be included.

She listens to all suggestions, accepting whatever kind of spoken dialect children use. After listening to the suggestions, she records them, using standard written English and imposing some kind of order and cohesion on them. She then reads aloud the sentences she has written. Because the teacher listens to the suggestions of many children and then records the "gist" but not the "exact words" of any child, the problem of recording and reading nonstandard usage does not occur.

How Shared Writing and Language Experience Develop Crucial Understandings

Both shared writing and language experience are valuable tools to use with children whose reading and writing experiences at home and at school have been limited. In most classrooms, the content of the writing relates to a topic the children are learning about. Often, they summarize important concept-building experiences such as field trips or science experiments. Children's background knowledge and concepts are extended through these experiences.

As children watch the teacher record their ideas, they notice the left-to-right, top-to-bottom, and other print conventions used in writing. They also hear print jargon being used as the teacher says,

"Let's write another *sentence* about your dog."

or

"It took a lot of *words* to write that long *sentence* about the weather."

As with shared reading, children begin to note patterns of repeated letters and sounds in the language experience and shared writing texts. The teacher can explicitly point out words that begin with the same letter and have children identify them. For example, the teacher might ask children to come to the dictated text and underline all words that begin with *m*. Saying the *m* words one after another with an emphasis on the beginning sound helps to build connections among the letters and sounds of our language. Many teachers create a typed copy of dictated text and make multiple copies to use with children. Making multiple copies allows teachers to do some word- and sentence-matching activities. It also encourages the development of sight words through repeated exposures to the words. Children learn words by seeing and using them many times in many ways.

Of course, children who engage in language-experience and shared-writing activities get excited about writing. They want to learn to write so they can tell about all the things they know. As they read the texts they have helped create, they develop self-confidence in their own abilities to learn to read and write.

Accommodations and Adaptations Using Language Experience and Shared Writing

FOR INCLUSION

Some children have a great deal of difficulty learning to track print. In spite of the group reading and writing activities they participate in, they don't learn how you must move from left to right and so forth. Often, these are the same children who don't learn any of the concrete words included in the shared reading and shared-writing stories. These children can learn to track print and learn some concrete words with some focused individual language-experience activities. Here is what one teacher does with the one or two children each year who don't learn to track print or don't learn any words from the group activities.

Day One

1. Sit down with the individual child and begin a simple book. (This book can be constructed with half sheets of ditto paper stapled between half-sheet construction-paper covers.) Explain to the child that she is going to make a book about herself. Talk with the child and decide on one sentence to go on the first page. Try to have a sentence long enough that it takes two lines to write. Write that sentence as the child watches.

2. Help the child read the sentence by moving her hand under each word. Read it together, pointing to each word until the child can read it and point to the words by herself.

3. As the child watches and says the individual words, write the sentence again on a sentence strip. Have the child read the sentence from the sentence strip, pointing to each word.

4. As the child watches, cut the sentence from the strip into words. Mix these words up and have the child put the words in order to make the sentence, using the sentence in the book to match to.

5. Put all the cut-up words in an envelope and label both the envelope and the page of the book with a 1.

6. Let the child draw a picture to illustrate page 1 of the book.

Day Two

1. Reread the sentence on page 1. Take the words from the envelope and put them in order by matching them to the book sentence.

2. Together, compose another sentence about the child for page 2. Write that sentence as the child watches.

3. Have the child read the sentence with you several times, helping the child to point to words while reading them.

4. Write this sentence on a strip, cut it apart, have it matched to the book sentence, and put it in an envelope labeled 2. Let the child illustrate page 2 of her book.

Day Three

1. Reread the sentences on pages 1 and 2. Take the words from the envelopes and put them in order by matching to both sentences.

2. Have the child find any duplicate words and decide that they are the same word and what that word is.

3. Come up with a third sentence for page 3. Use the same procedures of writing this sentence on the sentence strip, cutting, matching, and illustrating.

Day Four through Book Completion

Continue adding a page each day, matching the words and looking for repeated words. Read the whole book each day, but when you have five or more pages, match just the two or three most recent preceding ones. Look for duplicate words and observe which ones the child is learning. When the book is finished, have the child read the whole book and ask her to find words from the envelopes that she can read. Most children learn to track-print and accumulate eight to ten words through doing one twelve- to fifteen-page book. A few children need to do a second book, using the same procedure. Help the child construct the second book in the same way on a topic the child is particularly interested in.

FOR CHILDREN ACQUIRING ENGLISH

Picture modules are shared-writing selections that are built around a high-interest picture. The teacher allows students to select a picture from a group of pictures. The picture is glued to the upper left-hand corner of a sheet of chart paper. A paragraph about the picture is written on the lines beside and below the picture.

The class names the objects, people, and animals in the picture and the teacher writes them beside what was named. Relationships among objects and characters are also discussed ("The hat is on the head of the dog," "The girl is beside her sister") as well as describing the setting ("They are at the circus," "It is a sunny day"). Words are written next to the objects of characters ("dog," "hat," "sister," "sun") to remind students of key vocabulary. If necessary, the teacher could also write the words in the child's primary language as well as a bridge to remembering the English ("el perro," "el sombrero," "la hermana," "el sol").

After a thorough discussion and labeling of characters, objects, and setting, students talk about why the characters are where they are and what they are going to do. The "student of the week" (or some other student) gives the first sentence for the teacher to write. The teacher helps shape the sentence through questioning so that the student comes up with a topic sentence that the whole paragraph will be about. The teacher listens to suggestions and writes simple sentences using student ideas to complete the paragraph. Later in the school year, students might help construct a story (with a problem and solution) for the picture module. The picture module will get longer as the year goes on, too.

Having Children Write Supports Emergent Literacy

Until relatively recently, the theory was that if children were allowed to write before they could spell and make the letters correctly, they would get into "bad habits" that would be hard to break later. This argument does not hold up to scrutiny when you actually look at what children do before they come to school. Just as children from literacy-oriented homes read before they can read by pretend-reading a memorized book, they write before they can write. Their writing is not initially decipherable by anyone besides themselves, and sometimes they read the same scribbling different ways. They write with pens, markers, crayons, paint, chalk, and with normal-sized pencils with erasers on the ends. They write on chalkboards, magic slates, paper, and—alas—walls.

They write in scribbles, which first go anywhere and then show a definite left-to-right orientation (for children in English-language homes; the pattern may be different with another language). They make letter-like forms. They let single letters stand for entire words. They draw pictures and intersperse letters with the pictures. They make shopping lists by copying words off packages. They copy favorite words from books. They write love letters ("I love Joshua") and hate mail ("I hate Joshua").

Did You Know That?

Some parents question whether or not we should encourage young children to use invented spellings (also referred to as "temporary spelling" or "phonic spelling"). Experience and research in the last decade have shown us that literacy is not impeded by allowing children to write before they can spell. Rather, they learn many important concepts and develop the confidence that they can write. Children encouraged to use invented spellings become better decoders and spellers than children not allowed to use them.

Teachers can encourage and support students' own writing in numerous ways. While Chapter 8 more fully develops what you need to know to encourage as well as teach writing in your classroom, here are some activities that promote writing with emerging writers.

Model Writing for the Children

As children watch you write, they observe that you always start in a certain place, go in certain directions, and leave space between words. In addition to these print conventions, they observe that writing is "talk written down." Every classroom affords numerous opportunities for the teacher to write as the children watch, and for the children to help with what to write.

In many classrooms, the teacher begins the day by writing a morning message on the board. The teacher writes this short message as the children watch. The teacher then reads the message, pointing to each word and inviting the children to join in on any words they know. Sometimes, teachers take a few minutes to point out some things students might notice from the morning message.

"How many sentences did I write today?"

"How can we tell how many there are?"

"What do we call this mark I put at the end of this sentence?"

"Which words begin with the same letters?"

"Which is the shortest word?"

These and similar questions help children learn conventions and jargon of print and focus their attention on words and letters.

Provide a Variety of Things to Write with and On

Children view writing as a "creation" and are often motivated to write by various media. Many teachers grab all free postcards, scratch pads, counter checks, pens, and pencils, and haunt yard sales, always on the lookout for an extra chalkboard or an old but still working typewriter. A letter home to parents at the beginning of the year asking them to clean out desks and drawers and donate writing utensils and various kinds of paper often brings unexpected treasures. In addition to the usual writing media, young children like to write with sticks in sand, with paintbrushes or sponges on chalkboards, and with chocolate pudding and shaving cream.

Help Children Find Writing Purposes through Center Activities

Children need to develop a basic understanding that writing is a message across time and space. Once they have that understanding, they are able to identify a purpose for a piece of writing. For most young children, the purpose of writing is to get something told or done. Children will find some real purposes for writing if you incorporate writing in all your centers. Encourage children to make grocery lists while they are playing in the housekeeping center. Menus, ordering pads, and receipts are a natural part of a restaurant center. An office center would include various writing implements, a typewriter, or computer, along with index cards, phone books, and appointment books.

Children can make birthday cards for friends or relatives or write notes to you or one of their classmates and then mail them in the post office center. They can make signs ("Keep Out! Girls Only!") and post them as part of their dramatic play. When children put a lot of time into building a particularly wonderful creation from blocks or other construction toys, they often don't want to have it taken apart so that something else can be built. Many teachers keep a large pad of tablet paper in the construction center. Children can draw and label records of their constructions before disassembling them. Once you start looking for them, there are numerous opportunities for children to write for real purposes as they carry out their creative and dramatic play in various centers.

Provide a Print-Rich Classroom

Classrooms in which children write have lots of print in them. In addition to books, there are magazines and newspapers. There are charts of recipes made and directions for building things. Children's names are on their desks and on many different objects. There are class books, bulletin boards with labeled pictures of animals under study, and labels on almost everything. Children's drawings and all kinds of writing are displayed. In these classrooms, children see that all kinds of writing are valued. Equally important, children who want to write "the grown-up way" can find lots of words to make their own.

Accept the Writing They Do

Accepting a variety of writing—from scribbling to one-letter representations to invented spellings to copied words—is the key to having young children write before they can write. Teachers should talk with students the very first day of school about the forms they can use for writing. Show them examples of other children's scribbles, pictures, single letters, vowelless words, and other kinds of writing children use. Tell them they all started out at the scribble stage, and they will all get to conventional writing. For now, they should use the stage of writing that is most comfortable to share the message they have, and you will help them move along to the next stage.

Sometimes it is the children and not the teacher who reject beginning attempts. If more advanced children give less advanced children a hard time about their "scribbling," the teacher must intervene and firmly state a policy such as this:

> "There are many different ways to communicate through writing. We use pictures and letters and words. Sometimes we just scribble, but the scribbling helps us remember what we were thinking. We use all these different ways in this classroom."

Without this attitude of acceptance, the very children who most need to explore language through writing will be afraid to write.

How Writing Develops Crucial Understandings

Encouraging young children to write has many benefits. As children write, they learn the print concepts of left to right and leaving space between words. (Even when children are scribbling, they usually scribble from left to right and stop occasionally to write a new scribble.) Children often write about themselves and each other and copy names of favorite foods, restaurants, and places from the print in the classroom. From these writing opportunities, they learn concrete, important-to-them words. As they stretch out words to "put down the sounds they hear," they are developing phonemic awareness. We are all more apt to remember things we actually use. As children use what they are learning about letters and sounds to try to spell words, they are applying their phonics knowledge. Writing is perhaps our best opportunity for developing young children's print concepts, concrete words, phonemic awareness, and knowledge of letters and sounds.

The Theory and Research Base for Emergent Literacy

The first edition of this book contained no chapter on emergent literacy but, instead, a chapter on reading readiness. Readiness—or lack of readiness—for reading and writing instruction was the dominant view until the mid-1980s. The change characterized by the shift from readiness to emergent literacy is much more than just a change in terminology. Indeed, preliteracy, a term you might also find in the current professional literature, is a synonym for emergent literacy, whereas readiness is not. The use of the term "emergent literacy" represents a fundamental change in how we view literacy and the years leading up to independent reading and writing. To help you understand what an important and drastic change has occurred in our thinking, we will briefly summarize the readiness and emergent literacy theories.

For most of this century, educators believed that reading instruction should be delayed until children reached a certain level of mental readiness. They believed that for most children, this level of readiness would be achieved when they were about six years old. The most influential study (Morphett & Washburne, 1931) actually specified a mental age of 6.5 years as the right age to begin reading instruction. Many educators believed that writing should be delayed until reading abilities were firmly in place and recommended that children begin writing when they were eight or nine years old.

To determine which children were ready to read, most first-graders were given readiness tests after six weeks of first grade. These readiness tests tested the skills believed to be critical for success in beginning reading instruction. Most tests included the skills of visual discrimination ("Find the shape that is just like the first shape"), auditory discrimination ("Find the two pictures whose names begin with the same sound"), letter naming, matching pictures with their beginning sounds, high-frequency word knowledge, and measures of oral language and meaning vocabulary.

First-graders who scored high on these readiness tests were put into groups, and reading instruction—usually with a basal reader—was begun. There were two schools of thought about how to proceed with children who scored poorly on the readiness tests. Some schools and teachers felt it was best to wait for the readiness to develop. Other schools and teachers taught the skills—visual discrimination of shapes, auditory discrimination of sounds, letter names, and so forth—in an attempt to develop readiness.

Emergent literacy research began with the work of Charles Read (1971, 1975) and his mentor, Carol Chomsky (1970). Read's work described for many of us at the time what we were seeing with the writing of young children. It was not uncommon, prior to his research, to hear parents and early primary teachers say, "Isn't that cute?" of children's spellings of words. Read taught us that young children's spellings were not "cute" but were developmental and could be predicted based on an analysis of consonant and vowel substitutions students consistently made. Chomsky's article "Write First, Read Later" (1970) was seminal in helping to shift instruction toward the field that came to be known as emergent literacy. Henderson and Beers (1980) and Henderson and Templeton (1986) extended Read's work and devised a usable scale for teachers of developmental stages of writing that continues to be the basis for describing children's developmental writing characteristics.

We also found emergent literacy research beginning in the homes of young children. The research traces the literacy development of young children from birth until the time that they read and write in conventional ways (Heath, 1982; Harste, Woodward, & Burke, 1984; Teale & Sulzby, 1986; Sulzby & Teale, 1991). From this observational research, it became apparent that children in literate home environments engage in reading and writing long before they begin formal reading instruction. They use reading and writing in a variety of ways and pass through a series of predictable stages on their voyage from pretend and scribbling to conventional reading and writing. When parents read to children, interact with them about print they see in the world (signs, cereal boxes, advertisements), and encourage and support early writing efforts, reading and writing develop along with listening and speaking—concurrently rather than sequentially.

In short, the observational and experimental research on how young children learn to read and write debunked the readiness/mental age theories on which we had operated for half a century. Rather than needing to learn skills (auditory discrimination, letter names and sounds, etc.) before they began reading and writing, children exposed to lots of print experiences learned skills as they began reading and writing. Readiness to read has more to do with experiences with books than with any subset of skills or mental age.

This chapter is based on the emergent literacy research that shows the kinds of literacy behaviors young children engage in that result in their developing understandings essential to successful independent reading and writing. Whether kindergartens should be primarily for play and socialization or for more academic work has long been debated. Emergent literacy research supports neither kindergartens in which children play and socialize while we wait for literacy development nor kindergartens in which children work on isolated readiness skills. Rather than wait or teach separate skills for children who have not had these early literacy experiences before coming to school, kindergartens and other early school experiences should simulate as closely as possible the "at home" experiences observed in the research. We call these kindergartens "literate home simulations."

L o o k i n g   B a c k

For most teachers, learning to read and write were relatively easy, pleasant, and early activities. The ease with which most teachers learned to read probably reflects that most teachers grew up in literate home environments in which reading and writing were modeled, encouraged, and supported. Emergent literacy observational research has shown us the tremendous impact of these early literacy experiences. This chapter presented the practical implications of the emergent literacy research. It discussed five key ideas:

1. Emerging readers and writers develop seven crucial understandings about print.
2. Reading to children supports emergent literacy.
3. Shared reading with predictable Big Books supports emergent literacy.
4. Shared-writing and language-experience activities support emergent literacy.
5. Having children write supports emergent literacy.

Add to Your Journal

What do you remember about your early literacy experiences at home and at school? Did you come to school with many of the seven crucial understandings already established? Did you know why people read and wrote? Did you have a big vocabulary that represented lots of background knowledge and concepts? Could you track print as you pretended to read a book, and did you know common jargon—word, letter, sound, sentence? Could you read some important-to-you words like your own name, the names of other family members, pets, favorite restaurants? Could you name lots of the alphabet letters, and did you know the sounds for some of these? Did you know that words were made up of sounds, and could you mentally take words apart and put them back together again? Were you one of those children who just couldn't wait to learn to read?

Use the eight thinking processes—connect, predict, generalize, organize, image, self-monitor, evaluate, and apply—described in the previous chapter to think about the crucial understandings and the four activities presented in the chapter. If you teach young children, what role will these four activities play in your classroom? If you teach older children, how could you adapt these for children for whom literacy is a struggle or for children just learning to read in English?

Application Activities

Try It Out

Find or make a predictable Big Book and use it with a group of children. (When choosing your book, consider the three criteria: the book should be very predictable and appealing and should help children develop important concepts.) Try some of the activities suggested for *Hattie and the Fox* as well as others that fit your book better. As you read and reread the book with the children, be sure that you encourage their participation in the talking as well as the reading. Help them make connections and predictions and express their feelings. Encourage the whole range of thinking children can do with books. If possible, find a way for them to act out the book. Once the children have read and enjoyed the book several different times in different ways, do some activities that help them to focus on words and letters. As you plan and carry out your Big-Book activities, decide which of the seven crucial understandings are developed in each activity. (Of course, several understandings can and probably will be a part of each activity.) Summarize what you did and how the various activities developed each of the crucial understandings.

Try It Out

Do a shared-writing activity with a group of children. Choose a stimulus from the list that began that section or come up with one of your own. Encourage lots of talking by the children and then let them help you come up with good sentences. Once the piece is written, let children help you read it. What word and letter activities similar to those described under shared reading could you do once the shared writing is completed? Plan your activities to include as many of the critical understandings as you can. Summarize what you did and which of the critical understandings were fostered by the activities.

Listen, Look, and Learn

Visit a classroom for young children. Spend the whole day if possible. Look for evidence of the four emergent literacy-promoting activities. What evidence is there that reading and talking with the children about books is an everyday—more than once a day—occurrence? Are shared reading and shared writing important parts of the daily routine? What evidence is there that children write? Are there lots of writing utensils? Is writing incorporated in center activities? Would you describe the classroom atmosphere as print-rich? Consider all the activities you observe in light of your knowledge about the seven critical understandings. Which of these understandings is most and least promoted by the classroom instruction and environment you observe? What would you change if you were suddenly the teacher in this classroom?

References

Adams, M. J. (1990). *Beginning to read: Thinking and learning about print.* Cambridge, MA: MIT Press.

Allen, R. V., & Allen, C. (1966). *Language experiences in reading: Teachers' resource book.* Chicago: Encyclopaedia Britannica Press.

Chomsky, C. (1971). Write first, read later. *Childhood Education, 46,* 296–299.

Harste, J. E., Woodward, V. A., & Burke, C. L. (1984). *Language stories and literacy lessons.* Portsmouth, NH: Heinemann.

Heath, S. B. (1982). What no bedtime story means: Narrative skills at home and school. *Language and Society, 11(2)*, 49–76.

Henderson, E., & Beers, J. W. (Eds.). (1980). *Developmental and cognitive aspects of learning to spell: A reflection of word knowledge.* Newark, DE: International Reading Association.

Henderson, E., & Templeton, S. (1986). A developmental perspective of formal spelling instruction through alphabet, pattern, and meaning. *Elementary School Journal, 86,* 305–316.

Morphett, V., & Washburne, C. (1931). When should children begin to read? *Elementary School Journal, 31,* 495–503.

Read, C. (1971). Pre-school children's knowledge of English phonology. *Harvard Educational Review, 41,* 1–34.

Read, C. (1975). *Children's categorization of speech sounds in English.* Urbana, IL: National Council of Teachers of English.

Roser, N., & Martinez, M. (1985). Roles adults play in preschoolers' response to literature. *Language Arts, 62,* 485–490.

Routman, R. (1991). *Invitations.* Portsmouth, NH: Heinemann.

Stauffer, R. G. (1980). *The language-experience approach to the teaching of reading,* 2nd ed. New York: Harper & Row.

Sulzby, E., & Teale, W. (1991). Emergent literacy. In R. Barr, M. Kamil, P. Mosenthal, & P. D. Pearson (Eds.), *Handbook of reading research* (vol. 2, pp. 727–757). White Plains, NY: Longman.

Taylor, D. (1983). *Family literacy.* Portsmouth, NH: Heinemann.

Teale, W. H., & Sulzby, E. (Eds.). (1986). *Emergent literacy: Writing and reading.* Norwood, NJ: Ablex.

Children's Books/Materials Cited

Are You My Mother? by P. D. Eastman, Random House, 1960.
The Bear Scouts, by S. Berenstain & J. Berenstain, Random House, 1967.
Best Word Book Ever, by R. Scarry, Golden Press, 1980.
Brown Bear, Brown Bear, What Do You See? by B. Martin, Jr., Holt, Rinehart & Winston, 1970.
Goodnight Moon, by M. Brown, Holt, Rinehart & Winston, 1969.
Hattie and the Fox, by Mem Fox, Simon & Schuster, 1988.
Hop on Pop, by Dr. Seuss, Random House, 1987.
The Ocean Alphabet Book, by J. Pallotta, Charlesbridge Publishers, 1991.
One Fish, Two Fish, Red Fish, Blue Fish, by Dr. Seuss, Random House, 1960.
There's a Wocket in My Pocket, by Dr. Seuss, Random House, 1974.

Additional Readings

- These books and chapters give an overview of emergent literacy research findings, as well as some appropriate strategies and activities.

Honig, B. (1996). *Teaching our children to read: The role of skills in a comprehensive reading program.* Thousand Oaks, CA: Corwin Press.

Strickland, D. S., & Morrow, L. M. (Eds.). (1989). *Emergent literacy: Young children learn to read and write.* Newark, DE: International Reading Association.

- This article explains the theoretical basis for the importance of phonemic awareness to reading development and suggests appropriate instructional activities.

  Lundberg, I., Frost, J., & Petersen, O. P. (1988). Effects of an extensive program for stimulating phonological awareness in preschool children. *Reading Research Quarterly, 23,* 264–284.

- Kindergartens that foster emergent literacy are the focus of these two practical books.

  Fisher, B. (1991). *Joyful learning: A whole language kindergarten.* Portsmouth, NH: Heinemann.

  Walmsley, B. B., Camp, A. M., & Walmsley, S. A. (1992). *Teaching kindergarten: A developmentally appropriate approach.* Portsmouth, NH: Heinemann.

- Reading Recovery is a highly successful tutoring program for young children who experience difficulty in beginning reading and writing. These books describe the Reading Recovery instruction and assessment as well as a holistic theory of emergent literacy.

  Clay, M. M. (1991). *Becoming literate: The construction of inner control.* Portsmouth, NH: Heinemann.

  Clay, M. M. (1993). *An observation survey: Of early literacy achievement.* Portsmouth, NH: Heinemann.

  Clay, M. M. (1993). *Reading recovery: A guidebook for teachers in training.* Portsmouth, NH: Heinemann.

  DeFord, D. E., Lyons, C. A., & Pinnell, G. S. (1991). *Bridges to literacy: Learning from reading recovery.* Portsmouth, NH: Heinemann.

  Fountas, I. C., & Pinnell, G. S. (1996). *Guided reading: Good first teaching for all children.* Portsmouth, NH: Heinemann.

Fluency

Looking Ahead

Fluency is the ability to read most words in context quickly, accurately, automatically, and with appropriate expression. Fluency is critical to reading comprehension because of the attention factor. Our brains can attend to a limited number of things at a time. If most of our attention is focused on decoding the words, there is little attention left for the comprehension part of reading—putting the words together and thinking about what they mean. When children are just beginning to read, their reading cannot be fluent because they must pause to identify each word. To become fluent readers, children must learn to recognize high-frequency words immediately and automatically, engage in some repeated reading of text, and do lots of easy reading.

When you are reading or writing, your brain is busy constructing meaning and is simultaneously identifying or spelling words. Most of the time, you don't even know that you are identifying or spelling words because you have read or written these words so many times that their identification and spelling has become "automatic." Automatic means without any conscious effort or thought. The concept of automaticity is critical to your understanding of the words-meaning construction relationship because your brain can carry out many automatic functions simultaneously (perhaps you have some background music on right now and are listening automatically as you identify words automatically too), but the brain can do only one nonautomatic function. Meaning construction is the nonautomatic function. When your brain is stopped by a word you can't immediately and automatically identify or spell, the brain's attention is diverted from meaning to words. In order to read and write fluently, readers and writers must be able to recognize and spell the vast majority of the words immediately. This chapter contains four key ideas:

1. Fluency is a bridge between word identification and comprehension.
2. Children must become automatic at reading and spelling high-frequency words.
3. Fluency develops as children engage in various types of repeated readings.
4. Children become fluent readers and writers when they do lots of reading and writing throughout the school day.

Fluency Is a Bridge between Word Identification and Comprehension

As you learned in Chapter 1, reading is a complex behavior that builds on language and requires both and promotes thinking. Listening also builds on language and requires and promotes thinking. Reading differs from listening, however, because you must also identify the printed words and translate them into their spoken component. The words in the next sentence are written backwards. Read this sentence aloud and think about how you sound as you read it:

ouy t'nac dear yltneulf nehw lla rouy troffe si deriuqer ot yfitnedi eht sdrow.

You can read the sentence but you can't read it fluently. You read it slowly, one word at a time, and your reading lacks expression and phrasing. To understand what the sentence means, you would probably have to read it once or twice more so that your attention could be freed up from decoding the words and available for comprehending the meaning. Fluency is the ability to identify words quickly and automatically. Fluent reading is not saying one word at a time. Fluent reading puts words together in phrases and has the expression you would use if you were speaking the words. Fluency is a bridge between word identification and comprehension.

Developing fluency needs to be one of the major goals of a balanced literacy program. When children are first starting to read, their reading is apt not to be fluent. They must stop at almost all the words and take a second or two to recognize the word or figure it out. It is important when children are beginning to read that the text they are reading contain words they have already seen many times and can recognize instantly. In English, words such as *in, and, the, have, they* and many others occur in almost every text we read. These words are called "high-frequency" words because they occur so often in everything we read. To read fluently, children need to recognize these high-frequency words instantly.

In addition to making sure that children are learning to recognize high-frequency words, we must also make sure that the first texts children read do not contain too many words and that important words are repeated. A child reading a book about bikes would have to stop and identify the words *bike, helmet, handle-*

bars, and similar bike-connected words the first few times these words were encountered. By the end of the book, however, the child would probably be able to identify these words quickly. Because children learn to recognize words that are repeated more rapidly as they encounter them several times, children's reading of the second half of books is usually more fluent than their reading of the first half.

Rereading is critical for the development of fluency. Teachers of beginning readers use activities such as choral and echo reading and other rereading techniques to ensure that children reread text several times. The first time they may read word by word, but by the time children have read something several times, their reading is usually fluent—words are identified quickly and automatically and read with appropriate phrasing and expression.

Children also become fluent readers by reading and rereading lots of easy books. Most children who have favorite books at home in their own personal libraries read these books over and over. This rereading of favorite books contributes greatly to the development of fluency, and teachers of beginning readers need to provide time for children to read and reread favorite books as part of the school day.

Fluency is also important for writing. When you are writing, you have many things to think about, including what you want to say, how to begin, what the best words are, when you are at the end of a sentence, and what kind of punctuation that sentence needs. These and many other decisions vie for the attention of every writer. Writers also have to decide how to spell the words they have chosen to represent the ideas they want to convey. For young writers, "How do you spell it?" takes a lot of their attention. Any attention or energy devoted to thinking about how to spell words takes attention away from all the other things writers must juggle. Being able to spell high-frequency words automatically is as important to fluent writing as being able to recognize these words instantly is to fluent reading.

The classroom that helps all children develop fluency is one in which attention is paid to high-frequency words, there are many and varied opportunities for rereading, and a great deal of reading and writing is done throughout the school day. The remainder of this chapter will describe practical activities for making sure these goals are met, thus developing fluent readers and writers.

Did You Know That?

By the end of first grade, the average child reads about sixty to ninety words per minute (wpm) when reading material at first-grade level. Average reading rates increase across grade levels and are estimated as follows:

> *Grade 1 = 60–90 wpm*
> *Grade 2 = 85–120 wpm*
> *Grade 3 = 115–140 wpm*
> *Grade 4 = 140–170 wpm*
> *Adult = 250–300 wpm**

*These estimates are from Harris and Sipay (1990).

Children Must Become Automatic at Reading and Spelling High-Frequency Words

In order to read and write, children must learn to recognize and spell the most common words quickly and automatically. These are usually meaningless, abstract, connecting words (*of, and, the, is,* etc.). Children use these words in their speech, but they are not aware of them as separate entities. Read these sentences in a natural speech pattern and notice how you pronounce the italicized words.

> *What do* you see?
>
> I want that piece *of* cake.
>
> What are *they*?

In natural speech, the *what* and the *do* are slurred together and sound like "wudoo." The *of* is pronounced like "uh." The *they* is tacked on to the end of *are* and sounds like "ah-thay." All children use the very frequent words such as *what, of,* and *they* in their speech, but they are not as aware of these words as they are of the more concrete, tangible ones such as *want* and *pie.* To make learning to read and write even more difficult, many of these high-frequency words are not spelled in a regular, predictable way. *What* should rhyme with *at, bat,* and *cat. Of* should be spelled *u-v. They,* which clearly rhymes with *day, may,* and *way,* should be spelled the way many children do spell it: *t-h-a-y.*

Given that most frequent words are meaningless, abstract, and therefore not recognized by children as separate words, together with the fact that many of these words are irregular in spelling and pronunciation, it is a wonder that any children ever learn to identify and spell them! In order to read and write fluently, however, children must learn to recognize them instantly and spell them automatically.

Did You Know That?

Ten words—the, of, and, a, to, in, is, you, that, and it—account for almost one-quarter of all the words children read and write. Half the words can be accounted for by just over 100 words!

Since these words occur so often, children who read and write will encounter them in their reading and need to spell them as they write. Many teachers have found it effective to display the high-frequency words in a highly visible spot in their classrooms and provide daily practice with these words. Teachers often refer to the place where the words are displayed as their word wall (Cunningham, 2000).

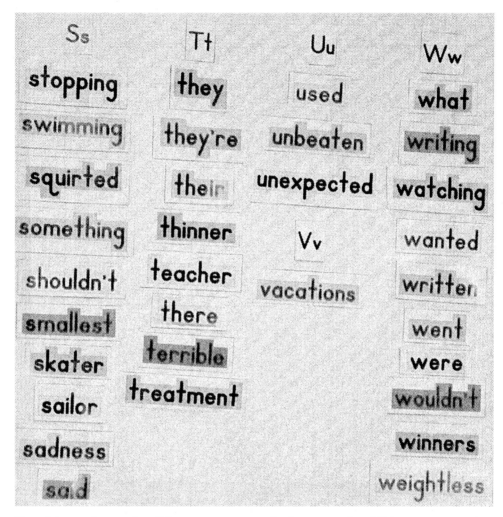

Here is part of a word wall from an upper-grade classroom. In addition to commonly misspelled words, this teacher has included words with common prefixes and suffixes.

How to Do a Word Wall

Select five words each week and add them to a wall or bulletin board in the room. The selection of the words varies from classroom to classroom, but the selection principle is the same. Include words that students will need often in their reading and writing and that are easily confused with other words. First-grade teachers who are using a reading series often select some high-frequency words taught in that series. Others select high-frequency words from Big Books or trade books that they are reading to children or that the children themselves are reading. After reading and enjoying *Brown Bear, Brown Bear, What Do You See?* (Martin, 1970), a first-grade teacher added the high-frequency words *what, do, you, see,* and *at* to the classroom word wall. Children knew these words from the *Brown Bear* book and used them frequently in their own writing.

Another way to know which words to put on the wall is to look in the first-draft writing of the children for commonly misspelled words. A look at the writing of some typical third-graders will often find these common misspellings: *thay, peeple, waznt,* and *freind,* along with confusions about homophones such as *their/there/they're, to/too/two,* and *wood/would.* Add words to the wall gradually, no more than five per week. Write the words on different-colored pieces of paper with a thick black permanent marker. Place the words on the wall next to the alphabet letter they begin with.

Word Wall Activities

Most teachers add five new words each week and do at least one daily activity in which the children find, write, and chant the spelling of the words. The activity takes longer on the day you add words, because you will want to take time to make sure students associate meanings with the words, and to point out how the words are different from words they may be confused with. Many teachers also do a hand-writing lesson with the five words on the day these words are added.

To do the daily practice, have students number a sheet of paper from one to five. Next, call out the five words, putting each word in a sentence. As you call out each word, have a child find and point to that word and have all the children clap and chant its spelling before writing it. When the children have written all five words in a numbered list, point to the words and have volunteers spell each word as students check and fix their own papers.

On the day you add words, call out the five new words. During the rest of the week, however, call out any five words from the wall. You should call out words the children need to practice a great deal almost every day. In addition to calling out five words and having the children chant, write, and check them, many teachers do an additional two-minute on-the-back activity with the words. Children who have written the wall words *go, want, look, ride,* and *talk* on the front may be asked to write the words *going, wanted, riding, looked,* and *talking* on the back. This provides practice with endings and required spelling changes. Children who have written the wall words *big, ride, night, nice,* and *came* on the front may be asked to write the rhyming words *twig, flight, slide, twice,* and *shame* on the back. This activity helps the children to see that words you know can help you spell rhyming words, which often have the same spelling pattern.

Word Walls Support Fluent Reading and Writing

Children who write *motorcycle* as *motrsikl* are not in danger of spelling *motorcycle* that way forever because they don't need to write the word *motorcycle* too often.

Unlike *motorcycle,* however, words like *they,* which children spell *thay,* are written so often that if they misspell them initially, many children become automatic at spelling them incorrectly. Things become automatic if you do them over and over until they require none of your conscious attention. Words on the wall are words we don't want children to invent-spell, and in most classrooms the rule is, "If it's up on our word wall, we have to spell it correctly!"

Once you have a word wall growing in your room, your students are sure to use it as they are reading and writing. You will see their eyes quickly glance to the exact spot where a word they want to write is displayed. Even when children are reading, they will sometimes glance over to the word wall to help them remember a particularly troublesome word.

about	from	my	then
after	fun	new	there (here)
again	get	night	they
all	girl	no	thing
am	give	not	this
an	go	now	time
and	good	of	to
are	had	off	too (too late)
at	has	old	two (2)
be	have	on	up
because	he	one	us
been	her	or	very
before	here	other	want
best	him	our	was
big	his	out	we
boy	house	over	went
but	how	people	were
by	I	play	what
call	if	ride	when
can	in	said	where
can't	into	saw	which
come	is	see	who
could	it	she	why
day	like	so	will
did	little	some	with
do	look	talk	won't
don't	made	tell	would
down	make	than	you
each	many	that	your
find	may	the	
for	me	their	
friend	more	them	

125 High-Frequency Words Often Found on Primary Word Walls (with clues to distinguish homophones)

about	excited	probably	very
again	favorite	really	want
almost	first	right (wrong)	was
also	friends	said	wear (t-shirt pic)
always	getting	school	weather (rain pic)
another	have	something	we're (we are)
anyone	hole (donut pic)	sometimes	went
are	I'm	terrible	were
because	into	that's	what
before	it's	their	when
buy (sell)	its	then	where
by	knew	there (here)	whether
can't	know	they	who
could	laugh	they're (they are)	whole
didn't	let's	thought	with
doesn't	maybe	threw (caught)	won
don't	myself	through	won't
enough	new (old)	to	wouldn't
especially	no (yes)	too (too late)	write
everybody	off	trouble	your
everyone	one (1)	two (2)	you're (you are)
everything	our	until	
except	people	usually	

90 High-Frequency Commonly Misspelled Words Often Found on Intermediate Word Walls (with clues to distinguish homophones)

A word wall provides children with an immediately accessible spelling dictionary for the most troublesome words. Because these words are added gradually, stay in the same spot forever, are alphabetical by first letter, are visually distinctive by different colors of paper, and are reinforced with daily practice, most children learn to read and spell almost all of them. Because the words you selected are needed constantly in reading and writing, children learn to recognize them automatically and can then devote their attention to less frequent words and to constructing meaning as they read and write.

Accommodations and Adaptations to Teach High-Frequency Words

FOR INCLUSION

Some children have a great deal of difficulty learning the function words, particularly the confusable ones such as *that, they, them, then, with, will, of, for,* and *from.*

"The Drastic Strategy" (Cunningham, 1980) summarized here was developed for teaching these hardest-to-learn words.

Step 1: Select a function word and write it on a vocabulary card for each child. Locate a story for storytelling, or spontaneously create a story, in which you use the word many times. Before you begin your story, instruct the children to hold up their card every time they hear the word printed on their card. As you tell the story, pause briefly each time you come to the word in the text.

Step 2: Ask children to volunteer to make up a story using the word on their card. Listeners should hold up their card each time they hear their classmate use the function word.

Step 3: Ask the children to study the word on their card. Next, go around to all the children and cut the word into letters (or have them do it for themselves). Have the children try to arrange the letters to make the word. Check each child's attempt for accuracy. They should mix up the letters and try to make the word again several times. Each child should be able to do this before moving on to the next step. Put the letters into an envelope and write the word on the outside. Children should be encouraged to practice making the word during free time.

Step 4: Write the word on the chalkboard and ask children to pretend their eyes are like a camera and to take a picture of the word and put it in their mind. Have them close their eyes and try to see it in their mind. Next, they should open their eyes and check the board to see if they correctly imagined the word. They should do this three times. The last activity is for them to write the word from memory after the chalkboard has been erased and check their spelling when it is rewritten on the chalkboard. This should be repeated three times.

Step 5: Write several sentences on the board containing a blank in place of the word under study. As you come to the missing word in the sentences, invite a child to come to the board and write the word in the blank space provided.

Step 6: Give children real books or text in which the function word appears. Ask them to read through the story, and whenever they find the word being studied, they should lightly underline (in pencil) the new word. When they have done this, read the text to them, and pause each time you come to the word so that the students may read it.

❉ ❉

Fluency Develops as Children Engage in Various Types of Repeated Readings

One of the major ways in which we become fluent readers is to read something over several times. The first time, a lot of our attention is on identifying the words. The second time, we are able to read in phrases as our brain puts the phrases together into meaningful units. The third time, we read more rapidly, with good expression, and in a seemingly "effortless" way. There are a variety of ways to include repeated readings as part of your classroom routines. In this section, we will describe five ways many teachers have found work well with children across the elementary grades: echo reading, choral reading, timed repeated reading, paired repeated reading, and taped reading/listening.

Echo Reading

One teacher had been doing echo reading for months when a child suddenly asked, "What's an echo?" When the teacher tried to explain it, he discovered that many children hadn't heard an echo. After some "field research," the teacher located a spot in the auditorium where sound would echo, and the class all got to hear their voices echoing back to them. Echo reading made a lot more sense to them after that, and they tried to "be the echo." It is easy to forget that our children don't know some of the basic concepts we know. If your children haven't heard an echo, you might try to find a place to take them where they can have firsthand experience with echoes.

Echo reading is usually done one sentence at a time. We often do echo reading with short, easy text that has only one sentence on a page. Echo reading is fun to do when the text has different voices. *Brown Bear, Brown Bear* (Bill Martin, Jr., 1970), *Hattie and the Fox* (Mem Fox, 1988), and *I Went Walking* (Sue Williams, 1990) are favorites for echo reading. Echo reading also works well for stories such as *There's an Alligator under My Bed* (Mercer Mayer, 1987) in which one boy is telling the story. We call these stories told in the first-person format, "I" stories. When we echo-read "I" stories, we try to sound the way the voice would sound. When we read,

> When it was time to go to sleep, I had to be very careful because I knew he was there.

we read it in a careful, frightened way. When we read,

> So, I'd call Mom and Dad.

we shout it. When we read,

> I followed him down the stairs.

we whisper it.

Children love to use different voices, and reading "I" stories aloud using an echo-reading format is one of their favorite ways to read. You will be amazed how many "I" stories there are when you start looking for them. Some of our favorites are *My Friend* by Taro Gomi (1990), *One of Three* by Angela Johnson (1991), and *Enzo the Wonderfish* by Cathy Wilcox (1993).

Echo reading is also appropriate for reading plays. We read the whole play in an echo-reading format first, using different voices for the different characters. As we read, we ask children to think about each character and which character they would like to be as we read the play again. We usually move from an echo-reading format into a playschool group format in which the children read their parts in small groups. Children love plays, and teachers tell us they would use more plays if they had multiple copies of easy plays. This is one of the few good uses of copying machines. You can easily take a favorite story of your children and turn it into a play script. All of the fairy tales make good and easy plays. Children love reading and playing *The Little Red Hen, The Gingerbread Man, The Three Pigs,* and *The Three Billy Goats Gruff.* The nice thing about writing out and copying simple scripts for these classic stories is that you can let the children take them home. Make their homework assignment to gather as many actors as they can and read the play at home. Parents love helping with this kind of homework and say they wish they had had homework like that when they were in school.

Choral Reading

Choral reading works best for poetry, refrains, and books with lots of conversation. Either have the whole class read, or assign groups and parts. Teachers use old favorites, including nursery rhymes and finger plays. "Itsy Bitsy Spider," "Five Little Pumpkins," "Rudolph the Red-Nosed Reindeer," and "Peter Cottontail" are naturals for choral reading. Choral reading is a wonderful way to reread books such as *The Lion and the Mouse* and *Brown Bear, Brown Bear,* in which characters talk to each other. Choral reading should be used throughout the grades, because rereading provides children with the practice needed to build fluency and self-confidence.

We are going to illustrate here a variety of choral reading activities with nursery rhymes and traditional poems, chants, and songs. These are all in the public domain—which means that the author is unknown or that they are no longer copyrighted—and thus we can reproduce them in this book. We would also recommend using lots of contemporary poetry, which can be found in poetry collections, reading texts, children's magazines, and at various websites; most of this is copyrighted material that cannot be freely reproduced in this book. Take these ideas and apply them to the wealth of materials you have available to you.

Nursery rhymes and other rhymes and finger plays are naturals for choral reading. Begin by reading the rhyme to the children. You may want to echo-read it with them once or twice. If you have the rhyme in a Big Book, use that. If not, reproduce it on a chart. After reading it together, children enjoy pantomiming the rhymes while other children read them.

Humpty Dumpty
Humpty Dumpty sat on a wall.
Humpty Dumpty had a great fall.

All the king's horses and all the king's men
Couldn't put Humpty together again!

For "Humpty Dumpty," you might have your children simply count off—1-2-3-4-5—
and then get together by numbers. Read the rhyme five times; each time a different-
numbered group reads a line or acts it out. Attach sticky notes to the lines, and
change the number each time. The first time, put the sticky notes in order. Everyone reads the title. Then, the children in the "1" group read the first line, those in
the "2" group read the second line, those in the "3" group read the third line, those
in the "4" group read the fourth line, and the "5" group acts it out. Move the sticky
notes five times, and everyone will get to read each line and act it out. Quick, easy,
fun, and fair! The same count-off procedure (with one group for each line plus the
actors) will work nicely for "Jack and Jill"; "Hickory, Dickory, Dock"; "Little Jack
Horner"; "Hey Diddle Diddle"; "Hop, Hop, Hop"; and many other short rhymes.
Children's fluency is built as they read the lines of the poem several times.

With longer rhymes and poems, you may want to assign children to verses
rather than lines. We always begin by reading the poem to them and then having
them read it with us several times. Then we assign reading parts and a pantomiming group. Counting off and letting each numbered group read every verse and be
the actors works well with most rhymes that have actions you can pantomime.
Count off by fives to read and pantomime "The Squirrel."

> ***The Squirrel***
> Whisky, frisky,
> Hippety hop,
> Up he goes
> To the tree top.
>
> Whirly, twirly,
> Round and round,
> Down he scampers
> To the ground.
>
> Furly, curly
> What a tail!
> Tall as a feather
> Broad as a sail!
>
> Where's his supper?
> In the shell,
> Snappity, crackity,
> Out it fell.

Once you get into "choreographing" your choral readings, you will find it easy
to assign parts. For "Five Little Monkeys," put the children in groups of five. The
first time you do the rhyme, call up one group of five to be the monkeys, assign an-

other group to say the doctor's lines, and have the rest of the children read all the other lines. Continue until all the groups have gotten to be monkeys and doctors.

Five Little Monkeys
Five little monkeys jumping on the bed.
One fell off and bumped his head.
Momma called the doctor and the doctor said,
"No more monkeys jumping on the bed!"

Four little monkeys jumping on the bed.
One fell off and bumped his head.
Momma called the doctor and the doctor said,
"No more monkeys jumping on the bed!"

Three little monkeys jumping on the bed.
One fell off and bumped his head.
Momma called the doctor and the doctor said,
"No more monkeys jumping on the bed!"

Two little monkeys jumping on the bed.
One fell off and bumped his head.
Momma called the doctor and the doctor said,
"No more monkeys jumping on the bed!"

One little monkey jumping on the bed.
He fell off and bumped his head.
Momma called the doctor and the doctor said,
"No more monkeys jumping on the bed!"

No little monkeys jumping on the bed.
None fell off and bumped his head.
Momma called the doctor and the doctor said,
"Put those monkeys back in bed!"

For "The Ants Go Marching," give your children index cards numbered 1 through 10, with each number written once little and once normal size. The child with the little number will be the one who does the action each time. So the child with the little "1" will jump and run, the child with the little "2" will tie his shoe . . . and the child with the little "10" will shout "The End!" All the children read until it is their turn to join the march. As everyone reads, the two ants designated "1" march in and the child with the little "1" does the appropriate action. Then the two designated "2s" join them as everyone else reads. Then the two "3s" join in, and so on until you have twenty marching ants. By now, you won't have very many readers! Have the pairs switch cards so that the other marching partner is now the little one and do it again. If you are fortunate enough to have less than twenty children, designate a stuffed animal to be one of the numbers that does not have an action, and let the partner number march it in. If you have more than twenty, do the whole thing again, letting those who didn't get numbers the first time pick their numbers and then letting some children do it again.

To save space and time in writing this, write the first verse on a chart and then write the parts that change—two by two; three by three . . . to jump and run, to tie his shoe . . . on sentence strips and cut to fit. Have the readers stop after each verse and wait for you to insert the appropriate words.

The Ants Go Marching

The ants go marching one by one.
   Hurrah! Hurrah!
The ants go marching one by one.
   Hurrah! Hurrah!
The ants go marching one by one;
   the little one stops to jump and run,
And they all march down into the ground.
   Boom, boom, boom!

The ants go marching two by two.
   Hurrah! Hurrah!
The ants go marching two by two.
   Hurrah! Hurrah!
The ants go marching two by two;
   The little one stops to tie his shoe,
And they all march down into the ground.
   Boom, boom, boom!

The ants go marching three by three.
   Hurrah! Hurrah!
The ants go marching three by three.
   Hurrah! Hurrah!
The ants go marching three by three;
   The little one stops to catch a bee,
And they all march down into the ground.
   Boom, boom, boom!

The ants go marching four by four.
   Hurrah! Hurrah!
The ants go marching four by four.
   Hurrah! Hurrah!
The ants go marching four by four;
   The little one stops to jump and roar,
And they all march down into the ground.
   Boom, boom, boom!

The ants go marching five by five.
   Hurrah! Hurrah!

The ants go marching five by five.
　Hurrah! Hurrah!
The ants go marching five by five;
　The little one stops to jump and dive,
And they all march down into the ground.
　Boom, boom, boom!

The ants go marching six by six.
　Hurrah! Hurrah!
The ants go marching six by six.
　Hurrah! Hurrah!
The ants go marching six by six;
　The little one stops to pick up sticks,
And they all march down into the ground.
　Boom, boom, boom!

The ants go marching seven by seven.
　Hurrah! Hurrah!
The ants go marching seven by seven.
　Hurrah! Hurrah!
The ants go marching seven by seven;
　The little one stops to chase a hen,
And they all march down into the ground.
　Boom, boom, boom!

The ants go marching eight by eight.
　Hurrah! Hurrah!
The ants go marching eight by eight.
　Hurrah! Hurrah!
The ants go marching eight by eight;
　The little one stops to roller-skate,
And they all march down into the ground.
　Boom, boom, boom!

The ants go marching nine by nine.
　Hurrah! Hurrah!
The ants go marching nine by nine.
　Hurrah! Hurrah!
The ants go marching nine by nine;
　The little one stops to read a sign,
And they all march down into the ground.
　Boom, boom, boom!

The ants go marching ten by ten.
　Hurrah! Hurrah!
The ants go marching ten by ten.
　Hurrah! Hurrah!

The ants go marching ten by ten;
The little one stops to shout
"THE END!!"

Choral reading of songs, rhymes, poems, and finger plays is an enjoyable activity for teacher and students. More important, it provides children with opportunities for repeated readings, which help build reading fluency. Just as for echo reading, many teachers duplicate the choral-reading material read in class for children to take home for homework. Rounding up family and friends to do choral reading at home is a homework assignment that is generally appreciated by all involved.

Taped Reading/Listening

Another way teachers provide opportunities for children to do repeated readings is to provide children with opportunities to read along with an audiotape of a book or story. There are lots of variations on this activity and lots of different names for it, including imitative reading, tape-assisted reading, and automated reading. Regardless of what it is called, the procedures are similar. Material is chosen that is at or near the instructional level of the reader. The child listens to and reads along with the tape as many times as it takes until the child can read it fluently without the aid of the tape. Then another book is chosen and the child listens/reads this book until fluent with it. Several students can participate in taped listening/reading simultaneously, each one with a different book. The limit is defined by how many tape recorders are available.

Dowhower (1989) describes how several schools in Madison, Wisconsin, used taped listening/reading as part of their reading program. The libraries had a large collection of books and audiotapes. Children went to the library to select their books. Before checking out the book/tape, the child read a short selection of the book to the librarian, teacher, or library aide. Children were shown how to choose books that were not too easy and not too hard. If the book was too easy, the child would already be able to read it fluently and this would defeat the purpose of the taped listening/reading activity. On the other hand, if the book was too hard, the child would not be able to achieve the goal of fluent reading after a reasonable number of times listening and reading along. The criterion used in the Madison schools was at least 85 percent accuracy of word identification on the tryout selection or the book was too hard.

Two important factors in the success of the Madison taped listening/reading program were that the children chose the books they wanted to learn to read fluently and that they were only allowed to practice with "just right" books. In Chapter 1 we saw how important success is to motivation and engagement. When children choose the books they want to be able to read fluently and are helped to choose a book they can succeed with, they are motivated to persevere and achieve the goal of reading the book fluently. This success in turn motivates them to approach the next book with enthusiasm and confidence.

Timed Repeated Reading

For timed repeated reading, a passage of probable interest to the student that is also at the student's instructional level is used. The passage should be short, no more than 150 words. Give the student the passage and tell him or her to read it silently and to get ready to read it orally with few errors and at a comfortable rate. Have the student read the passage to you after reading it silently, count the oral reading errors (the three most frequently occurring errors are words left out, words changed, and words added in), and time the reading. If the student made more than ten errors per hundred words, the passage is too difficult to use, and an easier one should be chosen. If there were fewer than ten errors per hundred words, help the reader correct the errors and tell him or her the time it took to read it. Next, have the reader practice reading the material silently again. Have the reader read the passage to you a second time after some more silent practice, and time the reading again. Once again, do not interrupt the reading, but correct any errors afterwards and tell the reader the time. Repeat this process until the student has read the passage three or four times and can do so fluently.

Many teachers use timed repeated reading with a small group of students. Some students are practicing while others are doing their timed oral reading with the teacher. Timed repeated readings are popular with children who enjoy "beating their time." Children see that rereading can help them read more easily and rapidly and they experience what it feels like to read fluently, rather than in a word-by-word fashion.

Paired Repeated Reading

Another popular technique for providing children with repeated reading practice is to pair children up and have each partner take turns reading the selection. Often the teacher models the reading of the selection first and may include the children in a second reading done in an echo- or choral-reading fashion. Children then read together as partners to "perfect" the reading of the passage. The partners take turns reading the selection, with each partner reading the piece two or three times. The listening partner helps the reading partner with word identification and phrasing. Many teachers partner up struggling readers with more able readers and designate the more capable partner to do the first reading. Even when partnerships are randomly formed, however, children are often able to help each other. They might make an equal number of errors—but they are usually not the same errors! The old adage that "two heads are better than one" is proved over and over in classrooms that partner children up for paired reading.

Often poems, play, or chants are chosen for paired repeated reading. Once the children have practiced reading them in pairs, they enjoy "performing" them for each other or for younger children. Duplicating the material and sending children home to read it to friends and family gives children a chance to "show off" their fluent reading skills.

Accommodations and Adaptations for Fluency

FOR INCLUSION AND CHILDREN ACQUIRING ENGLISH

Cross-Age Tutoring

You probably noticed that in all the techniques suggested for repeated readings, it is important to choose "just right" material for the reader to practice. With older struggling readers, this is easier said than done. After all, older children do not want to read "baby books." Many schools have solved this problem by setting up reading buddy programs in which older children read to younger children. Some of these "buddy" programs have "big kids" paired with kindergarten children. Once a week, the big buddies come to the kindergarten and read a book (which they have practiced ahead of time) to their little buddy. Arranging such a partnership allows your older poor readers to become reading models, but the buddy system also serves another critical function: it legitimizes the reading and rereading of very easy books. Once you have a buddy system set up, you can have the kindergarten teacher send up a basket of books from which each of your "big readers" can choose. Tell them that "professional" readers always practice reading a book several times before reading it to an audience. Then let them practice reading the book—first to themselves, then to a partner in the classroom, and finally to a tape recorder.

Webster Magnet school in Minnesota set up a tutoring program in which older struggling readers tutored younger struggling readers (Taylor, Hansen, Swanson, and Watts, 1998). Fourth-graders who were reading at beginning third-grade level tutored second-graders, most of whom were reading on primer level. The second-graders were all participating in an early intervention program in their classroom in which they read books at their level. The fourth-graders spent forty-five minutes on Mondays and Tuesdays with the reading coordinator or with their classroom teacher preparing for their twenty-five-minute tutoring session on Wednesdays and Thursdays. On Mondays, the fourth-graders selected a picture book to read to their second-graders and practiced reading the book. They also practiced word recognition prompts they would use when their second-grader was reading to them. On Tuesdays, they practiced again and developed extension activities to develop comprehension strategies, including story maps and character sketches. They came up with several good discussion questions based on the picture book they were planning to read.

On Wednesdays and Thursdays, the fourth-graders met with their tutees. During this session, they listened to their second-graders read the book currently being read in their classroom early intervention program. While listening, they helped their second-graders identify words by giving them hints such as, "Look at the picture," "It starts with *pr*," and "Sound it out in chunks. What would this part be (covering all but the first syllable)?" Next, they read the picture book they had chosen, built meaning vocabulary from the book, led a discussion based on their discussion questions, and did the comprehension extension activity.

On Fridays, the fourth-graders had debriefing sessions with their teacher in which they discussed how their tutees reacted to the book, how well their word recognition prompts were working, the success of their discussion and comprehension activities, and the problems they encountered and progress they observed. They also each wrote a letter to project coordinators detailing their successes and problems that week, to which they received a response the following Monday.

Data reported on this project show that both the second- and fourth-grade struggling readers made measurable progress. This is not surprising, because this program combines all of the elements essential for reading growth. Second-graders were getting daily guided-reading instruction in materials at their level in their classrooms. In addition, during the tutoring session, they were reading material at their level to someone who knew how to help them with word recognition. They were also increasing their knowledge stores and comprehension strategies as they listened to their fourth-grade tutors read the picture book to them and engaged in the discussion and comprehension activities. Fourth-graders were getting lots of repeated reading practice in material on their instructional level as they practiced reading the picture book, and they were learning word recognition and comprehension strategies as they prepared and carried out the tutoring with their second-graders.

Cross-age tutoring programs that partner older struggling readers with beginning readers give older children legitimate purposes for rereading easy books. The older children not only gain in reading ability but also in self-esteem and self-confidence. Clever teachers find creative ways to accomplish what needs to be accomplished!

Children Become Fluent Readers and Writers When They Do Lots of Reading and Writing throughout the School Day

Imagine that in this new millennium, when all kinds of technological wonders are being invented and mass-marketed, someone invents a readowritometer. This marvelous device, when implanted in a child's brain, would tally up the number of words that child read or wrote across all the home and school hours—school days and weekends. Imagine that various children had their readowritometers constantly running for their first three years of school. At the end of these three years, the children would all be given a test that would determine how many words they could immediately recognize and how quickly and accurately they figured out how to pronounce and spell unfamiliar words. The number of words read and written would be a strong predictor of each child's word fluency. Children who read and wrote a lot would instantly recognize huge numbers of words and would decode and spell much faster and more accurately than children who read little. The first and most important component of good word instruction is large doses of successful reading and writing. To achieve this, we make four recommendations.

Schedule Time Every Day for Self-Selected Reading

Self-selected reading is a critical daily component of a balanced reading program in any classroom. Some significant amount of time every day in every classroom should be devoted to allowing children to choose something to read and then settling down to read it. Self-selected reading is often promoted in terms of the motivation and interest children develop as they have time to pursue their own interests through books. Remembering from Chapter 1 the big idea that *feeling is the energizer of reading and writing* should convince you that self-selected reading is a critical component of how children develop positive attitudes toward reading. In later chapters, you will find descriptions of ways in which teachers at different grade levels make self-selected reading a daily reality in their classrooms. In the context of this chapter, whose purpose is to describe ways to help children become fluent readers and writers, we want to emphasize that the amount of reading children do is the biggest variable in their word fluency and that children who engage in regular self-selected reading read a lot more than children who don't.

Provide Lots of Time and Opportunities for Writing

In addition to lots of reading, lots of writing helps children become better readers and writers. This is especially true when young children are encouraged to invent-spell the words they need but haven't yet learned to spell. Clarke (1988) compared the decoding ability of children completing first grade and found that those who had been encouraged to invent-spell were better at decoding words than those from classrooms that emphasized correct spelling.

Not surprisingly, children who are explicitly given time to write each day write more than children who aren't. Children who are encouraged to invent-spell words they need as they write have daily opportunities to put to use what they are learning about letters and sounds. Writing is important for many reasons, described in more detail in Chapter 8. In this chapter, we want to point out that in addition to all its other benefits, daily writing helps children become better decoders and spellers.

Coach Children to Use Strategies during Oral Reading

Most of the reading children do should be silent reading in which they focus on understanding and enjoying what they read. It is also helpful and fun for children to read aloud on occasion. Young children like to read aloud, and as they do so, teachers have a chance to see how they are using their strategies and to coach them.

When children read aloud, they always produce a few misreadings. It is these misreadings that allow teachers a "window on the reading process" of the reader, and responding to them gives teachers a chance to coach children into strategic reading. Following are some suggestions for making oral reading an enjoyable and profitable endeavor.

Have Children Read to Themselves before Reading Orally. Making sure that silent reading for comprehension precedes oral reading will help students remember that reading is first and foremost to understand and react to the meaning of the printed words. Young children who are just beginning to read should also read material to themselves or with a partner before reading it orally to a group or the teacher. When beginning readers read, however, it is seldom silent. They don't yet know how to think the words in their minds, and their reading to themselves can be described as "mumble" or "whisper" reading.

Use Easy Material for Oral Reading. Material that students read orally should be sufficiently easy that they will make no more than five errors per hundred words read. If the average sentence length is seven words, this rate would amount to no more than one error every three sentences. It is very important for children not to make too many errors, because their ability to cross-check drops dramatically when they are making so many errors that they can't make sense of the material.

Don't Let Children Correct One Another. Allowing students to interrupt and correct one another inhibits their ability to self-correct and forces them to try for "word-perfect reading." While it might seem that striving for word-perfect reading would be a worthy goal, it is not, because of the way our eyes move when we read.

When you read, your eyes move across the line of print in little jumps. The eyes then stop and look at the words. The average reader can see about twelve letters at a time—one large word, two medium words, or three small words. When your eyes stop, they can see only the letters they have stopped on. The following letters are not visible until the eyes move forward and stop once again. Once your eyes have moved forward, you can't see the words you saw during the last stop. As you read orally, your eyes move out ahead of your voice. This is how you can read with expression, because the intonation and emphasis you give to a particular word can be determined only when you have seen the words that follow it. We call the space between where your eyes are and where your voice is your eye-voice span. Fluent readers reading easy material have an eye-voice span of five to six words.

Good readers read with expression because their voice is trailing their eyes. When they say a particular word, their eyes are no longer on that word but rather several words down the line. This explains something that all good readers do. They make little non–meaning-changing errors when they read orally. They read *can't* when the actual printed words are *can not*. They read *car* when the actual printed word was *automobile*. Non–meaning-changing errors are a sign of good reading!

They indicate that the eyes are out there ahead of the voice, using the later words in the sentence to confirm the meaning, pronunciation, and expression given to previous words. The reader who says *car* for *automobile* must have correctly recognized or decoded *automobile,* or that reader could not have substituted the synonym *car.* However, the word *automobile* can no longer be seen because the eyes have moved on.

Good readers make small non–meaning-changing errors because their eyes are not right on the words they are saying. If other children are allowed to follow along while the oral reader reads, they will interrupt the reader to point out these errors. If children are allowed to correct non–meaning-changing errors, children learn that when reading orally, you should keep your eyes right on the very word you are saying! This fosters word-by-word reading. Too much oral reading with each error corrected by the children or the teacher will result in children not developing the eye-voice span essential to all fluent readers. Constant interruptions by the teacher or other children also prevent the reader from developing appropriate cross-checking strategies and spontaneous self-corrections.

Eliminating interruptions by other children is not easy, but it can be accomplished by having all the children who are not reading put their fingers in their books and close them! In other words, when one child is reading, the others should not be "following along" with the words. Rather, they should be listening to the reader read and "following along with the meaning." Instead of correcting the reader, teach students to say, "I didn't understand that part. Would you read that again?" *Ignore errors that don't change meaning.* Small, non–meaning-changing errors—like "can't" for "can not"—are a sign of good eye-voice span and should not be corrected, even by the teacher!

When the Reader Makes a Meaning-Changing Error—Wait! Control the urge to stop and correct the reader immediately. Rather, wait until the reader finishes the sentence or paragraph. What follows the error is often the information the reader needs in order to self-correct. Students who self-correct errors based on subsequent words read should be praised because they are demonstrating the skill of cross-checking while reading. Students who are interrupted immediately never learn to self-correct. Instead, they wait for someone else to correct them. Without self-correcting and self-monitoring, children will never become good readers.

If Waiting Doesn't Work, Coach for Strategies Needed. If the reader continues beyond the end of the sentence without correcting a meaning-changing error, the teacher should stop the reader by saying something like,

> "Wait a minute. You read, 'Then the magician stubbled and fell.' Does that make sense?"

The teacher has now reinforced a major understanding all readers must use if they are to decode words well. The word must have the right letters and make sense. The letters in *stubbled* are very close to the letters in *stumbled,* but *stubbled* does not make sense. The teacher should pause and see if the reader can find a way to fix it. If so, the teacher should say,

"Yes, *stumbled* makes sense. Good. Continue reading."

If not, the teacher should point out the *m* before the *b,* or suggest a known rhyming word such as *crumbled* or *tumbled.*

Oral reading provides the "teachable moment," a time for teachers to help students use the sense of what they are reading and the letter–sound relationships they know. When teachers respond to an error by waiting until a meaningful juncture is reached and responding first with a "Did that make sense?" question, children focus more on meaning and begin to correct their own errors. The rest of the group hear how the teacher responds to the error. As they listen, they learn how they should use "sense" and decoding skills as they are actually reading. Feedback that encourages readers to self-correct and monitor their own reading sends a "You can do it" message.

Promote Word Fluency in All Subjects

In most elementary classrooms, at least two hours of the instructional day are devoted to reading and the other language arts. During the rest of the day, children study other subjects such as math, science, and social studies. Although we often don't think of it, these content-area subjects provide perfect opportunities to help children build their word fluency skills. In order to read and write in subject areas, they must learn fairly specialized vocabulary. Often, the words to be learned are big words that the children need help learning to recognize and spell. There are many ways teachers can promote word fluency as they teach a variety of topics. Many teachers reserve one of the bulletin boards in their room for use as a topic word board. As they teach science and social studies units, they identify fifteen to twenty-five words that are key to understanding and write these on large index cards with a thick black permanent marker. Rather than overwhelming students by presenting all the words at once, they add three or four each day as these words are introduced. As the words are added to the board, the students chant the spelling (cheerleader-style) of each word. Then they close their eyes and chant the spelling again. Many teachers then have them write one sentence (that makes sense) that uses as many of these words as possible.

Once the words are displayed on the board, the teacher draws students' attention to these words as they occur in reading, lectures, videos, experiments, or discussions. As students write about what they are learning, they are encouraged to use the words and to refer to the board for correct spellings. Students will develop positive attitudes toward learning big words if you point out that every discipline has some critical words, the use of which separates the pros from the amateurs.

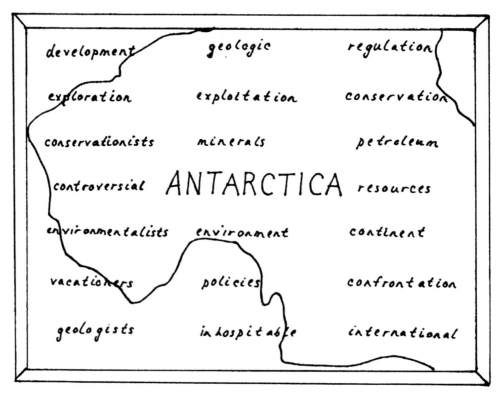

development   geologic   regulation

exploration   exploitation   conservation

conservationists   minerals   petroleum

controversial   ANTARCTICA   resources

environmentalists   environment   continent

vacationers   policies   confrontation

geologists   inhospitable   international

Here is a topic board containing words students will need to read and write about Antarctica.

The Theory and Research
Base for Fluency Instruction

Good readers recognize most words automatically, that is, quickly and with little or no effort, as a unit (Logan, 1997; A. Cunningham, Perry, & Stanovich, 2001; Gustafson, 2001; Lee, Honig, & Lee, 2002). Readers who automatically recognize most words in a text and can simultaneously do the other things that reading requires (J. Cunningham, 1993) are reading that text with *fluency*. Fluency is the ability to read most words in context quickly, accurately, automatically, and with appropriate expression. Fluency is critical to reading comprehension because of the attention factor. Our brains can attend to a limited number of things at a time. If most of our attention is focused on decoding the words, there is little attention left for the comprehension part of reading—putting the words together and thinking about what they mean. The NRP summary explains this relationship between reading comprehension and fluency thus: "If text is read in a laborious and inefficient manner, it will be difficult for the child to remember what has been read and to relate the ideas expressed in the text to his or her background knowledge" (p. 11).

Fluency is not something a reader has or doesn't have. In fact, how fluent a reader you are is directly related to the complexity of the text you are reading. If you are reading a text with lots of words you have read accurately many times before, you probably recognize those familiar words immediately and automatically. All your attention is then available to think about the meaning of what you are reading. If you are reading a text with lots of words you have never encountered in print before, you will have to stop and decode these words in some way—using the letter–sound and morphemic patterns you know to turn the printed letters into sounds and words. In order to comprehend what you have decoded, you may have to reread the text once or even twice so that your attention is freed from decoding and available for comprehending.

In English, approximately 300 words make up 85 percent of the running words in almost all the text we read (Samuels, 2002). Recognizing these high-frequency words accurately and automatically promotes fluent reading. While some practice with these high-frequency words in isolation can help children learn these words, that learning will not necessarily transfer to the ability to read the words in text unless lots of practice in reading interesting and meaningful text is provided (J. Cunningham, Koppenhaver, Erickson, & Spadorcia, in press).

Put Reading First (Armbruster, Lehr, & Osborn, 2001) recommends two activities for increasing reading fluency: reading aloud to children and engaging children in repeated readings of instructional-level text. "By listening to good models of fluent reading, students learn how a reader's voice can help written text make sense. . . . By reading effortlessly and with expression, you are modeling for your students how a fluent reader sounds during reading" (p. 26).

Even more important than the teacher modeling good oral reading is having the children read instructional-level texts more than once to improve how fluently they read them. To accomplish repeated readings without boredom setting in, *Put Reading First* recommends the use of plays and poetry using such formats as adult-then-student reading (echo reading), choral reading, tape-assisted reading, partner reading, and readers' theater. When meaning is emphasized during repeated readings, children can also be taught how to read with better expression (Erekson, 2001).

The amount of reading and writing children do is crucial in helping them recognize and spell high-frequency words immediately, create good models of expressive oral reading, and engage in repeated reading. Samuels (2002) recommends independent, silent reading but emphasizes that if this type of reading is going to increase the amount of reading done by poor readers, teachers should help students with book selection so that they don't choose books that are too hard and stop reading. He also stresses that students should read books they find enjoyable so that they are motivated to read further. Samuels concludes: "Increasing the amount of reading students do is important, because as words are encountered repeatedly there are a number of beneficial outcomes, such as improvements in word recognition, speed, ease of reading, and comprehension" (p. 174). Share (1999) reviewed the research evidence for his contention that self-teaching of word recognition occurs while a reader is decoding words during independent reading and concluded that readers teach themselves to recognize many words as they read for enjoyment.

L o o k i n g   B a c k

Fluency is the ability to read most words in context quickly, accurately, automatically, and with appropriate expression. Fluency is critical to reading comprehension because of the attention factor. When children are just beginning to read, their reading cannot be fluent because they must pause to identify each word. To become fluent readers, children must learn to recognize high-frequency words immediately and automatically, engage in some repeated reading of text, and do lots of easy reading. This chapter discussed four key ideas:

1. Fluency is a bridge between word identification and comprehension.
2. Children must become automatic at reading and spelling high-frequency words.
3. Fluency develops as children engage in various types of repeated readings.
4. Children become fluent readers and writers when they do lots of reading and writing throughout the school day.

Add to Your Journal

This chapter has presented a lot of information, some of which is probably new to you and some of which probably contradicts what you remember about learning to read. Did you realize how important fluency is and that it is a bridge between word identification and comprehension? Did you realize that just a small number of high-frequency words account for most of the words we read and write and that these words often do not follow phonics and spelling patterns? Were you aware of how important rereading is? Did you realize that the amount of reading and writing children do correlates strongly with how fluently they read? Respond to each of the key ideas in this chapter by using some or all of the eight essential thinking processes. What connections, predictions, and generalizations can you make? What images do these key ideas produce? How do you organize all this information? Monitor your own understanding by deciding if there are parts of this chapter about which you are still confused. Evaluate these ideas by deciding what your opinions about fluency instruction are. Most important, how will you apply these ideas to your classroom?

Application Activities

Try It Out

Find a child or a small group of children and try out two of the repeated reading techniques—echo reading, choral reading, taped listening/reading, timed repeated readings, paired repeated reading. Be sure the material you choose is at the "just right" level for your children. Of the two you try, which seems to be more successful with your child/children? What kind of fluency growth could you notice? How did the child/children respond to these techniques?

Listen, Look, and Learn

Interview a teacher at the grade level of your choice and determine what that teacher does about fluency. How does the teacher ensure that children are learning to read and spell high-frequency words automatically? What opportunities for repeated readings are used, and how often are they included in the classroom literacy instruction? For how much of the school day are the children actually engaged in reading and writing?

Do It Together

Talk with other teachers or future teachers at the grade level you teach or plan to teach. Come up with a plan for fluency instruction tailored to your grade level and school system. Be as specific as possible about how you will implement the key ideas described in this chapter.

References

Armbruster, B. B., Lehr, F., & Osborn, J. (2001). *Put reading first: The research building blocks for teaching children to read: Kindergarten through grade 3.* Washington, DC: The Partnership for Reading.

Clarke, L. K. (1988). Invented versus traditional spelling in first graders' writings: Effects on learning to spell and read. *Research in the Teaching of English, 22,* 281–309.

Cunningham, A. E., Perry, K. E., & Stanovich, K. E. (2001). Converging evidence for the concept of orthographic processing. *Reading and writing: An interdisciplinary journal, 14,* 549–568.

Cunningham, J. W. (1993). Whole-to-part reading diagnosis. *Reading and Writing Quarterly, 9,* 31–49.

Cunningham, J. W., Koppenhaver, D. A., Erickson, K. A., & Spadorcia, S. A. (in press). Word identification and text characteristics. In J. V. Hoffman & D. Schallert (Eds.), *Texts, tasks & teaching reading in elementary classrooms.* Mahwah, NJ: Erlbaum.

Cunningham, P. M. (1980). Teaching were, with, what and other "four-letter words." *The Reading Teacher, 34,* 160–163.

Cunningham, P. M. (2000). *Phonics they use,* 3rd ed. New York: Longman.

Erekson, J. A. (2001). Prosody and performance: Children talking the text in elementary school. (Doctoral dissertation, Michigan State University, 2001). *Dissertation Abstracts International, 62,* 947A.

Gustafson, S. (2001). Cognitive abilities and print exposure in surface and phonological types of reading disability. *Scientific Studies of Reading, 5,* 351–375.

Harris, A. J., & Sipay, E. R. (1990). *How to increase reading ability,* 8th ed. New York: Longman.

Lee, C. H., Honig, R., & Lee, Y. (2002). Phonological recoding of mixed-case words in the priming task. *Reading Psychology, 23,* 199–216.

Logan, G. D. (1997). Automaticity and reading: Perspectives from the instance theory of automation. *Reading and Writing Quarterly, 13,* 123–146.

National Reading Panel. (2000). *Teaching children to read: An evidence-based assessment of the scientific research literature on reading and its implications for reading instruction* (National Institute of Health Pub. No. 00-4769). Washington, DC: National Institute of Child Health and Human Development.

Samuels, S. J. (2002). Reading fluency: Its development and assessment. In A. E. Farstrup & S. J. Samuels (Eds.), *What research has to say about reading instruction* (3rd ed., pp. 166–183). Newark, DE: International Reading Association.

Share, D. L. (1999). Phonological recoding and orthographic learning: A direct test of the self-teaching hypothesis. *Journal of Experimental Child Psychology, 72,* 95–129.

Taylor, B. M, Hansen, B., Swanson, K., & Watts, S. (1998). Helping struggling readers in grades two and four: Linking small-group intervention with cross-age tutoring. *The Reading Teacher, 51.*

Children's Books/Materials Cited

Brown Bear, Brown Bear, What Do You See? by Bill Martin, Jr., Holt, Rinehart & Winston, 1970.

Enzo the Wonderfish, by Cathy Wilcox, Ticknor & Fields Books, 1993.

Hattie and the Fox, by Mem Fox, Simon & Schuster, 1988.

I Went Walking, by Sue Williams, Harcourt Brace, 1990.

My Friend, by Taro Gomi, Chronicle Books, 1990.

One of Three, by Angela Johnson, Orchard Books, 1991.

There's an Alligator under My Bed, by Mercer Mayer, E. P. Dutton, 1987.

Additional   Readings

- These sources provide a variety of practical strategies for assessing and developing fluency.
  Allington, R. L. (2001). *What really matters for struggling readers.* New York: Longman.
  Rasinsky, T. V., & Padak, N. D. (2001). *From phonics to fluency.* New York: Longman.

- Reading easy text is critical for the development of reading fluency. This book contains an extensive list of books, their reading levels, and a summary of each.
  Gunning, T. G. (1998). *Best books for beginning readers.* Boston: Allyn & Bacon.

- Word wall activities and grade-level lists of words can be found in these books:

Cunningham, P. M. (2000). *Phonics they use: Words for reading and writing,* 3rd. ed. New York: HarperCollins.

Cunningham, P. M., & Hall, D. P. (1997). *Month by month phonics for first grade.* Greensboro, NC: Carson-Dellosa.

Cunningham, P. M., & Hall, D. P. (1997). *Month by month phonics for upper grades.* Greensboro, NC: Carson-Dellosa.

Cunningham, P. M., & Hall, D. P. (1998). *Month by month phonics for third grade.* Greensboro, NC: Carson-Dellosa.

Hall, D. P., & Cunningham, P. M. (1998). *Month by month phonics for second grade.* Greensboro, NC: Carson-Dellosa.

Phonics and Spelling

English is an alphabetic language. The letters represent sounds. Unlike Spanish, however, in English, one letter does not represent one sound. In English, the sound of letters is determined by the other letters around it. Small words are made up of onsets and rimes. The onsets are all the letters up to the vowel and the rimes are the letters from the vowel to the end of the word. In the word glaze, *the onset is* gl *and the rime is* aze. *Readers decode and spell unfamiliar words by using spelling patterns—onsets and rimes—known from other words. For longer words, the letter patterns are morphemes—roots, prefixes, and suffixes This chapter describes practical activities for helping children learn patterns they can use to decode and spell new words.*

*I*magine that while reading you encounter the word *desufnoc.* When your eyes see the letters of a word you have never seen before, your brain cannot immediately identify that word. You must stop and figure out the word. This figuring out may include figuring out the pronunciation for the word and the meaning for the word. In this case, you can probably pronounce *desufnoc,* but since no meaning is triggered by your pronunciation, this word can't just join the others in working memory and help them construct some meaning to shift to long-term memory. Your reading is "stalled" by the intrusion of this unknown word. You have to either figure out what it is and what it means or continue reading, hoping the other words—the context—will allow you to continue constructing meaning even though you don't know the word *desufnoc.* A bit confused (which of course is *desufnoc* backward), you press forward!

1. Readers use patterns to decode and spell new words.
2. Beginning readers must develop phonemic awareness and learn some letter names and sounds.

3. Children must develop strategies for decoding and spelling unknown words.

4. Knowledge of morphemes is required for multisyllabic words.

Readers Use Patterns to Decode and Spell New Words

In addition to learning to recognize and spell the most frequent words instantly, children must learn how to figure out the pronunciation and spelling of words they do not know. All proficient readers have the ability to look at regular words they have never seen before and assign probable pronunciations. Witness your ability to pronounce these made-up words:

cate   frow   perdap   midulition

Now of course you weren't "reading" because, having pronounced these words, you couldn't construct any meaning. But if you were in the position of most young readers who have many more words in their listening/meaning vocabularies than in their sight-reading vocabularies, you would often meet words familiar in speech but unfamiliar in print. The ability you demonstrated to figure out rapidly the pronunciation of these words unfamiliar in print would enable you to make use of your huge store of words familiar in speech and thus create meaning.

Before we go on, how did you pronounce the made-up word *frow?* Did it rhyme with *cow* or with *snow?* Because English is not a one-sound, one-letter language, there are different ways to pronounce certain letter patterns, but the number of different ways is limited and with real words, unlike made-up words, your speaking vocabulary lets you know which pronunciation to assign.

Not only do readers use their phonics knowledge to read words they have not seen before, this same knowledge enables them to write. If the four made-up words had been dictated to you and you had to write them, you would have spelled them reasonably close to the way we spelled them.

All good readers and writers develop this ability to come up with pronunciations and spelling for words they have never read or written before. Many poor readers do not. When good readers see a word they have never before seen in print, they stop momentarily and study the word, looking at every letter in a left-to-right sequence. As they look at all the letters, they are not thinking a sound for each letter, because good readers know that sounds are determined not by individual letters but by letter patterns. Good readers look for patterns of letters they have seen together before and then search their mental word banks looking for words with similar letter patterns. If the new word is a big word, they "chunk" it, that is, they put letters together to make familiar chunks.

Based on their careful inspection of the letters and their search through their mental bank for words with the same letter patterns, good readers try out a pronunciation. If the first try doesn't result in a word they have heard and stored in their mental word bank, they will usually try another pronunciation. Finally, they produce a pronunciation that they "recognize" as sounding like a real word that they know. They then go back and reread the sentence that contained the unfamiliar-looking word to see if their pronunciation makes sense given the meaning they are getting from the context of surrounding words. If the pronunciation they came up with makes sense, they continue reading. If not, they look again at all the letters of the unfamiliar word and see what else would "look like this and make sense." Imagine a young boy reading this sentence:

The dancer came out and took a bow.

Imagine that he pauses at the last word and then pronounces *bow* so that it rhymes with *low*. Since that is a real word that he remembers hearing, his eyes then glance back and he quickly rereads the sentence. He then realizes, "That doesn't make sense." He studies all the letters of *bow* again and searches for similar letter patterns in his mental word store. Perhaps he now accesses words such as *how* and *now*. This gives him another possible pronunciation for this letter pattern, one that is also recognized as a previously heard word. He tries this pronunciation, quickly rereads, realizes his sentence now "sounds right," and continues reading.

From this scenario, we can infer the strategies this good reader used to successfully decode a word unfamiliar in print:

1. Recognize that this is an unfamiliar word and look at all the letters in a left-to-right sequence.
2. Search your mental store for similar letter patterns and the sounds associated with them.
3. Produce a pronunciation that matches that of a real word that you know.
4. Reread the sentence to cross-check your possible pronunciation with meaning. If meaning confirms pronunciation, continue reading. If not, try again!

Had this word unfamiliar in print been a big word, the reader would have had to use a fifth strategy:

5. Look for familiar morphemes and chunk the word by putting letters together that usually go together in the words you know.

Beginning Readers Must Develop Phonemic Awareness and Learn Some Letter Names and Sounds

You learned in Chapter 2 that phonemic awareness is one of the crucial understandings children must develop if they are to become successful readers and writers. Along with phonemic awareness, children who will become successful readers know some letter names and can tell you the sounds represented by some of these names. When they see the letter *m*, they can tell you its name and make the sound *m* makes—mmmm—or tell you some words they know that begin with the letter *m*, perhaps *mommy* and *McDonalds*.

These three goals—phonemic awareness, letter names, and letter sounds—are the foundation for developing decoding and spelling skills. Many of the activities described in the previous chapter—shared reading, shared writing, and children writing—promote the development of phonemic awareness and the learning of letter names and sounds. This section will describe some other activities that focus specifically on these three critical understandings.

Sing Rhymes and Read Lots of Rhyming Books

Rhymes and jingles have always been a part of early childhood classrooms. Little did we know that while we were reciting "Jack and Jill" and singing about "Five Little Pumpkins Sitting on a Gate," we were helping children develop phonemic awareness. Many children come to school with well-developed phonemic awareness abilities, and these children usually have come from homes in which rhyming chants, jingles, and songs were part of their daily experience. These same chants, jingles, and songs should be a part of every young child's day in the classroom.

Many wonderful rhyming books exist, but because of their potential to develop phonemic awareness, two deserve special mention. Along with other great rhyming books, Dr. Seuss wrote *There's a Wocket in My Pocket* (1974). In this book, all kinds of Seussian creatures are found in various places. In addition to the wocket in the pocket, there is a vug under the rug, a nureau in the bureau, and a yottle in the bottle!

Books Too Good to Miss

Among the many other wonderful rhyming books that can be used to develop phonemic awareness, a few of our favorites are:

Any rhyming book by Dr. Seuss.
"I Can't," Said the Ant, by P. Cameron, Coward, 1961.
Jake Baked the Cake, by B. G. Hennessey, Viking, 1990.
Pretend You're a Cat, by J. Marzollo, Dial, 1990.
Ape in a Cape, by F. Eichenberg, Harcourt, 1952.
Catch a Little Fox, by Fortunata, Scholastic, 1968.
Buzz Said the Bee, by W. Lewison, Scholastic, 1992.
Moose on the Loose, by C. P. Ochs, Carolrhoda, 1991.
Down by the Bay, by Raffi, Crown, 1987.
There's a Bug in My Mug and *My Nose Is a Rose,* by K. Salisbury, K. McClanahan, 1997.

After several readings, children delight in chiming in to provide the nonsensical word and scary creature that lurks in harmless-looking places. After reading the book a few times, it is fun to decide what creatures might be lurking in your classroom. Let children make up the creatures, and accept whatever they say as long as it rhymes with their object:

"There's a pock on our clock!"

"There's a zindow looking in our window!"

"There's a zencil on my pencil!"

Another wonderful rhyming book for phonemic awareness is *The Hungry Thing* (and the sequel *The Hungry Thing Returns,* is equally good for this purpose) by Jan Slepian and Ann Seidler. In the first book, a large friendly dinosaurlike creature (you have to see him to love him) comes to town, wearing a sign that reads,

Feed Me.

When asked what he would like to eat, he responds,

"Shmancakes."

After much deliberation, a clever little boy offers him some pancakes. The Hungry Thing eats them all up and demands

"Tickles."

Again, after much deliberation, the boy figures out he wants pickles. As the story continues, it becomes obvious that the Hungry Thing wants specific foods and that he asks for them by using a rhyme for what he wants. He asks for *feetloaf* and gobbles down the meatloaf. For dessert, he wants *hookies* and *gollipops.*

The Hungry Thing is a delightful book, and in many classrooms, teachers have made a poster-size Hungry Thing, complete with his sign that reads "Feed Me" on one side and "Thank You!" on the other. Armed with real foods or pictures of foods, the children try to feed the Hungry Thing. Of course, he won't eat the food unless they make it rhyme. If they offer him spaghetti, they have to say, "Want some bagetti?" (or zagetti, or ragetti—any silly word that rhymes with spaghetti). To feed him *Cheerios,* they have to offer him *seerios, theerios, or leerios.*

Once you have found some wonderful books with lots of rhyme, follow these steps to ensure that your children are learning to recognize and produce rhymes:

1. Pick a book with lots of rhyme that you think your children will "fall in love with." Read, enjoy, and talk about the content of the book, and let children become thoroughly comfortable and familiar with the book. Remember that children who are lucky enough to own books want books read to them again and again.

2. Once the children are very familiar with the book, reread it again and tell them that the author of this book made it "fun to say" by including lots of rhymes. Read the book, stopping after each rhyme, and have children identify the rhyming words and say them with you.

3. For the next reading, tell children that you are going to stop and have them fill in the rhyming word. Read the whole book, stopping each time and having children supply the rhyming word.

4. The activities in steps 2 and 3 have helped children identify rhymes. We also want children to produce rhymes. Depending on the book, find a way to have children make up similar rhymes. Producing rhymes was what children were doing when they made up rhyming items like "the zencil on the pencil" and tried to feed new things like *"theerios"* to the Hungry Thing.

Recognizing and producing rhymes form two of the critical components of phonemic awareness. Children who engage in these kinds of activities with wonderful rhyming books will develop the concept of rhyme.

Play Blending and Segmenting Games

In addition to hearing and producing rhyme, the ability to put sounds together to make a word—blending—and the ability to separate out the sounds in a word—segmenting—are critical components of phonemic awareness. Blending and segmenting are not easy for many children. In general, it is easier for them to segment off the beginning letters—the onset—from the rest of the word—the rime—than it is to separate all the sounds. In other words, children can usually separate *bat* into *b-at* before they can produce the three sounds *b-a-t*. The same is true for blending. Most children can blend *S-am* to produce the name *Sam* before they can blend *S-a-m*. Most teachers begin by having children blend and segment the onset from the rime and then move to blending and segmenting individual letters.

Many games children enjoy can help them learn to blend and segment. The most versatile is a simple riddle-guessing game. The teacher begins the game by naming the category and giving this clue:

> "I'm thinking of an animal that lives in the water and is a f-ish (or f-i-sh, depending on what level of blending you are working on)."

The child who correctly guesses "fish" gives the next riddle:

> "I'm thinking of an animal that goes quack and is a d-uck (or d-u-ck)."

This sounds simplistic, but children love it, and you can use different categories to go along with units you are studying.

A wonderful variation on this guessing game is to put objects in a bag, let children reach in the bag and stretch out the name of an object they choose, and then call on someone to guess, "What is it?" Choose small common objects you find in the room—a cap, a ball, chalk, a book—and let the children watch you load the bag and help you stretch out the words for practice as you put them in.

Children also like to talk like "ghosts." One child chooses an object in the room to say as a ghost would—stretching the word out very slowly—"dddoooorrr." The child who correctly guesses "door" gets to ghost-talk another object—"bbbooookkk." The ghost-talk game and the guessing game provide practice in segmenting and blending as children segment words by stretching them out and other children blend the words together to guess them.

You can even help children learn to blend and segment words by stretching out their names slowly as you call them to line up, come to the circle, and do other things. You could read the lunch menu to them, stretching out some of their favorite foods such as "cccaaakkkk" and "mmmiiilllkkk." As children stretch out words and blend sounds together to form words, they develop the understanding that sounds are manipulated to form words, an understanding critical to the ability to learn to decode and spell words.

Use Books with Lots of Alliteration and Tongue Twisters

In addition to concepts of rhyme, blending, and segmenting, children must learn what it means that words "start the same." This understanding must be in place before children can make sense of the notion that particular letters make particular sounds. Many children confuse the concept of words beginning or starting with the same sound with the concept of rhyme, so many teachers like to wait until the concept of rhyme is firmly established for most children before focusing on whether or not words begin with the same sound. Just as for rhyme, we would build a lot of our work with words that start the same by choosing wonderful books such as *All about Arthur (an Absolutely Absurd Ape)* by Eric Carle. Arthur, an ape who plays the accordion, travels around the country meeting lots of other musicians—including a bear in Baltimore who plays a banjo and a yak in Yonkers. The classic *Dr. Seuss's ABC,* in which each letter of the alphabet has a sentence such as "Many mumbling mice are making midnight music in the moonlight," is another excellent example of an appealing book that helps children understand what it means to "start the same." In using alliterative books, we would follow the same steps followed with rhyming books:

1. Read and enjoy the book several times.
2. Point out that the author used some "start the same" words to make the book fun to say, and identify these words.
3. Let the children say the "start the same" words with you as you read the book again.
4. Have the children come up with other words that "start the same" that the author could have used on that page.

Books Too Good to Miss

Here are some wonderful tongue-twister books:

Faint Frogs Feeling Feverish and Other Terrifically Tantalizing Tongue Twisters, by L. Obligada, Viking, 1986.

Dr. Seuss's ABC, by T. S. Geisel, Random House, 1963.

The Biggest Tongue Twister Book in the World, by G. Brandeth, Sterling, 1978.

Alphabet Annie Announces an All-American Album, by S. Purviance & M. O'Shell, Houghton Mifflin, 1988.

A Twister of Twists, A Tangler of Tongues, and *Busy Buzzing Bumblebees and other Tongue Twisters,* by A. Schwartz, HarperCollins, 1972.

Six Sick Sheep, by J. Cole, Morrow, 1993.

Animalia, by G. Base, Abrams, 1987.

Some Smug Slug (1996), *Four Foolish Foxes and Fosdyke* (1997), and *Dinorella* (1997), by P. D. Edwards, Harper.

Another source of alliterative words is a book of tongue twisters such as *Faint Frogs Feeling Feverish and Other Terrifically Tantalizing Tongue Twisters.* Once you have read and enjoyed several tongue-twister books, why not create a tongue-twister book for your class. Let the children help you make up tongue twisters, and add two or three to the book each day. Turn the tongue twisters into posters or bind them into a class book and let the children read them with you several times—as slowly as they can and as fast as they can. Help the children understand that what makes tongue twisters hard to say fast is that the words all start the same and you keep having to get your mouth and tongue back into the same place. The same first sound repeated over and over is also what makes them so much fun to say. Here are some to get you started. You and your children can surely make up better ones. Be sure to use children's names from your class when they have the right letters and sounds.

Billy's baby brother bopped Betty.
Carol can catch caterpillars.
David dozed during dinner.
Fred's father fell fifty feet.
Gorgeous Gloria gets good grades.
Hungry Harry hates hamburgers.
Jack juggled Jill's jewelry.
Kevin's kangaroo kicked Karen.
Louie likes licking lemon lollipops.
Mike's mom makes marvelous meatballs.

Naughty Nellie never napped nicely.
Patty prefers pink pencils.
Roger Rabbit runs relays.
Susie's sister sipped seven sodas.
Tom took ten turtles to town.
Veronica visited very vicious volcanoes.
Wild Willis went west.
Yippy yanked Yolanda's yellow yoyo.
Zany Zeb zapped Zeke's zebra.

As you work with books with lots of words that begin the same and tongue twisters, begin by emphasizing the words that start the same. This is the phonemic awareness understanding that underlies phonics knowledge. When your children can tell you whether or not words start with the same sound and can come up with other words that start that way, shift your instruction to which letter makes which sound. You can use the very same books and tongue twisters again, this time emphasizing the sound of the letter. Books with alliteration and tongue twisters can help your children develop the "starts the same" component of phonemic awareness and can help them learn some letter sounds.

Sing the Alphabet Song and Read and Make Alphabet Books

"The Alphabet Song" (sung to the tune of "Twinkle, Twinkle, Little Star") has been sung by generations of children. Children enjoy it, and it does seem to give them a sense of all the letters and a framework in which to put new letters as they learn them. Many children come to school already able to sing the alphabet song. Let them sing it and teach it to everyone else. Once the children can sing the song, you may want to point to alphabet cards (usually found above the chalkboard) as they sing. Children enjoy "being the alphabet" as they line up to go somewhere. Simply pass out laminated alphabet cards—one to each child, leftovers to the teacher—and let the children sing the song slowly as each child lines up. Be sure to hand out the cards randomly so that no one gets to be the *A* and lead the line or has to be the *Z* and bring up the rear every day! You can also teach them to sing the alphabet song to other familiar tunes like "I've Been Working on the Railroad," "This Old Man," "Mary Had a Little Lamb," and "This Is the Way We Wash Our Clothes." Repetition with variety is a basic learning principle.

Lots of wonderful alphabet books are available to read and enjoy. Many of these fit into your themes or units. Research shows that the simple books with not too many words on a page and pictures that most of the children recognize are the most helpful to children in building their letter–sound and letter–name knowledge. Once the book has been read and reread several times, children will enjoy reading it during their self-selected reading time. It is very important that children have time to choose and read books each day, and simple alphabet books

Books Too Good to Miss

Here are a few alphabet books that meet our "not too many words, familiar pictures, kids love to read them" criteria:

The Peek-a-Boo ABC, by Demi, Random House, 1982.
A to Z Sticker Book, by J. Pienkowski, Random House, 1995.
It Begins with an A, by S. Calmenson, Hyperion, 1993.
Alphabet Puzzle, by J. Downie, Lothrop, 1988.
Dr. Seuss's ABC, by T. S. Geisel, Random House, 1963.
The Alphabet Tale, by J. Garten, Random House, 1964.
Easy as Pie, by M. Folsom & M. Folsom, Houghton Mifflin, 1986.
Eating the Alphabet, by L. Ehlert, Harcourt, 1989.
By the Sea: An Alphabet Book, by A. Blades, Kids Can Press, 1985.
The Accidental Zucchini, by M. Grover, Harcourt, 1993.
NBA Action from A to Z, by J. Preller, Scholastic, 1997.

that have been read together provide books children can read on their own before they can read books with more text.

There are too many wonderful alphabet books to name them all here, but a few just have to be mentioned. *The Peek-a-Boo ABC* has little doors that you open. Inside the door to the barn is a bear. A clown appears as you open the door to the car, and lions can be found in the lunchbox. When reading this one with children for the second or third time, we pause before opening each door to see if they remember that it is salami in the sandwich and a watermelon in the whale. Another novel alphabet book that children adore is the *A to Z Sticker Book*. Each page has three or four pictures along with the words, and one word with no picture. On the *d* page, you see the words *donkey, dinosaur* and *dolphins* along with pictures of these. The word *drum* has a space next to it, and you have to find the sticker on the sticker pages in the middle of the book. Stickers peel off and go back to their spots when the book is read, so that the whole process can be done again and again.

Once you and the children have read several alphabet books, you might want to make a class alphabet book and/or have each child make one. Work on a few pages each day, and use all your resources—alphabet books you read to them, things in the room, places children like to eat—to brainstorm a huge list of the possible words for each page. Depending on your class, you may want to put just one word and picture on each page or several words and pictures for each letter. If children are making individual books, let them choose the order in which they will select the letters for the books as well as the words for their pages. They will most often choose the letters they know best first. Knowing that can help teachers identify what it is that children know.

Various pieces of software can help children learn letter names and sounds and develop phonemic awareness. Here are just a few examples of the kind of software currently available. Be sure to be on the lookout for "newer" and "better" because this is a rapidly growing area:

Peet's Talk/Writer (Hartley) and *Special Writer Coach* (Tom Snyder) are word processing programs that say words once they have been typed in. Both provide many opportunities for children to learn letter names and sounds.

The Big Bug Alphabet (Spectrum, Holobyte, 1994) is a CD-ROM in which Buzzy the Bug takes children on an alphabetic trip through a circus. Many wonderful rhyming, alliterative, and alphabet books are available on CD-ROM if you have the technology to use them.

Remember that tape recorders, though low tech, are wonderful ways to provide the multiple readings that many children need to develop phonemic awareness and learn letter names and sounds. As you are reading favorite rhyming, alliterative, and alphabet books, let children chime in with the parts they know. Tape-record the reading; children love to listen to tapes they participated in making.

Alphabet books help children learn letter names and sounds. Children who already know many of the letters and sounds begin reading the simple words and sentences in these books and are launched on their way to successful reading. Finally, alphabet books help children develop their language and concepts as they begin adding more words to their meaning vocabularies.

Establish Key Words for Sounds

Once your children are moving along in their phonemic awareness, have learned many of the letter names, and are beginning to learn some of the sounds, you can help them consolidate this knowledge by deciding with them on one key word to represent each sound. Many publishing companies and reading series include some key words for the common letter sounds, but often children call the word something other than what is intended—"puppy" for *dog* or "bunny" for *rabbit,* for example—and the key words confuse rather than support their learning of letter sounds. Our suggestion is that you work with your class to come up with a key word that works for you. Let all the children have a say in this, and spend some time discussing which word would be most helpful and which word they like best. Remember that "liking something" is very important to young children! You may want to use some of the wonderful examples from alphabet books, some of the names of your children when they are clear examples for the sound, and some favorite foods and places familiar to all your children. For the vowels, you may want two examples—one for each of the common sounds. Try to use "pure" sounds—a word with just *f*, not *fr* or *fl*—because separating these blended sounds is difficult for children in the beginning. Here are the key words one class decided they liked. The names are all names of children in the class or of famous people. Use this as an example of the kind of chart your children might help construct, but remember this only works if the children have ownership in choosing the words and if they like their choices!

A a	apple, ape		N n	nose
B b	boys		O o	octopus, Oprah
C c	cookies		P p	Pizza Hut
D d	dinosaur		Q u	quarter
E e	elephant, Ethan		R r	red
F f	fun		S s	soup
G g	girls		T t	Taco Bell
H h	Hardees		U u	underwear, unicorn
I i	insect, ice cream		V v	Vicki
J j	Jessica		W w	Wendy's
K k	K-mart		X x	x-ray
L l	Latecia		Y y	yellow
M m	McDonald's		Z z	zoo

Accommodations and Adaptations for Phonemic Awareness, Letter Names, and Sounds

FOR INCLUSION

Some children find it very difficult to segment words into sounds. Many teachers have found success using a technique called sound boxes (Elkonin,1973) in which children push chips, pennies, or other objects into boxes as they hear the sounds. In the first lessons, children have a drawing of three boxes.

(continued)

The teacher says familiar words composed of three sounds, such as *cat, sun, dog, pan.* Often children are shown pictures of these objects. After naming each object, the teacher and children "stretch out" the three sounds, distorting the word as little as possible "sssuuunnn." Children push a chip into each box as they say that part of the word. It is important to note here that the boxes represent sounds—phonemes—not letters. *Cake, bike,* and *duck* have three sounds, but four letters. These words would be segmented into three sound boxes. Once children get good at segmenting words with three sounds, they are given a drawing with four boxes, and they stretch out some four-phoneme words such as *truck, crash,* and *nest.*

Sound boxes are used extensively to develop phonemic awareness in children in Reading Recovery™ (Clay, 1985). (Reading Recovery™ is a highly successful one-on-one tutoring program that works with first-graders in the bottom 20 percent of the class.) Once children can push the chips to represent sounds, they can push letter cards into boxes. From the letters *m, b, s, t,* and *a,* the teacher could ask the children to push these letters to spell words such as *sat, bat, mat, bam, Sam, tab, bats, mats, tabs,* and *stab.* Children only work with letters in the sound boxes after they have developed some phonemic awareness and are working on learning letter names and letter sounds. Later on, children actually write the letters in the boxes as they are attempting to spell words they are writing.

Remembering letter names and sounds is particularly difficult for some children. In addition to all the activities already suggested, teachers use a variety of songs and rhythmic activities that help some children remember these letter names and sounds. In some classes, children sing "Old McDonald Had a Farm" and hold up the letters *e, i, e i, o* when they sing this part. They sing, "There was a man who had a dog, and Bingo was his name-o" and hold up the letters as they spell *B-i-n-g o.* The traditional jump-rope song, "A My Name is Alice," can be adapted to both boys and girls, and children can take turns making up verses which all follow a pattern you determine, such as the following:

> B. My name is Bobby.
> My sister's name is Beth.
> We live in Boston and
> We eat beans.

P. My name is Patty.
My brother's name is Peter.
We live in Pennsylvania and
We eat pie.

For two very different but delightful variations on this, see *A My Name Is Alice* (Byars, 1984) and *Alphabet Dreams* (Brown, 1976).

Finally, some children experience a great deal of difficulty with letters such as the lowercase *b* and *d*, which differ only on which side of the line the circle is. Some teachers report that even children who have had b/d confusions for years can get them straight if you teach them to close in the top of the letter they are confusing—lightly with a pencil at first and later in their minds—and see if they have a capital *B*. Children who can visualize the lowercase *b* turned into a capital *B* will have an independent way of determining which letter is which.

FOR CHILDREN ACQUIRING ENGLISH

Alphabet books not only provide children learning English with clear and many examples of English-language letter sounds, but the pictures help children simultaneously learn English vocabulary because they support the word meanings. The same suggestions given for inclusion would also support children learning English. Elkonin boxes help them to hear the unfamiliar sounds of English, and versions of the alphabet song allow them to learn the names of the English alphabet so that they bring a recognition of letter names to other literacy tasks.

Languages differ, and children are tuned into their primary home language sounds and patterns. The more familiar teachers are with the child's primary home language, the more easily they can help the child see relationships that exist between the languages and find the areas that might cause trouble. For example, when teachers know that the Spanish *j* has the English *h* sound, they can help their students with the sounds of both letters. They will know that /j/ is going to be difficult for these students to produce. If you don't know the language, ask for help from someone in your district, the parents (if they know English), or a community member who speaks the language.

Children Must Develop Strategies for Decoding and Spelling Unknown Words

Once children have developed some phonemic awareness and learned some letter names and sounds, they are ready to begin to apply the phonics and spelling to decoding new words they encounter in reading and spelling words they need while writing. This section describes four activities—Using Words You Know, Making

Words, Word Sorting and Hunting, and What Looks Right?—that elementary teachers use to help children develop strategies for decoding and spelling new words.

Using Words You Know

"Using Words You Know" is an activity designed to help students learn to use the words they already know to decode and spell lots of other words. Here are the steps of a "Using Words You Know" lesson.

1. Show students three to five words they know, and have the class pronounce and spell these words. For our sample lesson, we will tell students that some of the ways they travel—including bikes, cars, vans, and trains—can help them spell other words.

2. Divide the board, a chart, or a transparency into four columns and head each column with *bike, car, van,* or *train.* Have students set up the same columns on a piece of paper and write these four words.

3. Tell students that words that rhyme usually have the same spelling pattern. The spelling pattern in a short word begins with the vowel and goes to the end of the word. Underline the spelling patterns *i-k-e, a-r, a-n,* and *a-i-n* and have students underline them on their papers.

4. Tell students that you are going to show them some words and that they should write them under the word with the same spelling pattern. Show them words that you have written on index cards. Let different students go to the board, chart, or transparency and write the words there as all other studentes are writing them on their papers. Do not let the students pronounce the words aloud until they are all written on the board. Help the students pronounce the words by making them rhyme. Here are some words to use.

| pain | Spain | pan | jar | sprain |
| hike | Fran | spike | than | star |

5. Explain to students that thinking of rhyming words can help them spell also. This time you will not show them the words. After you say a word, the students will have to decide which word it rhymes with and then use the spelling pattern to spell it. Here are some words you might pronounce and have them spell:

| strike | stain | clan | hike | far |
| strain | bran | brain | scar | Mike |

6. End this part of the lesson by helping students verbalize that, in English, words that rhyme often have the same spelling pattern, and that good readers and spellers don't sound out every letter but rather try to think of a rhyming word and read or spell the word using the pattern in the rhyming word.

For the second part of the lesson (probably on the next day), use the same four key words and procedures again.

1. Head the board, chart, or transparency with *bike, car, van,* and *train.* Have students head four columns on their paper with these words and underline the spelling patterns. Explain to the students that using the rhyme to help you read and spell words works with longer words too.

2. Show students these words written on index cards and have them write them under the appropriate word. Once the word is written on the board or chart, have them pronounce the word, making the last syllable rhyme:

guitar	motorbike	complain	maintain	orangutan
suntan	dislike	entertain	hitchhike	Superman

3. Now say these words. Have students decide which word the last syllable rhymes with and then use that spelling pattern to spell it. Give help with the spelling of the first part if needed.

Batman	lifelike	restrain	remain	boxcar
unchain	contain	trashcan	hijack	began

4. Again, end the lesson by helping students notice how helpful it is to think of a rhyming word they are sure how to spell when trying to read or spell a strange word.

In doing "Using Words You Know" lessons, we always choose the words students will read and spell. We don't ask them for rhyming words because, especially for the long vowels, there is often another pattern. *Crane, jane,* and *rein* also rhyme with *train,* but we use only words that rhyme and have the same pattern. Later, when your students are quite accustomed to reading and spelling by pattern, do some "What Looks Right?" lessons that will help them determine which pattern to use. You can do "Using Words You Know" lessons with any words children can already read and spell. To plan your lessons, select known words that have lots of rhyming words with the same spelling pattern. A rhyming dictionary, such as *The Scholastic Rhyming Dictionary* (Young, 1994) is a great help in finding suitable rhyming words.

Making Words

"Making Words" (Cunningham, 2000) is a manipulative activity in which children learn how to look for patterns in words, and changing just one letter or where to put a letter changes the whole word. Each "making words" lesson has three parts. First, children manipulate letters to make ten to fifteen words—including a "secret" word made from all the letters. Next, they sort the words into patterns. Finally, they learn how to transfer their phonics knowledge by using rhyming words they have made to decode and spell some other rhyming words.

To plan a "making words" lesson, we begin with the "secret" word. We choose the secret word because it fits in with something we are studying or it has letter patterns we want to work with. The word for this lesson is *Martin.* The children have been learning about famous African Americans, including Martin Luther King, Jr. The words we make from the letters in *Martin* allow us to sort for the *t-r* blend and lots of rhymes. Using the letters in *Martin,* we choose ten to fifteen words that will give us some easy and harder words and several sets of rhymes. We then decide on the order in which words will be made, beginning with short words and building to larger words. We write these words on index cards to use in the sorting/transferring parts of the lesson.

As the children make each word in their holders, we choose one child who has made it correctly to come and make it in the pocket chart. As the lesson begins, the letters **a i m n r t** are in the pocket chart. The children have the same letters and a holder. The teacher leads them to make words by saying:

"Take two letters and make **am.** 'I *am* your teacher.'

"Now, change just one letter and you can spell **at.** 'We are *at* school.'

"Add a letter to make the three-letter word **rat.**

"Now change just one letter and **rat** can become **mat.** 'In kindergarten you slept on your *mat.*' Everyone say **mat.**

"Change a letter again and turn your **mat** into a **man.**

"Now change just one letter and **man** can become **tan.**

"Change **tan** into **ran.**

"Now change one letter and change **ran** into **ram.** 'Our high school's mascot is a *ram.*' Everyone say **ram.**

"Let's make one more three-letter word: **rim.** 'The top edge of something like a glass is called a *rim.*' Everyone say **rim.**

"Now, we are going to make some four-letter words. Add one letter to **rim** and you will have **trim.** Trim is another word for decorate. 'At Christmas, we *trim* the tree.' Stretch out the word **trim** and listen to the sounds you hear yourself saying.

"Change **trim** to **tram.** 'You can ride in a *tram.*' Everyone say **tram.**

"Take all your letters out and start over and make another four-letter word: **main.** You can only hear three sounds in **main** but it takes four letters to spell it. Think about what letter you can't hear and where to put it.

"Now change just one letter and **main** can become **rain.**

"Now, let's make a five-letter word. Add just one letter to **rain,** and you will have a **train.**

"Has anyone figured out the secret word? I will come around to see if anyone has the secret word."

Children often have trouble figuring out the secret word when it is a name—even though all their letters have a capital letter on one side. For this lesson, no one had figured out the secret word and the teacher gave them a hint:

"It's the name of one of the African Americans we have been studying."

Several children quickly figured out their letter could spell **Martin,** and a child who had spelled it correctly—with a capital M—in her holder went up and made it with

In the pocket chart are all the words made from the word *spider*. As children make words in their little holders, one child comes to the pocket chart and makes it with the big letters.

the pocket chart letters. Then everyone made **Martin** in their holders to finish the first part of the lesson.

For the sorting part of the lesson, we put the words on index cards in the pocket chart. The first sort in this lesson is for beginning sounds. The teacher tells the children to sort out all the words that don't begin with a vowel and put them together in columns with all the same letters up to the vowel. The children are used to sorting for all beginning letters and quickly arrange the pocket chart index cards so that these words are grouped together:

rat	mat	tan	trim
ran	man		tram
ram	main		train
rim	Martin		
rain			

The teacher and children pronounce all the words, paying special attention to the three *t-r* words. They "stretch out" *trim, tram,* and *train* and agree that you can hear both the *t* and the *r* "blended together."

Next we help them sort the words into rhymes:

am	at	man	main	rim
ram	rat	tan	rain	trim
tram	mat	ran	train	

Once the words are sorted into rhymes, we remind the children that rhyming words can help them read and spell words. We then write two new rhyming words on cards and have them place these words under the rhyming words and use the rhymes to decode them:

swim   Spain

Finally, we say two rhyming words and help them use the rhyming words to figure out how to spell them:

clan   Spam

"Making Words" is a versatile format for learning about how words work. We can make the lessons easier by using fewer letters and harder by including more letters. Our first "Making Words" lesson contains only five letters and one vowel. From the letters *a, d, h, n,* and *s,* we can make the words *an, ad, had, sad, Dan, and, sand, hand,* and *hands.* We can then sort them out by beginning letters and notice that the words that begin with the same letters begin with the same sounds. The final sort is always for rhyming words. Once we have the rhyming words sorted, we can use them to read a few new words—*bad* and *stand*—and spell a few new words—*land* and *plan.*

Steps in Planning a "Making Words" Lesson

1. Decide what the secret word will be. In choosing this word, consider child interest, the curriculum tie-ins you can make, and the letter–sound patterns you can draw attention to through the sorting at the end.

2. Make a list of other words that can be made from these letters.

3. From all the words you could make, pick twelve to fifteen words, using these criteria:

   Words that you can sort for the pattern you want to emphasize.

   Little words and big words so that the lesson is a multilevel lesson. (Making the little words helps your struggling students; making the big words challenges your highest-achieving students.)

   "Abracadabra" words that can be made with the same letters in different places (*seal/sale; bale/able*) to remind children that when spelling words, the ordering of the letters is crucial.

   A proper name or two to remind them that we use capital letters.

   Words that most students have in their listening vocabularies.

4. Write all the words on index cards and order them from smallest to biggest.

5. Once you have the two-letter, three-letter, etc., words together, order them so that you can emphasize letter patterns and so that changing the position of the letters or changing/adding just one letter results in a different word.

6. Choose four "transfer" words, words you can read and spell based on the rhyming words.

7. Store the cards in an envelope. Write on the envelope the words (in order), the patterns you will sort for, and the transfer words.

Harder lessons have more letters and make some more complex words. From the letters *a, a, e, b, b, l, l, s,* we can make *all, lab, slab, blab, ball, bell, sell, seal, sale, bale, able, sable, baseball.* After sorting the words into rhymes, we can use these rhyming words to read *cable* and *swell* and spell *crab* and *whale.*

Letters on strip:	e i c k n r s s
Make:	in ski ice nice rice rink sink/skin sick rise risen/rinse skier sicken Snickers
Sort for:	related words: ski, skier; rise, risen; sick, sicken
	rhyming words: in, skin
	ice, nice, rice
	rink, sink
Transfer words:	advice Berlin shrink price

Letters on strip:		e e i o c h r s
Make:		is his rich hero echo core score shore chore cheer sheer heroes echoes riches Cheerios
Sort for:	related words:	hero, heroes; echo, echoes; rich, riches (es ending)
	rhyming words:	core, score, shore, chore
		cheer, sheer
		is, his
Transfer words:		reindeer adore restore steer

Letters on strip:		e e l r p s t z
Make:		set pet pets/step/pest rest zest steep sleep slept reset spree pester seltzer pretzels
Sort for:	related words:	set, reset; pest, pester; sleep, slept
	rhyming words:	set, pet, reset
		pest, rest, zest
		steep, sleep
Transfer words:		request invest upset jeep

"Making Words" is lots of fun if you keep it fast-paced. The approximately fifteen words should all be made in no more than fifteen minutes. Take another six to eight minutes for sorting and transferring and you are finished while they are still eager to make other words with the letters. Here are a few more lessons. It is fun to plan your own and tailor them to your units and the interests of your students.

Did You Know That?

Just thirty-seven rhymes will allow children to read and spell over five hundred primary grade words (Wylie & Durrell, 1970). These high-frequency rimes are

ack	*ail*	*ain*	*ake*	*ale*	*ame*	*unk*
an	*ank*	*ap*	*ash*	*at*	*ate*	
aw	*ay*	*eat*	*ell*	*est*	*ice*	
ide	*ick*	*ight*	*ill*	*in*	*ine*	
ing	*ink*	*ip*	*it*	*ock*	*oke*	
op	*ore*	*ot*	*uck*	*ug*	*ump*	

Word Sorting and Hunting

"Word Sorts" (Henderson, 1990) have long been advocated as an activity to help children know what to attend to and to develop the habit of analyzing words to look for patterns. There are a variety of ways to do "Word Sorts," but the basic principles are the same. Children look at words and sort them into categories based on spelling patterns and sound. Children say the words and look at how they are spelled. They learn that to go in a certain category, the words must "sound the same and look the same." After sorting words chosen by the teacher, children hunt for other words in books, magazines, and other print around them and then sort these additional words for the patterns as well. Word hunts are not word searches. In word searches, children search through the letters laid out on a grid, looking for embedded words. In word hunts, teachers help students identify the patterns and then direct children to locate those patterns as they occur naturally in other print sources.

In many classes, different groups of children are working on different levels of sorts. Many teachers do a directed sorting lesson with a group of children first, and then the children continue sorting and hunting in their groups or in partner formats. Here is one example of how one teacher manages several different levels of spellers using a variety of sorting formats.

The teacher is meeting with a group of children who need to work with the various spellings of the vowel *a*. She has divided a transparency into four columns, and the children have all divided their papers into four columns. The teacher heads each column with a vowel pattern and a word the children know that has that pattern. The children set up their columns just like those on the transparency. Question marks are put in the last column to indicate the place to put other words with *a* that don't fit in the first three columns.

a	ai	a-e	???
cat	rain	make	are

As children write each word, the teacher helps them focus on the sound of the *a* and the spelling. *Cat* has just an *a*, and the *a* sounds like the *a* in *apple*. *Rain* has an *ai* and is pronounced like *ape*. *Make* is spelled with an *a*, a consonant letter, and an *e*, and the *a* is also pronounced like *ape*. *Are* looks like *make* but does not sound like *make* so it heads the ??? column. The teacher then shows children words with *a* and has them read each word and decide which column it goes in. To go in a column, it must both look the same and sound the same. The first four words the children see and pronounce are *map, name, paid,* and *pad*. The children pronounce them, stretching out the sound of the vowel, and write them in the appropriate column. The teacher writes them in the column on the transparency:

a	ai	a-e	???
cat	rain	make	are
map	paid	name	
pad			

The next word is *have*. The children immediately want to write it under *make*, but the teacher has them stretch it out, and they decide that it looks like *make* but sounds like *cat.* It has to go into the ??? column (which some teachers label odd-balls, or tricks). The teacher continues showing them words containing the letter *a*, which they pronounce and then write in the correct column. They have some trouble with *taste* because there are two consonants between the vowels, but the teacher explains that the pattern is *a* and one or more consonants and the *e*, and they decide it can go with *make*. They decide that *saw* and *park* have to go in the ??? column along with *was*. Here is what their papers and the transparency look like when fifteen words have been sorted.

a	ai	a-e	???
cat	rain	make	are
map	paid	name	have
pad	wait	taste	saw
fast	brain	rate	park
jazz		safe	was

On the following day, this group works alone. One member of the group is the leader and gets to play teacher. He shows each word (on index cards prepared by the teacher from word hunt words), has the group pronounce the word, and then writes it on the transparency after the group members have written it on their sheets. If there is disagreement about which column a word should go in, the leader does not write it anywhere but puts it aside to ask the teacher about when the teacher returns to check their work. At the end of this second day, their papers and the transparency look like this:

a	ai	a-e	???
cat	rain	make	are
map	paid	name	have
pad	wait	taste	saw
fast	brain	rate	park
jazz	jail	safe	was
lamp	main	crane	Paul
crash	fail	date	want
brag	bait	case	
pant	drain	place	

Meanwhile, on the second day while this group is working on their own with a designated teacher, the real teacher is doing a word sort introduction with a group of children who are working with spelling changes when *s* is added to words. This group's papers and transparency have these three columns:

s	es	I	ies
cats	churches	babies	

Working with this group, the teacher shows them words, which they pro-nounce and then write in the appropriate column. At the end of the first day, their columns look like this:

s	es	ies
cats	churches	babies
animals	boxes	ladies
whales	lunches	puppies
crabs	branches	berries
cameras	ashes	parties
cars	taxes	countries

The only word that is difficult for this group is *whales*. Some children think it should go in the "es" column because it ends with *es*, but they decide that they should focus on is what was added, and since the word *whale* ends in *e*, only the *s* was added.

On the next day, the group working with *a* works with partners to find more words with *a* for their group to sort on the fourth day. Each set of partners is given ten index cards and told to find "ten terrific words with *a*." They write the word they find in big letters on one side of the card and then print the key word to show what column they think it goes in (in teeny letters) on the other side, Meanwhile, the *s, es, ies* group is doing its "play teacher day," and the real teacher is doing a sort introduction with another group of students who are sorting words with vowels fol-lowed by *r* into these columns:

ar	or	er	it	ur
car	for	her	bird	curl
work				

After sorting with the teacher today, this group will work in a "play teacher" group on the second day, work with partners on the third day to find "ten terrific words," and then write them on index cards for their group to sort on the fourth day.

Children in every grade are at all different levels in their spelling abilities. Teachers who are good "kid watchers" look at how children spell words in their first-draft writing to decide what spelling patterns children are ready to learn. They then form some spelling groups, which change as teachers notice different things in their writing. The arrangement just described shows how teachers might work children on a number of different spelling levels. In this classroom the procedure for each group went like this:

Day 1. Teacher-directed introduction of a new sort.

Day 2. Group continues to sort words created by teacher under the direction of a "play teacher."

Day 3. Partners work together to find ten terrific words for their group to sort tomorrow. Teacher checks their cards before their group convenes again.

Day 4. Group convenes and each partnership gets to "play teacher" by presenting ten terrific words to the group to be written in the correct columns.

Day 5. Children in group hunt for more words or choose words they really like for each pattern and copy them into a page in their spelling notebooks, putting words in the correct columns.

Word sorting and hunting are wonderful activities to develop spelling and decoding skills because children are actively involved in discovering "how words work." Many teachers post charts with the categories the class has worked on, and children are encouraged to add words that fit the pattern anytime they find them in anything they are reading. Some children keep word notebooks and add words that fit particular categories as they find them throughout the year. In classrooms in which word sorting and hunting are regular activities, children love meeting a "new word" and thinking about where it might fit in all the various categories they have worked on. Most children love collecting things—word sorting and hunting encourage word collecting.

What Looks Right?

"What Looks Right?" is an activity through which children learn that good spelling requires visual memory and discover how to use their visual memory for words along with a dictionary to determine the correct spelling of a word (Cunningham, 2000). In English, words that have the same spelling pattern usually rhyme. If you are reading and you come to the unknown words *plight* and *trite*, you can easily figure out their pronunciation by accessing the pronunciation associated with other *ight* or *ite* words you can read and spell. That there are two common spelling patterns with the same pronunciation is not a problem when you are trying to read an unfamiliar-in-print word, but it is a problem when you are trying to spell it. If you were writing and trying to spell *trite* and *plight*, they could as easily be spelled *t-r-i-g-h-t* and *p-l-i-t-e*. The only way to know which is the correct spelling is to write it one way and see if it "looks right," or check your probable spelling in a dictionary. "What Looks Right?" is an activity that teaches these two important self-monitoring spelling strategies.

Here is a sample lesson for the *oat-ote* pattern. Using an overhead or the board, create two columns and head each with an *oat-ote* word most of your students can both read and spell. Have the children set up two columns on their paper to match your model:

coat   vote

Have your students pronounce and spell the words, and lead them to realize that the words rhyme but have a different spelling pattern. Tell them that many words

Technology Tips

A number of computer programs, such as *Wiggle Works* and *Simon Sounds It Out*, help children learn how to decode and spell using patterns.

rhyme with *coat* and *vote,* and that you can't tell by just saying the words which spelling patterns they will have. Next, say a word that rhymes with *coat* and *vote* and write it both ways, saying, "If the word is spelled like *coat,* it will be *g-o-a-t,* but if it is spelled like *vote,* it will be *g-o-t-e.*" Write these two possible spellings under the appropriate word.

Have your students decide which one "looks right" to them and write only the one they think is correct. As soon as they decide which one looks right and write it in the correct column, students should use the dictionary to see if that spelling can be found. If they cannot find the one that looked right, then have them look up the other possible spelling. Cross out the spelling you wrote that is not correct and continue with more examples. For each word, say something parallel to, "If it is spelled like coat, it will be *g-o-a-t,* but if it is spelled like vote, it will be *g-o-t-e.*" Write the word both ways and have each child first write it the way that looks right and then look in the dictionary to see if the word is spelled the way the child thought.

Here is what your columns of words would look like after several examples:

coat	*vote*
goat	~~gote~~
boat	~~bote~~
float	~~flote~~
~~doat~~	note
~~quoat~~	quote
throat	~~throte~~
bloat	~~blote~~

To make your lesson more multilevel, include some longer words in which the last syllable rhymes with *coat* and *vote.* Proceed just as before to write the word both ways and have children choose the one that looks right, write that word, and look for it in the dictionary. For the *coat-vote* lesson, here are three longer words you might use.

~~promoat~~	promote
~~devoat~~	devote
~~remoat~~	remote

Here is a lesson for the *ait-ate* pattern, notice that several of these pairs are both words. Children should find both *gate/gait* and *plate/plait*. This is an excellent time to talk about homophones and how the dictionary can help you decide which word to use. Also notice the words written at the bottom. Whenever we think of common words such as *great, eight, weight,* and *straight,* which don't follow the pattern, we point these out to children, explaining that most—but not all—words that rhyme with *date* and *wait* are spelled *a-t-e* or *a-i-t.*

date	*wait*
~~bate~~	bait
fate	~~fait~~
hate	~~hait~~
skate	~~skait~~
gate	gait
plate	plait
state	~~stait~~
rebate	~~rebait~~
debate	~~debait~~
donate	~~donait~~
hibernate	~~hibernait~~

***straight   eight   weight   great

"What Looks Right?" is an active every-pupil response activity that teaches a variety of important concepts. Words that rhyme usually have the same spelling pattern, but sometimes there are two common spelling patterns and you have to write it and see if it looks right or use the dictionary to check your spelling. The dictionary can also help you decide which way to spell a word when there are two words that sound the same but have different spellings and meanings. "What Looks Right?" is a versatile strategy and can be used to help children become better spellers of longer words. Here are words for the *tion/sion* pattern.

motion	*pension*
action	~~acsion~~
station	~~stasion~~
~~mantion~~	mansion
mention	~~mension~~
lotion	~~losion~~
nation	~~nasion~~
~~tention~~	tension
attention	~~attension~~

ext~~en~~tion	extension
divition	division
multiplication	multi~~pli~~casion
tele~~vi~~tion	television
vacation	vaca~~si~~on
col~~li~~tion	collision

Knowledge of Morphemes Is Required for Multisyllabic Words

You may have been taught to decode multisyllabic words by learning a set of syllabication and accent rules. Do you remember learning to divide between two consonants unless the consonants are a digraph or a blend? Did you learn that the next-to-the-last syllable is often accented? Syllabication and accent rules have been the traditional strategies taught to help students figure out multisyllabic words. Unfortunately, research (Canney & Schreiner, 1977) reports that although students can learn the rules, knowing the rules is not related to the ability to decode polysyllabic words.

The patterns in words of three or more syllables are not onsets and rimes. Rather they are morphemic units—meaning-bearing portions of words—commonly referred to as roots, prefixes, and suffixes. English is the most morphologically complex language. Decoding and spelling polysyllabic words requires that students understand how words change in their spelling, pronunciation, and meaning as suffixes and prefixes are added. The *g* in *sign* seems quite illogical until you realize that *sign* is related to *signal, signature,* and other words. Finding the *compose/ composition* and *compete/competition* relationship will help students understand why the second syllables of *composition* and *competition* sound alike but are spelled differently.

Did You Know That?

From fifth grade on, the average student encounters 10,000 new words each year— words never before encountered in print. Most of these words are big words, words of seven or more letters and two or more syllables. Many of these words are related semantically through their morphology. A child who knows the words hunt, red, fog, *and* string *will have little difficulty with the meanings of* hunter, redness, foglights, *and* stringy. *Meaning relationships exist between* planet *and* planetarium, vicious *and* vice, apart *and* apartment, *but these will probably not be apparent to most children unless they are pointed out. However, if readers understand these more complex morphological relationships, they will know six or seven words for every basic word (Nagy & Anderson, 1984).*

In order to decode and spell polysyllabic words, students must learn to see roots, prefixes, endings, and suffixes. Sometimes, these word parts also help you figure out meanings for words. When you *re*place something, you place it back. Other times, as in *reward* and *refrigerator,* the *re* is just the first chunk of the word. Students should learn to recognize the most common morphemes and to see them as helpful chunks for spelling and pronouncing words. They should also learn that sometimes these chunks provide you with clues to figuring out the meaning of words "you never heard of." Below is a list of common prefixes with examples of words in which the prefix helps with meaning, and others in which the prefix is only helpful for spelling and pronouncing the word.

Prefix	Meaning	Meaning Chunk	Spelling/Pronunciation Chunk
re	back	replacement	refrigerator
re	again	rearrange	reward
un	opposite	unfriendly	uncle
in (im, ir, il)	opposite	independent	incident
		impossible	imagine
		irresponsible	irritate
		illegal	illustrate
in (im)	in	invasion	instant
		impression	immense
dis	opposite	dishonest	distress
non	opposite	nonliving	—
en	in	encourage	entire
mis	bad, wrong	misunderstand	miscellaneous
pre	before	prehistoric	present
inter	between	international	interesting
de	opposite/ take away	deodorize	delight
sub	under	submarine	subsist
fore	before/in front of	forehead	—
trans	across	transportation	—
super	really big	supermarkets	superintendent
semi	half	semifinal	seminar
mid	middle	midnight	midget
over	too much	overpower	—
under	below	underweight	understand
anti	against	antifreeze	—

The "Unpeelable" Prefixes

In addition to the above prefixes, which can be understood by taking them off the root word and then combining the meanings, other common prefixes do not leave recognizable words when they are "peeled off." The prefixes *con/com, ex, em,* and *per* add meanings to words, but you have to have a rather advanced understanding of Latin/Greek roots to see the meaning relationships. It is probably best just to help students see how these are predictable spelling/pronunciation chunks rather than try to show them how to analyze these words for meaning clues. Here are some other examples for these "unpeelable" prefixes:

Unpeelable Prefix	*Examples*
com/con	Communities, competition, communism
	composer, computer, compassion
	continuous, construction, conclusion
	conversation, constitution, concrete
em	employee, embassy, embryo
ex	expensive, excitement, explain
per	performance, permanent, personality

Suffixes, Endings, and Spelling Changes

For suffixes and endings, we want students to focus not on a meaning change but on a change in how and where the word fits into a sentence. Students need to realize that "when you employ someone, you have given them employment and you become their employer and they become the employee." We also want them to notice how the spelling of the root word often determines the spelling of the suffix. On the next page is a list of the most common endings and suffixes, along with example words whose meaning is familiar to most children.

Suffix/Ending	*Examples*
s/es	heroes, musicians, signatures
(y-i)	communities, discoveries, countries
ed/ing	unfinished, performed, misunderstanding
(drop e)	nonliving, replaced, continuing
(double consonant)	swimming, forgetting
er/est	richest, craziest, bigger
en	forgotten, hidden, chosen
less	hopeless, careless, penniless
ful	beautiful, successful, pitiful

able	valuable, portable, incurable
ible	irresponsible, reversible, horrible
tion	transportation, imagination, solution
sion	invasion, impression, permission
ly	unfriendly, hopelessly, happily
er	composer, reporter, robber
or	governor, dictator, juror
ee	employee, referee, trainee
ian	musician, magician, beautician
ance	performance, attendance, ignorance
ence	independence, conference, persistence
ment	encouragement, punishment, involvement
ness	happiness, goodness, business
y	discovery, jealousy, pregnancy
ity	electricity, popularity, possibility
ant	unpleasant, tolerant, dominant
ent	different, confident, excellent
al	international, political, racial
ive	expensive, inconclusive, competitive
ous	continuous, humorous, ambitious
is	prehistoric, scenic, specific
ify	classify, beautify, identify
ize	deodorize, modernize, standardize
ture	signature, creature, fracture

The Nifty Thrifty Fifty List

In the previous section, you learned that children learn to decode and spell new words based on patterns they know from other words. Because the patterns in big words are the morphemes, students need to know some example words with the most common prefixes, endings, and suffixes. On pages 115–116 is a list of fifty words that most intermediate-aged children have in their meaning vocabularies and that provides examples for all the common prefixes, suffixes, and endings, including common spelling changes. Because these fifty words will help you with so many other words, we have named them "The Nifty Thrifty Fifty." You may want to use the word wall activities described earlier in this chapter to help your students learn to read and spell these words. You can then help them use these words to decode, spell, and access meaning for other words they encounter in their reading or need to spell as they are writing (Cunningham, 2000).

The Nifty Thrifty Fifty

Word	Transferable Patterns	
antifreeze	anti	—
beautiful	—	ful (y-i)
classify	—	ify
communities	com	es (y-i)
community	com	—
composer	com	er
continuous	con	ous
conversation	con	tion
deodorize	de	ize
different	—	ent
discovery	dis	y
dishonest	dis	—
electricity	—	ity
employee	em	ee
encouragement	en	ment
expensive	ex	ive
forecast	fore	—
forgotten	—	en (double t)
governor	—	or
happiness	—	ness (y-i)
hopeless	—	less
illegal	il	—
impossible	im	—
impression	im	sion
independence	in	ence
international	inter	al
invasion	in	sion
irresponsible	ir	ible
midnight	mid	
misunderstand	mis	
musician		ian
nonliving	non	ing (drop e)
overpower	over	
performance	per	ance
prehistoric	pre	ic

prettier		er (y-i)
rearrange	re	
replacement	re	ment
richest		est
semifinal	semi	
signature		ture
submarine	sub	
supermarkets	super	s
swimming		ing (double m)
transportation	trans	tion
underweight	under	
unfinished	un	ed
unfriendly	un	ly
unpleasant	un	ant
valuable		able (drop e)

Point Out Patterns in Words When Introducing Content-Area Vocabulary

Savvy teachers seize the opportunity when introducing vocabulary in a subject area to model for students how you figure out the pronunciation of a word. Modeling is more than just telling them pronunciation, it is sharing the thinking that goes on when you come across big words. Here is an example of how you might model for students one way to decode *international*.

Write the word you are introducing in a sentence on the board or overhead:

The thinning of the ozone layer is an *international* problem.

Then say to the class:

Today, we are going to look at a big word that is really just a little word with a prefix added to the beginning and a suffix at the end. (Underline *nation*.)

Who can tell me this word? Yes, that is the word *nation*. Now, let's look at the prefix that comes before *nation*. (Underline *inter*.)

This prefix is *inter*. You probably know *inter* from words like *interrupt* and *interview*. Now, let's look at what follows *inter* and *nation*. (Underline *al*.) You know *al* from many words such as *unusual* and *critical*. (Write *unusual* and *critical* and underline the *al*.)

Listen as I pronounce this part of the word. (Underline and pronounce *national*.) Notice how the pronunciation of *nation* changes when we put *a-l* on it. Now let's put all the parts together and pronounce the word *inter nation al*.

Let's read the sentence and make sure *international* makes sense. (Have the sentence read and confirm that ozone thinning is indeed a problem for many nations to solve.)

You can figure out the pronunciation of many big words if you look for common prefixes such as *inter,* common root words such as *nation,* and common suffixes such as *al.* In addition to helping you figure out the pronunciation of a word, prefixes and suffixes sometimes help you know what the word means or where in a sentence we can use the word. The word *nation* names a thing. When we describe a nation, we add the suffix *al* and have *national.* The prefix *inter* often means "between or among." Something that is *international* is between many nations. The Olympics are the best example of an *international* sports event.

This sample lesson for introducing the word *international* demonstrates how a teacher can help students see and use morphemes to decode words needed for content-area learning. Notice that the teacher points out words students might know that have the same parts. In addition, meaning clues provided by the morphemes are provided whenever appropriate.

The Theory and Research Base for Phonics and Spelling Instruction

Phonemic awareness has many levels, including the ability to decide whether or not spoken words rhyme, to know what spoken word you would have if you removed a sound, to segment words into sounds, and to blend separate sounds into words. Phonemic awareness seems to develop gradually for most children through lots of exposure to nursery rhymes and books that promote wordplay (Yopp & Yopp, 2000).

Phonemic awareness is one of the best predictors of success in learning to read (Bryant, Bradley, Maclean, & Crossland, 1989; National Reading Panel, 2000). Perhaps because it is such a good predictor of beginning reading, some schools and teachers have overemphasized phonemic awareness. Devoting large amounts of time to phonemic awareness activities each day means neglecting other activities important to literacy, such as the development of oral language and meaning vocabulary, listening comprehension, and print concepts. In fact, *Put Reading First* (Armbruster, Lehr & Osborne, 2001) makes the specific recommendation that, "Over the school year, your entire phonemic awareness program should take no more than 20 hours" (p. 9).

Few instructional studies have compared different types of phonics instruction, and those that have done so have often compared systematic phonics instruction with "hit or miss" phonics instruction. From these studies, we can conclude that any kind of well-organized and efficient phonics instruction is generally better than little or no phonics instruction that leaves learning phonics to chance. Stahl, Duffy-Hester, and Stahl (1998) reviewed the research on phonics in-struction and concluded that there are several types of good phonics instruction and that there is no research base to support the superiority of any one particular type. The National Reading Panel (NRP) (2000) reviewed the experimental research on teaching phonics and determined that explicit and systematic phonics is supe-rior to nonsystematic or no phonics, but that there is no significant difference in the effectiveness of the different kinds of systematic phonics instruction. They also found no significant difference in effectiveness among tutoring, small-group, or whole-class phonics instruction.

Newer approaches to teaching phonics often use guided and independent spelling activities to teach letter–sound relationships and their application (Stahl, Duffy-Hester, & Stahl, 1998; Cunningham, 2000). A number of studies support inte-grating phonics and spelling instruction for young children (e.g., Cataldo & Ellis, 1988; Ehri & Wilce, 1987; Ellis & Cataldo, 1990). For instance, Clarke (1988) found that first-grade programs that included invented spelling produced better decoders than first-grade programs that included only traditional spelling. Uhry and Shepherd (1993) also found that incorporating spelling into the word instruction first-graders receive improved their decoding. More recently, Davis (2000) found that spelling-based decoding instruction was as effective as reading-based decoding instruction for all her students, but more effective for the children with poor phonological awareness.

Early on, word identification and spelling seem to be strictly separate processes (Bryant & Bradley, 1980). By the end of first grade, however, they have become closely related to each other (Bryant & Bradley, 1980; Gough, Juel, & Grif-fith, 1992). Correlations between the two are quite high (Zutell, 1992; Ehri, 1997), in spite of weakening from the well-known fact that most children can identify words they are unable to spell (Bosman & Van Orden, 1997; Perfetti, 1997). The strong relationship appears to derive from research showing that in fact children beyond the beginning stage of reading can almost always pronounce a word accu-rately if they can spell it correctly (Hall, 1991).

Juel and Minden-Cupp (2000) observed that the most effective teachers of chil-dren who entered first grade with few literacy skills combined systematic letter–sound instruction with onset-rime compare-contrast activities instruction; in addi-tion, they taught these units for application in both reading and writing.

Phonics and spelling instruction for multisyllabic words has not been much investigated, but some understanding about the new words encountered in upper grades gives us some instructional direction. In 1984 Nagy and Anderson pub-lished a landmark study in which they analyzed a sample of 7,260 words found in books commonly read in grades three through nine. They found that most of these words were polysyllabic and that many of these big words were related semanti-cally through their morphology. Nagy and Anderson hypothesized that if children knew or learned how to interpret morphological relationships, they would know six or seven words for every basic word known. To move children along in their decoding and spelling abilities in upper grades, instruction probably needs to focus on morphemes—prefixes, suffixes, and roots—and how these morphemes help us decode, spell, and gain meaning for polysyllabic words.

Looking Back

The nature of English demands that children pay attention to patterns of letters to decode and spell new words. For small words, the patterns are onsets—all the letters up to the vowel—and rimes—the letters from the vowel to the end of the word. For longer words, the letter patterns are morphemes—roots, prefixes, and suffixes. This chapter described a variety of practical activities for helping children learn patterns they can use to decode and spell new words. It discussed four key ideas:

1. Readers use patterns to decode and spell new words.
2. Beginning readers must develop phonemic awareness and learn some letter names and sounds.
3. Children must develop strategies for decoding and spelling unknown words.
4. Knowledge of morphemes is required for multisyllabic words.

 Add to Your Journal

This chapter has presented a lot of information, some of which is probably new to you and some of which probably contradicts what you remember about learning to read. Did you realize that those rhyming games, chants, and jingles you enjoyed as a preschooler contributed to your phonemic awareness and consequently to your success in learning to read and write? Do you remember having to memorize a lot of rules for "sounding out words"? How does the information in this chapter fit with what you have read about "phonics" in newspaper and magazine articles? Respond to each of the key ideas in this chapter by using some or all of the eight essential thinking processes. What connections, predictions, and generalizations can you make? What images do these key ideas produce? How do you organize all this information? Monitor your own understanding by deciding if there are parts of this chapter about which you are still confused. Evaluate these ideas by clarifying your opinions about words, phonics, and spelling. Most important, decide how you will apply these ideas to your classroom.

Application Activities

 Add to Your Resource File

This chapter suggested many wonderful books and games to help children develop phonemic awareness and learn letter names and sounds. Find six more books—especially recent ones—that build the critical concepts of rhyme, alliteration, and letter names and sounds. Include complete bibliographic information for each book and summarize in a paragraph what it does and how it will build these crucial concepts. Find or devise four other devices—songs, games, chants, and others—that you could use with children. Describe each one and tell how it would be helpful.

Try It Out

Pick two of the formats described for helping children learn to decode and spell ("Using Words You Know," "Making Words," "Word Sorting and Hunting," and "What Looks Right?"). Plan two lessons—one for each format—using the examples from this book as models but focusing on different words. Write out the exact steps you would use to teach each lesson in about fifteen to twenty minutes. Teach these lessons to a group of children and write a summary of how the lessons went. (Round up neighborhood children or offer to babysit if necessary to find some real children.)

Listen, Look, and Learn

Observe a class during the time the teacher indicates that phonics, decoding, or spelling are being taught. Write down what the teacher does and what the children do. Compare and contrast what you saw with what is suggested in this chapter. Reconcile the differences. What did you see that you thought was more effective than our recommendations? What would you like to have seen that you didn't see? If you were a child in that classroom or the parent of a child, would you be satisfied with the phonics/decoding/spelling instruction being provided?

Do It Together

Working with one or two colleagues, decide on a method of modeling for students how to figure out a way to pronounce, spell, and establish meanings for the following big words:

ingratitude	disarmament	capacity	conversion	pretentious
misleading	modification	unqualified	resistant	multitude

Identify any prefixes, suffixes, root words, and endings (including spelling changes) that you see in these words. Plan a lesson in which you introduce these words and help students both use their morphemic knowledge from words they already know and add to their morphemic knowledge based on these multisyllabic words. List the words with morphemes that would help them that you think they might already know, and list a few other words they probably don't know for which the new morphemes would help them.

References

Armbruster, B. B., Lehr, F., & Osborn, J. (2001). *Put reading first: The research building blocks for teaching children to read: Kindergarten through grade 3.* Washington, DC: The Partnership for Reading.

Bosman, A. M. T., & Van Orden, G. C. (1997). Why spelling is more difficult than reading. In C. A. Perfetti, L. Rieben, & M. Fayol (Eds.), *Learning to spell: Research, theory, and practice across languages* (pp. 173–194). Mahwah, NJ: Erlbaum.

Bryant, P., & Bradley, L. (1980). Why children sometimes write words they cannot read. In U. Frith (Ed.), *Cognitive processes in spelling* (pp. 356–370). London: Academic Press.

Bryant, P., & Bradley, L., Maclean, M., & Crossland, I. (1989). Nursery rhymes, phonological skills and reading. *Journal of Child Language, 16,* 407–428.

Canney, G., & Schreiner, R. (1977). A study of the effectiveness of selected syllabication rules and phonogram patterns for word attack. *Reading Research Quarterly, 12,* 102–124.

Cataldo, S., & Ellis, N. (1988). Interactions in the development of spelling, reading and phonological skills. *Journal of Research in Reading, 11*(2), 86–109.

Clarke, L. K. (1988). Invented versus traditional spelling in first graders' writings: Effects on learning to spell and read. *Research in the Teaching of English, 22,* 281–309.

Clay, M. M. (1985). *The early detection of reading difficulties,* 3rd ed. Portsmouth, NH: Heinemann.

Cunningham, P. M. (2000). *Phonics they use,* 3rd ed. New York: Longman.

Davis, L. H. (2000). The effects of rime-based analogy training on word reading and spelling of first-grade children with good and poor phonological awareness (Doctoral dissertation, Northwestern University, 2000). *Dissertation Abstracts International, 61,* 2253A.

Ehri, L. C. (1997). Learning to read and learning to spell are one and the same, almost. In C. A. Perfetti, L. Rieben, & M. Fayol (Eds.), *Learning to spell: Research, theory, and practice across languages* (pp. 237–269). Mahwah, NJ: Erlbaum.

Ehri, L. C., & Wilce, L. (1987). Does learning to spell help beginners learn to read words? *Reading Research Quarterly, 22,* 47–65.

Elkonin, D. B. (1973). Reading in the USSR. In J. Downing (Ed.), *Comparative reading* (pp. 551–579). New York: Macmillan.

Ellis, N., & Cataldo, S. (1990). The role of spelling in learning to read. *Language and Education, 4,* 47–76.

Gough, P. B., Juel, C., & Griffith, P. L. (1992). Reading, spelling, and the orthographic cipher. In P. B. Gough, L. Ehri, & R. Treiman (Eds.), *Reading acquisition* (pp. 35–48). Hillsdale, NJ: Erlbaum.

Hall, D. P. (1991). Investigating the relationship between word knowledge and cognitive ability (Doctoral dissertation, University of North Carolina at Greensboro, 1991). *Dissertation Abstracts International, 52,* 2873A.

Henderson, E. H. (1990). *Teaching spelling,* 2nd ed. Boston: Houghton Mifflin.

Juel, C., & Minden-Cupp, C. (2000). Learning to read words: Linguistic units and instructional strategies. *Reading Research Quarterly, 35,* 458–492.

Nagy, W. E., & Anderson. R. C. (1984). How many words are there in printed school English? *Reading Research Quarterly, 19,* 304–330.

National Reading Panel. (2000). *Teaching children to read: An evidence-based assessment of the scientific research literature on reading and its implications for reading instruction: Reports of the subgroups* (National Institute of Health Pub. No. 00-4754). Washington, DC: National Institute of Child Health and Human Development.

Perfetti, C. A. (1997). The psycholinguistics of spelling and reading. In C. A. Perfetti, L. Rieben, & M. Fayol (Eds.), *Learning to spell: Research, theory, and practice across languages* (pp. 21–38). Mahwah, NJ: Erlbaum.

Stahl, S. A., Duffy-Hester, A. M., & Stahl, K. A. D. (1998). Everything you wanted to know about phonics (but were afraid to ask). *Reading Research Quarterly, 33,* 338–355.

Uhry, J. K., & Shepherd, M. J. (1993). Segmentation/spelling instruction as part of a first-grade reading program: Effects on several measures of reading. *Reading Research Quarterly, 28,* 218–233.

Wylie, R. E., & Durrell, D. D. (1970). Teaching vowels through phonograms. *Elementary English*, 47, 787–791.

Yopp, H. K., & Yopp, R. H. (2000). Supporting phonemic awareness development in the classroom. *The Reading Teacher, 54*, 130–143.

Young, S. (1994). *The scholastic rhyming dictionary.* New York: Scholastic.

Zutell, J. (1992). An integrated view of word knowledge: Correlational studies of the relationships among spelling, reading, and conceptual development. In S. Templeton & D. R. Bear (Eds.), *Development of orthographic knowledge and the foundations of literacy* (pp. 213–230). Hillsdale, NJ: Erlbaum.

Children's Books/Materials Cited

Alphabet Dreams, by J. G. Brown, Prentice Hall, 1976.

A My Name Is Alice, by J. Byars, Dial, 1984.

Brown Bear, Brown Bear, What Do You See? by B. Martin, Jr., Holt, Rinehart, & Winston, 1970.

Additional Readings

- These books and articles review existing research on how we learn to read words.

  Adams, M. J. (1990). *Beginning to read: Thinking and learning about print.* Cambridge, MA: MIT Press.

  Stahl, S. A., Duffy-Hester, A. M., & Stahl, K. A. D. (1998). Everything you wanted to know about phonics (but were afraid to ask). *Reading Research Quarterly, 33*, 338–355.

- These articles present a balanced view of reading and writing and the role of phonics in that instruction.

  Spiegel, D. L. (1993). Balance. *The Reading Teacher, 46*, 38–48.

  Stahl, S. A. (1992). Saying the "p" word: Nine guidelines for exemplary phonics instruction. *The Reading Teacher, 45*, 618–625.

- This book has lots of practical strategies for helping children of all ages learn about words. It is particularly helpful for planning word-sorting and hunting activities.

  Bear, D., Invernizzi, M., Templeton, S., & Johnston, F. (2000). *Words their way: Word study for phonics, vocabulary, and spelling instruction,* 2nd ed. Englewood Cliffs, NJ: Prentice Hall.

- These sources provide a variety of practical strategies for assessing and teaching phonemic awareness.

  Ericson, L., & Juliebo, M. F. (1998). *The phonological awareness handbook for kindergarten and primary teachers.* Newark, DE: International Reading Association.

  Fitzpatrick, J. (1997). *Phonemic awareness: Playing with sounds to strengthen beginning reading skills.* Cypress, CA: Creative Teaching Press.

  Opitz, M. (2000). *Rhymes & reasons: Literature and language play for phonological awareness.* Newark, DE: International Reading Association.

Chapter 5

Prior Knowledge and Meaning Vocabulary

L o o k i n g   A h e a d

Reading and writing performance increases and decreases according to students' knowledge of what they are reading or writing about. Students who activate their prior knowledge in preparation for literacy tasks have advantages over those who do not. Along with activating prior knowledge, readers and writers access the meanings of countless words. Effective elementary teachers provide numerous opportunities throughout the school day to help students activate and build prior knowledge and word meanings.

Imagine trying to read or write a passage when you know practically nothing about its topic. For example, many would be frustrated reading a technical manual on subatomic particles that discusses quarks, baryons, kaons, and leptons without explaining them. Writing an essay about these units of physics also would be torturous. Many of us simply don't know enough about subatomic particles to make sense of them. We lack the necessary prior knowledge and meaning vocabulary.

Like all readers and writers, elementary school students require appropriate prior knowledge and meaning vocabulary to make sense during their reading and writing. For instance, a child who chooses a book about the atom might find it too complex if the author uses terms like charm and quantum to explain current atomic theory and the child knows only a little about molecules and electrons. The child's failure to comprehend would be due to a lack of background information rather than a lack of interest, intelligence, or literacy. This chapter, which addresses prior knowledge and meaning vocabulary, contains six key ideas:

1. Activate prior knowledge when presenting new ideas.
2. Introduce vocabulary in meaningful settings.
3. Select vocabulary for intensive teaching.
4. Represent word meanings multiple ways.
5. Develop independence in vocabulary learning.
6. Promote vocabulary in all subjects.

Activate Prior Knowledge When Presenting New Ideas

When planning instruction, many educators add the word *prior* to *knowledge* to re- mind themselves that learners already know something about the new things they will be encountering. There always are familiar dimensions to the unfamiliar (Bruner, 1961). A child in the southern United States might not know much about the desert but probably does know a lot about the outdoors and dryness. The student's fa- miliarity with these concepts would be a good stepping stone to exploring unfamil- iar aspects of the desert. Prior knowledge would be the bridge to new knowledge.

Those who view reading as a constructive process place prior knowledge as a prerequisite to making sense of print (Spivey, 1997). According to this view, read- ing is like constructing a building. Readers, like builders, follow a blueprint to transform raw material into new structures. The raw material that readers use is prior knowledge. Readers shape prior knowledge, that is, what they know already, in large part according to authors' plans. Consequently, activating prior knowledge before and during reading to make maximum use of it is an indispensable part of the reading process.

Another view of the value of prior knowledge involves students' misconcep- tions about the world (Chinn & Brewer, 1993; Guzzetti, Snyder, Glass, & Gamas, 1993). Students' prior knowledge sometimes interferes with learning, because in- correct preconceived ideas often override verifiable content. For instance, many young students believe that prehistoric people lived during the time of the di- nosaurs, that wild animals are always ferocious, that heavier objects fall faster than lighter ones, that a ball released from a curved track will continue to curve, and that summer is warmer than winter because the earth moves closer to the sun. Stu- dents might become confused by or simply discount science passages containing alternative concepts. To counteract this situation, students should call up their prior knowledge. Once students are clear about what they believe, they can com- pare it with conflicting information and form reasoned judgments.

Finally, activating prior knowledge motivates learners. Children naturally want to know about their worlds. They want to make sense of what often seem to be chaotic situations. Children become motivated when they realize the possibility of increasing their competencies and extending their previous understandings (Wig- field, Eccles, & Rodriguez, 1998).

For these and other reasons, successful teachers devote attention to prior knowledge when preparing students to read and write. Practically every classroom lesson begins with what students already know about the topic under consideration. Five ways to activate prior knowledge are commonly used: brainstorming, questioning, predicting, writing, and discussing.

Brainstorming

Brainstorming is perhaps the most basic way to call up what is already known. Brainstorming frequently is a first step toward the exploration of a topic or a book. When brainstorming, learners spontaneously associate ideas, linking thoughts in a free-wheeling manner. Brainstormed ideas can be just talked about, or they can be jotted down on paper at students' desks, on a whiteboard, or on an overhead transparency. If students were preparing for the topic of Africa, they might call out concepts related to the land, the people, and the plants and animals. Items associated with the land might include jungle, the Sahara, dry grasslands, Congo River, Nile River, and rain forest. Calling up and talking about such items enhances students' readiness to learn more about the topic.

Questioning

Students who ask and answer questions before reading and writing have an advantage over those who simply begin reading and writing. For instance, the topic Africa could be posted and presented briefly, and students could then have free rein to pose questions about it. Searching their minds and available resources for questions to answer activates students' prior knowledge. After an introduction to the topic of Africa, students might pose questions such as the following:

Who are the Bedouins, the Boers, and the Bantu?

How does Africa's climate compare with North America's?

What animals are found only in Africa?

Why were European countries able to colonize Africa?

What are some common features of traditional African folktales?

Using what they already knew, students first would answer one or more of these questions as completely as possible. Then they would explore whatever resources were available to build on what they had.

Predicting

Making predictions about what will happen in a story is another time-honored knowledge activation strategy. Teachers might inform students that a story about to be shared is an African folktale and ask what to expect from it. Later in the title, students can predict the characters' next logical moves.

Predictions about informative passages are also appropriate. When studying African land forms, students might access what they know about waterfalls and mountains to predict what they will learn about Victoria Falls and Mount Kilimanjaro. Using what they know about the Rocky Mountains' effect on the U.S. climate, students might predict how the Atlas Mountains affect Africa. Teachers frequently record the predictions while moving through a passage and then have students confirm or negate them after reading.

Writing

The prior knowledge activation strategies listed above could include writing, but they do not emphasize it. Brainstorming, questioning and predicting might include writing mainly to list items for future reference. Here we emphasize writing as a way to compose complete coherent thoughts.

Students who write from the perspective of a story character before reading about the character go far in activating prior knowledge. Students might assume the role of a young Masai hunter in Kenya and describe impressions of his first hunt. Then they would read a passage describing such a hunt. Students might write to convince outsiders that they should live in the tropical rain forests of central Africa. Writing brief entries on this topic before investigating it further would access what is already known and prepare students for new leanings.

Discussing

Discussions consisting of free-flowing exchanges of ideas are especially useful for exploring problematic or controversial issues. Unlike recitations, discussions do not presume a single correct answer; rather, there is a give-and-take dialogue. Discussions based on prior knowledge related to Africa might center on the following assertions:

> Preserving the environment is Africa's biggest problem.
>
> The colonization of Africa was disastrous for the African people.
>
> African stories are more enlightening than American ones.

Talking about the issues that the statements address prepares students for future reading. They refine their grasp of the issues and stimulate efforts at comprehension. They become ready for what textbooks, library materials, Internet resources, and assorted pamphlets offer to inform future discussions.

Introduce Vocabulary in Meaningful Settings

Along with activating prior knowledge, literate successful students understand and use extensive vocabularies. Reading and writing occur in part by associating meanings with corresponding printed words. Many—but not all—of the difficulties readers have can be traced to difficulties they have with vocabulary. It is difficult to paraphrase the sentence, "His hirple was becoming steadily worse" if you don't know that a *hirple* is a lame walk, or hobble. Indeed, students' vocabulary knowledge and passage comprehension scores correlate reliably and substantially (Graves, 1994). Students with access to thousands of word meanings succeed inside and outside school.

Learning word meanings is a lot like getting to know people. As with words, you know some people extremely well, you are well informed about others, you have only vague ideas of still others, and so on. Knowledge of people depends on the experiences you have with them. You know some people, such as family members, extremely well because you have spent most of your life in their company. You have participated with them regularly in situations that have been intense and emotional as well as routine. Similarly, your best friends are intimate acquaintances, so you know their actions, personalities, and foibles. On the other hand, think of friends of friends that you have only heard about, as well as historical figures such as Charles Darwin and Catherine the Great and current public figures such as politicians and entertainers. You might have heard of them and seen illustrations, pictures, and videos of them, but these people are known only through the secondhand reports of others. Your knowledge of people that you know indirectly through secondhand information is limited in comparison to those you know directly through firsthand experience. In brief, learning words—like coming to know people—varies according to how much time you spend with them and the types of experiences you share.

Now think of how you make new friends. Social gatherings such as parties and meetings are excellent opportunities for getting to know others. When you move through a gathering on your own, you strike up conversations and get to know new people in part as a function of your motivation and your social skills. However, having a host, hostess, friend, or group of friends introduce you to people tends to expedite the process. Once you have made new contacts, you might get to know them better as you meet again in other settings. Don't forget the power of social networking: the more people you know, the more opportunities you have for helping each other out and meeting even more people.

Levels of knowledge about people and the dynamics of getting to know them are comparable in many ways to learning words. When given the opportunity, students learn many new words on their own, depending on their motivation and literacy skills. Additionally, students benefit from direct introductions and intensive interactions with a few new words. As students learn new words well, their opportunities for learning additional ones increase exponentially. The remainder of this chapter describes specific vocabulary practices along these lines.

Perhaps the best way to begin vocabulary instruction in your classroom is to introduce words in meaningful settings. Settings are meaningful when they relate to students' worlds, when they tap individuals' interests and concerns, when they are relevant. Students in meaningful settings want to acquire new words for a genuine purpose. They intend to apply what they learn. They acquire vocabulary while engaging their minds fully in worthwhile ideas.

Enthusiasm is another characteristic of meaningful settings. Teachers project enthusiasm about words by conveying their eagerness to learn more about unfamiliar ones and by sharing fascinating ones they encounter outside the classroom. Word enthusiasts express their appreciation of authors who arrange poetic and powerful word combinations. Children are often enthusiastic about new words, repeating them over and over, enjoying the sound of language and marveling at the meanings being expressed. Encourage this natural tendency in your classroom. Open your class to wondering about words, to spontaneous questions about unfamiliar words, to judgments about the sounds and values of words, and to comments about how what is being studied compares with what is already known.

In meaningful settings, students use the rich natural language that is provided by books, guest speakers, field trips, informative media, and classmates to extend their performance in and knowledge of the world. These settings are the opposite of antiseptic ones filled with lists of unrelated words to define, synonyms to match, and rote drills to perform. Two specific classroom practices that can be especially meaningful and appropriate for introducing vocabulary are wide reading and listening, as well as theme studies.

Wide Reading and Listening

Wide reading and listening is a premier setting for learning vocabulary (Sternberg, 1987; Elley, 1989). Reading self-selected materials and listening to someone read aloud provides a rich source of new words. Students who are regularly engaged with interesting and important materials infer meanings of unfamiliar words while reviewing and refining meanings of familiar ones. They add to their funds of knowledge what will be recalled and connected to more difficult materials they will encounter in the future. Chapter 6, "Reading and Responding to Literature for Children," describes types of materials appropriate for wide reading and listening and explains how to set up and manage opportunities for reading aloud and self-selected reading.

Theme Studies

We seldom, if ever, know a word without knowing other words that relate to it. Take the word *clock,* for example. People who are familiar with the word don't just know it as a piece of machinery for measuring and showing time. People with deep understandings of this word know other concepts and words related to it. Most people know uses for clocks (maintaining a schedule, keeping appointments, measuring events) and measurement units of time (hour, minute, second, A.M, P.M.). They know about dial and digital clock faces as well as about pendulum-driven, spring-driven, electric, and atomic mechanisms. They know where different timepieces are generally found (alarm clocks in bedrooms, watches on people's wrists, grandfather clocks in living rooms). Some people know historical devices for measuring time (sundial, hourglass, water clock), and some know the names for different parts of different kinds of clocks (stem, mainspring, chip).

Another example of learning words in relation to others involves the word *hot*. Think of children's encounters with hot when they touch something that has been cooking. Young children learn "hot" in relation to other ideas and terms. The experience and conversation that ensue from biting into extremely hot food help build understandings of *cook* ("Never touch anything that has just been cooked") and *burn* ("See how hot things burn?"). Thus, knowledge of the related terms *hot*, *cook*, and *burn* is developed simultaneously through a single experience.

Theme studies are instructional units that center on core ideas. By addressing plants, explorers, holidays, careers, discoveries, friendship, community, and identity—among other things—theme studies focus on related ideas. They present the big picture before focusing on details, so students have something to help organize all the new words they encounter. This whole-to-part approach enhances vocabulary development.

Select Vocabulary for Special Attention

Making new words available and accessible through meaningful settings like wide reading and listening and theme studies is necessary for vocabulary growth, but more needs to be done. Learners also benefit from direct introductions to words and their meanings, just as they do from direct introductions to people. Examining a few words in depth pays off because students retain them better and longer. Such examinations also develop students' word consciousness, their watchful attentiveness to vocabulary. Students become able to discern the meanings of related terms (*benefit, beneficial, beneficiary*) by learning certain ones well. Moreover, readers model how to access the meanings of unfamiliar words when examining some in depth. Selecting vocabulary for special attention and intensive study involves several considerations.

Number of Words

The number of words to select depends on factors such as your students' grade and age, their language and academic proficiencies, the difficulty and relatedness of particular terms, and your curriculum standards. In general, teaching a few words well pays off because, through your teaching, students learn what to pay attention to in words and can then learn many words on their own. A rule of thumb is to introduce about ten new words per week for each subject you teach. This number is meant to serve only as a rough estimate of what is most productive. Trial and error and ongoing monitoring of your instruction will help determine how many words to select for the intensive study that most effectively promotes students' vocabulary learning.

Student Selections

Determining who selects words for special attention is another important consideration. Enlisting students in this process emphasizes choice and ownership.

Students who decide what they should learn often invest more of themselves in their learning.

Students in many classrooms maintain literary response journals with sections devoted to vocabulary. Students enter into these sections portions of text that contain words they believe are important to know and want to share. During wide reading, students sometimes look for language gems, especially vivid or apt phrases that exemplify fine writing. Students often cite author, text, and page number for each item they record. They might explain the words' meanings as used in the passage. Students share these entries with classmates during discussions and with the teacher during conferences.

During small-group discussions of literature, some teachers assign discussants a role that centers on vocabulary. For instance, in small groups of four, one child can serve as a vocabulary researcher while others serve as discussion director, literary luminary, and secretary-checker (Fisher, Blachowitz, & Smith, 1991). Students fulfill each role during one day of discussion before circulating to another role. The vocabulary researcher selects about five or six words from the chapter being discussed, typically focusing on unfamiliar or interesting words (e.g., *brusque, adobe, rummaged*). During group work, the volcabulary resercher directs group members to the portions of text containing the words and helps them try to derive the meanings from the context. The vocabulary researcher confirms the meanings group members produce or provides appropriate ones. All students record the words and their meanings in journals.

Students can also select words to learn during theme studies. For instance, they might examine materials to be read for the purpose of listing two words they consider relatively unknown yet important for learning content information (Haggard, 1986). Students meet in two- or three-member teams to decide words to nominate before the whole class. Teachers guide the nominations by writing words on the board, explaining their meanings with student input, and assessing their importance.

Teacher Selections

In classrooms with balanced literacy instruction, teachers select words for special attention along with their students. They present the words and their meanings as students encounter them in particular passages or lessons. Since you cannot adequately address every word that deserves intensive study, you need to select only ones that meet certain criteria. Here are some criteria for deciding what to include:

- Is the word unfamiliar to most class members?
- Will students need help learning the word?
- Is the word necessary for understanding the particular passage or theme study under consideration?
- Are students likely to encounter the word regularly in the future?
- Will learning the word contribute substantially to learning other words?
- Will students find the word interesting?

Weigh the relative advantages of each word against the others when producing a final set. Adjust the selections so that not all words are extremely complex and unfamiliar. Be sure to include a few for their interest factor. If the passage has few words deserving special attention, you and your class can add related terms.

When to Teach Words

Planning when to teach the words you select is an important decision. Before a guided reading session, teachers often present a few unfamiliar words that are crucial for understanding the passage and are not explained well in it. Teaching only a few vitally important yet unexplained terms before students read is a good way to balance vocabulary and passage understandings. You can address the remainder of the selected words after students have read a passage. During theme studies, naming unfamiliar words that are coming up and then teaching their meanings in depth when presenting them during lessons is effective.

Teachable moment is a time-honored phrase referring to incidents when students' readiness to learn is at a peak. Conditions are just right for instructional input as learners feel an authentic and acute need to know something. Teachable moments can be cultivated, but they are by nature difficult to specify beforehand. Teachers might be completely ready to teach, but learners might not be so ready to learn. Teachable moments begin with learners' openness to new ideas.

Much vocabulary is selected and taught "on the fly" during teachable moments. When teachers read aloud to the class, many words come up that students want to know. For instance, in Leo Lionni's *Frederick* a "chatty family of field mice" are said to have their home "not far from the barn and the granary." If students express an interest in knowing what a granary is, then you have a teachable moment. Briefly explain granary, then move on. Students might be reading and discussing Jean Fritz's *And Then What Happened, Paul Revere?*, which notes that ships in the Boston harbor "were constantly coming and going, unloading everything from turtles to chandeliers." If students express an interest in *chandeliers,* then that is the time to lift it from the passage, teach it, and move on. When studying Thanksgiving, students might want to know where cranberries grow. If you mention that cranberries grow in *bogs,* then you might explain even more about bogs consisting of wet, spongy ground.

While language-rich classrooms consistently offer new words and teachable moments, caution yourself about overdoing it. Too much attention to new words disrupts the flow of lessons and language. For instance, be cautious about explaining every unfamiliar word you encounter when reading orally. When the story character Frederick told wintertime stories to his appreciative family of field mice, "he told them of the blue periwinkles and the red poppies in the yellow wheat." Stopping to explain the meanings of *periwinkles* and *poppies* runs the risk of ruining the story for the children. In addition, stopping and teaching these words would be counterproductive because the terms are not crucial for understanding the passage, the children probably can determine for themselves the word meanings from the picture clues and the story, and they probably will learn more about these flowers at a more opportune time. Not all moments available for teaching words on the fly are teachable moments.

Displaying the Selected Words

Displaying words enhances learning by calling attention to particular terms and signaling the importance of learning them. Teachers typically display sets of words for a week or two as students are reading passages or studying topics that embed them. The displays take several forms:

Topic Boards

Topic boards are effective tools for calling attention to words and their meanings. Words are displayed on a wall or bulletin board so that all students can see them. Once the words are up, students can visit and revisit them to learn their meanings.

Word Books

Many students make word books to record new vocabulary. Students may use a notebook or sheets of paper stapled together and decorated with an interesting cover. Words are usually entered according to their first letter, but in the sequence in which they are introduced. Depending on the age of the children and the type of word being studied, the following types of information can be recorded:

- The sentence containing the target word
- A definitional sentence ("Frigid means very, very cold.")
- A personal example ("Frigid is a February day when the thermometer hits 20 degrees and the wind is blowing.")
- A phonetic respelling ("frij id") to help students remember the pronunciation of words
- A contrasting word ("Frigid is not hot.")
- Morphemic word families ("My grandparents have a Frigidaire refrigerator.")
- Origins of words ("Frigid comes from rigid, which is what things are when they're frozen solid.")
- Pictures or diagrams

Journal/Learning Log Sections

Writing in literature response journals or learning logs is a common practice that can help students increase their vocabulary stores. Students might informally record their impressions of a passage they just listened to, notes about a topic, predictions about a story ending, memories of past events, and so on. In many classrooms, a special section of the journal or log is reserved for vocabulary.. Students record new words and meanings, along with the types of information suggested above for word books.

Books Too Good to Miss

Some books for children call special attention to words by presenting them in humourous or unusual ways. For instance, countless children have delighted in Amelia Bedilia's literal attempts to dress a chicken and draw the drapes. Some more recent books that highlight wordplay are

Brian Wildsmith's Amazing World of Words, by B. Wildsmith, Millbrook Press, 1997.
Dear Dr. Silly Bear, by D. C. Regan, New York: Holt, 1997.
Double Trouble in Walla Walla, by A. Clements, Millbrook Press, 1997.
Tangle Town, by K. Cyrus, Farrar, Straus & Giroux, 1997.
Night Knight, by H. Ziefert, Houghton Mifflin, 1997.

Represent Word Meanings Multiple Ways

Vocabulary development is such a complex enterprise that multiple actions are needed for maximum effects (Stahl & Fairbanks, 1986). Most words we know have been encountered on a number of occasions in various situations. Perhaps you first experienced the word *hot* when you burned your finger touching food that came right from the stove. As you cried out, your mother repeated, "Hot! I've told you never to touch anything hot from the stove. Even when the food is out, it stays hot for a long time. You see how hot things burn. Never, never touch hot things again." This experience and the word *hot* are not likely to be forgotten. But at this point, you have only a limited concept of "hot." This concept will be broadened as you hear that word in relationship to multiple experiences—a hot summer day; the car's engine overheating; the desert heat portrayed in a movie. Related meanings of the word also become apparent in various situations ("The team is hot," "Coach got hot because no one was following directions," "The spicy food is hot"). These experiences broaden and delineate your grasp of this simple word by representing it multiple ways. Just as you come to know friends well after sharing varied public and private life experiences, you come to learn words well by experiencing their meanings represented multiple ways.

Classrooms that represent word meanings multiple ways allow learners plentiful access to vocabulary. They help students broaden and deepen their hold on words, resulting in elaborated knowledge. They demonstrate how word meanings change according to how they are used. Multiple representations also provide diverse learners opportunities to use the visual, auditory, and social modes of learning they prefer. Especially when presenting vocabulary intensively, word meanings can be represented through direct experience, media, dramatization, making connections, and categorization.

Direct Experience

Children often develop their vocabularies best when they directly experience what words depict. Children benefit from talking about their hands-on experiences. A sports topic could lead to you or your students bringing in the equipment noted in a passage, playing the game, and talking about the concepts that are involved. Garden implements, attempts to grow flowers or vegetables, and ongoing conversations could accompany stories and passages about growth. If primary-grade students are addressing shoes, students could match shoe pairs, talk about when and why different types of shoes might be worn (dress shoes, sport sneakers, pool sandals, work boots), and have a salesperson present what he or she knows about footwear and does for a living. If actual events, objects, or models of objects are not possible, bring in representative pictures and talk about them. Labeling and talking about direct experiences is an especially important teaching-learning practice for children learning English.

As you and your students move through passages, seize opportunities to experience directly what words portray. If the word *ledge* appears, point out any window or table ledges within sight. *Pierce* can be connected with students' pierced ears, or you might punch a little hole in a piece of paper to demonstrate piercing.

Media

Many young children have a concept for mountain even if they have never been in the presence of a mountain. Most young children can recognize zebras, elephants, and monkeys even though they may never have been to a zoo, circus, or other place with these animals. Many children who have never sailed or been in a canoe know what canoes are. How did this learning occur? Did someone explain to them what a mountain was? Was the dictionary definition of monkeys read to them? Did some adult attempt to explain or define a canoe? In most cases, when children have concepts for objects and realities they have never directly experienced, they have seen these objects or realities portrayed on television, in movies or videos, in pictures or picture books, and in computer simulations.

Teachers often introduce word meanings as the terms are encountered through audiovisual media; then they refer to those representations continually when later talking about the words. Many primary-grade classrooms contain displays of colors, numbers, foods, animals, furniture, transportation devices, and so on, along with the word that corresponds to each item. A related practice is for students to gather pictures from magazines, newspapers, and catalogs. Having students first label the items and then show and describe what they produced allows them to extend their vocabulary through media in a meaningful social situation.

Word posters are another form of media that children can produce. Students select one word and illustrate it on a poster. You can have students sign up for words so that no two posters are about the same word, or you can let repetition occur where it will. Both approaches have their advantages and disadvantages. In either case, the students may first use whatever textual or human sources are available to determine an understanding of the word chosen and then look for or draw pictures that illustrate the word. In addition, a student may use a short caption for each picture to add to the poster's clarity in representing the word. Word posters are a meaningful homework assignment.

Dramatization

Word dramatizations involve physical performances that represent particular word meanings. Most word dramatizations involve relatively brief skits. Depending on the age and sophistication of the students, either the teacher or small groups of students make up skits. To make up a skit, take a word from a book or theme study and develop a two-minute scenario in which students extemporaneously act and speak so that the meaning of selected words becomes clear. Act out the skit in front of the class; then talk about both the skit and the wprd being taught. For instance, imagine that you wish to teach a class of first-graders the word *curious*. Consider how acting out the following skit might serve as a good introduction:

> A girl and a boy pretend to be a boy and his mother walking down a street. Two children pretend to be playing hopscotch at one place along the street. Two more children pretend to be brothers and sisters arguing over whose turn it is to help clean up after dinner. As the "mother and son" walk down the street, the boy keeps listening to each conversation, or watching the game, asking questions to try to find out who's winning or what someone said. All this time, the mother keeps trying to get him to come along, for she is in a hurry. The mother and everyone else keep remarking how curious the boy is.

When the actors finish the skit, the teacher asks the audience what curious means. Most children have had direct experience being curious, even if they did not attach the word *curious* to the experience. The teacher can help children activate their prior knowledge by asking, "What have you been curious about? Have you ever been in a situation where someone got into trouble for being too curious? Do you know someone who is a really curious person? Have you seen really curious animals?" While not providing children with the direct experience of *curious*, these questions help children call up from their experience a situation in which they were curious and connect the term to the experience.

Students often pantomime the actions of poems, short stories, or informational passages that are being read aloud. In a total physical response setting, after reading or listening to a passage, students respond with their body to directives such as the following:

> Point to the picture of the horse.
>
> Move like an elephant.
>
> Show how Pat feels panicked when she loses her money.

As with skits, there is follow-up talk about the vocabulary represented in the dramatization.

Making Connections

If a child asks you, "What does cancel mean?" you might respond by saying something like, "Sometimes school is canceled because of bad weather. It means to end something." In this case, the child could connect prior knowledge and experience with an unknown term to make sense of it. As explained in our presentation on the connect thinking process and on prior knowledge, learners constantly associate familiar ideas with unfamiliar ones. Teachers who explain unfamiliar words and ideas in terms of familiar ones go far in promoting vocabulary. Connecting vocabulary with learners' prior knowledge is a top priority in effective classrooms.

A common way to connect vocabulary with prior knowledge is to explain how two concepts are alike and different. Children come to school with thousands of well-developed concepts built through firsthand experience, and these funds of knowledge grow especially well in meaningful settings during the school years. A big part of a teacher's job is explaining how the knowledge gained from previous experiences relates to the new words students encounter. For instance, if you were teaching the term *magma*, you might compare it with tar:

> Magma is like tar. Do you remember the tar that was put on the roof last year? Magma is like tar because they are both sticky and slow-moving liquids when they are hot. When they cool, they both become extremely hard. Magma is different from tar because magma consists of melted rocks and is found beneath the earth's crust, whereas tar comes from plants.

An important point about comparing and contrasting concepts is that your students must know what is being used to teach the unfamiliar concept. If students don't know what tar is, the connection presented above will not be effective. Explaining that the British game of rounders is a lot like cricket is not helpful if you don't know the game of cricket.

One way to extend thinking about how two concepts are alike and different is to have students produce the links. First, teach the meanings of new words as well as you can; then have students produce similarities and differences. You might say, "Write down events that were planned and then *canceled*," "What do you know that is like *magma*?," and "Select a sport and explain how it is similar to and different from *rounders*." Students could produce examples individually or in small groups and then share them as a class. Individuals could make their own comparisons and contrasts every day when reviewing the vocabulary displayed on a topic board. Selected examples could be recorded in word books or the vocabulary sections of journals.

Vocabulary can be connected with learners' prior knowledge in ways that go beyond comparing and contrasting concepts. When students in your presence encounter unfamiliar words, ask, "What do you know that can help you understand and remember this word?" In addition, the suggestions above for what to include in word books and vocabulary sections of journals are good possibilities. Students connect ideas when they call up personal experiences with what a word refers to ("I remember a time when I was 'exhilarated'") and when they generate morphemic word families, sometimes in sentence form ("Bakers bake baked goods in bakeries"). Asking what images new words elicit also taps prior knowledge ("What do you think an osprey looks like?").

Other types of connections highlight the associations of one word with another more than the relationships among words and prior experiences and knowledge. Speaking and writing are wonderful opportunities for students to make connections between words. Producing stories, poems, and informational passages by definition entails putting words together. Children who think about or ask, "What's a good way to describe the playground?" and "What's another way to say that my friend is friendly?" are connecting concepts and words. When they plan their writing with others, they talk about how they will connect words in print ("I'm going to say she was 'humorous,' then say why").

A word-connecting activity that includes both speaking and writing is Capsule Vocabulary. This technique stresses social aspects of word learning by having students purposely, yet informally, talk about related sets of words and their meanings (Crist, 1975). Capsule Vocabulary emphasizes practice and application of vocabulary in supportive social settings. Students take a set of about ten terms that have been introduced and intentionally work them into a conversation with classmates. Students working as pairs seem to do best with this activity. The partners record the words that have been used. After each partner talks through the set of words, they individually write a summary of the topic containing the terms, exchange papers, and comment on each other's word usage. Set aside a certain time, perhaps fifteen minutes, for this entire activity.

Still another way to emphasize word associations throughout the year is with cloze. Cloze involves students supplying words for ones that are deleted in sentences and passages. The deletions can occur any way:

1. I went to the store and saw a _____.
2. I went to the _____ and saw a banana.
3. I went to the store and _____ a banana.
4. I _____ to the store and saw a banana.

Any of the deletions would lead students to fill in the blank with words they associate with the surrounding words. For sentence 1, students name what they see in stores; for sentence 2, they name where they might go and see bananas; and so on.

Along with sentences, students can examine short passages such as the following that are constructed either just for the lesson or taken from a passage the students are reading:

A tree grew in the _____. Pat was _____ when he saw it. He _____ to the tree and began climbing it. Before he got too far, he _____.

Again, students complete sentences such as the above with words they associate with the surrounding ones. For the first blank, you might support students' efforts by asking, "Where do trees grow that someone named Pat might see?" As you can see, cloze calls on students to attend to passage grammar as well as associate words.

A teaching practice called "Can These Two Go Together?" is also a good way to direct attention to word relationships. Put two words together in a question that students can answer only with *yes* or *no.* You or your students can be the ones to make up the sentences. The responses can be written or stated orally, and hands can be raised for yes and then for no. For instance, the following questions might be asked about words associated with *volcanoes*:

1. Do *igneous* rocks come from *magma?*
2. Are *volcanoes* made from *lava?*
3. Would you find *igneous* rocks around *volcanoes?*
4. Is *magma* the same thing as *lava?*

Be sure to talk about students' reasons for deciding whether or not two things can go together as stated in controversial sentences. For instance, in sentence number 4, students could argue convincingly for or against the truth of the proposition. Acknowledging their valid points would help represent the meanings of the target words.

Categorization

Categorizing words is one specific way of connecting words that also requires students to organize. Category names can be produced before or after the groupings. If you provide category names before students group the words, correct answers would be expected. If students are allowed to invent their own categories, correctness is based on the students' explanations for the categories.

For instance, if primary-grade children were reading about food, they might categorize the following items:

apple	pizza	ice cream
hamburger	cake	peach
orange	hot dog	pie

Many times children like recording each word on a separate slip of paper in order to physically manipulate and group the words. Additionally, you might produce one or more category topics and then have students supply examples such as

Fruit	Dessert	Meat Dish

You and your class might display the categories in a graphic organizer or web according to their relationship with one another (see pages 201–203 of this text).

Displaying terms in main idea–detail or sequential arrangements promotes deep understandings of the relationships among vocabulary. It is like producing a map of a topically related group of words.

Accommodations and Adaptations for Vocabulary

FOR INCLUSION

All children need a variety of activities to increase their prior knowledge and vocabulary stores. For children who are hearing impaired and children with various physical problems that limit their mobility, prior knowledge and vocabulary development are especially crucial. Many of the concepts we have and words we know were learned in incidental ways as we went through our daily activities. Conversations during trips to the grocery store and Sunday afternoon outings are not intended to develop children's prior knowledge and word stores, but they do. Many hearing-impaired children have to have their attention focused on the speakers and their hearing aids turned on in order to make sense of speech. Many children with physical disabilities have not been taken along on the normal "outings" of life. These two groups of children need huge doses of activities that build prior knowledge and meaning vocabulary. If these children are part of your classroom, make extra efforts to include as many direct experiences as possible. Buddy these children up with another child who can demonstrate and explain unfamiliar concepts. Children with hearing and physical impairments do not need different prior-knowledge/meaning-vocabulary activities, but they do need a lot more of them.

FOR CHILDREN ACQUIRING ENGLISH

Many children have limited English vocabularies because English is their second— or even third or fourth—language. Perhaps the main guideline regarding vocabulary instruction with these students is to honor all languages. Let students know that you respect their native language and that you expect them to learn English, too. Display words written both in children's dominant languages and in English. Have students interact with specific terms in their native language and in English. Have students name concepts in their primary language and connect the names with their English counterparts.

Accept children's accents, focusing on word meanings more than word pronunciations. Focus on what children are communicating more than the form. Correct language miscues gently and quickly, and after first attending to the content of children's messages. Encourage students who are less proficient in English to participate in school activities with students who are more proficient; both students will benefit from the language interactions.

Develop Independence in Vocabulary Learning

Selecting and intensively teaching particular words pays off in students learning a few words well and in developing students' word consciousness. However, presenting words one at a time—even in related sets—never would provide students what they need for proficient reading and writing. Students need opportunities to encounter on their own thousands of words in meaningful contexts, along with the means to take advantage of those encounters. They need to be able to capitalize on the opportunities language-rich environments offer. Students require the ability to go it alone in understanding and remembering words. Students require independence in vocabulary learning.

Many of the practices described in this chapter so far promote independent learning of vocabulary. Students who regularly activate their prior knowledge, enthusiastically engage in word learning, select words from their reading for group consideration, consistently connect what they already know with new ideas, and represent word meanings multiple ways enhance their independent learning of new words. Some additional specific practices that promote independence in vocabulary learning are discussed below.

Using Context

Using context refers to determining the meaning of an unfamiliar word by noting the way it is presented in a passage. Passages frequently provide clear, direct explanations of unfamiliar words, so students should learn to pay attention to those explanations. For instance, a passage might contain these sentences: "All rocks that were formed from fiery hot magma, whether they cooled above or below the earth's surface, are called igneous rocks. Igneous means 'fire-formed.'" Focusing students' attention on these sentences during a comprehension lesson would go far in teaching the meaning of *igneous,* and—perhaps more important—in teaching how passage contexts can reveal word meanings.

One caution about relying on context is that it does not always directly reveal the meanings of unfamiliar words. For example, the sentence "The chiaroscuro was excellent" does not provide enough information about *chiaroscuro* to enable you to form an adequate meaning. You know that *chiaroscuro* is something that can vary in quality, but that is all. Consequently, inform students that many word meanings can be inferred from context but many cannot. The strategy of using context to determine word meanings is best summarized as follows: "When there's a hard word in the sentence, look for other words that tell you more about that word" (Cantine, Kameenui, & Coyle, 1984, p. 198).

Model how to use context at the beginning of the year when reading aloud passages and guiding students' reading. Then support students' use of context during their self-selected and guided-reading experiences.

Using Morphemes

As described in Chapter 4 morphemes consist of prefixes, roots, and suffixes, which are meaningful parts of words. *Morphemic analysis* consists of identifying prefixes, roots, and suffixes found in derived words; it also consists of identifying meaningful parts found in compound words and contractions. Morphemes differ from syllables because morphemes are portions of meaning, and syllables are portions of sound. For instance, *disagreeable* contains three morphemes (*dis/agree/able*) and five syllables (*dis/a/gree/a/ble*). Analyzing the three morphemes in *disagreeable* helps readers determine its meaning.

Teaching students to note morphemes is a valuable way to remember words and to determine independently the meanings of unfamiliar words. To do this teaching, analyze the parts of derived words as presented in Chapter 4. That is, if *international* is a word selected for intensive teaching, point out how *inter* and *al* are attached to *nation*, and describe the effect the affixes have on the root.

A powerful way for students to grasp morphemic analysis is to understand the power of morphemic word families. A morphemic word family consists of words derived from the same root, or base. For instance, *volcano, volcanoes,* and *volcanic* make up a morphemic word family; *igneous, ignite, reignite,* and *ignition* make up another.

To teach students morphemic word families, take a selected word from a passage or unit and write its derived forms in a column. Underline the common word part and tell students its meaning. Present each word in a sentence or short paragraph so that students learn how the meaning of the common element remains constant even though the derived words are different.

Accommodations and Adaptations for Morphemic Analysis

FOR CHILDREN ACQUIRING ENGLISH

Language learners tend to transfer some of the knowledge and skills of their native language to the language they are learning. In the case of Spanish-speaking students, cognates seem to be one aspect of their language that has much potential for help with English (Nagy, Garcia, Durgunoglu, & Hancin-Bhatt, 1993). Cognates are words derived from the same form. These are some Spanish-English cognates:

naturalmente	naturally
clima	climate
curioso	curious
novelas	novels
decidir	decide

Instruction in Spanish-English cognates should follow the guidelines for instruction in using morphemes described above. Indeed, a shared morpheme is what makes up a cognate pair. Students who are sensitive to meaningful parts of words can decide whether or not the parts are related across languages. Systematic relationships

(continued)

(e.g., reality-realidad, exactly-exactamente) are especially good candidates for special attention. Many Spanish and English words beginning with the letter *v* are cognates.

* *

Using the Dictionary

Look at the following word and notice how incredibly fast a meaning pops into your mind:

Purple

Now think of the definition of purple. Are you finding that instead of having a definition of purple memorized, you are having to use your understanding of purple to make one up? In other words, your understanding of words can be used to construct definitions, but your understanding of words is not a set of definitions. In fact, your understanding of words is often a set of nonverbal sensations (images, memories of events) and related words. Generally, the only words for which you have memorized definitions stored in your memory are those words that you do not understand. For years, one of us kept trying to understand *existentialism* as a philosophy or school of thought. He never understood it, but then, and to this day, he always remembered the definition: "The philosophy that existence precedes essence." Perhaps had he ever come to understand *existentialism*, he would have forgotten that definition.

Having students memorize definitions of words as a means of building their meaning vocabularies cannot succeed, because understanding a word means that you do *not* have a definition stored in memory for it. Reading dictionary definitions can remind us of meanings we already understand or can refine or add precision to meanings we already have. Expecting a definition to provide the package of related words necessary to understanding a word meaning to the point of usefulness is like expecting a photograph to be an adequate substitute for getting to know someone.

Think back to your elementary school days. Do you remember looking up words and copying their definitions? If the word had several definitions (as most words do), which one did you copy? The first one? The shortest one? What did you do if the dictionary definition contained a word for which you didn't know the meaning? Most of us have had the experience of looking up words, copying the definition (first or shortest), and then memorizing it for a test, regardless of whether we understood it. As soon as the test was over, however, most of the really unfamiliar words were forgotten. Those words for which you already had some associations were remembered, however, and their meanings were probably broadened by the experience of checking the dictionary definition. Consequently, have students use the dictionary to check or add to a word's meaning. Do not allow students to copy definitions.

Students Teaching Key Words

After teachers have intensively taught selected words a few times, students should know how to present new vocabulary. They can work individually or in pairs to prepare their own lessons to the whole class or to small groups. They might bring in a concrete representation of what the word means; find a picture, slide, or other media; create a skit; and explain how their prior experiences relate. Students will need some initial help with this work, but as time goes on they become more adept. As students teach their lessons, remind them that they can perform some of these activities whenever they meet a word for which they do not have meaning. "Where could I find a picture? I wonder if there is one in my text," "Is this like anything I already know?," and "What can I do to understand and remember this word?" are models for how students should think when faced with an unknown, important vocabulary.

Promote Vocabulary in All Subjects

Vocabulary instruction goes on all day every day during effective elementary school teaching of different subjects. One of the primary goals, especially of social studies and science, is to help children develop rich concepts for events, places, people, and phenomena. Field trips that take children out of the classroom and guests and objects brought into the classroom provide direct experiences for concept development. Teachers should make maximum use of these opportunities by preparing the children ahead of time for what they will experience and by leading them through discussions and other language-oriented activities after the experience. This helps children sort through the experience, connect appropriate words with the information they encounter, and store what they learned for later use.

Having students learn what an informational passage says about terms such as *magma, lava, igneous rocks,* and *volcanoes* is valuable. Reading materials in all subjects include sources such as informational books and periodicals along with textbooks. Reading helps children understand and better organize the world in which they live; informational books provide a wonderful way to do that. They are often more interesting than textbooks, because the authors of children's informational books know that their products will be purchased and read by children only if the children enjoy them. But learning word meanings through direct experience and media is also appropriate. For instance, you could bring in examples of igneous rocks, watch a video about volcanoes, and demonstrate volcanic action.

Videos, DVDs, and CD-ROMS are other sources that many teachers use to help children develop concepts for things that they have not directly experienced. The common classroom sharing period in primary grades presents meaningful settings for vocabulary development. Questions related to the objects brought to share such as "What is this object made of?," "Is this object more than one foot long?," "Where would we find these objects?," and "Can anyone think of other objects that are usually this color?" help focus the children's attention on vocabulary development as it relates to the objects the children are directly experiencing. Group discussions and writing foster vocabulary development as children clarify concepts by talking and writing about them.

The instructional strategies presented so far in this chapter apply to the prior knowledge and vocabulary emphasized in all school subjects. Teachers and students maintain topic boards, produce word posters, dramatize word meanings, and use morphemes with terms from science, social studies, and mathematics. The teaching suggestion that follows, scavenger hunts, activates prior knowledge and develops vocabulary by emphasizing media and direct experience. We present scavenger hunts as an example of a way to highlight and teach the extensive vocabularies encountered during subject matter instruction.

Scavenger hunts are a way of gathering objects and pictures to represent concepts that need developing (Vaughn, Crawley, & Mountain, 1979). Imagine that you are about to begin a science unit on weather. You look through the passages your students are going to read; preview videos and other teaching aids; and make a list of the unfamiliar vocabulary you will teach as you increase their store of information on the topic of weather. Your list includes *evaporation, condensation, cirrus clouds, cumulus clouds, stratus clouds, precipitation, temperature, humidity, barometer, thermometer, cyclone, tornado, hurricane, meteorologist, wind vane, rain gauge,* and a variety of other words. Of these words, some can be represented by pictures (indirect experience) and objects (direct experience). Other's, such as *evaporation, condensation, precipitation, temperature,* and *humidity,* cannot be represented directly or indirectly. Take all of the words on your list that can be represented by pictures or objects—*cirrus clouds, cumulus clouds, stratus clouds, barometer, thermometer, cyclone, tornado, hurricane, meteorologist, wind vane,* and *rain gauge*—and add to these terms some familiar, picturable words related to the topic of weather such as *snow, rain, ice, lightning, fog, frost,* and *rainbow* until you have a list of twenty to twenty-five picturable words that relate to the topic of weather. You now have your list of things for which your students will scavenge.

Assign your students to teams of four or five and provide each team with the list. Set a date (a week or two from when the list is provided) on which the teams are to bring a picture or object representing as many of the items on the list as they can find. To the students' inevitable question, "How can I bring a hurricane?" your response will be, "You can bring a *picture* of a hurricane." Two points are given for each object and one point for each picture. Pictures can be illustrations, photographs, tracings, or drawings, as long as they actually represent the word. Allow the team time to discuss what the different words mean and who might be able to find an object or picture representing each. If some of the words are truly unfamiliar to your students, a question such as "What's a rain gauge?" may arise. Depending on the maturity of your students and on whether this is their first or their tenth scavenger hunt, you may choose to respond by explaining what each word means or by saying, "I guess you will have to look it up somewhere. It's hard to find a picture or object that represents something if you don't know what that something is." This response should send your teams to their dictionaries or other reference sources.

Allow the teams to meet several times during the time they are scavenging. They should check things off the list as pictures and objects are found. Do not, however, allow any pictures or objects to come to school before the appointed date. Teams should be cautioned to keep secret what they find and where they found it. On the appointed day, each team will assemble and show their pictures and objects. The teacher will total the points for each team (two for each object, one for each picture—only one picture and object per word per team). The team with the most points is the winner. Because winners like to get a prize, what better prize than being allowed to create the bulletin board? What bulletin board? The weather bulletin board! You would not want to let all of those pictures go to waste. The winning team, therefore, should design the bulletin board so that each word is printed in large letters and the different pictures that represent it are displayed with the word. (A word without any pictures might be displayed by itself—a challenge to someone to find a picture.) What about the objects? Any objects that are valuable, dangerous, or live must be taken back home. But the rest can be displayed on the table you place underneath the bulletin board. Also, you will need to say in big bold letters somewhere, *"Weather bulletin board created by winners of weather scavenger hunt,"* and include a list of the winner's names.

You are now ready to begin your unit on weather. More important, your students are now ready. Having spent the previous week or two collecting objects and pictures related to the topic of weather, they have increased their general knowledge of that topic (perhaps they talked to the local meteorologist, or watched the weather report, or even read an intriguing section of the reference book from which they traced their picture of cirrus clouds) and have a much greater interest in the topic of weather. You also have a marvelous bulletin board with representations of the portion of your meaning vocabulary that can be represented by objects and pictures. Some of your meaning vocabulary that could not be directly or indirectly represented can be easily understood with reference to the pictures and objects: *precipitation* is a form of moisture such as *rain* or *snow; temperature* is measured with *thermometers.*

Now that the children have enjoyed their first scavenger hunt and have begun their actual study of weather, what next? Perhaps you plan to study Mexico soon, and your Mexico topic includes words such as *Copper Canyon, pyramids,* and *desert;* maybe you are developing a unit on animals, and words such as *polar bears, cobras,* and *gerbils* are part of it. The children will certainly be ready for another scavenger hunt. This time, having learned how to hunt for objects and pictures, how to find out what unfamiliar words mean, and how to create a bulletin board, they will be much more ready to get right to work on locating these representations.

The Theory and Research Base for Prior-Knowledge Activation and Vocabulary Instruction

For quite some time, educational researchers have realized that readers and writers rely on prior knowledge (Herbart, 1898) and meaning vocabulary (Thorndike, 1921). Research in the 1980s and 1990s on these topics worked to specify how students use prior knowledge and meaning vocabulary and how to promote this practice. Some research focused on writing (DeGroff, 1987), but most was devoted to reading comprehension.

To date, the best general explanation of how prior knowledge facilitates reading comprehension is still the 1984 review of schema theory by Anderson and Pearson. In this review, prior knowledge is said to provide a schema, which is a framework or knowledge structure that facilitates thinking. For instance, readers familiar with sports can predict that a passage about a baseball game will have nine players on each side, the players will field different positions, some will be better than others, one team will win and another will lose, and so on.

Prior knowledge also allows readers to assimilate information readily. Readers map ideas from a text onto preexisting ideas. Sports-minded readers can readily understand and remember the progress of a baseball game because they have a general idea of what should happen.

In addition, prior knowledge helps readers perform inferential elaboration; it helps readers "fill in the blanks" left by authors. Authors assume their readers share common understandings, so they do not thoroughly explain everything in a passage. For instance, baseball fans have an advantage understanding snide comments about designated hitters' fielding abilities because they know that these players are expected only to bat and not to field.

The role of prior knowledge explained through schema theory does not account for the entire reading comprehension process (Sadoski, Paivio, & Goetz, 1991; Carver, 1992). For instance, schema theory does not explain readers' images nor readers' seemingly effortless apprehension of ideas contained in easy-to-read materials. But it explains enough to warrant educators' attention to prior knowledge.

Stahl and his colleagues (Stahl, Jacobson, Davis, & Davis, 1989; Stahl, Hare, Sinatra, & Gregory, 1991) investigated the roles prior knowledge and meaning vocabulary play in passage comprehension. These studies showed that students' knowledge of a passage's topic affected comprehension differently than did their knowledge of a passage's vocabulary. Prior knowledge influenced their understanding of the gist of a passage, whereas vocabulary knowledge affected their comprehension of details. These studies showed that teachers should attend to both prior knowledge and meaning vocabulary because each plays an independent role in reading comprehension.

Educational researchers conducted and reported numerous vocabulary studies during the 1980s and early 1990s, but this attention waned in the middle 1990s. To illustrate, Hiebert and Raphael (1996) devoted only one paragraph to this topic in forty-two pages of text reviewing psychological perspectives on literacy research. Three excellent reviews of the earlier research are by Baumann and Kameenui (1991), Beck and McKeown (1991), and Graves (1986). Additionally, the *Encyclopedia of English Studies and Language Arts* contains three consecutive entries on vocabulary that are quite informative (Blachowicz & Fisher, 1994; Graves, 1994; Scott & Nagy, 1994). Among other things, these reviews clarify distinctions between teaching specific words and teaching students how to learn words independently.

Another point to remember from these reviews is that vocabulary instruction should emphasize motivational aspects. Teachers should help students develop a sense of curiosity about words, an appreciation for their nuances of meaning, and an enjoyment and satisfaction in their wise use.

Looking Back

Reading and writing performance is strongly affected by students' knowledge of what they are reading and writing about. Thus, prior knowledge activation is a crucial part of preparing to read and write, and it can be accomplished many ways. Along with activating prior knowledge, students require access to word meanings when reading and writing. This access too can be accomplished many ways. This chapter developed six key ideas:

1. Activate prior knowledge when presenting new ideas.
2. Introduce vocabulary in meaningful settings.
3. Select vocabulary for intensive teaching.
4. Represent word meanings multiple ways.
5. Develop independence in vocabulary learning.
6. Promote vocabulary in all subjects.

Add to Your Journal

Think about the six key ideas presented in this chapter. What connections can you make to your own vocabulary learning in school? What images do these ideas evoke? What conclusions or generalizations can you draw from this information? Use some or all of the eight thinking processes to think about each of these key ideas. Be sure to include your evaluation of these ideas and your plans for applying them in your classroom.

Application Activities

Listen, Look, and Learn

Observe at least one class session in which students are encountering new concepts, such as the introduction to a new unit of study or to a new topic within an ongoing unit. Note how students' prior knowledge is activated. What did they do to call up and connect what they already knew with what they were preparing to learn? Ask the teacher how he or she prefers activating prior knowledge. What techniques does the teacher prefer? How do they compare with the ones suggested in this chapter?

Try It Out

List three to five words that you have learned in the past few months. Distinguish between words that you were taught and ones that you learned entirely on your own. Describe the situations in which you encountered the words, how you came to understand them, and why you remembered their meaning. Did you learn these words through direct experience, media, dramatizations, making connections, categorizing, or some combinations of all these activities?

Add to Your Resource File

The Books Too Good to Miss section in this chapter listed some books that help children enjoy words. Find three more books, particularly recent books, that promote children's fascination with and enthusiasm for words. Give a complete bibliographic reference for each and a summary including how you think this book would promote "word wonderment."

Do It Together

Pick a topic you might teach and select five words that would be critical to learning that topic. Plan a lesson in which you teach these five words using some of the activities in this chapter.

References

Anderson, R. C., & Pearson, P. D. (1984). A schema-theoretic view of basic processes in reading comprehension. In P. D. Pearson (Ed.), *Handbook of reading research* (pp. 255–291). New York: Longman.

Baumann, J. F., & Kameenui, E. J. (1991). Research on vocabulary instruction: Ode to Voltaire. In J. Flood, J. M. Jensen, D. Lapp, & J. R. Squire (Eds.), *Handbook of research on teaching the English language arts* (pp. 604–632). New York: Macmillan.

Beck, I., & McKeown, M. (1991). Conditions of vocabulary acquisition In R. Barr, M. L. Kamil, P. B. Mosenthal, & P. D. Pearson (Eds.), *Handbook of reading research* (vol. 2, pp. 789–814). White Plains, NY: Longman.

Blachowicz, C. L. Z., & Fisher, P. J. L. (1994). Vocabulary instruction. In A. C. Purves (Ed.), *Encyclopedia of English studies and language arts* (vol. 2, pp. 1244–1246). Urbana, IL: National Council of Teachers of English.

Bruner, J. (1961). *The process of education.* Cambridge, MA: Harvard University Press.

Carnine, D., Kameenui, E., & Coyle, G. (1984). Utilization of contextual information in determining the meanings of unfamiliar words in context. *Reading Research Quarterly, 19,* 188–204.

Carver, R. P. (1992). Commentary: Effect of prediction activities, prior knowledge, and text type upon amount comprehended: Using rauding theory to critique schema theory research. *Reading Research Quarterly, 27,* 165–174.

Chinn, C. A., & Brewer, W. F. (1993). The role of anomalous data in knowledge acquisition: A theoretical framework and implications for science instruction. *Review of Educational Research, 63,* 1–49.

Crist, B. J. (1975). One capsule a week—a painless remedy for vocabulary ills. *Journal of Reading, 19,* 147–149.

DeGroff, L. (1987). The influence of prior knowledge on writing, conferencing, and revising. *Elementary School journal, 88,* 105–118.

Elley, W. B. (1989). Vocabulary acquisition from listening to stories. *Reading Research Quarterly, 24,* 174–187.

Fisher, P. J. L., Blachowitz, C. L. Z., & Smith, J. C. (1991). Vocabulary learning in literature discussion groups. In J. Zutell & S. McCormick (Eds.), *Learner factors/teacher factors: Issues in literacy research and instruction* (pp. 201–209). 4th Yearbook of National Reading Conference. Chicago, National Reading Conference.

Graves, M. (1986). Vocabulary learning and instruction. In E. Z. Rothkoph (Ed.), *Review of research in education* (vol. 13, pp. 49–90). Washington, DC: American Educational Research Association.

Graves, M. (1994). Vocabulary knowledge. In A. C. Purves (Ed.), *Encyclopedia of English studies and language arts* (vol. 2, pp. 1246–1248). Urbana, IL: National Council of Teachers of English.

Guzzetti, B. J., Snyder, T. E., Glass, G. V., & Gamas, W. S. (1993). Promoting conceptual change in science: A comparative meta-analysis of instructional interventions from reading education and science education. *Reading Research Quarterly, 28,* 116–159.

Haggard, M. R. (1986). The vocabulary self-collection strategy: Using student interest and world knowledge to enhance vocabulary growth. *Journal of Reading, 29,* 634–642.

Herbart, J. (B. C. Mulliner, Ed. and Trans.). (1898). *The application of psychology to the science of education.* London: Swan Sonnenschein.

Hiebert, E. H., & Raphael, T. E. (1996). Psychological perspectives on literacy and extensions to educational practice. In D. C. Berliner & R. C. Calfee (Eds.), *Handbook of educational psychology* (pp. 550–602). New York: Macmillan.

Nagy, W. E., Garcia, G. E., Durgunoglu, A. Y., & Hancin-Bhatt, B. (1993). Spanish-English bilingual students' use of cognates in English reading. *Journal of Reading Behavior, 25,* 241–259.

Sadoski, M., Paivio, A., & Goetz, E. T. (1991). Commentary: A critique of schema theory in reading and a dual encoding alternative. *Reading Research Quarterly, 26,* 463–484.

Scott, J. A., & Nagy, W. E. (1994). Vocabulary development. In A. C. Purves (Ed.), *Encyclopedia of English studies and language arts* (vol. 2, pp. 1242–1244). Urbana, IL: National Council of Teachers of English.

Spivey, N. N. (1997). *The constructivist metaphor.* New York: Ablex.

Stahl, S., & Fairbanks, M. M. (1986). The effects of vocabulary instruction: A model-based meta-analysis. *Review of Educational Research, 56,* 72–110.

Stahl, S. A., Hare, V. C., Sinatra, R., & Gregory, J. F. (1991). Defining the role of prior knowledge and vocabulary in reading comprehension: The retiring of number 41. *Journal of Reading Behavior, 23,* 487–508.

Stahl, S. A., Jacobson, M. G., Davis, C. E., & Davis, R. L. (1989). Prior knowledge and difficult vocabulary in the comprehension of unfamiliar text. *Reading Research Quarterly, 24,* 27–43.

Sternberg, R. J. (1987). Most words are learned from context. In M. G. McKeown & M. E. Curtis (Eds.), *The acquisition of word meanings* (pp. 89–106). Hillsdale, NJ: Erlbaum.

Thorndike, E. L. (1921). *The teacher's word book.* New York: Columbia University, Teachers College.

Vaughn, S., Crawley, S., & Mountain, L. A. (1979). A multiple-modality approach to word study: Vocabulary scavenger hunts. *The Reading Teacher, 32,* 434–437.

Wigfield, A., Eccles, J. S., & Rodriguez, D. (1998). The development of children's motivation in school contexts. In P. D. Pearson & A. Iran-Nejad (Eds.), *Review of Research in Education* (vol. 23, pp. 73–118). Washington, DC: American Educational Research Association.

Children's Books/Materials Cited

See box on page 133.

Additional Readings

- Attention to unfamiliar words before reading helps activate prior knowledge, which this article details.

  Wood, K. D., & Robinson, N. (1983). Vocabulary, language, and prediction: A prereading strategy. *Reading Teacher, 36,* 392–395.

- These articles offer perspective and strategies for helping students learn words independently.

  Hillerich, R. L. (1989). Developing independence in word meaning. *Teaching PreK–8, 20,* 26–28.

  White, T., Sowell, J., & Yanagihara, A. (1989). Teaching elementary students to use word-part clues. *Reading Teacher, 43,* 302–308.

  Buikema, J. L., & Graves, M. F. (1993). Teaching students to use context cues to infer word meanings. *Journal of Reading, 36,* 450–457.

- A consideration of the complex relationships among vocabulary knowledge and passage comprehension is offered here.

  Ruddell, M. R. (1994). Vocabulary knowledge and comprehension: A comprehension-process view of complex literary relationships. In R. B. Ruddell, M. R. Ruddell, & H. Singer (Eds.), *Theoretical models and processes of reading* (4th ed., pp. 414–447). Newark, DE: International Reading Association.

- Practical activities with lots of real classroom examples can be found in this book.

  Blachowicz, C., & Fisher, E. (1996). *Teaching vocabulary in all classrooms.* Englewood Cliffs, NJ: Prentice Hall.

- Many educational authorities over the years have researched and written about developing vocabularies for reading and writing. Three classic publications are as follows:

  Gray, W. S., & Holmes, E. (1938). *The development of meaning vocabularies in reading.* Chicago: University of Chicago.

  Johnson, D. D., & Pearson, P. D. (1984). *Teaching reading vocabulary.* New York: Holt, Rinehart & Winston.

  Petty, W. T. (1968). *The state of knowledge about the teaching of vocabulary.* Champaign, IL: National Council of Teachers of English.

Chapter 6

Reading and Responding to Literature for Children

L o o k i n g   A h e a d

In the galaxy of literature, a world of books exists for children. Some of these books achieve literary and artistic recognition. Various awards presented to the authors and illustrators of high-quality children's books include the John Newbery Medal, the Randolph Caldecott Medal, the National Book Award, and the Boston Globe–Horn Book Award. However, not all literature for children has been in contention for these awards. Many past generations of readers grew up with book series such as Nancy Drew or the Hardy Boys; young children of other eras have enjoyed the Henry Huggins and Ramona stories. Although efforts such as these are rarely singled out as exemplars of the writer's and illustrator's craft, they are ones that children search out, benefit from, and enjoy. Additionally, children read a wide range of magazines that include worthwhile fictional and informational text.

$\mathcal{H}$ere we purposely use the terms *literature for children* and *children's books* to refer to critically acclaimed as well as popular publications for young people. In this chapter we introduce children's books and present classroom uses of them. This chapter contains six key ideas:

1. Welcome the diverse world of literature.
2. Use literature to promote thinking and feeling.
3. Link reading and writing instruction with children's books.

4. Schedule daily self-selected reading.
5. Celebrate book response projects.
6. Enrich all subjects with literature.

Welcome the Diverse World of Literature

Children's books exist for all ages and interests. There are books about all kinds of people, places, and topics. There are books that entertain, enchant, and inform. They contain exciting stories, stimulate children's imaginations, present valuable ideas, and evoke novel experiences. They transport children to new worlds. The categories of literature for children presented below suggest some of what is available. These categories, or genres, only hint at the richness of the world of children's books; you need to spend time exploring these genres with young people to appreciate all they have to offer.

alphabet books	modern and historical fiction
biography	multicultural literature
concept books	mystery
counting books	poetry
fables, myths, and epics	picture books
fairy tales	realistic fiction
fantasy	science fiction
folk literature	wordless books
informational books	

Three of the genres presented above—folk literature, fantasy, and informational books—may not be familiar by the titles we have used. Because of this, we describe these three somewhat fully. At the same time, by realizing how broad these three genres are, you can see that all genres might contain more possibilities than you suspect.

Folk literature encompasses fairy tales, folktales, epics, myths, and fables. Although modern fairy tales such as *Dove Isabeau* and *The Rainbabies* may be written, we normally think of fairy tales as part of folk literature. Folk literature consists of tales for which there is no identifiable single author or for whom authorship is in doubt because the stories have been in existence for so long. Cinderella stories are common tales in all culture groups, and many of us grew up with tales of the "threes": pigs, goats, and bears. These stories were first part of the oral tradition and written down only much later.

Fantasy is also a broad genre. It includes both classic fantasies (such as *Alice's Adventures in Wonderland* and *Charlotte's Web*) and modern ones (such as *Jumanji, Polar Express,* and *Tuesday*) as well as science fiction and science fantasy. The distinction between the last two may be somewhat blurry. But essentially, science fiction books contain scientific facts that have the possibility of being extrapolated from reality; science fantasy books involve the supernatural or are so futuristic that currently known scientific facts do not allow the extrapolation that occurs. A good example of science fiction is *This Time of Darkness,* whereas *A Wrinkle in Time* embodies the essence of science fantasies.

Another type of book is the *informational book.* This category contains factual materials for science, social studies, cooking, and other content areas, as well as "concept books" for the very young dealing with the alphabet or relationships of time, space, and amount (such as *The Handmade Alphabet, Exactly the Opposite,* and *Of Colors and Things*). When we think of informational books, often an image of dull, pedantic, sterile writing comes to mind. If that ever were characteristic of informational books, it certainly is no longer. The illustrations and photographs of many current informational books enrich the text and are high quality; the writing is lively and entertaining.

Informational books explain something to children or teach them how to do something. For example, there are many children's cookbooks, such as *Kitchen Fun for Kids: Healthy Recipes and Nutrition Facts for 7- to 12-Year-Old Cooks.* Other books that explain the human body to children in clear yet interesting ways include *The Brain: Our Nervous System, Sleep Is for Everyone,* and *Why Can't I Live Forever?* Children learn about life in prehistoric times with *Dinosaur Valley* and learn how to make many fun and interesting objects in *Nature Crafts* and *Papier-Mache Project Book.* Books such as *Bears* describe the life cycle of a particular species of animal.

Welcoming folk literature, fantasy, and informational books into your classroom—as well as all the other genres—is an essential preliminary step toward effective reading instruction. Different types of readings address different aspects of the world and appeal to different children. One book does not fit all. An array of genres in your classroom goes far in meeting children's interests and needs as you move through the year.

Technology Tips

Websites provide good information about current children's books. The following sites are worth checking:

Children's Book Council (www.cbc.books.org)

Children's Literature (www.parentsplace.com/readroom/index.html)

Children's Literature Web Guide (www.ucalgary.ca/~dkbrown)

The Children's Bookstore (www.iquest.net/cbooks)

Use Literature to Promote Thinking and Feeling

Involving children with the literature you welcome into your classroom promotes many outcomes. You learned in Chapter 1 that thinking is the essence of reading and writing and that feeling energizes reading and writing. Classrooms in which literature pervades the day are classrooms in which literacy, thinking processes, and feelings combine and mutually develop each other.

Literature Links to Thinking

Children's books can provide excellent opportunities for thinking in general, and reading and writing strategies in particular. For instance, *The Very Hungry Caterpillar* promotes children's reading countless ways by supporting their efforts at making sense of it. The initial pictures set the stage for the story, so early readers get off to a good start with the poetic opening line, "In the light of the moon a little egg lay on a leaf." The author's presentation of the caterpillar progressing through each day of the week offers a familiar structure that supports early readers' grasp of the story line. Repetition of the phrase "was still hungry" offers a predictable language pattern for readers to lock onto. Actual holes in the pages vividly depict just how hungry the caterpillar was. The ending of the book, "That night he had a stomach ache," registers with young children who also have eaten too many rich foods.

Along with supporting readers through books, well-written literature extends reading strategies by providing models of structure and style. For instance, children have ready access to figurative language when reading about the "carpet of snow" and the "white statues" presented in *Owl Moon*. Their grasp of multiple-meaning words is developed by the Amelia Bedelia books when she literally "dusts the furniture" and "draws the drapes." Themes become readily apparent in the *Fables* that Arnold Lobel presents. Books like *Meanwhile Back at the Ranch* and *Fortunately* foster the organized thinking process by relating textual ideas in quite comprehensible ways, yet ones that differ from conventional chronological or main idea-detail progressions.

Literature promotes the connect process when authors directly tie textual information to children's worlds, and when children form their own connections with ideas they encounter. Children's books readily allow readers to form images and tap into other sensory associations by providing abundant illustrations, pictures, and vivid language. Literature for children also presents ready examples of vocabulary, characterization, main ideas, plots, and so on. Books support and extend students' thinking and literacy proficiencies.

Literature Links to Positive Feelings

Readers respond emotionally to what they read. This response is important to keep in mind when planning instruction because the intellectual side of reading is frequently emphasized over the emotional side, though both deserve attention. Literature for children goes far in promoting positive feelings.

The experience of reading is emphasized when readers become deeply absorbed in books' ideas, as well as in the manner by which those ideas are presented. When the experience of reading is positive, children enjoy reading for its own sake, for the joyful satisfaction of being with print. For instance, countless young children have positively experienced "The Elephant's Child," absorbing the language cadence and rhythm, the imagery, the ideas, and the identity of the young elephant who runs away to "the great grey-green, greasy Limpopo River."

One way to understand literary experience as a positive feeling is to realize the need for the literary work itself (Rosenblatt,1938/1983). In activities such as learning facts from a biology textbook, an exact paraphrase of the book can be as useful and have as much impact as the original. However, for literary experiences to accentuate positive feelings, readers need to encounter the actual work firsthand. Consider the following poem by Langston Hughes (1932):

April Rain Song
Let the rain kiss you.
  Let the rain beat upon your head with silver liquid drops.
  Let the rain sing you a lullaby.
  The rain makes still pools on the sidewalk.
  The rain makes running pools in the gutter.
  The rain plays a little sleep-song on our roof at night,
  And I love the rain.

A paraphrase or summary of this poem would destroy its essence because the beauty and nuances of the language would be lost. The full experience of reading involves qualities of language beyond the direct, specific meanings denoted by words.

Literature for children also promotes imaginative release. The Dr. Seuss books, *Winnie-the-Pooh*, and *Frog and Toad Together* are examples of books that exist mainly for the joy of reading. Escaping into a good mystery or fantasy can provide the release many children need to cope with the pressures of the outside world. Children can identify with Max in *Where the Wild Things Are*, who is sent to his room but who escapes through his imagination to the land of the Wild Things. After holding a wild rumpus, Max leaves the land of the Wild Things and returns to his real-life home and finds dinner still hot and waiting for him. Like Max, children often need to escape to other worlds and let their imaginations run free.

Some reading programs devote exclusive attention toward teaching students how to read. That is, young students work daily on developing their word identification and comprehension strategies by reading short instructional passages and by completing study sheets related to the passages. The problem with these programs is that they fail to show students why they should read. The strategy work is frequently done at the expense of developing feelings about reading, and the result is students who can read but have no desire to do so. Linking reading and writing instruction with children's books fosters a love of reading that is as important as—if not more important than—acquiring any particular set of strategies.

Accommodations and Adaptations— Just the Right Book

FOR INCLUSION

Books do so many things for all children that children with special needs are sure to find a variety of books they will enjoy and relate to. There are, however, some particular books you should know about. Books written about challenging life situations promote children's resiliencies in light of such situations. Books about children who face physical challenges, children whose families are having problems, and children who feel different from everyone else are too numerous to list here, but you should know that a large variety exist. The following bibliographies are good starting points for identifying books that address challenging situations:

Bibliotherapy with Young People, by B. Doll & C. Doll. Englewood, CO: Libraries Unlimited, 1997.

Books to Help Children Cope with Separation and Loss (4th ed.), by M. K. Rudman, K. D. Gagne, & J. E. Bernstein. New York: R. R. Bowker, 1993.

Portraying Persons with Disabilities, by J. G. Friedberg, J. B. Mullins, & A. W. Sukiennik. New Providence, NJ: R. R. Bowker, 1992.

Sensitive Issues: An Annotated Guide to Children's Literature, by T. V. Rasisnski & C. S. Gillespie. Phoenix, AZ: Oryx, 1992.

FOR CHILDREN ACQUIRING ENGLISH

Children acquiring English benefit from culturally responsive classrooms, environments bridging home and school that provide a sense of belonging. These classrooms affirm children's membership in school by displaying pictures and phrases and by inviting community members to share food, music, and other customs that reflect all students' heritages. Along these lines, culturally responsive classrooms contain books reflecting and celebrating students' particular cultural backgrounds. The following references describe some of these books:

A Hispanic Heritage, Series 4: A Guide to Juvenile Books about Hispanic People and Cultures, by I. Schon. Metuchen, NJ: Scarecrow Press, 1991.

Connecting Cultures: A Guide to Multicultural Literature for Children, by R. L. Thomas. New Providence, NJ: R. R. Bowker, 1996.

Multiethnic Children's Literature, by G. Ramirez & J. Ramirez. Albany, NY: Delmar, 1994.

Our Family, Our Friends, Our World: An Annotated Guide to Significant Multicultural Books for Children and Teenagers, by L. Miller-Lachmann. New Providence, NJ: R. R. Bowker, 1992.

The Literature Connection: A Read-Aloud Guide for Multicultural Classrooms, by B. A. Smallwood. Reading, MA: Addison-Wesley, 1991.

Link Reading and Writing Instruction with Children's Books

Effective teachers link reading and writing instruction with children's books. They often use stories in their district's reading series as jump-offs to engage children with whole books. If, for instance, a story in their reading series is an excerpted chapter from a novel, they will read the novel aloud to the children or break away from the series and guide the children's reading of the novel. Other times, they have groups of children read particular books because of common interests. Effective teachers often provide instruction and assess children's progress through individual conferences.

These teachers feel compelled to ensure that their students are taught the strategies their reading series lays out, but they don't believe that they must have the children read all of the stories in a particular reader. They know that the strategies can be taught in a variety of ways and with a variety of materials.

Effective teachers frequently read aloud chapter books so that children have the opportunity to see characters develop through a long work and because the teachers know that children enjoy a long piece and look forward to coming to school to find out what will happen in the next chapter. They also read informational books, biographies, mysteries, and books about sports heroes, because they believe that a child who doesn't like to read is just a child who hasn't yet discovered the perfect book—and that *perfect* is a very personal matter. These teachers always read at least once a day to their students, and most weeks they find that they have read more than once a day.

Effective teachers ensure that all students engage in daily self-selected reading by scheduling it as a regular event. Effective teachers have many tapes of books. Children who can't read very well yet but would like to read a particular book follow along in the book as they listen to the tape. These children also spend time actually reading easier books that are within their range.

Effective teachers believe that it is important to have a classroom library that will encourage independent reading by children. They are constantly looking for ways to increase their libraries, such as having children bring some of their own books to school to lend to the room library for a few weeks. Their libraries include a variety of books at many different reading levels and interests, and they try to make the area conducive to reading by providing rugs and floor pillows. These teachers attract children to the area by reading aloud some of the books, by talking about them, and by displaying books on a specific topic or by featuring an author or illustrator of the month.

Children are expected to share and refine their responses to what they read with the teacher during individual conferences. The children might record their thoughts in journals or discuss them with classmates. They occasionally produce, within a certain range, somewhat elaborate response projects. Effective teachers offer projects to choose from, as well as encouraging students to come up with projects of their own. The types of response projects that are offered vary, although effective teachers know that responses involving expressive language—writing and speaking—have more impact on literacy achievement than drawing, so art projects tied to books are completed at home and during free time in school.

As the description above shows, classrooms that link literacy with children's books balance opportunities for meaningful reading and writing with instruction on how to read and write meaningfully. Here are some specific practices effective teachers use to link their reading and writing instruction with children's books.

Reading Aloud to Children

No matter what the grade level, exciting, well-read books capture the class's attention. Listening to written language read well encourages students to read, promotes thinking, builds language, and promotes a positive attitude toward books. In many classrooms, the teacher reads to students twice a day. Reading early in the morning seems to begin the day with a positive tone, and reading just before school is out ends the day on a similar note. Other transition times corresponding to recess, lunch, and special classes are appropriate for reading aloud, too.

Selecting the books you intend to present and the order in which you will present them are an important aspect of reading aloud. Primary-grade teachers reread favorites such as *Corduroy* and *The Giving Tree* several times so that students can respond to them at different levels. This practice is similar to bedtime or lap story reading practices wherein children experience the identical book many times. Many teachers present clusters of books by the same author or illustrator, or they find others on the same topic. The topic is often tied to the subject matter being presented in social studies or science; for instance, *Out of the Dust* and *Potato* are shared when studying the Great Depression.

Selecting books that stretch students' imaginations and concepts is an important part of a read-aloud program (Hoffman, Roser, & Battle, 1993). You can share materials with children that they would have difficulty reading on their own. School librarians will suggest books appropriate for oral reading, and they might be able to tell you which books teachers in other grades read aloud to their children so that you can avoid overlap.

Children of all ages benefit from listening to passages read aloud by an accomplished reader. Teachers, aides, and parents can be the ones to read to children. When reading aloud, your voice and gestures should convey enthusiasm and positive feelings for the book. Since familiarity with the passage is essential for effective oral reading, first read to yourself what you will later read orally to your students. Teachers generally introduce a book to a class by connecting its author, illustrator, or contents with materials the children already know. If the book contains pictures, share them with the children when appropriate. Follow-up discussion, writing, or art projects are appropriate when used in moderation. Also, reading comprehension techniques are appropriate for listening comprehension. Finally, you might encourage students to borrow a book they enjoyed hearing read to read it for themselves.

Book Talks

Teachers and librarians frequently promote literature through book talks. Book talks encourage reading by presenting brief summaries of parts of books, oral readings of excerpts, and comments about the contents. Those who present book talks share the contents of the materials in intriguing ways so that students want to read the entire work; book talks are like attempts to sell the book. After talking about books and showing them to the audience, make the materials available so that students have access to the ones they want as soon as possible.

Having students present book talks to their classmates is a good variation on having only teachers and librarians present them. Children often position themselves in a special reader's chair when they try to sell their book to the rest of the class. They follow the same book-talk pattern as the adults, reading a small portion or two of the book, summarizing parts, and sharing their opinions on the book.

Book Displays

Like book talks, book displays entice children to read selected materials. Book displays are advertisements for a particular cluster of reading materials. Bulletin boards, pictures, decorations, and concrete objects are used to draw readers to the books, just as department stores set up displays to attract consumers to their products. Teachers and librarians frequently choose an author or illustrator, learn the month when that person was born, and then set up displays promoting the person's work during that month. As is done with book talks, the materials to be promoted in book displays might be grouped because they are new, relate to a certain topic, have general wide appeal, or were produced by the same person.

Many teachers enlist groups of students to create book displays, knowing that classmates often trust—or at least are interested in—each other's opinions. A good variation on traditional book displays is a classroom bookboard. Divide a bulletin board into forty to fifty spaces for intermediate-grade students; then write the title of a promising book in each space. Next, designate three sticky-note colors to represent degrees of approval. Green might mean "Super, two thumbs up!" Yellow might mean "OK, one thumb up." Red could mean "Terrible, two thumbs down!" After reading a book listed on the bookboard, students sign a colored note representing their rating and post it in the space. Teachers conduct weekly discussions of the books' ratings, noting ones that are rated consistently and those that are not.

Literature Response Journals

Many teachers find that an easy and natural way to connect reading and writing with literature is to have students keep response journals (Routman, 1991). Children are encouraged to take some time after reading each day and record their thoughts, feelings, and predictions (see Figure 6.1 for examples). Teachers

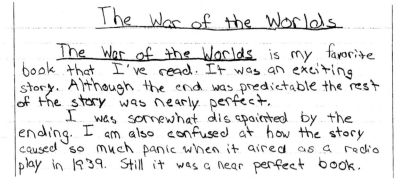

book Meanwhile back at the ranch.

I like meanwhile back at the ranch a lot it Makes me laugh cuse rancher hicks goes out to sleepy gulch and elnas gettin evry thing!

Book: *Meanwhile Back at the Ranch.* I like *Meanwhile Back at the Ranch* a lot. It makes me laugh 'cause Rancher Hicks goes out to Sleepy Gulch and Elna's getting everything!

The War of the Worlds

The War of the Worlds is my favorite book that I've read. It was an exciting story. Although the end was predictable the rest of the story was nearly perfect.

I was somewhat disapointed by the ending. I am also confused at how the story caused so much panic when it aired as a radio play in 1939. Still it was a near perfect book.

Figure 6.1 These two examples were taken from the literature response journals of a first-grader and a fourth-grader.

model this by recording some of their personal responses. From time to time during teacher–student conferences, children and their teachers can share the responses they have written. Thus, students come to conferences with their books as well as their journals. This is often a good time for promoting discussion of divergent responses to stories and clearing difficulties.

Sudduth (1989) reported that many of her third-graders didn't really know what to record in their literature journals. This was especially true of those children who were finding learning to read difficult. She outlined the step-by-step instruction she took them through:

1. At first, have the students read the same book. They can read this silently or with a partner or listen to a tape recording or to a teacher reading aloud. Have specific stopping points in the reading, and help the children to verbalize what they are thinking and feeling.

2. On chart paper or the overhead, record some of the students' responses and have children copy the ones they agree with into their logs. Use sentence frames such as:

I was surprised when . . .

I predict that _____ will happen next because . . .

The story reminds me of . . .

3. As students understand the various open-ended ways in which they can respond to literature, move them toward independence. Continue the discussions but don't write down what they say. Rather, have them write their own personal entries following the discussions. Have the class brainstorm a list of log topics and frames and display these so students can refer to them when they need starters.

4. Have students choose books they want to read and produce their own response journals. You might divide the time available for self-selected reading into reading time and journal-writing time, perhaps twenty minutes to read and ten minutes to write. Once children are reading individual books, provide time each week for sharing in small groups what they have written.

Perhaps the greatest contribution of producing responses in a journal is that they enable students to determine for themselves how thoroughly and imaginatively they comprehended a piece of literature. To produce an overt response to what has been read, students need to step back and sort out their thinking. If they find their comprehension to be inadequate, they can rethink and reread the passage to obtain a deeper insight. Without such response activities, students often become stranded at superficial levels of comprehension.

Journal response activities also get students into the habit of processing literature thoughtfully (Hancock, 1992). That is, as you regularly help students interpret and evaluate literature, they can learn to interpret and evaluate it on their own. Students then become used to expecting insight from what they read, and they are not satisfied until such insight is obtained.

Literature Discussion Groups

Literature discussion groups—often called literature circles or book clubs—provide children with opportunities to share and refine their responses in the company of others (Gambrell & Almasi, 1996; McMahon & Raphael, 1997). Teachers meet with the groups from time to time and model discussions with the whole class, but the emphasis in discussion groups is on students interacting with each other. Young people act like adults participating in real-life book clubs sponsored by community agencies, churches, or informal circles of friends.

Book discussions give children the chance to talk about what they have read, sharing what they know and investigating what is vague or unknown. Book discussions offer children a chance to explore their ideas about books. Young people work together to uncover new meanings in literature and support their interpretations with ideas and facts from the materials. The idea is to construct responses first to what has been read and then to the constructions themselves. Ideal discussions consist of conversations between students, as opposed to question-and-answer recitations.

To begin literature discussion groups, address the social skills needed for productive interactions. Model the skills in whole-class situations, being quite explicit about what they are and why they are important. One teacher relies on a single guideline, "No ugliness" (Sierra-Perry, 1996, p. 20), to direct students' book club interactions. After participating in effective discussions as a whole class, students might produce a somewhat specific Looks Like/Sounds Like/Feels Like chart (Vogt, 1996) such as the one below to remind them of the social skills needed in small groups:

Looks Like	*Sounds Like*	*Feels Like*
• People face each other.	• One person at a time talks.	• Others take my ideas seriously.
• People concentrate on what others are saying.	• No one dominates.	• I learn new ideas from what others say.

The books to be discussed can be selected several ways. The whole class might have one book read aloud to them, or the class all might read copies of the same book. Children then break into small groups to talk about portions of text that have been covered. You might pull together sets of about eight copies each of particular books, describe each collection to the class, and then have students sign up for a group to read and discuss the book according to their interest. These sets can be related to a single theme. You might also form small groups of students who individually select their own materials for discussion.

When students gather for literature discussions, they might begin with one person reading aloud from his or her response journal. Another entry to discussion involves generic, open-ended questions such as the following:

What will you remember most about the passage?

What is the most important word, sentence, or section?

What have you read that is similar?

What did the characters learn?

What did you learn?

What should others know about the passage?

What part of the book do you wonder about?

If you rewrote this book, what would you change?

How did the author hold your attention?

What parts made you feel the strongest?

Why would you like or not like to read other books by this author (and illustrator)?

To maintain the discussion in response to questions such as the ones above, say, "Tell me more about that," and "What else can be said?" If the students' comments are unclear or fragmentary, ask for restatements or clarifications with questions such as "What do you mean?"

Questions that fit only the story being discussed are also appropriate. For instance, the Junior Great Books Program suggests that its discussion leaders begin a second-grade discussion of *Jack and the Beanstalk* by asking whether Jack succeeds mainly by luck or by his own abilities (Kuenzer, 1978).

An important rule for teachers and students to follow throughout these discussions is to ask only those questions that have more than one correct answer. When the questioner is certain of the answer to a question, the discussion becomes a closed search for what is in that person's mind rather than an open exploration of ideas.

Schedule Daily Self-Selected Reading

Because daily self-selected reading is typically the centerpiece in successful efforts to link reading and writing instruction with children's books, we highlight it here with a major heading of its own. Practically every effective literacy program includes daily self-selected reading in some fashion, centering it as the core to reading aloud to children, book talks, book displays, literature response journals, and literature discussion groups.

Self-selected reading involves students with materials of their choice. Self-selected reading requires extensive, varied reading materials because all class members read. Thus, a wide selection of books, magazines, newspapers, and pamphlets is needed. Self-selected reading is characterized by free-reading time, a quiet place, and abundant materials. Ensuring that students read large quantities of material enhances their opportunities to expand their strategies, knowledge of the world, attitudes about reading, and feelings on topics. The power of self-selection lies with children investing themselves fully in whatever they choose to do.

> ## Did You Know That?
>
> *If students read just seventy-five minutes a week, their word knowledge, fluency, and comprehension increase noticeably (Anderson, Wilson, & Fielding, 1988). Seventy-five minutes a week, or fifteen minutes each school day, is a small investment for a large return.*

Because all students deserve an opportunity to read self-selected materials, we recommend setting aside a regular time of the day for this. A common practice is to encourage students to read on their own after they have completed their assigned schoolwork. Students take out a book and read at their desks or in a designated area. This practice is helpful for students who finish quickly, but it discriminates against those who seldom finish early—the same students who are most in need of extra reading.

Setting Up Self-Selected Reading

To begin self-selected reading in your classroom, collect a large assortment of reading materials. Some collections are stored in a classroom library corner of the room, some are divided among boxes or baskets and placed on groups' tables, and some are scattered about the room in various learning centers. Change the collections according to criteria such as the topics being studied in class, children's developing interests and proficiencies, what the popular media are emphasizing, what genres have been underrepresented, what is newly published, and what is available from the school and public libraries. Include multiple copies of old favorites. Highlight promising new materials when adding them to the collection.

Once reading materials are obtained, each child chooses what to read from the collection. Set aside about twenty minutes of the school day for private or buddy reading of the self-selected materials. Some teachers set aside the time immediately after breaks in the day such as lunch or recess because self-selected reading typically settles children down. Specify an exact amount of time for this activity, and keep your class to that time. Many teachers use a timer to signal the end of reading time. The time spent reading can be gradually increased as your students become better able to stay with a sustained reading task. Some teachers start off lower primary-grade children with five minutes a session and gradually increase it to fifteen minutes by the end of the year. Other primary teachers find that their students can sustain self-selected reading for longer periods. Teachers should try out different times during the first couple of weeks in school to determine a starting point.

Before beginning a self-selected reading session, ensure that each child has gathered material to read. Most classrooms have a few students who require help selecting and staying with a book. You will need to pay special attention so these students have materials they like plus clear guidelines to follow. After allowing a few minutes to select materials, inform your class that everybody is to read silently for the specified time. Many teachers hold individual conferences with students about their self-selected reading choices. In some classrooms, the self-selected reading time ends each day, with a few children sharing their books and reactions to them with others.

Teacher–Student Conferences

In many classrooms, teacher–student book conferences accompany daily self-selected reading. Teachers schedule brief meetings—three to five minutes—with individual students. Many teachers designate certain students for Monday, others for Tuesday, and so on, to ensure that they meet all students within a week. Students bring to the conference one book they would like to share. Typically they read a short segment and then talk with the teacher about how that portion of text fits the overall passage, explaining why they chose it to read. This practice allows teachers to converse with students about what they are reading while simultaneously noting (often on an ongoing record form) students' reading strategies and skills. Teachers remain updated on what children are reading independently and the progress being made. They can support children's efforts with encouragement and specific suggestions about strategies. They can suggest additional books children might like on the same topic or by the same author. Conversely, students have a special personal time to talk with their teacher about books. They can check in with their teacher, asking questions and gaining insights into sophisticated reading expectations and ways of talking about books.

Some teachers go to where the children are reading and confer with them there. Other teachers sit at a table and call students to them. Most teachers ask children to read a page or two from their chosen books to determine the levels of difficulty they are handling. They also pose a general question or two, choosing from those listed above in the section on literature discussion groups or asking some of the following:

> Why did you choose this book?
>
> Have you read any other book by this author?
>
> Is your book fiction (made up) or nonfiction (informational)?
>
> What do you think will happen next?
>
> How did the author make the facts interesting in this book?

All children like to tell you what they think. We use open-ended questions to help them form and tell us about their reading preferences:

> What did you like about this book?
>
> Who was your favorite character?

Was there anything you didn't like about this book?

What was your favorite part?

Did the book have any pictures you really liked?

What was the most interesting thing you learned in this book?

What was the funniest (saddest, most surprising, silliest, strangest) part of this book?

As you think about your conferences with children on books, keep in mind that no one likes to be interrogated! View the conference as a conversation between you and the child. Using questions such as those above will move the conversation forward.

Building a Classroom Library

To have a successful self-selected reading program requires time, commitment, and a large collection of all kinds of reading materials readily available in the classroom. The problem many teachers (particularly beginning teachers) face is how to acquire a sufficient quantity of such materials. Stocking a classroom with bright, new books purchased with school-district money is too often a distant dream. Nevertheless, we encourage you to search for book monies among the labyrinth of school budgets, district grants, and outside grants. School administrators generally don't advertise that they have extra funds available, but if you present a specific, already prepared book order that requires only a signature and a school purchase order, you might be pleasantly surprised. However, if that doesn't work, or if it does work but you need still more books to fill a classroom library, consider the following options.

Borrowing from Libraries

Sharing books among classrooms and borrowing a quantity of books at one time from the school library are ways to bring literature into your classroom. Rotating books this way allows you to get the most mileage out of what is currently available at your school. Furthermore, a close working relationship with your school librarian can do wonders toward acquiring and promoting children's literature. Most schools have scheduled times for classes to visit the library and check books out, but inviting the librarian to come into your classroom to promote books that have just arrived can work also. Another important service that the school librarian can perform is to compile books that relate to a certain unit or theme that you are exploring with your class. Literature can be collected at your city or county library and brought into your class for a specific period too. Up to twenty books at a time usually may be acquired this way.

Involving Parents

The PTSA and other groups of concerned people can be mobilized. Parents often want to help out, but they don't know what to do. Asking them to gather, borrow, and buy literature for children directs them toward a worthwhile goal. When Christmas arrives and you prepare to receive presents from your class, you might suggest books. Perfume, handkerchiefs, and neckties are nice, but you probably would do better with a good, new item of children's literature to share with your class. Another way to stock your classroom library is to have children bring in books from their personal collections to share with the class. Children enjoy reading their favorite books to their peers and then placing that book in the library.

Building Children's Personal Collections

Helping students acquire books for their personal collections at home also deserves attention. Book fairs can be held at which representatives from one or more book companies come to your school and display their books for sale. Although book fairs are designed ostensibly to sell books, they also seem to sell enthusiasm and interest in reading. Watching young students move among all of the new books as they prepare to purchase one confirms this second outcome. In addition, the money earned from book fairs can go toward purchasing materials for your classroom library.

Another way to help students build a personal collection is to participate in book clubs such as Lucky, See Saw, and Troll. Such clubs typically mail teachers invitations to participate. In book clubs, students' orders are sent to a specific company. The bonus books that come with a minimum order are good additions to the classroom library.

Subscriptions to children's periodicals such as *Your Big Backyard, Kids Discover, Disney Adventures,* and *Zoobooks* are good ways to build children's collections of reading materials. Few techniques seem better at encouraging children to read than receiving magazines through the mail.

Student-run bookstores are a relatively new way to help students build personal collections. Students and their sponsor order books (at a substantial discount), organize inventory, advertise, and manage workers. Students not only learn the essential elements of running a small business but also provide a service for the school by making a wide range of inexpensive books readily accessible to large numbers of students.

Celebrate Book Response Projects

Teachers and students moving through the school year in effective classrooms punctuate their everyday instructional routines by celebrating book response projects. Celebrations are enjoyable occasions set aside to honor others' efforts publicly; in this case, teachers and students honor the creative compositions class members produce in response to what they read. These occasions are meant to enliven and energize readers even more than usual. Teachers rarely assign grades when celebrating book response projects, preferring to comment only on positive aspects and informally noting whether or not individuals invested reasonable

efforts. If everyday practices such as daily self-selected reading and literature response journals are the bread and butter of instruction, then celebrations of book
response projects are the delicacies.

Book response projects conducive to celebrations are often related to what students read during their self-selected reading time, although they can be parts of
subject-matter study. They involve somewhat elaborate productions, often encom-
passing more than a week's effort and involving the help of classmates, family
members, or friends. Students might work on their projects on a daily basis, but individuals or groups present their final products to an audience only during special
occasions. Some classrooms have a daily time set aside for celebrating what has
been produced as individuals and groups come forward to present their efforts to
the whole class.

Children often choose the project they wish to pursue in response to a book.
The two categories we have found most effective include story retellings/recreations
and visuals.

Story Retellings/Re-Creations

Retelling and re-creating stories help children respond to literature by sharing what
they have read or listened to in dramatic form. Dramatization is a powerful
medium for constructing interpretations of favorite stories (Heinig, 1992). Dramatic story retellings and re-creations consist of activities such as puppetry, story
acting, lap stories, flannel boards, acetate stories, and readers' theater.

Some general guidelines are appropriate for conducting story retellings and re-
creations. The following steps are the framework for retelling or re-creating a story:

1. Have students read the story knowing that it will be performed or written
   about later.
2. Describe the key characters, summarize the key events, and block scenes.
3. List props for the performance or written retelling; prepare props, if needed.
4. Narrate the story and have children supply the dialogue while manipulating
   the props, or have children write it in play or story form.

When the teacher performs the narrator's role, control over the presentation is
maintained. The children who are performing certain roles can be readily directed
to speak when their turn arises. If a child does not know what to say, the teacher
may help out as long as the designated child actually speaks for the character.
Memorizing dialogue or reading directly from a script while manipulating story
characters might be appropriate in certain situations, but having students produce
dialogue as needed seems to promote better understanding of passages.

Numerous variations or innovations of folk and fairy tales exist in children's literature. Western (1980) and Worthy and Bloodgood (1993) describe numerous activities to engage children in comparisons of folk-literature variants. The innovations
that children read act as models for their own creations. Additionally, higher-order

thinking is required of children as they compare variants. You might elect, for example, to engage children in variants of *The Three Little Pigs*. You would bring into your classroom titles such as *The Three Little Pigs* (Galdone and Zemach versions), *The Three Little Javelinas, Three Little Pigs and the Big Bad Wolf, The True Story of the Three Little Pigs,* and *The Three Little Wolves and the Big Bad Pig.* Western details the steps in comparing story structure elements across variants. Worthy and Bloodgood list several comparison tasks for children to engage in. Having children write innovations once they have read and analyzed numerous examples is a logical next step. Of course, children could also create a production for their variation instead.

Children would also enjoy hunting for variants if you start them with a single title such as *How Many Spots Does a Leopard Have? and Other Tales* or *The Stinky Cheese Man and Other Fairly Stupid Tales.* Many children also enjoy creating innovations of friends' original stories in the classroom.

Puppets

Children can and will make puppets out of any material. We found that having some books on how to make puppets (e.g., Currel, 1980) and having boxes that contain raw materials such as socks, paper-mache, colored paper, and other colorful materials provide enough for children to produce puppets for story retellings. Large and small stages are needed for children to crouch behind to present their stories. Many teachers simply turn a table over on its side to create a puppet stage.

Acting It Out

With very few props, children can act out stories that have been read. Teachers often allow groups of children who particularly enjoyed a story to dramatize it, and others have children in a reading group act out a story. It is best to begin story acting with small segments that children mime as the story is read aloud. A simple passage with only a few events should be used at first. Later, you can move to more complex passages containing several characters and much action. Dialogue can be added when the children seem ready.

Lap Stories

The lap story requires a small painted or covered board that will fit in your lap and sheets of unlined paper to tear into the shapes of story characters and props. If you desire, clay can be used for molding, though it takes much longer to complete the story. Ask, "Who is in this story?" and as a child names a character, give the child a sheet of paper or a lump of clay. Direct the child to create the character by tearing the paper or molding the clay into a representative form. No drawing or cutting is allowed. However, if children are tearing paper, they can be given colored markers to add details after the tearing is done. Although clay can be used to make the characters, we believe it is best to have children tear paper into shapes because it seems to reduce anxiety about art. We've had children say, "I can't draw a bear," but practically everyone can *tear* a bear, and the children know it. For this activity, we want to decrease the emphasis on art and increase the emphasis on storytelling.

After various children have been given paper or clay for the creation of characters, ask them, "What else do we need for this story?" Children should identify needed major props such as the bridge for *The Three Billy Goats Gruff* or three porridge bowls, three chairs, and three beds for *Goldilocks and the Three Bears*. Children may also want to include nonessential props such as the forest or other items of furniture. The only limitation you have is based on how much your lap can hold and how much your hands can manipulate. We have gotten ourselves into a pretty pickle on occasion by allowing all the children to create items for the lap story, only to find a lap insufficient to hold it all.

With younger children, partially prepare the paper in advance for certain stories. For *The Three Billy Goats Gruff*, for instance, three sizes of paper are provided so that the goats don't end up being the same size. When the lap story is finished, the characters and props can be placed in a large envelope, labeled with the story name, and placed in a learning center or story box. Then children can get the envelope and retell the story whenever they wish. Even when the paper shapes become tattered, we have found that it is no great problem. For one thing, they represent very little time or money investment, and children can easily replace the tattered forms with new ones. Finally, we take the salvageable shapes from several envelopes (tossing out the ruined ones) and put them together in a "Make a New Story" envelope to derive even more use.

Lap stories are more easily done with small groups of children, but they also work well with entire classes. The only caution is to seat the children close enough to you so that all can see and enjoy the story.

Flannel-Board Stories

Another type of story retelling that is common in the elementary school classroom is done with the use of the flannel board. Story retellings can be done with a surface covered with a material with a nap (such as felt or flannel) and objects representing characters and props that will stick to the surface of the flannel board. The size of the surface used for flannel boards ranges from very large, heavy easels that are virtually untransportable to small, cardboard stationery or pencil boxes with hinged lids that children can use individually at their seats.

Some people make all their characters and props from colorful felt pieces and glue on contrasting felt or draw details with colored markers. Others cut out paper characters from books or draw paper characters that they seal with clear adhesive paper to protect the figure and give it more substance. A small piece of felt or sandpaper is glued onto the back of these paper figures so that they will adhere to the surface of the flannel board. Again, these characters are manipulated by the teacher as narrator, with children providing the dialogue; alternatively, children use the flannel boards by themselves to retell familiar stories.

Acetate Stories

Acetate stories call for the creation of miniature transparencies of story characters and props. Place a sheet of acetate, such as that used to make overhead transparencies, over the illustrations in the book you want to use for story retelling. It is important that the pictures are not too large; an overhead projector enlarges what it projects, and you may have a wall full of dragon without room for any other characters or props on the screen.

When the acetate has been carefully placed over the desired picture, trace around the shape of the illustration with a thin-line, permanent-ink transparency marker. It is important to use the permanent-ink markers because water-based ink will not adhere to the acetate. After the shapes and internal details are outlined, fill them in with thin-line, permanent-ink markers in various colors. After the acetate pictures have dried (it takes only a few moments), peel back part of the backing from a sheet of clear, adhesive plastic. Place the side of the acetate you just colored on the sticky side of the plastic. Cut around the edges of your characters and props so that you have the tiny acetate figures to go with a story the children know. What remains is a little transparency that can be projected on a screen for you and your children to use in story retellings.

Readers' Theater

Most children like to read plays. However, locating and affording quantities of plays appropriate for classrooms are difficult tasks, so many teachers turn to readers' theater as an alternative. Many variations of readers' theater are available (Sloyer, 1982); the following is a basic explanation of how to produce a readers' theater in a busy classroom.

Readers' theater consists of designating readers as particular story characters or the narrator and having them orally read the appropriate dialogue and narrative of a story. When introducing this technique for whole-class participation, have the students follow along in a story as a small group demonstrates the technique. Another way to introduce readers' theater is to reproduce part of a story on an overhead transparency or the chalkboard and demonstrate how a group would orally perform the selection.

To refine readers' theater presentations, sound effects and simple props might be used. Some teachers tape-record the presentations to allow later critiques of the performance. Older students who become enthused about readers' theater might form groups, select a passage, prepare it, and then present it before the class as a special project.

Young and Vardell (1993) not only describe the process and benefits of readers' theater; they tell how to adapt scripts. Their major focus, however, is on moving readers' theater out of "reading" time and into other parts of the curriculum.

Visuals

Visuals such as collages, posters, and book jackets are another category of book response projects that can be celebrated readily. Visuals help students form mental images of what they read, manipulating and developing ideas through artistic forms of expression. Creating visuals is the mainstay of many response activities in primary-grade classrooms because young students can often put into a picture what they cannot put into writing.

When this option is followed, make sure there is a balance between the amount of reading or writing done by the student and the amount of time spent on the visual. When primary students spend five minutes writing and a half hour illustrating, there is an imbalance. Perhaps having students complete the illustrations as homework will balance literacy efforts. The following visuals are nonverbal book response projects that can be readily celebrated.

Illustrations

Students often draw pictures of characters, scenes, or locations they encounter in literature. The criteria for deciding what to illustrate can depend on what your students consider to be their favorite, most important, or most exciting topic. In addition, students frequently design posters and bulletin boards in response to what they read.

Collages

Assembling a group of pictures, cloth or wood pieces, and other materials in response to what has been read is a favorite activity of older students. They especially seem to enjoy hunting through magazines, catalogs, and newspapers for just the right pictures or printed phrases that symbolize a character or the general theme of a novel.

Maps

Showing where a character went in a story requires careful reading. After deciding what locations to represent, students map them out on paper, label them, and often illustrate them for greater detail. Maps can depict story characters' travels in any area. For example, the locations within a single house as well as the locations within a community, state, nation, or world can be mapped.

Time Lines

Time lines comprise a set of illustrations that portray the key events of a passage. Different groups of students can be responsible for individual illustrations, or one student can complete the entire project. The illustrations may be separated on different pieces of paper for others to arrange in correct sequence, they can be placed in different segments of a single sheet, or they can be drawn on poster paper to make a mural.

Comic Strips

This activity combines aspects of several other activities described here. Students depict a series of story events in a time line and produce dialogue for the story characters within that time line. Retelling a story through this comic strip format is a somewhat advanced task.

Book Jackets

Designing a book jacket that differs from the original directs students' thinking toward the central focus of the book. To choose a character or scene to portray on the cover, students need to judge what deserves emphasis. This is a high-level reading task.

Display Ads

Creating a display ad is similar to creating book jackets; however, display ads openly attempt to convince readers to buy a certain book. They generally include more information about a book than its jacket does, and they include brief pieces of persuasive writing along with examples of what to expect.

Choosing Appropriate Activities

When choosing literature response activities such as the ones described, consider several points. First, matching the right activity with the right book and the right student is an uncertain undertaking. The best method we know for making proper matches might be termed enlightened trial and error. You simply try certain activities that seem right for certain students and then pay attention to the results. If your students work comfortably with the project and if they gain insight into the material they have read, you have evidence that a worthwhile match was made. If the results you obtain are not so positive, try another activity.

Second, response activities can be viewed as products for instruction or as products for testing. For example, questions can be instructional when they are used to expand students' thinking about certain aspects of a story. In the children's novel *Number the Stars,* children can explore the horrors of the Nazi occupation of Denmark, the bravery of the resisters, and the terror felt by the Jewish children hiding from their occupiers. Children can discuss issues related to whether or not they might risk their lives and the lives of their families in order to protest atrocities

Technology Tips

The Internet offers wide-ranging references on using children's books while offering children material to read. Here are some references worth examining to sample some of the best that is available:

Integrated Curriculum (www.smplanet.com/bookclub/bookclub.htm)

Magic School Bus (www.scholastic.com/MagicSchoolBus)

Peggy Sharp (www.peggysharp.com)

Whales Unit (curry.edschool.Virginia.EDU/~kpj5e/Whales/Contents.HTML)

against others. Questions about reasons for the Nazis' treatment of Jews, gypsies, and the physically and mentally challenged can stimulate thinking and discussion. At the other extreme, students' answers to such questions can be written down and then graded with no constructive feedback. When response activities such as questioning are used as a product only to be graded and not discussed, commented upon, or elaborated in some way, they are being misused.

Third, overt responses are important because they elicit active thinking and allow students to receive feedback, but time spent reading is important too. Discussing ideas, writing down ideas, and creating artistic responses can be counterproductive. We caution against "killing the butterfly." The beauty of books and the beauty of butterflies come from viewing their intricacies, their form, and their color in their entirety. Consequently, it is important to preserve children's feelings for the wholeness and overall impact of pieces of literature. Well-written and well-illustrated books, like butterflies, fall apart when their parts are dissected and overanalyzed.

Literature can be presented during self-selected reading with no teacher intervention, and children will enjoy and respond to it on their own. Anyone who has seen a child cry when reading or listening to *Stone Fox* knows what we are talking about. Because of this, knowing when *not* to require overt responses to literature is as important as knowing which response activities are most appropriate for special occasions. Also, don't forget to allow student choice for response projects. When you only assign response projects, you are denying students' own personal choices in response projects you had not even considered.

Enrich All Subjects with Literature

Because literature for children develops knowledge of the world, it should be used to enrich all school subjects. Books expand children's learning by presenting to them people, events, and locations that are beyond the possibility of face-to-face contact. Literature allows children to learn about people such as Marco Polo and Clara Barton, events such as the Crusades and the first landing on the moon, and locations such as the Amazon and the inside of human lungs.

Literature transports young readers to other times and places and allows them to learn new things. They can learn about life on the American prairie during the late 1800s in *Sarah, Plain and Tall,* they can travel to America with a Japanese immigrant in *Grandfather's Journey,* and they can appreciate the inspiration of Dr. Martin Luther King, Jr.'s "I Have a Dream" speech. Additionally, children can learn that they are not alone in their wishes, successes, and rejections. The insights they gain about characters' dilemmas and reactions to dilemmas allow them to broaden their understandings of human relationships.

Literature not only expands children's knowledge of the world; it also deepens knowledge. When children identify with story characters, they can experience the events more deeply than if they read about the events only in a textbook. Children who read *Roll of Thunder, Hear My Cry* learn well what life was like for rural African

Americans in the South during the Great Depression. This learning takes hold and becomes meaningful because readers share Cassie's anger at her and her family's persecution; readers do not simply read a catalog of problems that people in those circumstances had to face. As readers enter into the world suggested by an author, they deepen understandings of what they read. Two instructional arrangements for enriching all subjects with literature include theme studies and book studies.

Theme Studies

When planning theme studies, teachers establish concepts such as *plants, explorers, states,* and *weather* as the curricular focus. Sometimes they focus on more abstract ideas such as *friendship, patterns,* and *identity.* Or they might pose questions such as "Why do people hurt others?" or "What is a balanced diet?" Selecting books that contribute to students' understandings then follows. For example, if the class is studying the U.S. Southwest, books such as *Desert Dwellers, Anasazi,* and *The Apaches* might be brought in when examining indigenous people, *Storm on the Desert* when considering the land, and *Abuelita's Heart* when viewing today's cultural groups.

When planning theme studies, decide how you will use different books. Reserve a few to read aloud to the class. Gather others for daily self-selected reading, inquiry projects, and book projects. Decide if you want groups of students to read copies of one particular book and discuss it in book clubs. School media centers typically have collections of books and other resources such as videos and reference materials that can be brought to classrooms during theme studies.

Book Studies

Many children's books work well as the curricular focus. With book studies, planning progresses from individual books to associated themes and related learning outcomes. For example, while reading aloud *Turn Homeward, Hannalee* to children, one teacher helped the class plot Hannalee's journey on the prison train from Athens, Georgia, to Indiana and the return home to her mother through the war-torn South. Children who read any Laura Ingalls Wilder book usually become eager to learn more about prairie life and the settlement of our country. Children who read stories about young people in other countries typically become curious about those countries.

As students read and enjoy *The Very Hungry Caterpillar,* mentioned earlier in this chapter, they can count and add all the things this caterpillar eats on its way to becoming a butterfly. They can also note fraction concepts related to the parts of foods the caterpillar eats. Many teachers connect this book with science concepts such as growth, changes, and life cycles.

In *Ten, Nine, Eight* a father helps his daughter get ready for bed, and they count down from 10 small toes all washed and warm to 1 big girl all ready for bed. This book emphasizes counting and has African American characters. *Dad's Diet* is a hilarious description of Dad's attempts to lose weight. Dad ends up weighing only six-sevenths of his previous weight. Since this book takes place in Australia, map study is appropriate. Additionally, Dad's weight is given in kilos, so work with fractions and with measurements can stem from this book. Children will enjoy figuring their own weights and the weights of their family and friends in kilos and determining how much each would weigh if they lost six-sevenths of their mass.

The Theory and Research Base for Reading and Responding to Literature for Children

Children who read and respond to literature attain numerous personal and educational outcomes. In a respected compendium on children's literature, Huck, Hepler, and Hickman (1987) cite research indicating that young readers can be expected to achieve personal values such as pleasure, vicarious experiences, and insights into and understanding of human actions and interactions. The studies they cite also document the acquisition of educational outcomes such as language development, story structure, oral reading fluency, and literary heritage. These days, teachers need not work hard justifying literature in classroom reading programs.

Most inquiries into literature for children in the 1980s and early 1990s emphasized children's responses. Response-oriented researchers focused on what individuals say or write about a literary passage, giving secondary attention to the work itself. Current conceptions of literary response began with the work of Louise Rosenblatt (Beach & Hynds, 1991), who published her first major work in 1938 (Rosenblatt, 1938/1983). Rosenblatt suggests that authors, like painters and sculptors, elicit aesthetic responses from their patrons. Students can focus on the quality of these experiences as much as on the contents of the object that stimulated them. According to this view, readers do not uncover the meaning that resides in a literary work; readers construct meaning in response to a work (Spivey, 1997). The common question people ask of each other when puzzling over something, "What do you make of it?" aptly expresses the constructivist principle that people produce—rather than receive—meaning.

Readers construct their responses in part according to the social norms and standards of their communities (Bleich, 1978; Fish, 1980), and school classrooms are major entities with authority over what counts as appropriate responses to reading (Many & Wiseman, 1992). When classroom communities are student centered, students tend to produce alternative critical interpretations of texts (Hickman, 1983). However, most classrooms still adhere to traditional views of authority and are characterized by teacher-led recitations of factual information lifted from texts (Weinstein, 1991).

A central recommendation for enhancing readers' construction of responses involves talking with others (Martinez & Roser, 1991). When social interactions involving books become "grand conversations" (Eeds & Wells, 1989), students might share personal events related to a passage, question what they read, and report what they liked about the author's writing. When discussing stories independently in literature groups, students can engage the text at high levels of thinking, construct multiple meanings for it, and participate in conversations that have a natural structure (Leal, 1992).

Many prominent studies have examined the effects of culture on readers' interactions with texts and with each other. Among other things, researchers have reported how instructional practices that differ from cultural expectations alter literary response. For instance, individuals who expect collaborative participation when retelling stories tend to shut down when teachers call for them to isolate themselves and retell stories on their own (Au, 1980; Heath, 1983). Students who expect authoritarian statements from assertive leaders often become confused and anxious during leaderless discussions (Barrera, 1992). Additionally, readers who find material unfamiliar due to cultural differences (e.g., wedding customs, family relations) often produce limited responses (Steffensen, Joag-Dev, & Anderson, 1979; Reynolds, Taylor, Steffensen, Shirey, & Anderson, 1982).

Critical researchers of the 1990s are focusing on how students might question, resist, and talk back to books that position them in subordinate ways (Rogers & Soter, 1997). Critical theorists claim that overemphasizing personal responses to literature actually fosters inequities that oppressed groups encounter in school. Keeping response within individual realms of experience makes differential status in society seem natural and preordained. Accentuating only the personal does not empower individuals to reflect on societal situations that position them on the margins, nor does it promote conditions for change.

Although literary response and critical theory researchers emphasize readers' articulated statements about their experiences, unarticulated experiences also merit consideration. In a study of readers who lose themselves in books, Nell (1988) described engaged reading as something done for its own sake. This type of response is a flow experience wherein individuals find reading intrinsically motivating and totally absorbing, and the experience is its own reward.

Looking Back

This chapter presented a rationale and a plan for using children's literature in the classroom. Various genres of literature and ways to respond to literature were described, and a variety of ways in which to think about the many ways in which literature might be part of the elementary curriculum were discussed. This chapter presented six key ideas:

1. Welcome the diverse world of literature.
2. Use literature to promote thinking and feeling.
3. Link reading and writing instruction with children's books.
4. Schedule daily self-selected reading.
5. Celebrate book response projects.
6. Enrich all subjects with literature.

Add to Your Journal

Are you a reader? A reader is not just someone who can read; a reader is someone who chooses to read—who reads a chapter or two of a good book before turning off the light and looks forward to that week at the beach partly because of the sustained reading time it will permit. If you are a reader, how did that happen? Did you have teachers who read to you? Did you get to choose some of your own books to read in school? Did you participate in some interesting literature-response activities? If you are not a reader, what can you do to ensure that the children you teach have the opportunities in your classroom to become readers? What will be the role of literature in your classroom? How often will you read to your students and what will you read to them? How will you provide for daily self-selected reading? What kinds of response activities will you engage them in? Think about the potential of books to enrich people's lives—throughout their lives—in a variety of ways and decide what role books will play in your instruction. Use some or all of the thinking processes—connect, generalize, image, organize, monitor, predict, evaluate and apply—to respond to each of the key ideas in this chapter.

Application Activities

Do It Together

Work with a small group to construct a short questionnaire—eight to ten questions—that will allow you to find out about experiences adults have had with books at school and at home. Your questions should reveal whether the person interviewed likes to read, books they remember reading in childhood, read-aloud experiences remembered from home and school, positive encounters with books, negative encounters, etc. Once your group has constructed the questions, each group member should interview two adults—friends, neighbors, relatives, colleagues. Reconvene the group and tally up responses. What did your group discover about how adults feel about books and their home and school experiences?

Listen, Look, and Learn

Visit a classroom and interview the teacher about the various ways children in that classroom respond to literature. Do the children keep any kind of response log? How are discussions conducted? Are there any readers' theater activities? What kind of story retellings and recreations are used? Do the children create visual responses to books? How is the decision made about what kind of response activities will be used for particular books? Do the students have some choice about how they will respond? Is there variety in the response options? Summarize what you learned and decide how you can relate this to your own classroom.

Add to Your Resource File

Find five children's books you think will appeal to children you teach (or will teach) and will enrich the science, social studies, or math curriculum. Explain why you chose these books and how you anticipate using them. List thematic connections you could make between these books and these curricular areas.

References

Anderson, R. A., Wilson, P. T., & Fielding, L. G. (1988). Growth in reading and how children spend their time outside of school. *Reading Research Quarterly, 23,* 285–303.

Au, K. H. (1980). Participation structures in reading lessons: Analysis of a culturally appropriate instructional event. *Anthropology and Education Quarterly, 11,* 91–115.

Barrera, R. B. (1992). The culture gap in literature-based literacy instruction. *Education and Urban Society, 24,* 227–243.

Beach, R., & Hynds, S. (1991). Research on response to literature. In R. Barr, M. Kamil, P. B. Mosenthal, & P. D. Pearson (Eds.), *Handbook of reading research* (vol. 2, pp. 453–488). White Plains, NY: Longman.

Bleich, D. (1978). *Subjective criticism.* Baltimore: Johns Hopkins University Press.

Currel, D. (1980). *Learning with puppets.* New York: Play, Inc.

Eeds, M., & Wells, D. (1989). Grand conversations: An exploration of meaning construction in literature study groups. *Research in the Teaching of English, 23,* 4–29.

Fish, S. (1980). *Is there a text in this class? The authority of interpretive communities.* Cambridge, MA: Harvard University Press.

Gambrell, L. B., & Almasi, J. F. (Eds.). (1996). *Lively discussions! Fostering engaged reading.* Newark, DE: International Reading Association.

Hancock, M. R. (1992). Literature response journals: Insights beyond the printed page. *Language Arts, 69,* 36–42.

Heath, S. B. (1983). *Ways with words: Language, life, and work in communities and classrooms.* Cambridge, UK: Cambridge University Press.

Heinig, R. B. (1992). *Improvisation with favorite tales: Integrating drama into the reading/writing classroom.* Portsmouth, NH: Heinemann.

Hickman, J. (1983). Everything considered: Response to literature in an elementary school setting. *Journal of Research and Development in Education, 16,* 8–13.

Hoffman, J. V., Roser, N. L., & Battle, J. (1993). Reading aloud in the classroom: From the modal to a "model." *Reading Teacher, 46,* 496–503.

Huck, C. S., Hepler, S., & Hickman, J. (1987). *Children's literature in the elementary school,* 4th ed. New York: Holt, Rinehart, & Winston.

Hughes, L. (1932). April rain song. *The Dream Keeper and Other Poems,* Alfred Knopf.

Kuenzer, K. (1978). Junior Great Books: An interpretive reading program. *School Library Journal, 24*(2), 32–34.

Leal, D. (1992). The nature of talk about three types of text during peer group discussions. *Journal of Reading Behavior, 24,* 313–338.

Many, J., & Wiseman, D. (1992). The effect of teaching approach on third grade students' response to literature. *Journal of Reading Behavior, 24,* 265–287.

Martinez, M. G., & Roser, N. L. (1991). Children's responses to literature. In J. Flood, J. M. Jensen, D. Lapp, & J. R. Squire (Eds.), *Handbook of research on teaching the English language arts* (pp. 643–654). New York: Macmillan.

McMahon, S. I., & Raphael, T. E. (Eds.). (1997). *The book club connection: Literacy learning and classroom talk.* New York: Teachers College Press.

Nell, V. (1988). *Lost in a book. The psychology of reading for pleasure.* New Haven, CT: Yale University Press.

Reynolds, R. E., Taylor, M. A., Steffensen, M. S., Shirey, L. S., & Anderson, R. C. (1982). Cultural schemata and reading comprehension. *Reading Research Quarterly, 17,* 353–366.

Rogers, T., & Soter, A. O. (Eds.). (1997). *Reading across cultures: Teaching literature in a diverse society.* New York: Teachers College Press.

Rosenblatt, L. (1938/1983). *Literature as exploration,* 4th ed. New York: Modern Language Association.

Routman, R. (1991). *Invitations.* Portsmouth, NH: Heinemann.

Sierra-Perry, M. (1996). *Standards in practice, grades 3–5.* Urbana, IL: National Council of Teachers of English.

Sloyer, S. (1982). *Readers theatre: Story dramatization in the classroom.* Urbana, IL: National Council of Teachers of English.

Spivey, N. N. (1997). *The constructivist metaphor.* New York: Ablex.

Steffensen, M. S., Joag-Dev, C., & Anderson, R. C. (1979). A cross-cultural perspective on reading comprehension. *Reading Research Quarterly, 15,* 10–29.

Sudduth, P. (1989). Introducing response logs to poor readers. *The Reading Teacher, 42,* 452–454.

Vogt, M. (1996). Creating a response-centered curriculum with literature response groups. In L. B. Gambrell & J. F. Almasi (Eds.), *Lively discussions! Fostering engaged reading* (pp. 181–193). Newark, DE: International Reading Association.

Weinstein, C. S. (1991). The classroom as a social context for learning. In R. Rosenzweig & L. W. Porter (Eds.), *Annual review of psychology* (vol. 42, pp. 493–525). Palo Alto, CA: Annual Reviews.

Western, L. E. (1980). A comparative study of literature through folk tale variants. *Language Arts, 57,* 395–402, 439.

Worthy, M. J., & Bloodgood, J. W. (1993). Enhancing reading instruction through Cinderella tales. *Reading Teacher, 46,* 290–301.

Young, T. A., & Vardell, S. (1993). Weaving readers theatre and nonfiction into the curriculum. *Reading Teacher, 46,* 396–406.

Children's Books/Materials Cited

Abuelita's Heart, by A. Cordova, Simon & Schuster, 1997.

Alice's Adventures in Wonderland, by L. Carroll, Franklin Watt, 1966.

Anasazi, by L. E. Fisher, Atheneum, 1997.

The Apaches, by V. D. H. Sneve, Holiday, 1997.

Bears, by I. Stirling, Sierra Club Books for Children, 1992.

The Brain: Our Nervous System, by S. Simon, Morrow, 1997.

Charlotte's Web, by E. B. White, Harper & Row, 1952.

Corduroy, by D. Freeman, Viking, 1985.

Dad's Diet, by B. Comber, Ashton Scholastic, 1987.

Desert Dwellers, by S. S. Warren, Chronicle, 1997.

Dinosaur Valley, by M. Kurokawa, Chronicle, 1992.

Dove Isabeau, by J. Yolen, Harcourt Brace Jovanovich, 1989.

"The Elephant's Child" in *Just So Stories,* by R. Kipling, Doubleday, 1952.

Exactly the Opposite, by T. Hoban, Greenwillow, 1990.

Fables, by A. Lobel, HarperCollins, 1983.

Fortunately, by R. Chirlip, Aladdin, 1993.

Frederick, by L. Lionni, Pantheon, 1967.

Frog and Toad Together, by A. Lobel, Harper & Row, 1972.

The Giving Tree, by S. Silverstein, HarperCollins, 1987.

Grandfather's Journey, by A. Say, Houghton Mifflin, 1993.

The Handmade Alphabet, by L. Rankin, Dial Books, 1991.

How Many Spots Does a Leopard Have? and Other Tales, by J. Lester, Scholastic, 1989.

I Have a Dream, by M. L. King, Scholastic Press, 1997.

Jumanji, by C. Van Allsburg, Houghton Mifflin, 1981.

Kitchen Fun for Kids: Healthy Recipes and Nutrition Facts for 7- to 12-Year-Old Cooks, by M. F. Jacobson & L. Hill, Henry Holt, 1991.

Meanwhile Back at the Ranch, by T. H. Noble, Turtle, 1992.

Nature Crafts, by S. Lohf, Children's Press, 1990.

Number the Stars, by L. Lowry, Houghton Mifflin, 1989.

Of Colors and Things, by T. Hoban, Greenwillow, 1989.

Out of the Dust, by K. Hesse, Scholastic, 1997.

Owl Moon, by J. Yolen, Philomel, 1987.

Papier-Mache Project Book, by M. Elliot, Chartwell Books, 1992.

Polar Express, by C. Van Allsburg, Clarion Books, 1991.

Potato, by K. Lied, National Geographic, 1997.

The Rainbabies, by L. K. Melmed, Lothrop, Lee, & Shepherd, 1992.

Roll of Thunder, Hear My Cry, by M. Taylor, Dial Books, 1976.

Sarah, Plain and Tall, by P. MacLachlan, Harper & Row, 1985.

Sleep Is for Everyone, by P. Showers, HarperCollins, 1997.

Stellaluna, by J. Cannon, Harcourt Brace Jovanovich, 1993.

The Stinky Cheese Man and Other Fairly Stupid Tales, by J. Scieszka & L. Smith, Viking, 1992.

Stone Fox, by J. Gardiner, Harper & Row, 1980.

Storm on the Desert, by C. Lesser, Harcourt, 1997.

Ten, Nine, Eight, by M. Bang, Greenwillow, 1989.

This Time of Darkness, by H. M. Hoover, Viking, 1980.

The Three Little Javelinas, by S. Lowell, Northland Publishing, 1992.

Three Little Pigs and the Big Bad Wolf, by G. Rounds, Trumpet Club, 1992.

The Three Little Pigs, by M. Zemach, Sunburst Books, 1990.

The Three Little Pigs, by P. Galdone, Scholastic, 1970.

The Three Little Wolves and the Big Bad Pig, by E. Trivizas, Macmillan, 1993.

The True Story of the Three Little Pigs, by J. Scieszka & L. Smith, Viking, 1989.

Tuesday, by D. Wiesner, Clarion Books, 1991.

Turn Homeward, Hannalee, by P. Beatty, Morrow, 1984.

Two Bad Ants, by C. Van Allsburg, Houghton Mifflin, 1988.

The Very Hungry Caterpillar, by E. Carle, Putnam, 1989.

War of the Worlds, by H. G. Wells, Watermill Press, 1980.

Where the Wild Things Are, by M. Sendak, Harper & Row, 1963.

Why Can't I Live Forever? by V. Cobb, Lodestar, 1997.

Why Do Volcanoes Erupt: Questions about Our Unique Planet Answered by Dr. Philip Whitfield with the Natural History Museum, by Viking Penguin, 1990.

Winnie-the-Pooh, by A. A. Milne, Dutton, 1926.
A Wrinkle in Time, by M. L'Engle, Farrar, Straus, & Giroux, 1962.

Additional Readings

- Approximately 3,500–5,000 children's books are published each year. If only 10 percent of these publications are excellent books, you would have to read more than one book a day to have read all the best new books produced for children. Because staying abreast of the best new children's books is so demanding, teachers often rely on their school media specialists for suggestions. Additionally, many educators subscribe to professional journals—and join the journals' sponsoring organizations, when available—for updates on children's books. The following publications are especially good at highlighting new titles for classroom purposes:

  Book Links. 434 W. Downer Pl., Aurora, IL 60506.

  Childhood Education. Association for Childhood Education International, 11501 Georgia Ave., Ste. 315, Wheaton, MD 20902.

  Cricket Magazine. Open Court Publishing Co., 1058 Eighth St., LaSalle, IL 61301.

  Language Arts. National Council of Teachers of English, 1111 Kenyon Rd., Urbana, IL 61801.

  School Library Journal. P.O. Box 1978, Marion, OH 43306.

  The New Advocate. 480 Washington St., Norwood, MA 02062.

  The Reading Teacher. International Reading Association, 800 Barksdale Rd., P.O. Box 8139, Newark, DE 19714.

- Two excellent presentations of reading aloud to children and recommended titles for reading aloud are as follows:

  Freeman, J. (1992). *Books kids will sit still for: The complete read-aloud guide,* 2nd ed. New York: R. R. Bowker.

  Trelease, J. (1995). *The read-aloud handbook,* 4th ed. New York: Penguin.

- The following provide excellent descriptions of magazines for children:

  Richardson, S. K. (1991). *Magazines for children: A guide for parents, teachers, and librarians,* 2nd ed. Chicago, IL: American Library Association.

  Stoll, D. R. (1994). *Magazines for kids and teens: A resource for parents, teachers, librarians, and kids.* Newark, DE: International Reading Association.

- Numerous publications list children's books appropriate for theme studies. The first reference describes nonfiction authors and books that address different subject matter; the remaining references exemplify what currently is available for three particular subjects:

  Wyatt, F. R., Coggins, M., & Imber, J. H. (1998). *Popular nonfiction authors for children: A biographical and thematic guide.* Englewood, CO: Libraries Unlimited.

Mathematics

Griffiths, R., & Clyne, M. (1991). *Books you can count on.* Portsmouth, NH: Heinemann.

Braddon, K. L., Hall, N. J., & Taylor, D. (1993). *Math through children's literature. Making the NCTN standards come alive.* Englewood, CO: Teacher Idea Press.

Rommell, C. A. (1991). *Integrating beginning math and literature.* Nashville, TN: Incentive Publications.

Science

Butzow, C. M., & Butzow, J. W. (1989). *Science through children's literature.* Englewood, CO: Teacher Ideas Press.

Kenney, D. M., Spangler, S. S., & Vanderwerf, M. A. (1990). *Science and technology in fact and fiction: A guide to children's books.* New York: R. R. Bowker.

Social Studies

Adamson, L. G. (1998). *Literature connections to American history, K–6: Resources to enhance and entice.* Englewood, CO: Libraries Unlimited.

Adamson, L. G. (1998). *Literature connections to world history, K–6: Resources to enhance and entice.* Englewood, CO: Libraries Unlimited.

Barr, C. (1998). *From biography to history. Best books for children's entertainment and education.* New Providence, NJ: R. R. Bowker.

Perez-Stable, M., Cordier, M. (1994). *Understanding American history through children's literature: Instructional units and activities for grades K–8.* Phoenix, AZ: Oryx.

Chapter 7

Comprehension

Reading comprehension requires much on the part of students. Readers actively think about what is on the page and what they already know, and this thinking is colored by how interested they are in reading about the topic. Teachers develop students' reading comprehension proficiencies by planning and implementing various activities throughout the school day. Teachers provide students with time and motivation for individual reading and for exploring information in subject-matter materials. One activity, comprehension strategy lessons, is designed to teach students directly how to comprehend. Knowing the principles of effective comprehension strategy lessons informs decisions about how to guide and support children's comprehension. There are many comprehension lesson frameworks you can use to meet the comprehension needs of all your students. But studying requires comprehension and something more—taking extra steps to remember more than one ordinarily does from just reading.

*S*ay the following words silently or aloud:

experiments	strategy	structural
presentations	dyslexics	atypical
nonverbal	normals	laterality
randomized	stimulus	strategical
blocked	predict	
verbal	hemispheric	

You were probably able to pronounce all of these words, but read the following paragraph containing the same words to see how well you understand it:

> The experiments employed randomized or blocked presentations of verbal and nonverbal materials to determine whether previously reported differences between dyslexics and normals were due to structural hemispheric differences or to stratigical processing differences. The results indicate that if dyslexics are unable to predict the nature of the stimulus, then they behave as normal readers. Their atypical laterality emerges only when they adopt a strategy in anticipation of a specific type of stimulus. (Underwood & Boot, 1986, p. 219)

Did the click of comprehension occur as you read this paragraph? Could you close the book and then retell the paragraph in your own words to a friend? Could you give examples that illustrate what the authors were explaining? Although word identification is important, we hope this exercise convinces you that for readers to comprehend, they must do much more than simply pronounce printed words and listen to what they are saying. Furthermore, as noted in Chapter 6, "Reading and Responding to Literature for Children," response-oriented educators concentrate on readers' aesthetic reactions to literary texts, giving less attention to readers' learning of text content. But as the above example shows, readers' grasp of text content is also a compelling concern. Educators who share this concern concentrate on reading comprehension, giving less attention to literary response. We include chapters on literary response and comprehension in this book because both aspects of reading deserve classroom attention. This chapter on comprehension explores five key ideas:

1. Reading comprehension requires word identification, prior knowledge, strategies, and engagement.
2. Comprehension can be developed with all kinds of materials in all subjects.
3. Comprehension strategy lessons engage students before, during, and after reading.
4. A variety of before- and after-reading activities can be used to teach comprehension strategies.
5. A variety of reading formats can be used to make guided reading multilevel.

Reading Comprehension Requires Word Identification, Prior Knowledge, Strategies, and Engagement

Reading comprehension is an incredibly complex process. Comprehending is essentially thinking, and the act of thinking has mystified scholars since antiquity. Although a complete account of the reading comprehension process is not available,

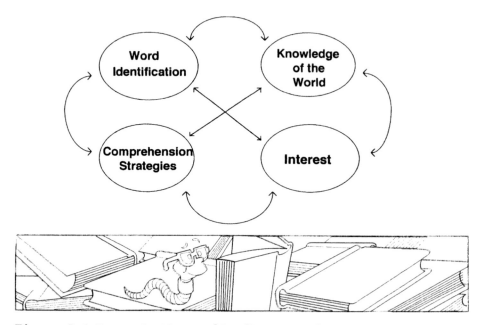

Figure 7.1 Interactive Nature of Reading Comprehension

a general explanation is this: reading comprehension results from an interaction among word identification, prior knowledge, comprehension strategies, and engagement.

Comprehension occurs as the result of an interaction (Rumelhart,1985). This means that parts of the process act upon one another; one part influences another, and influenced parts double back to influence the parts that first influenced them. This interactive cycle then continues forward. Figure 7.1 contains a model of the comprehension process that emphasizes its interactive nature. The two-way arrows indicate that readers continually move from one component to another in a flexible sequence.

Comprehension is an interactive process of at least four major components. However, each component is described most clearly one at a time. What follows is a portrayal of each one.

Word Identification

Chapters 3 and 4 present a thorough view of word identification, so only two additional points are made here. The first point is that word identification is necessary for readers to comprehend. The second point is that comprehension is necessary to help readers self-monitor their identification of words.

Word identification facilitates comprehension by signaling certain thoughts. When you see the following symbols, you are unable to comprehend the message they represent:

({+#(@)(#&##$

However, if you knew the code well, you would have little trouble with this message. The code is simple:

Coded Symbol		Letter
)	=	a
#	=	e
{	=	i
&	=	d
$	=	p
(	=	r
@	=	s
+	=	v

Working back from these symbols gives the trite message: *rivers are deep.* This demonstration shows that word identification facilitates comprehension. Readers must identify words to derive meaning from print. However, this role of word identification probably seems obvious to you.

The effect of comprehension on word identification is not so obvious. Nevertheless, children who read a lot with good comprehension become better able to identify words as they progress through a passage. To appreciate this phenomenon, read the following short paragraph:

The hunter set his trap and began moving away. He did not get far when he heard a sudden metallic snap. He knew he had caught something. He quickly returned to his hotel to see what he had.

Did you mentally do a double take when you came to the word "hotel" in the paragraph? Did you look at the word for an extra few milliseconds to make sure you had identified it correctly? If so, you were using your reading comprehension to self-monitor your word identification.

Young readers need to learn phonics so that they can figure out unfamiliar words when they read, but phonics is far from a perfect science. Learning to apply phonics properly is like learning to do anything else that is complicated—it requires much practice with regular feedback on how one is doing. Comprehension provides the incentive to do the necessary practice and also provides much of the feedback needed. Whenever a child employs phonics to decode a word during reading, the child receives instant feedback as to whether that word sounds familiar, fits into the syntax of the sentence, and makes sense—given what has been read previously. The more young readers use their phonics during reading comprehension, the more they receive the feedback they need to fine-tune their understanding and application of letter-sound relationships. Comprehension doesn't teach phonics, but it helps readers refine what they know about phonics so that they can apply it better and more quickly.

The positive effect that comprehension has on the development of word identification is important to remember. This effect necessitates an instructional program that balances attention to words with attention to meaning to produce the best possible readers. Emphasizing one of these aspects of reading at the expense of the other is counterproductive because the two work together.

Prior Knowledge

Along with word identification, comprehension depends in part on how knowledgeable readers are about the content of the passage being read (Anderson & Pearson, 1984). Think about the difficulty you had with the passage presented earlier about the experiments. To understand the passage, you needed to know about specific concepts such as *blocked presentations* of materials, the difference between *verbal* and *nonverbal* materials, and *laterality*. You also needed to have some general knowledge about the type of research being reported. Knowing that psychological studies frequently present tasks to different groups of readers to determine their intellectual differences would have provided some perspective for interpreting this particular study. As Chapter 5 indicated, prior knowledge is important because writers assume that their readers share certain understandings.

Having knowledge of the world is essential for comprehension, but prior knowledge is still useless if it is not connected to the passage being read. Readers need to know something about what they are reading; they also need to realize when their knowledge fits the particular passage they are reading. To appreciate this point, read the following sentence:

The notes were sour because the seams split.

This sentence probably seemed incomprehensible to you. The individual words made sense, but they most likely did not hang together for you. You might be able to repeat the sentence verbatim, but you would only be parroting sounds. However, if you had known that the sentence was about bagpipes, you would have thought it quite comprehensible. Knowing that this particular sentence is about bagpipes is just as important as knowing about bagpipes in the first place; connecting knowledge of the world to a passage is just as important as having knowledge of the world (Bransford & McCarrel, 1974).

Again, as with word identification, there is a reciprocal relationship between prior knowledge and reading comprehension. Not only does prior knowledge help enable reading comprehension to occur, but reading a lot with good comprehension is one of the most important ways of building one's prior knowledge.

In brief, prior knowledge is crucial for comprehension. Students require a great deal of information before they can understand what is presented in books. Students also require the ability to connect what they know to the upcoming ideas in a passage. Simply having knowledge of the world is not enough; readers need to activate and apply it when they read. For students to have the prior knowledge that comprehension will require in future grades, they must be reading a lot now with good comprehension.

Comprehension Strategies

Word identification and prior knowledge are only part of the comprehension process; comprehension strategies are also crucial (Paris, Wasik, & Turner, 1991). Strategies are tactics, or procedures, that are employed to achieve certain goals. To appreciate the role of strategies, solve the following word puzzle:

0

BA

MA

PhD

Readers who are familiar with this type of puzzle have no difficulty determining that this one stands for *three degrees below zero*. However, if you did not already know what the puzzle represented, and if you did not know how to figure it out, you would be stuck. You might ask someone, "How do you do these puzzles? What's the trick?" You would be wanting some word-puzzle strategies. An astute friend might explain his or her tactics this way: "First, look at the puzzle and come up with one directional word like *over, through,* or *between.* Then say that word along with what the other words and letters represent. Keep combining these words in different order until you produce a well-known saying or familiar phrase." With this strategy for solving word puzzles, you would be able to figure out that *you just me* represents *just between you and me* and *side side* stands for *side by side.* After a while, you would not need to think about the word-puzzle strategy when you met unfamiliar puzzles because you would apply it automatically. In fact, this process might become so automatic that you might be unable to describe the strategy if someone asked you about it.

Comprehension strategies are like word-puzzle strategies in that they provide tactics to derive meaning. Sometimes children have to think explicitly about a strategy in order to apply it, and sometimes children apply it automatically. Whatever the case, comprehension strategies are considerably more numerous and complex than word-puzzle strategies. Here are some of the comprehension strategies frequently listed in school curriculum guides, instructional materials, and professional articles:

Having and connecting relevant background knowledge

Predicting what the passage will contain

Focusing on important ideas

Following story structure (e.g., setting, goal, outcome)

Following expository structures (e.g., cause-effect, comparison-contrast, topic-detail)

Determining the author's purpose

Self-monitoring understanding

Distinguishing facts from opinions

Evaluating passage contents

Good readers perform the strategies listed above as well as the thinking processes presented in Chapter 1. In fact, the thinking processes and comprehension strategies are closely linked. Obviously, you use the connecting thinking process when you have and connect relevant background knowledge to what you are reading. You predict what the passage might be about and where the text is taking you. You organize in order to follow text structure. You generalize as you determine the most important ideas and figure out what the author's purpose is. Self-monitoring understanding during reading is obviously one kind of the self-monitoring thinking process. When you evaluate passage content, you are using the thinking process of evaluating to form your own judgment. How much imaging and applying you do depends on the passage and your purpose for reading it.

As a teacher, you must determine which strategies students need to understand the passage they are reading currently, as well as strategies they will probably need in the future. Many teachers select strategies from lists provided by their schools to address their students' needs. You should also include any strategies you know are crucial for comprehension that might be missing from the curriculum list. Once you know which strategies you need to focus on, you can plan strategy lessons using the lesson planning features described later in this chapter.

Engagement

As we noted in Chapter 1, feeling is the energizer of reading and writing. Among other things, this means that interest influences readers' comprehension. Different readers will come away from an identical passage with different understandings, partially because their interest in the topic varies (Baldwin, Peleg-Bruckner, & McClintock,1985; Wade & Adams, 1990).

Interest attracts readers to certain materials. Students who are particularly interested in animals or superheroes will tend to understand passages about those topics better than students who are more interested in romantic fiction or biographies. Even within a particular type of literature, some passages exert a greater attraction than others. Everyone has favorite reading materials. Some materials engage readers' attention and cause them to become concerned with the content. For instance, readers tend to identify emotionally with some story characters more than others, and this identification influences the message readers take from the passage. It seems clear that teachers must consider the role of interest as they consider how to develop comprehension.

As helpful as it can be to provide children with reading materials that match their interests, they must also become engaged with the broad variety of materials that school requires them to read and learn from. Ensuring success in comprehension and teaching comprehension strategies can also help students become more engaged in what they read, even when it is not about something that especially interests them.

When we consistently give students the instructional support they need to achieve satisfactory comprehension with a reasonable effort, we are protecting them from experiences that undermine self-confidence in their ability to comprehend and to learn to comprehend better. Students who experience regular failure to understand what we ask them to read cannot be expected to continue to put forth an effort.

Teaching comprehension strategies well to students helps them attribute the success or difficulty they have to those strategies and not to their general competence or lack thereof. As a result, they can be expected to pay more attention in the future when we try to teach them new strategies, since they have reason to believe that those strategies will actually help them improve their comprehension.

Again, as before, engagement increases comprehension, and comprehension increases engagement. Success precedes motivation and motivation leads to more success.

Comprehension Can Be Developed with All Kinds of Materials in All Subjects

The elementary classrooms in which almost all children become avid readers and good comprehenders usually have a teacher who knows that "you don't work on reading just during reading time." The most successful elementary teachers develop comprehension by the way in which they guide students' comprehension as they read about "Pollution" during science and "The Pilgrims" during social studies. Integrating reading and writing instruction with topics being studied is commonly called "content-area reading and writing" or "reading and writing across the curriculum."

When you explore subjects with your students, you have countless opportunities to extend their reading and language abilities (Fulwiler & Young, 1982). For example, during the study of the weather, your class can read newspaper weather reports, listen to radio announcements, talk about how rain occurs, draw pictures of various cloud formations, and write about experiences during various types of weather disturbances. You can use the textbook along with informational trade books, Weather Service brochures, and pamphlets. Charts can be developed to show wind currents and pressure systems. Maps that indicate weather patterns can be interpreted, and tables that report the temperatures of various cities can be consulted. Experiments with water evaporation can be conducted and reported. CD-ROMs, websites, and videos that explain weather changes can be examined and then discussed or written about. As students develop understandings of facts and ideas related to a topic with your help, they also develop ability to read and write about facts and ideas.

We have the responsibility to teach students how to comprehend a wide variety of reading materials. It is important to use all genres in comprehension lessons—stories, poetry, plays, and informational texts. Here are some of the more common sources of good passages to use for comprehension lessons in the elementary grades:

- Current reading series
- Science and social studies textbooks
- Old reading series
- Leveled readers
- Multiple subscriptions to *My Weekly Reader, Scholastic,* or *Time for Kids*
- Big Books
- Multiple copies of trade books
- Reproducible materials—plays and poetry
- Internet reproducibles

While no classroom or school will have access to all these types of materials, the list serves to show that only using one source of passages for comprehension lessons is missing opportunities to teach a broader range of material that will interest a greater percentage of our students. This key idea doesn't take long to explain or justify, but comprehension will definitely be improved by the effort to develop it with all kinds of materials in all subjects.

Comprehension Strategy Lessons Engage Students before, during, and after Reading

Comprehension strategy lessons teach students how to comprehend. These lessons emphasize the ideas contained in the book or story along with the ways students can go about understanding those ideas. Comprehension strategy lessons occur during three time frames—before, during, and after reading. To improve students' comprehension, the preparation done before reading is as important as the activities that occur after reading.

To present comprehension strategy lessons, we wrote a model plan that accompanies a folktale. The steps of this lesson apply to all strategies and passages, but the specifics of the plan presented here apply to only one comprehension strategy and passage.

One of our lesson plan features is that the actual wording for the lessons (i.e., a script) is provided. The point to remember about the script is that it is a model for teachers to follow. The lesson plan script presented here is intended to demonstrate the types of things teachers might say when conducting a lesson; the script is not meant to be followed verbatim.

Before reading the following model, you need some additional perspective. First, the following is a lesson *plan;* it is a bare-bones framework designed to start actual lessons. The actual dialogue between teachers and students during a comprehension would be much richer. Finally, the wording for this model lesson plan is presented three ways: (1) directions to the teacher are in italic print—*like this;* (2) the actual words suggested for teachers to say to students are in regular print—like this; and (3) the possible responses from students are included in brackets—[like this]. What follows is a model comprehension strategy lesson plan and corresponding story. After showing you how the lesson might go, we explain more about the special features of each step.

Model Comprehension Strategy Lesson Plan for *The Farmer's Crowded House*

This comprehension strategy lesson guides students through reading a story that they enjoy and that makes them think. The strategy, finding a central story problem and its solution, is an appropriate one to teach using this story. It is also a strategy that will help students comprehend many of the stories they will read in the future.

Before Reading
Activate Prior Knowledge and Teach Specific Vocabulary.

The story we will read today is titled *The Farmer's Crowded House.*

The Farmer's Crowded House is a folktale. This means it began when people told stories aloud rather than writing them. Folktales are meant to entertain people and present a lesson about life at the same time.

The Farmer's Crowded House contains some words that you will need to know. *Crowded:* The title of this story suggests that a farmer had a house that was crowded. This means that the house was filled. Think of the times you have been in a crowded place. Tell us about being crowded and what you did about it. *Have a few students share their experiences being crowded in places such as their homes, cars, school assemblies, and shopping malls.*

Miserable: The word *miserable* is related to the word *misery:* People who are miserable, who have a lot of misery, are very uncomfortable. In this story, the farmer is miserable because his house is too crowded. Who can tell about a time when you were miserable? *Have a few students share their experiences.*

Wise man: A wise man is someone who is very knowledgeable about life. Listen to this description: "My father was a very wise man. He could listen to a problem and do the right thing to solve it. If my brother and I fought over who could have a toy, my father would take it away for a week. We soon learned to stop fighting over toys." Why was the speaker's father a wise man? [He solved problems well. For instance, he took away toys if two children were fighting over the same one.] The farmer in this story talks with a wise man about his crowded house. *Mansion:* Here is a picture of a mansion. As you can see, it is a house. It is a special type of house because it is especially large and well built. The farmer's crowded house is not a mansion. *Advice:* Let's say you have a problem and don't know how to solve it. A friend keeps borrowing your things and not returning them. You might ask someone what they suggest you do. You ask someone for advice. In this story, the farmer asks the wise man for advice about what to do with his crowded house.

Engage Students in the Purpose for Reading.

Now get ready to read *The Farmer's Crowded House.* This is a story, so it has a problem and a solution. Based on the title of the story and what I've said, what do you think the story problem is? [The farmer has a crowded house.] What should you know at the end of the story? [How the farmer solved the problem of his crowded house.] Read to learn how the farmer solves his problem.

The Farmer's Crowded House

Once there was a farmer who lived with his wife and their ten children in a very small farmhouse. The farmer and his family were miserable. They were always bumping into each other and getting in each other's way. When the children stayed inside on rainy days, they fought all the time. The farmer's wife was always shooing children out of the kitchen so she could cook. The farmer had no place to sit quietly when he came in from work. The farmer finally could stand it no longer. He said to his wife, "Today I am going into the village to talk with the wise man about our crowded house. He will know what to do."

So the farmer walked to the village and told the wise man his problem. The wise man listened and then asked, "How many animals do you have?"

"I have ten chickens, eight pigs, six goats, four donkeys, two cows, and one horse," replied the farmer.

"Good," said the wise man, "go home and move all your animals inside your house. Come back and talk with me in one week."

The farmer returned to his family and told them to gather together the chickens, pigs, goats, donkeys, cows, and horse and bring them inside the house. When this was done, the house became more crowded than ever. The children fought all the time, even when it was not raining. The farmer and his family ate their meals off the cow's back because they could not reach the kitchen table. After a week the farmer returned to the wise man.

"The animals take too much room!" cried the farmer. "We are too crowded!"

The wise man answered, "Now go home, move the animals back into the farmyard, and come see me again in one week."

The farmer did as he was told. When he returned to the wise man one week later, he exclaimed, "Our house seems like a mansion now that the animals are gone! I will never complain again about our crowded house. Thank you for your advice."

During Reading
Use a Reading Format That Supports Your Struggling Readers and Makes Guided Reading Multilevel.

I want you to read *The Farmer's Crowded House*. Each of you take two of these sticky notes. When you think the farmer is doing something that will solve his problem, put a sticky note right on that sentence in the book. You have only two sticky notes, so think carefully about where to put them. Keep reading until you finish the story.

After Reading
Follow Up the Purpose for Reading.

How was the farmer's problem solved? [Following the advice of the wise man, the farmer and his family lived with all the animals in the house for one week. When the animals were put back outside, the house did not seem crowded.]

The steps of a comprehension strategy lesson plan can be applied to any passage. Once you learn this pattern, you can develop lessons for chapters of paperback novels and passages contained in commercial reading series, subject-matter textbooks, library books, and magazines.

As noted earlier, the pattern of a comprehension lesson plan consists of three time frames: before, during, and after reading. Teachers prepare students for a selection before they read it, guide students during the reading, and follow up afterward. Figure 7.2 contains a list of guidelines pertaining to each of the steps of comprehension lesson plans. These guidelines are explained in the next section.

Comprehension Strategy Lesson Plan Steps

The same steps followed in the model comprehension strategy for *The Farmer's Crowded House* can be followed in any comprehension strategy lesson.

Before Reading
Activate Prior Knowledge and Teach Specific Vocabulary. This step of a comprehension lesson plan is designed to teach students general background along with certain words and their meanings. As mentioned earlier in this chapter, readers require knowledge of the world. To decide the particular background knowledge and word meaning to teach, you need to know the passage to be read and the

Activate Prior Knowledge and Teach Specific Vocabulary

Decide what background knowledge and word meanings to teach by considering what students need to know to fulfill the purpose for reading.

Teach no more than ten vocabulary words for any one selection.

Tap thinking processes when teaching vocabulary.

Do not do this step if it contradicts the purpose for reading. For example, if the purpose for reading has students predict before reading, this step would undermine the comprehension strategy being taught.

Engage Students in the Purpose for Reading

Establish one clearly stated purpose for reading.

The purpose should require students to read and think about the entire selection.

Model and directly teach the students how to read for the stated purpose.

Use a Reading Format That Supports Your Struggling Readers and Makes Guided Reading Multilevel

Select a way of grouping the students that supports your struggling readers and makes the lesson as multilevel as possible.

Select how the students will read the selection, whether the selection is in little-book or big-book form, and other aspects to support your struggling readers and make the lesson multilevel.

Vary the format from lesson to lesson so that you are not privileging the same children every day.

Follow Up the Purpose for Reading

Determine if students have fulfilled the purpose for reading.

Discuss the comprehension strategy if needed.

Figure 7.2 Comprehension Strategy Lesson Plan Guidelines

purpose to be met. Then ask yourself, "What do my students need to know to fulfill this purpose?"

To determine the problem and solution of *The Farmer's Crowded House,* students would need to realize that the story was a folktale. Knowing that *The Farmer's Crowded House* allowed unusual happenings would help them accept the idea of a farmer going to a designated "wise man" who suggested moving animals into the house. Students who expected only realistic stories probably would be confused by these events.

Only five words and their meanings were presented in the model lesson. We recommend teaching no more than ten words during each lesson. Teaching a few words well is better than teaching many words superficially. To select the words to be taught, decide which ones your students probably do not know well, are not clarified by the passage, and are the most important for fulfilling their purpose for reading. We selected *crowded, miserable, wise man, mansion,* and *advice* because they met these criteria. Limit the words to be taught by holding them to the criteria of being unfamiliar yet important for understanding the passage.

Various thinking processes were tapped to teach the five terms that were selected. Connecting was used to teach *crowded* ("Think of the times you were in a crowded place") and *advice* ("Let's say you have a problem and you don't know how to solve it. A friend keeps borrowing your things and not returning them. You might ask someone what they suggest you do. You ask for advice"). To teach *mansion,* imaging was tapped ("Here is a picture of a mansion") along with organizing ("It is a house. It is a special type of house because it is especially large and well built"). When first presenting vocabulary, connecting, imaging, and organizing are the thinking processes that should be tapped regularly because they are most feasible and powerful.

Notice that students did not use their dictionaries or glossaries to look up the meanings of the five words introduced in *The Farmer's Crowded House.* Such an activity keeps students busy, but it results in little long-term retention of word meanings. Dictionaries are best used as resources to check meanings and to clarify or embellish word meanings already known. For instance, if students wanted to know more about why a mansion was a special house, teachers might have students locate the word in a dictionary and discuss the meanings that were provided. Young students require initial instruction in how to use dictionaries and glossaries.

The guidelines for this step are summarized as follows:

1. Decide the background knowledge and word meanings to teach by determining what students need to know to fulfill their purpose for reading.
2. Teach no more than ten new vocabulary terms for each passage.
3. Tap essential thinking processes when teaching vocabulary.
4. Use dictionaries and glossaries only to confirm or clarify word meanings.
5. Do not do this step if it contradicts the purpose for reading.

Engage Students in the Purpose for Reading. The purpose set in this step was a single, clearly stated reason for reading ("Read to learn how the farmer solves his problem") that required the strategy, finding a central story problem and its solution. Setting a purpose, monitoring students' performance, and guiding students to acceptable performance are designed to teach students one comprehension strategy. Even though good comprehenders perform many comprehension strategies simultaneously when they read a passage of appropriate difficulty, new comprehension strategies are best taught and learned one at a time. In the example, students were being taught how to determine story problems and solutions, so the reason for reading was to determine the solution to the problem raised in the story.

Another characteristic of this step, setting the reading purpose in the sample lesson, is that it focused on implied information that was obtained only from reading the entire selection. Stated simply, students would need to read between the lines, and they would need to read the whole story to fulfill the purpose. Setting this type of reading purpose is important, because it promotes a comprehension strategy that is seldom taught. A purpose that called for finding a specific fact from the passage would promote only superficial scanning. A purpose that called for an entirely creative response (e.g., "If you were a farmer who lived in a crowded house, how would you solve your problem?") would not compel students to read the passage carefully. Students with a broad purpose that taps implied information can monitor their comprehension readily throughout the passage. Students can continually ask themselves, "How did the farmer solve his problem?" Students direct their attention meaningfully when reading for broad implied purposes. The point of directing students to a specific purpose is to make it possible for them to apply a comprehension strategy to their reading that they may otherwise be unable to apply. Once they have applied the strategy successfully several times with your modeling and direction, they should be able to apply the strategy independently. Three guidelines relative to setting purposes were presented here:

1. Establish one clearly stated purpose for reading.
2. Regularly establish a purpose that focuses on implied information that is obtained only from reading an entire selection.
3. Model and directly teach the students how to read for the stated purpose.

During Reading

Use a Reading Format That Supports Your Struggling Readers and Makes Guided Reading Multilevel. Historically, guided reading (sometimes called directed reading) was instruction provided by the teacher to help children improve their oral reading fluency and silent reading comprehension as they read different kinds of texts (Harris & Hodges, 1995). Today, some people use the term "guided reading" in a narrower sense to refer only to the teacher guidance given to a small group of readers as they read material at their level. We, however, use the term in its broader sense. For us, guided reading occurs when a teacher guides some students—whole group, small group, or individual—through an activity designed to help them apply their word identification and/or comprehension strategies.

Reading level is not a static entity like height. Interest, prior knowledge, type and amount of instruction, type of support, and rereading all matter to what children can successfully read. Now, there are limits to how readable you can make a particular text for a particular child—regardless of these other variables. A child whose reading level is end of first grade will not be able to read a selection written at fifth-grade level, even if that selection is on a high-interest, high-prior-knowledge topic like dinosaurs and she gets good prereading instruction, her partner helps her with some words, and she is reading it for the second time. Four grade levels is just too much of a leap! But most children whose measured reading level is end of first grade could read and understand that same selection on dinosaurs with all the same conditions if that selection were written at a late second-grade or even early third-grade level.

Conversely, a student whose measured reading level is fifth grade but who has little knowledge about or interest in dinosaurs and minimal prereading instruction might read this fifth-grade level text on dinosaurs by himself for the first time and not understand much of what he read. Many grade-level readers develop reading problems in intermediate grades when faced with boring text and little instructional support. When considering whether or not something a child is reading during guided reading is on that child's reading level, we can't just look at the reading level of the child and the reading level of the text. We must consider factors within the child such as interest and prior knowledge as well as the type and amount of instruction and support we can provide.

The reading format includes all the specifics of how the students will read the selection during a particular comprehension strategy lesson. Figure 7.3 presents three of the dimensions along which reading formats vary.

The teacher plans the reading-format step of a comprehension strategy lesson to accomplish two goals. First, a reading format is selected to support the struggling readers who will participate in the lesson. Second, a reading format is selected to make the lesson *multilevel,* that is, to maximize the range of students who can benefit from it.

While no reading format can meet the needs of everyone during a single lesson in a typical class or reading group, using a variety of reading formats (and a variety of reading materials at different levels) over time can help everyone benefit from your comprehension strategy lessons.

Grouping While Students Are Reading:

• Teacher-guided whole group

• Teacher-guided small group

• Peer-guided small groups

• Partnerships

• Independent (self-guided)

• A mixture

Oral Reading, Silent Reading (Reading to Yourself), or Silent Followed by Oral

Big or Little Book ("Big Book" also includes any time the selection to be read is projected on a wall or a screen)

Figure 7.3 **Some Ways Reading Formats Differ**

Three guidelines pertain to the use of reading formats to guide and support student reading during comprehension lessons:

1. Select a way of grouping the students that supports your struggling readers and makes the lesson as multilevel as possible.

2. Decide how the students will read the selection, whether the selection is in Little-Book or Big-Book form, and other aspects of guidance and support that will support your struggling readers and make the lesson multilevel.

3. Vary the way you group students and the other aspects of the format from lesson to lesson so that you are not privileging the same children every day.

After Reading

Follow Up the Purpose for Reading. This step of a comprehension strategy lesson exists for one simple reason—the before-reading step that engages students in the purpose for reading would have no value without it. This before- and after-reading activity teaches comprehension because it changes the way students read and think. Imagine that you are going to read a selection. Before you read it, we tell you that you will be given a closed-book test on it after you read it and that we will pay $100 for each correct answer on the test. Now, imagine that you read the same text, but that before you read it we tell you that we want you to write a summary of it afterwards with the book open. Would you read it and think about it the same way both times?

However, for our before-reading activity to have an effect on your reading more than one time, we would have to do what we told you we would after you read or the next time you would pay no attention to what we told you before you read. Also, what we told you before reading would have to be clear to you and something you could keep in mind while reading; it couldn't be too complicated or have too many aspects to remember. It would help if it were written on the marker board or displayed, so that you could refer to it while you read.

When the teacher engages students in a purpose for reading before they read that helps them apply a particular comprehension strategy *while* they read, they will be able to show after reading that their thinking and reading were improved. As long as we follow up the purpose for reading after the students read, engaging students in the purpose for reading before they read will influence how they read and think.

The following guidelines will help the after-reading part of the before- and after-reading activity have its maximum influence:

1. Always follow up the purpose for reading that the students were engaged in before they read. For example, don't have them predict what will happen in a story before they read and then have them complete a story map after they read. When the after-reading activity fails to follow up on the before-reading purpose, students will be wise to ignore the purpose for reading next time.

2. While an occasional exception may be called for, ordinarily have students read without being able to take notes. The reason is simply that the latest research on the comprehension process identifies comprehension with the construction of

memories for the text. When students are not allowed to write anything down during reading, they are more likely to try to remember what they read. This guideline is not actually a part of the after-reading step, but it will influence how effective the after-reading step is.

3. As you follow up the purpose for reading after your students have read the selection, they should usually have their books closed. That is, they should answer any questions, engage in any discussion, and perform any task you set for them from memory, rather than by leafing through the pages of what they have read. If there are disagreements among them or they cannot remember something you ask them about, they can open their books to the selection and find the information. However, they should close their books again to complete the step.

A Variety of Before- and After-Reading Activities Can Be Used to Teach Comprehension Strategies

Now that you have a fleshed-out idea of what a comprehension lesson looks like and understand what you can do before, during, and after reading to teach comprehension, we want to broaden your concept of a comprehension lesson by sharing with you several before- and after-reading activities. The lesson is structured in the case of each activity, but they all share the common goal of helping students learn how to make sense of their reading.

Graphic Organizers

A popular before- and after-reading activity for comprehension lessons involves having the students construct or fill in a graphic organizer after they read. Webs are the most commonly used graphic organizer at the elementary level. They are wonderful ways of helping readers organize information when their reading gives lots of topic/subtopic information. Imagine that your class is going to read an informational selection about Africa. Figure 7.4 shows a web that you might use to begin to help them organize the information they will be learning.

The comprehension strategy you want them to work on is determining important information and organizing that information. You set up the graphic organizer with them before reading and use it as you accomplish the before-reading steps of a comprehension lesson.

You activate prior knowledge and teach specific vocabulary as you and the students set up the web, using the key words and connecting students' prior experiences to them. You let students know their purpose for reading—they should read to find information to add to the web and decide where the important information should go.

Then, students read the text about Africa. They could read it individually, with partners, or in small groups. As they read, you go around and remind them (as needed) of their purpose.

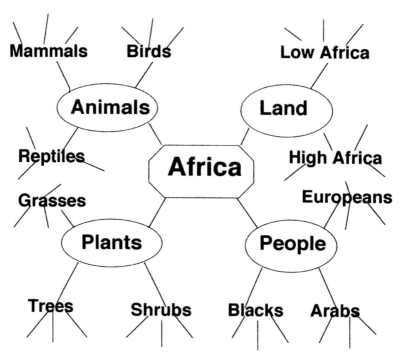

Figure 7.4 Web for Africa

"Have you found anything yet that you think we need to add to our web? Where should we put it? Be sure you are looking for the things we are trying to find out about Africa."

When the time allotted to reading is up, students gather back with you and help complete the graphic organizer begun before reading. If there are disagreements or gaps, students return to the text and try to find the missing information.

Webs are an efficient graphic organizer for topic/subtopic information, but there are many other ways to show types of relationships. Data charts (McKenzie, 1979) are another way of helping children organize information that compares and contrasts members of the same category. In one example, McKenzie's data charts begin with a series of questions that you search for information to answer. For Africa, for example, the questions might be "What animals live there?" "What do they eat?," "Who are their enemies?," and "What plants grow there?" Usually there is also an "Other Interesting Facts" box. Figure 7.5 shows a data chart used to record information about the various regions in Africa.

Webs and data charts are the most popular graphic organizers used in elementary classrooms, but they are not the only possibilities. Time lines are wonderful graphic organizers to help students determine important information and

Regions	People	Plants	Animals	Land
Desert				
Semiarid				
Tropical				

Figure 7.5 Data Chart for Africa

organize that information sequentially. Time lines are the graphic organizer of choice when reading history, historical fiction, and biography.

Of course, this is just a sampling of graphic organizers and is just to get you thinking about how you can help students see important relationships by considering how you would graphically depict those relationships. When you determine that what you want students to think about as they read is how text is organized, or to show topic/subtopic, compare/contrast, or time/order relationships, a graphic organizer is often the most efficient format for supporting their reading strategy use. Regardless of which graphic organizer you construct, the activities that go on before, during, and after reading follow those outlined in the model lesson.

Before Reading

Construct the skeleton graphic organizer in front of the children. Build background knowledge and vocabulary as you write key words on the graphic. Give examples and elicit examples from your students for the concepts represented by the words on the organizer. Before they begin reading, be sure that they know that they are reading to ferret out important information and to decide where it should go in the graphic organizer.

During Reading

Use a reading format that supports struggling readers and makes the guided reading multilevel.

After Reading

Have them work with you to add information to the organizer. Once all information is added, let them go back to the text to clarify, prove, disprove, or add important information.

KWL

KWL is a flexible and popular way to guide students' thinking when they are reading informational text (Ogle, 1986; Carr & Ogle, 1987). The letters of KWL stand for what we *K*now, what we *W*ant to find out, and what we have *L*earned.

Imagine that your class is about to study Washington, D.C. You might begin the lesson by pointing out Washington, D.C., on a map and asking if any students have been there. Share some pictures and picture books of this city. Then begin a KWL chart on the board, overhead, or chart paper, explaining the headings as you set them up.

Washington, D.C.

What we know	*What we want to find out*	*What we have learned*

Have students brainstorm what they know about Washington, D.C., and write their responses in the first column. When the children have brainstormed their prior knowledge, the chart might look like this:

Washington, D.C.

What we know	*What we want to find out*	*What we have learned*
capital		
White House		
president lives there		
lots of drugs		
cherry blossoms in spring		
cold in winter		
near Virginia		
near Maryland		

Next, direct the students' attention to the second column and ask them what they would like to find out about Washington, D.C. List their questions in the second column:

Washington, D.C.

What we know	*What we want to find out*	*What we have learned*
capital	How old is it?	
White House	How big is the White House?	
president lives there	What is in D.C.?	
lots of drugs	Where is the IRS?	

cherry blossoms
   in spring
cold in winter
near Virginia
near Maryland

What kind of government do they have?
Why is it not a state?
How many people live there?
What do people do there?

Once the questions are listed, students read in some format in order to see which of their questions can be answered and to find other information they think is important. After reading, the teacher begins by determining which of the questions were answered and writes these answers in the last column. Next, the teacher leads the students to add other interesting facts. This information is also recorded in the third column. All members of the class are encouraged to contribute to this adding of information learned. Sometimes, a fact that someone wants to add is disputed by other class members. The teacher adds this fact—but marks it with a question mark.

After recording this first draft of what the class has learned, the children go back to the text to clarify, prove, or fill in gaps. When someone wants to prove, clarify, or disprove a disputed fact, we have them read the relevant parts aloud and help them explain their thinking. When the information on the chart is complete and accurate, there is a general feeling of satisfaction in the entire class, a kind of "Look how much we learned!" attitude.

Story Maps

Story maps draw children's attention to the structural elements of stories. Stories have characters and a setting. The characters usually have some goal they want to achieve or some problem they need to resolve. The events in the story typically lead to some solution or resolution. Sometimes stories have implicit morals or themes. Here is a story map based on a model created by Isabel Beck (Macon, Bewell, & Vogt, 1991):

Main characters

Setting (time and place)

Problem or goal

Event 1

Event 2

Event 3

Event 4

Event 5

Event 6

Solution

Story theme or moral

Here is the story map from above filled in for *The Three Little Pigs:*

Main characters: Mother pig, three little pigs, big bad wolf.

Setting (time and place): Woods, make-believe time and place.

Problem or goal: Pigs want to be independent and have own houses.

Event 1: Mother pig sends three little pigs out to build their own houses.

Event 2: First little pig gets some straw and builds a straw house. Big bad wolf blows the straw house down.

Event 3: Second little pig gets some sticks and builds a stick house. Big bad wolf blows the stick house down.

Event 4: Third little pig gets some bricks and builds a brick house. Big bad wolf cannot blow the brick house down.

Event 5: Big bad wolf runs off into woods (or gets scalded/cooked coming down the chimney—depending on how "violent" the version of the story is).

Solution: Pigs live happily ever after in strong brick house.

Story theme or moral: Hard work pays off in the end!

You can see how the story map would make a good before- and after-reading activity for a comprehension lesson. As the teacher sets up the map with children, both prior knowledge and vocabulary and the purpose for reading would be made clear. As children read, the teacher could remind them as needed that in a few minutes they would be helping to complete the story map. After reading the story, the teacher and class would complete the map. In addition to filling in the information, the teacher would ask questions such as "How did you know that?" This would allow children to "make public" their thinking. Once the map was completed, the children would be asked to share other reactions to the story.

Sketch to Stretch

Sketch to Stretch (Harste, Short, & Burke, 1988; Whitin, 1996) is different from the before- and after-reading activities discussed thus far because it engages students in drawing—sketching—rather than relying just on words to think about and respond to what they have read. Sketch to Stretch is intended to "stretch" students' thinking beyond the literal and into what the selection they read "means" to them. Here is an example of a Sketch to Stretch lesson based on Tomie dePaola's *Tony's Bread* (1988).

Sketch to Stretch lessons concentrate on how children use drawing to respond to stories after they read. Harste, Short, and Burke do not specify what you might do with children before reading to build prior knowledge and teach vocabulary. We think the best prior-knowledge-building activity for *Tony's Bread* would be to take students on a "picture walk" through the book. A picture walk is simply a way of using pictures that accompany the selection to help students build and access prior knowledge and specific vocabulary. It is most appropriate for selections with rich illustrations and in which some of the unfamiliar concepts are clearly depicted in the pictures. The picture begins with the teacher and children looking at the first two pages in the story and the teacher asking questions such as the following:

What do you see in these pictures?

Does this story look as if it takes place in our time or long ago?

Where do you think the story is taking place?

The children realize that the setting for this story is a long-ago, faraway place based on the dress of the people, the look of the buildings, and the way the bread is baked and displayed. The teacher then tells them that they are correct and that the setting for this story is long ago in northern Italy. Italy is quickly located on a globe (always available for quick access), and the teacher and children go on to the next pages.

After talking about the funny illustrations, the teacher asks the children to point to a strange-looking phrase in the second sentence. Together, they find the phrase

una piccola bambina

With the teacher's help, they pronounce this funny phrase, conclude it is Italian, and read the translation next to it:

a little girl

The children are now eagerly seeking out the other italicized Italian phrases, pronouncing them and reading the English translations:

una principessa—a princess; *dolci*—sweets; *Che bella donna*—What a beautiful woman!

Impressed with themselves for their ability to "read Italian," the children continue to talk about all the pictures and identify all the Italian words. Led by the teacher they decide the following:

There are letters to read that the characters write to each other.

The baker bakes a funny loaf of bread in a flower pot!

This bread has red and green things in it. All the people love this bread!

Two of the characters get married at the end.

After engaging in the picture walk, the children are eager to read the story. Before letting them begin, the teacher makes clear their purpose by explaining what they will do after reading. The teacher says something like this:

I know you are going to enjoy this story, and I want you to share your reactions to it by sketching something to show "what it meant to you." I am going to have you read it together with a small group, and when you are finished, I want you each to come get a piece of this paper and get your crayons out and draw something that shows what you thought the story meant (or is about). Don't just draw your favorite part. Don't worry about a finished "work of art." Just sketch out something that shows what you think the story means. You can draw a picture that is easily recognizable (representational art) or an abstract picture of shapes or objects."

As the children read the story in some format, perhaps together in groups of three or four, the teacher circulates and reminds each group to think about what the story means and how they could sketch that.

When each child finishes reading and begins to sketch, the teacher circulates again and tells them that there will be many different meanings in this story and many different ways to show this.

All your sketches will be different, and you can use pictures, words, shapes, colors—anything that helps you show what the story means to you.

As the students finish their sketches, the group takes turns looking at one student's sketch at a time. They tell the artist what they think the artist is saying about the story. Only then can the artist tell what is meant by the drawing. The second student in the group then shows the picture and others interpret it as before. This continues until several group members have had their pictures interpreted and had the chance to explain their own drawing.

The teacher emphasizes how different the sketches all are, that stories have different meanings for different readers, and that there are many different ways of sharing those meanings.

Stretch to Sketch is very popular with children. Using it to structure the comprehension lesson when it fits the selection being read stretches children's thinking beyond the literal. It also provides for children who are not the fastest "verbal thinkers" to share their thinking through a visual medium. Gardner (1993) suggested that children have "multiple intelligences." Sketch to Stretch appeals to many children but is invaluable for children whose intelligence is strongly visual.

For more ideas about and examples of before- and after-reading activities, see *Guided Reading the Four-Blocks Way* (Cunningham, Hall, & Cunningham, 2000).

Accommodations and Adaptations That Develop Comprehension

FOR INCLUSION

All the frameworks discussed so far benefit all the students you teach, including those who struggle with reading. One lesson framework, however, has special benefits for students whose major difficulty with reading is comprehension. QARs help the "literal reader," the student who thinks "if I can't find the sentence that says that, how am I supposed to know?" Their lack of comprehension is not because they can't identify the words or because they lack prior knowledge, strategies, or interest. They simply get so focused on "saying the words" that they don't simultaneously focus on "getting the meaning."

QARs

QAR stands for Question–Answer Relationships (Raphael,1982). QARs help children learn that much of the information they gain from reading is not "right there" on the page. In QAR, students learn that there are three basic types of questions:

1. Right There questions
2. Think and Search questions
3. On My Own questions

To teach about the three types of questions, write a paragraph or two about one of the students in your class, such as the following:

> The morning got off to a bad start when David turned off his alarm clock, rolled over, and went back to sleep. He barely made the bus, and he had to sit next to Jennifer! When David got to school, he realized that he had forgotten his lunch money and his homework. He borrowed lunch money from Jennifer and had to do his homework over again during the after-lunch recess. The long day finally ended, and David boarded the bus to go home. "One down, four to go," he thought as the bus slowly made its way to his street.

After the students read this paragraph, ask two questions that are explicitly answered in the paragraph:

> Who did David sit next to on the bus?
>
> What two important things had David forgotten?

The children should be able to find the answers to these literal questions, and you can easily illustrate why this type of question is labeled "Right There."

Next, ask two questions that do not have answers right there but have clues to appropriate responses. Explain to the students that they will be able to answer these questions only if they search for clues in the paragraph and think about what would make sense.

> What were the other children doing while David did his homework over?

(continued)

On what day of the week did this story take place?

Help your students realize that you must "Think and Search" for clues in order to answer these questions.

> Because it was recess time, the other children were probably outside playing.
>
> Because David said "One down, four to go" as he was riding home, it was probably Monday, leaving four more days of the school week.

The children should conclude that you can find support for answers to these questions, but you cannot find the answers stated right there on the page.

Finally, ask two questions that do not necessarily have a right answer, such as:

> What will David do when his alarm goes off on Tuesday morning?
>
> If David's mother asks him, "What kind of day did you have?" what words might he use to describe his day?

Help children to see that there are many possible answers to these questions and that the answers come not from the story but from their own experiences and their own thinking. We label these questions "On My Own."

Once children understand the differences among the three types of question-answer relationships, use all three types in a before- and after-reading activity. Do not label the questions, but have the students classify each type of question after they answer them. When students are able to distinguish the three types of questions, have them work together in groups to make up questions of each type to ask other groups of students.

QARs can be used with both stories and informational text. Their value lies in the message their regular use conveys to children. Reading is not just saying words and looking for answers that are right there. Reading is also searching for clues and thinking about what the clues lead to, and reading is using your own ideas and experiences to make predictions, generalizations, and evaluations.

FOR CHILDREN ACQUIRING ENGLISH

The comprehension lessons described in this chapter are suitable for children acquiring English, especially when they are using culturally relevant reading materials. Culturally relevant materials center on settings, events, and characters that students recognize and with which they identify. These books' pictures portray people and places that are like the people and places of the children's communities. Providing access to materials grounded in students' cultural heritages honors their backgrounds and links home with school. It goes far in helping children gain comfort and proficiency in a new language.

Interpreting pictured information is a way to build on nonverbal expression. The Sketch to Stretch lesson framework presented earlier, which calls for children to illustrate and talk about their illustrations in response to reading, is especially appropriate for children whose primary language is not English. Emphasizing the pictures of a book (e.g., "Show me the sidewalk. What is happening here?") supports entry into a new language.

Teachers also support second-language comprehension during ongoing classroom interactions. Effective teachers recognize cultural sources of students' behaviors and adjust instruction accordingly. For instance, students' ways of taking turns when talking during text-based discussions might differ from their teacher's. If students are used to interrupting others and the teacher is not, then the situation should be addressed. Get the issue out in the open and talk about it. The case could be that students view interruptions as ways for group members to express togetherness and collectively produce a message, whereas teachers view interruptions as takeover attempts by outspoken individuals. Whatever the case, teachers might promote talk about text that follows students' expectations, or they might promote students' self-monitoring so that they can try out different behaviors in different talk about text situations.

Effective teachers also accommodate the uncertainties and pressures second-language learners typically experience. Realizing how vulnerable language users can feel when acquiring a new language, teachers promote risk-free nonthreatening learning climates. They make it clear to the class that spoken miscues are expected and are considered opportunities to learn from, rather than mistakes to be shunned. They allow second-language learners ample time to reply to questions, and they repeat and rephrase questions that appear unclear. They encourage students to initiate questions about what has been read. They elicit comments from all students in whole-class and small-group settings so that more than just a few vocal individuals participate.

A Variety of Reading Formats Can Be Used to Make Guided Reading Multilevel

Reading formats are the various ways children are grouped and asked to read during guided reading. Remember that each reading format is one way we support and guide the "during reading" part of a comprehension strategy lesson. A full comprehension lesson requires combining a before- and after-reading activity with a (during-) reading format. Under this key idea, we briefly describe a few of the reading formats we use to make guided reading as multilevel as possible for a wide range of children.

Shared Reading of a Big Book

Shared reading is a term used to describe the process in which the teacher and the children read together. For beginning readers, the best kinds of books to use with shared reading are predictable books. Predictable books are those in which repeated patterns, refrains, pictures, and rhymes allow children to "pretend read" a book that has been read to them several times. Shared reading of predictable books allows all children to move successfully into the acquisition of literacy, develop some reading and print concepts, learn some words, and above all develop confidence in their ability to learn to read.

Shared reading can also be used as the reading format to solve a common problem encountered by teachers of older children. Many children who are otherwise good readers have trouble reading science and social studies textbooks. These books often have a table of contents, illustrations with captions, diagrams with labels, maps, charts, a glossary, and an index. Many children don't know what to do when they encounter these elements in their books, so they just ignore them. Informational books often have structural and special features that are different from stories. Children usually need to slow down their reading rate and pay attention to more than just the words in order to comprehend informational text.

It is difficult to guide children's reading and thinking about the special features of informational text when they are all looking at their own copies of the book. An informational Big Book (or informational text projected on the wall or screen) allows us to focus our students' attention on what we are teaching them. The teacher and students can use a pointer, highlighting tape, and other attention getters to make sure everyone's eyes are in the right place! Most teachers know that they need to teach students how to use the special features of informational text and that learning to read and use these features would greatly increase student confidence and comprehension of informational text. Unfortunately, because of the difficulty of accomplishing this goal when students have their own copies of textbooks, many teachers have quietly given up on it. Shared reading of informational Big Books is a format that encourages many teachers to give it another try!

How Shared Reading Is Multilevel

A good shared-reading lesson has something for everyone! As we read predictable books from which most beginners are learning such basic concepts as how to track print and what reading actually is, advanced readers are learning many—if not all—of the words. After several rereadings of a predictable Big Book and some ac-

Informational Big Books

There are many wonderful, engaging, informational Big Books being published today. Textbook publishers often provide some Big Books along with their pupil editions of science and social studies texts. National Geographic, Modern Curriculum Press, and Shortland Publications all publish a large variety of informational Big Books. Some magazines, among them *My Weekly Reader* and *Scholastic*, include "big magazine" versions with a class subscription.

companying comprehension and word activities, all children feel that they really can read. A few children are just reproducing memorized sentences; many children are reading some words and filling in the rest from what they remember; our most advanced readers usually learn most of the words. As we continue to do shared reading with predictable books, more and more children move from the "pretend reading" stage to the "reading the words stage" that is real reading.

When we use informational books for shared reading with older students, there are also multiple skills to be learned. The main purpose of using these books is to teach the important comprehension strategies needed for informational text. Every reader—struggling as well as advanced—can learn how to preview informational text; how to get the most information from the pictures, maps, charts, graphs, diagrams, and accompanying quicktext; and how to use the table of contents, index, and glossary. We choose informational Big Books that connect to our science and social studies units so that every child can learn some new science and social studies content and vocabulary. Of course, our advanced readers will learn the most—they will probably be able to read and have meanings for all the new words in the informational Big Book! Multilevel instruction does not mean that everyone learns the same things or the same amount. Rather, multilevel activities always include multiple things that can be learned. Multilevel activities are structured so that everyone can engage in them, learn something, and thus feel successful. When students experience success in an activity, they engage that activity more energetically the next time. This success triggers the upward spiral of success→motivation→engagement→learning→success.

ERT . . . (Everybody Read To . . .)

Although practice of taking turns reading aloud, commonly known as "round-robin reading," has been criticized and condemned for decades, still it persists in many classrooms. When teachers continue to do something in spite of numerous and almost unanimous criticism, there must be a reason! We think the reason teachers still close their door and do round-robin reading is that sometimes they want to guide the whole class or a small group through the reading of a selection, making sure that the students are attending to certain critical concepts and that everyone is getting important information. By having the selection read out and asking questions to make sure everyone is paying attention, the teacher feels assured that everyone is involved in some way in the reading of the selection.

Round-robin reading is not a multilevel activity in which everyone feels successful and during which there are multiple things to be learned! The ERT format is a way of guiding the whole class (or a small group) through the reading of a selection. We use ERT (rhymes with *shirt*) when we want the students to do the initial reading on their own but prefer to keep them together to provide a lot of guidance and support. Here is how we use the ERT format.

We lead students through the text, setting purposes for each page or two-page spread. Some of these purposes are literal and some are inferential. We cue them to the type of question by asking students to "find out" when the answer can be found right there on the page, and "figure out" when the answer is not directly stated but you have to figure it out based on what is said and what you know already. In ERT, students are asked to read to find out or figure out a variety of things. When they have found them or figured them out, they raise their hand and continue reading until they finish the page or pair of pages. When most hands are raised, we call on one child to tell the answer and another child to read the part where the answer was found or cite the clues that "helped us figure it out."

When children do the reading to find or figure out answers to our questions, that reading is done silently or—if children still need to hear themselves reading—in a "whisper voice." We usually include one or two "two handers" in each lesson, an ERT that has two questions. Students love these because they get to raise one hand and then the other and usually need to hold the book open with their elbows—providing a bit of a balancing challenge, a chance to stretch their muscles, and an opportunity to present a comical image!

ERT can be done with both story and informational text. Here are some literal and inferential purposes set for students reading a social studies selection on Mount Vesuvius.

"Everybody read these two pages to figure out why Pompeii was a good place to live and what Vesuvius was compared to."

[Students read and raise first one hand and then the other for this "two hander." Teacher reminds those whose hands are raised to finish reading the section and then calls on one student.]

"Who figured out why Pompeii was a good place to live? Jack, can you tell us?"

[Jack gives an appropriate answer, and the teacher calls on a different student to read some of the clues.]

"Who can read some of the clues that let Jack figure out that Pompeii was a good place to live?"

[Teacher asks the second question students were asked to figure out an answer for and then asks for another volunteer to read some of the clues.]

"Who figured out what Vesuvius was compared to?"

"Who can read some of the clues you could use to figure out what Vesuvius was compared to?"

[Teacher sets a literal purpose for the next page.]

"On this page, I want everyone to read to find out if the people knew what was going to happen."

[Students read, and many hands are raised. Teacher calls on a student.]

"Josh, did the people know what was going to happen?"

[Josh answers that the people didn't know and the teacher calls on another student to read the part where Josh found the answer. That student proudly reads,]

"The people did not know what was going to happen."

How ERT Is Multilevel

An activity is multilevel if many different levels of readers can feel successful in the activity and if multiple things can be learned from it. ERT is a very multilevel format if you strictly follow a few rules. First, make sure that you include about equal numbers of inferential "figure out" purposes and literal "find out" purposes. Make your "find outs" very literal. In the Vesuvius example, in which everyone was asked to "find out if the people knew what was going to happen," one sentence stated the following:

The people did not know what was going to happen.

By including some very literal purposes, your struggling readers will soon discover that, although they may not be able to read all of the text, they can find the answers to many of the questions, raise their hands, and proudly give the correct answer! Remember that children who "won't try" are children who are convinced they can't do it. When they experience some very obvious success, they try harder. As they listen and actually try to read the pages, they (and the teacher) usually discover they can read more than they thought they could.

By understanding more than they probably would ordinarily from reading the text, and from hearing the answer given by others to the "figure outs," even the struggling readers will probably be able to succeed with the after-reading activity that teaches the comprehension strategy for today's lesson.

In addition to including some very literal questions, many teachers have students repeat the purpose before they read. As students respond that they are reading "to find out if the people knew what was going to happen," they attend to what they are saying. This greatly increases the probability that struggling readers will recognize those very same words as they turn their attention to reading the page.

In ERT, the person who gives the answer to a question is never the same person who reads the part where the answer was found or the clues that let you figure it out. This ensures the participation of many students in the lesson and is also important for the participation of the struggling readers. Many struggling readers can read enough to find out and figure out some answers, but their oral reading would be choppy or hesitant. Many older struggling readers would never volunteer to answer a question to which they knew the answer if they thought they would then be called on to read aloud. After a few ERT lessons in which the teacher makes it clear that the child who gave the answer will NEVER be the one who reads aloud (even if he or she wants to), struggling readers "figure out" that it is "safe" to answer questions and begin to participate in the activity (instead of just sitting there waiting for it to end!).

Many teachers experience so much success with ERT that they are tempted to use it every day. Resist the temptation! ERT is fun for the students if used judiciously, but any format becomes boring if you do it every day. Many teachers use ERT as the format for reading the first chapter in a book, or the first part of a selection. The first part of any selection is always the hardest to read, because it is where major characters are being introduced or major concepts are being built. Once your readers are successfully launched into a selection, consider using some of the other formats such as partner reading, playschool groups, or coaching groups to provide students with the support they need to continue experiencing success and learning from the selection.

Partner Reading (Two Heads Are Better than One!)

Partner reading is a format that allows your children to learn to read better and faster, and for many children, reading it with a friend is just more fun! We have worked with teachers for many years to help them make partner reading a fun, productive, successful, multilevel format. We would like to share our most important "Dos" for successful partner reading.

1. *Do think about who you will—and won't!—partner up with whom.* Children whose families have been feuding for generations probably won't make good partners. The best reader in the class is probably not the best partner for the worst reader. If they are at the "can't stand the girls" stage, it is probably best to do same-gender partnerships. Think about your struggling readers first and who would be the best partners for them. Ask yourself, "Who would be patient and not just tell them all the words?" "Who would be insightful and would be able to coach them and get them to talk about their reading?" In most classrooms, there are a couple of very nurturing children who would love to help some of their struggling classmates. These are the children to try out as partners for your most struggling readers.

2. *Do make sure your partners KNOW their purpose for reading.* We all work more "purposefully" when we know exactly what we are trying to do. The comprehension strategy underlying the purpose for reading is what students are trying to learn how to do, and the after-reading activity is what they should be ready to contribute to. If they are going to "do the beach ball" after reading, the partners should be reading to find answers to the beach ball questions. If they are going to add things to the KWL chart, they should be reading to find things to add. Remember that comprehension strategy lessons are where we teach children how to think about text—the comprehension skills and strategies. As they begin reading with partners, it is important to remind the children of the purpose for reading with which you engaged them in the before-reading part of the lesson.

3. *Do set a time limit for reading.* Before children begin reading, tell them exactly how long they have to read it. Make it a reasonable time—but don't give them longer than most of them will really need. Most behavior problems during partner reading happen when children have time to fool around. Don't give them the same amount of time each day, because some selections are longer and some rereading of selections can be done in less time. But set a time—write it on the board and/or set a timer. When the time is up, tell them that you are sorry if they didn't finish but you need them to join the group—or tell them that if they haven't finished, they can finish and then join the group—it doesn't matter, but be consistent and enforce your time limits. You will be amazed how much more they can read and how much better they behave when the "clock is ticking."

4. *Do make sure they have something to do if they finish before time is up.* Always give them a "filler"—what they should do if they finish before time is up. Relate this "filler" as closely as you can to the purpose for reading. If they are reading to answer the questions on the beach ball, tell them that if they finish before the time is up, they should take turns asking each other the questions on the beach ball and come up with "awesome" answers. If they finish before time is up and are reading to find information to add to the KWL chart, they should begin to write some of these things down. If the after-reading activity is going to be "doing the book" and they have a few minutes, they should decide which character they would like to be and practice what they will say and how they will act.

Having something they are to do if they finish early is absolutely essential for successful partner reading: if they don't, some of the partners will rush through and then create problems because they're "all done!" Children are not in such a rush to finish first when they have to think and prepare. (Don't turn the filler into a requirement for everyone, or have them turn it in, or give them time to finish it; you are then right back in the same old "they don't all finish at the same time" bind. It is probably not a good idea to call what you give them to do a "filler," but that it is important for you to remember that this is what it is!)

5. *Do teach your students how you want them to read with their partners.* Role-play and model for them what partners will do and how they should help each other and correct each other nicely. Demonstrate how to ask good questions. Here are some of the different ways we teach partners to read—depending on their age and our purpose for reading that day.

> *Take turns.* One partner reads the first page, the other partner the second page, and so on. This is the most common way of partner reading—but not necessarily the most productive.
>
> *Read and point.* One partner points to the words on one page while the other partner reads; then they switch reader/pointer roles on the next page. This is particularly helpful in the beginning, when print tracking is a big issue for some children. You will be surprised at how quickly some of your children will pick up print tracking when a nurturing helpful partner is pointing to their words and then making sure they point to the words correctly when it is their turn. We would not recommend this once children become more fluent, however, because it does slow children down and can take their focus away from the meaning.
>
> *Ask questions.* Both children read each page—silently if they can or chorally if they need help. They then ask each other a "good question" about what they have read.
>
> *Say something.* Say something is also a good partner working strategy. The simple notion is that after you read a page, you "say something." If you don't

have anything to say, you may have been concentrating too much on the words and not enough on the meaning. You may need to reread the page, thinking about what you might say about it. Some teachers have partners taking turns reading a page and saying something. On other days, partners can be told to read the page together or silently and then each say something.

Echo reading. Once they know how to echo-read, they will enjoy echo reading some sections. Give the child who is the echo in each partnership something to designate his or her status or have both partners read the selection twice, then switch first-reading and echo-reading roles. Make sure struggling readers are the echo on the first reading.

Choral whispering. Choral whispering is a variation of choral reading. Children whisper with their partner. Children use a "whisper" voice so that their voice will not distract partners seated nearby.

ERT. Children love doing ERT . . . with each other. It is particularly effective as a rereading strategy when they know what the selection is about and need a good purpose for rereading. Even children who are not very fluent readers can usually find the answer to a question and pose a good question for their partner when they have already read the selection and this is a rereading.

6. *Do use the partner reading time to assist and monitor the reading of your children.* Many teachers who are accustomed to conducting instruction in small groups worry that when they use a variety of multilevel formats, they won't have time to listen to individual children read and won't know who is getting it and who isn't. Partner reading is a wonderful opportunity for teachers to circulate around and both assist and monitor the reading of individual children. Many teachers tell the children that they will be coming around to most of the partnerships and listening in on the reading and discussion that is going on.

> "When I join your partnership, I may interrupt and ask each of you to read a little aloud for me so that I can hear how well you are growing in your reading ability. I may ask you to retell or summarize what you have read so far. I will write some notes here on my clipboard so that I have a record of how well you are reading and how you are all becoming such good thinkers about your reading. If I don't get around to all the partners today, I will make a note of that too and make sure I get to listen to the rest of you read and tell about your reading next time we read in partners."

Many teachers use partner reading as the reading format one or two days each week. They use their time while partners are reading to monitor and coach the children on word and comprehension strategies.

How Partner Reading Is Multilevel

Working together on something is a natural arrangement in real life. Children are used to helping each other and teaching each other all kinds of things. Most children learn how to ride a bike and how to play a new game from their friends. When you use partner reading, you significantly increase the number of teachers in your classroom. You also increase the amount of time children spend reading orally, especially your struggling readers.

Coaching Groups

On some days, the teacher meets with a small group and coaches them to use their word and comprehension strategies. Who is included in the coaching group changes from time to time, but struggling readers are included more often than advanced readers. We do, however, include some children who are not struggling each time we do a coaching group. Including some better readers guarantees that the coaching group will not see itself or be seen by others as the "dumb readers," makes sure that we have some good reading models in the group, and allows everyone to learn to be a word coach.

We explain coaching groups to the children by making analogies to sports teams. Children understand that first you practice various soccer moves and then the coach watches you play in a game format, stopping you from time to time to coach you to use the skills you have practiced. Once children understand how to coach, we let them play the role of word coach. Before long, they learn how to use their coaching skills when reading in partners or playschool groups. We choose something to read that is at the reading level of most of the children we have decided to include in this group. We have the children read parts of the selection to themselves first. Then we ask someone to read aloud so that we can demonstrate what a word coach does.

Coaching Steps

Before the children start to read, we remind them of the strategies they can use to figure out an unfamiliar word. We post a chart of the steps we review each time before children begin reading.

How to Figure Out a Hard Word
1. Put your finger on the word and say all the letters.
2. Use the letters and the picture clues.
3. Look for a rhyme you know.
4. Keep your finger on the word, finish the sentence, and pretend it's the covered word.

Here is how we coach each step and why each step is important.

1. *Put your finger on the word and say all the letters.* When a child comes to words he does not know, we have her put her finger on the word and say all the letters. It is very important here that the child says the letters. Saying the letters is not sounding out the word by saying individual sounds. English is not a sound-it-out-letter-by-letter

language, and the worst readers are the ones why try to do it letter by letter. We want them to say all the letters so that we know that they have indeed looked at them all in the right order; having them say them is the only way to know for sure. We also want them to say the letters because there is strong evidence that retrieval from the brain's memory store is auditory. If you are just looking at letters and searching in your brain for that word or a rhyming word, it is apt to be harder to find than if you say the letters so that the sound goes through the brain's auditory channel.

In our experience, if children are reading at the right level and say the letters of an unfamiliar word aloud, they will sometimes correctly pronounce that word immediately. Proof positive that they needed that auditory channel for retrieval! When they say all the letters and then successfully pronounce the word, cheer! They have scored a goal. "See, it was in there. You just had to say it so that your brain could find it!" If, after they say all the letters, they still don't know the word, we give them one of the next three cues, depending on the word.

2. *Use the letters and the picture clues.* Pictures often provide clues to words. The child who sees the word *raccoon,* says all the letters, and then glances at the picture may indeed see a picture of a raccoon. The picture, along with the letters we know he has looked at because he just said them, will often allow him to decode the word. So once the child has said all the letters aloud, if there is something they should have noticed in the picture, we cue them to that.

"I see an animal in the picture that looks to me like a r-a-c-c-o-o-n."

3. *Look for a rhyme you know.* In our words activities, we teach children to decode and spell words based on rhyming patterns. If the unknown word has a familiar rhyming pattern, we cue the child to some of the rhyming words he might know.

"We know that w-i-l-l is *will* and s-t-i-l-l is *still.* Can you make t-h-r-i-l-l rhyme with *will* and *still*?"

4. *Keep your finger on the word, finish the sentence, and pretend the word is the covered word.* Guess the Covered Word is an activity that helps children use beginning letters, word length, and context to figure out words. If the picture is no help and we can't think of rhyming words that would help, we cue them like this:

"Keep your finger on the word, finish the sentence, and pretend it's the covered word." This is the cue we use when the others won't work. Reading on and going back interrupts the reading, and we want children to look at and process unknown words as soon as they encounter them. But when they need the clues provided by the rest of the sentence to decode the word, we want to coach them to use them.

Coaching a Missed Word

The procedure just described is what we do when a child stops on a word. If, instead of stopping, the child misreads a word, we let her finish the sentence and then bring her back to that misread word. Imagine, for example that the child read

"There was not a cold in the sky."

In fact the sentence said

There was not a cloud in the sky.

When the child misread "cold" for *cloud, cold* did make sense. By the end of the sentence, however, she should realize that the sentence didn't make sense and go back and try to fix something. We let children finish the sentence so that they will develop their own self-monitoring system. If, however, they don't notice and just continue reading, we stop them and say something like,

"That didn't make sense. Let's look at this word again. Say all the letters in this word."

We then give them the appropriate cue to help them figure out the word.

When We Do Coaching Groups

Many teachers run coaching groups while the children not in the coaching group are reading with partners. Some teachers find time in their weekly schedule to meet with coaching groups outside the guided reading time. In some classrooms, the teacher meets daily with an "After Lunch Bunch" and does coaching at that time. We include all children in the After Lunch Bunch activities across the week, but we include the struggling readers almost every day and the others less frequently. In some classrooms, teachers have a center time each day and do a coaching group that we call a "Fun Reading Club" during that time. Coaching groups only last ten to fifteen minutes. We don't do before- and after-reading activities to teach comprehension, since children included in our coaching group were also included in our guided reading comprehension lessons. We don't introduce high frequency or teach decoding strategies, as this is our focus during our words activities We simply choose some material at the instructional level of most of the children we intend to include and begin reading it. We want to simulate what children must do during self-selected reading when they tackle text on their own. As they read and encounter problems, we coach them to apply what they have learned when they actually need to use it.

In some classrooms it is the special teachers or assistants who run coaching groups with children. If you have help coming and many children who need coaching, you might schedule self-selected reading at that time and have the helper coach children in their self-selected books. Many teachers like to schedule guided reading when they have help coming. The helping teacher can coach children through the selection if it is close to their instructional level or can read that selection to them and then coach them in material at their level.

Finding the time, people, and reading materials needed for coaching groups is not easy. But when you put some regular coaching in instructional-level material on top of all the good instruction struggling readers receive throughout the day, you will be amazed at the rapid progress these poorer readers can make.

How Coaching Groups Are Multilevel

In coaching groups, we stress that all children are learning to become word coaches. We call them together and model what a word coach does. Then we let different children volunteer to be word coaches and we coach them on how to coach. We do include struggling readers in coaching groups, and we choose material at the appropriate level for those children who need coaching. Every group includes some more able readers, however, and the membership in coaching groups changes regularly. Because the coaching group is just one of the formats we use to make our guided reading time multilevel, and because we group children together for all different kinds of reasons, these groups are not viewed by others or the children in them as "low" reading groups. For more ideas about and examples of multilevel reading formats, see *Guided Reading the Four-Blocks Way* (Cunningham, Hall, & Cunningham, 2000).

The Theory and Research Base for Comprehension

In 1979, Delores Durkin published a landmark study demonstrating that there was little if any reading comprehension instruction happening in most classrooms and that the little bit that did occur was "mentioning" rather than teaching. Having children answer comprehension questions to assess their reading comprehension was the most widely practiced activity. This finding shocked the reading community and probably propelled much of the reading comprehension research that has occurred since. Unfortunately, more recent research (Beck, McKeown & Gromoll, 1989; Pressley & Wharton-McDonald, 1998) indicates that reading comprehension instruction is still a rare commodity in most elementary classrooms.

One important type of reading-comprehension research has focused on the characteristics of good comprehenders. Duke and Pearson (2002) summarize what good readers do, here is our summary of their summary. Good readers

- are active and have clear goals in mind.
- preview text before reading, make predictions, and read selectively to meet their goals.
- construct, revise, and question the meanings they are making as they read.
- try to determine the meanings of unfamiliar words and concepts.
- draw from, compare, and integrate their prior knowledge with what they are reading.
- monitor their understanding and make adjustments as needed.

- think about the text's authors and evaluate the text's quality and value.
- read different kinds of text differently, paying attention to characters and settings when reading narratives, constructing and revising summaries in their minds when reading expository text.

Knowing that good readers have and use them, many researchers have investigated the effects of teaching students a variety of comprehension strategies. According to the National Reading Panel (NRP) report (2000), there is substantial evidence to support the teaching of the following six comprehension strategies:

1. Monitoring comprehension.
2. Using graphic and semantic organizers.
3. Answering questions.
4. Generating questions.
5. Recognizing story structure.
6. Summarizing.

According to the NRP report, there is also some research support for two other strategies:

7. Using prior knowledge.
8. Using mental imagery.

Duke and Pearson (2002), in their review of research, identify six research-based strategies:

1. Prediction/activation of prior knowledge.
2. Think-alouds (which includes monitoring comprehension).
3. Using text structure.
4. Using/constructing visual representations (including graphic organizers and imagery).
5. Summarization.
6. Answering questions/questioning.

A comparison of their list with the NRP list shows remarkable agreement on which strategies, if taught, produce measurable gains in reading comprehension.

The final question to be considered is how these comprehension strategies can be most effectively taught. Again, we find a great deal of consensus. Both the NRP and the Duke and Pearson reviews suggest that explicit teaching, including an explanation of what and how the strategy should be used, teacher modeling and thinking aloud about the strategy, guided practice with the strategy and support for students applying the strategy independently are the four steps to effectively teaching any comprehension strategy.

Earlier reviews of research on teaching reading comprehension found that a number of specific lesson frames can improve reading comprehension ability (Tierney & J. Cunningham, 1984; Pearson & Fielding, 1991). Most of these lesson frames include guidance throughout and links among before-, during-, and after-reading activities. They each teach one or more strategies that appear in one of the lists cited above.

Duke and Pearson also found that it is better to teach a variety of comprehension strategies rather than relying on one or a few. For example, they cite a research base for SAIL (Students Achieving Independent Learning). Comprehension strategies taught in SAIL (Pressley, Almasi, Schuder, Bergman, Hite, El-Dinary, et al., 1994) include predicting, visualizing, questioning, clarifying, making associations between the text and the reader's experience, and summarizing. In SAIL, students observe teacher think-alouds and then practice applying these strategies to a variety of texts.

L o o k i n g   B a c k

Comprehension is a complex process that requires readers to juggle many sources of information. Students learn to control this process during many encounters with print inside and outside classrooms. Teachers plan and implement comprehension lessons to teach students directly to control their comprehension. There are many different before- and after-reading activities and reading formats that teachers can match to their various goals and students' needs. This chapter presents this information under five key ideas:

1. Reading comprehension requires word identification, prior knowledge, strategies, and engagement.
2. Comprehension can be developed with all kinds of materials in all subjects.
3. Comprehension strategy lessons engage students before, during, and after reading.
4. Use a variety of before- and after-reading activities to teach comprehension strategies.
5. Use a variety of reading formats to make guided reading multilevel.

Add to Your Journal

This chapter presents four aspects of reading comprehension: word identification, prior knowledge, comprehension strategies, and engagement. Do you think anything else belongs in a description of the dynamics of reading comprehension? What else do you think might be involved in the process of constructing meaning from print? The special steps of comprehension lesson plans present a rather detailed view of lesson planning. Compare this lesson format with others you have encountered. What is the same? What is different? How might you combine their positive features? What attention to your reading during subject-matter study do you recall? How do you intend to incorporate comprehension instruction with subject-matter study? Respond to each of the key ideas in this chapter by using some or all of the eight essential thinking processes. What connections, predictions, and generalizations can you make? What images do these key ideas produce? How do you organize all this information? Monitor your own understanding by deciding if you are still confused about any parts of this chapter. Evaluate these ideas by deciding what your "opinions" about comprehension are. Most important, how will you apply these ideas to your classroom?

Application   Activities

Add to Your Resource File

A variety of comprehension lesson frameworks (before- and after-reading activities) were described in this chapter, but there are many more we didn't have space to include. Search through journals, textbooks, or "the Net" and find another before- and after-reading activity you like. Write a description of what a lesson in this framework would look like, including what you would do before, during, and after reading and how this framework would satisfy many of the guidelines given for comprehension lessons. Be sure to include a complete bibliographic reference so that others can locate your source.

Try It Out

Plan a comprehension lesson and teach it to some "real kids" or to a small group of peers. Write out a description of your lesson that tells exactly what you would do for each step. Try to include in your lesson something that shows you have incorporated the guidelines listed under each step. After you teach the lesson, write a self-evaluation in which you describe what went particularly well and what you would change if you were going to teach this lesson again.

Listen, Look, and Learn

Observe a comprehension lesson—either in a real classroom or on a video. Describe what you saw the teacher and students doing. Compare this lesson to the comprehension strategy lesson framework. What steps did you see? What guidelines were followed? What was missing? What did you like about this lesson? How would you adapt it, given what you have learned about comprehension lessons?

R e f e r e n c e s

Anderson, R. C., & Pearson, P. D. (1984). A schema-theoretic view of basic reading processes in reading comprehension. In P. D. Pearson (Ed.), *Handbook of reading research* (pp. 255–291). White Plains, NY: Longman.

Baldwin, R. S., Peleg-Bruckmer, Z., & McClintock, A. H. (1985). Effects of topic interest and prior knowledge on reading comprehension. *Reading Research Quarterly, 20,*497–504.

Bransford, J. D., & McCarrel, N. S. (1974). A sketch of a cognitive approach to comprehension. In W. B. Weimer & D. S. Palermo (Eds.), *Cognition and the symbolic processes* (pp. 189–229). Hillsdale, NJ: Erlbaum.

Beck, I. L., McKeown, M. G., & Gromoll, E. W. (1989). Learning from social studies texts. *Cognition and Instruction, 6,* 99–158.

Carr, E., & Ogle, D. (1987). K-W-L plus: A strategy for comprehension and summarization. *Journal of Reading, 30,*626–631.

Cunningham, P. M., Hall, D. P., & Cunningham, J. W. (2000). *Guided reading the four-blocks way.* Greensboro, NC: Carson-Dellosa.

Duke, N. K., & Pearson, P. D. (2002). Effective practices for developing reading comprehension. In A. E. Farstrup & S. J. Samuels (Eds.), *What research has to say about reading instruction* (3rd ed., pp. 205–242). Newark, DE: International Reading Association.

Durkin, D. (1979). What classroom observations reveal about reading comprehension instruction. *Reading Research Quarterly, 14,* 481–533.

Fulwiler, T., & Young, A. (1982). *Language connections: Writing and reading across the curriculum.* Urbana, IL: National Council of Teachers of English.

Gardner, H. (1993). *Multiple intelligences: The theory in practice.* New York: Basic Books.

Harris, T. L., & Hodges, R. E. (Eds.). (1995). *The literacy dictionary: The vocabulary of reading and writing.* Newark, DE: International Reading Association.

Harste, J. D., Short, K. G., & Burke, C. (1988). *Creating classrooms for authors: The reading–writing connection.* Portsmouth: NH: Heinemann.

Macon J. M., Bewell, D., & Vogt, M. (1991). *Responses to literature.* Newark, DE: International Reading Association.

McKenzie, G. (1979). Data charts: A crutch for helping students organize reports. *Language Arts, 56,*784–788.

National Reading Panel. (2000). *Teaching children to read: An evidence-based assessment of the scientific research literature on reading and its implications for reading instruction: Reports of the subgroups* (National Institute of Health Pub. No. 00–4754). Washington, DC: National Institute of Child Health and Human Development.

Ogle, D. (1986). K-W-L: A teaching model that develops active reading of expository text. *The Reading Teacher, 39,* 564–570.

Paris, S. G., Wasik, B. A., & Turner, J. C. (1991). The development of strategic readers. In R. Barr, M. L. Kamil, P. B. Mosenthal, & P. D. Pearson (Eds.), *Handbook of reading research* (vol. 2, pp. 609–640). New York: Longman.

Pearson, P. D., & Fielding, L. (1991). Comprehension instruction. In R. Barr, M. L. Kamil, P. B. Mosenthal, & P. D. Pearson (Eds.), *Handbook of reading research* (vol. 2, pp. 815–860). White Plains, NY: Longman.

Pressley, M., Almasi, J., Schuder, T., Bergman, J., Hite, S., El-Dinary, P. B., et al. (1994). Transactional instruction of comprehension strategies: The Montgomery County, Maryland SAIL Program. *Reading and Writing Quarterly, 10,* 5–19.

Pressley, M., & Wharton-McDonald, R. (1998). The development of literacy, Part 4: The need for increased comprehension in upper-elementary grades. In M. Pressley (Ed.), *Reading instruction that works: The case for balanced teaching* (pp. 192–227). New York: Guilford.

Raphael, T. (1982). Question-answering strategies for children. *The Reading Teacher, 39,* 186–190.

Rumelhart, D. E. (1985). Toward an interactive model of reading. In H. Singer & R. B. Ruddell (Eds.), *Theoretical models and processes of reading* (3rd ed., pp. 722–750). Newark, DE: International Reading Association.

Tierney, R. J., & Cunningham, J. W. (1984). Research on teaching reading comprehension. In P. D. Pearson, R. Barr, M. L. Kamil, and P. Mosenthal (Eds.), *Handbook of reading research* (vol. 1, pp. 609–655). White Plains, NY: Longman.

Underwood, G., & Boot, D. (1986). Hemispheric asymmetries in developmental dyslexia: Cerebral structure or attentional strategies? *Journal of Reading Behavior, 18,* 219–228.

Wade, S. E., & Adams, R. B. (1990). Effects of importance and interest on recall of biographical text. *Journal of Reading Behavior, 22,* 331–353.

Whitin, P. E. (1996). *Sketching stories, stretching minds.* Portsmouth: NH: Heinemann.

Additional Readings

- Both these sources provide good introductions to teaching text structure:

  Beck, I., McKeown, M., Hamilton, R., & Kucan, L. (1997). *Questioning the author: An approach for enhancing student engagement with text.* Newark, DE: International Reading Association.

  Armbruster, B. B., Anderson, T. H., & Osterta, J. (1989). Teaching text structure to improve reading and writing. *The Reading Teacher, 43,* 130–137.

- These two articles on how to teach comprehension strategies offer additional perspectives.

  Pressley, M., El-Dinary, P. B., & Gaskins, I. W. (1992). Beyond direct explanation: Transactional instruction of reading comprehension strategies. *Elementary School Journal, 92,* 513–555.

  Rosenshine, B., & Meister, C. (1992). The use of scaffolds for teaching higher-level cognitive strategies. *Educational Leadership, 50,* 26–33.

- These two practical books present a variety of comprehension lesson frameworks made real by lots of classroom examples.

  Graves, M., & Graves, B. (1994). *Scaffolding reading experiences.* Norwood, MA: Christopher Gordon.

  Yopp, R. H., & Yopp, H. K. (1992). *Literature-based reading activities.* Boston: Allyn & Bacon.

Writing

Looking Ahead

No area of the elementary school curriculum has undergone more change than the way in which children are taught to write. The self-selected and process approaches to teaching writing have spread until they are now widely used. This chapter helps teachers understand how elementary schools can teach both self-selected and focused writing, in both their single-draft and process versions, as well as how traditional concerns with writing mechanics and usage can best be met.

Back when they were first called "The Three Rs," *reading* usually meant oral reading, *arithmetic* meant computation, and *writing* meant handwriting. In recent decades, reading has increasingly come to include and emphasize silent reading comprehension and response to literature, arithmetic to include and emphasize problem solving, and writing to include and emphasize composition. Still, until the recent process-writing revolution, more stress in writing instruction was placed on spelling, mechanics, and usage than on the ability to organize and express ideas.

Contemporary society increasingly communicates through writing. Listen to those who work in large businesses or agencies today. Their constant complaint seems to be the amount of paperwork they must do. Some of that paperwork is the completion of simple forms, but more and more it also consists of writing memoranda, reports, brochures, business letters, and professional e-mail. Word processing is ubiquitous, and almost everyone appears to want or need to leave "a paper trail" in his or her wake.

Like the learning of reading and mathematics, learning to write takes several years of good instruction, each of which builds on what was previously learned. In this chapter, we present to you a balanced approach to help children become writers through the elementary school years. This chapter presents five key ideas:

1. Self-selected writing promotes engagement.
2. Students should learn to produce certain types of writing.
3. Reading can support writing, and writing can support reading.
4. Students should apply conventions in their writing.
5. Students should write in all subjects.

Self-Selected Writing Promotes Engagement

From the very first day of each year's writing program, K–5, individual children should have the responsibility of deciding what topics they will write about and how they will approach them. That is where the term *self-selected writing* comes from. Having children come up with their own topics is an essential characteristic of an effective beginning writing program for four main reasons, all having to do with increasing or maintaining student engagement in writing. First, every language user began by wanting to make others understand. Having something to say serves as the motivation for acquiring the ability to say it. Success in communicating is the reward for trying to learn how to communicate. Consequently, when children are introduced to writing, it does them little good for someone else to tell them what to write about. That removes the main motivation for them to do the hard, sometimes frustrating work of trying to be understood by others. Second, people communicate best when they have knowledge of the topic they are speaking or writing about. When students decide on the topic of their writing, they almost always select something from their experience. When provided with a topic by someone else, they often lose the advantage their prior knowledge of a personally derived topic would have given them. Third, self-selected writing is an area where we can take advantage of an excellent opportunity to use the multicultural backgrounds and perspectives of an increasingly diverse student population. When students write about topics we assign them, we miss that opportunity. Fourth, when children write about the same topic and share their writings, the differences in their writing ability are obvious to one another, attacking the self-confidence of all but the most proficient. When children write about different topics and share, the differences in their writing ability are much less apparent because the emphasis is on the topic rather than how it is handled. Self-selected writing is the single most important tool for promoting engagement in writing.

At first, you can use single-draft, self-selected writing to help children who lack self-confidence and intrinsic motivation to write become engaged with writing. Later, you can use self-selected process writing (usually called writers' workshop) to continue increasing children's engagement with writing and also to help them become able to produce more sophisticated final drafts. Still later, after children have acquired the necessary engagement and skills, you can use focused process writing to help them become successful with the more difficult and less en-gaging tasks of writing to specified topics in specified forms.

Children Share Their Writing with Other Students

Once individual students are writing several times a week about topics of their own choosing in their own ways, it is an essential characteristic of a self-selected writing program that the students share what they have written with each other. If the chief motivation for learning to write is to communicate with others, the writer must have a supportive audience who reads or listens to what was written. Self-selected writing programs use other students rather than the teacher as that audience. Writers must understand and be able to relate to their audiences. A child writer is more likely to understand other children and be better able to relate to other children than to an adult, particularly a teacher who is responsible for grading and discipline. When the teacher is the only one who reads or hears student writing, much less sharing goes on and it is often delayed. If sharing is to have maximum value for establishing writing as communication, the amount of sharing must be substantial and come soon after pieces are written. Having students regularly share their writing with one another is the best way to achieve substantial and timely communication through writing.

For sharing to play its role in helping children develop as writers, the children must respond as readers and listeners, not teachers or critics. They must respond to the ideas of what is written, not its form, and positively, rather than negatively. Fortunately, when students choose their own topics for writing and approach those topics in their own way, it is much more likely that sharing can be kept positive and centered on ideas. In our experience, children are usually quite tolerant of major differences in sophistication among pieces of writing by different children as long as those pieces address different topics in somewhat different ways.

As children improve in their willingness and ability to express their ideas in writing, sharing serves an additional role. These shared writings become models for other children to follow and adapt as they make decisions and solve problems about what they want to say and how they want to say it.

Teachers Teach Minilessons

As long as they are careful not to intimidate students with their sophistication or quantity of writing, teachers can also provide modeling to children by sharing what they write. When teachers plan aloud what they are going to write and then actually write it on the overhead projector while students watch and read what is being written, that kind of teacher sharing is called a *writing minilesson*. Minilessons are extremely valuable tools for showing children how to think of a topic and how to go about deciding the way one approaches writing about a topic one has chosen. Each minilesson has a single teaching point that is emphasized by the teacher (e.g., choosing a topic, looking around the room to find letters to write down, phonic spelling, using the word wall, deciding what an audience needs to be told). When a writing minilesson is followed immediately by a time of student writing, the teacher can often see students improve in the use of whatever planning or writing strategies the teacher modeled during that minilesson. Of course, teachers can also write while the children are writing and occasionally share what they have written during sharing time afterward. The emphasis during sharing time, though, must be on the children sharing their writing with each other.

Children Spell Some Words Phonetically

The most controversial feature of self-selected writing is that students must spell words phonetically (use their developing understanding of letter sounds and patterns to spell words) while writing. It is feared by some that students who spell words phonetically will develop bad habits and fail to discover the importance of correct spelling. Both concerns are legitimate, but overstated. If self-selected writing is seen as the way we *introduce* writing to children, the tolerance for incorrect spellings in children's writing is as natural and harmless as our tolerance for the beginning speech patterns of two-year-olds. Phonic spelling has two main values that make it an essential component of a self-selected writing program. Its greatest value is that it enables children to write before they have mastered spelling. If children who have not learned to spell well are held accountable for correct spellings on their first drafts, they will write very little and will write that very slowly. They will resist writing words unless they are sure how to spell them correctly. They will wait to write a word until the teacher or another child tells them how to spell it. If you try to get them to use a dictionary instead of asking you, writing must be postponed until children have learned alphabetization and the other skills necessary to use one efficiently. Without phonic spelling, beginning writers will not write enough for a self-selected writing program to succeed.

A less well understood value of phonic spelling is that it is an important activity to help children develop the phonological skills on which later phonics and spelling abilities are based. That is why we prefer the name "phonic spelling" for the practice, rather than the term "invented spelling." When children are encouraged and required to spell words phonetically, they must listen for the sounds of the words in order and represent those sounds as best they can with letters. This process requires them to focus on letter–sound relationships in an intense way and provides them with an excellent application activity for the phonemic awareness and phonics they are learning elsewhere during the day. Their attempted spellings reveal to the teacher how well they are progressing in their acquisition of sound-letter knowledge.

Three practices mitigate the possibility that children will develop any long-term problems as a result of phonic spelling: (1) Teachers can place the most frequent and least phonetic words on the wall so that children can see them from wherever they sit in the room. This "word wall" eventually becomes internalized by students as they refer to it during writing, so they learn to spell the most frequent words correctly without having to interrupt their writing to ask someone or consult a dictionary. (2) Teachers of process writing can also require students to have correct spellings in any final drafts they "publish," for example, those displayed on a bulletin board in the hall or sent home with them. The amount and kind of support that students will need in order to meet this standard for the words not on the wall will vary depending on a student's sophistication. This requirement teaches the importance of correct spelling without requiring it on first drafts, which would reduce the amount and enjoyment of writing itself. (3) Teachers can teach conventional spellings of words other than those on the word wall as part of a formal spelling program and expect that students will eventually spell those words correctly in their first drafts without being told to do so. Again, this instruction teaches the importance of correct spelling without requiring it on first drafts.

Children Revise Some of What They Have Written

Once children are writing regularly without your suggesting topics or spelling words for them and sharing with one another regularly what they have written, they are ready to move from single-draft self-selected writing to self-selected process writing (writers' workshop). This move maintains the advantages of self-selected writing while adding the advantages of process writing. Process writing is much more effective when the students are engaged with writing, because revising and editing require hard work, which unmotivated children will often be unwilling to do.

In a process-writing program, at first children write several times a week on topics of their own choosing and share what they have written by reading it aloud to the class, a sharing group, or another student. During sharing (sometimes called *peer conferencing*), teachers help students be content oriented and positive in their comments about each other's writing. After several weeks of this kind of writing and sharing, children's apprehensions and negative associations with writing diminish or even disappear. Most look forward to writing and sharing what they have written.

When writing has become a regular, positive occurrence for students, process-writing teachers begin having students do some targeted rewriting of selected first drafts. The impetus for students to rewrite at first is usually that they are going to write a "book." Having students rework and extend a first draft, illustrate it, and bind it with the teacher's help makes writing incredibly exciting for children and gives them a purpose for working hard on what they have written. Actually, it is the several phases of publishing a piece of writing that gives the *process* approach its name (Dyson & Freedman, 1991).

As each student plans first drafts, writes first drafts, and selects a first draft from his or her working portfolio to revise for publication, the teacher does very little other than to encourage, model, and help students be open and positive toward each other's efforts. Once a student has selected a first draft to revise, however, the teacher's guidance becomes much more important. Even if revisions are to be based on suggestions made during peer conferences, the teacher needs to be involved to maximize the feeling of accomplishment that the student achieves from the publication. It is usually a good idea for the teacher to read the draft each student has selected and then meet individually with that student for a few minutes to help the child develop a plan and reasonable expectations for what the published piece will be like. If the child is going to produce a book, will the book have illustrations? Who will do them? What size will they be? Will they be drawn and colored, or cut from magazines? Will the illustrations be done first? Will the book be bound? Will there be a dedication? Who will copy the text onto the book pages: the student or the teacher? Whether or not the published draft will have illustrations or take the form of a book, will the spelling, capitalization, punctuation, and so forth have to meet certain standards? If so, what are they? Will it be the student's responsibility to meet those standards, or will the teacher make any required corrections that need only be copied?

Obviously, the teacher must carefully oversee this process to maximize both students' learning and their feelings of success. Teacher observation of student writing is the crucial factor in guiding how the teacher will use revision and editing to help each student improve.

Why Self-Selected Writing Is Essential

Traditionally, prior to the late 1970s, students did very little writing other than copying or responding to short-answer questions until they wrote their first report in social studies, science, or health, around the fourth grade. Even that first report was often largely copied from an encyclopedia. What little "creative writing" was done in elementary school was often on a voluntary basis, as part of a writing contest or during leisure time. Those students who most needed writing opportunities were, of course, the least likely to volunteer. Does the contrast between this tradition and the self-selected writing approach mean that self-selected writing is new? Not really.

Most of the children who became good writers in the traditional elementary school had engaged in something like self-selected writing at home. Perhaps a chalkboard or marker board was purchased for the child when he or she was about three years old. The letters of the alphabet were probably displayed at the top of that board. Perhaps magnetic letters were purchased and placed on the front of the refrigerator so that the child could manipulate them. Alphabet blocks and even soup or cookies were probably also made available to the child.

From age two, the child was probably allowed to "write" on paper with pens, pencils, or crayons as long as he or she did not write on floors or walls. At age three or four, the child was probably taught how to print his or her first name. Since the parents often wrote letters and shopping lists at home, the child pretended to write letters and shopping lists as well.

As these children received formal handwriting, reading, phonics, and spelling instruction in the primary grades, they gradually incorporated some of what they had been learning in their "play" writing at home. Perhaps they were encouraged to write an occasional letter to Santa Claus or Grandma or a friend who had moved away. Perhaps they were then encouraged to put foods or things they needed for school "on the list." Perhaps they were asked to make a birthday list or Christmas list of presents they wanted to receive.

Without necessarily intending to do so, many families provided and still provide occasional self-selected writing experiences over a five- or six-year period for their children. During these experiences, children are usually permitted to "write" without the parents caring whether they spell words correctly or make their letters just so. Unlined paper and colored writing implements are used without penalty. Communication and enjoyment are the only important features of most of these out-of-school writing activities.

The growth of the self-selected writing approach in schools over the past twenty years is based on two basic insights. First, if some children are already doing self-selected writing at home (including phonic spelling), it cannot hurt them to do it at school. Second, if some children have not been doing self-selected writing at home, they may never learn to write well without it. Indeed, it has been our experience that even students in fourth or fifth grade who have not engaged in regular self-selected writing before will demonstrate the same growth in willingness and ability to write from regular self-selected writing as do kindergartners and first-graders.

Establishing a Self-Selected Writing Program in Your Classroom

It is not difficult to establish a self-selected writing program in your classroom as long as you meet the following requirements:

You are committed and patient.

You encourage and eventually require phonic spellings.

You do not correct or grade first drafts.

You encourage and eventually require sharing.

You insist that students respond positively to one another's writing.

The Four Steps

Early in kindergarten or first grade, many teachers teach students "the four steps": draw a picture, write something, write your name, copy or stamp the date (Fisher, 1991). At first, the teacher carries out a minilesson to model the four steps. Using an overhead projector placed on the floor so as not to obstruct anyone's view of the screen, the teacher actually does the four steps while the children sit together on a rug and watch. The teacher is careful to draw a very simple and primitive picture that will not intimidate the children into thinking they must be artistic. While drawing, the teacher tells them what he or she is trying to draw. Then the teacher prints something about the picture (e.g., "This is my new car" or "I went to see a baseball game") while saying it out loud. There are no lines on the acetate for the teacher to write on. At this point, the teacher explains to the students that, since they have not been taught how to write yet, they may just write some letters they know. The children are told that whatever they write will be okay. Some teachers model for the children what their writing might look like. Then the teacher writes his or her name. Again, the children are told that it is all right if they cannot write their names; they should just put some letters they think might be in their names. Finally, the teacher copies the date (e.g., 9/10) off the chalkboard. Immediately after this minilesson, the children are given paper and writing implements and encouraged to do the four steps at their seats. The teacher walks around the room, encouraging children to do whatever they can. This minilesson, followed by having students do the four steps, is repeated every day in an atmosphere of patience and encouragement until all students are attempting to do the four steps.

Sustained Silent Writing

When children come to second grade or higher and have not engaged in much self-selected writing before, the teacher often uses Sustained Silent Writing (SSW) as the means of getting students to write regularly without fear of failure or fixation on form. This same method is sometimes called "Can't Stop Writing." The children are given a minute or two of quiet time to think individually of what they want to write about. Then, using a kitchen timer with its face turned away, the teacher sets an amount of time during which everyone, including the teacher, must write without interrupting anyone. At first, most teachers set the timer for three minutes. When the timer bell rings, students are allowed to finish the sentence they are writing and then they must stop.

Teachers often introduce students to SSW by modeling it in a minilesson. The teacher first does a teacher think-aloud to model the choice of a topic (e.g., "Let's see . . . what have I seen in the last day or two that was interesting? Oh, I know. On the way home yesterday, I saw firefighters trying to put out a fire in a field. I think I'll write about that."). The teacher picks up the kitchen timer, sets it for three minutes, and writes on the overhead while the children sit and watch. It is important to keep it simple and to write slowly so that the students are not intimidated by the teacher's superior writing facility. They do not talk while they write, so the students try to read what the teacher is writing while it is being written. When the timer bell rings, teachers finish the sentence they are writing and stop. They then read aloud to the children what they have written. If the children want to talk positively about the ideas briefly, teachers permit that discussion.

Immediately following this minilesson, the children are given a minute or two to think individually about what they want to write about; a three-minute SSW session for the entire class, including the teacher, then follows. SSW is done regularly until all the children are sustaining their writing for three minutes. Gradually, a minute is added to this time until children are able to sustain their writing for six or seven minutes. Once children are writing willingly and enjoying it for six or seven minutes or longer, SSW has probably outlived its usefulness. Rather than a means to get students comfortable just writing to their own topics with phonic spelling, timing actually becomes counterproductive. How long will it take to increase a class's SSW from three to six or seven minutes? It depends on how much writing the students have done the previous year.

Of course, it is not always possible to determine how much the children have engaged in regular self-selected writing in previous years, especially the prior year, so it is a good idea to observe carefully. If children moan when it is writing time, complain that they can't think of anything to write about, and ask you to spell words for them, they are almost certainly not ready to write longer. If children seem familiar with writing, write without asking you for topics or spellings, and some-times even complain that they want more time to write, a minute should be added to the timer. In short, SSW may be used for a few weeks or a few months, depend-ing on what the students seem to need.

Phonic Spelling

Phonic spelling is always encouraged from the beginning in a self-selected writing program. Before students write on the first day, they are told that their papers will not be corrected or graded for spelling. They are told that if they share what they have written, they will do so by reading it aloud. A few days into the program, the teacher does a minilesson before students write in which she or he models phonic spelling (sometimes called "ear spelling") for the children. Whenever children ask how to spell a word, they are told "to write down any letters you hear." The teacher may do a guided phonic spelling lesson in which the students guess several differ-ent ways a given word might be spelled before finding out how it is spelled correctly.

Sharing

From the beginning of a self-selected writing program, children are also invited to volunteer to share what they have written. Usually, the student who has just shared is allowed to call on two or three children to make a comment or ask a question about what they have just read or heard shared. The teacher is always prepared to guide and encourage positive responses about the content of what was shared. As voluntary sharing increases, the teacher may eventually choose an equitable way of having students take turns sharing, if that becomes necessary.

Book Publishing

Once these components of a self-selected writing program are operating smoothly, it is easy to get the students to select a piece of writing from their writing folder that they want to turn into a "book." Each day for a while, the children move through the stages of book publishing: conferencing with one or more other students, rewriting, conferencing with the teacher, illustrating, copying or having the teacher copy their writing onto the illustrated pages, making a dedication page, creating a cover, and binding the cover and pages together into a book. These stages are usu-ally conducted in centers or at stations. The most effective writers' workshop class-rooms have the children working at different points in the book-publishing process. When a child has published a book, the child shares that book with the entire class from the "Author's Chair."

Grades

If children must be graded, we recommend that they be given a single grade for reading/language arts. However, if children in a self-selected writing program, whether single-draft or process, receive a separate grade on their report cards for writing, their grade can be based on two factors. (1) Their grade can reflect their progress in terms of their readiness to write during writing time, their willingness to spell words phonetically, their desire to share, and their effort when preparing a "book" for publication. This factor has nothing at all to do with what they write, only with their participation and cooperation in the program itself. The rationale is simple: children must be actively involved in the self-selected writing program to benefit from it, and parents can be informed whether children are so involved. (2) Once you begin doing self-selected process writing (writers' workshop) with them, their grade can also be based on the quality of their final drafts, to the extent that their contributions to that draft can be clearly differentiated from yours. Here the distinction in grades should not be between pass and fail but between satisfactory and excellent. The rationale: all children who are actively involved in a self-selected process-writing program should make satisfactory progress, or the program should be modified until they do.

Accommodations and Adaptations That Develop Writing

FOR INCLUSION

Dialogue Writing

While self-selected writing is generally successful with the widest range of students, some teachers use dialogue writing with children who can write well enough for you to read it but are reluctant to share what they have written with others. In dialogue writing the child turns in each first draft to the teacher. The teacher writes a simple, personal response to what the child has written. When the child writes next time, he or she can write on a new subject or can respond to what the teacher wrote. This dialogue in writing between teacher and child can do wonders in motivating a child to write and in teaching that child the true nature of writing as communication. Later, the teacher can pair two children with whom he or she has been doing dialogue writing and let them do dialogue writing with each other. Before long, these children will probably be willing to share what they have written with the rest of the class.

FOR CHILDREN ACQUIRING ENGLISH

Especially in the early stages of English acquisition, children understand much more than they can produce. These children orally express much more in their first language than they can in English. Consequently, teachers support these children's efforts at writing in English to a considerable degree.

(continued)

An especially effective support is having children collaborate with others in their first language and in English. Children acquiring English might be paired with a classmate who is slightly more proficient in the language, and they might have access to paraprofessionals, upper-grade students, and family and community volunteers who speak both languages. Teachers occasionally organize the class so that they work individually or in groups with children acquiring English.

When writing is self-selected, children acquiring English collaborate with others several ways. They review class expectations and contents in their first language and in English. Using both languages, they talk through what they want to write. They might produce one draft in their first language and then collectively translate it into English. To maintain writing fluency, children sometimes combine languages by inserting first-language terms for unknown English ones; later they might revise the draft with someone to contain only English.

Students Should Learn to Produce Certain Types of Writing

Over the years in our work with teachers and schools, we have found it useful to draw a distinction between self-selected writing, as discussed above, and what we call *focused writing*. Like self-selected writing, focused writing has two versions—a process and a single-draft version. Unlike self-selected writing, the single-draft version of focused-writing instruction is more challenging than the process version. That is because there are no standards other than willingness to write independently in single-draft, self-selected writing. In focused writing, however, students always have standards to meet, so it is easier to meet them in multiple attempts than in a first draft that is also a final draft.

A number of important distinctions exist between self-selected writing as we have so far delineated it and what we refer to as focused writing. In self-selected writing, students choose their own topics and how to address them; in focused writing, the teacher gives the class a writing prompt that constrains their writing in one or more ways. In self-selected writing, the time before students begin a first draft is spent on individual planning—deciding what to write about and how; in focused writing, students also do some individual planning, but depending on the prompt, students may additionally be taught background knowledge for the topic, the role, and the audience, as well as for the form (type of writing). They may also be guided to do some inquiry or research on the topic before writing about it. In self-selected writing, the emphasis is on having students learn to revise and edit as part of the writing process so that they can learn individual writing skills and strategies and be able to produce more sophisticated final drafts. In focused writing, the emphasis is on helping students develop automaticity with writing skills and strategies so that they can move away from process writing to be able to produce more sophisticated first drafts.

Important differences also exist between focused writing and traditional school writing (how writing was generally taught, when it was taught, before 1970). In traditional school writing, students were given a writing assignment and allowed to ask some questions about it; in focused writing, for each prompt, the teacher guides students through a planned, prewriting phase. In traditional school writing, the emphasis was usually on mechanics and usage; in focused writing, mechanics and usage have value, but the emphasis is always on the ideas and type of writing. In traditional school writing, students were often taught about a particular form by examining a good example of it; in focused writing, students examine good models but are also taught how to do a particular form by being put in a writing situation that naturally elicits that type of writing. The prompt and any inquiry or research they do are designed to help students develop the strategies a particular type of writing requires. In traditional school writing, students learned about a type of writing, tried to produce a piece of that type, and were graded on it; in focused writing, students do a large number of pieces of a type of writing and self-evaluate how well they did on each one until they become successful at composing that type of writing.

Both self-selected and focused writing are crucial if most students are going to learn to write well. Process writing is essential to enable children to write without being held accountable for skills and strategies that are as yet not automatic for them. Used regularly over several years, focused-writing activities are particularly helpful to students in learning to produce many different types of writing. *Type of writing* is the term we use with elementary students instead of the terms *genre* or *mode of discourse.* Specific types of writing that elementary teachers talk about with their students often include friendly letter, business letter, story, narrative, description, and persuasion.

A Lesson Framework for Focused Writing

Although focused-writing activities can vary significantly, each one can be seen as an instance of a general lesson framework with mandatory and optional phases and steps:

Focused-Writing Lesson Framework

I. Focused-Prewriting Phase
    Step 1. Teach or review background knowledge for the prompt.
    Step 2. Present the prompt.
    Step 3. Have students engage in inquiry or research (optional).
    Step 4. Have students individually plan their writing.

II. Writing Phase
    Step 5. Have students produce a first (and possibly final) draft.

III. Sharing Phase (optional)
    Step 6. Have each student share the draft with at least one other student.

The heart of a focused-writing lesson is the prompt. Constructing a good writing prompt is the first thing a teacher does when planning a focused-writing lesson. The prompt that will be given to the students in step 2 of the lesson determines what background knowledge needs to be built in step 1 and what inquiry or research—if any—students will do in step 3. The writing prompt is simply a brief, written statement of the writing assignment. If it is not written down so that the students can refer to it while planning and writing, it is not a prompt.

Your ability to construct good writing prompts will come from practice, trial and error, and understanding your particular class of students. It will also help you to think critically about each prompt you construct if you *analyze* it before using it in a focused-writing lesson. Analyzing a prompt consists of breaking it down into its elements.

A writing prompt may have as many as four elements:

audience	=	to whom the writing should be directed
role	=	who should be "speaking" the words
topic	=	what the piece of writing should be about—its content
type of writing	=	the general form the piece of writing should take

Since the main goal of the focused-writing approach is teaching students how to produce different types of writing, the most important aspect of the prompts used in the approach will be the element that specifies or implies the type of writing students are to do.

A writing prompt may also contain specifications as to how long the piece of writing must be or can be and when it is due, but these are not really considered elements of the prompt. These specifications may be written at the end of the prompt or simply told to the students. Students are often informed as to what will be done with the drafts after they are finished, that is, shared, taken up and graded, self-evaluated, or filed in a working portfolio, but that information is not considered an element of the prompt either. It may also be written at the end of the prompt or told to the students. The prompt itself, the four elements combined in a brief paragraph, must always be written and made accessible to the students during planning and writing.

Imagine that you have constructed the following prompt for your fourth-grade class:

> Pretend you are a fourth-grade teacher. Write a business letter to the director of the state's history museum. Ask him or her when the museum is open for visitors and how to schedule a visit for a class.

Now, let's analyze this prompt into its elements:

audience	=	the director of the state's history museum
role	=	a fourth-grade teacher
topic	=	asking when the museum is open for visitors and how to schedule a visit for a class
type of writing	=	a business letter

When analyzing a prompt, try to put every important word in one of the four elements. Do not put any word from the prompt in more than one element. If one or more of the elements are not specified in the prompt, just leave them blank. Since the students will never see the elements broken out separately, it is not necessary to word the elements in complete sentences.

After you have broken a prompt into its elements, you can readily see which elements you need to build background for and whether you want to have students do inquiry or research on the topic, role, or audience. If it appears that a lot of background building may be necessary for concepts that are not really your focus, you may want to modify those elements to make the prompt more targeted to your objectives for the students.

In the sample prompt above, both the state's history museum and the concept of a visit to the state capital could require some background building or research, depending on how much you think your students already know about one or both. Certainly, the teacher would have to provide students with the name and address of the director of the state's history museum. The emphasis in the background-building step (step 1) should, however, be on the form of a business letter. The best tack to take is probably to display or distribute a model of a business letter that the students could follow when formatting their letters. This model should *not* be a letter to the director of the state's history museum. We want the children to apply the model when writing, not merely to copy down its formatting.

This sample prompt will probably work best if students are also guided through an inquiry step (step 3) in which they work together in pairs or small groups to examine a couple of sample business letters that ask for information. By discussing how two or three different letter writers went about asking for information, they could decide how they might go about asking for information in their letters.

Consider a second sample prompt for a third-grade class:

> Pretend you are your mother or father [or some other caregiver]. Tell a story about what it was like when you were in the third grade.

audience	=	
role	=	your mother or father [or . . .]
topic	=	what it was like when you were in the third grade
type of writing	=	a story

This lesson will probably require background building on what a story is, depending on how elaborate you want their stories to be. By "story" you may just mean "an interesting event" or you may mean a narrative. You do not mean a fictional short story. Letting them see or hear a couple of "stories" like those you have in mind would be helpful. Providing two or three models and helping students think about them is always a good way to build background for a particular form you are teaching children how to produce. You may choose to tell them a story about what it was like when you were in the third grade.

Let's say your step 1 also has the students brainstorm interesting things that they have done or that have happened this year in third grade. In step 2, you present the prompt and allow students to ask questions and make comments. A few of the children may already know some stories about their parents' childhood experiences, and you may choose to allow a few of those to be told. In step 3, you first put the students together in small groups to plan an interview they will use to get one of their parents to tell them about what third grade was like for them. During or after this inquiry activity, you have each student make a copy of the interview that the small group composes. Then you assign students to complete their interview (conduct their research) by a certain day. On that day, students could carry out step 4 of the lesson in class by individually webbing the story each intends to write. At this point in the lesson, you could refer them to the prompt and remind them to tell the story in the first person. In step 5, they would write their stories at the same time in class, at different times during the school day, or at home. If you have a step 6 in this lesson, children would share their stories in pairs, small groups, or as a whole class.

Analyzing each prompt you have constructed should stimulate this kind of decision making before you teach the focused-writing lesson containing that prompt. A good prompt and good decisions about what to do at each of the four mandatory steps and two optional steps, if anything, make for a successful focused-writing lesson. The more focused-writing lessons you teach, the better you and your students will become at doing them.

Once you become proficient at crafting good prompts and teaching successful focused-writing lessons based on those prompts, you have a powerful tool to help your students learn how to produce any type of writing you need or want to teach them. There is tremendous flexibility in the focused-writing lesson framework. Step 1, for example, could consist of an entire reading/ literature lesson that would ordinarily stand alone. Now, however, you could integrate writing and reading by using that lesson as the background knowledge step of a focused-writing lesson in which your students learn to produce the type of writing exemplified by that piece of literature. Moreover, during step 3, the students could work together in inquiry groups to discuss what about that piece of literature made it so interesting, beautiful, inspiring, gripping, or whatever. In step 4, they could be led to plan individually what each would do to make his or her attempt at that type of writing interesting, beautiful, inspiring, gripping, or whatever.

Developing a Writing Scale

No single focused-writing lesson ever teaches students how to produce a particular type of writing. A series of focused-writing lessons, all specifying or eliciting the same form, has a better chance of teaching students how to achieve that form. However, the combination of teaching a series of focused-writing lessons on the same form *and* teaching students to self-evaluate their writing with a writing scale developed for that form is the most effective means of teaching students how to produce a particular type of writing.

A writing scale is a list of rules or questions to answer that students are taught how to use to evaluate their own papers. A writing scale for a type of writing has a list of rules or questions to answer that focus on the key features of that form. Developing a writing scale for a type of writing is tantamount to making explicit what you, as the teacher, look for in deciding whether a particular piece of student writing is a good example of an assigned or elicited form. Providing students with a writing scale based on a type of writing is the only way to effectively teach them to self-evaluate their writings as instances of that type of writing. Through this self-evaluation, they will eventually internalize a sense of that form. See Figures 8.1 and 8.2 for samples of different types of writing.

There are two subtle but important differences between a writing rubric and a writing scale. First, writing rubrics are usually instruments that lead to a grade or

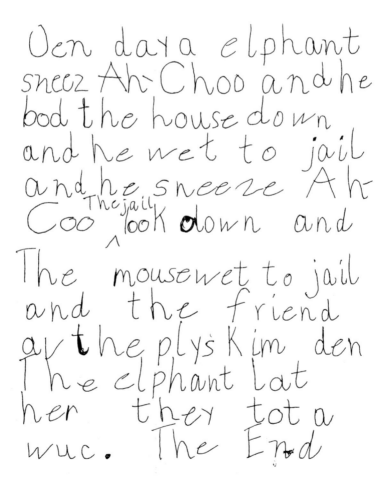

Figure 8.1 First-Grade Narrative Writing

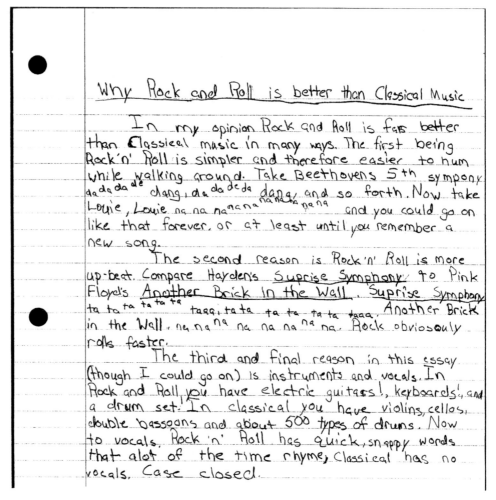

Why Rock and Roll is better than Classical Music

In my opinion Rock and Roll is far better than Classical music in many ways. The first being Rock'n' Roll is simpler and therefore easier to hum while walking around. Take Beethovens 5th sympony da da da dã chang, da da de da dang, and so forth. Now take Louie, Louie na na nanana na na na na na and you could go on like that forever, or at least until you remember a new song.

The second reason is Rock'n' Roll is more up-beat. Compare Hayden's Suprise Symphony to Pink Floyd's Another Brick In the Wall. Suprise Symphony ta ta ta ta ta ta taaa, ta ta ta ta ta ta taaa, Another Brick in the Wall, na na na na na na na na na. Rock obviosouly rolls faster.

The third and final reason in this essay (though I could go on) is instruments and vocals. In Rock and Roll you have electric guitars!, keyboards!, and a drum set! In classical you have violins, cellos, double bassoons and about 500 types of drums. Now to vocals, Rock 'n' Roll has quick, snappy words that alot of the time rhyme, Classical has no vocals, Case closed.

Figure 8.2 **Fourth-Grade Persuasive Writing**

holistic score being placed on a paper. As such, writing rubrics may be used by teachers and shared with students. Unfortunately, some schools are so oriented to the extrinsic motivators of grades and test scores that they try to teach children to use a writing rubric themselves to get a certain score. This process undermines intrinsic motivation to write because it focuses student attention on the grade or score rather than on what they are learning how to do better when they write. On the other hand, a writing scale focuses student attention on a few specific aspects of their writing that they are trying to learn how to improve in order to be better writers. Second, writing rubrics are usually too complex and subjective for students to use well. Because a writing scale has a few very specific, "yes or no" standards, intermediate elementary students can learn to apply those standards to their own papers.

The first criterion or question on a form-based writing scale should help students learn to address the prompt when there is one. Here is a question that gets at whether the student's paper addresses the prompt for each type of writing:

1. Does the paper have the same topic as the prompt?

Give students papers from another year's class, without names on them, that do and do not have the same topic as the prompt the students were writing to. Help them understand that writing well to a prompt means having the same topic as the prompt.

The second criterion or question on a form-based writing scale should probably deal with the unity of the writing. Every kind of writing has a subject that needs to be maintained throughout the piece. Here are second questions that get at the unity of the piece that students can be taught to answer about each of three types of writing:

2. Is the paper clearly about just one character, person, place, or event? [narrative writing]

2. Is the paper clearly about just one person, place, thing, or feeling? [descriptive writing]

2. Is the paper clearly arguing for just one opinion? [persuasive writing]

Again, give students examples of papers that would provide obvious answers to this second question. Help them see that better papers maintain unity of focus throughout.

When students become able to produce first drafts that consistently allow their readers to be able to answer yes to both of these questions, they have learned how to address the prompt and maintain unity of subject in the particular type of writing they are learning.

The trickiest part of developing a form-based writing scale is formulating questions that get at the basic structure of ideas in that form. Here are possible third and fourth questions for each of the three examples we are using:

3. Does the paper tell exactly what happened?

3. Does the paper talk about several major features of the person, place, thing, or feeling?

3. Are at least three different reasons given to support the opinion?

4. Is it clear what happened first, what happened after that, and what happened last?

4. Is there a good explanation of each major feature?

4. Are the reasons good ones that might convince the readers?

Once students come to understand the basic logic of a form, their chief failing in carrying out that form is usually the lack of elaboration. Here is the fifth question for each of the three examples that helps students gradually improve their elaboration:

5. Are there enough details to help readers clearly imagine each thing that happened? Are we helped to see, hear, smell, taste, and feel in our minds?

5. Are there enough details to help readers clearly imagine the person, place, thing, or feeling? Are we helped to see, hear, smell, taste, and feel in our minds?

5. Is each reason supported and explained well?

Finally, every form-based writing scale needs to have some questions that get students to self-evaluate how well they carry out that type of writing. We can use the same questions for all three examples:

6. Does the paper have a good beginning, or does it "start in the middle"?

7. Does the paper have a good ending, or does it "leave us hanging"?

8. Does each sentence nicely connect to the next one, or do we sometimes have to say "huh"?

Our form-based writing scale for narrative, descriptive, or persuasive writing would consist of the corresponding eight questions. A form-based writing scale for any other type of writing that intermediate elementary students might be taught to write would probably be similar.

At first, students should be given only the first question to answer about a draft, and they should probably answer it for each other's drafts. The teacher should not add the second question to the writing scale until the class is comfortable answering the first question. After the second question is added, it must not be assumed that the first question was mastered. Now students should use both questions to evaluate each other's or their own drafts. Eventually, students will be able to self-evaluate their drafts using all the questions on the scale. During this time, when you respond to the form of a student's draft, you should use the same questions on the writing scale that the students are currently using. Occasionally having students rewrite a paper to get yes for all the questions on the writing scale to that point helps them understand and internalize the characteristics of that type of writing.

When students involved in focused writing are graded on writing, that grade should be based on pieces of writing done in class in response to new prompts. Children should be allowed ample time to plan and write during these "tests," because quality of writing is not a function of time spent writing. Some great writers have been very prolific; others have labored long to produce a little. The grade each paper receives should be based on (1) its conformity to the prompt, (2) its consistency with the form-based writing scale, and, possibly, (3) its correct spelling of the words on the wall.

It is not a mystery why students generally did not learn how to produce many different types of writing from traditional writing instruction. Most of them had not previously engaged in two or three years of self-selected writing. If they had done that, then most of them did not attempt each form often enough. When they attempted a form, they did not write to a well-crafted prompt, and they were not systematically taught how to evaluate their own attempts at a form by answering a limited set of clearly stated questions. They rarely if ever revised, and when they did so, they did not revise to improve their papers relative to a form-based writing scale.

Accommodations and Adaptations That Develop Writing

FOR INCLUSION

Adapting Writing Scales

Sometimes it is necessary for a teacher with a wide range of children to add new questions to the form-based writing scale, even though one or two students are really not ready for them to be added. When this happens, it is important and easy for the teacher to require some children to evaluate or revise their papers based on the specific questions the teacher knows they can handle. For example, if the teacher has five questions on the writing scale, that teacher may require one or two students to use the first three questions on the writing scale while requiring most students to use all five. The downside of this practice is that public awareness of these differences can undermine the self-confidence of those given fewer standards to meet, so it should probably be done only if necessary.

FOR CHILDREN ACQUIRING ENGLISH

Children acquiring English benefit from collaboration during focused writing just as they do during self-selected writing. Working with others in their first language and in English, they clarify class expectations and contents, plan their drafts, and translate what is needed. Just as with reading comprehension, children acquiring English benefit from cultural relevance when writing. Topics, roles, audiences, and forms fit students' backgrounds. For instance, focused writing might address food, dress, music, and holiday customs that have commonalities among cultures but vary significantly. Students might write in response to the messages that community members representing different cultural groups share with the class. They might also produce pamphlets, posters, or brochures portraying aspects of their homelands.

Another good way to support children acquiring English during focused writing involves language patterns. Give students structured phrases, sentences, or longer

(continued)

units of language to follow when expressing their own ideas. The following present possible patterns:

- *Phrases:* in the . . .
- *Sentences:* She was surprised when she saw . . .
- *Paragraphs:* Pat went . . . She was surprised to see . . . So she quickly . . .
- *Poetry:* Brown Bear, Brown Bear, what do you see? I see . . .
- *Story plot:* Change "The Three Little Pigs" to "The Three Little Cats."
- *Song lyrics:* Change "I'm a Little Teapot" to "I'm a Little Tractor."

Reading Can Support Writing, and Writing Can Support Reading

Reading and writing are closely related. The phonics knowledge that enables a reader to predict the pronunciation of an unknown word also enables a writer to predict the spelling of an unknown word. The syntactic maturity that enables a reader to process more sophisticated sentences also enables a writer to produce more sophisticated sentences. The mastery of directionality in written language that enables a reader to move effortlessly through print left-to-right, swing-back-to-the-beginning-of-the-next-line, top-to-bottom, front-to-back also enables a writer to inscribe letters and words smoothly on paper left-to-right, swing-back-to-the-beginning-of-the-next-line, top-to-bottom, front-to-back.

Beyond basic structural relationships such as these, reading and writing also share a dependence on higher aspects of literacy. A sense of author helps readers comprehend and respond to books just as a sense of audience helps writers plan, compose, and revise their drafts. Engagement is as important and as dependent on self-confidence, attributing success to strategies, and experiencing pleasure in reading as it is in writing. Prior knowledge of what a reader is reading about is as necessary and as facilitative as prior knowledge of what a writer is writing about.

Because there are so many links between reading and writing, reading can promote children's writing development, and writing can promote their reading development. The materials children read provide models for the materials they write. The children benefit from comprehension lessons and literature discussions that help them make the most of these models. When students learn to control a particular aspect of writing, they are usually better able to negotiate that same aspect when reading. In fact, because writing is ordinarily more difficult than reading, writing is "overlearning" for reading. In other words, to gain control over an aspect of writing means to learn it better than reading requires that aspect to be learned. Consequently, writing instruction leads to fluency in reading in the areas taught during writing. For example, phonic spelling in kindergarten and writing in first grade help children benefit from their phonics instruction better than they would have without these experiences (Clarke, 1988).

For another example, sentence-combining instruction in writing leads to improved sentence comprehension in reading.

In a complete and balanced reading program, writing instruction is really another method of teaching reading. Some children will learn how to read better from good writing instruction than they will from any other reading instructional method. All children will transfer some of their increased writing ability to their reading.

In a complete and balanced writing program, reading comprehension instruction and literature discussion will help some children understand how writers write and motivate them to want to be authors themselves. All children who are writing regularly will transfer some of their increased reading ability to their writing.

In addition to the general cross-fertilization that will inevitably occur between reading and writing in a successful literacy program, there are special lesson frameworks that strengthen the mutually supportive relationships between reading and writing.

Reading-Writing Lessons

A reading-writing lesson is simply a response to literature activity (see Chapter 6) or a comprehension lesson (see Chapter 7) followed by a focused-writing lesson that builds on or extends that activity or lesson. The model comprehension strategy lesson plan for *The Farmer's Crowded House* is actually a reading-writing lesson. Here are the parts of the focused-writing lesson that would require special planning during a reading-writing lesson.

I. Focused-Prewriting Phase

Step 1. Teach or review background knowledge for the prompt. The comprehension lesson can also be seen as this step. If the comprehension lesson the focused-writing lesson is based on took place one or more days ago, aspects of that lesson to be built up should probably be quickly reviewed.

Step 2. Present the prompt. The prompt must be crafted to build on or extend the comprehension lesson. For example, if the comprehension lesson consisted of completing a discussion web after reading a piece of literature, then the prompt must have a clear and direct link to that web.

> Decide whether you think the *Two Bad Ants* should have stayed at the house or not. Write a letter to the ants telling them what you think.
> Tell us whether you think Mother Bird should have reared *Stellaluna* as a bird or not. Explain why you think the way you do.

Step 3. Have students engage in inquiry or research (optional). If the comprehension lesson left students with questions still unanswered, the focused-writing part of the reading-writing lesson can use this step to have them try to go beyond the original selection to answer those questions. The answers they find would then be included in the writing they produce in response to the prompt. For example, after the KWL comprehension lesson on Washington, D.C., from Chapter 7, the students could be directed to other sources to find out what they wanted to know about Washington, D.C., but were not told in the single selection they read for that lesson. The writing they did would include some of the new information they gathered during this inquiry/research step of the focused-writing lesson.

Of course, the focused-writing lesson that is the second part of a reading-writing lesson can target type of writing rather than topic, but that would require the introduction comprehension lesson to target some aspect of the author's craft rather than the content of the reading selection.

Writing-Reading Lessons

A writing-reading lesson is simply a focused-writing lesson followed by a comprehension lesson of some kind. The most common reason for a writing-reading lesson is to increase student interest in the reading they will be asked to do during the comprehension lesson. For example, if students were going to read a story set in the Arctic or Antarctic Circle or an article about one or both of those regions, a focused-writing lesson could serve to pique the students' interest in that story or article. The focused-writing lesson could have this prompt:

> Explain why you think some people choose to live in the coldest places on earth.

The background building for this prompt should probably include using a globe to teach the concepts *Arctic Circle* and *Antarctic Circle.* However, it should also include teaching less important but more intriguing concepts such as the *30–30–30 Rule* ("When it is 30 degrees below zero Fahrenheit and the wind is blowing 30 miles per hour, human flesh freezes solid in 30 seconds"). Such a writing lesson has value for improving writing, but it can also prepare students to read with more interest and curiosity during a comprehension lesson than they might otherwise.

Students Should Apply Conventions in Their Writing

Back when elementary students did very little writing other than copying or responding to short-answer questions, they were taught writing rules in isolated exercises from the language book or on worksheets. There were probably several reasons that this practice persisted. Traditional standardized and teacher-made language tests assessed writing rules in isolation from writing. Because many students have trouble transferring what they have learned to new situations, experienced teachers usually have their teaching activities resemble the test the students will be given. Traditional teachers tended to teach writing rules in isolation, at least in part because they tested them in isolation. This tendency increased when teachers were held accountable for student performance on tests. In addition, behaviorism used to be the worldview of most educators, and to behaviorists, all learning was habit formation. Teachers taught children writing rules before letting them write much, in part because they did not want them developing bad habits. Finally, because teachers had been taught writing rules in isolation when they were children, they in turn taught them in isolation, out of tradition.

Of course, teaching writing conventions in isolation was an unsuccessful practice, as indicated by middle and high school students' writing. Their lack of proficiency in capitalization, punctuation, formatting (margins, placement of headings, indention, etc.), and usage (subject-verb agreement, consistency of tenses, pronoun-antecedent agreement, knowledge of verb conjugations, etc.) was the constant complaint of middle and high school teachers and administrators. The solution? More isolated work on mechanics and usage, but no more writing. Isolated work on mechanics and usage in writing became the modern equivalent of bleeding: when the patient died it was *in spite of* being bled, and when the patient recovered it was *because of* being bled. When most students did not become proficient at writing by the rules, it was assumed that they had been hopeless anyway or that even more isolated work should have been done. When some students did become proficient at writing by the rules, the isolated work was credited with their success. In other words, the more isolated teaching of mechanics and usage elementary teachers did, the more they were criticized for not having done enough!

As writing tests were developed that required students to actually write, as behaviorism gave way to the cognitive revolution, and as dissatisfaction with traditional educational achievements grew, more and more educators began to face what the research had always indicated: teaching writing mechanics and usage in isolation does not work for most students. Today, the most successful teachers of writing emphasize ideas and type of writing over mechanics and usage, while using writing scales and other supports to help students gradually learn mechanics and usage rules through applying them in their writing.

Writing Rules on the Wall

When a teacher is establishing a self-selected writing program in his or her classroom, that teacher's goals are to get the students to write regularly about their own topics in their own ways, to spell words phonetically while writing, and to respond positively to the ideas of each other's writings while sharing. In kindergarten, achieving these three goals for all students will probably take the entire year. In first grade, depending on how much self-selected writing the children did in kindergarten, achieving these three goals for all students may take as long as the entire first semester. Beyond first grade, regardless of how much self-selected writing students have done previously, it is important to establish at least six weeks of self-selected writing early in the school year, because it builds an atmosphere of trust and a supportive relationship between the students and the current teacher.

Once children in first grade or above are writing regularly, usually generating a reasonable quantity of writing, spelling words phonetically, and sharing appropriately, many teachers begin helping them apply a few basic mechanics rules in their writing. Sometimes teachers call the writing scale consisting of these rules a *writing checklist*. Because we advocate that this writing scale be posted so that all children can see it from anywhere in the classroom, we call it *writing rules on the wall*.

Sometimes the first rule or two on the wall chart do not deal with mechanics or usage but communicate to the children the more basic notion that what they write should have a message:

Every sentence should make sense.

Every sentence should keep to the topic.

When the writing scale on the wall consists of either or both of these two rules, the word *sentence* should be not interpreted strictly or grammatically. At this stage, if it makes any sense when read aloud, it's a sentence! The second of these rules requires a loose understanding of *topic* as "what the paper is about." Many teachers find that these two rules are unnecessary to post, because most students who write and share regularly will automatically apply them without being told to do so. Teachers observe the sharing that students are doing to determine if it will be necessary to post either or both of these rules when the first writing rule is placed on the wall.

The first (or next) writing rule on the wall is often this:

Every sentence should begin with a capital letter.

Again, if it makes sense when shared, at this point it's a sentence. The trick here is to avoid discussions of whether a sentence is complete. Instead, help children see that every question mark, period, and exclamation point they write (except in the final sentence) should be followed by a word beginning with a capital letter. This focuses their attention on this rule rather than the later rule that will deal with sentences needing to be complete.

As with all writing scales, no new rules are added until most students consistently apply those already posted. When a new rule is added, it is taught to the students in several ways. Most teachers like to post the first or new rule on the wall and then immediately teach a minilesson focusing on that new rule.

A rule-based minilesson proceeds with the teacher writing a brief piece on the overhead projector while students watch and read along. The teacher purposely writes in such a way that there are a number of opportunities to apply the new rule on the wall. The first few times, the teacher applies the rule correctly but then makes sure to violate (fail to apply) the new rule several times by the end of the composition. After writing, the teacher asks the children to help determine whether the teacher kept the new rule throughout. As a child points out an error on this new rule, the teacher asks someone to say what should have been written or lets the child correct the error on the overhead. At the end of this minilesson, the children immediately write on topics of their choosing. The teacher reminds them of the new rule as they begin writing.

The same rule may be modeled in several minilessons, if necessary. After students have written several times with the new posted rule, they practice proofreading their own or each other's papers for all the posted rules, including the new one. Sometimes when students proofread for the writing rules on the wall, they also correct their papers for those rules, and the teacher takes up the papers to check them for those rules. Many teachers have children skip every other line when writing to make it easier for them to correct errors when editing.

After students become consistent in beginning their sentences with capital letters, they are ready to learn to put appropriate punctuation at the end of their sentences. Only two rules, taught one at time, are necessary:

Every question should end with a question mark.

Sentences that are not questions should end with a period or an exclamation point.

The first rule requires a question mark after a question. The second of these two rules lets students decide whether a sentence should have a period or an exclamation point. Exclamation is really in the mind of the writer rather than the teacher. It is unusual for a student to make an error when placing an exclamation point instead of a period at the end of a sentence. The only common error concerning exclamation points is overuse.

Here the trick is to get students to "listen" to each "sentence" they have begun with a capital letter and now want to end to see whether it should have a question mark or not, and if not, whether it should have an exclamation point or not. Any discussion of whether the sentence is complete will distract students from listening for the intonation clues that determine ending punctuation. Such discussion still needs to be postponed. If it makes sense, it's a sentence. If not, it should be changed so that it makes sense—that is one of our first writing rules on the wall.

While using minilessons, proofreading practice, and editing practice to teach the rules on the wall, teachers also use other activities and exercises to help students understand and remember a rule. These other activities and exercises will be effective, however, only if they simplify rather than complicate the rule, and if they do not take much time away from time spent applying the rule in actual writing.

Now, finally, students are ready for this rule:

Every sentence should be a complete sentence.

You have delayed talking about what a complete sentence is or isn't. Instead, you have concentrated on getting students to divide their writing up into units that begin with a capital letter; end appropriately with either a question mark, period, or exclamation point; and make sense when read aloud. Now, you and your students reap the reward of this lengthy process in that you find most of their written sentences to be complete without the need for you to explain to them the difference between a complete and an incomplete sentence—surely one of the most complex understandings children can ever be asked to grasp. Posting this rule at this time will not be as confusing or frustrating, because they already are following the rule much of the time.

From the time a self-selected process-writing program is well established, this method of teaching writing rules on the wall gradually helps students learn to apply the basic mechanics and usage conventions of writing. When writing rules on the wall are used in the intermediate grades, it may or may not be necessary to include basic mechanics rules like the six discussed above.

Beyond these basic four to six rules, a number of other writing rules will probably be important enough to teach by the end of fourth grade:

Indent the beginning of every paragraph.

Combine short, choppy sentences together.

Do not use run-on sentences.

Use commas after words in a series.

Punctuate quotations correctly.

Use *I* and *me, we* and *us, he* and *him, she* and *her,* and *they* and *them* correctly. (This rule could be broken out into five separate ones, if necessary.)

Do not use double negatives.

Some rules are difficult for children to apply because they lack a prerequisite ability. Children above first grade often write in run-on sentences because they are trying to produce longer sentences. They compose run-on sentences because that is the only way they know how to produce longer sentences. Putting a rule on the wall that says "Do not use run-on sentences" is really telling such children to produce short, choppy sentences. Many of them will refuse to do that because they associate it with being younger. Sentence-combining activities can teach such children how to achieve longer sentences without making them run on. The wise teacher will try to figure out why children are having trouble applying a rule and will try to teach them any prerequisite abilities they lack.

If children in a self-selected process-writing program receive a separate grade for writing, their application of the writing rules on the wall can be considered in their grades. Students' willingness to proofread and correct their papers according to the rules on the wall constitutes an aspect of their overall involvement in the process-writing program. Students' ability to apply the rules on the wall in their final drafts also constitutes an aspect of the overall quality of those drafts.

If children engaged in focused writing receive a separate grade for writing, their application of the writing rules on the wall can also be considered in their grades. If students are to be held accountable for applying the rules on the wall when taking a writing "test," they must be told so in advance. It will then be up to them whether they want to be concerned with those rules on the first draft or to leave themselves time to proofread and edit their first drafts before handing them in.

Whether they are engaged in self-selected or focused writing, children must not be graded in such a way that they lose sight of what is most important in writing. Mechanics and usage should always be less important than the ideas and type of writing. If a grading system is giving children a different idea, it must be modified, or that grading system is undermining the entire writing program.

Even though the ideas and type of writing continue to be the main emphases of the writing program, mechanics and usage conventions can be successfully taught to children through the systematic use of writing rules on the wall, rule-based minilessons, supporting exercises and wall charts, and proofreading and editing practice.

Students Should Write in All Subjects

Whether students are involved in self-selected writing or focused writing, as we have distinguished them, they receive additional benefits from engaging in that same kind of writing across the curriculum. Not only do the increased opportunities to write in different contexts help children learn to write better, but writing also helps children learn more social studies, science, health, and literature. Teachers at upper levels of schooling have always recognized that writing is the best means to get students to think about whatever they are learning. In recent years, educators have realized that the same holds true for content learning in the elementary grades.

Again, it should be noted that many teachers naturally extend writing into all content areas without making a distinction between that writing and what the students have been doing previously. The distinction between *writing* and *writing across the curriculum,* like that between self-selected and focused writing, has been useful for us in helping teachers. Many teachers, perhaps most, refer to it all as just "writing."

Self-Selected Writing in the Content Areas

Although some students in a self-selected writing program may naturally choose to write about what they are learning in science, social studies, health, or reading/literature, it is not likely they will. Consequently, a teacher often needs to make a modification in self-selected writing when using it to elicit student writing in a subject area. Specifically, when they engage in self-selected writing in a content subject:

Children choose their own subtopics.

When doing self-selected writing in a subject, individual children still have the responsibility of deciding what they will write about and how they will approach it, with one exception: each must choose a topic having to do with the particular content area in which the writing occurs (e.g., science). Once students are comfortable with self-selected writing, it is not difficult to get them to do self-selected writing in any subject. After a particularly interesting or stimulating experience during a content lesson, the teacher can readily say something like, "That was amazing. Now, I would like you to write what you think about that."

Otherwise, when they engage in self-selected writing in a subject:

Children still share their writing with other students.

Children still spell words phonetically.

Teachers still do not correct or grade first drafts.

When they are ready to benefit from process writing, children still revise some of what they have written.

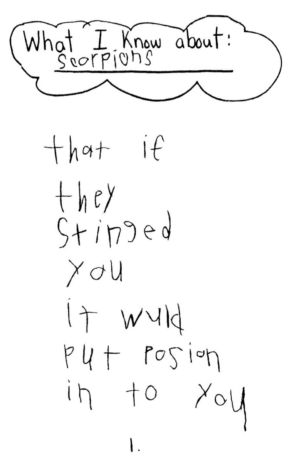

Figure 8.3 First-Grade Science Learning Log

The major application of the self-selected writing approach to subject areas takes the form of *learning logs*. Learning logs are a type of journal writing in which students summarize what they have learned and how they feel about it. Children can keep learning logs in any subject and can add to their logs daily, weekly, or after the teacher completes a unit. Sometimes, the teacher responds in writing to a student's learning log entry, making the learning log into a dialogue journal. If so, the teacher always responds positively to the ideas, rather than negatively to the form, and no grade is given. The purpose of the teacher's written response is to help students think more and more deeply about what they are learning. (For examples of entries in learning logs, see Figures 8.3 & 8.4.)

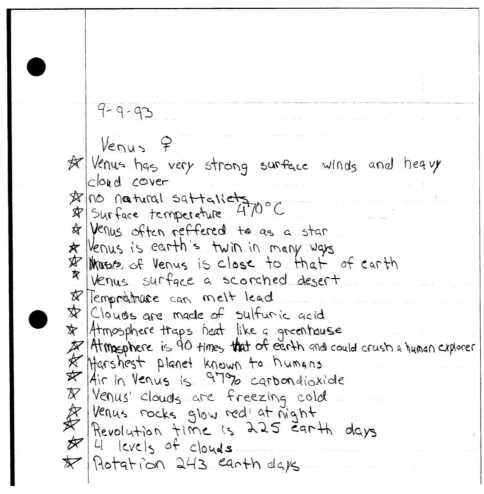

9-9-93

Venus ♀
☆ Venus has very strong surface winds and heavy cloud cover
☆ no natural sattaliets
☆ Surface temperature 470°C
☆ Venus often reffered to as a star
★ Venus is earth's twin in many ways
☆ Mass of Venus is close to that of earth
☆ Venus surface a scorched desert
☆ Temprature can melt lead
☆ Clouds are made of sulfuric acid
☆ Atmosphere traps heat like a greenhouse
☆ Atmosphere is 90 times that of earth and could crush a human explorer
☆ Harshest planet known to humans
☆ Air in Venus is 97% carbondioxide
☆ Venus' clouds are freezing cold
☆ Venus rocks glow red! at night
☆ Revolution time is 225 earth days
☆ 4 levels of clouds
☆ Rotation 243 earth days

Figure 8.4 Fourth-Grade Science Learning Log

During self-selected writing in subject areas, teachers should leave on the wall any writing rules, words, and other supports that they use during writing/language arts time. However, children should not spend time during science, social studies, or health proofreading or editing their papers or journals. The students' concern and attention in self-selected writing in a subject area should always be on content. The grade a piece of self-selected writing in a content area receives should be based solely or primarily on the content of a final draft.

Self-selected writing in subject areas increases the quantity and variety of self-selected writing that students do. It also encourages students to self-monitor and evaluate what they are learning in their content subjects, and to think interpretively about that new learning.

Focused Writing in the Content Areas

After students have engaged in self-selected writing across the curriculum for an extended period of time, they are ready to benefit also from focused writing across the curriculum. The main difference between focused writing and focused writing across the curriculum is that the former concentrates on teaching students to do one or more types of writing, while the latter focuses on specific subject matter. The increased structure of focused writing across the curriculum can help students better learn social studies, science, health, or literature.

A Content-Writing Lesson Framework

Exactly the same focused-writing lesson framework can be used when focusing student writing in a content area. What differences there are lie in how the steps of a lesson are carried out.

The background-building step (step 1) of a focused-writing lesson almost always focuses on the type of writing that will be specified in the prompt when it is presented in step 2; step 1 of a content-writing lesson almost always focuses on building background for the role, audience, or topic that will be specified in the prompt. The prompt (step 2) and inquiry/research (step 3), if any, of a focused-writing lesson are designed to enable the students to be successful at producing the type of writing specified in the prompt; the prompt and step 3, if any, of a content-writing lesson are designed to enable the students to be successful at understanding and interpreting the content they are writing about.

As with focused-writing lessons, planning good prompts is the key to having effective content-writing lessons. This ability comes only with effort and experience but is helped when teachers analyze a prompt before using it with students.

Imagine that you have constructed the following prompt for your fourth-grade social studies class:

> Pretend that you are President Abraham Lincoln. Write a speech for fourth-graders explaining why no one should have slaves.

audience	=	fourth-graders
role	=	President Abraham Lincoln
topic	=	why no one should have slaves
type of writing	=	a speech that explains

In this sample prompt, both President Lincoln and the topic of slavery could require background building or research, depending on how much you have previously taught your students about one or both. If you are more interested in students' affective responses to slavery at this point, you might read them a book or story or show them a video about life as a slave before teaching this particular lesson. If you are more interested in students' knowledge about the institution of slavery, you might have them take notes from encyclopedias during step 3 and then allow them to use these notes during steps 4 and 5.

For this example, students should need very little, if any, background built about the nature of a speech or lecture. The emphasis of this lesson is on the content, not on teaching students how to compose a speech.

Here is a sample prompt for a content-writing lesson in science:

Why do bees fly from flower to flower? Does this help or hurt flowers? How?

audience	=	
role	=	
topic	=	why bees fly from flower to flower and how this helps flowers
type of writing	=	

This second sample prompt is very assumptive. It assumes that students have been regularly sharing what they have written with one another so that they have developed a sense of the audience as their peers rather than you, the teacher. If not, a number of students will probably be pretty sketchy about what they write, and when you ask them why, they will reply that you already knew the answers! The sharing phase of a focused-writing/content-writing lesson is optional only if students have done enough sharing previously to develop a sense of the audience as their peers.

Of course, this second sample prompt also assumes that students have done enough self-selected writing and focused writing to have developed their own voice (self as role). Knowledge of the topic is probably too involved to be developed in step 1. Either this writing lesson should follow a study of cross-pollination in plants, or it should require research on that topic in step 3. The second sample prompt is fine, but it assumes a lot of previous experience with writing and also either assumes knowledge of the topic or requires a research step.

As with self-selected writing across the curriculum, the students' concern and attention in focused writing across the curriculum should always be on the content.

The grade for a piece of focused writing in a content area should be based solely or primarily on its content.

Again, the flexibility of the focused-writing lesson used across the curriculum should be noted. For example, a focused-writing lesson can be taught both for its own sake and to prepare students to read a particular piece of literature in a subsequent reading lesson. Specifically, to heighten students' understanding and interest, they could write to a prompt that elicits persuasive writing from them before reading a piece of persuasive writing during literature class. Focused-writing lessons can serve as content-writing lessons in a great variety of ways: preceding the reading of literature and integrated with it, following the reading of literature and integrated with it, or in any of several roles in a thematic unit.

The Theory and Research Base for Writing Instruction

Most of the research on writing over the past thirty years has been in three areas: the uses of writing—emphasizing how literacy functions in various communities and cultures; the processes of writing—emphasizing how writers actually write; and the development of writing—emphasizing how writers mature and progress over time, both overall and in particular aspects (Dyson & Freedman, 1991). This third area includes writing instructional research but has concentrated more on stages writers may move through in their writing and writing-skills development. This complex body of research on writing is probably best reflected and applied in the excellent and highly influential books on teaching writing by Atwell (1990), Calkins (1994), Graves (1983), Newkirk (1989), and others.

While there have been many classroom applications of the research on writing, these applications have generally stressed four components. Because one of the major areas of recent writing research has focused on how literacy functions in various communities, applications of this writing research are usually marked by *authentic writing* and *collaboration*. Because research has also focused on how writers write, classroom applications are usually marked by an emphasis on *process* rather than product. Moreover, because the third major area of research has focused on how writers develop, applications usually emphasize stages that children move through while involved in a writing program. The most common aspect of student writing that teachers examine from a developmental perspective is *phonic/invented spelling*.

The notion that children's writing in school should generally be authentic follows largely from research on the role of writing in various communities (e.g., Heath, 1983) and as engaged in spontaneously by children (Dyson, 1985). Writing is said to be authentic when it is done for real purposes. When authenticity is a component of the writing program, children choose their own topics, write to communicate with others and for enjoyment, and write across the curriculum. Isolated writing-skills instruction and artificial writing assignments are kept to a minimum.

The research on the uses of writing has also led to the insight that communities often collaborate when planning to write, when writing, or when responding to what has been written. Real writers who function well in communities ordinarily produce "reader-based" rather than "writer-based" prose (Flower, 1979/1990). Sharing writing with other students and peer conferencing, along with training in responding positively to ideas rather than negatively to form, are the means teachers usually employ to achieve the collaboration that in turn helps writers become more reader based. By these means, the teacher attempts to establish a community of writers in the classroom.

The process (or processes) of writing, on the part of both adults and children, has probably been the major focus of the research on writing since 1970. How writers actually write, rather than how they should, has served as the impetus for the process-writing revolution. Eliminating standards for first-draft writing and regularly involving students in revising what they have written are the two means teachers usually employ to involve students in the writing process. In combination with the other components that follow from recent writing research, process writing has represented a concerted effort to help children become and see themselves as authors.

Since the pioneering work of Read (1971) and Beers and Henderson (1977), young children's incorrect attempts to spell words while writing have been recognized as powerful indicators of their developing phonemic awareness and knowledge of sound–letter relationships (Adams, 1990; Henderson, 1990). The research on spelling indicates that phonic spelling is an important part of an effective spelling and phonics program in the primary grades. Spelling is not merely right or wrong. Students' incorrect spellings can be studied for what they indicate about the development of their awareness of sound–letter relationships and phonemic sequencing (Gentry & Gillet, 1993). This work does not, however, suggest that correct spelling has no place in these same grades. On the contrary, Clarke's study (1988) suggests that the combination of phonic spelling and correct spelling is what helps children most.

Research on writing instruction prior to the 1970s was largely limited to studies of the efficacy of formal grammar instruction. Formal grammar instruction has traditionally consisted of teaching children to identify the parts of speech; to determine whether a sentence is simple, compound, or complex; to diagram or otherwise identify the function of each word, phrase, or clause in a sentence (e.g., subject, indirect object); to state rules for capitalization and punctuation; to conjugate regular and irregular verbs, especially *to be;* and so on. From as early as 1903 (Palmer, 1975), a number of researchers compared groups of students taught grammar with groups not taught grammar on the correctness of their writing. A number of studies during this era also examined the correlation between students' knowledge of traditional, formal grammar and the correctness of their writing. Braddock, Lloyd-Jones, and Schoer (1963) summarized all of the research to that point:

> In view of the widespread agreement of research studies based upon many types of students and teachers, the conclusion can be stated in strong and unqualified terms: the teaching of formal grammar has a negligible or, because it usually displaces

some instruction and practice in actual composition, even a harmful effect on the improvement of writing. (pp. 37–38)

Others summarizing those same studies, along with the research conducted since 1963, including attempts to teach newer grammars such as structural or transformational, have agreed with Braddock et al. (Palmer, 1975; Hillocks, 1986; Linden & Whimbey, 1990). It can now be stated in no uncertain terms that grammar instruction of the kind we all experienced does not teach students how to write "grammatically" (i.e., conventionally correctly). Common sense should have told us what this body of research has repeatedly confirmed. We do not expect children to learn to play the piano by learning rules or memorizing the names of the parts of it. We do not expect children to learn to swim or ride a bicycle properly without actually engaging in those activities. Why did we think we could teach children to write conventionally correctly from instruction that involved little or no actual composition?

So if formal grammar instruction has been a failure because it is taught separately from writing, how can students be taught to write mechanically correctly while they are learning to write? The traditional approach was to assign an occasional piece of writing, mark errors on students' papers, and return those papers with a grade that reflected the number of errors made. In his landmark overview of research on teaching writing, Hillocks (1986) summarizes the research on this practice:

> Teacher comment [written on students' compositions] has little impact on student writing. None of the studies of teacher comment . . . show statistically significant differences in the quality of writing between experimental and control groups. Indeed, several show no pre-to-post gains for any groups, regardless of the type of comment. (p. 165)

Teachers who wish to increase student ability to write mechanically correctly will not rely on either formal grammar instruction or marking errors on student papers. These two methods have nothing but tradition to support them.

The major examination of instructional writing research was conducted by Hillocks (1986). His meta-analysis did not focus on formal grammar instruction or on the uses, processes, or development of writers through stages. Rather, he synthesized the best available research on how to teach writing, including how to teach students to write mechanically correctly. The distinction in this chapter between self-selected, focused, and traditional writing is similar to Hillocks's distinction between the natural-process, environmental, and traditional modes of writing instruction. The use in this chapter of form-based writing scales and writing rules on the wall is based on his discussion of the research on teaching students to evaluate their own writing with writing scales.

The research on writing supports a balanced program that begins with self-selected writing, gradually incorporates a writing scale for conventions, moves into focused writing, uses form-based writing scales, and extends writing across the curriculum.

Looking Back

A balanced writing program for the elementary school begins with single-draft self-selected writing, extends self-selected writing across the curriculum, adds the writing process to self-selected writing, builds on self-selected writing with focused writing, extends focused writing across the curriculum, and helps children move beyond dependence on the writing process. From the time children become comfortable writing and sharing what they have written, conventional spelling, mechanics, and usage are supported with wall charts and gradually taught by having students learn to apply them a little at a time in their writing. This chapter discussed five key ideas:

1. Self-selected writing promotes engagement.
2. Students should learn to produce certain types of writing.
3. Reading can support writing, and writing can support reading.
4. Students should apply conventions in their writing.
5. Students should write in all subjects.

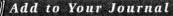
Add to Your Journal

In this chapter, teaching methods regarding self-selected and focused writing have been contrasted with each other and with traditional writing instruction. What was your experience with these different approaches? Compose a brief memoir of your development as a writer. Describe particularly the writing experiences and instruction you remember having at home and in elementary school. How did you feel about the kind and amount of writing instruction you received? How do you feel about it now? When you teach writing in an elementary classroom, how do you intend to go about it? Use the thinking processes to respond to each of the five key ideas.

Application Activities

Try It Out

Plan a focused-writing lesson for a particular grade level of students. Come up with a prompt, considering audience, role, topic, and type of writing. Then decide what you will do for all six steps of your lesson.

Do It Together

Meet with three or four of your peers and connect with your memories of writing. Did you engage in self-selected writing as well as some focused writing lessons? Were you taught the rules in ways that you could apply to your own writing? Was writing something you looked forward to or dreaded? Summarize the collective experiences of your group with writing and compare what you experienced to what you have read so far in this chapter.

Listen, Look, and Learn

Interview a teacher you respect about his or her writing program. Ask questions that will help you determine if self-selected writing, focused writing, or traditional writing are used regularly. Remember that people use other terms for these types of writing, so phrase your questions so that you can determine what kind of writing is actually being done and how often. See if you can determine whether self-selected writing or focused writing is being used to support learning in different content areas. Ask to see some first drafts along with published writing samples. Summarize what you learned from your interview. What changes would you make in the writing program if you were the teacher?

References

Adams, M. J. (1990). _Beginning to read: Thinking and learning about print._ Cambridge, MA: MIT Press.

Atwell, N. (1990). _Coming to know: Writing to learn in the intermediate grades._ Portsmouth, NH: Heinemann.

Beers, J. W., & Henderson, E. H. (1977). A study of developing orthographic concepts among first graders. _Research in the Teaching of English, 11,_ 133–148.

Braddock, R., Lloyd-Jones, R., & Schoer, L. (1963). _Research in written composition._ Champaign, IL: National Council of Teachers of English.

Calkins, L. M. (1994). _The art of teaching writing,_ 2nd ed. Portsmouth, NH: Heinemann.

Clarke, L. K. (1988). Invented versus traditional spelling in first graders' writings: Effects on learning to spell and read. _Research in the Teaching of English, 22,_ 281–309.

Dyson, A. H. (1985). Research currents: Writing and the social lives of children. _Language Arts, 62,_ 632–639.

Dyson, A. H., & Freedman, S. W. (1991). Writing. In J. Flood, J. M. Jeusen, D. Lapp, & J. R. Squire (Eds.), _Handbook of research on teaching the language arts_ (pp. 754–774). New York: Macmillan.

Fisher, B. (1991). Getting started with writing. _Teaching K–8,_ 49–51.

Flower, L. (1979/1990). Writer-based prose: A cognitive basis for problems in writing. _College English, 41,_ 19–37. Reprinted in T Newkirk (Ed.), _To compose_ (pp. 125–152). Portsmouth, NH: Heinemann.

Gentry, J. R., & Gillet, J. W. (1993). _Teaching kids to spell._ Portsmouth, NH: Heinemann.

Graves, D. H. (1983). _Writing. Teachers and children at work._ Portsmouth, NH: Heinemann.

Heath, S. B. (1983). _Ways with words: Language, life, and work in communities and classrooms._ Cambridge, UK: Cambridge University Press.

Henderson, E. H. (1990). _Teaching spelling,_ 2nd ed. Boston: Houghton Mifflin.

Hillocks, G., Jr. (1986). *Research on written composition: New directions for teaching.* Urbana, IL: ERIC Clearinghouse on Reading and Communication Skills; National Conference on Research in English.

Linden, M. J., & Whimbey A. (1990). *Why Johnny can't write.* Hillsdale, NJ: Erlbaum.

Newkirk, T. (1989). *More than stories: The range of children's writing.* Portsmouth, NH: Heinemann.

Palmer, W. S. (1975). Research on grammar. A review of some pertinent investigations. *High School Journal, 58,* 252–258.

Read, C. (1971). Pre-school children's knowledge of English phonology. *Harvard Educational Review, 41,* 1–34.

A d d i t i o n a l   R e a d i n g s

- These books have excellent suggestions for setting up self-selected writing in classrooms.

  Bromley, K. (1994). *Journaling: Engagements in reading, writing, and thinking.* New York: Scholastic.

  Fiderer, A. (1994). *Teaching writing: A workshop approach.* New York: Scholastic.

  Routman, R. (1988). *Transitions.* Portsmouth, NH: Heinemann.

  Routman, R. (1991). *Invitations.* Portsmouth, NH: Heinemann.

- Suggestions for writing in all subjects can be found in these books and articles.

  Atwell, N. (1998). *In the middle: New understandings about writing, reading, and learning,* 2nd ed. Portsmouth, NH: Boynton/Cook & Heinemann.

  Cudd, E. T. (1989). Research and report writing in the elementary grades. *The Reading Teacher, 43,* 268–269.

  Cudd, E. T., & Roberts, L. (1989). Using writing to enhance content area learning in the primary grades. *The Reading Teacher, 43,* 393–404.

  Moore, D. W., Moore, S. A., Cunningham, P. M., & Cunningham, J. W. (1998). *Developing readers and writers in the content areas K–12,* 3rd ed. New York: Longman.

- Ways to integrate reading, literature, and writing are the topics of these two journal articles.

  Shanahan, T. (1988). The reading–writing relationship: Seven instructional principles. *The Reading Teacher, 41,* 636–647.

  Wahnsley, S. A., & Walp, T (1990). Integrating literature and composing into the language arts curriculum. *Elementary School Journal, 90,* 251–274.

Assessment

Looking Ahead

To teach anything, teachers must have some knowledge about what learners already know and can do. Each day, teachers diagnose the abilities, attitudes, and prior knowledge of their class as a whole and individual students within that class. Based on this diagnosis, they make decisions about where to begin instruction and how to pace that instruction. They then monitor how well students are progressing toward meeting particular goals. This monitoring of instructional progress is referred to as assessment. Some people think of assessment and testing as being synonymous. But testing is only one means of assessing progress. Teachers assess when they observe how children read from a particular book, respond to a question, complete an assignment, or carry out an experiment or project. Teachers make records of these observations and look at these observational records across time to see how children are progressing.

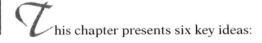his chapter presents six key ideas:

1. Be sure your assessment is reliable and valid.
2. Determine instructional reading levels by observing how your students read.
3. Use observation and anecdotal records as the cornerstone of your assessment.
4. Include students' attitudes and interests in your assessment.
5. Create portfolios to monitor and demonstrate progress.
6. Beware of standardized tests.

Be Sure Your Assessment Is Reliable and Valid

A person is said to be reliable if that person can be depended on, time and time again, to do whatever he or she is expected to do. J. C. Nunnally (1967) stated that "reliability concerns the extent to which measurements are *repeatable*" (p. 172). An assessment measure is said to be reliable if it can be depended on, time and time again, to do what it is expected to do. If a measure is very reliable, it will yield approximately the same results today as it will tomorrow or next week. You can rely on the consistency of the response. A scale is a reliable indicator of your weight if, when you neither gain nor lose pounds, it indicates the same weight each time you weigh yourself.

Test makers achieve reliability in a number of ways, one of which is by including many different items to measure each ability. A student may miss one of the items because of confusion, inattention, or fatigue but may get most of the other items correct. Another student may correctly guess the answer to an item but show the true deficiency by responding incorrectly to the remainder of the items. The scores of both students will be fairly reliable if a number of items test the same ability, because judgment is not likely to be made based on one chance mistake or guess.

Teachers achieve reliability in a similar manner. Judgments are never based on one observation or on one test item. Rather, teachers make decisions based on several observations or testings. In addition, once decisions are made, teachers continue to observe, evaluate, and constantly rethink their decisions based on new information.

The concept of validity is somewhat harder to explain than the concept of reliability. Nunnally (1967) stated that "in a very general sense, a measuring instrument is valid if it does what it is intended to do." Validity of measurement refers to the match between the concept or skill to be measured and the means by which it is measured. A measure is valid to the extent that it measures what it was intended to measure. This distinction may seem academic and superfluous because we ought to be able to assume that any instrument will measure what it is intended to measure. This assumption, however, is often questionable. An example should clarify both the meaning of validity and the difficulty of achieving it.

Imagine, for example, that a reading skill important for beginning readers is associating consonant letters such as *b*, *m*, and *s* and the sounds commonly associated with these letters. Creating a valid test of this knowledge would appear to be simple. One could create a test that contained some pictures and ask students to write the letter they thought the picture began with. Is this a valid measure of their knowledge? When the tests have been scored, will the teacher know which students have this initial consonant knowledge and which don't? The answer is perhaps. Imagine, for example, that some students don't know, or can't remember the names for, or have different names for some of the pictures. A student who looks at a picture of a dog, calls it a puppy, and writes the letter *p* under the picture has the wrong answer and the right knowledge. Imagine another child who writes the letter *b* under the picture thinking that he or she has made the letter *d*. This student, too, has marked the test item incorrectly but has the knowledge that the test was designed to evaluate. Another student may be able to spell dog and thus will write the letter *d* under the picture. If this response was generated by a memorized spelling, the correct response does not indicate that the child has achieved the desired letter–sound associations. To create a valid test of students' consonant letter–sound knowledge, the test creator would have to be sure that most of the stimulus pictures were familiar to the children, called by the desired name, and not familiar enough to have their spellings memorized. Moreover, even this test would be valid only for students who could write all their consonants correctly.

There is, however, a much more serious problem with the test procedure just described. This problem is related to the issue of why it is desirable for students to be able to associate consonant letters with sounds. This knowledge, in and of itself, is useless. It becomes useful only when the student can *use* this knowledge and the context of what is being read to decode an unfamiliar word. What we really want students to do is to *apply* their knowledge of letter–sound relationships as they read. The previously described test procedure is aimed at testing the student's letter–sound association knowledge, not the application of this knowledge in real reading. So if the desired skill is the ability to use this knowledge in reading, how can this skill be measured validly? The answer to this question is obvious and simple. Put the children in a "real" reading situation and observe what they do.

Because these observations occur as a natural part of the lesson, children are able to demonstrate their true ability unconfounded by the anxiety, panic, and inability to understand directions that often result from the awareness that one is taking a test. Because you have structured the observations so that decisions are based on the correct or incorrect response of the children, you view these responses in an objective, unbiased way. Because these observations are conducted in the context of "real reading," you can observe not only whether students have learned certain associations but also whether they can apply what they have learned as they read. You have achieved validity by objectively measuring what you chose to measure in a context that simulates as closely as possible the tasks children are actually required to perform as they read. You will achieve reliability if you make tentative decisions about how well different children are using strategies but suspend judgment in any final sense until you have had a chance to observe the children's responses for another day or two.

Determine Instructional Reading Levels by Observing How Your Students Read

A child's instructional reading level is simply the level of difficulty of material that the child will most benefit from reading. Over the years, research, common sense, and professional experience have shown that children learn to read best by reading material that is neither too difficult nor too easy for them. To determine a child's instructional reading level, you need some materials that get increasingly more difficult. Some teachers use an IRI—Informal Reading Inventory—to determine this level. An IRI contains passages of increasing difficulty and comprehension questions. Most reading series have IRIs that you can administer to determine the appropriate level of materials in that series. There are also a number of commercially published IRIs. Many states and school systems have come up with benchmark books for each grade level. Teachers in these states have children read to them from increasingly harder levels of these benchmark books to determine the appropriate instructional level for each child.

Regardless of whether you are using an IRI from a reading series, a published IRI, or a group of graded benchmark books, you need to determine instructional reading levels; you need to have the child read aloud to you and mark any errors (sometimes called miscues) the child makes. Next, you should have the child close the book and ask the child comprehension questions or ask the child to retell what was read in order to determine how well the child is comprehending. The instructional reading level is the highest level of material in which the child makes no more than 5 errors per 100 words and has 75–80 percent comprehension.

There are various systems for recording miscues. Figure 9.1 shows one possible marking system. When a word is skipped or omitted by the child, we circle that word. When the child inserts a word, we write a caret (∧) beneath the text line and

Once there was a farmer who lived with his wife and their ten children in a very small farmhouse. The farmer and his family were miserable. They were always bumping into each other and getting in each other's way. When the children stayed inside on rainy days, they fought all the time. The farmer's wife was always ~~shooing~~ *shooting* children out of the kitchen so she could cook. The farmer had no place to sit ~~quietly~~ *sc quickly* when he came in from *his* work. The farmer (finally) could stand it no longer. He said to his wife, "Today I am going ~~into~~ *to* the village to talk with the wise man about our crowded house. He will know what to do."

Figure 9.1 **An Oral Reading Record of One Child's Reading of This Passage**

insert the word that was added. When a word is not decoded accurately or when another word is substituted for it, we write what the child said above it. If a child goes back and successfully corrects a miscue, we leave the miscue marked but write *sc,* for self-correction. Anything the child self-corrects is not counted as an error. The child's dialect is usually ignored when marking miscues. If a child reads a word the way he or she would have pronounced it in conversation, the child has read the word correctly.

Looking at the reading we see in Figure 9.1, we count four errors. The child said "shooting" instead of *shooing,* inserted the word *his,* left out *finally* and said "to" instead of *into.* The child also read *quietly* as "quickly" the first time but then went back and self-corrected. We mark self-corrections but do not count them as errors. Since there are just over 100 words in this passage, the child's oral reading accuracy is in the correct range for instructional level. We would then take the passage from the child and have him retell the passage, or we would ask him questions. If his comprehension was 75–80 percent, we would consider this to be an appropriate level for this child. This passage might not be the child's instructional reading level, however, because we want the highest level of material that the child can read with at least 95 percent accuracy and 75–80 percent comprehension. If we wanted to find the highest level, we would have to have the child continue to read harder passages until he is unable to meet the oral reading accuracy or comprehension criteria.

Use Daily Observation and Anecdotal Records as the Cornerstone of Your Assessment

The most reliable and valid way to assess children's progress is to observe them in daily reading and writing activities and make records of your observations. Anecdotal records are the written records that teachers keep on individual children based on their ongoing observation of and interaction with them. A classroom in which children are involved in comprehension lessons, self-selected reading, responding to what they have read, discussing what they have read, writing, inquiring, researching, writing about what they have read, sharing what they have written, proofreading, and correcting what they have written, making words, using wall charts that support their reading and writing, and so on provide the teacher with hundreds of opportunities each day to form or modify judgments about how individual students are learning. Unfortunately, no teacher can systematically and objectively process this wealth of information. Fortunately, because there is so much of it, sampling from it in a systematic and objective manner will still provide a rich portrait of each child across the weeks and months.

Why is it necessary to keep timely, written records of a teacher's observations of each child? There are several reasons. First, experienced teachers know that if they do not keep written records, they will remember very little of all they witness. For some children, they will remember almost nothing. Second, we all have personalities and preferences that match us better with some students than others. We may naturally respond better to girls than to boys, or vice versa. We may interact more with children who are highly verbal than with those who are quiet. Unless we keep systematic written records of some kind, it will be very difficult for us to observe every student enough to maintain a truly reliable and valid assessment of that child's engagement, success, and achievement with each major type of instructional activity. Third, if we write anecdotal records, we can subsequently sit in a quiet place to examine what we have observed about a single child and decide what we want to observe in the future to round out our developing picture of that student.

There are probably a large number of ways in which a teacher can efficiently record and update written observations about individual students. Here is the one we have found to be the most practical.

Any school supply or office supply store sells adhesive file-folder labels by the sheet. The user types or writes on a label, peels it off the sheet, and affixes it to the tab of the file folder being labeled. These labels are also perfect for recording brief comments about children's understanding and engagement, success, or achievement with instructional activities.

We place one or more sheets of these labels on a clipboard we carry with us in the classroom. When interacting with or observing students, we will occasionally witness a significant indicator of the child's learning or lack thereof. It is quick, easy, and unobtrusive to record the child's nickname, the date, and a brief comment on one of the labels on the sheet attached to the clipboard. After school, we take a few minutes to affix each label used that day onto a page for that subject in the child's anecdotal records folder.

When planning an instructional day, teachers using this system can analyze the anecdotal records for two or three of the children. At this pace, every student's anecdotal records can be analyzed every two weeks. The analysis of a child's anecdotal records consists of determining how much support there is in the folder for evaluative statements that would be written in a narrative description of the child's learning or shared with a parent at a conference. It is during these analyses that teachers often realize that they have not actually recorded enough observations about how well the child is doing in some important area of the literacy program. In such cases the teacher writes the child's nickname or initials on one of the file-folder labels on the sheet on the clipboard along with a one- or two-word description of the observation needed for that child. While moving through the school day, the teacher then has several labels on the sheet as a reminder to obtain particular observations of certain children.

If anecdotal records are collected regularly and systematically, and if they consist of objective and specific descriptions of children's engagement, success, or achievement with actual instructional activities, there is no more reliable or valid means of diagnosing or evaluating students' ongoing learning. These records can then serve to support any summative statements that the teacher needs or cares to make to anyone about the child's progress.

Assessing Emergent Literacy

Chapter 2 described many activities for "building the foundation" for literacy and concluded that there are seven signs of emergent literacy. These seven signs are the reading behaviors we look for as indicators that each child is moving successfully into reading and writing. These behaviors form the basis for our assessment of beginning readers. We assess these behaviors as children are engaged in their daily literacy activities. Many teachers of young children keep a checklist such as that in Figure 9.2. Each day, they put the checklists of two or three children on their clipboard and observe and talk with these children as they are engaged in self-selected reading and writing to determine how they are developing the critical behaviors. Teachers often use a simple system of putting a minus (–) to indicate that the child does not have that behavior; a question mark (?) when the behavior is erratic or it is unclear that the child has it; and a plus (+) to indicate the child does seem to have developed that behavior. Three pluses on three different dates is a reliable indicator that that child has indeed developed that behavior.

Assessing Word Strategies

The goal of fluency, decoding, and spelling instruction is to teach children words and strategies they actually use when they are reading and writing. What we want to know is not how children spell words during the daily word wall activity or on the test but how quickly they recognize these words when reading and how correctly they spell these words when they are writing.

There are many opportunities throughout the day to make these observations. During our weekly conferences with children during self-selected reading, we ask them to read aloud to us a short part of what they have chosen to share with us. We don't do a formal oral reading record at that time, but we do listen for how fluently they read, how automatically they identify the word wall words, and how they use cues like patterns and context to figure out unknown words. When children are partner-reading during a comprehension lesson, we circulate to the different partnerships and ask them to read a page to us. Again, we can note how they use what we are teaching them about words as they actually read text. Another opportunity to observe their sight word recognition, word identification, and fluency is when we meet with small coaching groups. We observe their spelling behaviors by periodically looking at samples of their first-draft writing, by analyzing their spelling in writing samples we collect three times each year, and in our revising/editing/ publishing conferences with individual children. As with emergent literacy behaviors, the "– ? +" system easily allows us to record what we observe on each child's word behavior checklist (see Figure 9.3).

Assessing Comprehension Strategies

Chapter 5 described comprehension strategies and a variety of activities to use before and after reading that teach comprehension and foster thoughtful literacy. As with emergent literacy behaviors and word strategies, we monitor and assess chil-

---

Emergent Literacy Behaviors

Name _____   Dates Checked (– ? +)

"Pretend reads" favorite books, poems, songs and chants   __ __ __ __ __ __ __

"Writes" and can and "read back" what was written   __ __ __ __ __ __ __

Tracks print   __ __ __ __ __ __ __

    left page first

    top-bottom

    left-to right

    return sweep

    points to each word

Knows reading "jargon"   __ __ __ __ __ __ __

    identifies one letter, one word, and one sentence

    identifies first word, first and last letter in a word

Reads and writes some "concrete" words   __ __ __ __ __ __ __

    own name and names of friends, pets, family

    favorite words from books, poems, and chants

Demonstrates phonemic awareness   __ __ __ __ __ __ __

    counts words

    claps syllables

    stretches out words in an attempt to spell

    blends and segments words

    identifies rhymes

Demonstrates alphabet awareness   __ __ __ __ __ __ __

    names some letters

    knows some words that begin with certain letters

    knows some common letter sounds

Figure 9.2 **Emergent Literacy Checklist**

dren's development of these behaviors as we interact with them during comprehension lessons and in our self-selected reading conferences. Because comprehension is so dependent on prior knowledge and interest, in this context we are unable to feel as secure in our judgments of whether a child can—or cannot—use a particular

Sight Word, Decoding, and Spelling Behaviors

Name _____   Dates Checked (– ? +)

Identifies word wall words automatically when reading   — — — — — — —

Spells word wall words correctly in first-draft writing   — — — — — — —

Uses letter patterns, picture and sentence cues to decode   — — — — — — —

    beginning letters of word (br, sh, f)

    rhyming patterns (at, ight, ain)

    endings (s, ed, ing)

    prefixes (un, inter) suffixes (able, tion) for big words

    combines letter cues, picture cues, and sentence cues

Uses letter patterns to spell words   — — — — — — —

    beginning letters of word (br, sh, f)

    rhyming patterns (at, ight, ain)

    endings (s, ed, ing, er, est)

    prefixes (un, inter) suffixes (able, tion) for big words

Self-monitors   — — — — — — —

    self-corrects when meaning is distorted

    self-corrects when nonsense word is produced

    rereads to correct phrasing

    rereads for fluency

Reads fluently   — — — — — — —

    with phrasing

    attending to punctuation

    with expression

Writes fluently   — — — — — — —

    writes words quickly

    handwriting not slow and laborious

    focused on meaning

Figure 9.3 Sight Word, Decoding, and Spelling Checklist

comprehension strategy. Often, children recall much information and respond to that information in a high-level way when the topic is familiar and of great interest but demonstrate very little comprehension of less familiar, uninteresting topics. We can use some checklists to indicate general use of comprehension strategies, but anecdotal records are also helpful because the teacher can include comments about prior knowledge and interest as well as comprehension strategies. Figure 9.4 and 9.5 present two checklists—one for story and one for informational text—that many teachers find useful.

Assessing Writing

The best way to determine how well students write is to engage them in the writing process from the first day of school. You can observe many aspects of writing as you move among the class. Is handwriting easy for them? Do they have a store of high-frequency words they can write automatically? Do students struggle with trying to identify a topic for writing? When asked to write, who does some planning first? Do students move confidently through a first draft? Do students revise and edit some as they write, or do they wait to be asked to do it?

Many teachers like to take a focused writing sample during the first week of school. The teacher gives the children a prompt that all the children can relate to,

---

Comprehension Strategies—Story

Name _____   Dates Checked (– ? +)

Names and describes main characters   — — — — — — —

Names and describes settings   — — — — — — —

Describes the goal or problem in the story   — — — — — — —

Describes major events that lead to resolution   — — — — — — —

Describes the resolution to the story   — — — — — — —

Makes inferences and predictions   — — — — — — —

Makes connections   — — — — — — —

    to self

    to world

    to other texts

Expresses a personal reaction/opinion   — — — — — — —

Monitors comprehension and uses fix-up strategies   — — — — — — —

Figure 9.4 **Story Comprehension Checklist**

Comprehension Strategies—Information

Name _____   Dates Checked (– ? +)

Describes major ideas   — — — — — — —

Summarizes important information   — — — — — — —

Accurately recalls important facts/details   — — — — — — —

Organizes ideas appropriately   — — — — — — —

    sequence/chronology

    topic-subtopic

    comparisons

    cause-effect

    problem-solution

Makes inferences   — — — — — — —

Makes connections   — — — — — — —

    to prior knowledge and experience

    to information from other texts

Expresses a personal reaction/opinion   — — — — — — —

Monitors comprehension and uses fix-up strategies — — — — — — —

Figure 9.5 **Informational Text Comprehension Checklist**

such as "What Third Grade Is Like" or "My Most Favorite and Least Favorite Things." The teacher then analyzes the sample to determine where individual children are in their writing development and what the class as a whole needs to work on. The sample is then put away, and halfway through the year the teacher asks the children to write on the same prompt again. Once the children have written the second time, the teacher returns the first sample and lets each child analyze his or her writing growth. The teacher then analyzes the second sample, comparing it to the first for each child and again looking for indicators of things the class needs to work on. The same procedure can be repeated once more at the end of the year.

    Writing is a very complex process. No matter how good we get, there is always room for growth. Because writing is complex, it is easy to see only the problems children still exhibit in their writing and not the growth they are making. Having three writing samples on the same topic across the school year provides tangible evidence of growth to both teacher and student.

Include Students' Attitudes and Interests in Your Assessment

Throughout this book, we have emphasized that reading is affective. The way you feel about what you read and what you do during reading instruction matters. If students read well but don't choose to read, we have not accomplished what we want to accomplish. In this text, we have suggested numerous activities and ways of organizing for instruction that should produce students who like to read and read for information and pleasure. We cannot, however, take it for granted that this will occur and should demonstrate our concern for reading attitudes by periodically assessing how our students feel about reading. Here are some suggestions for monitoring the progress your students are making toward becoming lifelong readers.

Did You Know That?

According to a survey by the Book Industry Study Group (Lehr, 1985), 96 percent of the U.S. population aged sixteen and older read books, magazines, or newspapers. Fifty-six percent of these adults read books. A larger percentage read newspapers and magazines. Although the results of the overall survey were encouraging, the results for young adults aged sixteen to twenty-one were discouraging. Only 63 percent of the sixteen- to twenty-one-year-olds surveyed reported that they were readers. This number represented a 12 percent decline from 1978, when 75 percent of this age group reported that they were readers. Achievement-test scores indicating how well children and young adults read generally rose from 1978 to 1983. The combined achievement-test scores and results of the BISG surveys indicate that students were reading better but liking it less.

Early in the year, try to determine what your students like to read and how they feel about reading. You may want to make a homework assignment for everyone to bring to school on a specified day: "The three best books you read all summer." Encourage the students to go back to the library to check out a book previously read. Even if they can no longer find the book, ask them to tell why they thought it was such a good book. Young children should bring favorite books they like to have read to them. When the children bring their books, let each child tell why he or she liked the books. You may want them to do this book sharing in small groups. As they share, note the titles of the books they bring and their reasons for liking them. This will tell you what current reading interests you should encourage and also where you need to try to broaden interests.

You may have some children who don't bring three books or who bring books but don't really have anything to say about them and may not really have read or liked the books. This tells you a lot about the current interests and attitudes of these children and lets you know that all of the efforts you plan to make to encourage and support reading are truly important and needed.

You might want to follow up this "best books" assignment with another homework assignment to bring in magazines and parts of the newspaper they read. Again, follow up this assignment with group sharing and make notes about what each child brought (or didn't bring). Record your results on a "Beginning Interests and Attitudes Summary" such as that shown in Figure 9.6. In addition to noting what each child shared, summarize the interests of the class by noting which top-

Children's Names	Books Shared	Magazines/ Newspapers	Current Interest (none, little, some, much)
Carol	Ramona the Pest Charlotte's Web	none	some
Sheryll	3 Bobbsey Twins mysteries	none	some
Sue Ann	Whales Dinosaurs Runaway Horse	U.S.A Today	much
Travis	none	Sports page	little
Ray	none	Fishing	little
David	3 Star Trek books	Sports Illustrated	some
Jason	Cannonball Death at High Noon Dirty Dozen	Time	some

Topics of interest to many children:

Sports, fantasy

Types of books read:

✓Realistic fiction	✓Science fiction	Historical fiction
✓Mystery	Myths/legends	Folk/fairy tales
Fantasy	Biography	Autobiography
✓Informational	Other _____	

Figure 9.6 Beginning Interests and Attitudes Summary

ics and types of books were shared most. You have now diagnosed your students' entering interests and attitudes toward reading and can plan how much and what kinds of motivational activities you will do.

Just as with any kind of assessment, your assessment of reading interests and attitudes should be ongoing. By linking your assessment directly to your instruction, you ensure that your assessment is valid. By assessing interests and attitudes on a regular schedule, you get a more reliable indicator than if you assess only once or twice a year. Also, as in any assessment, you can use a variety of methods to assess interests and attitudes. One of the best methods of assessing is to observe what your students actually do. Figure 9.7 is an example of a checklist you might use to observe systematically the growth in reading attitudes. To make this less of a burden, you might fill out one of these checklists each week for a fourth of your class. At the end of the month, you will have observed and focused on the reading attitudes of everyone. If you do this all year, you should have eight or nine indicators of reading attitude throughout the year and should be able to document which students have better attitudes at the end of the year than they did at the beginning.

Child's   Name_____   **Date**____

Over the last two weeks, has the child

	Yes	No
1. Seemed happy when engaged in reading ?	____	____
2. Seemed happy when engaged in writing?	____	____
3. Talked about reading at home?	____	____
4. Talked about writing at home?	____	____
5. Brought a book from home to share with the class?	____	____
6. Checked out and read books from the library?	____	____
7. Read a piece of writing to the class?	____	____
8. Published a piece of writing?	____	____
9. Shown enthusiasm during a reading conference?	____	____
10. Shown enthusiasm during a writing conference?	____	____
11. Chosen to read rather than engage in another pleasurable activity?	____	____
12. Chosen to write rather than engage in another pleasurable activity?	____	____

Figure 9.7 Observation Checklist to Assess Literacy Attitudes

Create Portfolios to Monitor and Demonstrate Progress

A portfolio is a collection of student work. The idea of a student portfolio comes from the practice of painters, photographers, architects, interior designers, and other individuals who maintain an assemblage of their work as a means of demonstrating their professional ability and accomplishments.

When teachers use student portfolios to diagnose or evaluate reading or writing, they maximize the reliability and validity of those assessments. If done well, portfolio assessment is reliable for individual students because the teacher bases each judgment on multiple indicators. It is also valid because the teacher bases each judgment on how well students perform on the actual activities being used to teach them reading or writing.

Working Portfolios

A working portfolio is simply all the student's work of a particular kind. Neither the teacher nor the student has screened the samples that are placed in a working portfolio. As long as the student is at least temporarily finished with a piece of work, it is dated and placed in the working portfolio for that kind of work. For example, if students write a first draft two or three times a week, that draft is filed in the student's working portfolio for writing as soon as the student finishes writing or sharing it. Of course, the teacher or the student may later select a first draft from the working portfolio to confer about, or for the student to proofread, edit, or revise. When additional work on the piece is completed, all subsequent drafts are also dated and filed along with the first draft in the working portfolio. For another example, the teacher may have each student record an oral reading each week. The same cassette tape could be used for each child. Each oral reading sample should begin with the date. By listening to the tape, the teacher can readily hear children's improvement or lack thereof in their oral reading, as long as the passages are of comparable difficulty and length. The tape itself could stand alone as the oral reading portfolio for that child, or it could become one item in the child's more diverse reading portfolio.

Showcase Portfolios

Tierney, Carter, and Desai (1991) have eloquently argued the advantages of having students develop a sense of ownership over their own portfolios. Involving them in evaluating their own progress and accomplishments builds students' independence, increases their motivation to work and learn, and helps them develop insights about reading or writing that cannot be taught directly. The purposes of a showcase portfolio are to grant students ownership and involve them in self-assessment.

While the teacher may set a minimum or maximum number of items that the student must choose, the student independently selects and periodically updates the pieces of work that go into that student's showcase portfolio of reading or writing. It is the process of student selection rather than the particular products chosen by the student that has instructional value. As students examine all their dated work in order to choose a few samples, their sense of themselves as readers or writers is fostered in a powerful and personal way. They develop pride and ownership over their work as they remember the occasions when the work was produced. Examining their work in order cannot fail to show them that they are improving and learning.

The instructional value of having students maintain showcase portfolios is enhanced by having them caption the pieces they select and allowing them to share their showcase portfolios with the class. When professional photographers and others put together their showcase portfolios, they generally caption each piece in the portfolio with a brief statement that explains why that piece was selected or what is special, important, or unique about it. Teachers often require students to use one side of a 3" × 5" lined index card to caption each piece of work chosen for the showcase portfolio. Teachers may guide the captioning process somewhat by suggesting that students begin their captions with "I chose this piece because . . ." or "When I did this piece, I was trying to . . ."

Several approaches to the sharing of showcase portfolios can be taken. Each week, for example, one of the students in the class could be Reader or Writer of the Week. A bulletin board could display the student's photo graph and various biographical or personal facts on it. Books that the child has read or previously published could also be affixed to this bulletin board. One day during the week, time could be set aside for the child to share his or her showcase portfolio with the class, explaining why each piece was chosen and telling what the child hopes to accomplish in the future. By the end of the school year, every child in the class could have had one week each semester devoted to his or her work.

For showcase portfolios to provide their potential benefits to students, adequate time must be set aside for students to select, caption, and share. These processes must be conducted in a truly student-centered manner. Teachers should also be careful not to base report card grades on showcase portfolios. Few students in elementary school are sophisticated enough to choose work that will maximize their grades or otherwise put their best foot forward to an adult audience. Showcase portfolios are designed to help children learn to self-assess, not to grade them on how well they are able to self-assess. When elementary students are to be graded, it is the responsibility of the teacher, not the children, to select the work that most fairly and accurately determines those grades. This point leads us to a discussion of the third type of portfolios.

Growth Portfolios

What does a teacher want more than anything else for his or her students? Growth. Every literacy teacher wants students to grow in their willingness to read and write, their effort to read and write well, their enjoyment of reading and writing, and their ability to read and write. Portfolios have the potential to help teachers reliably and validly assess growth on all of these dimensions. Teachers can also analyze samples to diagnose why more growth has probably not occurred and what might be done about it.

A growth portfolio is the collection of student work samples and other items that a teacher selects or elicits in order to conduct the diagnosis or assessment the teacher has decided to perform. First, the teacher selects samples for a student's growth portfolio from the student's working and showcase portfolios. The teacher may also elicit new work from or administer special tasks to the student for the growth portfolio in order to answer specific diagnostic or assessment questions. The chief characteristic of a growth portfolio is that items are selected or elicited to shed light on specific aspects of reading or writing learning and development. For example, a teacher concerned with student improvement in focused writing could choose to compare writing samples done several months apart in response to similar prompts on the same topic. Teachers sometimes design parallel prompts to contrast student growth in producing a type of writing such as a story, biography, letter, or description. For another example, a child's growth portfolio in reading or writing may contain three or four dated entries from that child's reader-response journal on poetry.

Instead of captioning each piece of work in a growth portfolio, most teachers write a narrative description of the child's strengths, weaknesses, and changes as manifested by the samples. This description can be shared with the child or with parents during a conference to inform them of progress and to get their input on future goals. If necessary, the teacher can assign a grade or grades to one or more aspects of the growth portfolio and justify the evaluation by referring to specifics in the samples.

In many schools, some or all of the pieces in the growth portfolio go to next year's teacher. Teachers usually agree on the amount and kinds of items to be included. Sometimes groups of teachers design parallel reading or writing situations to highlight certain facts of long-term growth in literacy. Often children help the teacher decide on some of the work that will be placed in the student's growth portfolio. The growth portfolio can be a real source of pride and accomplishment on the part of an upper elementary student who can readily discern the tremendous progress he or she has made over the years.

Many teachers broaden the concept of portfolio to include anecdotal records and records of observation. If so, a child's growth portfolios in reading or writing would contain those kinds of records as well.

Beware of Standardized Tests

When most people think of assessment, they think of standardized tests. Except as a screening device, standardized, group tests have *no* place in the assessment of individuals. Standardized reading tests may tell you how well groups of children are achieving. They do not tell you very much about individual children even though, unfortunately, they do print out scores for individual children. How can this be? If a child scores in the 44th percentile on a standardized reading achievement test, what does that mean? Does that mean this child is a better reader than a child who scores in the 14th percentile? Probably. Does that mean that a child who scores in the 74th percentile is a better reader than this child? Probably. Does that mean this child is a better reader than a child who scores in the 40th percentile? Possibly, but almost as probably not. There is quite a good chance that the child who scores in the 40th percentile is a better reader than the child who scores in the 44th!

All tests have what is called "standard error." *Standard error* is the term used to describe how much the child's true score is apt to vary from the test score. Standard error comes from sources such as the fact that some children get really "up" for tests and perform much better for the test than they ever could on a day-in, day-out basis, whereas other children panic and don't do nearly as well as they do on a day-in, day-out basis. Standard error also exists because some children don't feel well on the day of the test. Moreover, some test-wise children make great guesses. Others are easily frustrated and quit when they get to a hard item. Finally, some children are just lucky. All standardized tests have a standard error, and the test manual will tell you how much the standard error is for each part of the test.

Standardized, group tests are developed to be reliable for a group of students. Give a standardized test, as directed, to a group of thirty or more students who are the kind of students the test was designed for, and the average score of those thirty children will be extremely reliable. The problem is that the score of any one of those students will not be reliable: that's what the standard-error measurement is telling you. On a very reliable test, for every child in a group who scores better than he or she should, another child out of the group is likely to score worse than he or she should, so it evens out. The problem is that the teacher wants to diagnose and assess each individual student, and it is impossible to know whether an individual student scored above or below his or her true score (what the child's score would have been on a perfect test) and by how much. Each child's true score will fall within the range described by the child's actual score plus or minus the standard-error measurement 68 percent of the time. To be 95 percent sure that the child's true score lies within a certain range, you have to add two standard-error measurements to the child's actual score to get the top of the range and subtract two to get the bottom of the range. If one child had a particularly bad day and another a good one, four standard-error measurements could separate their actual scores when their true scores are the same!

And what about the validity of standardized, group tests? Let's say schools gave every child thirty different forms of the standardized reading test each spring (no doubt dramatically increasing the burnout rates for teachers, children, and parents!). Each child's average score across the thirty testings would certainly have a standard error that approached zero. What would each child's highly reliable average score mean? It would tell you how well the child could and would do on the kind of reading task the test employed. The question is, how much is the test's reading task like the reading tasks you had your children engage in during the year (curricular validity), and how much is it like the reading tasks your children are apt to engage in outside school over the years to come (authenticity)? To the extent that the reading test has your children do tasks that resemble your instruction and your long-term goals for them, you will probably think it yields valid scores. Otherwise, you will probably conclude that the test lacks validity.

These same problems exist with statewide writing tests. Such tests usually require students all over the state to write at one time to the same prompt. Again, looking at the average score of a large number of students on this writing test will tell you with reliability how well that group as a whole did on the test. However, anyone who has been involved in administering these tests will know that an excellent writer can often score very poorly on these tests and that a mediocre writer can sometimes do quite well. It seems to matter a lot how much an individual child knows or cares about the subject matter of the prompt. Other factors such as sickness, test anxiety, test wiseness, student frustration, and so on also play their customary roles. Moreover, the test is usually scored on the basis of whether a student's writing product conforms to a kind of formulaic writing. Children who were taught to write to the formula sometimes do better than children who were involved in a more authentic writing program. Still, these tests represent progress over an era when "writing" was tested without the children actually doing any writing.

Most schools and school districts administer standardized, group tests and use them to evaluate the reading and writing abilities of their students in general, or even classroom by classroom. The best standardized tests are reliable enough to be used in that way, but their validity is often questionable. Sadly, many schools also make decisions about individual child placement in special programs or even about promotion versus retention based on a single score on a standardized, group test. Experienced teachers have learned, however, that such tests of reading or writing really tell them almost nothing of value about their individual students or how to teach them better.

The Theory and Research Base for Assessment

Psychometrics is the science of measuring mental abilities, processes, and states. Of course, that definition includes measuring the relative strengths and weaknesses within a student's overall profile of reading or writing capabilities (diagnosis). It also includes measuring how well a student reads or writes at a particular point in time (assessment). From its beginnings a century or so ago, psychometrics has gradually given us a sophisticated body of theory and research on scientific concepts of measurement. Any teacher would certainly benefit from an increased knowledge of psychometrics, especially a practical understanding of the notions of validity and reliability in educational tests and measurement.

While psychometrics has developed into a science with much to teach us, most educational applications of psychometrics have been in the production of standardized tests of various kinds. These tests have generally been used in what Calfee and Hiebert (1991) call "externally mandated assessments": Federal, state, or local agencies, laws, or pressures, acting from without, compel schools and teachers to administer certain assessments in certain ways at certain times. The value of these "high-stakes tests" remains a matter of considerable controversy, but there seems to be a consensus among literacy educators that "internal assessment" (Calfee & Hiebert, 1991) holds much more promise for helping teachers improve student literacy.

Other terms for internal assessment include *curriculum-based assessment* (Fuchs & Fuchs, 1989), *assessment designed for instruction* (Calfee & Hiebert, 1991), *constructive evaluation* (Johnston, 1992), and *teacher-directed assessment* (Calfee & Hiebert, 1991). These various terms, and others like them, all imply that successful teachers of reading and writing evaluate their students continually in order to modify how they are teaching them. In addition, these terms imply that, whatever their value, externally mandated assessments can never be as useful to teachers as quality internal assessments that they administer and interpret for their own instructional purposes. Developing the ability to direct their own assessments is probably one of the most valuable professional skills teachers of literacy can acquire.

Actually, the notion of teacher-directed assessment has a long history in reading education. Betts (1946) advocated the individual informal reading inventory, administered and interpreted (and even constructed) by the teacher, some fifty years ago. Today, teachers can select from a number of commercially available informal reading inventories (Woods & Moe, 1999; Johns, 2001; Leslie & Caldwell, 2001; Silvaroli & Wheelock, 2001). Each of these inventories relies on teachers to decide when and whom they will test, how they will score the various subtests, and how they will interpret those scores.

Likewise, in writing education, there has been for several decades a tradition of teacher-directed assessment. Teachers of writing have been taught to achieve reliability and validity of assessment through either analytical or holistic scoring of student papers (Spandel, 1990). In Chapter 8 the discussion of writing scales as an evaluative tool subsumes both analytical and holistic systems for scoring writing. Rule-based writing scales are equivalent to analytic scoring systems used by students; form-based writing scales are equivalent to holistic scoring systems used by students. Teachers who use writing scales typically assess students' writing in their growth and cumulative portfolios with regard to the criteria on one or the other of the two kinds of writing scales.

A separate but related movement in recent theory and research on educational measurement has argued for more authentic measurement practices, both in externally mandated and teacher-directed assessment. "The aim of authentic assessment is to assess many different kinds of literacy abilities in contexts that closely resemble the actual situations in which those abilities are used" (Valencia, Hiebert, & Afflerbach, 1994, p. 9). It may be said that the move toward more authentic assessment involves increasing teacher-directed assessment and making externally mandated, high-stakes tests more like teacher-directed assessment.

L o o k i n g   B a c k

◦ ◦

If all children were alike, or could be taught as if they were, this chapter would not have been written. In order to meet the needs of all students, teachers must use the most reliable and valid assessments to determine reading levels, assess student learning, and monitor progress. This chapter discussed six key ideas:

1. Be sure your assessment is reliable and valid.
2. Determine instructional reading levels by observing how your students read.
3. Use observation and anecdotal records as the cornerstone of your assessment.
4. Include students' attitudes and interests in your assessment.
5. Create portfolios to monitor and demonstrate progress.
6. Beware of standardized tests.

 Add to Your Journal

What experience have you had working with children? Have you taught for several years? Do you have children of your own? Have you student-taught? Have you visited classrooms, been a counselor at a summer camp, taught Sunday school, or been a lifeguard? What do these experiences tell you about the need to observe children carefully? Can engagement, success, and achievement with instructional activities, as well as attitudes and interests, be observed? What do you remember about assessment? Was it synonymous with tests and grades? Make a plan for classroom assessment of literacy based on your experiences and on what you have learned in this chapter.

Application Activities

 Try It Out

Have a child select a piece to read to you. Do an oral reading analysis as the child reads, and then ask the child some questions to determine comprehension. Have the child continue reading passages until you find the highest-level passage in which the child can read 95 percent of the words and comprehend 75 percent of the ideas. This is the child's instructional level.

Try It Out

Find one child who writes regularly and work with that child to assemble a showcase that illustrates growth in writing. Let the child select what will go into the showcase portfolio and have the child caption those pieces. You should decide what will go into the growth portfolio and write a narrative description of what you included and what it demonstrates about the child's writing development.

Listen, Look, and Learn

Interview a teacher you trust at a grade level you would like to teach. Ask the teacher to show you what he or she does about assessment. Are anecdotal records kept? Are checklists used? Are writing samples collected and analyzed to determine instructional needs and document growth? What role do portfolios play in the assessment? If it seems appropriate, share some of the assessment ideas from this chapter. Compare and contrast what you learn about assessment from this interview with what you learned in this chapter.

References

Betts, E. A. (1946). *Foundations of reading instruction.* New York: American Book Co.

Calfee, R., & Hiebert, E. (1991). Classroom assessment of reading. In R. Barr, M. L. Kamil, P. B. Mosenthal, & P. D. Pearson (Eds.), *Handbook of reading research* (vol. 2, pp. 281–309). White Plains, NY: Longman.

Fuchs, L. S., & Fuchs, D. (1989). Curriculum-based assessment. In C. Reynolds & R. R. Kamphaus (Eds.), *Handbook of psychological and educational assessment of children: Vol. 1. Intelligence and achievement.* New York: Guilford.

Johns, J. L. (2001). *Basic reading inventory: Pre-primer through grade ten,* 8th ed. Dubuque, IA: Kendall/Hunt.

Johnston, P. H. (1992). *Constructive evaluation of literate activity.* White Plains, NY: Longman.

Lehr, F. (1985). A portrait of the American as reader. *Journal of Reading, 29,* 170–171.

Leslie, L., & Caldwell, J. (2001). *Qualitative reading inventory,* 3rd ed. Glenview, IL: Scott, Foresman.

Nunnally, J. C. (1967). *Psychometric theory* (p. 172). New York: McGraw-Hill.

Silvaroli, N. J., & Wheelock, W. H. (2001). *Classroom reading inventory,* 9th ed. Dubuque, IA: William C. Brown.

Spandel, V. (1990). *Creating writers: Linking assessment and writing instruction.* White Plains, NY: Longman.

Tierney, R. J., Carter, M. A., & Desai, L. E. (1991). *Portfolio assessment in the reading-writing classroom.* Norwood, MA: Christopher-Gordon.

Valencia, S. W., Hiebert, E. H., & Afflerbach, P. P. (1994). *Authentic reading assessment: Practices and possibilities.* Newark, DE: International Reading Association.

Woods, M. L., & Moe, A. J. (1999). *Analytical reading inventory,* 6th ed. Columbus, OH: Merrill.

Additional Readings

- If you are going to read one book on reading assessment, we highly recommend Joanne Caldwell's *Reading Assessment: A Primer for Teachers and Tutors.* We learned a lot from reading this book and enjoyed all her lively examples and analogies. It is clearly the most wonderfully written and practical book on reading assessment we have seen.

  Caldwell, J. *Reading Assessment: A primer for teachers and tutors.* New York: Guilford, 2002.

- These books have lots of practical suggestions for portfolio and other authentic assessment devices.

  Batzle, J. (1992). *Portfolio assessment and evaluation: Developing and using portfolios in the classroom.* Cypress, CA: Creative Teaching Press.

  DeFina, A. A. (1992). *Portfolio assessment: Getting started.* New York: Scholastic.

  Graves, D. H., & Sustein, B. S. (Eds.). (1992). *Portfolio portraits.* Portsmouth, NH: Heinemann.

  Jasmine, J. (1993). *Portfolios and other assessments.* Huntington Beach, CA: Teacher Created Materials.

- For detailed examples of running records and a wealth of other excellent diagnosis by observation instruments, see these two recent books by Marie Clay.

  Clay, M. M. (1993). *An observation survey: Of early literacy achievement.* Portsmouth, NH: Heinemann.

  Clay, M. M. (1993). *Reading recovery: A guidebook for teachers in training.* Portsmouth, NH: Heinemann.

- This article contains a wonderfully practical attitudes survey using the popular Garfield character.

  McKenna, M. C., & Kear, D. J. (1990). Measuring attitudes toward reading: A new tool for teachers. *The Reading Teacher, 43,* 626–639.

Planning and Organizing

Looking Ahead

Classrooms are complex environments in which one teacher and twenty to thirty children must carry out a variety of activities. There is always too much to be done and not enough space or time in which to do it. The fact that all children are different and come with their own personalities and learning preferences/difficulties further complicates the orchestration. Being a successful teacher requires a high level of knowledge of literacy development and instruction as well as an unswerving commitment to and love of children. In addition to knowledge and commitment, however, successful teachers must be good planners, observers, and organizers. In this chapter, we will help you think about the "nitty-gritty" issues of planning and organizing that sometimes make or break a teacher.

The key ideas presented in the previous chapters provide you with the major concepts and teaching strategies you need to create a classroom in which a variety of different children make steady progress toward the critical goal of becoming literate adults. To make all this work, however, you must develop some critical planning and organizing strategies. Beginning and veteran teachers alike report that classroom organization and management issues often get in the way of their accomplishing the goals they know they should and could accomplish. This chapter presents four key ideas:

1. Start your year with a plan.
2. Use a variety of grouping structures.
3. Engage parents as partners.
4. Enlist the help of others to meet the needs of all your students.

Start Your Year with a Plan

Planning is at the heart of successful teaching. Planning is thinking ahead, setting goals, and determining how much time you can allot to various activities. Successful teachers plan on at least four different levels—yearly, unit, weekly, daily—and each level of planning serves an important function. Planning at any of these levels requires that teachers observe their children analytically and make plans that consider their unique talents, needs, and interests.

Planning the Year

One of the most rejuvenating parts of teaching is that every year you get to start again! Most of us are convinced that "next year will be the best year ever!" Most teachers do a lot of thinking and planning between the time one year's class leaves for the summer and the next year's class arrives in the fall. Veteran teachers evaluate how well certain strategies, units, activities, and so on worked and plan to modify some, continue others in pretty much the same form, and drastically overhaul or dump others. Beginning teachers—or teachers who change grade levels—also engage in yearly planning and goal setting. The plans and goals of beginning teachers may have to be adjusted more quickly and more frequently, but having some idea where you are going is still preferable to the aimless day-by-day, minute-by-minute existence some beginning teachers complain characterized their first year of teaching.

There are, of course, a variety of ways to approach the yearly planning, and the approach you take will vary depending on your own learning style and your level of experience. Here are some possibilities for you to consider in making your own yearly plans.

List in simple language your most important literacy goals for your students. What do you want your students to do, think, feel, and experience related to reading and writing? This is the time to think about the big, important, obvious (and consequently often overlooked) goals:

They should come to see books and reading as enjoyable.

They should learn to use informational books to find out answers to questions they have and topics they wonder about.

They should learn to love poetry.

They should all publish some books.

They should learn how to read their social studies books.

They should read a variety of genres and come to know lots of different authors.

They should learn to revise and edit their own writing.

This is just a sampling of the big goals teachers might have, and what these goals are will depend on your own experience, your view of literacy, and your teaching situation. The important thing is not that the list be perfect or complete, but that it exist. In teaching, it is very easy to lose sight of the forest for the trees; one leading reading educator/professor who took off a year to teach in an elementary classroom and get back in daily contact with kids put it this way: "When you're up to your neck in alligators, it is hard to remember that you came in to drain the swamp!"

Your big goals will help you make the thousands of little decisions about time, materials, and so forth. Many teachers write their big goals on a large index card and tape it to a prominent spot on their desks. A quick glance at these goals is sometimes enough to help you get back on track.

Look through the curriculum guides and standards your school uses. Once you know what your personal goals for your students are, it is time to find out what goals your school or school system has set. Although there is a lot of variety across the different schools, most school systems and some states have written down somewhere the major topics, concepts, strategies, and so on that students should experience at each grade level. Curriculum guides can be very helpful if they are relatively short, practical, and up to date—or not helpful if they are long, detailed, and out of date. But helpful or not, if they exist, you need to know about them and consider them in your long-range planning. Once you find them and look through them, you will need to decide how much your instruction should reflect the established goals. In the fortunate event that your goals and teaching beliefs match much of what you find in the guides, your planning will be much easier. If you

Technology Tips

State standards can be found in a number of places on the Internet. One site that we have found useful is

www.putwest.boces.org/Standards.html

This site lists standards for all states that have them available. Other information is often available at these individual state sites, such as the state's assessment plan.

Examine the standards set by the International Reading Association and the National Council of Teachers of English for classrooms, and compare them to the other external standards you have examined. Familiarize yourself with both these professional groups by reading their journals and other publications. IRA also publishes an electronic journal, *Reading Online*. For additional information and resources, visit their websites:

www.ira.org

www.ncte.org

don't agree with what you find, ask (diplomatically) another teacher you respect and trust how closely he or she follows the guide. (If that teacher's response is "What guide? I don't remember us having a language arts guide," you can probably put the guide back where you found it.)

Look at all the materials/books/teaching aids you have available. This is a big job and not one you will be able to do thoroughly and carefully. But at least you should know what materials you have and how much you can use them to support your own goals and those you developed based on the curriculum guides. Once again, if your materials support the kind of literacy program you believe in, you are in luck! If not, you will need to ask your trusted friend how closely you are expected to stick to what is in the books and where other materials can be found.

List the big topics, goals, and strategies you will focus on and make some initial time allocations. Right now you are not setting a schedule or deciding minute-by-minute allocations, but you should decide such things as these:

How much time to give to each subject area you have to teach.

What integration you could do across subject areas so that you can "kill two birds with one stone."

How many weeks you can spend on each topic—science, health, social studies, math—allotting more time to more important topics but making sure you won't have six critical topics left over for May.

Yearly planning includes first deciding what your important goals are, what school system and state goals are, and what materials you have available and then coming up with some time allocation decisions so that you have some initial plan for the impossible task of getting it all done. Teachers who plan how they will do it all don't always meet all the various goals, but they come much closer than teachers who don't know all the big things they need to try to accomplish in one short year.

Unit Planning

After yearly planning, the next biggest chunk of planning most teachers do is planning certain units of instruction. This is usually a yearlong process in which teachers look at what needs to be taught and consider how to use the time and resources available to accomplish a variety of goals for a variety of students. Units can take a variety of forms. Sometimes, units are topically arranged. This is often the case in the content areas where energy or Australia or drugs might be the unit focus. Literacy units are also sometimes organized around a topic. Students in first grade might spend a few weeks reading lots of bear books—both fiction and nonfiction—while older students might spend time reading a variety of stories and books related to the Old West. Literacy units sometimes revolve around a particular author such as Eric Carle or Katherine Patterson, a particular theme such as courage or ethnic differences/similarities, or a particular genre such as mysteries, poetry, or historical fiction. In addition to reading that supports the focus of the unit, writing helps students focus on the unit. Students might write about a particularly coura-geous person they have known, write a poem in the style of a poet being studied, or write a mystery for classmates to solve.

Sometimes literacy units revolve around particular strategies. Students might read lots of different stories and use these to discuss story elements such as setting, character, story problem, or theme. Students might then compose stories and work on these story elements in their own writing. Students might read informational texts and learn how to sort out the main ideas from the details and perhaps how to web or outline the most important ideas. The writing component of this informa-tional text structure unit would teach students how to write well-formed para-graphs and eventually how to combine these into longer informational pieces.

In many classrooms today, unit planning cuts across the curriculum. Teachers planning a science, health, or social studies unit find materials for the students to read and identify writing tasks that not only help the children learn the science in-formation but also provide real purposes for reading and writing. Sometimes, teachers begin the unit with the literature they want children to read and then see how that literature leads students into discoveries in other parts of the curriculum.

Unit planning varies greatly according to the focus of the unit, the needs of the students, and the purposes and beliefs of the teacher. Good unit planning, however, requires that the teacher list the major goals for the unit, provide for a variety of materials and activities within the unit that will meet the needs and abilities of a wide range of children, and plan some assessment activities that will allow both students and teacher to see how much was learned.

Weekly and Daily Planning

Most schools require that teachers have weekly plans, and some schools require that these plans be turned in to the office before teachers leave on Friday afternoon. Some schools require that plans be written in a specific format, and other schools leave it to each teacher to determine how best to write down these plans. (Check with your trusted, respected teacher friend.) Generally, beginning teachers need to write down more detailed plans than do veteran teachers who "carry all that wealth of information around in their heads."

Weekly planning is a much easier task when it has been preceded by some yearly and unit planning. The time allocations across the week should reflect those you decided based on a careful consideration of important goals and topics during yearly planning. A three-week unit on mysteries might involve the whole class of students in reading and discussing the same mystery the first week, choosing one of three mysteries to read and discuss in a literature circle the second week, and collaboratively writing mysteries the third week. If you have two weeks to do a sci-ence unit on energy, the first week might be spent on sharing beginning informa-tion and ideas together as a whole class, and the second week might be spent having the students do experiments and gather information in small groups. The final day would be spent in having children share what they learned and assessing with them the success of the unit.

Weekly planning also requires that the time you decided should be given to re-curring activities is actually devoted to those activities. If children are going to write something every day, when is this going to happen? If children are going to engage in self-selected reading every day, when is this going to happen? If you believe you should read aloud to children several times during the day, when is this going to occur?

Daily planning usually involves looking at what was accomplished—and what wasn't accomplished—today and then adjusting tomorrow's plan based on your evaluation of today. Often teachers include the children in daily planning. Many teachers sit down with the children during the last fifteen minutes of each day and have a class meeting in which they discuss a variety of things, including a look back at what the class, small groups, and individuals accomplished and a preview of what the class will be trying to accomplish tomorrow. Teachers who involve the students in planning—including some weekly and unit planning as the year goes on—find that children are more motivated to meet the goals and accomplish the tasks when they have some say in determining what those goals and tasks will be and how and when they will get done.

Use a Variety of Grouping Structures

Think back to your reading experiences in elementary school. What did reading time look like? Some of us remember the teacher assigning us to a selection that we read silently and independently, completing a worksheet when ready. Many of us recall sitting in a circle with the teacher. We took turns reading aloud in a group of chil-dren of similar ability. Others of us recall the teacher calling on students as we sat in our seats—often placed in rows—to read aloud before the whole class. Our role, when not reading aloud in these last two instances, was to follow along with the reader. A few of us will recall that we were allowed to select our own reading mate-rials daily to read silently and then discuss with the teacher or a group of other stu-dents who were reading the same thing. Believe it or not, you would see very similar things happening today during reading time in American schools. Grouping pat-terns should be selected to accomplish specific goals. Teachers can accommodate a wide range of instructional purposes by matching the grouping with the purpose. The following descriptions of four grouping structures—teacher-led whole group, teacher-led small group, cooperative groups/partnerships, individuals—allow teach-ers to accomplish any goal they set.

Teacher-Led Whole Group

Teacher-led, whole-group instruction is selected when the teacher knows that most of the students do not have the experience, concept, strategy, or skill. When the teacher reads aloud to students daily, that is a type of teacher-led, whole-group les-son. The teacher also frequently conducts whole-group lessons when introducing or culminating a unit of study. Teachers may introduce a selection of reading materials to the whole group with a book talk to familiarize students with the books they can choose from for their student-led, small-group lessons. Teachers often conduct whole-class focus lessons, which target a particular comprehension or writing skill that most of the students do not yet have.

When teachers conduct whole-group lessons, however, the tendency is to teach to the middle of the group. The best whole-group lessons recognize that there is a range of student abilities and provide multilevel instruction to accommodate the range. When lessons are multilevel, teachers are able to engage the students rather than leaving them behind or boring them with too much repetition. Modifying questions is one way to provide multilevel instruction. Rather than asking "Who can find a word that begins with c on our chart?" a teacher may ask students "What do you notice about the letters and words on our chart?" This type of question opens up the response options to many more students and allows for even more literacy learning with the expanded responses you'll get. The chapters in the second part of this book present numerous examples of how teachers make whole-group instruction multilevel.

Teacher-Led Small Groups

Teacher-led, small-group instruction is structured so that the teacher assigns the groups and specific duties or requirements for the different members of the groups. If several students have similar reading levels, it is not always necessary to teach these students individually. The teacher may sit with a group that is reading from the reading series, for example, and guide children's reading of the text. Guided reading is one of the most common examples of teacher-led small groups. The major concern with teacher-led small groups is that they be flexible, rather than static. These groups should form around a short-term purpose and dissolve after the purpose is met.

Cooperative Groups/Partnerships

Cooperative groups come in lots of forms. A "group" might be five students or a pair. The old saying that "two heads are better than one" has proved true in classrooms. A whole body of research under the heading of "cooperative learning" demonstrates that when children work together on something, all children learn more (Johnson & Johnson, 1985). There are many opportunities in every classroom every day for children to work together on something. At other times, teachers may let the children choose a subject or activity of interest, and the groups will be formed by children who chose the same thing. Groups can research questions, share and respond to each other's writing, prepare a play for the class, make a mural, or do any number of other activities. When the teacher structures the classroom so that working together in school is as normal as it is in real life, there are many "little teachers" in the class.

Children can work together on many activities. Children like to read to each other in a reading center or to read each other's writing in a writing center. Young children enjoy partner reading, in which they take turns reading or rereading the pages of a favorite book. Children can work together in research groups to find information and plan how to make reports.

Children can even do worksheets together. Assign two children of similar ability who like working together to be worksheet partners. To be sure that both children are working and thinking, assign one partner to be the "thinker" and the other partner to be the "writer." The thinker's job is to read each question and tell what he or she thinks the answer is. The writer's job is to write the answer if the writer agrees and to explain to the thinker why the answer is wrong and what the right answer would be if the writer does not agree. If they cannot reach agreement on the correct answer, they write both answers with their initials next to them. As you can imagine, a lot of learning goes on as the two children try to convince each other why their answer is correct. If they cannot reach agreement, they are eager to bring their worksheet to the group to see who was right. The next day the children switch roles. The thinker becomes the writer and the writer becomes the thinker.

Literature Circles and Book Clubs are two very popular types of student-led small groups. In these configurations, students who have selected the same material read it together and complete assigned activities together. The format of Literature Circles and Book Clubs parallels what real readers do when they get together to talk about books with friends on their own.

Individuals

For some portion of each day, children should be working on their own. Children read on their own during Self-Selected Reading time. They write on their own when they are writing first drafts. Teachers work with individuals when they conference with them about their Self-Selected Reading and when they work with them in publishing conferences. Teachers also pull individual students to do some assessment or some individual tutoring. The teacher may have identified a particular student who just needed that little extra boost in order to understand the content that was presented in one of the group settings. The teacher finds ten minutes when others are engaged in seatwork, are at a center, or are in cooperative groups. That ten minutes of focused instruction can be very powerful in student learning.

Effective teachers use all these grouping patterns across a school day to accomplish different purposes. Using a variety of grouping structures is one of the major ways in which teachers can accommodate that wide range of student interests and abilities found in every classroom.

Engage Parents as Partners

Teachers can capitalize on parental interest and take the opportunity to update parents on how schooling is a new and improved version of what they remember. Always begin your year with a parent meeting that explains your goals, your curriculum, and your instructional practices. To help parents understand what you intend and why, engage them as actively as you can during the meeting. You will have more effect on their understanding of how you will develop phonics skills if you take them through a "Making Words" lesson than if you just tell them about it. Give them the letters *a, e, n, p, r, s,* and *t* and have them make *at, pat, sat, set, pet, pets, pest, rest, rent, sent, spent,* and finally see if they can guess the secret word—"parents!" Show them how you can sort for rhyming words and then use these rhyming words to decode and spell more words such as *bent, vet, brat,* and *chest.* After going through this lesson, parents will much more clearly understand how engaged their children will be in learning and one of the ways you will go about teaching them to read and write. Showing, not telling, is a good teaching principle to use with parents as well as students.

Parent conferences offer another opportunity to show parents what you are teaching and how well students are learning. Sometimes teachers involve students by asking them to provide entries and comments on the teacher-selected entries for a folder that will be shared with parents. Sometimes students even join in for part or all of the conference to ensure that all parties hear and understand the same information. Most often, though, the teacher alone prepares a folder that is to be both snapshots of the child at points in time and a plan for learning for the remainder of the year. These conferences are time-consuming in preparation and in meeting time. However, it is one part of the current school routine that neither parents nor teachers wish to surrender because the face-to-face dialogue (meaning both parents and teacher share freely) has the potential for making a real difference for children and their learning.

Staying Connected with Parents

You can connect with parents and enlist their support and involvement in numerous small ways. Divide your class number by the number of weeks in the month and make positive phone calls each week to those homes. Making a call or two a day after school to tell parents about something their children learned that day or something difficult that you noticed they accomplished is well worth the small amount of time it takes. When you have to make a call enlisting their support later on with an issue that must be resolved, the receptivity to your request is much higher than it would be if that were your first call to those parents.

Another simple way to connect with parents is sending newsletters, checklists, or notes home on a regular basis. Many teachers prepare a standard, one-page newsletter that outlines the week's work and upcoming special events. They leave a spot on the newsletter for a special comment about each child in order to personalize the newsletter. Sentence stems that some teachers find helpful in creating those personal comments are similar to these:

> (Name) worked really hard on this project and did great work.
>
> Be sure to ask (Name) what she found most interesting in our science unit.
>
> I was really surprised when (Name) (asked about, did, figured out something).

(Name) made some major contributions to our class discussions this week.

(Name) is very helpful to others in the class.

(Name) set really high expectations for himself this week and met them.

A third kind of simple connection to make with parents is with a set of color-coded bookmarks that accompany books sent home each day. These bookmarks can be made from laminated construction paper to help them last longer (and to keep them from "bleeding" if they get wet) or from colored tagboard. The red bookmarks all say, "Read to me." Tell parents that when that bookmark comes home in a book, you would like them to sit and read that book to their children at least once. Other family members or the childcare provider might also read the book to the child. The blue bookmarks say, "Read together." This bookmark is put into books that you think have parts easy enough for the child to read sections of (like repetitive phrases) or to read when some cues are given by parents ("Look at the picture to see if that helps," or "What starts that way that makes sense here?"). The parent may alternate pages with the child as another way to get through the book. The third bookmark, a yellow one, says, "I can read this myself." Parents should listen to children read and provide cuing if needed. However, this level of book has likely been practiced at school and is meant to be read independently to an audience. Teachers sometimes write some short reminder on the back of the bookmarks to help parents remember what their role is to be with each kind of book. On the back of the red bookmark for reading to the child, for example, the teacher might include a suggestion for cuddling into a chair together and encourage the parent to read expressively and use different voices for the various characters. The bookmark might also suggest questions that could be asked during the reading, like "Why would he do that?," "What is going to happen now?," and "Can you smell the mud (feel the pebbles, hear the waves, etc.)?" Parents who read to their children develop positive attitudes about reading and background information; parents who discuss what they are reading with their children also build an understanding of how to make sense of print.

Helping Parents Know the Role to Play

Knowing what role to play can be very confusing for today's parents. What kind of help can they give their children? Is it "cheating" to work on a big project together? Shouldn't children do their homework alone? When teachers clarify their expectations to parents about the kinds and amount of involvement they can have, children, parents, and teachers all benefit. You might want to have these discussions with teachers at your grade level, or the school may want to publicize some schoolwide expectations. Even if the school or your grade-level teachers are unwilling to state expectations, *you* must. Ask yourself what helped you to be the learner you are. Likely you will remember that your mom never let you watch television until you had finished your homework. Or you might remember that you always did your homework at the kitchen table while your parents cleaned up the dinner dishes, making it handy to ask them a homework question that you were puzzling over. Perhaps you remember that your dad always went over your homework to check it before he declared you to be done. You possibly remember how that big Egyptian project became a family affair as both parents aided you in locating and constructing objects while also guiding the development of the accompanying report. None of this was cheating. None of this pre-empted your work. Rather, you became a stronger student with these kinds of supports in place to help you understand your work better. Isn't that what you want for all of your students, too? Do you remember a classmate who didn't have those kinds of supports at home? We do. Most of those students didn't do as well in school as we did. While we may have chafed at having dad always check the homework, there was some security in knowing that we would not be taking poor work to school.

Teachers of our own children have been very good about clarifying the role they expect us to play. When a project is due, the project expectations and criteria (even point values) are identified from the beginning. There is a place for indicating who helped with the project and what kind of help they provided. This "up front" acknowledgment that some parents are going to help (and that it is okay to do so) sends a message to all parents that they can help with the project, just in case they thought they weren't allowed to. With all types of assignments, both daily and long-range, specify the parental role clearly.

Enlist the Help of Others to Meet the Needs of all Your Students

Most elementary teachers sometimes feel like the Little Red Hen. They have to do everything and no one wants to help. Although we all feel that way on "down" days, it usually is not true. You have grade-level colleagues, special teachers, and volunteers who can help you in various ways so that you can meet the needs of all your students.

Getting by with a Little Help from Your Friends

Your colleagues at your grade level are an obvious first resource. Informal conversations happen before and after school and at grade-level planning sessions. You can formalize some of this talk by asking if a part of each of your grade-level meetings can be devoted to individual students each of you is struggling with, either because they are having trouble learning or you are having trouble providing enough challenge. "I'm kinda worried about . . . " sessions focus on students and help bring teachers' thinking back to the reason they are working on the new unit of instruction or selecting instructional materials as their main meeting agenda.

Some teachers have developed a formal structure across grade levels to provide instructional and management suggestions for teachers prior to calling in the district-level psychologist and other specialists to the structured "Child Study Team" meeting. The Child Study Team is a structure that provides input from parents, teachers, and specialists (like the special reading teacher, special education teacher, school psychologist, speech pathologist, occupational or physical therapist, and others as appropriate) who have observed and assessed the student. These sessions must be requested and planned, usually many months in advance.

At some schools, teachers decided to provide an intermediary step that is highly focused, not so time-consuming, and more immediate for the teacher to use. A group of teachers, selected for the year, meets together with the classroom teacher when he or she identifies a child who may need a Child Study Team later on. They have found this group to be highly effective. Many students who would have been referred to Child Study in the past are helped by the interventions teachers' colleagues suggest, and the teacher is provided with suggestions from an expert group who may have taught a child very much like that one.

Coordinating with Special Teachers

When you have a need for additional help, and after you have talked with grade-level colleagues, you might seek the help of the school's special reading teacher or special education teacher if you have these services at your school. These teachers have received additional training and often have a lot of experience dealing with struggling students. Be prepared for them to ask you questions such as the following:

> "How does her listening comprehension compare to reading comprehension?
> "What is his instructional reading level?
> "What types of comprehension seem easy? Hard?
> "What are her strengths in literacy? What is the hardest thing for her to do?
> "What strategies does he regularly use when decoding?"

These specialist teachers may be able to provide you with resources or strategies to use for a particular child. They can also be a resource for general literacy information for school or grade-level inservice sessions.

In some schools, classroom teachers and specialist teachers work together by sharing lesson plans. The classroom teacher shares lesson plans for reading and language arts with the special program teacher, who uses that as one source of information in planning instruction. Even better than simply sharing the plans is to sit together and jointly create the lessons to be offered in both situations. Of course, this requires finding time for both teachers to meet, but in some schools that recognize how crucial classroom and specialist teacher collaboration is, joint planning time is being built into the schedule.

These specialists also count on you to provide them with feedback on students they have in your class, just as they keep you informed about that student's work while with them. Some classroom and specialist teachers communicate with regular notes or checklists that identify areas of instruction as well as strengths and limitations that have been identified. Some teachers send a notebook back and forth with the child that each one can write in to inform the other. In the notebook, the classroom teacher simply notes the classroom material being used and the focus of the lesson that day. In addition, the classroom teacher might jot down a comment about the child's performance (e.g., Tim had difficulty following the story line) or a particular skill or strategy needing additional attention (e.g., Tim has real difficulty with long words. He seems not to know how to break them down into more manageable components). The special program teacher jots notes back to the classroom teacher and returns the notebook with the child after their instructional session. The point is that the notes do not have to be long or complicated, especially if they are jotted down regularly. The more closely the classroom and special area teacher can work together, the better for the student. When classroom and intervention program instruction are aligned, students make more progress.

In an increasing number of schools, special program teachers provide their instructional support in the regular classroom rather than in a location down the hall. The fundamental goal of these "in-class" instructional support models is to improve classroom instruction through developing shared knowledge and creating more coherent instructional interventions. In addition, students should lose less instructional time in transition from one setting to another.

Volunteers

Finally, consider volunteers—older children, parents, senior citizens. In some schools, parents who bring their children to school or who pick them up stay an extra half hour or come a half hour early and provide individual attention to children who need it. These volunteers can provide some valuable instruction through simple activities such as listening to a child reread a familiar book, helping the child write a story, or supporting a child's writing on a computer. Computers offer some wonderful opportunities for children who have coordination problems or are terrible spellers. When equipped with spelling checks and other writing-support programs, these children can often produce writing they can be proud of.

In many schools, the oldest children in the school volunteer a half hour each day in a younger grade. Upper-grade struggling readers provide tutoring to younger students as part of the intervention for the older student. Tutors frequently learn more than the ones being tutored. When older struggling readers read regularly to kindergartners or first-graders, they have a legitimate excuse for reading and rereading "easy" books. Older children who help younger children practice their math facts usually get some practice themselves. Older children who know how to write on the computer can teach younger children how to do this and increase their fluency with the computer at the same time.

The Theory and Research Base for Planning and Organization

Numerous analyses of teaching recognize the significance of planning. For instance, Danielson's (1996) framework places *Planning and Preparation* as one of the four essential domains of professional practice, along with *Classroom Environment, Instruction,* and *Professional Responsibilities.* Research from the 1980s showed how teachers' deliberative thinking before instruction differed from their immediate decision making during instruction. Reports by McCutcheon (1980) and Clark and Yumger (1987) clearly demonstrated teachers planning at different levels such as yearly, unit, weekly, and daily. These reports explained how a process of problem finding and problem solving affected decisions made at one level, which in turn affected decisions at other levels.

Instructional decisions about grouping are another important aspect of teachers' plans. Teachers and students perceive distinctive teaching-learning opportunities when students work individually, in pairs, in small groups, and as a whole class (Elbaum, Schumm, & Vaughn, 1997; Moody, Vaughn, & Schunun, 1997). Oral reading, listening to stories, and analyzing words are among the activities that bring students together (Cunningham, Hall, & Defee, 1998; Pardo & Raphael, 1991; Radencich & McKay, 1995). Groups are complex and powerful teaching tools that contribute to numerous intended and unintended social, emotional, and intellectual consequences (Webb & Palincsar,1996).

Home-school connections are especially important (Cohn-Vargas & Grose, 1998; Comer & Haynes, 1991; Epstein, 1995), and numerous home-school programs that address literacy have been studied. For instance, parents who share with teachers knowledge of their children's literacy development have been shown to help teachers design better instruction (Lazar & Weisberg, 1996). A model called the "ABC's of Cultural Understanding and Communication" (Schmidt, 1998) helped teachers expand students' opportunities for reading and writing. Family literacy programs can assist parents, children, and other adults in the house to mutually support each others' reading and writing (Edwards, 1990).

L o o k i n g   B a c k

If all children were alike, or could be taught as if they were, this chapter would not have been written. In order to meet the needs of all students, teachers must plan. Next, they must organize, using the time they have as effectively as possible by considering which group structures are most efficient for which activities. Finally, successful teachers don't try to "go it alone." They communicate with and enlist the support of parents, other teachers, and volunteers. This chapter presented four key ideas:

1. Start your year with a plan.
2. Use a variety of grouping structures.

3. Engage parents as partners.

4. Enlist the help of others to meet the needs of all your students.

A p p l i c a t i o n   A c t i v i t i e s

Do It Together

Work with others at your grade level to make a plan for reading and writing instruction for one year. Don't get too specific, but do list your big goals and consider grade-level goals and standards in the school or district you will be teaching in. Consider major units you will teach and look at materials to see what is available and what you need to cover in a year's time. Try to come up with some estimates of how long you can spend on particular topics and units.

Listen, Look, and Learn

Interview a classroom teacher you respect about how that teacher plans for the year, unit, week, and each day and how that teacher assesses students' needs and abilities in reading and writing. What kind of observational records are kept? Are portfolios part of the assessment? Are the children learning how to self-assess their progress? Finally, ask the teacher about organization. What kinds of different group structures are used for what? How does the teacher enlist the support of parents and other individuals?

R e f e r e n c e s

Clark, C. M., & Yinger, R. J. (1987). Teacher planning. In J. Calderhead (Ed.), *Exploring teachers' thinking* (pp. 84–103). London: Cassell.

Cohn-Vargas, B., & Grose, K. (1998). A partnership for literacy. *Educational Leadership, 55(8),* 45–48.

Comer, J. P., & Haynes, N. M. (1991). Parent involvement in schools: An ecological approach. *The Elementary School Journal, 91,* 271–277.

Cunningham, P. M., Hall, D. P., & Defee, M. (1998). Nonability-grouped, multilevel instruction: Eight years later. *The Reading Teacher, 51,* 652–665.

Danielson, C. (1996). *Enhancing professional practice: A framework for teaching.* Alexandria, VA: Association for Curriculum and Supervision Development.

Edwards, P. A. (1990). *Parents as partners in reading.* Chicago: Children's Press.

Elbaum, B. E., Schumm, J. S., & Vaughn, S. (1997). Urban middle-elementary students' perceptions of grouping formats for reading instruction. *The Elementary School Journal, 97,* 475–500.

Epstein, J. L. (1995). School/family/community partnerships: Caring for the children we share. *Phi Delta Kappan, 76,* 701–712.

304 Part One * Reading and Writing . . .

Johnson, D. W., & Johnson, R. T. (1985). Cooperative learning and adaptive education. In M. C. Wang & H. J. Walberg (Eds.), *Adapting instruction to individual differences*. Berkeley, CA: McCutchan.

Lazar, A. M., & Weisberg, R. (1996). Inviting parents' perspectives: Building home–school partnerships to support children who struggle with literacy. *The Reading Teacher, 50,* 228–251.

McCutcheon, G. (1980). How do elementary school teachers plan? The nature of planning and influences on it. *The Elementary School Journal, 81,*4–23.

Moody, S. W., Vaughn, S., & Schumm, J. S. (1997). Instructional grouping for reading: Teachers' views. *Remedial and Special Education, 18,* 347–356.

Pardo, L. S., & Raphael, T. E. (1991). Classroom organization for instruction in content areas. *The Reading Teacher, 44,* 556–565.

Radencich, M. C., & McKay, L. J. (Eds.). (1995). *Flexible grouping for literacy in elementary grades.* Boston: Allyn & Bacon.

Schmidt, P. R. (1998). The ABC's model: Teachers connect home and school. In T. Shanahan & F. V. Rodriguez-Brown (Eds.), *47th yearbook of the National Reading Conference* (pp. 194–208). Chicago: National Reading Conference.

Webb, N. M., & Palincsar, A. S. (1996). Group processes in the classroom. In D. C. Berliner & R. C. Calfee (Eds.), *Handbook of educational psychology* (pp. 841–873). New York: Simon & Schuster Macmillan.

Additional Readings

- These books are excellent sources of information for organizing classrooms for balanced literacy instruction.

  McVitty, W. (Ed.). (1986). *Getting it together: Organizing the reading-writing classroom.* Portsmouth, NH: Heinemann.

  Wong H. K., & Wong, R. T. (1998). *The first days of school,* 2nd ed. Sunnyvale, CA: Wong Publications.

- This book is a good source of authentic, holistic reading and writing activities for children with special needs.

  Rhodes, L. K., & Dudley-Marling, C. (1988). *Readers and writers with a difference: A holistic approach to teaching learning disabled and remedial students.* Portsmouth, NH: Heinemann.

. . . In *Elementary* *Classrooms*

The Retreat

Mr. Topps looked over the agenda for the faculty retreat on teaching reading and writing. Getting the money for stipends for the whole faculty had taken some finagling, but he was a problem-solving principal! A district-level grant and some money his site council had raised provided the funding he needed to add two workdays to the school year just ended. He believed a retreat was needed because he and his faculty had never really taken the time to work on instructional principles for literacy. Though the teachers were ready for their summer break, everyone had agreed it was better to do major work like this now so that they had the summer to plan the coming year.

In preparation for the retreat, Tip had papered the room with posters he called his "brainwashings." These were the things he believed in and that helped guide his daily practice as an instructional leader in the school. He knew the teachers were somewhat familiar with them, because he regularly brought them up during his conferences with them after observing their teaching.

They can ALL learn to read and write.

More children are "instructionally disabled" than "learning disabled."

You are a gifted teacher of gifted children.

Teach children not the curriculum.

Think outside the box!

As the first group of teachers began to arrive, Mr. Topps put them to work distributing markers, paper, note cards, and other supplies they were going to need for their work together. Some teachers had also gathered around the brainwashings, and as he walked around distributing copies of the agenda, he heard them wondering whether they were all supposed to subscribe to these ideas. He also overheard conversational bits as teachers arrived and glanced over the agenda. Someone at Helen Launch's table of kindergarten teachers remarked that there was no way this agenda was going to take all the time scheduled for the retreat; but when he passed by the third-grade teachers' table, he heard Vera Wise say that there was no way they could finish all the agenda in the time scheduled for the retreat. He hoped the truth was somewhere in between.

Mr. Topps welcomed the group of teachers before him and told them he had always wondered about the word "retreat" because his intent for these few days was to make progress, but when he asked for funding for a "progress" nobody bit. After the light laughter died down, he placed an overhead transparency on the projector and read it aloud.

> I am only one.
>   Still I am one.
>   I cannot do everything.
>   Still I can do something.
>   Because I cannot do everything,
>   I will not refuse to do the something I can do.
>   Edward Everett Hale

After a pause, he continued, "These are some of the words I try to live both my professional and personal life by. Imperfectly, at times, I admit. Hale's poem causes me to accept responsibility and not to give up in the face of overwhelming circumstances. Take a bit of the problem and deal with that. At least try, he says to me. I'd like each of you to take a file card and write down some words you use to help guide your life. We will be sharing these in a few minutes." Mr. Topps leaned against the table and watched the group. At the end of three minutes he told them to share their guiding words with their grade-level group. Then he called on some of the teachers who volunteered to share with the whole group.

"Well," began Helen Launch, "I had never really thought about it like this before, but when I was in college I read some of Haim Ginott's work, and one thing really stuck with me. He said, 'Treat every child as if he already is the person he is capable of becoming.' I know I try to live those words as I teach children. I really do believe they can all learn to read and write, and I know if I act that way, in my behaviors, the language I use with each child, and in the instructional choices I make, then they all will learn." The murmurs around the room showed how impressed her colleagues were with Helen's explanation.

Yetta Maverick chimed in from the fourth-grade teachers' table. "Helen, I didn't know that quote before, but I copied it down on my card right next to Hale's poem. It just feels right to me! Oh, Tip? How many cards are we each allocated? Anyway, what I wrote was a quote attributed to Martin Luther. He purportedly said, 'Even if I knew certainly the world would end tomorrow, I would plant an apple tree today.' What Luther says, to me anyway, is similar to Hale's poem—do something, don't just sit there, but it goes further than Hale. Be hopeful; there's always a chance; don't give up; make the world different because you were here."

Frank Lee piped up to say, "You know, the words that have meant the most to me are, 'Every child has a right to a safe and orderly environment in which to grow into a physically and mentally healthy adult who is an eager lifelong learner.' These are the words that have meant the most to me as I teach," Frank finished as the room erupted in laughter to hear their school's mission statement used in this context.

The sharing of guiding words continued for several more minutes before Mr. Topps cut into the lively discussions and told them they had to get on to other agenda items. Anyone who wanted to share their guiding words with the whole group could put them in the center of the table, and he would have Ms. Mainstay, the school secretary, type them up for everyone. He suggested that teachers take their own guiding words (and any that were appropriate from others) and put them on posters in their classroom next year. "Start the year by sharing the words with the students and telling them how you live out the words in your daily life," Tip suggested.

Next, Tip directed them to his posters. "Some of you recognize these things from conversations we have had. I call these my brainwashings because I really like them. Talk with your grade level about any relationships you see between the guiding words everyone shared and the brainwashings. Also decide if any of the brainwashings make sense for your grade level. If not, why not? If so, how?"

After this activity, Mr. Topps helped the teachers think about what makes avid readers and writers. "You all know avid readers; you may even be one. Take an index card and write the names of five avid readers—yourself, children you have taught, anyone."

"Only five, Tip?" queried Will Minter, a second-grade teacher, with a grin.

"Only five," he responded.

Mr. Topps paused for them to jot down names. "Now, circle one name. On the back of the card, write down how you know that person is an avid reader." He again paused to allow them to respond. "Now, talk with the others at your table about the person you selected and the evidence of avid reading you have observed."

Tip listened in on the discussions at various tables. When he heard them winding down, he switched on the overhead again. "Tell me what you notice about avid readers," he asked. Tip began to record their comments on the overhead transparency.

stacks of books around	always has a book
talks about books	has a good vocabulary
knows lots of stuff	owns lots of books
gives books as presents	wants books as presents

"Now write the names of five avid writers you know, and we'll go through the whole process again."

"Do we have to have five names, Tip?" asked Will.

"Try," Mr. Topps responded.

The teachers settled back down to brainstorming names, selecting one name, and then finding evidence of avid writing. Sadly, many teachers could not think of five avid writers they knew. As the process continued, they also discovered that the evidences of avid writing were not as clear to them either. They did finally produce a short list, which Tip compiled on a transparency too. They discussed why it was harder to know who writes a lot and enjoys it. They decided that readers are more likely to talk about what they are reading than writers are to talk about their own writings. While both reading and writing may be solitary endeavors, writing is even more so, and the joy of writing less obvious to the observer.

Mr. Topps continued, "If this is what avid readers and writers are like, let's keep this in mind as we do our curriculum planning. Everything we do ought to be with the goal in mind of creating avid readers and writers. Use these behaviors to gauge your students against. Are you helping to shape avid readers and writers with each instructional decision you make?"

A quick glance at the clock showed him that the morning was already over. The salad-and-sub-bar lunch was quickly set out, including some cheesecake that Frank Lee's sister Sara had sent, and the group settled into talking about the morning's activities and their upcoming summer plans.

When the teachers returned after lunch, they found that name tags had been placed on all the tables. "Ah ah ah!" Tip waggled his finger as Linc Toomey and Ed Dunn tried to get their name tags together at a table by trying to trade places with Vera Wise. "No trading! You think I went to all this trouble so you could mix them up any way you want?" He grinned to take the sting out of his comment.

"Gee, Tip. Ed and I need to be together. We're working on that big tech project in his room, y'know," Linc implored. No soap! Ed and Linc gave in to the inevitability of the grouping and went around warning others of the dire consequences that would befall switchers.

"What do you notice about the people sitting with you at your table this afternoon? Isn't that a good multilevel question, Helen?" Tip asked a kindergarten teacher as they were starting the session.

"It is a good multilevel question, Tip! I noticed we are from different grade levels," said Rita Wright, her first-grade self squeezed into a space between a fourth-grade and a kindergarten teacher.

"Exactly so," he responded. "For this afternoon's work, we need thinkers representing different experiences and understandings about a range of student abilities, ages, and curricula. The instructional principles we formulate must reflect our whole school, and if you only worked with your grade level, you would be less likely to consider the full range of students we deal with. Our students come to us with a range of individual, cultural, and language differences. We must teach all of them. Among us we ought to have a pretty good idea of what that will take.

"That is not to say we must all teach reading and writing alike. Shared instructional principles simply means we have agreed to some overall guidelines that give our program continuity and integrity. You all know how much I believe that teachers are professionals, and as such, you should have freedom to select instructional materials, methodologies, and practices that fit your unique perspectives, abilities, and philosophies. However . . . " Tip paused for effect, then continued, "However, we must agree to some instructional principles because we have a responsibility to do our best to ensure that all students learn to read and write as well and as much as they can.

"Each table has a sheet of chart paper. Designate a scribe for your group. The writer will put 'Children learn literacy best . . . ' at the top. Also designate a speaker who will explain your list to the whole group. Your group, including the writer and speaker, is to generate as many things as you can think of that finish that sentence stem. Use the brainwashings around the room, any other products we created this morning, and your own understandings and experiences. For example, were I in your group, I would suggest that we write, 'Children learn literacy best when actively engaged.' I would also suggest that we include 'Children learn literacy best through repetition with variety.'"

Teachers talked together, generated lists, posted their lists on the wall, and then shared information about their lists. The activity took them up to their break time. When they returned from break, they found another blank sheet of chart paper on their tables.

"This time I want you to think about the instructional implications of all these wonderful things you believe about how children learn literacy best. If you believe that children learn literacy best when actively engaged—which, by the way, I see made it onto every group's list—if you believe that, then what must teachers do to ensure that this occurs? Writers, label this sheet 'Teachers should . . . ' Now, spend twenty-five minutes again creating your chart. First fifteen minutes on talking, last ten finalizing language and writing it out."

"That's harder!" protested one table.

The sharing by groups of the ideas on the second chart took them up to the end of the day. Mr. Topps introduced Sue Port, the district curriculum supervisor, in case any teachers had not met her. She was going to join them for the next day's sessions. The teachers hung their "Teachers should . . . " charts on the wall and headed home.

The next day, Tip kicked off the session. "Okay. Ready for the next step. We are going to work on this all morning. Your group needs to schedule your own fifteen-minute break. Agree first when that will be. Second, start generating a list of the literacy instructional principles every classroom teacher in this school ought to be guided by. For example, in the past we have agreed as a school that we would all have self-selected reading daily. Maybe you think we should keep that or maybe you think it should be history. We have always said that we believe in having high expectations and that all children can learn to read and write. Do we still believe that? Do you get the level of specificity and language I am asking for here?

"Again, designate a scribe—get someone else this time—and begin talking through what we are going to all agree to. Spend at least a half hour trying to integrate the various posters and charts with your own experiences and expectations. What does our community expect? Come up with no more than twenty to twenty-five instructional principles max. Put these on file cards, one principle per card. Once you have identified your set of instructional principles, start sorting them into categories and paring them down to the most essential ones. By lunchtime, you must have a list of about ten items that you all understand and any one of you could explain to the whole group this afternoon. Sue and I will be sitting in with different groups so we can hear what the issues are and what you are thinking about them."

Each group settled in to work. To give them time to get started, and to orient Sue to what had gone on the previous day, Tip showed her the agenda and explained the wall hangings, handouts, and some of their discussions. Then they split up and began to sit in with groups of teachers, asking clarifying questions and encouraging them to consider additional issues before moving onto another group. When they had all left for lunch, Tip began to clean up the area, set up the room, and put out materials for the afternoon. He couldn't help but read the lists that had been left on the tables. He was pleased to see the instructional principles they were formulating and how much similarity there was across tables. This afternoon would be much easier than it could have been!

After lunch, Tip gave directions for their work up to break time. Tables of teachers had been paired to form half the number of this morning's tables. Their task was to resolve their two lists to devise one list of instructional principles between them. Same rules, no more than ten instructional principles, which the groups would post on chart paper. After break, the groups would resolve the list into one final set of instructional principles and give three examples of instruction that reflected each principle. They got to work. Tip and Sue circulated again, listening in on the discussions.

Comment: "Okay, so we agree. All of us think it is a nobrainer that we need daily writing and that we need time every day for us to read to kids and for them to read to themselves."

Another comment: "How can we *not* put on there that we will have a safe school environment? If it isn't safe to be at school, nothing else can happen."

"Do you mean safe emotionally or physically?"

Another group: "Reading and writing *are* thinking, feeling, and language. I mean, what else could you put there?"

"I'm not disagreeing, but why? What does it mean? What does it mean for our teaching? How do we teach so that reading and writing are thinking, feeling, and language?"

Another group: "But reading and writing are learned in a variety of ways. If there were only one way, we would have found it a long time ago. Because kids come to us different in individual, cultural, and language ways, we have to have a range of approaches."

Another comment: "I cannot imagine how we would set schoolwide literacy instructional principles and not address decoding and spelling. Those two are crucial for kids to become independent with literacy tasks."

"I didn't say they were not important. You know how much time I spend on both in my room! However, the issue is should they be separate instructional principles or are they included within other areas?"

Another comment: "We have to say something about grading or report cards or something. Parents want to know how their children are doing. They want grades."

"Yeah, they want grades because they think they know what an A means."

"But don't you think what they really want is to know 'Is my kid doing okay or should I be worried here?' "

Overheard elsewhere: "I don't see the need for a goal on having groups. I lived through the bluebirds, redbirds, and buzzards era. I don't want to go back to that."

"I'm not talking about ability groups. There is something other than ability grouping and whole-group teaching. Doesn't it frustrate you that some kids already know what you're teaching and others are left in the dust? Whole group usually just teaches to the middle."

Throughout these discussions, Sue and Tip made notes on the issues that were coming up at the various tables. At their meeting during the break, they would take the literacy instructional principles identified by the teachers and the issues they were currently struggling with and create some inservice topics to offer during the year. Both were very impressed with the quality of the discussions and the professionalism with which the teachers handled the areas of disagreement or misunderstanding.

Following the break, groups began to reconcile the instructional principles from their various charts. Tip told them, "The final list can be no longer than twelve items—it must fit on a single sheet of paper. The final list must be in plain and clear language we can share with parents and school board members who don't know educationese. Let me first, though, go across the charts and find those items that are on all the charts." He began circling items that were similar and then rewriting those onto a clean piece of chart paper.

The groups worked hard for the rest of the afternoon. While the teachers worked, Tip removed all the posters, except the final list, from the walls, leaving plenty of room for their products. When Sue and Tip perched at different tables, they heard teachers saying over and over, "Yes, but when you . . . , you have to . . . ," and "But what I thought that meant was . . . " Even though these very smart and dedicated teachers all agreed on the same instructional principles, their personal interpretations of what that meant or how it looked in the classroom varied a lot. The three examples of instruction that reflected each principle were really a selection from the ones each group had written during their various deliberations.

At the end of the session, the teachers gathered up their personal items and said their good-byes, making arrangements to meet for additional planning or for social events. Tip took down the twelve charts the teachers had created. He loved the tone of his school. There was a positive atmosphere that reflected the learning attitude of the teachers. But to help all of this happen, he, Sue, and the teachers had a lot of work ahead of them.

1. Provide a balanced Literacy program.

   Use a variety of methods to meet one goal.

   Balance teacher-led and student-centered activities.

   Build on children's multiple intelligences.

2. Make instruction multilevel.

   Let students make choices whenever possible.

   Use a variety of whole class, small group and partner arrangements.

   Use a variety of materials on different levels.

3. Use language as the foundation for reading and writing.

   Speaking and listening should often precede reading and writing.

   Use a variety of oral language strategies like discussion, sharing, and dramatization.

   Help children know that reading, writing, listening, and speaking are social and cultural.

4. Teach reading and writing as thinking.

   Teach students that the essence of reading and writing is thinking.

   Model essential thinking processes of connect, self-monitor, predict, organize, generalize, image, evaluate, and apply.

   Use these thinking processes all day, every day.

5. Use feelings to create avid readers and writers.

   Use student interest to engage them with reading and writing.

   Help students realize their success comes from their effort and procedures, rather than their ability or luck.

   Ensure success with appropriate reading and writing materials and tasks.

6. Connect reading and writing to all subject areas.

   Provide real rather than artificial purposes for reading and writing.

   Help students to develop their own purposes for reading and writing.

   Have them read and write a variety of different kinds of text.

7.
Read aloud to students daily.
Select high-interest books and articles.
Select a variety of authors, genres, and topics.
Read expressively.

8.
Schedule daily self-selected reading.
Set aside time just for self-selected reading.
Teachers must help students get better at choosing books they will like.
Teacher conferences with individuals or groups during self-selected reading.

9.
Have students write every day.
Teach and use self-selected writing.
Teach and use focused writing.
Provide opportunities for students to respond to one another's writing.

10.
Teach the decoding and spelling strategies reading and writing require.
Stress transfer in all activities.
Assess by what they actually use in reading and writing.
Help students develop "word wonder".

11.
Use observation to assess learning and plan instruction.
Assess, evaluate, plan, then teach.
Adjust instruction based on student strengths, limitations, and needs.
Track student progress by observing their task performance and evaluating their work samples.

12.
Inform parents of expectations and progress.
Meet with parents in conferences.
Hold a parent curriculum night at beginning of year.
Make positive phone calls and send notes home once a month per student.

Miss Launch: Kindergarten

The Parent Meeting

Over at last! Helen Launch glanced at her watch and noted with surprise that it was only 9:00 P.M. As she moved about the room, collecting materials and getting out other supplies for the next day, she thought over what had taken place. She had talked to the parents about her program for approximately half an hour, and then some of them had asked questions. To her amazement, many parents had stayed longer for a private chat. But now, even they had gone, leaving her to her reflections. She decided she would also need to contact the absent parents at a later time to discuss her kindergarten program with them.

She had known that this should be one of the most important encounters she would have with parents this year, and that this meeting would set the tone for all future parental cooperation. Mr. Topps had told them all to relax—these meetings went much more smoothly if they were informal and casual. To Miss Launch, with her penchant for food, that meant cookies and coffee! While the parents were assembling in the classroom, she had announced that refreshments were in the rear of the room, as was a sign-in sheet for their names.

Miss Launch firmly believed kindergarten to be an essential and integral part of the total school program. She had told the parents that kindergarten was *not* playtime for which she was the baby-sitter. Further, she had emphasized that the foundation for all future school success was laid in kindergarten.

She had outlined some of the experiences that the children would have in her room and the reasons for them. This had been an important part of her presentation, for she wanted and needed parental support and cooperation. She had pointed out to the parents the various centers for learning. In addition to providing the traditional block, art, and house corners, she had included other areas that she felt would enhance the educational program for the children. There was an animals area, an area for puppets and plays, one for reading, and a things-to-do corner that would include activities ranging from math, to science, to cooking and other topics. Much of the learning would take place in these centers.

Learning would also occur outside the classroom. Miss Launch had told the parents that she had planned two field trips a month to various places in the school and community. Follow-up activities for these field trips would include making thank-you cards, drawing pictures, and having shared writing/language-experience lessons about what they learned. These field trips would make up most of the social studies curriculum of her kindergarten program as well as some science and much reading, writing, and math.

Miss Launch had also informed the parents of her concern with oral language development. She said that there would be many and varied opportunities for the children to talk and listen to one another. One of the mothers questioned why talking was important.

"Miss Launch, I don't know much about how they do school now, but when I was in school they didn't take learnin' time for talkin'. I don't see how that can help Chip learn to read! Readin' and talkin' are two different things as I see it!"

Miss Launch had replied calmly to Mrs. Moppet. "Not so different as you might think. The language children can speak and listen to is the foundation we build on to teach them to read and write. Children are already speaking many thousands of words when they enter kindergarten. They will be able to read all of those words within the next few years and spell most of them. In addition, they will be reading and writing other words that they do *not* yet know. But almost without exception, those new words they will learn to read and spell will also be words that they have used in speech. If they do not learn to *say* new words, or if they do not learn to use old words in new ways, then they will read and spell only at the level at which they now speak. That is why I do so much with oral language development. In reading and writing, I want to build from what the children know to what they need to know. That is another reason, by the way, for the two monthly field trips. Not only will the children become more familiar with their community, but these trips will also expose them to new words and new ideas that they will need later for reading, writing, and other subjects."

She had gone on to say that there would be much dramatization and storytelling. Some of the children's stories would be written on chart paper, some might appear in individual storybooks, and still others might become part of one of the class books of original stories. Each day, before the children left, she would sit with them and discuss all the activities engaged in that day. She felt that this discussion would help them develop a sense of sequence, the recognition of main ideas, and a memory for things they had accomplished—all important requisites for reading and writing. Besides, she had said, when parents ask children what they did in school all day, she wanted to prevent the old "Oh, nothing!" response that children often give.

Miss Launch explained to parents that she wanted to give the children many experiences in identifying, sorting, and classifying. These activities help children develop vocabulary and see conceptual relationships. They would work with letters, colors, numbers, their own names, and many other concepts that would help them learn to do the thinking crucial for success in reading and writing.

Miss Launch indicated that she would use a variety of techniques to prepare children for the very important idea that one reads with the expectation of understanding what is read. They would construct charts of their animals' activities, of the weather, and of other things they knew about or could observe. They would be dictating stories and "reading" them to one another and to her. They would cook in the classroom and follow simple recipes. While she did not believe that kindergarten is the place to establish reading groups and use commercial reading programs, she did believe that each child should have constant exposure to things that can be read.

Miss Launch told them that she would read to the children to develop their listening skills. ("Good luck," she heard Butch's mother mutter.) During these listening lessons, she would model for the children her thinking processes as a reader. While reading good children's books, she would model how to connect, organize, self-monitor, predict, image, generalize, apply, and evaluate. She showed them a copy of a Big Book of nursery rhymes she would be reading to the children the first week of school. Parents exclaimed over the size and joined in as she modeled how she would do these shared book readings with the children. Even parents in the back row could see the words as she pointed to them.

She planned to read to the children a great deal, and she expected them to "read" to her. For some children, this reading would consist of picture interpretation; for others, actual words would be read. Everyone would be reading when they were in the reading center and, later in the year, during their self-selected reading time. By the end of the school year, they would be able to read to themselves for several minutes each day. She had also planned many literature response activities for the children. These activities would be extensions of stories read to them, and they would be tied into other classroom activities such as music, art, and cooking.

> **Miss Launch:** Children first of all need to develop a desire and purpose for reading. Reading is a difficult task at best, but without proper motivation, it is even more so. We're all going to read, read, read in this class and not just during reading-center time or self-selected reading. I will read to the children and they will "read" to me and to one another. Even if they're only reading pictures, they are still acquiring abilities they will need to be good readers. They can determine the sequence of story events, what the important ideas in the story are, and what might happen next in the story. We will write and, I hope, receive letters. We will label things around the classroom and set up a post office for messages. We'll make books of all kinds. Some will have only pictures, like Mercer Mayer's "Frog" books, and others will have words. We'll follow recipes for purposeful reading. In addition, we'll be working with rhyming patterns and letter names and sounds. As I said earlier, I believe that a firm background of oral language is the most important contribution I can make to your child's future success in reading, so I will

do much with that. I have lots more planned, but I hope that you have the general idea.

Horace's mother held up her hand. "Could you explain that in a little more detail, Miss Launch? I'm not quite sure that I understand what our children will be doing."

Miss Launch: Children who are ready to begin reading and writing have certain characteristics. They know why people read and write, they have a broad background of knowledge and concepts, they know that words are made up of sounds, and they know many letter names and sounds. They know how print works and how we describe print, they know twenty to thirty sight words, and they want to learn how to read and write. Children are at all different places with these critical knowings; I'll be working to make sure I develop them during the school year. The main activities I use are reading to the children shared book experiences such as I modeled earlier, language experience and shared writing, and having the children write. Through these activities and many others, I will be helping your children to better understand how words, letters, and sounds work.

Mr. Martin: You've mentioned cooking in kindergarten a couple of times now, and I can't for the life of me figure out what cooking has to do with reading and writing. Can you explain it to me?

Miss Launch: Would you believe that it's really because I like to eat? [Chuckles around the room] Actually, I do justify it educationally, though I must admit that I enjoy the food too! Cooking in this room will be done for several reasons. First, since children eat what they prepare, they learn that it is important to follow directions carefully; second, the food produced is the incentive to do the work well, so there is meaning to doing it; third, there is always more language produced as we discuss why a particular sequence is necessary and why certain ingredients are added, what they do together; and fourth, new science concepts are observed and dealt with, such as the evaporation of liquid, or the nature of change as we observe it with popcorn. Maybe I should add a fifth one—because it's fun, and if language, literacy, and science learning can all result from an enjoyable activity as well as it can from a pencil and paper task, well, I'm all for it!

Mrs. Penn: I recently read an article about . . . is it phonemic awareness? What is that anyway? The article made it look like that was just about all that mattered in kindergarten.

Miss Launch: Yes, it is important, though not more important than other critical knowings. *Phonological awareness* is the term that phonics researchers have used to refer to whether children are conscious of the elements in the language they speak and hear. So, *word awareness* concerns whether children are conscious of the individual words in the oral language around them. All children who can talk can speak and understand separate words—

the question is, are they aware of those separate words? The reason word awareness is important is simple. How could a child learn to read and spell a word unless you could link the word up to the separate pronunciation that word has in oral language? *Syllable awareness* concerns whether children are conscious of the separate syllables in spoken language. *Rhyme awareness* concerns whether children can tell whether two spoken words rhyme, as opposed to when they don't sound alike or when they sound alike at the beginning rather than the end. Finally, the *phonemic awareness* you asked about, Mrs. Penn, concerns whether children are conscious of the smallest individual sounds in the words they speak and hear. Phonemic awareness seems very important as children are learning phonics. Obviously, they cannot learn to associate sounds with letters unless they are conscious of the sounds in spoken language. This year, we will do a number of activities to help your children develop these different kinds of *phonological awareness*. It is one of the critical knowings I talked about a few minutes ago.

Mr. Martin: Will the children be studying a letter each week, the way my older children did when they were in kindergarten?

Miss Launch: No, because I have not found that to be a particularly effective approach. By the end of kindergarten, children should recognize almost all capital and small-case letters and know almost all of their names; they should know the sounds of almost all the consonant letters; and they should be able to form almost all of their capital and small-case letters on unlined paper. If we try to teach everything about a letter during a single week, we miss the wonderful opportunity of revisiting the same letter over and over again throughout the year, which all the children will benefit from. Programs that teach a letter a week often have children who really don't remember much about the letters they studied earlier in the year. Also, when we teach letter names and letter sounds together, children are more likely to confuse them. Letter formation is harder than letter recognition, so it is better taught several months later.

Miss Launch then explained that there would be at least two parent conferences this year, and that at the end of the year, parents would receive a written appraisal of their child's performance in various areas.

Mr. Graham: I have no questions as such, but I just want you to know that I am amazed that so much can be done with kindergartners! You have a very ambitious year mapped out. Is there anything we can do to help you?

Miss Launch: Is there ever! Thanks so much for asking, because I was just about to ask for your help. I can use parents and other relatives to help with taping stories, typing books, helping children write, field trips, cooking, and all sorts of things. I'll be sending a request-for-help letter home soon, giving you the opportunity to volunteer. Some of the jobs can be done at home, so that even if you don't have a lot of time, you can still help me out. As to all that the children can do, I have found that many adults tend to underestimate the capabilities of young children, and for that reason we do not help them to attain their full potential. I hope to help them do so without the attendant pressure that we sometimes place on children.

As Miss Launch evaluated the evening, she found that the meeting had gone rather well. Many of the parents had remarked to her that they were pleased that the emphasis would be on learning through creative means. She was certain that she would have a great deal of support from the parents whenever she might need it. She hoped she had convinced them that kindergarten was "real school," but not like first grade. Oh, well, if not now, then by the end of the year they would be aware of it! She glanced around the room. Yes, all was ready for tomorrow morning. She allowed herself the luxury of a stretch and a yawn; then she turned off the lights and left for home.

Monthly Logs

September

September is always a bit of a shock to my system. Each year I am taken aback at how small and shy the entering kindergartners are. I quickly realize that I am using the children of the previous spring as my criteria. How much they do grow and change in one year's time! It always takes so long to deal with some of the school socialization processes, such as how to use the water fountain and what "line up" means. Those can be difficult areas for children to deal with for the first time. Fortunately, most of them are already "housebroken"!

Starting the year is the difficult task, and as I look over the list of all I have set out to accomplish, I wonder somewhat at my audacity. The twelve instructional principles we formulated at our retreat in June have been in my mind ever since. I know that a certain road is paved with good intentions and that if I don't structure myself, I will probably not do all that I now plan to. Therefore, I have taped a list of seven critical knowings inside my plan book so that I will be reminded to include specific activities for each in my planning. These knowings are my way of turning the twelve instructional principles into a form that will guide my kindergarten program throughout the year.

The Seven Critical Knowings

1. Children need to know why people read and write.
2. Children need to have a broad background of knowledge and concepts.
3. Children need to know that words are made up of sounds.
4. Children need to know many letter names and sounds.

5. Children need to know print conventions and jargon.

6. Children need to know twenty to thirty concrete words.

7. Children must want to learn how to read and write.

Daily Instruction to Accomplish the Knowings

Read to and talk with children.

Use shared book experiences.

Use shared writing and language experience.

Have children write regularly.

Help children understand how letters and sounds work.

My class of twenty-five includes some very interesting young people, I can tell already! The list of children follows:

Alex	Daphne	Mike
Alexander	Hilda	Mitch
Anthony	Horace	Mort
Betty	Jeff	Pat
Butch	Joyce	Paul
Carl	Larry	Rita
Chip	Mandy	Roberta
Daisy	Manuel	Steve
Danielle		

One child was so withdrawn that I was immediately aware that his problem was more than fear of coming to school for the first time. Paul wouldn't speak to me or any of the others for three class sessions, and then he merely uttered his name in a group game. When this happened, we were so excited that we gave him a "silent cheer" (that is, we raised our hands into the air, shook them up and down, and formed our mouths as though we were cheering). Paul cried often during those first two weeks, but they were strange, silent tears that rolled down his cheeks. There was no sobbing or screaming—just a sad, sad look and those tears running down his cheeks. (I have asked the school social worker to investigate the home situation. Something is drastically wrong; perhaps we can discover what it is and then remedy the situation.) Alex and Daphne began to sniffle when they saw this (tears are among the most contagious of childhood afflictions), but Hilda simply told them to be quiet, that she had looked around and it was obvious that there was nothing to be afraid of! The sniffling subsided, but Paul continued his silent crying despite all my efforts to comfort or distract him.

Although he is quite friendly and willing to play with the other children, Manuel apparently does not speak one word of English. He may understand a few words from watching television, but even there I am not sure. So far, he gets along with the others because he relates well nonverbally, but I feel the challenge of teaching him what kindergarten exists to impart.

I read to the children every day, usually more than once a day, and sometimes the whole morning is built around one book. First the book is read to them, and then we do other activities to tie the book into the other curricular areas. As an example, one of the first books I read to them was Mirra Ginsburg's *Mushroom in the Rain.* After reading it, we talked about their favorite parts of the story, and they drew with crayons or painted at the easel the one thing they had enjoyed the most. We hung these up and let children tell what the part was and why they had chosen it. The fox section was the most popular of all, for children like to be scared just a little. Then we dramatized the story by playing the parts of the various animals. When I asked the children what we could use for a mushroom, they cleverly decided to use an umbrella that they would open out more and more as the various animals came under. In addition, we counted the number of animals in the book. We looked for certain colors ("Find all the red things on this page"). We made up a song that we could sing to the tune of "Are You Sleeping?":

> Is it raining,
>   Is it raining,
>   Little Ant?
>   Little Ant?
>   Hurry to the mushroom!
>   Hurry to the mushroom!
>   Drip, drop, drip.
>   Drip, drop, drip.
>   Is it raining,
>   Is it raining,
>   Butterfly?
>   Butterfly? (etc., for all the animals up through the rabbit. Then:)
>   Here comes Foxy!
>   Here comes Foxy!
>   Poor Rabbit! (two times)
>   "No, he is not here, Sir." (two times)
>   "Go away." (two times)
>   See the rainbow. (two times)
>   In the sky. (two times)
>   Now the sun is shining. (two times)
>   Warm and bright. (two times)

We tested the hypothesis that mushrooms grow in the rain, and we planned additional adventures for the characters in the book. We talked about who else might have come to the mushroom, what might happen next, where Ant would go when the rain finally stopped, and what other scary things might happen to the other animals. After we did a lap story with *Mushroom in the Rain,* I placed the characters, props, and the book in the puppets and plays center so that the children can retell the story individually or in small groups over and over.

At their seats, they drew a picture about another animal that might try to get under the mushroom. I encouraged them to write a word or more on their paper that would tell others about their idea. Then I had them think of a statement to dictate about their picture, and I circulated among their work tables, writing statements for them on the page. I can really see how it might help to have a parent volunteer help me with this part! Chip seemed not ever to have seen a crayon, and so Danielle helped him learn how to hold it and mark with it. Paul could not come up with an animal to draw or a word to say. Most children drew but did not try to write any words. Larry wrote his own sentence!

(An elephant tried to get under the mushroom.)

We have established a daily pattern or schedule. Establishing a routine that children can depend on is a critical aspect of school. The morning is mainly spent on math and language arts, so I have only three hours in which to do a lot of things. Here is the morning schedule:

8:30	Attendance, sharing, read a story or poem
9:00	Work time—centers, oral language lessons, etc.
10:00	Physical education—outside if possible
10:15	Snack and story
10:30	Work time
11:15	Group together for review of work sessions

Most mornings at 9:00, we begin by singing the alphabet song. In addition to having a book- and print-rich classroom, I have had the capital letters displayed large over the marker board and at eye level two or three places around the room since they entered my classroom on the first day. For a few minutes each morning, I use an empty can, carton, or wrapping of a product I think the children may be familiar with. I ask if anyone knows what it is—someone usually does. One of the first packages I hold up is an empty Cheerios box. After we share briefly about whether we have had them, like them, or prefer another kind, I ask them to volunteer to come up one at a time and point to something on the box they notice that no one else has noticed yet today. Some children point out a color, some a picture, and some a letter. Rather than asking who can point to the letter C or who can point to the color yellow, I use this multilevel task because it helps every child be successful. After the children are finished, I "notice" anything else on the box that I want to draw their attention to but which no child pointed out. I emphasize letters during this activity, making sure that every child is paying attention when a letter is noticed and noticing any myself that the children did not.

During the third week, at work time the children were to find pictures of red things in magazines and catalogs. Larry, who is already reading, I've discovered, found the word *red* also. We pasted the things they found on a chart labeled "Red Things." Most of the children could already identify the colors without help, but some could not. I paired Joyce (who could) and Chip (who couldn't), so she could help him find red things. Daisy, Jeff, Paul, and Butch also worked with other children to find red objects. Once Manuel understood what we were looking for, he was able to find pictures of red things independently.

We took the first field trips of the year right in our own school area. It is important for children to become oriented to the building, the grounds, and the personnel as soon as possible. The first day the children came to school, we spent part of the morning walking through those parts of the building we *had* to know—the restrooms, the office, and the janitor's room—so that when (not *if,* but *when*) a child throws up I can stay with the child while someone else asks the janitor to bring a mop. We have our own kindergarten-sized playground equipment, and that also had to be shown. We went to the office on subsequent days and met the secretary, Mrs. Mainstay, and the principal, Mr. Topps. I prepared for these trips by first going there myself and making sure that someone who knew precisely what it was I wanted children to learn about that particular place would be on hand. I prepared the children by telling them the highlights of each place, alerting them to what to look and listen for, and urging them to try to remember everything, so that we could talk and write about it when we got back to the room. Upon our return, I asked them to tell what we had seen and done. As each child made a contribution, I wrote it down on chart paper with the child's name after it, so that he or she could see the very words contributed. I repeatedly drew their attention to the chart by reading aloud what I wrote while I wrote it. Afterward, I wrote the sentences on sentence strips, cut these into words and let children glue them back on another piece of paper in the proper order. Finally I read it all back to them and they agreed that they had done a fine job!

It has also been a busy month with some of the activities that I have been doing with the children to help develop visual discrimination of letters. We have learned to play some new games. I wrote out six copies each of the capital forms *P, H, A,* and *R.* I made each one about six inches high so that the children could readily see them from across the room. They are on sheets of oak-tag and covered with clear plastic adhesive paper so that they are durable. The first game was one that the whole class played together. I shuffled the cards and gave out one to each of the children. I told them to find the other children who had the same letter. When two children got together, they had to stay together while searching for other children who matched them. If they thought that they had found one that was a match, they carefully looked at the parts to see if they were correct. After all groups had been formed, I checked them: perfect the first time, just as I had known it would be, for the abler ones helped those who could not yet match. (I had set the timer for three minutes. They enjoy the timing—it gives activities a little added excitement.)

It was interesting to observe the differences among the children as they formed their groups. Paul stayed put and was found by Mandy and Horace, who also had *P*s. They dragged him along with them until they found or were found by the other *P*s. Daisy dashed wildly around the room, ostensibly looking for the other *A*s, but in fact making it only more difficult for them to track her down. Mort sat in a chair, apparently not wanting to exhaust himself, being fully confident that the *H*s would get to him in time. Chip and Manuel held hands and went from group to group checking the letters, even though Chip was an *A* and Manuel an *R*. I suppose they just needed the extra confidence that gave each other. The children begged to do it again, so we shuffled the cards and went through the same process. This time, Hilda tried to organize the thing a little more by shouting out, "A! A! A!" apparently as a clue to those who might know the name of the letter. Larry formed his hand into the letter *P* and said, "Do you look like this?" Ingenious children I have!

For another game I used the same cards and placed three cards of the same letter on the chalkboard tray with one that was different. I arranged the cards like this for ease the first time: *A A A P*. I then asked Rita to come find the ones that were the same. She chose the first three. "Terrific! Let's all give Rita a silent cheer!" (The silent cheer is a good reward for children, and it's also easy on the teacher's eardrums.) I continued the game with other children, making the letter combinations harder or easier depending on a child's capabilities. I then put the cards into the things-to-do center and suggested that they were available to play with.

October

October is over—I didn't think Halloween would *ever* arrive, and neither did the children! Every day it seemed they asked if it were here yet. Well, at least I was able to channel some of that interest toward school activities. Many of the books I selected to read to them and ones they chose themselves were about Halloween or monsters. One of my favorites, *Where the Wild Things Are*, was one of those with which we did literature response activities. The children made monster masks, and we had a "wild things" parade. We also had a word gathering for scary words—I asked them to tell me all of the scary things they could think of. Since this was our first word gathering, the children had trouble getting started. After only a few suggestions by other children, everyone joined in. Even Paul gave me one—*night*. When they started to bog down, having given me several words and phrases, I asked them for scary colors, then for scary smells, sounds, and looks. This is their completed list. Leo Lionni's Frederick the mouse, the original word gatherer, would be very pleased with this compilation.

Scary Things

blood	monster	bad dream	nightmare
howl	bloody	black cat	Boo!

ghost	scream	witch	mummy
giant	storm	red	fire
dogs	growl	night	orange
purple	blue	scared	afraid

something touching me in the dark

when my night light burns out

footsteps in the dark

my mom's closet without the light on

my window with the curtains open

noises outside in the dark

After we had completed the list, I read the words back to the children, running my hand under each word or phrase as I said it so that they would have more opportunity to observe left-to-right progression with the return sweep to the next line. "Now," I told them, "we are going to write a poem!" I had read many poems to them and they did enjoy poetry. Now it was our turn to produce. I used a concrete format since it is the simplest one I know. I drew a random number and arrangement of lines on the chalkboard, and the children helped me to fill them in with words and phrases. To show them what I wanted us to do, I had them count the number of lines I had drawn, and I told them that I was going to use some of the words from our scary things chart to help me make up the poem. There would be only one word written on each line, so since we had counted twenty-one lines, I needed to write twenty-one words. This is what they saw:

____ ____

____ ____ ____ ____ ____ ____

____ ____

____ ____ ____ ____ ____

____ ____

____ ____ ____ ____

The children were intrigued, particularly when they saw me begin to write words on each of the lines. This is my finished poem:

I felt
  something touching me in the dark.
  I knew
  my window curtains were open.
  I screamed.
  Bad dream go away.

We counted the number of words that were on each of the rows of lines. Mort pointed out that the first line in the second row had nine words on it! At that point, to help them distinguish between words and letters, we talked about how some words have one letter (pointing out "I" in the poem) and that some words have more than one letter. The word *something* has nine letters. I wrote *Mort* on the board. "What is that word?" I asked. He did know his name and told me that it said *Mort*. "This is one word and that word is your name. But your name has four letters in it." Of course, it was necessary to do the same with the names of several other children, since all of them wanted their names written. But it was also important to count the letters in the names of several children in order to show children the concept of *letter* versus *word* in lots of examples. Obviously they didn't all get it this time around, but with lots of examples throughout the year they should all have the idea by the time they hit first grade (I hope!). With a little help, this is what the class was able to come up with:

One Night
Black cat scream, black cat howl!
Why do you make that noise?
Growl, purr, growl, purr
Dog and cat
fight.

I copied both my poem and their poem onto sheets of chart paper and hung them near the scary things chart. I find it fascinating that Danielle will steer her wheelchair over and pore over the poems with Roberta and Alex. They seem fascinated with the idea that there is one word on each of the lines, and they try to count how many letters are in each of the words. Occasionally Mort will wander over and watch them for a while. I heard him say, "But how do you *know* which ones are words and which ones are letters? I don't get it. I think you're making it all up." Clearly, there is a range of abilities within this classroom.

We also did a concrete poem on the color black. First we had a word gathering of black words, sounds, and smells to get them prepared.

Black
Black, black is the night,
blacker than black
is
my window.

While we were gathering black words (which was, of course, the color chart they were working on that week), a discussion took place. The children were coming up with all kinds of black things when Butch contributed three words: *Joyce, Danielle,* and *Jeff.* Some of the children turned around and looked at those children as if they had never seen them before. Others started murmuring—this *was* a revelation!

Larry said, "No, I don't agree. Some people call them black, but I think they are actually more brown."

The three were asked by another child what color *they* thought they were. Joyce responded, "Well, what color do you think *you* are?" There was a general comparing of arms, but little agreement. Finally Jeff said proudly, "Well, I don't care what color I look like; I'm black." So his name went up on the chart, and though he tried to hide it from them, he smiled! Later I saw him tracing the letters of his name on the chart. He was the only child to get listed on the chart.

I sent a letter to all my parents at the beginning of October to solicit help. Parental response to the letter was overwhelming. For the most part, parents want to be involved in their children's education and will volunteer if there is something specific that they feel confident in doing. In some cases, parents prefer to or *must* do things at home. For example, Chip's mother must stay home to take care of an elderly aunt and uncle who live with them. She thus offered to cut out things for me if I would send the materials to her. *Where* it's done matters not to me! I'm just delighted that parents are willing to do it at all!

I have labeled many things around the room: window, door, mirror, desk, table, chair. Children seem to enjoy finding labeled objects that have letters like those in their names. I was working with each of the children so that they would recognize their own names. I wrote each name about three inches high on unlined paper. I then took each child's hand and traced over the name with two fingers. All the time we did that, I said the name over and over with the child. Then, after we had done that a few times, I let them go to the chalkboard where they could write it, using the paper as a model. I stayed with each child until the name was mastered and then went to work with the next one. With that technique, almost all of the children can recognize their names when they see them, and several can write their own names without looking at a model. As a further incentive, I labeled the bulletin board with their names and then asked them to draw a picture of themselves and tell me where to hang it. Mort, Paul, and Daisy were the only three who needed extra help. Mort got confused because of all the names that began with *M*, as did Daisy with three *D* names. Paul just didn't have a clue! Another activity they like is to dip one-inch paint brushes into clear water and write on the board with those. They have fun, they learn, there is no erasing to do, and at the end, the chalkboard is clean.

A device I started this month to also help the children identify their own and each others' names, as well as to help them develop responsibility, is a *job chart*. There are always many tasks to be done in a classroom, and by this time of the year I try to involve the children even more than previously. There are enough jobs for everyone, even though several children have the same job simultaneously, as the cleaners do. So that children have a variety of jobs during the year, the job assignments rotate weekly. Some jobs can be done by the children only if their teacher instructs them. For instance, they must be told how much water to give the plants that are so important for the science we teach in kindergarten. One tip that I found helpful was to color-code plants to soup cans used for watering. I draw a line inside the soup can with permanent marker to indicate how much water is needed for a plant. A small square of color on the plant container that matches the line drawn in the can will clue children so that they will have a hard time going wrong. I learned, however, that with a color-blind child like Butch, you may have a drowned cactus and a droopy ivy! Using this kind of a coding system is the beginning of learning to follow "written" instructions. Though no words are used, children learn to decode the meaning of the symbol being used (in this case, color) in order to follow some specific instructions.

Here is the job chart for one week. Every week new assignments are made:

Water plants	Chip	Paul	Anthony		
Room cleaners	Betty	Butch	Daisy	Rita	Hilda
Messengers	Manuel	Daphne	Alexander		
Mail	Larry and Danielle (they knew all of the names)				
Line leader	Mort				
Group work leaders	Roberta	Horace	Carl	Alex	
Feed animals	Pat	Mike	Steve		
Special helpers	Mitch	Joyce	Mandy	Jeff	

I now have the capital letters of the alphabet also spread out on a wall of the room, and I have placed the first names of all of the children by the letter that begins their name. I wrote each name on a sentence strip made of colored tagboard. They are large enough to read from anywhere in the room. All the activities I do with children's names help them become aware of letters and words. These activities are highly motivating, because children are always interested in their own and other children's names. I often see them standing alone or in pairs or triples near the job chart or name wall, looking at or talking about one or more of the names.

Another popular hangout is the "Words We Can Read" bulletin board. Children have been bringing in words from advertisements that they can read. Of course, if "the golden arches" are missing, Betty can't really say "McDonald's." Nevertheless, being able to read the word with the logo is a beginning step for successful later reading. They love bringing in words, which they share with the class during our morning opening time, pinning them to the bulletin board. Along with this, the children are making their own *Words I Can Read* books by pasting logos and words to pages. I often see them reading their books to other children.

During work time, I frequently ask the class to go one at a time to the "Words We Can Read" bulletin board and point to one word we know and say it. I ask them to point to one no one else has pointed to today, which helps them try to pay attention to what others are doing. We have done several other activities during work time this month.

We have used Cheerios to "count" the words in oral statements. I give each child six Cheerios. After modeling for them several times, I make a statement to them and ask them to push out a Cheerio for each word they hear. In the statement "I love you," they should push out three Cheerios. At this point, I don't use any words with more than one-syllable, and I don't use any statements with more than five words. I help the ones who are having trouble by "stretching" my statement, "I-love-you." This activity helps children acquire word awareness.

Instead of singing "The Alphabet Song," as we did regularly last month, this month I often have the class say the capital letters while I point to them in order with my yardstick. I pace it so they have to look at the letter to know when to say it, rather than just saying the alphabet without looking at the letters.

During teacher read-aloud time this month, I read lots of alphabet books to them. I made sure the book was a very simple one like *The Timbertoes ABC Alphabet* or *Alphabetics*. After I had read one of these a couple of times, I encouraged the children to consider where they had seen a particular letter or whether they had that letter in their name. Such discussions, though brief, help children become more aware of particular letters in their environment outside school.

Our two field trips this month were to places that supply us with food—the grocery store and the farm. I had taken my class to these same two places last year, and I made extensive notes to myself about the kinds of things I wanted them to notice and learn about. I spend a lot of time listing for myself what concepts and vocabulary I anticipate will be developed. After each visit, then, we make language-experience charts of things seen and learned.

I made arrangements for the manager of the grocery store to show us around at 8:45. I planned to spend half an hour there, so the children would be able to observe some shoppers but the store wouldn't be too crowded. I prepared the children for this trip by discussing with them the various services and goods the store has to offer. I put down things the children said, so after the trip they could look at their list and add to it. Upon our return, we wrote this summary that hangs on the bulletin board surrounded by all of the children's pictures.

We went to the store. (Daphne)

We saw lots and lots of food. (Daisy)

The fruits and vegetables are called *produce.* (Larry)

We saw lots of meat. (Chip)

There were sweet things to eat. (Carl)

The store man showed us many things. (Pat)

We had fun and learned a lot. (Rita)

My mother and Larry's mother drove. (Roberta)

In addition, the children drew pictures and wrote thank-you letters that I mailed along with a copy of their summary and a personal note of thanks from me. Some of the children were even able to write a few real words.

We did the same kinds of activities for our visit to the farm. So many children do not associate the farm with the grocery store that I made a special effort to talk about where butter, milk, meat, and vegetables come from. When I first asked them where milk comes from, Butch replied, "From the carton." But where did the milk for the carton come from, I persisted. Jeff told me that it came from the store! In the whole group, only four—Larry (no surprise!), Steve and Anthony (the science buffs), and Daphne (who lives on a farm)—knew that cows are milked and that is the source of milk.

We received several pumpkins from both the farm and the grocery store, so it seemed only reasonable to try out some of the recipe and craft ideas in *The All-Around Pumpkin Book*. Two of their favorite recipes were roasted pumpkin seeds and pumpkin milk (believe it or not!). Here's the adapted recipe for pumpkin milk, which they did in groups of six:

Pumpkin Milk
We Need:
>   2 cups of plain yogurt
>   ¾ cup pumpkin sauce
>   4 tablespoons honey
>   1½ teaspoons nutmeg
>   1½ cups milk
>   2 tablespoons wheat germ

We Do:
>   Put everything in the blender and turn it on.
>   Turn the blender on whip.
>   When it is all mixed up it will be all orange.
>   Turn off the blender and pour the pumpkin milk into 6 glasses.

I thought it turned out remarkably well. All the children except Anthony tried it. However, I was a bit chagrined to overhear Butch muttering, "I'd rather have some coffee."

We ended the month by starting to do "The Five Steps," my version of Bobbi Fisher's "Four Steps" (in her book *Getting Started with Writing*, 1991). The Five Steps are think; draw a picture; write something; write your name; copy (or stamp or get an adult to write) the date. At first, I do a minilesson to teach the Five Steps. Using an overhead projector placed on the floor so as not to obstruct any child's view of the screen, I do the Five Steps while the children sit together on a large rug and watch me.

I begin the minilesson by turning on the light to reveal a blank transparency with no lines on it. I say something like this:

> "Boys and girls, in a few minutes I want you to do the Five Steps. So you will know what I want you to do, I am going to do the Five Steps and let you watch me. Before I do that, repeat after me what the Five Steps are: think [they repeat as I raise a finger]; draw a picture [they repeat as I raise another finger]; write something [they repeat as I raise another finger]; write your name [they repeat as I raise another finger]; stamp the date [they repeat as I raise a fifth finger]. So, what's the first step? ['think.'] All right, the first thing I have to do is think about what I will draw today. Have I seen anything interesting in the past few days? Have I done something interesting that I would like to draw? Let me think."

At this point, I pause and then mention one or two things that I have done or seen lately that I might draw. I make sure they are things that the children can relate to. An example might be for me to say something like,

> "I know. We have a new baby in our neighborhood. I went over to see her when they brought her home from the hospital. Maybe I'll try to draw her asleep in her bassinet."

After mentioning a couple of examples like this one, I decide out loud to the class which one I will draw. Then, I say something like,

> "I've thought about what I'm going to draw. Now it is time for me to do the second step. What is the second step? ["draw a picture."] Right! Now I have to draw my picture."

I pick up a colored marker appropriate for use on acetate—any bright color but black—and begin drawing. I am careful to draw a very simple and primitive picture that will not intimidate the children into thinking they must be artistic to do this step. While drawing, I tell them what I'm trying to draw. I might also say something like,

> "I won't draw my picture too big, because I need to leave room to write something later."

It is important for me not to take too long drawing my picture. When I have finished drawing, I put down my colored marker. Then, I say something like,

> "I've thought about what I wanted to draw, and I've drawn a picture. Now it is time for me to do the next step. Does anyone remember what the third step is? ["write something"] Now it is time for me to write something about my picture."

Using a black marker, in my best handwriting, with correct spelling, capitalization, and punctuation, I write something about the picture I have drawn ("*I went to see the new baby.*") while saying out loud what I am writing.

At this point, I explain to the students that if they aren't sure what letters to use to spell the words, they should write some letters they know how to write. The children are told that whatever they try to write will be okay. I model for the children what their writing might look like by writing a few letters or squiggles near what I have printed.

I say something like,

> "It is time for me to do the next step. Does anyone remember the next step after we write something? Yes, now it is time for me to write my name."

I write "Miss Launch." I tell the children that it is okay if they are not sure how to write their whole names. They should just put any letters they know are in their first names. I model what theirs might look like by putting one or two letters from my name near where I have printed my name.

For the fifth step, I model for the children how I want them to get their paper dated after they have finished the first four steps. I use a date stamp to stamp the date on my writing.

Immediately after this minilesson, I give the children unlined paper and drawing implements and tell them to begin doing the Five Steps at their seats. Again, I have them repeat the Five Steps aloud chorally after me. For a couple of minutes at the beginning, I tell them they are to think about what they will draw today. During this time, I do not let anyone start drawing. After the couple of minutes have elapsed, I tell everyone to begin drawing their pictures. I walk around the room, encouraging individual children as they move through the steps.

If they ask me to spell a word for them, I encourage the children just to write letters on their paper. I also encourage children to look around the classroom in order to copy letters or words they find displayed there.

From the time the children begin the thinking step until I end the activity is about fifteen minutes. At the end of each Five Steps lesson, I make sure that I can read the name on each child's paper. If not, I turn the child's paper over on the back and write the name there. I do not have the children tell me what they were trying to write so I can write it down correctly, because I don't want them to compare what they did with what an adult can do. At this point, that would teach them nothing but frustration. I write down what they dictate to me during language-experience lessons, not during writing.

After the Five Steps lesson is over, the children often want to show me and any other adults in the room what they drew and wrote. I take a few minutes and look at what they produced. I encourage everyone but make sure to single out for praise the children who completed all five steps. I take up all the children's papers for filing in their individual writing portfolios.

I have the class do the Five Steps lesson at least two days a week at the beginning. I always start with a minilesson that has a teaching point. My teaching point for the first several minilessons is "what the Five Steps are" until I am sure that every child knows and understands the steps in order. After that, my minilessons have other teaching points such as "ear spelling" (phonic spelling) or "look around the room to find letters or words to put on your paper."

All of these activities seem to be helping Manuel learn English. It is amazing that he has already learned to say and read most of the other children's names and the names of certain objects around the room.

November

I have been having so much fun with Big Books! The other kindergarten teachers and I have a number of highly predictable big books to use during the first half of the year. Every week since the middle of September, I have been doing shared reading with the children, using one of these enlarged-print books. Because a Big Book makes it possible for all the children to see the print and not just the pictures of the same book, it is invaluable in helping children learn concepts about print. Left-to-right directionality is the first concept about print I emphasize during shared reading, and the concept of words is second. Of course, I sometimes have them do "One Thing I Notice" after shared reading, because that is a multilevel task that enables everyone to be successful, regardless of how much or how little they know about print. For example, one day Paul noticed a *P*, while Roberta noticed a question mark.

One week this month, I *made* a Big Book of Little Miss Muffet by using shapes to represent the characters and props: Miss Muffet was a red circle, the tuffet was a green square, the curds and whey were a yellow triangle, and the spider was a black rectangle. The book had five pages, with the appropriate shapes on each page.

I wrote the lines of the rhyme in very large print, so that children could read the book from about 12 feet away. I used white tagboard that was 18 by 24 inches. After gluing on the shapes, I laminated the book for durability.

I had also cut out pieces of felt, using the same shapes so that I could retell the story on the flannel board and show children how the spider moved beside her and how Miss Muffet ran away. In addition, I had duplicated the pages so that the children could create their own small book by pasting on the appropriate shapes as we went through the story page by page. Children helped one another at each table, and I had a parent helper in that day too. In about forty-five minutes, I had gone over the story with the Big Book several times, as children joined in, and with the flannel board once, and all of the children had completed their own books. They then went to Mrs. Wright's room to read to the children there.

Other creations like that took much less time. Now they know the process, and it is really much faster to make the small books. I guess we must have made a half dozen or so by now. The parents really love them!

Finally! Colors are finished! Our room looks like a rainbow gone crazy. Because Joyce and Danielle had finally declared themselves brown, I changed the order to the colors we were working on. We did brown the first week of November, and their names were the first words put on the chart. They helped me spell them, too, which made it even more important to them. We did purple and white things during the second and third weeks, which led to further discussion among the children of which ones were white. Some decided they were pink, some orange, and some light brown. Mike (of course!) declared himself purple and used some of the finger paints to prove his point. What an unexpected way to have gotten into such a serious issue—I think the children have a better idea now of how complicated the notion of skin color is.

Larry is able to read a great many of the things we have listed on our charts. I'm amazed that he can read so well. He often chooses the reading corner in which to spend his free time.

The reading corner is furnished with an old bucket seat from the car of a friend of mine. (My friends are well trained—they never throw any unusual items away without checking with me first. Over the years I have asked them for odd items, from popsicle sticks to eggshells.) The children love the car seat—two can sit together cozily, reading or looking at books. There are also a small rug, some pillows donated by parents, and a small table with three chairs. A shelf contains a variety of books, ranging from those with pictures only to those with quite a long story line. The children can sometimes choose books they want me to read to them, and often we do literature response activities with these books.

The blocks area is another one that the children enjoy and use frequently. It lends itself to all sorts of language experiences as the children build and discuss what they have done and why. Sometimes they ask me to write signs for them or write down stories that the constructions trigger. By the end of November we had enough of those stories to make a book, which we placed in the reading corner. The children were really pleased that I valued their work enough to put a cover around it and give it a title. Nearly everyone in the class had contributed something to the book, and even those who hadn't had worked in the block corner and could enjoy the stories and illustrations.

The art area has paint, easels, clay, crayons, colored chalk, *lots* of paper, odds and ends for constructions, and various other materials for artwork. I have a section of the bulletin board reserved for paintings and a small table nearby for displaying constructions. Very often, artwork acts as a stimulus for story writing. One of the children might ask me to write down his story about the horse he or a classmate had made of clay. I am often asked to label their work; not only is there further language concept development, but this labeling also seems to add value to the work.

I have never called the house corner the doll corner or dollhouse, as some of my kindergarten colleagues do, for lots of boys don't want to play there if it has that name. They learn too soon to shun the so-called feminine playthings. By calling it the house corner, there is a greater opportunity to draw boys in. They experiment with all sorts of housekeeping experiences, even arguing over whose turn it is to vacuum the floor. Of course, they get real cooking and dishwashing experiences from the cooking sessions we have.

For the time being, every time we do a language-experience chart, I underline and then point to each individual word with my finger as I read back the completed story to the children to emphasize the concept of a word. Our latest one dealt with one of our more disastrous cooking experiences.

We had a messy time cooking today. (Anthony)

We made cranberry-orange relish to take to our Thanksgiving dinner with the first-graders. (Danielle)

We got juice and seeds all over the floor. (Alex)

It tasted yucky. (Butch)

Nobody wanted to eat any but Miss Launch. (Carl)

After each language-experience chart, I usually have them do "One Thing I Notice." I am amazed at how well this activity reviews different concepts about print and letter names that we have covered, yet my students who know so much feel so successful in being able to notice things they really couldn't be expected to know for a few years yet.

Daphne's grandparents, with whom she lives, are farmers. In fact, it was their farm I have taken my class to visit each of the past two Octobers. They told me that they very much enjoyed having the children come to the farm and that they felt somewhat guilty they did not have enough time to come to the school and volunteer some of their time. Despite my protest that it was fine, they insisted that they wanted to help out in some way. Could I use two bushels of apples from their orchard? I love questions like that!

Need I tell you that every one of our cooking activities for the month of November involved apples? I did have to alter the cooking plan that I had made for the year, but it was worth it. One of their very favorite recipes came from *The Taming of the C.A.N.D.Y. Monster.*

Candy Apples
We Need:
  1 apple for each person
  1 popsicle stick for each person
  A bowl of honey
  Toasted wheat germ on waxed paper

We Do:
  Pull the stem off your apple.
  Push the stick in where you took out the stem.
  Dip the apple in the bowl of honey and turn it 2 times.
  Hold the apple over the bowl of honey until it stops dripping.
  Roll the apple in the wheat germ and eat it up!

All the children seem to know what the Five Steps are, in order, so now the teaching point of my minilessons before they write is no longer just what those steps are. I am now teaching them how to "stretch" words they want to write and listen for the sounds, so they can use one or more letters to spell out those sounds. This "invented spelling" or "phonic spelling"—what I teach the children to call "ear" spelling—is somewhat controversial, but an essential instructional activity in kindergarten and first grade.

First of all, I find it to be the best activity to help children develop phonemic awareness. By stretching words and listening for sounds, they increase their awareness of those sounds. Once they get in the habit of doing it regularly when they write, nothing can provide them more or better practice with phonemic awareness. Second, by stretching words and listening for sounds, they also increase their phonemic sequencing ability—the ability to hear the sounds in order from beginning to end. Third, ear spelling makes it possible for them to write more, to remember better what they wrote, and after they get pretty good at it, to write something I can actually read. Nothing is better at encouraging children's self-confidence and desire to learn to

*Ear Spelling

write than being able to write something someone else can read! Fourth, their ear spellings, and the writings those spellings make possible, provide me with an invaluable diagnostic and assessment tool. If, for example, a child writes:

Midg nm Sm

the child and I can each usually read it to say, "My dog is named Sam" or "My dog's name is Sam." From this writing, I can tell that child knows, among other things, that letters go from left to right when words are made, that many sounds have been matched with their letter forms, that letters are grouped to make words, and that there is an understanding that words are written so that others can read them. Clearly there are many things for the child still to learn; however, it is easier to teach from a base of what is known and gradually introduce new information than to try to teach everything at once or separated from real applications.

This month we continued to "count" words in oral statements by pushing out Cheerios or sunflower seeds. We began clapping or ruler-tapping the number of "beats" (syllables) in their names to help them develop syllable awareness. Each child loves it when we do his or her first or last name. Again, I praised the children who were getting it right and helped the others by stretching the words to make it easier to hear the separate syllables. I just started using the name wall with syllable-awareness activities—I ask the children to guess which child I mean when I make statements like, "The name is on the wall, begins with an R, and has three beats in it." They love these activities and are getting very good at using the number of syllables in a child's name as a clue.

The children continue to read the alphabet chorally as I point to each letter. Now, however, I have placed the small-case letter beside each capital, both above the marker board and at eye level around the room. I point to the small-case letter with the yardstick, even though both letters are there together. In addition, I put five letters in order on the marker board each day and had several children come one at a time and track (point to) each letter while saying its name. I carefully observed whether the children were pointing to the correct letter as they were saying it, or just saying the same five letters as the previous child.

The children have been working since the beginning of the year on matching uppercase letters to uppercase letters, and recently they have been matching lowercase letters to lowercase letters. I waited to have them do this until I felt I had taught the capital and small-case letter names well using alphabet books, choral reading of the alphabet while I pointed to each capital or small-case letter, and use of the name wall.

One of my tricks is to tell them that while they were outside, an elf came in and mixed up all those nice letters we had been playing with—could anyone help us to get them straightened out again? Of course, there are always several volunteers! We concentrate on three pairs at a time, which is a workable number for them. Also, I always begin with those upper- and lowercase letters that tend to resemble one another except for size (such as *S*s) to further ensure success.

I also play a game of "Memory" with the one capital and one small-case letter card for each of the three letters we are currently working on. I shuffle the six letter cards and place them face down in a two-by-three array. The children take turns selecting two of the letter cards to be revealed. They are then turned over. If they match, they keep the cards. If they do not match, the cards are turned back over to be chosen at a later time by someone who can remember the position of the letters.

December

Despite the holiday rush and clamor, we did manage to accomplish some things this month. It does seem to me, though, that the break can't come a minute too soon, for we have been in a holiday whirl since before Halloween!

We did another very easy poetry format this month. First, I asked the children if they knew what opposites were. Horace volunteered. "That's when my mom puts money into the bank."

"Pretty good guess," I replied. "That is called a *de*posit."

Larry said, "You know, they're words that mean just the different thing, just the, well, *opposite*, like hot and cold, wet and dry, up and down."

"Very good, Larry. Can you think of any other opposites, children?" They came up with several pairs: warm and cool, summer and winter, big and little. I asked them to choose a pair so that we could make up a poem. They chose up and down. I told them that this time we would start and end the poem with these words and fill in with others. We would put the words in one long column, one word per line. There was an uneven number of words, for the middle word, the transition word, had to have something to do with both of the opposites. Together we talked for a short time about some possible words for the slots in the poem. I chose from among their ideas to complete the poem that follows:

Up (Larry)
Sky, (Joyce)
Clouds, (Pat)
Flying, (Mike)
Swing, (Hilda)
Falling, (Butch)
Dirt, (Mitch)
Rocks, (Steve)
Down. (Larry)

I read their poem to them, phrasing it to make the most of the poetic elements. Notice that the middle word is the one where the transition is made between the opposites. The words from the top to the middle build images for the top word; the words from the middle down build images for the bottom word.

Rhyme awareness is considerably more difficult for children to acquire than word or syllable awareness. We began working on that this month. We did an occasional game with rhymes or riddles. Several times, we did the "Head or Knee" rhyming game. I had all the children stand, and then I would say a sentence containing a word that rhymes with either head or knee and then repeat just that word ("I fed the gerbil. Fed. Now, point . . ."). They respond by pointing to their head or their knee after I repeat the word. It is fun and helps them get the wiggles out.

Their favorite Big Book this month was *Brown Bear, Brown Bear.* I introduced it in the usual way, by showing the cover and having them predict what the story might be about. I asked them to image with me as I conjured up the bear lumbering through the forest, lifting his nose to sniff for honey. Then I began to read the story in a fluent and expressive way. I told children that this was my turn to read, and they should not try to join in with the reading yet. They were to listen to the story first. I read each page of the book, pausing to allow them to comment on the pictures and the story line. I used a pointer to touch each word as I said it. The second time I read it, I invited children to join in when they could. By the third reading, nearly everyone was chiming in. The fourth time I asked them to try to read it without my help, and I had to step in only a few times to help them.

After we read the book together for three days (the other two days took much less time), I gave the children small copies that they read together in pairs. They love this part the most! They really feel like readers as they go off together to a special corner and read with a friend. I have put capable and struggling children together so that the modeling continues for those who need it. They continue to read the book with their partner until they feel very comfortable with it. At that point they read it to me, and if they do well (which means they sound fluent, not that each word is necessarily perfect), they may check the book out to take home to read to their parents and others.

Predictable big books like *Brown Bear, Brown Bear* seem to be helping Manuel learn English. I believe that the repetitive sentence pattern, with different words being substituted that are illustrated in the pictures, is helping him learn English syntax. Certainly, he can help "read" these kinds of Big Books during shared reading time. I am just so pleased at how his self-confidence and interest in reading are growing along with his ability to speak and understand spoken English.

Since we began the Five Steps in late October, I have been loudly praising everyone who attempted to complete all five steps in the time allotted for writing. In minilessons, I have modeled looking around the room and copying letters and words children find, as well as modeling ear spelling—stretching a word you want to write, listening for letters, and writing down the letters you hear. By now, almost all of the children are doing all five steps most days.

I have been working on small-case letter names with the children even more this month. I have read to them several times a couple of alphabet books in which the small-case letter is prominently displayed on each page. We finished the classroom alphabet book we began in the middle of last month. I put a photo of every child on the page his or her first name begins with, and then we put a photo of an object from our classroom on the pages for the other letters.

This month we did one of our recipes as a chart very much like the ones that are in some of the children's cookbooks that I showed to the class. They had almost all seen cookbooks at home, but they had not really noticed how the recipes were written. The form we now use includes the headings *Ingredients, Utensils,* and *Preparation* (written with numbered steps). The recipe was for "Happy Holidays Egg Cones," a kind of egg salad that we scooped into ice cream cones. Recipes certainly help work on the essential thinking processes as we *connect* new and old cooking experiences; *generalize* about what we have learned about how to cook so far; *apply* reading as we cook different recipes; *image* how this might look, taste, feel, or smell; *organize* the directions in a logical sequence; *predict* what might be added next or what step to do next; *self-monitor* if the directions or proportions make sense; and *evaluate* the product.

This was one of our better experiences this year. The children learned so many things while putting together this recipe. For example, we looked at raw eggs and hard-cooked eggs and talked about how the cooking changed them from a liquid to a solid. We measured the water after the first batch of eggs had finished cooking. Evaporation was discussed when they noticed much of the water gone. This recipe format allowed the introduction of quite a few new words, such as *ingredients*. There was much more measuring than in other recipes we had tried. All in all, it did go well. It amazes me to realize the number of concepts being developed.

I feel better about my assessment this year than I ever have before. No longer am I concerned about what to report to parents during our conferences or on my written summary of progress sent home to them at report card times. I use my observations and samples of their work, particularly their writing portfolios, to characterize each child's current status on each of my seven critical knowings. I make sure to point out each child's main strengths and weaknesses and then to summarize how well I think the child is moving toward ultimate success in first grade and beyond.

January

The children seemed really glad to be back at school—two weeks is a long time to be away. I find, too, that they usually have become bored at home and come to miss the routine we have so carefully established. Furthermore, most of them are anxious to share their holiday "goodies" with the other children. Pat got her wish and received some new books, which she assured me she could read. I asked her to bring them in and show them to us and perhaps read them to the class. Pat brought in a predictable-language book, *The Napping House.* First she read it to me, and then I let her read it to the class.

This month I began self-selected reading. Most of the teachers in this school set aside a period during which the children silently read materials of their oven choice at their own pace. I explained to the class that I was going to set our timer for three minutes, and during that three minutes everyone was to be looking at a book. We went to the school library to select books just for self-selected reading. I aided some in their selections so that Larry, Roberta, and Danielle had books they could read, and Paul and Daisy had some bright picture books on topics they found interesting (a children's cookbook for Daisy!). At self-selected reading time, it all went rather well, considering that this was a first for them. After it was over, I pulled aside the children who had had an especially difficult time sitting with a book for three whole minutes. We discussed again how they could look at the pictures to try to figure out what the story was about or to name the colors they saw on the pages, or how they could go through and think of the names of as many things as possible pictured on each page. I encouraged these children to try to decide if they liked the book enough to want me to read it to the whole class. I had to do this several times with various children in the room (not always the same ones), but by the end of the month, all the children really could sit still with a book for three minutes.

Children are getting the idea that what is in books should make sense to them and to others. By "pretend reading" the books over and over, many of them are even able to identify some of the words that occur repeatedly in each book. Certainly the motivation of reading to their peers has helped some of the children to become more interested in reading and in words. They also are becoming exposed to a variety of different kinds of books.

There was a flood of stories from the children after our field trip to the fire station this month. *Now* everyone wants to be a firefighter! They tell gory stories about how brave firefighters save helpless people and little babies—the influence of television, I think, for the fire chief certainly did nothing that would have aroused such stories.

Our second trip, a visit to a restaurant, couldn't compare with the excitement of the trip to the fire station. The children were fascinated with the huge appliances in the kitchen, and they informed the chef that they too were cooks. He asked them what they could cook, and they proceeded to catalogue our entire year of cooking for him, complete with the description of the mess we had with the cranberry-orange relish!

I am still having problems with Alexander. He often removes his hearing aid so that he can get out of work by claiming he doesn't know what to do. He is one of the children most in need of the language activities we do. He still doesn't talk in sentences; mostly he grunts and points. I suspect he can understand more than he appears to, because his mother told me that they communicate this way at home often. He points and she fetches! He is really getting to be a pill! His hearing loss wasn't discovered until two years ago. He is so delayed in language because he missed so many important concepts. He really has the language development of a three-year-old child. Even Paul may be ahead in this area.

I have begun to check letter–name knowledge with the children. I have been calling them to me one at a time and showing letter cards with both the upper- and lowercase on the same card and asking the children to name the letter. Up to this point, the letter names that the children have learned have been through exposure to lists of their classmates' names, letters and words they have matched on the chart stories, and their writing. Eleven of the alphabet letters were easily learned by most of the children just because those letters begin the names of the twenty-five children. Paul is the only child who knows only two letters: *P* and *C* (for Paul and Carl). Larry, Danielle, Pat, Roberta, Hilda, Joyce, and Mandy can name all the letters, capital and small-case, very quickly. Rita, Betty, Horace, Alex, Steve, and Anthony know most of the fifty-two letter names with the exception of the least frequent ones. The other children are at varying points in the number of letters they can name and how quickly they can name them.

Sometimes, after I write a language-experience chart, I tell the children that I am going to cover up the chart with another sheet of paper and we're going to play the "How Many Words?" game. I peek at the first sentence so that I can say it aloud to the children. As I read it to them, they are to raise a finger for each word I say, so that they can tell me how many words are in a sentence. They tell me the number (or numbers!) and I remove the paper covering so that we can count the number of words. Then I count on my fingers with them so that they have a model for what we are doing, and we do another sentence on the chart the same way.

Distinguishing words that rhyme and coming up with rhymes is one of the major phonemic awareness abilities we work on. I find that children can begin to make sense of the concept of rhyme when I use one of my favorite books, *The Hungry Thing*. In this book, we meet the Hungry Thing and find that he will eat only silly rhymes for real words, so that if they want to feed him "noodles," they tell him he is eating "foodles"; "soup with a cracker" is "boop with a smacker," and so on. As we read the story, the children try to guess what the Hungry Thing is eating throughout the book. When we finish the book, I tell them it is our turn to feed the Hungry Thing. I tell them to think of their favorite food and then to try to find a silly rhyme for it, so that the Hungry Thing will eat it. They enjoy playing "Feed the Hungry Thing," and it is increasing their awareness of rhyme and ability to come up with rhymes.

I think that Big Books and the Five Steps have totally changed the way I view beginning reading and writing instruction. Everyone can have success, and I can tell so much more easily who is acquiring which of the critical knowings. In writing, we have begun a formal sharing time after the Five Steps. Before, I had been going around as they finished and let them share with me what they had done. This month, however, I started allowing four or five children to share each day. I have found in the past that nothing motivates kindergarten children to write like having an opportunity to share with the whole class what they have written.

Jeff burned himself slightly during a cooking adventure the other day, so I took him over to the plant shelf, broke off a piece of a leaf, and rubbed the cut end of the leaf over the burned area. Immediately a crowd grew around the scene, fascinated children observing that the juice of the plant had made the burn feel better. "What is that?" "How did you know to do that, Miss Launch?" "Wow! Magic!"

Ah ha! The teachable moment my college professors were always talking about! "Let's sit down and do a chart about this plant," I suggested. "Plants are really wonderful things. Not only do they look nice in our room, but some of them can be used for food, some for medicine, and some to make clothes and houses. What are some questions you have about this plant?" For the next five minutes, they asked questions and I wrote those questions on the chart.

Some of their questions were related to the name and characteristics of the plant (color, size, etc.), some dealt with the care of the plant, and some concerned how new plants were grown. After all their questions were on the chart, I cut them apart and we grouped them according to the type of question they had. Based on this grouping, I sent Danielle, Paul, and Horace to the library to bring back books on plants. I sent a note with them to Miss Page, the librarian, telling her we were trying to get information about the aloe plant. With books before us, we came up with the following chart about aloe plants.

The Aloe Plant

Our plant's name is "aloe vera." (Anthony)

Aloe vera means "true aloe" because there are more than one kind of aloe. (Larry)

Aloe vera is a succulent because it has fat leaves and likes water. (Danielle)

It can grow one or two feet. (Paul)

It is all green. (Chip)

It likes lots of light. (Carl)

You can make new plants by planting the baby shoots called suckers. (Steve)

Aloe is special because it can help the burn places on you. (Jeff)

I was impressed with how much they really got into the aloe plant. Now they keep asking me if the other plants we have are special in any way. We may be making our own book about our classroom plants. This was a highly successful science lesson, and I told the students so. I want them to see science as interesting and valuable knowledge.

Another really successful cooking experience was tied to one of the many books I read to the children each week. I had brought in several versions of the old story "Stone Soup," and we compared how the stories were alike and how they were different. After those discussions, I told them that we were going to make some stone soup in the slow cooker. Their reactions ranged from Butch's "Yuk!" to Hilda's "How fascinating!" Everyone was told to bring in a vegetable, any vegetable, the next day.

"But what do we need, Miss Launch? How can we cook if we don't know what we need?" asked a worried Betty.

"Well, in the book they didn't have a recipe. They just put in whatever was brought to them." That, clearly, was not very satisfying to Betty.

The next day most of the children had remembered to bring in a vegetable. We went out to the playground, and each person was to find one small stone to put in the soup. Alex was appalled! "But they're dirty. People have been walking on them, and I even saw Mort and Butch spitting on the rocks!" "Yuk too," I thought, though I dared not show it! "We will carefully wash each rock in hot, soapy water so that they are nice and clean for the soup," I told him. And wash we did. The rocks were then placed in the bottom of the slow cooker, and I added twelve cups of water and twelve beef bouillon cubes.

We began acting out the story with three children pretending to wonder what else they could put in the soup and how good it would be if only there were a carrot or two. In this way, we went through each of the vegetables the class had brought. Whoever had brought the vegetable had to wash it and cut it into pieces to put into the soup. I helped cut off the tops and bad places, but the children did most of the work. When all the veggies had been added, we put on the lid of the slow cooker and left it until nearly time to go home. Daphne gave it a stir with a big wooden spoon and put the lid on one more time. I took it home with me to continue cooking and then to refrigerate. The next day, we heated it up in the slow cooker by snack time. Needless to say, the soup was pretty good, much to Alex's amazement.

This month, I began systematically teaching the consonant letter sounds. We have been noticing sounds letters make in all our activities and particularly when I model for them how to "ear spell" words as they stretch them out to write them. I am now going systematically through the consonant letters. For each one, we identify all the children who have that letter in their name and stretch out the names to see if we can hear that letter's "usual sound." We are putting up key words for each letter—a favorite food and an action—a great teaching device I learned from Mrs. Wright. We have also read some tongue-twister books and are writing a class book of tongue twisters. The first ones we wrote use the names of the children, and later we will add some for those letters we don't have names for. In teaching the letter sounds, I don't go alphabetically, because *b* and *d* are so confusable, as are *m* and *n*. Rather, I pick ones that have very different sounds and for which I have name examples. This year, the first four I taught were *m, p, l,* and *j.* Here are the tongue twisters for them:

> Mandy, Mike, Mitch, Mort, and Manuel make meatballs.
>
> Pat and Paul pick peaches.
>
> Larry loves lemonade.
>
> Jeff and Joyce jump and juggle.

The children are learning these sounds quite easily. I attribute their success to all the work we did from September through December. Had I begun teaching these sounds in September, some of the children would simply have been unable to learn them, and almost all of the children would have had more difficulty.

February

Our poetry writing is coming along so well! I read Mary O'Neill's *Hailstones and Halibut Bones* to the children and discussed with them that O'Neill thought colors could represent things and feelings as well as thoughts. Then we did a poetry format (again as a group) that has this configuration:

> I feel _____
>
> I see _____

I hear _____

I smell _____

I taste _____

I feel _____

The unifying factor here is the repetition of the phrase "I feel." To help the children recognize the five senses the poem deals with, I told them that I would give them several days to work on a collage of pictures from magazines, newspapers, and other sources that portray the five senses. They were to find as many pictures as they could that would finish the phrases I listed. It was a messy assignment, but the children helped to create several poems and collages. In addition, the children were proud because the collages described *them* as individuals. I had the children work individually on this project, so I did have to help out some of the more unsure children such as Paul and Chip. Paul struggled—with my help—to find one example for each phrase. When some of the children wondered if they could finish the phrase with just one word or a picture, I told them that they could. Others complained that they couldn't do that—they needed to say more! I told them that the only rule was that they finished the phrases, no matter how many words they used.

Last month's interest in the plants did indeed result in a science book we made for the classroom and the school library about the plants we have. Steve, who has a remarkable eye for drawing nature objects, did the illustrations. Actually, he did the outlines in pencil and then asked certain students to do the coloring in. We made one book for our room and another for the library, since Miss Page had been so helpful all year.

I have been doing some "Think Link" listening comprehension lessons with the children recently. Sue Port, the curriculum supervisor, was in last month and complimented me on the way I asked children to use the essential thinking processes as I read through a story. She really liked relating the listening to those processes. But, she said, what about Paul and Chip and some of the others who never contributed to the discussion? It was clear that children like Larry and Danielle were dominating the discussions. I told her that this had concerned me too. "Give me a week," she said. "I've got an idea for another way to use those thinking processes that I'd like you to try out."

Well! Sue Port's idea has revolutionized my classroom listening lessons. She told me that she wanted to try out a "Think Link." In Think Links, the teacher models what she is thinking about by talking through the story, stopping at appropriate places to tell children which of the essential thinking processes were triggered by the text. In this way, children like Paul and Chip can get an insight into *how* people think, not just *what* they think. She asked if she could model a story with my class.

Sue Port began her lesson by telling the children that when they went on to first grade, people were going to be asking them to tell about things they were reading. She wanted to show them how she understood things she was reading by reading a story and telling them what her mind was thinking about throughout. She showed them the cover of *Swimmy* and said:

> "This book is called Swimmy, and it is by Leo Lionni. I know that I am probably going to like this book because I have liked other books by him. If I went into the library and found this book, I might pick it up and look at the cover and think, "Hmmm. Swimmy. I see a fish on the cover and since fish swim, I'll bet that's the name of the fish in this story. I wonder where the fish lives. Maybe a river. Maybe a lake. Maybe this fish lives in the ocean. Maybe Swimmy is a pet. I don't know yet if the fish is a girl or boy. I'd guess, though, that it's a make-believe story because Lionni writes a lot of make-believe stories."

She continued to go through each page of the book with the children, talking about "what my brain is telling me" as she read the text and looked at the pictures. I was particularly intrigued by her imaging with the children, because I had found that to be the hardest of the essential thinking processes for me to use with children. After reading about Swimmy's family being eaten and Swimmy going off on his own, she said:

> "I can just see Swimmy gliding through the water, slowly, sadly. His little tail is hardly swishing at all. Close your eyes. Can you see him swimming? Ooooh! The water is getting colder as he goes deeper. I'm shivering as I feel that cold water all around his body. Can you feel it? Close your eyes. Feel that cold water. Are you shivering?"

The children responded so well to what she was doing. Mike even said, "So that's how Larry knows so much! His brain is thinking of stuff!" As we talked later, Sue told me that she did not cover all of the thinking processes because not all of them were appropriate for that story. In fact, she really spent most of her Think Link on imaging and predicting, because the story fit those two quite well.

After she left, I dug out some books I had planned to use with the children and developed a skeleton of a Think Link for several of them. I plan to do Think Links once a week.

Self-selected reading continues to roll along smoothly. We are up to five minutes of reading time, now. We will hold at that level for a while, since Butch and Mort are at the upper limit of their ability to sit still. Larry and Danielle, however, continue to read after the class time is up. They both are reading almost a book a day. Danielle's father told me that he thinks Danielle is such a good reader because she was in the hospital for so long after the car accident in which she was hurt and her mother was killed. Her father, the nurses, and all her visitors read constantly to her and had her try to guess about story events, and they sat beside her so that she would always see the words as they were reading.

Again this year, I find it wonderful to see the consonant letter–sound relationships I am teaching show up in so much of the children's writing. Because I now require ear spelling of every child, when they stretch words to listen for letters to write down, they are naturally more likely to hear the sounds they have been learning to associate with particular beginning consonant letters. Often they hear them elsewhere in the word besides the beginning! Children's ear spellings during writing are the best means I can think of to assess children's developing phonemic awareness and phonics knowledge.

I praise the children who stretch words and listen for letters to write down during their writing. Moreover, I often point out to the other children when I can read a word or even a statement that a child has written using ear spelling. This not only encourages them to apply their developing phonics knowledge during writing, but it is part of my overall strategy to build their self-confidence to learn.

The first several months of the year, I wouldn't allow anyone to denigrate children's pretend reading or initial efforts at writing, even though they weren't really reading or writing. I wanted all the children to feel that they were doing exactly what I wanted them to without thinking they were inadequate, and I also wanted them to use these pretend experiences to begin to enjoy reading and writing as activities.

Beginning last month, however, and continuing on for the rest of the year, I am helping the children come to understand that how well they do is a result of their effort and how they go about it. So, when children use the pictures to figure out a word or part of the story, I not only praise them, but I point out what they did and how it helped them. Likewise, when children use the beginning letters of a word along with its context to figure out what the word is, or when they ear-spell a word so that I or another child can read it, I not only praise them, but I explain that their success on that word resulted from a good strategy that they made the effort to apply.

The favorite cooking experience this month was making whole-wheat pretzels. Children shaped the dough into letter names they knew and baked them. What fun and what motivation! Even Mort seemed to want to learn some more letters so he could make more pretzels.

March

I noticed this month that I don't even look at the seven critical knowings in the front of my plan book anymore. It has become so automatic to think of everything we do in terms of my knowings that I was well into the preparation of the cards for a game when it suddenly occurred to me that this simple game was facilitating some of my seven ingredients. In fact, all around me are opportunities to exploit learning!

I started this month with a game that the children really enjoyed. I told the children that we would be playing a game that might take all morning to finish, but that it didn't matter because they could play the game while they worked.

Surprise, surprise! Each child was going to have the picture of an animal pinned on his or her back, and they were to guess the animal. They could ask only two questions of each classmate, and the questions could only be answered yes or no. The purpose of this restriction was to encourage a maximum use of language on the part of the one guessing and to discourage unnecessary hints and clues. The children seemed very excited by the idea and were ready to begin immediately. I reminded them that they were to continue their work while trying to guess, and that it would be a good idea to think carefully before asking questions so that the questions wouldn't be wasted. I gave the following demonstration: "Mandy, will you please pin the picture of an animal to my back?" She did so, and I turned so that my back—and the picture—were toward the children. There was much giggling from some of the children.

"Okay. Steve, do I have hair? No? Hmmmm. Steve, do I have six legs? No? Thank you. Let's see now—Rita, do I have wings? No. All right, do I have scales? Ah ha! Now we're getting someplace. Mandy, do people catch me to eat? No, that means that I'm not a fish. Do I crawl? I thought I might. Horace, am I a snake?"

The children were amazed that I guessed the animal so quickly. I explained that animals are in groups and that I was trying to find which group my animal was in. One large group that includes bears, cats, dogs, beavers, and people was the one I was asking about first—they all have fur or hair. When I knew that the animal didn't have fur or hair, I knew that it had to be an insect or an amphibian (living both on land and in water) or a bird or a reptile (an animal with scales). "Listen carefully" was my last injunction before pinning on the animals. And the game was on! Larry, Hilda, Roberta, and Steve guessed theirs rather quickly, for they had paid attention to what I had told them and tried logically to figure out what to ask next. Daisy used up all her questions by running from person to person, asking questions like "Am I a deer? Am I a goat?" rather than trying to find the category and proceed logically. It took most of the children the entire morning to determine what they were. Paul managed to find out that he was a dog, though his guess was based on luck rather than system.

So many things are going on with this particular activity. Children are engaging in an identifying-sorting-classifying game that helps to develop further their understanding of animals and animal characteristics. They are developing the essential thinking processes of generalize, predict, and apply as they work on this background information. I think I'll do this again next week with forms of transportation or foods.

Anthony's mother has been riding me all year about making sure that I am teaching the children all they need to know to go into first grade. She and I have had a few points of departure this year in our assessments of his abilities. He is her brilliant, only child and she wants to make certain that he will be ready to attend MIT when the time comes! She has been taking books home from the school she teaches in for him to read with her. No wonder he is so intractable some mornings. She had told me that they have one hour of reading every night, and that she has been having him copy the words he doesn't know over and over. I told her that he had many opportunities and materials to explore and read at school. However, because he is so focused on science, she believes that we are not providing enough science stuff here. I haven't been able to budge her or she me. Oh, well!

All the things we do every day are moving along just as they should be for March. Self-selected reading is up to seven minutes, and all the children are writing about events or objects in their lives that they choose. Steve and Anthony have been trying some science experiments and writing down what they do and how it turns out (I am unable to read most of it, but they generously share what their markings mean).

The Big Books continue to be popular reading material with the children, and their favorite Big Books are the ones we made that were parallel to stories read in class. We wrote a version of *The Three Little Kittens* called *The Three Little Goats* who had lost their boats. They came up with some very nice ideas. I put it on the large tagboard and let the children illustrate the book. They worked in small groups so that every child got to add something to the book.

Manuel has come sung way! He is now able to converse with the other children fairly well, unless he is trying to explain something that happened at home. Even then, he often succeeds. A literacy- and language-rich classroom seems to be one thing a child learning English needs!

The third-graders from Mrs. Wise's class have been writing books for the children, as well as coming down to take dictation so that the kindergartners can get *their* stories into print. The third-graders have been studying bookbinding and have made some very handsome books for the children to take home or to put in our classroom library. To thank them for all their help, we invited them to come help us eat the peanut-butter cookies we made.

April

Spring, spring, spring!!! I love it. We've been outside a lot lately, which has been good for the children as well as for me. We do some of our work out there when we can, such as our lesson on poetry. The poetry we composed this month used an "I wish" format. I told the children that they were to think of four different things they wished for. The poem was to have lines beginning with the words *I wish*, but the first and the last lines were to be identical. Here is the large-group poem that we did before breaking up into small groups for more poetry writing using this format.

> I wish spring was here. (Steve)
> I wish that the sun was warm. (Manuel)
> I wish that the frogs would make noises. (Butch)
> I wish I could go out without my coat. (Alex)
> I wish spring was here. (Steve)

The children have been creating greeting cards all year long, but some of the birthday cards for Jeff were just too much! Someone got the notion that even if he couldn't give Jeff a present, he could *wish* to give him a present. I don't know who began it, but children began to write things such as "I wish you could have this" with their ear spellings. Some children became the "experts" at the table, offering their help to those who wanted to write messages. In walking around later, I noticed that they were cutting pictures out of our catalogues and magazines. The picture of a bike, swimming pool, motorcycle, or some other luxury item would appear at the bottom of the written message, which was then passed over to Jeff for his birthday. Jeff was grinning from ear to ear all day long!

I am still trying to help the children develop their reasoning and questioning abilities by such things as the "feely" box. I have constructed the feely box by cutting a hole in one end of a shoebox and attaching to the hole a sock with the toe end cut off. I placed a comb in the box and permitted the children to reach in through the sock and into the box where they could feel the object but not see it. Each child was permitted a few seconds to feel the object and then report what the object might be. I changed the objects frequently, so that the children would have many opportunities to use the sense of touch. The next project was somewhat harder for the children, for I had arranged the experiences in order of difficulty. This time a single child would feel the object, describe it in three different ways, and then guess what it was. The third kind of experience was to let a child see an object, describe it to the other children, and let *them* guess what was being described. The fourth task was even more complicated, for this time the child felt an object, described it to the other children, and they had to guess what it was that he or she had felt. Occasionally, as a variation, I would let several children feel the same object so that they could help one another with the description. The rest of the group had to try to guess what it was that was being felt. This worked out very well, particularly when Paul, Chip, or Joyce, who have a great deal of difficulty verbalizing, described the object. However, it is obviously easier for the group if the clues are clearly stated, a skill these three were unable to demonstrate yet.

The three gained from listening to the descriptions given by the more verbal children, however, for they experienced the same object and could compare their own perceptions with what was being said. The fifth task with the feely box was to have a child feel an object and then give a one-word clue, and so on. A particularly interesting game was one that took place this week. Steve reached into the box and felt the object. He said, "Prickly." There were guesses of *porcupine, cactus,* and *pins.* The next clue was "Woody." The children were stumped for a moment, until Larry guessed that it might be a plank from the workshop. The next clue: "Tree." Something from a tree that is wooden and prickly?

"Oh, I know, I know!" exclaimed Hilda, who had been putting all the clues together. "It's bark from the tree!" She sat back smug and confident.

"No, that's not it. 'Seeds.'"

The crestfallen Hilda began muttering, "Seeds? Seeds. Seeds! It's a pinecone! Am I right this time, Steve?" Steve's nod reassured her that her deduction skills had been well utilized.

The most difficult of all was the last project—identifying the object within a wrapped box by asking questions of me. They found this to be a very challenging task. They knew that it could not be a chair, for instance, for the package would not accommodate so large an object. The questioning techniques of the children had increased with the readiness activities that they had been doing for the few weeks prior to this exercise, and they did guess that the object was a shoe.

Our consonant letter–sound instruction is going quite well. I am seeing all the consonants occur in the ear spellings that almost all of the children are now including in their writing. Of course, I review, review, review these letter–sound relationships. When I first taught each consonant, I taught them a key action that begins with that letter and sound. "Leap" was our *l* action. Each day for a while, we would all stand by our seats and leap to help us remember the sound *l* makes. Likewise, I taught them key actions for each of the other consonants, along with the other means I used to help them remember the sound of the letter. Before long, one of the ways we reviewed each of the single onsets we had learned so far was for me to write either the capital or the small-case letter on the board and have them (on the count of three) perform the key action for that letter. I will continue this type of "action" review of the consonants until the year ends.

This month we began to study capital letter formation. Of course, all the children have been writing the capital letters all year, but with no standards to meet. Now, I am systematically teaching them how best to form each capital letter on unlined paper and having them practice writing them. Their previous writing makes it easy for them to learn to improve their letter formation, yet they haven't been writing so long without formal handwriting instruction that their habits are too ingrained to gradually change.

This month, we made "Ants on a Log" by cutting celery using a premeasured length and then filling the hole with peanut butter and putting on the ants (raisins). A great snack and E-A-S-Y, even for Paul at this point.

May

It is just amazing to me how much my children know about every aspect of reading and writing! That retreat last summer, and my translating what we agreed on into the seven critical knowings for kindergarten, has really paid off. I have never had a class end the year knowing so many letter names so fluently. I have never had a class with such a grasp of consonant letter–sound relationships. Yet I also have never had a class so turned on to reading and writing and with such developed language and thinking abilities.

This month we studied small-case letter formation. I didn't go straight through the alphabet, but rather taught the easiest ones first and separated the reversible ones—*b*, *d*, *p*, and *q*. This year, I have fewer students making letter, numeral, and word reversals, though you always have some with kindergarten children. I attribute this improvement to all the shared reading with Big Books, language-experience lessons and charts, and writing that the students have done. Directionality has to be learned, and contextualized reading and writing are the main tools for teaching it.

For the last field trip, I asked the two first-grade teachers if they would permit our children to visit their rooms to acquaint them with the teachers and also to give them some idea of what they could expect to see in first grade. Both teachers agreed and gave the children a fine overview of the first-grade program. Mrs. Wright had one of her students act as guide around the room, and she had others who explained the various things that they were working on. The kindergartners were quite impressed with the "big" first-graders who were so helpful to them, and all of them said that they wanted to be in Mrs. Wright's room next year.

After the children had finished their tour, I asked them how they would feel about doing something similar for the kindergarten class who would be arriving next fall.

"You mean you're going to have *more* kids here? I thought you just taught us," said Daphne.

"Now you know that there is going to be another group here. Remember the recent kindergarten round-up?"

"Yes, but we thought . . . I thought . . . I mean . . . "

"I will remember all of you. You don't have to worry about that. We care about one another, and when we care about people, we don't forget them. But you can't stay with me forever. You are ready to go on and learn more. You don't want to do the same things again. First grade is so exciting! You'll love it, but remember to say hello to me once in a while! But you still haven't answered. Shall we do something for the next kindergarten class like what the first-graders did?" Amid cries of "Yes! Yes!" there was one, Larry, who commented that that would be difficult, since we didn't know who the children would be.

"How about this?" I began, and outlined the plan for creating a mural depicting the various kindergarten activities. The children would put it up on the bulletin board and leave it there. When fall came, the new students would see some work done by "big" kindergartners telling them what to expect. The children loved the idea, and so did I. One of my pet peeves has always been that I begin the school year without any artwork from children on the walls—now there will be.

Self-selected reading has been highly successful this year. We're up to eight minutes a day as a class. However, some children continue reading after the timer rings. Mandy told me that she enjoys the idea of everyone reading at the same time.

I have found that I can do Think Links almost without thinking. It seems very easy to me now to examine a book for which one of the thinking processes can be highlighted and then to talk my way through the book. I have also found that by varying the kinds of materials I read—magazine articles with animal facts, books about other cultures, poems, and stories—I have thoroughly covered all of the thinking processes by this time. By now I have begun asking the children at several points to tell me what they are thinking and what caused them to have that thought. Even Chip and Alex are doing well with this now.

I did decide to risk making a whole meal at school, and it actually came off well! I had considered an early lunch for them to prepare, but I decided after one of our book sessions that nothing would do but to fix breakfast. The impetus for this decision, as you might have guessed, was Dr. Seuss's *Green Eggs and Ham!* The room was set up in stations for the big event. There were the measuring and mixing area, the scrambled eggs area, the toast area, the juice and milk area, and the cleanup area. Five children were in each of the areas, with clearly defined responsibilities.

The scrambled egg recipe was quite easy, although it did involve some high-level counting skills. For each person to be served, the children measured and mixed 1 egg, 1 tbsp. milk, and 2 tsp. diced ham. When it was all mixed together, they added the special ingredient: ½ tsp. blue food coloring! (We had quite a discussion about what color we should add to the yellow eggs.) The eggs were cooked in three electric skillets at the scrambled eggs area. Many cries of "Yuk!" and "Gross!" were heard and brought others to the scrambled eggs area to exclaim anew at the mess they saw before them.

Meanwhile, the people in "juice and milk" were pouring out servings into paper cups, and the people in "toast" were making four slices at a time. After the toast came out of the appliance, they used a plastic glass and pressed the top into the slice of toast, cutting out a circle. They made two heaps of toast: circles and slices with holes. The cleanup people, who would not have anything to do until after the breakfast was over, came to the toast area and placed one circle and one slice on each one of the paper plates. They carried the plates to "scrambled eggs," where a spoonful of green eggs and ham was put into the hole of the bread slice. They got their beverages and then their plates, and we all ate heartily!

My routine, lately, has involved sorting out materials and tossing away some of the accumulation. In doing so, I came across my very tattered copy of the critical knowings. I looked over the list yet again and thought back over all the activities I had been led to do using those seven factors as my guideline. I did indeed have children using shared book experiences and lots of writing. They dictated all sorts of language experiences to me. I read to them and talked with them a lot. Many of the activities, such as writing, fulfilled several of my goals at the same time. I wonder if it is possible to delineate all of the learnings that occurred in this room this year, or is there such an interaction of children, needs, and knowings that it would not be possible to construct two-dimensionally? I think I'll leave that one for contemplation at my beach retreat this summer!

As I look back across the year, I guess I am proudest of what Manuel has accomplished. I just never would have believed that he would have learned to listen, speak, read, write, and apparently think as much English as he has. He has a way to go, but he is definitely on the road to academic success. It makes me realize how much more he could have accomplished had we had an ESL teacher to work with him regularly each week. The combination of a literacy-rich kindergarten *and* a good ESL teacher would have ensured a speedy transition to English proficiency for Manuel. I know Mr. Topps is trying to get an ESL teacher for us in the future, but the number of children who need such a service is lower at our school than at several others in the district. I'll be sure to speak with Manuel's first-grade teacher about him at the beginning of next year.

The Curriculum Committee Meeting

Miss Launch sat at the large oval table, trying to restrain herself from tapping her pencil on the tabletop. She had been sitting at this same table every week for the last three months. Miss Launch had been very quiet during these meetings, feeling that, as a relative newcomer to the district, she should allow those who had been with the school system longer to do most of the talking.

As nearly as she could tell, this group of kindergarten teachers, all of those who taught in the school system, were divided into three distinct camps. Miss

Launch felt sorry for Sue Port, the curriculum supervisor, who had to chair the meetings. She had always found Ms. Port very facilitative and helpful. But these meetings must surely be a strain on her good nature!

"All right, people," interrupted Ms. Port, "let's try to get some consensus on this matter. Let me summarize what we have all agreed on." There was general laughter around the room, since they all knew that this would be a short summary.

"Our kindergarten curriculum guide is fifteen years old, and although it has some good aspects to it, it seems that some of the information and guidelines are outdated. It also seems that the guide is better the longer you have taught! This indicates to us that the guide is not very helpful to beginning teachers, since more experienced teachers have to fill in with materials and knowledge they already possess—not a problem for them, but it surely is to some others. The feeling among many of you is that you like the, shall we say, vagueness of the present guide because it allows a lot of freedom for individual teaching styles. But there is no choice, which is what I've been trying to get through to you these past many weeks; we are mandated by the school board to produce a new kindergarten curriculum guide by the end of the summer. Frankly, I'm getting worried! I see three factions in this group. Let me outline them for you so that we can try to bring this together today.

"We have one group of teachers who would like us to purchase one or more of the kits on the market. This group argues that the kits are complete with materials, teacher's guide, and objectives. I brought a few examples of kits today so that we could examine them more closely.

"Another group seems to want to develop a new curriculum guide that will be a kind of super-teacher's manual and to meet through the summer over salad lunches to put together the materials you'll need for the first few weeks. We would then meet regularly during the school year to produce additional materials and to add to the teacher's manual based on the actual teaching done with it.

"The third group is inclined to forget the whole thing." She paused as laughter interrupted. "But knowing we can't, they would like us to add a couple of things to the old guide and continue to ignore it and teach as they have always done."

"Wow," thought Miss Launch, "she's not pulling any punches today."

"That's not quite fair," spoke up the most vocal member of the third group. "We have been teaching for a long time, and nobody seems to have complained about what we've been doing. Why change now just to be changing? I know for sure that I can do a better job with the children I teach than if you made me use one of those kits over there! Those kits don't contain all the aspects that I deal with in my program."

"You know, Kay," said Ms. Port, "you just might be able to pull off the greatest program in the world. However, much as I'd like to think it, this school system just is not filled with Kay Longs. What about some of our teachers who just got out of college? What about teachers like Helen Launch who came to this school system from another, very different one? Don't we owe those people a chance to share in your expertise?

"One problem we face is that we have to have some consistency within our school system so that kindergarten means essentially the same thing no matter where one goes. Why, even within the same school I've noted great differences, substantive differences, in the kindergarten program. Another fact to face is that the instruction in kindergarten should help to facilitate the child's beginning reading and writing experiences, not hinder them. If we have some common goals toward which we are all working, then we should be facilitating beginning reading and writing. Right now, we only hope we are. We have some ideas about specific teaching emphases based on our experiences with the spring kindergarten screening we do. However, I've always felt *that* information is somewhat suspect because the situation in which the children are assessed is so strange to them. They are taken into a big room, the cafeteria or gym, and meet with many different people to perform many different tasks. You all know how hard it is to get a five-year-old to perform on command! So we know if they can see or hear, but I wonder how much valid information we get on their academic knowledge.

"I'm open to suggestion as to where we go from here. Yes, Helen, is that your hand I see?"

"Well, I've kept rather quiet through all of these discussions, but I wonder if I might be able to offer, just as a starting point, the guidelines I used to help me teach this year. Maybe we could look at the kits up there using these objectives, so that at least we would all be talking about the same things."

With Ms. Port's encouragement, Miss Launch put the seven critical knowings on the chalkboard in the room and then sat down and discussed each of them briefly. She noticed murmurs and nods of agreement among teachers from all three factions. No one could argue against any of them, because they did seem to be essential to beginning reading and writing success. However, the discussion turned lively when they began to examine the kits, using the knowings as guidelines!

"Hey, where are all the books? If we are to encourage children to read and listen to a variety of materials, and to immerse them in books so that they develop a desire to learn to read, then we're going to need more books than the five they have in this kit. Five books is an insult! Why put in any?"

"Look how flimsy all this stuff is! My kids would have these thin cardboard pictures destroyed in a week, even though they're pretty careful. And those puppets! Do you believe they are trying to pawn those off for classroom use? I give them three days!"

"Speaking of the pictures, just look at them closely. What's that a picture of? A dog? A beagle? A puppy? Pet? Stuffed animal? It's really hard to tell. The pictures are small and not very clear—too much distraction in them."

"Listen to this manual, you guys. This whole kit as well as the other two really hit phonics hard! But the instruction is too hard for my students, and they need a lot more repetition than these kits provide for. It says here we can 'add additional materials' from our own sources, if necessary. I thought this was supposed to be complete!"

These comments continued for some minutes as the teachers found that, even with their aura of professionalism, the kits were not complete sets of materials that would make teaching a breeze for the school year. More important, they didn't even come close to providing for all the learnings that adherence to Miss Launch's seven knowings called for. Ultimately, it was clear to Ms. Port that the consensus had indeed been found. Though much discussion about the details of pulling off the new curriculum guide remained to be gone through, basically the teachers agreed that Miss Launch's seven knowings should be the core of the new curriculum guide. They realized that they could produce their own curriculum, which would be much more complete than the kits they could purchase for the same money.

Helen and Sue left the room together, the last of the group to trail out. "Thank you for your help today," said Sue. "I think they see now that good learning and teaching can't be totally packaged, nor can it exist without structure. That was the breakthrough today. You've left your mark on this school system. I'm glad you're one of us!"

Miss Launch waved to the departing back of the smiling Ms. Port, marveling at what she had just said. "Me? I left a mark? I'm just trying to teach all the kids the best way I know how."

Children's Books/Materials Cited

Alphabetics, by Suse MacDonald, Bradbury Press, 1986.
The All-Around Pumpkin Book, by M. Cuyler, Scholastic, 1980.
Brown Bear, Brown Bear, What Do You See? by Bill Martin, Jr., Holt, Rinehart, & Winston, 1970.
Frederick, by Leo Lionni, Knopf/Pantheon, 1970.
Green Eggs and Ham, by Dr. Seuss, Random House, 1960.
Hailstones and Halibut Bones, by Mary O'Neill, Doubleday, 1990.
The Hungry Thing, by J. B. Slepian & A. G. Seidler, Scholastic, 1971.
Mushroom in the Rain, by Mirra Ginsburg, Scholastic, 1974.
The Napping House, by A. Wood, Harcourt Brace Jovanovich, 1986.
Swimmy, by Leo Lionni, Knopf Books for Young Readers, 1970.
The Taming of the C.A.N.D.Y. Monster, by V. Lansky, Book Peddlers, 1978.
The Timbertoes ABC Alphabet, by Highlights for Children, Boyds Mills Press, 1997.
Where the Wild Things Are, by Maurice Sendak, HarperCollins, 1963.

Mrs. Wright: First Grade

The Parent Meeting

Rita Wright sat in her first-grade classroom, awaiting the arrival of the parents for their orientation meeting. She remembered how nervous she had been at her first parent meeting years ago, and although there was still a little nervous flutter in her stomach, she had learned to approach these meetings with confidence. "The parents all want the best for their children," she reminded herself, "and I have learned so much since that first year about how to teach them." Mrs. Wright felt particularly confident and excited about this year because last year she had phased in a four-block approach to reading and writing (Cunningham, Hall, & Sigmon, 1999) that had resulted in accelerated progress for her top and her bottom students. She had worked out the "bugs" in this balanced approach and was beginning this year with a clear sense of how she would organize and what she might accomplish. Tonight, she hoped to explain to the parents, in simple terms, what this four-block approach was and how it would benefit all their children.

As parents began to arrive, Mrs. Wright rose to greet them and make sure they all put on name tags. She recognized several parents whose older children she had taught and chatted with them for a minute about how these children were doing. As parents introduced themselves and put on their name tags, she found herself noticing how like and unlike some of their children they were. Daphne's grandmother was there, and Mrs. Wright understood where Daphne got her nurturing, caretaking ways. Chip's grandfather came and he, just like Chip, was clean and presentable but dressed in old, threadbare clothes. Mike's father came and paced around restlessly, and Mrs. Wright could picture his constantly-in-motion son. Betty and Roberta's mother came, and Mrs. Wright could account for Betty's neat, orderly, pleasing style. She wondered if Roberta took after her father! These twins' differences had reaffirmed Mrs. Wright's belief that children come with their own personalities and do not all learn in the same way.

When everyone appeared to be there—Paul, Butch, and Alexander, three of her students she was most concerned about, had no parent or other relative present—Mrs. Wright began the meeting.

"I am just delighted that you took time out from your hectic schedules to be here tonight. School has been in session only a week, but your children and I are already hard at work here in our classroom. My goal is that all your children will learn to read and write and do math and learn more about the world in which we live. Accomplishing this with a diverse class of twenty-five children will take all our best efforts. Your making the effort to be here tonight lets me know that your children and the school have your support, and I will do my very best to teach all your children and keep you informed of their progress.

"Many of you know that the summer before last, we had a two-day retreat to really spend some extended time talking about what we believe and how to make our instruction consistent with out beliefs. Out of that meeting came this list of twelve guiding principles, which all the teachers at Merritt try to follow. I would like each of you to have a copy of this and as I talk, I will try to remember to point out how our classroom program reflects each of these principles." Mrs. Wright passed out the following statement of twelve principles.

At Merritt Elementary, we believe that all children can learn to read and write. We hold high expectations of every child. To make these expectations a reality, we all agree to have our instruction reflect twelve guiding principles:

1. Provide a balanced literacy program.

2. Make instruction multilevel.

3. Use language as the foundation for reading and writing.

4. Teach reading and writing as thinking.

5. Use feelings to create avid readers and writers.

6. Connect reading and writing to all subject areas.

7. Read aloud to students daily.

8. Schedule daily self-selected reading.

9. Have students write every day.

10. Teach the decoding and spelling strategies reading and writing require.

11. Use observation to assess learning and plan instruction.

12. Inform parents of expectations and progress.

"I would like you to look at our schedule, which is posted on this chart," Mrs. Wright continued. "When I explain to you what happens during each of these blocks of time, I think you will understand all we have to accomplish and how hard we will be working each day."

Here is the schedule for Mrs. Wright's first-grade class:

8:30–8:45	Morning meeting/Planning for the day
8:45–9:20	Writing block
9:20–9:50	Working with Words block
9:50–10:10	Break/Recess
10:10–10:45	Guided Reading block
10:45–11:30	Math
11:30–12:00	Lunch
12:00–12:15	Rest/Quiet Time
12:15–1:00	Science or Social Studies unit
1:00–1:30	Specials—P.E., Music, Library
1:30–2:00	Teacher Read-Aloud/Self-Selected Reading block
2:00–2:15	Summary/Review/Prepare to go home
2:15–2:45/3:00	Centers

Pointing to each of the time slots, Mrs. Wright explained what happened in each of these and what they were intended to accomplish.

"Although some children are in the room earlier, we start our official day at 8:30. The children check in when they arrive and indicate their lunch choices, so we don't waste time with attendance. In the first fifteen minutes, I try to accomplish a number of goals. We always do some activities with our calendar, such as determining what day and month it is, and counting the number of days to certain special days. This may seem simple enough to you, but many first-grade children are still unsure of important time concepts like days of the week, months, and seasons. We then look at our daily schedule, and we move the hands of this big clock to show what time we will do each activity. If there are any changes in our normal schedule, I point these out to the children and write them on a note that I attach to our schedule. Starting out each morning by orienting ourselves in this way helps the children have a real sense of orderliness and allays any fears they might have that we might forget one of the important parts of the day like recess or lunch or centers. It also gives us lots of opportunities to use math in real situations as we count days, months, and so on and work with the important first-grade math concept of telling time. We usually end this opening meeting by singing a favorite song, reciting a favorite rhyme, and doing a favorite finger play.

"At 8:45, we begin Writers' Workshop. Daily writing is a very important part of how children learn to write, and writing is also a major way in which children become readers. Each day, I do a minilesson in which I write something while the children watch me write. Then the children write. Right now, we are in what I call the 'driting' stage. The children both draw and write, often intermixing the two. I model this for them by drawing something each day and writing a little something

Red Honda
Accord

Mrs.
Wright

Merritt
Elementary
School

to go with my drawing. Here is the driting I did this morning." Mrs. Wright displayed the large piece of drawing paper on which she had created her drawing and word labels. Parents chuckled when they saw her artwork!

"As you can tell, my drawing skills are limited, but I try to turn this disadvantage into an advantage. My children never tell me that they can't draw. They know that they can all do as well as—and many better than—I do.

"After I draw and write a few words and tell the children about my driting, they all get a piece of drawing paper and they 'drite' something they want to tell about. I go around and encourage them, but I don't spell or write words for them. If they want to write a word, I encourage them to put down all the letters they hear, and write it just so that they can remember what they want to tell about."

At this point, Mrs. Wright was interrupted by Roberta and Betty's mother, who said "Mrs. Wright, this is something I have been worrying about. Betty told me that she wouldn't write because she can't spell all the words, and Roberta says that it doesn't matter if you spell them right as long as you know what you are saying. They are always fussing about this when they come home with their driting, and I don't know what to tell them. I always spell words for them at home. How are they going to learn to spell if no one spells words for them?"

Several parents were nodding their heads in agreement, and Mrs. Wright realized she would have to try to convince them that invented spelling was an important part of learning to spell correctly.

"I know that for many of you, letting the children spell words by putting down the letters they hear seems strange. That is certainly not the way things were done when I was in school and not the way I taught just a few years ago. But research has shown that children who are encouraged to put down the letters they hear as they are writing write more and better pieces and become better at sounding out words when they are reading. Think about it. If your child is trying to write *motor-cycle* and says *motorcycle* slowly, listening for the sounds in *motorcycle,* he might end up writing 'morsk,' which is not *motorcycle* but does have many of the letters heard in *motorcycle.* The difficulty with teaching children to use phonics to figure out words is not in teaching them the sounds made by letters but in actually getting them to use what they know about letters and sounds when they are reading and writing. Children who invent-spell as they write are using the phonics they are learning, and both the research and my experience during the last few years confirm that they write more and become better at figuring out how to read and spell unknown words. I can assure you that your children will not spell *motorcycle* 'morsk' forever. There is a problem with children invent-spelling the high-frequency words like *they, was,* and *want,* however. Let me finish talking about our Writers' Workshop, and then when we get to our Words block, you will see how we are going to handle that problem."

Mrs. Wright quickly finished talking about Writers' Workshop, saying less than she had intended, realizing that time was marching on and she wasn't even halfway through the morning yet.

"After the children finish their driting, we go around and let each child show and tell about what he or she drew and/or wrote. We will continue in the driting stage for a few more weeks. Meanwhile, during the Words block, children will be learning to read some words, and we will be doing some handwriting instruction. When most of the children know some words and can make most of the letters, we will move to writing on this paper I call half-and-half paper." Mrs. Wright held up a piece of paper with drawing space on the top and writing lines on the bottom. "I will continue to model for the children, but now I will write a sentence or two first and then do a little drawing at the top. When the children do their writing, I will ask them to write a sentence or two or a few words first and then draw. When almost all the children are able to write something readable, we will move to our writing notebooks. In my newsletter to you, I will announce that we are about to graduate to writing notebooks—a very advanced stage—and ask you to send a notebook like this one." Mrs. Wright held up a seventy-sheet composition book. "Once the children start writing in their notebooks, we will begin our editing and publishing process. Every three or four weeks, your child will pick one piece to publish. I will work with your child to edit that piece, and at that point we will fix the spelling. Your children will publish in various forms, including these books that they are so proud of. Here is one written by a child who moved unexpectedly last year and left this behind."

Mrs. Wright passed around the book, and she could tell that the parents were impressed and that their fears about spelling were starting to be allayed. She then explained the major goals for the Working with Words block.

"At about 9:20 each morning, we devote approximately thirty minutes to making sure your children are learning to read and spell the most common words and to developing their phonics and spelling skills so that they become increasingly able to read and spell new words. If you look here above the alphabet letters," Mrs. Wright said, pointing to the space above the chalkboard, "you will see the beginning of our word wall. Currently, as many of you have heard, we are adding the name of one of your children each day. Of course, all your children want their names up first, so to be fair, I have all their names written on different-colored paper scraps in this box. Each morning, at the beginning of our Words block, I close my eyes and reach in and pull one out. That child becomes our special child for the day, and the name gets added to the wall. As you can see, Horace, Manuel, Paul, Daphne, and Roberta were the lucky five whose names came out first, but in twenty more days, everyone's name will be up there, and they will all have been special for a day. Perhaps you know that our first social studies unit focuses on the idea that everyone is special and different and that we should celebrate these differences.

"Jumping ahead to our 12:15 to 1:00 slot for social studies or science, I read aloud many books and do other activities during that time to develop the notion that we are all different and special. One thing we do each day is to interview the special child whose name was added to the word wall and do a shared writing chart based on that interview. Once we get all the names up here, we will begin adding those common, hard-to-spell words I mentioned earlier, including *they, were,* and *want.* We will add five words each Monday, and we will spend our entire thirty minutes of Words time on Monday working with those five words. We will use them in sentences and have a handwriting lesson on them. On the other days, Tuesday, Wednesday, Thursday, and Friday, we will spend about eight minutes at the beginning of each Words block, practicing how to spell these important words. When the children tell you that they are chanting words and learning to be cheerleaders, they are referring to our daily word wall practice. I pick five words each day, and the children chant them cheerleader-style several times and then write them. You will be hearing more about our word wall because it is an important part of our total reading and writing program. Word wall is the main way I have of making sure your children can read and spell what we used to call 'sight words.' When children are writing, they stretch out words and spell them with whatever letters they know, unless it is a word wall word. Your children will get tired of hearing me say, 'If it's on our word wall, we have to spell it correctly!'

"As I said, word wall takes all our thirty minutes of Words block on Monday when we add the five new words, but only about eight minutes on the other days. We devote the remaining twenty-two minutes to activities that teach phonics and spelling." Mrs. Wright noticed some relieved faces and reminded herself that first-grade parents always need to be reassured that their children are learning phonics. "Currently, we are working with the sounds of the initial letters. If your children told you that *R* is their *running* letter and they ate raisins today because *raisins* begins with an *R,* you know that we are beginning our phonics instruction. The concept that words have beginning, middle, and ending sounds and that letters 'make' these sounds is a very difficult one for young children. I try to make it as concrete as possible by giving them an action and a food for each letter. I have duplicated for you the action and food we are going to do for each letter. One way you could help is by donating one of the foods on the list. We ate raisins today, and tomorrow we will all drink milk as we try to get a handle on the sound of *M.* There is no particular order in which the letters need to be taught, so I try to begin with letters that begin children's names that are already on the wall and to make the first letters taught very different in appearance and sound. By the end of this week, your children should be able to tell you that *R* is the *running* and *raisins* letter and the first letter in Roberta's name, that *M* is the *marching* and *milk* letter and the first letter in Manuel's name, and that *D* is the *dancing* and *donuts* letter and the first letter in Daphne's name. It is too bad that I don't have children's names for all the beginning letters! Here is a list of the actions and foods that you might use to remind your children when they are reading or writing and can't remember the letter that goes with a particular sound. I have tried to make the foods as healthy as possible. Let me know at the end of the meeting if you would be willing to donate one of these and we will talk about when we will need it." Mrs. Wright handed out the following:

Mrs. Wright's Action and Food List

b	bounce	bananas
c	catch	cookies
d	dance	donuts
f	fall	fish (we will do this on a day when fish is on our lunch menu)
g	gallop	gum (sugarless!)
h	hop	hamburgers (lunch menu)
j	jump	Jell-O
k	kick	Kool-Aid
l	laugh	lemonade
m	march	milk
n	nod	noodles (lunch menu)
p	paint	pizza (lunch menu)
r	run	raisins
s	sit	salad (lunch menu)
t	talk	toast
v	vacuum	vegetables (assorted, raw)
w	walk	watermelon
y	yawn	yogurt
z	zip	zucchini bread
ch	cheer	Cheerios
sh	shiver	sherbet
th	think	three thin things

"We also do many activities during the Words block that focus on the vowel spelling patterns. As you know, the vowels in English have more than one common sound and have different spellings. The *o*, for example, has the sounds you hear in *box* and *boat*. Perhaps you remember that we used to call these the 'short' and 'long' sounds. But *o* in combination with other letters represents many more than just two sounds. Think about *port* and *joy* and *cloud*. Then think about the fact that *boat* and *vote* rhyme but have different spelling patterns. The vowel sound spelled *o-y* in *joy* is spelled *o-i* in *soil*. The sound spelled *o-u* in *cloud* is spelled *o-w* in *cow*."

Mrs. Wright had been writing these words on the board as she said them, and you could tell from looking at the faces of the parents that most of them had never thought about how complicated a spelling system English has.

"The ability to figure out how to read or spell a word you have never seen before is a critical skill in becoming a good independent reader. We will spend most of our Words block every day helping children to learn these spelling patterns and how to use the patterns in words they know to help them figure out how to spell and read new words. Because English is a complex language, this will not happen overnight. We will make charts of rhyming words, and I will include some of these in my newsletters to you. We will also do an activity called Making Words a couple of times a week. The children will be bringing home some Making Words strips and challenging you to see how many words you can make from the letters on the strip. Be sure to encourage and praise them for their growing spelling and phonics skills, and be patient with us. By the end of the year, most of your children will be spelling wall words well and will be able to decode and spell almost any regular one-syllable word."

Mrs. Wright glanced up at the clock and realized she had less than ten minutes to explain the rest of the day. Quickly, she moved through the other time slots.

"After our Words block, we have our break/recess time. Fortunately, you all know what happens in the twenty minutes. Then we have our guided reading lessons. At this point, we are doing shared reading with Big Books such as these." Mrs. Wright quickly showed them *Mrs. Wishy Washy* and *The Very Hungry Caterpillar*. "We read the book together and do many activities related to the book. In October, we will begin reading in the books in our adopted reading series. These are the books adopted by the school system, and we will read these as well as real books whenever I can get my hands on enough copies."

At this point, Steve's father raised his hand and asked, "How will you do three reading groups in thirty-five minutes?"

Mrs. Wright hadn't intended to go into this tonight, but the question had been asked. "I won't have three reading groups. Reading groups are another mainstay of our school days that have been seriously questioned in recent years. The children who are put in the bottom group in first grade almost always remain in the bottom group throughout elementary school and almost never reach the point where they can read on grade level. Three groups are also a problem for children in the top group. You wouldn't believe how much difference there is between children in a top reading group. Some are just a little faster and further along than average readers, while others read at second- or third-grade level at the beginning of first grade. For truly top children, just putting them in a book a little above grade level doesn't even begin to meet their needs. The other problem with ability groups is what you pointed out—you can't do three reading groups in thirty-five minutes. If I were to put your children in three groups, I wouldn't really be meeting the needs of my most advanced readers or of those who need a lot more practice. I also wouldn't be able to give thirty-five minutes each day to writing, which is an approach to reading, thirty minutes to the Words block, and thirty minutes *here*," Mrs. Wright pointed to the 1:30–2:00 time slot, "to the critically important Teacher Read-Aloud/Self-Selected Reading time. At this time of the year, I usually read to the children for about twenty minutes, and they read to themselves for about ten minutes, but by February I hope to have that time divided more evenly so that the children are reading books of their own choosing for about fifteen minutes each day.

"Having three groups is an attempt to meet the needs of the whole range of diverse children that is found in any classroom. Unfortunately, it doesn't meet the needs very well, and doing three groups takes most of the reading/language arts teaching time. My instruction in reading takes place in all four blocks: the Writing block, the Working with Words block, the Guided-Reading block, and the Teacher Read-Aloud/Self-Selected Reading block. These blocks represent the competing methods that people are always arguing about—what is the 'best method.' My experience with the four blocks last year and the experience and research of others who have organized this way show that all children do not learn in the same way. We need a variety of methods going on simultaneously if we are to teach all children successfully. Think about two sisters you have known, born to the same family, growing up in the same house. Have you ever said, 'How can two sisters be so different?'"

At this point, Roberta and Betty's mother piped up with, "Maybe the sisters are even twins—born within minutes of each other!" The group of parents, many of whom knew Betty and Roberta, broke into laughter, and the point that not all children learn in the same way was brought home to everyone.

Mrs. Wright summed up. "If you would look at your list for just a minute, I want to try to show you how the four-block framework allows me to implement all twelve principles. To me a balanced literacy program, number 1 on your list, means first and foremost providing children with many different ways to learn to read and write—something for every personality. Within each block, I make the instruction as multilevel—that's principle number 2—as possible. Writing and Self-Selected Reading are the most multilevel blocks; there is no limit to how high the children can move. The Guided-Reading block is the hardest one to make multilevel because whatever we are all going to read has a level—which is too hard for some and too easy for others. I make this block multilevel by not sticking with the same level of material all week and by having the children sometimes read with partners. I also meet with flexible groups that meet for a few days or a week to read a particular story or book. In these groups, the more advanced readers might be reading something challenging together, and the children who need more easy reading might be reading something easy together. Last year was the first year I organized my language and reading instruction into the four blocks, and I have to tell you that the children who would have been in the bottom group made much more progress than in previous years, and that children who would have been in the top group really moved ahead."

Just then Mr. Topps popped his head in the door. A glance at the clock told Mrs. Wright that she was now ten minutes over and that all the other classes were probably already assembling in the cafeteria for refreshments and the general meeting.

She quickly finished up by saying, "I hope you see that numbers 7, 8, 9, and 10 get daily time and attention in this room. Number 3 is the reason that I focus so much on oral language and listening throughout the entire day. I try to promote thinking—number 4—all day, but I focus on this during Guided Reading when I teach the comprehension strategies and during Writing when I help them learn to think the way writers do. Number 5 is absolutely critical for first-graders. I want them to love books and to love telling their own stories through their writing, and I try to provide enough success so that everyone develops self-confidence. You will see evidence of number 6, the connections we make reading and writing, and science and social studies, in the first newsletter I will send home in a few weeks. This newsletter and the parent conferences we will be having soon are two of the major ways I meet number 12. I am always observing your children and making records of what they can do and what they need help on. Your children will soon be bringing home books they can read and their own published writing, as well as other samples of what they are doing, so that you too can observe their progress. If I have any particular concerns about any area of your child's development, I will call you, and I trust that you will call me if you have any concerns. Please let me know if you can bring any of the foods on the list. I look forward to seeing you all at parent conference time in eight more weeks and want to remind you that visitors and volunteers are always welcome in this school and in my class."

As the parents left, several offered to send food, and several others said they would love to come and see how "this four-block thing" worked. Mrs. Wright suggested that they wait a few weeks until she and the children could get the routines better established and then just send her a note telling her when they would like to come. She warned them, however, that there were never enough hands to help or ears to listen to children read, and that when they came, she would probably put them right to work!

Monthly Logs

September

Now I know why October is my favorite month—all month long I celebrate my survival of September! My supervising teacher from long-ago student-teaching days used to say, "I could teach first grade until I am eighty if someone would teach the first four weeks for me."

I got my group this year from Miss Launch. They are as ready and eager as a motley crew of six-year-olds can be. And a motley crew they are. I am most worried about Paul. It is a rare day on which Paul doesn't return to his seat, put his head on his desk, and sob. I have tried to contact his parents, but there appears to be no father at home and his mother works odd hours. Miss Grant, the social worker, says his home situation is "not supportive," so I will continue to do what I can for him here. Daisy presents a different set of problems. She doesn't want to do anything and doesn't get along with anyone! Her mother will be in next week for a conference. I hope we can work together to find ways to motivate Daisy.

Poor Chip! I have managed to stop most of the taunts and snickers directed at his tattered clothes, but I know Butch and Mort still bother him on the playground. He goes his own way, however, and pays as little attention to them as possible. I do admire the child.

Manuel's English is still not strong, but considering that he didn't speak any when he came last year, he is doing well. The children are all used to helping him understand, and I was surprised to know that they all can speak some Spanish! Miss Launch, apparently, appointed all the children "English teachers" and Manuel their "Spanish teacher." After all my years of teaching, she amazes me with the clever solutions she comes up with.

Larry, Danielle, Roberta, and Pat are reading quite well. The cumulative portfolios I got from Miss Launch indicate that Larry and Danielle were reading when they came to kindergarten, and that Roberta and Pat learned during the year. Larry has more general knowledge than anyone else. He is always adding some little-known (to the other children) fact to our discussions. The others listen in awe and amazement. Yesterday Hilda said, "Larry, how do you know that?" He responded, "I read it in a book," as if that were the most natural thing in the world, and I guess it is for him.

Alexander has a hard time sometimes dealing with me and the other children. The hearing aid he wears is supposed to give him enough hearing capacity to function normally if he is seated close to you, but his oral language and listening abilities are like those of a four-year-old. Miss Launch says I should have seen him when he came to kindergarten last year. He could hardly talk and wouldn't listen. Apparently, they didn't discover his hearing problem until he was over two years old and had yet to say "mama" or "daddy." I have assigned Steve to be his buddy for the time being and have talked with the children about what an important invention hearing aids are. One hundred years ago, Alexander would not have been able to hear at all! We try to treat Alexander as special and lucky, but he still gets frustrated sometimes and lashes out at us. Once in a while, I think he pretends (or chooses) not to hear—usually when I say, "Time to clean up," or "Where is your paper?" It is hard to know what to do. I want to treat him as normal, but he does need special consideration. The speech and hearing specialist works with Alexander on Wednesdays and Fridays. I will ask him for advice.

We have made good progress this year into our four-block instruction. We are still using drawing paper for our Writers' Workshop, but I think we will move to the half-and-half paper by the middle of October. Almost all the children are adding some letters and words to their drawings now, and Larry, Danielle, Roberta, Pat, and Hilda are often writing sentences along the bottom of their drawing paper. Even the children who are further behind have the idea of what reading and writing are and are adding some labels to their drawings. All but four of the children's names are now up on our word wall, and the children often draw pictures of themselves and other classmates and write the classmates' names next to their pictures. They also draw their pets and can usually spell their pets' names.

We are about finished learning actions and eating foods to go with the letters. Connecting the letter names and sounds with children's names, actions, and foods seems to be really helping all the children. I was reading them one of our many alphabet books before Self-Selected Reading yesterday, and the children were having trouble coming up with the name *porcupine*. Daisy piped up and said, "I don't know what it is but it begins like pizza!"

"And Paul," chimed in Chip.

"And paint," added Butch, acting out the painting action as he said it.

It is truly amazing to me how many different and fascinating alphabet books there are. The children adore the alphabet book *NBA Action from A–Z*, the singable rhymes in *ABC Bunny* by Wanda Gag, and finding the hidden animals in *Alphabeasts: A Hide and Seek Alphabet Book* by Durga Bernhard. I even found two alphabet books that tied in with our I Am Special social studies unit. *Ashanti to Zulu: African Traditions* by Margaret Musgrove allowed us to think about how special each of our heritages and traditions is, and *The Hand Made Alphabet* by Laura Rankin shows children how to finger-spell the letters along with some great pictures of objects beginning with those letters.

In addition to interviewing the special child each day and then writing a chart telling what was special about that child, I read them a book almost every day about a child, and we talk about what was special about the child in the book. We also talk about how the same things that make you special can be problems at times. They enjoyed old favorites like *The Hundred Dresses* by Eleanor Estes, as well as some new books including *I Hate English* by Ellen Levine, in which a Chinese girl, Mei Mei, tries to cope with life in a new country, a new school, and a new language. I also read them some books in which animal characters had special characteristics, including *The Biggest Nose* by Kathy Caple, in which an elephant is being teased by her hippo friend about having such a big nose. The elephant feels self-conscious until she realizes that her hippo friend has such a big mouth. My children are very aware of how they are physically different from one another, and talking about the differences is easier sometimes when characters in the book are humorous, lovable animals.

We have read several predictable Big Books during our Guided-Reading block, including *Ten, Nine, Eight* by Molly Bang, which portrays beautifully the relationship between an African American girl and her father. In addition to fitting into our I Am Special unit, this counting book tied in with our math. I don't know about the other teachers, but I find it very easy to put into practice the principle that we should connect reading and writing to the other subject areas.

Self-Selected Reading is also off to a good start. I think that is because I didn't take for granted that children knew how to enjoy books before they could actually read them. In the past, I have noticed my children with the fewest literacy experiences at home having great trouble settling down with a book. They would keep picking books up, flipping through them, and putting them back. I didn't mind that they weren't reading the books, but they weren't even really looking at them. This year it occurred to me that maybe they didn't know how you could enjoy a book even when you couldn't read it. I decided that some modeling and direct experience were called for. About the third week of school, as I sat down to read to them before their Self-Selected Reading time, I picked up a copy of *Are You My Mother?*—a book I had already read to them several times and one many of them had at home.

"You know," I began, "there is more than just one way to read a book. Usually, when I read to you, I read by saying all these words." I pointed to the words and read a few pages. "Saying all the words is one way to read, but there is another way to read. Let me show you how my son David used to read *Are You My Mother?* when he was just starting first grade."

I then unzipped my magic bag (this is a big canvas bag I carry around with me all the time. I call it my magic bag because I often keep things hidden in it and surprise the children with them when I pull them out. The children are always asking, "Got anything magic in that bag today?") and pulled out my son's favorite teddy bear and introduced Bare Bear to the class.

"Now, when my son David was just your age, he loved his Bare Bear and he loved *Are You My Mother?* Every night, I would read him two books, and he would always choose *Are You My Mother?* first. After I read to him, I would let him have ten minutes to look at his books before he had to turn his light out and go to sleep. I would go to the kitchen to clean up the dishes, and I could hear him reading *Are You My Mother?* to Bare Bear. This is how he read it."

I then read *Are You My Mother?* to them the way a young child pretends to read a memorized book. The children watched in amazement. When I finished, I asked them if I had read it the way I usually read to them by saying all the words, and got them to explain that I knew the story so well I could tell it and repeat the familiar parts.

Then I asked, "How many of you have a favorite book at home that someone has read to you over and over again and you can pretend-read that book to a little brother or sister or to your favorite stuffed animal?" Several hands went up, and I let the children tell me the title of the book they could pretend-read. I then invited them to bring these books the next day and show us how they could pretend to read the book. Betty asked if she could bring her Kitty that she read to. I asked if Kitty was stuffed or alive. Betty looked horrified and said, "Kitty's not alive. I wouldn't bring a live cat to school!" Her twin (in name only), Roberta, chimed in with, "I would!"

The next day Betty, Roberta, Harriet, Steve, and Anthony proudly walked in with books and stuffed animals. At Teacher Read-Aloud/Self-Selected Reading time, they "read" their books to their animals and to us. Betty "read" *The Ginger-bread Man,* Roberta "read" *Where the Wild Things Are,* Harriet "read" *Goodnight Moon,* Steve "read" *Over in the Meadow,* and Anthony "read" *Where's Spot?* On the following day, several more children brought in their favorite predictable books and "read" them to us. By the end of the week, all my children knew that there were two ways you could read a book. You could say all the words or you could retell the story of a favorite book, making up parts and saying the repeated parts you knew.

Last week, I introduced the third way we read books. Out of my magic bag, I pulled a whole stack of books about airplanes. I explained to the children that when David was their age, he loved airplanes. He wanted to be a pilot when he grew up or the owner of an international airline. He was always checking books about airplanes out of the library, and I bought him many airplane books with great pictures. I then proceeded to show them how David "read" the airplane books, not by saying the words and not by pretending to read them. I showed them that most of the books had a lot of writing and that David would have to be at least ten or eleven before he could even begin to read these books. There was also too much writing in these books to remember what the book said and pretend you were reading it. David read these books by talking to himself about the pictures. I then went through several of the airplane books with the children, and making no pretense at reading the words, I talked about the pictures as if I were a six-year-old.

> "Oh, look at that old airplane. Hard to believe that anyone would fly in something that rickety looking!"
>
> "What a neat fighter jet! I bet that one can go a thousand miles per hour!"

The children joined in and helped me talk about the pictures. After looking at several of the airplane books, I asked the children if any of them had books at home that they couldn't read or pretend-read but that had lots of wonderful pictures that they loved to look at and talk to themselves about. Several children volunteered that they had such books, and on the next several days they brought these books in and "read" them to us by talking about the pictures. Mitch brought in some books about trucks. He wants to be a truck driver like his father when he grows up. Steve brought in some books with all different kinds of plants in them. Larry surprised us all by bringing in a bunch of books about different countries and talking about the pictures and where he planned to travel when he was grown up.

"But, Larry," Hilda asked, "you can read! Why don't you just read the books instead of talking to yourself about the pictures?"

"I like the pictures," Larry explained. "That is a lot of words!" he said, pointing to the words on one of the pages.

"Even when you can read," I explained, "there are books you like to enjoy just by looking at them and talking to yourself about the pictures."

Now everyone in my class knows that there are three ways to read books, and the difference at Self-Selected Reading time is incredible. Even Paul, who doesn't participate in much of anything, ponders over the pictures in informational books and sometimes mumbles to himself. Most of my other children are pretend reading some favorite books, and some, of course, are really reading some of the books. While they read, I circulate around, stopping for half a minute to encourage each child. I notice how they are reading their book and join them in whatever kind of reading they are doing. I wish I had realized years ago that some children couldn't settle in with a book because they knew they couldn't read it and that is all they had ever seen anyone do with a book! Now that all the children know three ways to read and that all those ways are acceptable (how could they not be acceptable if geniuses like Larry and my son David did them?), they are all eager readers.

Next month will be a busy month. We will start writing on half-and-half paper, add high-frequency words to our word wall, and begin reading in our reading series. In our social studies/science time, we will do a unit on fall, spend some time discussing Halloween customs, and learn more about families around the world. Good thing October has thirty-one days!

October

To most first-graders, Halloween is second only to Christmas in generating excitement and distractions. I try to capitalize on their excitement and channel their energies. Our unit at the beginning of the month was on families. We extended the I Am Special unit from September into a Families Are Different and Special unit. The children talked about their families, but I was careful not to ask for too specific information. Fewer than half my class live in a family that contains both the father and the mother they were born to. We defined a family as the people you live with who love you and each other, and we defined an extended family as including all your relatives. We brought in pictures of our families and talked about how families have to work together, do fun things together, and sometimes they don't all get along perfectly. Paul had very little to say during the unit, but he did listen and seemed comforted to know that all families have problems they have to work through.

During Guided Reading, we read the Big Book *Families Are Different* by Nina Pelligrini, which explores all kinds of different families all held together "with a special kind of glue called love." I read aloud to them a number of books that featured various family groups, including *The Mother's Day Mice, A Perfect Father's Day,* and *The Wednesday Surprise*, all by Eve Bunting, who treats the issue of different families with extreme sensitivity. I also read them *Fly Away Home,*

Bunting's story of a boy and his dad who live in an airport while looking for a real home.

In addition to our family unit, we spent some of our afternoon science/social studies time on a unit about Weather and the Seasons.

Our Writers' Workshop is moving right along. We are now using half-and-half paper and pencils to write with, instead of drawing paper and crayons. I have made a transparency with lines like the bottom of the handwriting paper and left a little drawing space at the top. Each day, for our minilesson at the beginning of the Writing block, I sit down at the overhead and write two or three sentences and then draw a picture to go with them. Before I write, I think aloud about the topic I might write about:

> "Let's see. What will I write about today? I could write about seeing Anthony and his baby sister at the grocery store last night. She is so cute! I could write about what a time we had yesterday getting George back into his cage after someone left the door open. I know what I'll write about!"

By thinking aloud about a few topics that I don't write about, the children are reminded about some things they may want to write about. I don't write about running into Anthony and his baby sister, but Anthony might. I don't write about trying to recapture our pet gerbil, but many of the children involved in the chase yesterday are reminded of this and they might choose to write about it.

When I do write, I don't say the words as I am writing them. You will be amazed at how closely the children watch me write and how hard they try to figure out and anticipate what I will write when I am not saying it as I write it. I do say a few words aloud, however. Each day in my writing, I stretch out a few words and spell them by putting down the sounds I hear. I tell the children that this is how I used to spell the big words when I was their age. I also remind them that they will need to write many words that aren't on our word wall yet and that they can't spell yet, and that they should put down the letters they hear just as I do when I write the big words in my writing. When I finish writing, the children and I read it together.

I write all kinds of different things. On some days I write something related to what we are learning in science and social studies. Other days, I write about something that happened in our classroom. Sometimes, I write about something special that will happen that day or that week. I tell about children's lost teeth, new baby sisters or brothers, accidents, and upcoming birthdays. The children are always eager to see "what she will write today"! Probably their favorite thing for me to write is what I call the "When I Was Your Age" tales. Here is one I wrote just before Halloween.

The children love my "When I Was Your Age" tales and are always asking me if they are all true. It is a little hard even for me to imagine my middle-aged self going door to door in a fairy princess costume and craving Tootsie Rolls!

When I was your age, I loved Halloween. I went trick or treating dressed as a fairy prinses. My favrit candy was Tootsie Rolls.

I take no more than eight minutes to write and then read aloud my piece to make sure it makes sense. Then the children all get their half-and-half paper and I give them about fifteen minutes to write and draw. Some of my more advanced children, including Larry, Pat, Danielle, Steve, and Betty, are writing some fairly lengthy pieces, often taking several days to complete one piece. Other children are just getting a few words down. Paul wouldn't write anything for several days and now seems to be copying the names of the children from the word wall. Alexander is the other one who writes almost nothing. With his hearing loss, I am not sure he can hear any of the sounds in the words he might write. Mostly, he is still drawing. Mike is a surprise! He writes up a storm, putting a letter or two for each word and with no spaces between the words. No one else but Mike can read it, of course, but he draws wonderful monster pictures, and when he shares, he tells all about the monsters, and I guess that is what he is trying to write with his collection of letters. At any rate, the children all love his stories, and I see monster stories being written by other children. It is funny how these writing crazes catch on with six-year-olds. I worry about some of my children who just "go through the motions" during writing time. Mort, particularly, is always sitting there looking pained, and when I ask what he is thinking about writing, he just responds, "I don't really care!"

Finally, all the names are on the word wall, including mine and George's (our gerbil), which the children insisted had to be there. Once we got the names up, I added five words last week—*boy, girl, friend, like, is*—and five more this week—*play, school, good, come, go.* I added these words first because they are some of the words used in the first book in our series, which we began this month, and they are more concrete than the abstract connecting words such as *with, of,* and *they.* They are also words children use a great deal in their writing. I try to make sure that the first words begin with different letters and are different lengths. I use the scraps from the construction paper drawer, write the words with a thick permanent black marker, and then cut around their shape so that the length and shape become quite distinctive. I use only light colors and put easily confused words on different colors. *With* is on blue, so when I get ready to add *will, went,* and *want,* I will make sure I use different colors. The different colors and shapes make for an interesting display and help my children differentiate the confusable words.

On Monday, when I put the new words up, we do a lot with them, count the number of letters, use them in sentences, compare them to other words on the wall, and do a handwriting lesson with them. On the other days, I call out any five words from across the wall—including a name or two each day. I point to each word, and when all their eyes are glued to the word, we clap and chant it three times. Then they write it on handwriting paper as I write it on the board. When they have written all five words, they take out their red checking pens and check each word by making the shape around the word with their red pen. I do the same with my words on the board. Making the shape helps to emphasize which are the tall letters and which go below the line. Most children have written them as best they can, but if they do find something not correct when they are checking, they just go over that part with their red pen. The children are becoming better at their handwriting, but there are still huge differences in their ability to control those pencils and get them to do what they want them to do. I know that handwriting develops with practice, along with maturity and development—especially for my young boys—so I accept whatever they can do, as long as they appear to be making a good effort.

We have actions and food for all the initial consonants and *ch, sh,* and *th.* We are now using the twenty minutes of Words block after word wall to collect rhyming words. I have read them lots of *Hop on Pop* and *The Cat in the Hat* type books, and then we list on a chart a lot of words that rhyme. Our *Cat in the Hat* chart had *a-t* words all lined up with the *at* underlined in each. I do include words that begin with the blends, and we say them slowly, listening for the sounds of both beginning letters.

Our Guided-Reading block is going pretty well. We are now halfway through the first book in our reading series. I begin this block with the whole class gathered on the rug and introduce the selection first. We always preview each selection by looking at the pictures and talking about the meaning. As we turn each page, I ask questions like these:

What do you see in the picture?

What do you think is happening?

Why do you think everyone looks so mad?

What is that big brown animal called?

I usually lead them to look through the whole piece with me, and we talk about what we see in the pictures, naming the characters, animals, objects, places, and so on. We predict what might happen next and speculate about what is happening based just on the pictures.

After looking at the pictures one time and focusing only on meaning, we then look through the pages a second time, but this time I write an important word or two for each page on the board. They use what they know about letters and sounds and word length along with the picture on each page to try to figure out the word I have written. These words are not very difficult to figure out when you use all the clues you have. Once they have figured out the word, I have them search the page and put their finger on the word when they find it. This vocabulary introduction works well for the picturable words—*kangaroo, babies, pouch*—but, of course, doesn't work for other words.

I introduce the other words by writing some patterned sentences on the board, using the names of my children and the word I want to draw their attention to. For the word *is*, for example, I wrote these simple sentences:

Mandy *is* a girl. Mitch *is* a boy. George *is* a gerbil.

Because they know each other's names and because they love to have things written about them, they pay close attention and can more easily learn an abstract word like *is*. I then send them on an *is* hunt in the story they are going to read. They move their fingers along the line of print and try to count how many times they see the word *is*. I introduce a few more high-frequency abstract words in the same way, and these words are likely candidates to be added to the word wall next week.

Next, the children and I read the story. Sometimes we read it together, with everyone chiming in, still sitting there on the rug. After we have read each page, we talk about what we found out and add that to the meaning gained from looking at the pictures. On other days, we don't read it together first, but I send them off to read it with their partners. I have assigned all the children a reading partner, pairing up students who need help with friendly, helpful children who can help them but not do it for them. (I have paired Daphne with Paul and have quietly asked her to just read the story to him and let him read if he wants. She is such a little dear! She leads Paul off somewhere quiet and reads with him the way a mother would to a little child.) The children know that they and their partner should take turns reading pages, and that they should give each other clues when they get to words they don't know:

> "Remember the name of that animal who has the babies in her pouch."
>
> "It's that little word she used in the sentences about Mandy, Mitch, and George."

After they do partner reading, we gather together again for just a few minutes and talk about the piece, using "What else did we learn from reading the words that we couldn't figure out from just the pictures?"

We usually spend two or three days on each selection. If we partner read the first day, we often read it chorally the second day and then do some comprehension-oriented follow-up such as acting the story out or talking about the order in which things happened or discussing the characters, setting, problem, and solution. I focus on thinking throughout the school day, but I consciously model and have them use the thinking processes—connect, predict, organize, generalize, image, self-monitor, apply and evaluate—as part of my Guided-Reading instruction.

So far, the Guided-Reading block is going well. Of course, the reading is well below the level of my top readers like Larry, Danielle, and Pat. I would worry about their not being on the level they need to be on if Guided Reading were my total reading program. But my observations of them during the Writing block, Self-Selected Reading, and our science/social studies unit time assure me that they are working up to their advanced levels for a large part of the day.

November

Thanksgiving took much of our attention this month. I have always enjoyed all the holidays, and one of the fringe benefits of teaching first grade is that all the traditional holiday songs and activities are fresh and new to the children, and I get into the holiday spirit right along with them. We did many Thanksgiving activities, and I read aloud to them many Thanksgiving stories as well as some nonfiction books describing the first Thanksgiving and the early days of our country.

Our Writers' Workshop is moving along very well. I plan to ask all the parents to send notebooks next month so that we can start writing in our notebooks. I came up with an ingenious plan to limit the amount of time we spend sharing each day. At the beginning of the year, we had time for everyone to share because they were writing just a little and they could show their driting and tell about it. Now that they are writing longer pieces, however, it was taking twenty minutes each day for them all to share. This cut into our Words block time and put us about ten minutes behind schedule every day. In addition, as what they were sharing got longer, the children were not able to sit and be good listeners for everyone's piece!

I have designated all the children as days of the week. I did this somewhat arbitrarily, but with an eye to having some of the most prolific and reluctant writers spread across the days. Each day, we end the writing block with an Author's Chair, and the designated children get to sit in the rocking chair and read one piece they have written since the last time they shared. After they share their piece, they call on one person to tell them something they liked about their piece. This is working out quite well. With the exception of Paul, the children are all eager to read on their special day. The listeners listen better when they are listening to only five authors.

I have also extended this "Day of the Week" idea to other areas. The children whose day it is pass out and pick up things whenever that service is needed. They lead the line and get to do whatever other special things need doing. This has certainly cut down on the "But I never get to do . . . " and the occasional "You always let her do everything!"

I am also using these designations to do my anecdotal records on children. Last year, we moved to a report card /conference system that really stresses using observation and reading and writing samples to monitor and demonstrate progress. I have an anecdotal record sheet for each child, and I was walking around with twenty-five sheets on my clipboard and never able to pull out the right sheet at the right moment. Now, each morning I put on my clipboard only the sheets for the children whose day it is. I begin writing comments when they share in the Author's Chair, and then I glance at their writing, which they hand to me after they read. I continue to note how they do with our Words block activities, and I make sure to have them read a little bit to me during our Guided-Reading block. During Self-Selected Reading, I have the children come on their designated day for a conference. They read to me—in whichever of the three ways we read—two pages from a book they select. I write down the title of the book, which way they are reading it, and a comment about their comprehension, enjoyment, fluency, and so on. Since I carry around these sheets with me anyway, I am making some notes about their math skills, their contributions during our science/social studies unit time, and a note about what they choose to do during center time. By the time I got to report cards and conferences this month, I had a great deal of information about each and every child. This "Day of the Week" system is so simple, I can't figure out why I didn't think of it earlier.

We now have thirty words on our word wall in addition to the names. The children are continuing to respond well to our daily look, chant, and write practice, and they are obviously using the word wall when they are writing. As I write each day, in addition to modeling the invented spelling of a few big words, I also model looking up at the word wall and finding a word there that I need in my writing. As I do that, I think aloud, "If it's on our word wall, I have to spell it correctly!"

In addition to our word wall, which has high-frequency words, I am doing content boards related to our science or social studies theme. Along with pictures, I put important words children might need in their writing. Our Thanksgiving board has Thanksgiving pictures and the words *Thanksgiving, thankful, turkey, feast, Pilgrims, Indians, corn,* and *food*. Between the high-frequency words now on

Word Wall

Aa Bb Cc Dd Ee Ff Gg Hh Ii Jj Kk Ll Mm Nn Oo Pp Qq Rr Ss Tt Uu Vv Ww Xx Yy Zz

and — Alex — Betty
can — elephant — big — children — Bozo — Carl — Baby — Chip — Donald — red — Tom — George — Horace
here — have — Hilda
Tree — Joyce
Mr. — Flower — Mike — Marty — Milton — little — Mark — Barry — Mrs. — Morky — not
people — Paul — Pat
sad — Roberta — Kim — to — Rita — Steve — My
where — was — want — were

Today is _____

Schedule
8:30 – Arrival
8:45 – Writing
9:30 – Recess
10:00 – Reading
10:45 – Math
11:30 – Lunch
12:00 – Rest
12:15 – Science
1:00 – Spanish

380

our wall and the content words, every child is doing some writing. Last week Alexander wrote:

I like Thanksgiving. It is fun. I have a feast. I eat good food.

While this is hardly an award-winning piece, for Alexander, who still has not learned how you separate words into sounds, his ability to write something is remarkable. He is pleased with himself, too, and I think he now has a strategy for writing. With the word wall, the content boards, and their growing awareness of letter–sound patterns, all my children can and do write.

We are continuing to work on rhyming words, and our room is now filled with charts of rhymes. In addition, I have come up with a little activity that helps them apply their knowledge of initial letters and sounds. To prepare for this activity, I write four or five sentences using my children's names in each and cover up an important word in each sentence. Here are the sentences I used this week. (The food word in each sentence is covered with two sticky notes so that the children cannot read it.)

Butch likes to eat hamburgers.
Mitch likes to eat cheeseburgers.
Paul likes to eat spaghetti.
Mrs. Wright likes to eat lasagna.
George likes to eat carrots.

The children see the sentences when they first come in the morning, and they immediately begin trying to guess the words hidden under the sticky notes. (I put these high up on the board so they can't peek under!) Once we finish our daily word wall activity, we begin to guess what each person likes to eat. I write several possibilities they suggest on the board, and then we observe that "the word can be lots of different foods when you can't see any letters." I then remove the sticky note that covers the first letter or letters (all letters before the vowel). We then cross out any guesses that don't begin correctly, observing that the guesses made sense but didn't begin with the right letters. Next, we guess some more things that both make sense and begin with the revealed letters, and then we reveal the whole word.

We do sentences like this one or two days a week, and my children are becoming very good at realizing that when you come to a word you don't know, you can make a really good guess if you think of something that makes sense and starts with the right letters. We call this activity "Guess the Covered Word," and the children love it!

We are reading in the second book of our adopted series now. Before beginning this book, I had the children I was most worried about—Paul, Mike, Alexander, Mitch, Daisy, Mort, and Chip—read a few pages in the first selection to me. I took an oral reading record as they were doing this, and then I had them retell what they remembered. Using the 90 percent word accuracy criteria, Mort and

Chip just made it. Alexander, Mitch, and Jeff were less than 90 percent but better than 80 percent. All five of them had good comprehension, although it was hard to tell with Mort because he was so bored by the whole process that he didn't tell me much! Paul, Mike, and Daisy, however, were not even close. They are reading with us in the second book, but I am doing some individual work with them, rereading the first book. I have scheduled each of them for ten minutes with me. Paul is always here when I come to open up the room, so I have my ten minutes with him first thing. I take Mike during the after-lunch quiet time because Mike can't sit quietly under any circumstances, and I read with Daisy for ten minutes during centers.

I am doing repeated readings with them with the book we have already read and discussed. Each day, when it is time to read with one of them, we set the timer for ten minutes, and beginning on the first page each day, we see how far we can read in ten minutes. They read to me, and if they miss or don't know a word, I help them. Then I model fluent reading of the page, and they read it fluently, without error, before going on to the next page. We continue reading until they get stuck; then I help them, model fluent reading, and have them reread the page. When the timer signals the end of the ten minutes, we note down the page on which we stopped. On the first day, Mike got to page 5 in ten minutes. Starting again on page 1 the next day, he got to page 9. On the third day, he got to page 15. When he got to page 20, I stopped beginning on the first page each day but did back up about ten pages, beginning with the story that began on page 10.

This is working exceptionally well for Mike. He is much less distractable when I have just him to focus on, and he loves trying to beat the clock and seeing the progress he is making on his pages-read chart. Daisy is making some progress, but she doesn't particularly like giving up ten minutes of her center time, so she is not always very cooperative. Paul is sporadic. Some days, he does quite well, and other days, he won't read at all. I try to talk to him and assure him that he is making progress, and I give him a hug and tell him I love him. Some mornings, if he can't read, I just rock him and talk to him the way you would a crying two-year-old. I have yet to see his mother, but Miss Grant tells me the home situation is pitiful—whatever that means! I have referred him for psychological evaluation, but I don't know what they will tell me that will help. It just isn't right that children should be so emotionally upset and we can do so little for them! I have always found this the most frustrating thing about teaching first grade.

December

Finally—two weeks' vacation! Am I ever ready for it after this month. Every year I forget what a fevered state my little ones get into as they await the big day. Of course, much of what we do this month is related to the holidays. This year we celebrated Christmas, Hanukkah, and Kwanzaa! Many of my read-aloud books were holiday connected, including *A Picture Book of Hanukkah* by David Adler, *My First Kwanzaa Book* by Deborah Newton Chocolate, and *Happy Christmas, Gemma* by Sarah Hayes. Joyce's mother came and talked to us about the Kwanzaa celebrations they were taking part in. Mort's mom came and talked to us about their

Hanukkah customs. I thought Mort might perk up with his mother here, but he was his typical, uninterested, "Who cares?" self. I talked briefly with his mother about his apathy, and she says he is the same way at home and she doesn't know how to motivate him either!

Our Writing and Words blocks are moving along nicely. Of course, I put some holiday boards up in our room with words attached to them, enabling the children to write their letters to Santa, and so forth. Butch and Hilda insist that there is no such thing as Santa, and they tease some of the others about this. Yesterday, Butch had Rita in tears, so I decided to try to call a halt to it. I told them that I didn't know for sure that there was a Santa Claus, but that someone always left presents under my tree. Larry refuses to comment on the subject, but he wears a knowing look.

We did manage to finish the second book in our reading series this month, and again I had the children who are borderline read to me a few pages from the third book. All but Daisy, Paul, Mike, and Chip could read with at least 90 percent word accuracy. Mort read well, but I couldn't get him to tell me enough to be sure his comprehension is adequate. Chip was close enough and tries hard enough that I think he will be okay. I had Daisy, Paul, and Mike read to me the first selection in the second book—the one we just finished. Daisy and Mike read it with better than 90 percent word accuracy. Paul didn't meet the criteria, but he could read some, and he told me what was happening in the story and seemed to enjoy it. I plan to continue my ten-minute timed repeated readings with Paul, Daisy, and Mike in the second book and to make sure they have helpful partners or are included in a group with me during our Guided-Reading time.

I did get the psychological report back on Paul. He doesn't qualify for anything! His IQ is well below average but not low enough for him to be classified EMH. Of course, his IQ is too low for him to be classified as learning disabled. Although he has many emotional problems, he is not severely enough disturbed to meet the criteria for the emotionally disturbed class. The report recommended that he be given individualized instruction on his level and that adjustments be made for his slow learning rate and his periods of inattention. I will continue to work with him, but it is frustrating that more can't be done. So often with a child like Paul, you know he needs help, but he doesn't fit anywhere! Thank goodness for Daphne. She loves being his partner, and when I tried to rotate partners more, she quietly told me, "He reads a little with me, and I think I am helping him. Can't I still be his partner?"

Our afternoon Teacher Read-Aloud/Self-Selected Reading time is going exceptionally well. For many years now, I have suggested to parents that. if they wanted to send me a holiday gift, they could donate an "easy-to-read" book to our classroom library. I have stressed that I didn't expect a gift, but that if they wanted to buy something I would really appreciate, we could never have too many copies of the *Clifford* books; *One Fish, Two Fish, Red Fish, Blue Fish, Robert the Rose Horse;* or *The Gingerbread Man.* By now I have multiple copies of many of these easy-to-read classics. This month, I began reading them to the children. As I read, I made a tape of the reading. I signaled the children, and they clapped their hands when it

was time to turn each page. They also joined me in saying any repeated refrains—
"Run, run, as fast as you can. You can't catch me. I'm the gingerbread man!"

Once I had read this book and made the tape, I pulled out my many copies of
the book and put them in the Self-Selected Reading crates. The next day, I read another easy-to-read favorite of which I had multiple copies, making the tape with the
children's help. Again, I added multiple copies to the crates. By the end of the week,
I had read aloud and made tapes of five easy-to-read books of which I had multiple copies. These books are all out for the children now, and many children are
amazed to find that they can really read them. I overheard Roberta remark that she
was reading these books, not just pretend-reading! That, of course, was my plan. By
now most of them know enough to really read some of these old favorites, and they
are delighted with their newfound ability. It is one thing to be able to read in a
"schoolbook," but a real book that you can buy in a store or get through the book
club—that's reading!

Of course, I put the tape I made, along with a copy of the book, in our listening center. Each day from 2:15 to 2:45/3:00 (children leave on buses at stag-
gered times), we have our center time. I started this many years ago when I
realized that things would go well in our classroom for almost all day and then
fall apart in the last thirty minutes. It was almost always during this last half
hour that arguments would occur between the children, and I often found myself
losing my composure and yelling at someone. Yelling is not my style, and after
the children left, I would feel terrible and berate myself for not handling the situation better. "We were having such a nice day," I would think, "until it all fell
apart at the end!"

After many years of teaching, I decided that neither the children nor I could
give learning the kind of attention required by any subject after 2:15. I had been
doing some center activities in the morning on certain days, and I just decided to
pretend the day ended at 2:15—get the children all ready to go, notes distributed,
book bags on desks, and so forth, and then children could go to the centers. This is
a very nice way to end the day. The children all look forward to it, and because they
get to choose what they want to do and don't have to attend to me or each other,
there is almost no fussing or squabbling. (Mike does still have some problems during center time, but I give him one warning and then send him back to his seat, and
he is learning some self-control.) I enjoy this time because I get to circulate and talk
with the children individually, a luxury that I seldom have at any other time when
I try to keep up with twenty-five children.

Some centers stay with us all the time, and some centers change as we work
on different projects. We have a center board in our room, and the number of
clothespins there indicates how many children can go to each center at one time.
Each day at 2:15, the children choose their centers. We do this by days of the
week. On Thursday, the Thursday children go first to claim their clothespins, followed by the Wednesday, Tuesday, Monday, and Friday children. The Friday children who choose last on Thursday don't complain, though, because they know
that they will choose first on Friday. Children can change centers if there is a
clothespin available indicating space in the center they want to go to.

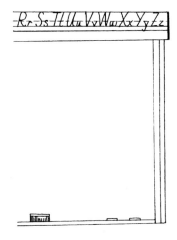

This month, the two most popular centers have been the art center and the writing center. In the art center, I put old greeting cards and the materials for making greeting cards. The writing center has, among other things, stationery on which to write to Santa and catalogues of many of the items on their wish lists. I was delighted to see many of the children going off to find a copy of one of their favorite books so that they could copy its title on their list. They aren't taking any chances when it comes to someone knowing exactly which book they are hoping to find among their holiday presents. They want to spell it right!

January

January is always one of my very favorite teaching months, and this year has been no exception. The fall is wonderfully exciting, with all the big holidays, but exhausting, too, as I get to know a new class of children and get them smoothly into reading and writing and the routines they need to follow. But when we come back after the holidays, they and I are rested, eager, and ready to move!

Over the break, I pulled out my list of guiding principles again, and I think I am doing very well with most of them. I definitely think that doing all four blocks every day gives children many avenues to literacy and provides them with a balanced literacy program. My Writing, Self-Selected Reading, and Words blocks are very multilevel. Guided Reading still worries me—not so much about Larry and the other exceptional readers, because they enjoy what we read and like helping their partners—but because I think we need some easier reading for Paul, Manuel, and the others who aren't quite where they should be. I decided to split up my week between grade-level guided reading and easier selections. I do have lots of sets of easy-reading books that I am going to use for Guided Reading on Thursdays and Fridays. I gave myself an "A" for teaching in ways that reflect the principle that language is the foundation of reading and writing and for emphasizing thinking. We always preview selections, connecting what we know and predicting what will happen or what we will learn. We do a lot of talking and acting out of what we read, and I am always asking the children what they think about the selections we read during Guided Reading. Language and thinking are readily apparent during our Writing block each day, and of course we do a lot of discussing and listening and concept development during our science and social studies units.

Number 6 is one I am going to work more on for the remainder of the year. I do try to get the children motivated and excited about reading and writing. Choice is a big part of motivation, and they choose what they want to write about and the piece they are going to publish, as well as what they read during Self-Selected Reading. They do choose their centers in the afternoon. I am going to try to find some places where I can give them more choices. I know that success plays a big part in how you feel about activities, and making the blocks as multilevel as possible helps provide success, but I need to do more to show my struggling students that they are growing and learning. My schedule means that I read aloud to them daily, and that they have daily time for Self-Selected Reading and writing. I definitely teach decoding and spelling, but I see them applying their phonics knowledge more when writing than when they are reading. I am going to work on getting them to use what they know as they are reading. I think having two days of easier reading each week during Guided Reading will help here, because children apply their phonics more when they only need to figure out a few words.

Assessment is always hard, but I do most of my assessment by observing what the children can actually do. I had the children pick some writing samples they wanted me to share with their parents during parent conferences this month, and they each made a tape recording of a book they liked and could read well. Next month, I am going to start being more systematic in what I do with each child during our weekly Self-Selected Reading conference and see if I can use this time to both encourage them in their reading and see what strategies they are using.

I think I do a good job of communicating my expectations to parents. The newsletter I send home every two weeks lets them know what we are working on and gives them suggestions for home activities that will support what we are doing here. Parents come in and help and visit whenever they want to. The conferences we hold at report card time allow me to talk to them about their child's individual progress. Unfortunately, the parents of the children I worry most about—Paul, Daisy, and Butch—are seldom seen or heard from.

We did a science unit on animals this month. Children love animals, and we took a trip to the zoo. This was a major adventure because the zoo is two hours away. The bus rolled out of our parking lot here at 8:00 and we returned about 6:00. I always do this trip on a Friday so that I have the weekend to recover. It was worth it, however. Most of my children had never seen any animals except for pets and some farm animals. Tigers, lions, bears, kangaroos, and penguins were just pictures in books and images from TV! Of course, we did a lot of research and reading and looking at videos before we went, and since we came back, many of the children have started writing about various animals.

Our Writers' Workshop is moving along quite well. The children are all writing in their notebooks now. On Fridays, I let them select one piece they have written and draw a picture to go with it, but on the rest of the days, they are spending their full fifteen minutes writing. I still do a minilesson each morning, but I am writing slightly longer pieces, just as they are. I have begun our editing checklist. As I was getting ready to write one morning, I told the children that now that they were all real writers—writing in their writing notebooks every day—they would need to learn how to help each other edit their pieces. We talked about editors and publishing books and how every book that I had read to them or that they had read had been written by an author, but the author had an editor's help to make the book as exciting and easy to read as possible. I told them a little about publishing companies and how books got published and the many different people who are involved in the publishing of a book. I then wrote on a half sheet of chart paper:

Our Editor's Checklist

1. Do all the sentences make sense?

I explained to the children that one thing editors always read for is to make sure that all the sentences make sense. Sometimes, writers leave out words or forget to finish a sentence, and then the sentences don't make sense. "Each day, after I write my piece, you can be my editors and help me decide if all my sentences make sense." I then wrote a piece and purposely left out a few words. The children, who were, as always, reading along as I wrote and often anticipating my next word, noticed my mistakes immediately. When I finished writing, I said, "Now let's read my piece together and see if all my sentences make sense." The children and I read one sentence at a time, and when we got to the sentences where I had left a word out, we decided that the sentence didn't make sense because my mind had gotten ahead of my marker and I had left out some words. I wrote the words in with a different-colored marker and thanked the children for their good editing help. I then had a child come and draw a happy face on my paper, because although my sentences didn't all make sense when I first wrote them, I checked for that and fixed them.

After I wrote my piece, the children all went off to their own writing. As they wrote, I circulated around and "encouraged" them. I don't tell them what to write, but I do engage them in conversations about what is happening in their worlds and remind them of some of the possibilities. I don't spell words for them, but I do help them stretch words out and put down the sound they hear.

When the fifteen minutes of allotted writing time is up, I point to the Editor's Checklist we have just begun. "Be your own editor now. Read your paper and see if all your sentences make sense. If you didn't finish a sentence or left a word out, take your red pen and fix it." I watch as the children do their best to see if their sentences make sense, and I notice a few writing something with their red pens. After just a minute, I say, "Good. Now, use your red pen to draw yourself a little happy face to show you checked your sentences for making sense."

Every day after that when I write, I leave a word or two out or don't finish a sentence. The children delight in being my editor and helping me make all my sentences make sense. Every day, when their writing time is up, I point to the checklist and they read their own sentences for sense. They don't find every problem, but they all know what they are trying to do, and I have noticed almost everyone picking up the red pen and glancing up at the checklist as soon as I ring the bell to signal the end of writing time. I am about to add to our checklist a second thing to read for:

2. Do all the sentences start with capital letters?

Once I add that, I will begin some sentences with lowercase letters and let them help me edit for sentences both making sense and beginning with capital letters. Of course, they will read their own piece for these two things also. We will then be at the "two happy faces" editing stage.

Our writing is going so well that next month we are going to start publishing some pieces. I hope that by the end of February all my writers will be published authors!

The Words block is going well. I add five high-frequency words each week to our word wall. We do about eight minutes of looking, chanting, and writing practice each day. Many of my children are learning to spell these words. Some children still have to find them to write them, but they have all learned to read them.

I continue to do some work with rhyming words, and one day a week, I do the Guess the Covered Word activity they enjoy so much. This month I also began our Making Words lessons (Cunningham & Hall, 1997). I usually do two Making Words lessons each week. For the first five lessons, I gave the children only one vowel. Here is how the very first Making Words lesson went.

The letters for this first lesson were *u, k, n, r, s,* and *t.* I made letter cards with the lowercase letter on one side and the capital letter on the other side for all the letters. The vowel letters are written with a permanent red marker and stored in large red plastic cups, one for each vowel. The consonants are written with a blue marker and stored in blue plastic cups. That morning, I appointed some of my early arriving children "holder stuffers." I put the cups containing the letters needed and a stack of holders on the back table. I then showed the holder stuffers how to take one letter from each cup and put it in a holder. (The holders are made by cutting file folders in half and folding up and stapling the bottom inch.) At the beginning of the lesson, I handed each child a holder, and they had all the letters needed. The next morning, I recruited some early arrivals to unstuff the holders.

I began the lesson by making sure the children had and could name all their letters. I held up the *u* card from the pocket chart and had them hold up their *u*. I told them that the *u* was red because it was the vowel, that every word needed at least one vowel, and that because their only vowel today was the *u*, they would need it for every word. I then held up the other letters, named each, and had the children hold up and name theirs. I told them that we would use these letters to make lots of words, and that at the end of the lesson, we would make a word that used all six letters. I then wrote a 2 on the board and told them that the first word would use only two letters. I asked them to take two letters and make *us*. I had them say the word *us* and watched as they decided how to spell *us*. I then asked Mike, who had made *us* correctly with his little letters, to come up and make it with the pocket chart letters. I then put the word *us*, which I had written on an index card, along the top of the pocket chart.

Next, I crossed out the 2 on the board and wrote a 3. I had the children hold up three fingers and told them that the next word would take three letters. I asked them to take three letters and make *run*. Again, I watched and sent someone who had made it correctly to make it with the pocket chart letters. I placed the word *run* next to *us* along the top of the pocket chart. "Change the first letter in *run* and you can change your *run* into *sun*." They made two more three-letter words, *nut* and *rut*, and then I crossed out the 3, wrote a 4 on the board, and said, "If you add a letter to *rut* you can change your *rut* into *ruts*. After it rains, my driveway has lots of ruts in it."

Once a child had come and made ruts with the big letters, I said, "Now, this is a real magic trick. Don't take any of the letters in *ruts* out of your holder and don't add any. Just change around where the letters are, and you can change your *ruts* into *rust*. Say *rust*. When we leave things made of metal out in the rain, they might rust." The children seemed amazed to discover that just changing the position of those last two letters could change *ruts* to *rust!*

We then made two more four-letter words, *tusk* and *stun*.

I crossed out the 4, wrote a 5, and said, "Now we are going to make a five-letter word. Take five letters and make *trunk*. We have been studying about animals, and we know that an elephant has a trunk. Say *trunk* slowly and listen to where you hear all those letters."

At the beginning of the lesson, when we were making *us* and *run* and changing *run* to *sun*, I had been monitoring my struggling children and sending them to make the word with the pocket chart letters, but the lesson had now moved to a challenging stage, and I was watching to see how Danielle and Pat were going to spell *trunk*. Pat got it spelled correctly, and as she did so, she also realized what word you could make with all the letters. "If you put the *s* on *trunk*, you have *trunks*," she exclaimed. "That's exactly right," I said. I then had her make *trunk* with the pocket chart letters, asked everyone to make sure they had made it right with their little letters, and let her show how adding the *s* made the word *trunks*. I asked the children if the word *trunks* was in any way connected to our animals unit. They quickly realized that we had seen elephants at the zoo and been amazed at the size of their trunks. Larry pointed out that trunks were also large suitcases for packing things, and Butch reminded us that cars have trunks.

Next, I had the children close their folders with the word *trunks* still in them and directed their attention to the words on index cards I had been placing along the top of the pocket chart. I had them read the words with me and talk about what we changed to make them:

us	run	ruts	trunk	trunks
sun	rust			
nut	tusk			
rut	stun			

I then had them sort out the rhyming words:

run	rut
sun	nut
stun	

The final step in any Making Words lesson is the most important step—Transfer. Children need to see how noticing rhymes and spelling patterns help them to decode and spell new words. For this step, I took a blank index card and wrote the word *shut* on it.

"What if you were reading and you came to this word?" I asked as I was writing *shut* on the card. "Don't say this word yet, if you know it," I warned, "but who can go put this word with the rhyming words that would help you figure it out?"

Manuel went up to the pocket chart and put *shut* under *nut* and *rut*, and we said all three rhyming words, making *shut* rhyme with *nut* and *rut*.

I then wrote another rhyming word—*bun*—and Roberta put *bun* under *sun*, *run*, and *stun*, and we pronounced *bun* to rhyme with the others.

"Thinking of rhyming words can help you figure out how to spell words too," I said, as I picked up a third blank index card. "What if Steve were writing about building a 'hut' in the woods. Which words rhyme with *hut?*" The children decided that *hut* rhymed with *nut*, *rut*, and *shut* and would be spelled "h-u-t." We then used *run*, *sun*, *stun*, and *bun* to help us decide how Joyce could spell *spun* if she were writing about Rumpelstiltskin.

That afternoon when the children were getting ready to go home, I gave them a take-home sheet. The sheet had the letters *u k n r s t* along the top and boxes for words. Most children immediately recognized that these were the letters they had used to make words. "For homework," I said, "take this sheet home and cut the letters apart and see if you can fill these boxes with words. Don't tell anyone else the secret word—the word that can be made with all the letters—but see if they can figure it out." I could tell that the children were going to enjoy seeing if they could stump their parents. I overheard Roberta warning Betty, "She told us not to tell, and you'd better not!"

We did several other lessons this month with just one vowel. From the letters *i, g, n, p, r,* and *s,* we made the words *in, pin, pig, rip, rips, nips, spin, pins, sing, ring,* and *spring.* From the rhymes we sorted, we decoded the new words *bring* and *chin* and figured out how you would spell *string* and *fin.* From the letters *o, g, n, r, s,* and *t,* we made *so, no, go, got, rot, not, song, sort, rots, snort,* and *strong* and used the rhymes to decode and spell *spot, long, trot,* and *shot.* From the letters *e, d, p, n, s,* and *s,* we made *Ed, Ned, end, pen, den, pens, dens, send, spend,* and *spends.* The transfer words were *then, bend, lend,* and *men.* From the letters *a, h, l, p, s,* and *s,* we made *Al, pal, lap, sap, has, ash, pass, pals, slap, slaps,* and *splash.* The transfer words were *trap, mash, clap,* and *smash.*

The children enjoy manipulating the letters to make words. Even Paul can successfully make the easier words in the lesson. Stretching out the words as we make them and sorting out the rhymes and saying the rhyming words to figure out the transfer words provide excellent phonemic awareness practice for children like Manuel, Paul, and Alexander, who still need it. My whiz kids love trying to figure out the word that can be made with all the letters. Using the rhymes to decode and spell new words helps children apply what they are learning about letters and sounds. Making Words is truly a multilevel activity. In one twenty-minute lesson, there is something for everyone! The parents tell me that their children love bringing home their Making Words sheets and often stumping them about what word can be made with all the letters.

February

In addition to all the Valentine's Day excitement, we have done units this month on African Americans in celebration of Black History Month, and we have learned about our nation's presidents, including Abraham Lincoln and George Washington. I read several biographies to them, including *If You Grew Up with Abraham Lincoln* by Ann McGovern, *If You Grew Up with George Washington* by Ruth Belov Gross, and *A Picture Book of Martin Luther King* by David Adler. We have talked about biographies and autobiographies. The children are fascinated with the idea of autobiographies, and with it being such a huge word!

I have modeled how you write biographies during some of my minilessons, and last week, when I wrote a "When I Was Your Age" tale telling about my first-grade boyfriend and the valentine I made for him, Larry observed, "If these 'When I Was Your Age' stories are true, you are really writing your autobiography!" I had never really thought about that before, but I had to admit that I was at least writing the six-year-old part of my autobiography. At any rate, many of the children are into writing biographies and autobiographies.

We have published one set of books, and the children are thrilled. Before we began, I showed them the book made last year by Jonathan, a boy in my room who moved and forgot to take his book. I read the book to them, beginning with the dedication page ("Dedicated to Mrs. Wright and all the people in my class"), reading the story about a soccer match between Jonathan's team and his cousin's team, talking about the illustrations that Jonathan had done to accompany his writing, and ending with the "About the Author" page on which I had written:

> Jonathan Marr is seven years old and is in the first grade at Merritt Elementary School. He loves to read and write and play soccer. This book tells the true story of his soccer team's biggest victory!

I then explained how Jonathan and my other first-graders last year had made the books. "They couldn't all make books at once," I explained, "because, as you know, books need editors and you can help each other edit, but I will be the editor-in-chief who approves final copy." No editor-in-chief could have twenty-five authors in the publishing stage at the same time! Because we had talked a lot about publishing companies and how books got published, the children knew that a book takes a lot of work after the first draft is written.

I explained how I had helped Jonathan's class and would help their class so that everyone would publish a book by the end of the month, but only one-third of the class would be publishing at a time. I then showed them the blank books that some parents had helped me assemble. The books were spiral-bound, with covers made from half sheets of construction paper. Inside each book were half sheets of paper. The first page of each book had a place for the title, author, and date. The second page said "Dedicated to" and had several lines on which the author could write the dedication. The last page said "About the Author" and had lines on which I would write something about each of them. The middle pages all had two writing lines at the bottom and the top half blank for the illustration. I showed the children that the parents had made books with eight, twelve, sixteen, and twenty pages and reminded them that some books were much shorter and some books much longer than others. We counted the pages in Jonathan's book and realized that he had published a twelve-page book! "Most of your books will probably be twelve pages, too," I remarked, "but some may be shorter and some longer." I could see by the looks on Larry's, Steve's, and Roberta's faces that they already had long books in mind.

I then explained to the children how we would go about getting everyone a published book by the end of the month. I had arbitrarily divided the class into thirds, making sure to put my weakest writers—Paul, Daisy, and Alexander—in different thirds, and my best writers—Larry, Hilda, and Pat—also in different thirds. I wanted Paul, Daisy, and Alexander in different cycles because I knew they would each require a lot of individual attention, and I wanted Larry, Hilda, and Pat in different cycles so they could help me edit. I showed them the list, and there were some grumblings from children who were not going to be first, but I told them that they would all have their turn and that those publishing later would have more time to work on a really good first draft. Roberta chimed in and said, "I don't care if I'm in the last group. I need the time because I am going to write a really long book."

Finally, I explained how we would make each book. The children who were in the first group had to decide by the next day which first draft they wanted to make into a book. We would work together to help each writer revise—make the meaning clear and the book as interesting and exciting as possible. Then children would work with partners to do a first edit. I would do a final edit, and the children would copy their piece into their book and do the illustrations. "By the end of the month, if we all work hard together, you will all have a published book like Jonathan's."

It was easier said than done, but we did do it! For the rest of the month, we continued beginning Writers' Workshop with my minilesson and ending it with the children whose day it was sharing in the Author's Chair, but during the fifteen to twenty minutes of writing time, two-thirds of the class were writing in their notebooks while I helped the other third edit and publish.

On the first publishing day, I sat down with Paul, Daphne, Pat, Rita, Horace, Danielle, Jeff, and Mike. I had each person read the piece he or she wanted to publish, and after they read, I and the other children made comments. As in Author's Chair sharing, we always began by telling the writer one thing we liked. Next, however, I modeled helping the author make the piece as clear and exciting as possible by comments such as, "Daphne, I loved your story about your grandmother, and I know she will love reading this book. You say she is very nice to you. Tell me some of the nice things she does."

Daphne had many examples of her grandmother's love and caring, and I suggested that she address these in her story. I told her to write these on another sheet of paper and then, when we edited, we would figure out where they should be inserted.

As each child read, I tried to listen for anything that was unclear or something that could be added to make the book more interesting and I suggested this. I also invited the suggestions of the other writers, and some of them had good comments. In the time we had that first day, five of the eight children read their first-draft pieces and listened to our comments on meaning. We finished this on the second day. I knew that Paul would not share his with the group, so I got him to tell me ahead of time what he wanted to publish, and then I explained this to the group. They were very supportive and said Paul's book about George, our gerbil, was going to be terrific! On the third day, the children worked on adding or changing anything they wanted to do based on our comments. They then chose someone to help them read their piece for the two things on our Editor's Checklist: Do all the sentences make sense, and do they all begin with capital letters?

While they did this, I worked with Paul. I explained that I wanted him to have a great book about George the gerbil, and I got him to tell me what he wanted to say. I then wrote his sentences on a clean sheet of paper and let him choose an eight-page book. I had him read his simple sentences to me several times and made sure he understood that he would copy them in his book and then illustrate them. I asked him who he wanted to dedicate the book to and helped him write *My Mom* on the "Dedicated to" page.

By the fourth day, Paul was working on his book, and I was ready to play editor-in-chief for my other writers. I talked with them first and helped them decide how many pages they needed in their book and about how much would go on each page. They wrote the page number on their first draft in red pen above what they thought would fit on each page. I told them that the sentences wouldn't all fit exactly on each page, and that it would be fine for sentences to go over to the next page. By knowing approximately what was going on each page, the children could begin their illustrations while I was helping each child edit. For the next three days, I worked with each child individually to edit his or her piece. I helped them fix up sentences that didn't make sense. I inserted needed punctuation and wrote the correct spelling of words above their invented spelling. After my editing, they copied their writing into their books and did their illustrations.

Seven days after I began with this first group, I had the second group sitting with me and reading their chosen piece so that we could give them feedback on their message. Children from the first group finished up their illustrations and then went back to their writing notebook first-draft writing. I helped Alexander, who was in this group, just as I had helped Paul, and he got a nice book written about his dog.

By the time I got to the final third, they were ready to go. The children who had already published had shared their books when it was their day in the Author's Chair, and the last third had a better idea than the others about what they were trying to accomplish. They worked hard, and by the very last day in February, all twenty-five of my children were published authors. I have put their published books in special baskets in our classroom reading center, and these are very popular choices for reading during Self-Selected Reading.

The children are already asking me when they can do another book! We are going to take a few weeks just for first drafts at the beginning of March, and then we will begin another book-publishing cycle. This is a lot of work, but the pride they take in their books and their clear sense that they are all real writers now makes it worth all the time and trouble.

Work in the other blocks has also moved along this month. We now have sixty-five words on the wall, besides our names. We continue to do work with rhyming patterns, Guess the Covered Word, and Making Words lessons.

We are now reading in the fourth book of our reading series for some of our Guided-Reading lessons. On Thursdays and Fridays, however, I am using easier books. Some weeks, if the easier book ties in with our comprehension strategy of the topic of what we read earlier in the week, we all read in the same easier selection. I partner up the children and remind them of how we help partners when they come to words they don't know by giving them clues instead of just telling them the word. Other weeks, I have three or four different titles, and following through on my decision to give children choices whenever possible, I let them make a first and second choice and then form flexible groups to read the book. I spend some time during Guided-Reading meeting with the groups and coaching them to use their decoding strategies. I meet with all the children across the week but spend more time with the children—Paul, Daisy, Mike, Chip, Alexander, Mort, Jeff, Carl, Butch, Manuel, and Alex—who need the most coaching. The groups change from week to week, and I never put all my struggling readers together in one group, but I often include more of them together—along with some good reading models—and give these groups more of my time.

Their burgeoning independent reading ability is really showing up during our afternoon Read-Aloud/Self-Selected Reading time. Currently, I am reading to them for fifteen minutes, and they are reading on their own for the remaining fifteen minutes. Even Mike is getting to the point where he actually settles down and reads most days. Now if I could just find something to motivate Mort and captivate Daisy!

March

We did a science unit on weather this month. We read two terrific Big Books, *What Will the Weather Be Like Today?* by Paul Rogers and *Caps, Hats, Socks, and Mittens* by Louisa Borden. I also read many other books to them. Their two favorites were both about snow—*The Snowy Day* by Ezra Jack Keats and *White Snow, Bright Snow* by Alvin Tresselt. We are up to the "three happy face" stage of our Editor's Checklist with the addition of

   3. Do all the sentences have ending punc (. ? !)?

Now in my writing, I make all three kinds of mistakes—but just one or two total in any one piece. On some days, I leave a word out, resulting in a sentence that doesn't make sense. Other days, I begin one of my sentences without a capital and stick a capital right in the middle of a word. I might write four or five sentences and forget the ending "punc" on one of them. The children are getting good at seeing my mistakes and helping me edit. At the end of their writing time each day, I remind them to read their sentences for sense, beginning capitals, and ending punctuation and to give themselves three happy faces.

We are halfway through our second book-publishing cycle. The third that had to wait until last to make their first books went first this time, and the first third has to wait until last. This publishing has gone much more smoothly because we all learned so much the first time through. They are producing some really terrific books. We should be able to get one more publishing cycle in, and then they will all have three published books to take home for the summer.

My children are getting so fast at chanting and writing their five words each day that I have added an "on the back" activity. After they have written the five called-out words on the front and checked them by tracing around them, I have them turn their papers over and we do an activity on the back. At least one day a week, I have them write their word wall word with an ending. I always preface this with "Sometimes when you're writing, . . . " because I really stress that the word wall is not there just so we can chant and write the words during our daily word wall practice but to help us when we are writing.

Last Tuesday, I had called out the five words: *play, go, come, give,* and *want.* When they turned their papers over, I said, "Lots of times when you are writing, you need to write a word that is on our wall but you need to add an ending. What if you were writing *I was playing baseball.* How would you spell *playing?*" I got them to tell me that you would spell *playing* p-l-a-y-i-n-g and then to write it on their papers. I continued, having them write *wanting, going, coming,* and *giving,* making sure they told me about dropping the *e* before adding *ing* before writing the last two.

On Wednesday, I called out the five words: *house, look, thing, those,* and *saw.* When they turned their papers over, I said, "Lots of times when you are writing, you need to spell a word that is not on our word wall, but if you can think of a word that is on our word wall that rhymes with the word you want to write, you might be able to use that word to help you spell your word. What if you were writing a story about a mouse; which word from the wall will help you spell *mouse?* I had the children tell me that "since *house* is spelled *h-o-u-s-e, mouse* is probably spelled *m-o-u-s-e.*" They wrote *mouse* on the back of their papers, and I continued in the same manner. What if you were writing about a crook? A rose? Some string? A house of straw? For each word, I had them tell me the word wall word that rhymed and how that might help them spell the word they needed, and then I had them spell it aloud before writing it. These on-the-back activities are taking only about two minutes each and are giving me a lot of good spelling practice beyond just the word wall words.

We are finishing the fourth book in our reading series and have continued our small-group reading of multiple copies of easier books on Thursdays and Fridays. This is working out remarkably well, and I plan to continue this through April and May. Many of my children are rereading during Self-Selected Reading the books we read during Guided Reading, as well as their old favorites that we earlier made tapes of. I forget from year to year what absolute delight first-graders take in being able to "really read!" And how much they enjoy reading books again and again, for the sheer pleasure of doing it!

This month, I have made a special effort to get my children actually using the letter–sound knowledge they have when they are reading. When they write, they have to represent the word in some way, so they do use their letter–sound knowledge to spell words. But getting them to look at the letters and use what they know to figure out a word in reading is harder.

I do several things to help them learn to apply their phonics skills. One thing I do is to model for them how I would decode an unknown word. Of course, I do this during Guided Reading, but I also do it during the afternoon science and social studies time as I am introducing words needed in our units.

This month our science unit was on weather. I wrote sentences on the board one at a time, underlining the words I wanted to introduce. I told the students that the underlined words were words they didn't know, but that if they used the letter sounds they knew and made sure the words made sense, they would be able to figure them out.

I read the first sentence and stopped when I got to the underlined word, *hot.* I then thought aloud, "Hmm, if I didn't know this word, how could I figure it out? I know that *h* usually has the sound it has in *hamburger* and *house.* I know that *n-o-t* spells *not* and *l-o-t* spells *lot. H-o-t* should be a rhyming word—*hot!* Yes, hot makes sense because it is a kind of weather."

Today is ————————

Sometimes the weather is <u>hot</u>.
Sometimes the weather is <u>cold</u>.
Some days are <u>rainy</u>.
Some days are <u>sunny</u>.
Some days we have bad <u>storms</u>.
On <u>stormy</u> days, we see
<u>lightning</u> and hear <u>thunder</u>.

I then had children read the other sentences, led them to figure out the underlined words, and helped them to explain how they might have figured it out. *Cold* was decoded based on the rhyming word *old.* The children knew the words *rain* and *sun* and pronounced "rainy" and "sunny" so that they sounded right in the sentence. *Storms* was decoded because "it starts with *st,* has *ms* at the end, and makes sense because storms are bad." *Stormy* was difficult, but when I pointed out how *rain* and *sun* became *rainy* and *sunny,* most of the children understood it. *Lightning* was decoded because "you see lightning on stormy days, and it has *light* as the first part." *Thunder* "begins with *th* and then has *un* like *fun* and *run* and ends like *her,* and you hear thunder in storms."

Next, I had the children read part of the weather chapter in their science books. I told them that there would be several new words they would have to figure out and reminded them of what they could do when they came to a word they didn't know. After they had read, I let several children write words on the board that they had figured out in their reading and explain how they had figured them out.

On the following morning, I gave each child a yellow index card and asked all of the children to try to find a word somewhere in their reading that day that they didn't know. They should write that word on the yellow card and then use the card to mark the page on which they found the word. At the end of the day, each child who found a word came to the board, wrote that word on the board, read the sentence in which the child had found the word, and tried to explain how he or she had figured it out. The children really seemed to like doing this, so I designated Wednesdays as official "word-busting" days. Every Wednesday the children get their yellow cards and are on the lookout for one new word they can figure out. I hope their enthusiasm stays high.

April

All year I have been concerned with providing direct experiences to promote concept development and increase the depth and breadth of my children's meaning-vocabulary store. I try to remind myself constantly that language really is the foundation of reading and writing. Adding words and concepts to their oral and listening vocabularies increases the number of words they can make sense of while reading and use in their own writing. Whenever possible, I bring real objects into the classroom and encourage them to bring objects in. We not only name each object, but we also describe and classify it and decide which attributes it shares with other objects and how it is different from other objects. Often these objects relate to the science or social studies unit we are studying, and in addition to talking about these objects, we write about them in shared writing charts. I also use many videos, picture books, and pictures to provide the students with visual experience with words and concepts for which we don't have real objects readily available. Years ago, I started a picture file for one of my methods courses, and I have added to it ever since. Currently my picture file categories include food, animals, plants, clothes, occupations, vehicles, holidays, city life, South America, Asia, Africa, United States, famous people, tools and utensils, and a huge and disorderly miscellaneous category. I have laminated most of the pictures I have collected, and I find my picture file an invaluable resource in concept and meaning-vocabulary development.

I also do many categorization activities with my children to help them clarify and extend meanings for words. One I particularly enjoy doing is a list, group, and label lesson originated by Taba (1967) for use in the social studies curricula. To do a list, group, and label lesson, you begin by asking children a question that will elicit many responses. Last week, as we were beginning our science unit on nutrition, I asked the children to list all the foods they could think of. As they named various foods, I wrote these food words on the board. From time to time, I stopped to read what was already listed on the board and encouraged them to think of more foods. Finally, when we had filled almost the whole board, I said, "Let's just have Mike, Roberta, and Horace tell me their foods, since they have their hands up. We will then have the whole board full of food." I then reread the whole list, letting the children read along with me if they desired. I then left the list on the board for the next day.

On the following afternoon, I pointed to our list of foods and told the children that I was going to read the list again and that this time they should listen and think, "Are there any foods on the list that seem to go together in some way?" I then read the entire list and asked if anyone had a group of foods that seemed to go together.

Mitch said that cake, cookies, chocolate pie, ice cream, and gingerbread went together. I wrote these five on a sheet of chart paper and asked him why he had put these foods together. He said, "Because you eat them all after the meal." I then asked him if he could think of a name or label for his group. He hesitated a moment and then said, "Desserts."

Steve put mushrooms, grapes, berries, rhubarb, and nuts together. I listed these five foods on the chart paper and asked him why he had put those particular foods together. He said it was because they all grew wild. I then asked him if he could give a name or label to that group. After some hesitation, he said, "Things That Grow Wild."

Chip put peanuts, chocolate candy, hamburgers, potato chips, soda, oranges, and tomatoes together. I listed them and in response to my "why" question, he said, "Because they are my favorite things to eat." When I asked him to give a name or label to this group, he couldn't. I said that that was fine, that we couldn't always think of names for groups, and went on to the next child.

While doing these lessons, I accept every child's response. During the listing process, everyone usually contributes something, but I call on the children with smaller vocabularies first, so that they have a chance to contribute. I usually save the grouping and labeling steps for the next day, so that the lessons don't take more than twenty-five minutes. When we form groups, each child who wants to organize a group tells me why those particular things are grouped together and then attempts to give a label to that group. This labeling step is difficult for many of my children, and if they can't do it, I simply accept that and go on to the next volunteer.

As you can see, the children have different categories and different reasons for grouping things together. Therefore, no child is allowed to add anything to another child's group. I also write the name of the child who labeled a group under that group. Objects from the list can be used over and over again as different children make groups. The children enjoy these lessons, and I can see that they have had an effect on their vocabulary and categorization skills.

We are through with our second book-publishing cycle, and everyone is going to publish one more book in May. The children are even more excited about this last book, and those children who have been in the second publishing third each time have already informed me that it is their turn to be first. I have added the fourth and final thing to our Editor's Checklist:

4. Do all the people and place names and I start with a capital?

I continue to write during the minilesson each day and the children help me fix my piece using the four items on the checklist. I have been amazed at how well all my children are writing. When I think back to my early teaching days, when I thought that children had to be able to read well before they could write independently, I am appalled! It is perfectly clear that with word wall and content board support, plus encouragement and modeling of stretching out words to spell them, all children can write, and for many of them, writing is their major avenue to reading. I consider all four blocks—Writing, Words, Guided Reading, and Teacher Read-Aloud/Self-Selected Reading—equally important, but I must admit that Writing is the block in which many of my lowest and highest achievers seem to make the most progress. I guess Writing is the most multilevel block.

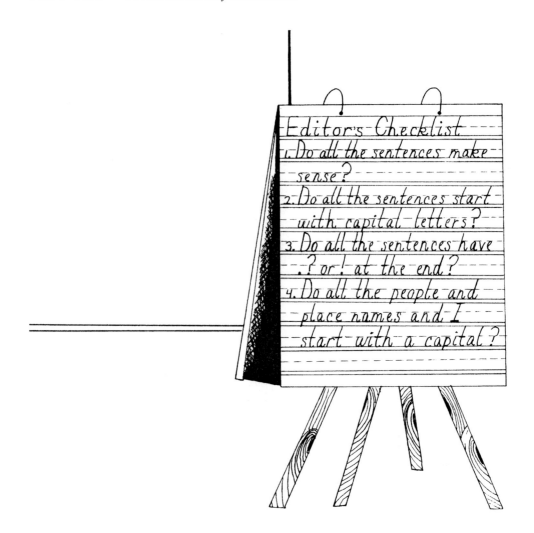

Editor's Checklist
1. Do all the sentences make sense?
2. Do all the sentences start with capital letters?
3. Do all the sentences have . ? or ! at the end?
4. Do all the people and place names and I start with a capital?

We now have 110 high-frequency words on the word wall, in addition to the names. I am not going to add any more words this year because I want to use May to really help them consolidate their knowledge of these critical words. I will, however, continue the daily practice with the words. On Mondays we are making up sentences, using only words on the wall or on our content word boards. This is quite a challenging task, but the children are enjoying it. After they make up the sentence, I locate all the words, and we all write the sentence. We are trying to make up big "fancy" sentences, and they are very clever at combining the words. Here are the three sentences they composed last Monday using the word wall and our nutrition board. (The underlined words are attached to our nutrition board. The others are on the word wall.)

Vegetables are very very good for you.

People should not eat too much *junk food.*

People should eat some *cereals* and *grains.*

I am continuing to do an "on-the-back" activity after we chant, write, and check five words on the front. In addition to adding endings to our wall words and spelling rhyming words, we have written some compound words, including *boyfriend, girlfriend, playhouse, without, cannot, someone, something, somewhere, everything, seesaw.* The children are very impressed with their ability to spell such big words! I am also occasionally having them put the five words they wrote on the front in alphabetical order on the back as we begin to learn some alphabetizing/dictionary skills.

We are continuing to do Making Words lessons at least twice a week. Whenever possible, I tie these into our science/social studies units or what we are reading during Guided Reading. This month we did three lessons in which the last word connected to nutrition. From the letters *a, o, c, r, r, s,* and *t,* we made the words *car, cat, rat, rot, cot, coat, cost, star, oats, coats, coast, roast, actor,* and *carrots.* We then sorted out the rhyming words and used them to decode *toast* and *flat* and to spell *pot* and *chat.* From the letters *a, e, o, g, n, r,* and *s,* we made *an, on, Ron, ran, rag, sag, gas, nose, rose, sore, snore,* and *oranges.* The transfer words we decoded and spelled were *core, bran, score,* and *chose.*

The word that no one could figure out was the word that can be made from the letters *a, a, e, o, l, m,* and *t.* They noticed immediately that they had more red letters—vowels—than blue letters and this had never happened before. I began by having them take three letters and make *eat.* Then I told them that they could just change their letters around and that, like magic, these same three letters could spell *ate.* When they had accomplished that trick, I told them that the same three letters in different places would spell the word *tea.* While they were still marveling at three words they knew spelled with the same three letters, I had them add a letter to *tea* and turn it into *team,* and then move the same four letters around to spell *tame, meat,* and *mate.* After changing *mate* to *late* and *late* to *lame,* I had them move the letters in *lame* around to spell *meal* and then *male.* The children are really getting the idea that where you put letters makes a big difference in what word you spell, and this lesson with so many "turn-around" words made a big impression on them. Next, they made *mole* and *motel,* and then, since no one had figured out the word that could be made with all the letters (and most of my children were convinced that there was no such word!), I got to show them how all their letters could be used to spell *oatmeal.* They hate it when I stump them like this, and I don't get to do it very often. (They did love taking home their Making Words homework sheet that night, however, and stumping all their parents.) Of course, we finished the lesson with some transfer words: *crate, cheat, game,* and *blame.* Most of my children's spelling is beginning to reflect what we do as we make words, sort out the rhymes, and use the rhyming words to decode and spell new words. Many of them realize that you often need letters you can't hear, and they are using rhyming words they know to figure out vowel patterns.

We are reading in the final book of our adopted series now along with books in sharing groups on Thursday and Friday. I had each of them come and read to me a few pages of a selection toward the end of their first reader, and all but Paul, Daisy, Mike, Butch, and Alexander met or exceeded the 90 percent word identification criteria I use when I make oral reading records of their reading. I then had these five read to me from a middle-first-grade-level book they had not read before, and all but Paul were successful with that. While I would love to have them all reading at or above grade level at the end of the year, I know that not everyone can accomplish that in one year's time. I am delighted that Daisy, Mike, and Alexander have moved as far as they have, and even Paul is not a nonreader. When he is having an "alert" day, he can read early first-grade material independently.

I have as I planned put a bit more structure into my weekly conferences with children during Self-Selected Reading. While I still allow them to "pretend read" familiar stories and "picture read" informational books, I ask them to bring to our weekly conference a book in which they can read most of the words. I also ask them to choose two pages that they want to read to me at the beginning of the conference. As they read, I observe whether or not they are correctly reading almost all the words, and I notice the strategies they use to figure out an unknown word. I also notice their self-correction strategies. When they have read the two pages to me, I point out what I have seen:

> "You have chosen a good book that you can read very well. I was very proud of the way you went back and reread this sentence when you realized that it didn't sound right and something must be wrong. You used the letters in the word you knew and the ideas from the rest of the sentence to help you figure out the word."

If a child has brought a book that is much too hard, we talk about how that child could pretend-read or picture-read that book—and then I steer the child toward books in which they can read almost all the words. I show that child how to read the first page or two and put one finger down for each word he can't figure out. "If you get all five fingers down on two pages, that book is too hard for you to read and bring to our conference. You need to find an easier one." I help the child find a suitable book to bring to our conference next week.

Some children—especially Mort and Daisy—seem just to grab any easy book. I try to steer them toward some books they haven't read yet and would like and that would be on their level but a little bit challenging. I have made a rule for everyone that you have to bring a different book each week after Mort brought the same easy book three weeks in a row! Does he think I don't notice, or does he not care?

During the conference, I make anecdotal notes about what each child read and how well they were reading. I note their use of picture clues, attempts to figure out unknown words, fluency, self-correction, and other reading strategies. I always ask them what they liked about the book they were reading, and sometimes I suggest another book that they might like. I try to make the conference more of a conversation than an "inquisition," but at the same time I do ask some questions that will let me know how well they are comprehending. Depending on the child and the book, I might ask two or three questions like these:

Why did you choose this book?

What did you like about this book?

What was your favorite part?

Who was your favorite character?

Did the book have any pictures you really liked?

What was the most interesting thing you learned in this book?

What was the funniest (saddest, most surprising, silliest, strangest) part of this book?

Can you tell me what happened at the beginning, middle, and end of your story?

What new facts did you learn about penguins (or whatever topic we have been learning about) from this book?

Is your book a fiction (made-up) book or nonfiction (informational) book?

What do you think will happen next?

How did the author let you know that the main character was scared?

Did you learn anything from this book that you can use in your own writing?

I am just delighted that all my children see themselves as readers and writers! That is one of the main benefits of not putting them in fixed-ability groups and of giving them multiple opportunities to read and write. The discouraged, defeated attitude that has taken hold by this time in the year for children in the bottom group is not evident in my struggling readers. I just hope they can make more progress next month, and I am going to do my best to encourage their parents to take them to the library and read with them this summer. I know Mike's mother will try. I am not sure about Butch's, Alexander's, or Daisy's parents, and I have yet to meet Paul's mother. I am also going to encourage Chip's and Carl's parents to make library trips and books a regular part of their summer. They are right on grade level now, but they probably won't be if they don't look at a book for three months!

May

Well, the year is almost over. Just one more week of school for the children and lots of report writing and finishing up for me. I always feel a little sad during the last weeks of school—so much yet undone. All in all, this has been an exceptionally good year. The children have all learned to read and write and do math, and I know they know a lot more about the world we live in than they did when they entered this classroom in September.

We finished the year with a social studies unit on friends and a science unit on water. I like to do the friends unit at the end of the year, because by now the children have so many friends here at school, and they also have friends in their neighbor-hoods and in the places they will visit this summer. We talk about what it means to be a friend and how most of us have friends who have moved away or whom we see only at certain times of the year. We locate on the map the places they will visit this summer, as well as places some of their friends have moved to. I modeled writing letters to some friends during my minilessons, and I did a few "When I Was Your Age" tales, in which I wrote about my friends when I was in first grade. Of course, I read them some books about friends and reread some of their old favorite *Frog and Toad* and *George and Martha* stories.

Our water unit was, as always, a lot of fun. Many of the children will vacation near some kind of water this summer, and the rest will spend some time at the community pool. We did lots of experiments with water, learned about water pollution and the need for water conservation, and realized how critical and huge a part water plays in our everyday lives. We read books about the ocean and other bodies of water and enjoyed some of the Jerry Pallotta alphabet books, including *The Ocean Alphabet Book* and *The Underwater Alphabet Book*. By far, the children's favorite book this month was *The Magic School Bus at the Waterworks*. Like the other books in Joanna Cole and Bruce Degan's science series, this book finds Ms. Frizzle and her class taking an incredible journey—this time right through the town's waterworks. The children marveled at what they found on this journey. They remarked longingly, "Wouldn't it be wonderful if we could really go inside things like they can on *The Magic School Bus*."

Fortunately, Ms. Maverick's class had foreseen the popularity of *The Magic School Bus* books and had ordered many copies of each title for their annual end-of-the-year book fair. My class was one of the first to go, and they bought up all the copies of *The Magic School Bus at the Waterworks* and a lot of the other titles. This book fair is a super idea, but I worry about the children who can't scrape together any money. Paul surprised me by bringing five dollars, which he spent with great care. Daisy had money but wouldn't spend it. The others teased her, saying that she was probably going to spend it all on candy! Chip was the only one who didn't bring any money, but I had anticipated that and had hired him to stay after school for several nights and help me do some of the end-of-the-year packing up, and then I paid him with books he had selected.

Last week, we had an experience in here! Sue Port came and asked me if I would spend a half day with all the first-grade teachers in the school system and explain to them my four-block approach to reading and writing. I protested that I couldn't possibly explain this in just a few hours' time, but she persisted. Then she had this brainstorm. "How about if I send our central office media person to make some videotapes of what is happening in here? That way, you could show them what is happening, and the teachers would really understand what a lively, varied day the children have and how well they are all reading and writing." Before I could convince her that I didn't want someone in my room taping everything we did during these last hectic days, she had bustled off to "set it up"!

The next morning Miss Media arrived, and she stayed for three days! Of course, the children were beside themselves on the first day, and I didn't think we would get any good tape. But on the second and third days, they settled down and started ignoring the camera—as did I—and although I haven't looked at it all yet, I do think we will have some parts that really show what is happening and how well the children are reading and writing. On the third day, Miss Media had each child bring a book he or she wanted to read and the last book he or she authored, and each child read a few pages of the favorite book and the entire authored book for the camera. This part we watched together as a class, and the children all did remarkably well. The books Danielle, Pat, and Larry read parts of were chapter books usually read by fourth-graders. Mike's authored collection of monster stories is extraordinarily clever! Even Paul had chosen a book he enjoyed reading and could read the book he wrote. I hate to admit it, but Sue was right. I am going to pick portions to show each block, as well as the children reading and writing. That all my children are reading and writing better than anyone could expect them to is undeniable when you see them doing it. Although I don't enjoy talking to groups of my peers, particularly other teachers I work with, I think I might actually look forward to this presentation!

The First-Grade Meeting

Sue Port called the meeting to order and introduced Mrs. Wright. "To most of you, Rita Wright needs no introduction. Rita has taught at Merritt Elementary School for more years than she likes to admit to. Rita has served on and, at times, chaired your grade-level curriculum committees. Rita is, and has been for many years, an outstanding first-grade teacher who uses all means at her disposal to get children off to a terrific start. Last year, Rita began implementing what she calls her four-block approach to reading and writing. She had read about this approach to organizing beginning reading instruction, and the idea that children do not all learn in the same way and that multiple methods were needed if all children were going to succeed was one she had believed in for many years. Another part of this organizational plan she agreed with was not putting children in leveled reading groups. Reading groups have been our major way of dealing with the differences children at entering literacy levels bring with them to school, but the effectiveness of reading groups has been seriously questioned in recent years. I don't want to take any more of Rita's precious time because, knowing Rita, I am sure she has this planned down to the minute, but I do want you to know that I have been impressed with what I have seen in Rita's classroom in the past two years, and it is at my insistence that she is here to share with you today."

The assembled teachers clapped in a restrained, polite way as Rita rose to speak. The anticipation she had felt earlier began to turn to anxiety as she looked out at the somewhat skeptical faces of some of her colleagues. She began by telling them that she felt a little uneasy talking to them about first grade. She knew most of them and knew that they were all terrific first-grade teachers.

"If you had asked me two years ago to tell you honestly how good a job I thought I was doing as a first-grade teacher, I would have told you that there were things I would like to change—mostly things about some of the kids." Some teachers nodded and laughed in agreement, and Mrs. Wright began to relax a little. "But all in all, I thought I was doing as well as anyone could, considering the wide range of children we have at Merritt and the lack of home support many of the children we teach today have. Two years ago this summer, however, I read an article by Cunningham, Hall, & Defee (1998), which Sue has had duplicated for you to take with you, and I got excited by what I read. A lot of what was in their article I was already doing, but the teachers who developed the four-block approach had put components together in what looked to me like a very workable, practical way. Last year, I tried out some of the parts of this approach, and this year, I jumped in feet first! I am the same teacher, teaching in the same school, teaching the same variety of children, using the same materials, working as hard as I always work, and my children—particularly the ones who came least prepared and the ones who came already reading—are reading and, writing much better than they have in all the other years. Since there are no other changes except for this new way of dividing up my time and organizing; my day, I have to assume that this approach is just better suited to the varied needs of my children. Let me begin at the end and show you some of my children reading and writing."

Mrs. Wright switched on the VCR and there on camera was Chip. Chip read a few pages from a "Curious George" book he had selected and then read and showed the illustrations of his last published book. Daisy was next to read, followed by Alexander, Mike, and finally Paul. When these five children had all read from selected books and their own published books, Mrs. Wright paused the tape and said, "Now I know that many of you are thinking these children are not unusually good readers and writers for the end of first grade, but these are my five lowest children. Chip can almost read on grade level. Daisy, Alexander, and Mike are on a good solid middle-of-first-grade level, and Paul is my lowest, but he can read easy books independently, and he can read the three books he has authored."

Mrs. Wright could tell that most of the teachers were looking at this reading and writing of these five children differently when they realized they were the below-level readers. Mrs. Wright then fast-forwarded through the rest of the class reading and writing, stopping once or twice so that the teachers knew that these children all read easily at first-grade level or above. She showed the tape at normal speed once again while Larry, Danielle, Pat, and Steve read aloud. All four of these children had chosen to read a couple of pages of chapter books usually read by fourth- or fifth-graders. The published books they shared also demonstrated writing abilities way beyond that of average first-graders.

When she stopped the tape, the teachers were all abuzz, talking to each other. Mrs. Wright mouthed a "thank you" to Sue for insisting on the three days of taping and on having all the children read for the tape. The teachers now had all kinds of questions:

Was Mrs. Wright sure that this was a normal class at the beginning of the year?

How far had she taken those last four students in their reading series?

How could a student like Paul write a book like the one he wrote?

Wasn't there a single child who was still a virtual nonreader/nonwriter?

Mrs. Wright laughed at this question and said, "I didn't hide any children or ask any of their parents to keep them home when the visitors came, as I hear used to happen in the old days."

Mrs. Wright then showed the teachers her daily schedule and showed clips of each of the four blocks. As she went through, she reminded the teachers that they were seeing the last few days of school, and that although she had done all four blocks from the beginning of school, what she and the children did in those blocks looked quite different in September and even in February from what they were seeing at the end of May.

She showed some tape of the Writing block and of her minilesson in which she wrote while the children watched. The teachers expressed amazement that she didn't say the words while she was writing them, but she had them focus on the children, and it was obvious that the children were all trying their best to read what she was writing. She also pointed out to the teachers that in her minilesson, she always looked for a word or two on the word wall, looked pleased to find it there, and commented, "If it's on our word wall, we have to spell it correctly."

When she got to the point where she spelled a couple of big words, stretching out the words and writing down the letters you could hear, she could tell from the shaking heads that some teachers didn't think a teacher should ever spell a word wrong. Leaving out some ending punctuation and capital letters did not please some either. As soon as Mrs. Wright finished writing, she pointed to the Editor's Checklist:

Editor's Checklist

Do all the sentences make sense?

Do all the sentences start with capital letters?

Do all the sentences have . ? or ! at the end?

Do all the people and place names and I start with a capital?

She took a different-colored marker, and the children helped her read for each item on the checklist and fix each and then draw a happy face. In addition she asked them which words she had stretched out to spell, and she underlined these, remarking that she would have to find the correct spelling for these words if this were the piece she chose to publish.

Next, the tape showed the children writing. Most children were writing in their notebooks, but a few were finishing up the copying and illustrating of their final first-grade published books. When Mrs. Wright rang the bell to signal the end of the writing time, five children lined up and read their chosen piece in the Author's Chair. Each child who read chose one child from the audience to tell something he or she liked about the piece.

Mrs. Wright stopped the tape, and there were a slew of questions!

How did she get them started writing?

Did she give them a topic for writing?

How did they know how to choose a topic?

How did she have time to help them all edit and publish?

Who made all the blank books?

Mrs. Wright tried to answer the questions, and then Sue Port jumped in to announce that it was time for a break, and that after the break, she wanted Mrs. Wright to show tapes of the other blocks. "I know that you all still have questions about the writing, and you will have questions about the other blocks, but we will have only an hour left, and I want you to get an overview of all four blocks. When we end this afternoon, I am going to ask you to write down the questions you still have, and then I will see what we can plan before the start of the next school year to help provide answers to your questions."

The teachers talked to each other and asked Mrs. Wright individual questions throughout the break, and Mrs. Wright was amazed at their enthusiasm. After the break, she did a whirlwind tour of the other blocks. She showed the word wall and explained about putting the names up one each day and having one child be the special child for the day. She told them how she had added five high-frequency words each week and explained that they took all the Monday Words time to work with and practice handwriting with the five new words. On the other days, five words were reviewed. The teachers watched the children clap and chant and write the words and then get out their red pens to trace around and check them. Then the children turned their papers over and Mrs. Wright led them to use their word wall words to spell rhyming words on the back. The tape then focused on their content board, which at this point had pictures of water and water words, and Mrs. Wright explained that between the word wall and the content boards, even children like Alexander, who still couldn't hear sounds in words very well, were able to write.

Next they watched a Making Words lesson in which the children used the letters *a, e, h, l, s,* and *w* to make the words *we, he, she, sea, was, saw, law, slaw, heal, seal, sale,* and *leash.* The teachers were amazed when Mrs. Wright got to the end of the lesson and asked, "Has anyone figured out what word we can make with all these letters?" At least a dozen hands went up from children who (unlike many of the teachers watching) had figured out that these letters could spell *whales*—an animal they were studying about as part of their water unit. Mrs. Wright then led the children to sort the words into patterns and they used the rhyming words to decode and spell *claw, steal, meal* and *thaw.*

The teachers again had all kinds of questions about the word wall and Making Words lesson, but Sue insisted that they write down their questions and pushed Mrs. Wright forward to show some of the Guided-Reading block. Mrs. Wright showed part of Wednesday's lesson in which they were all reading in partners from the adopted reader, as well as part of Thursday's lesson in which they were reading in small groups in the easier books.

Finally, Mrs. Wright showed just a little snippet of Thursday's Teacher Read-Aloud/Self-Selected Reading block. The teachers were all amazed at the ability of all the children to sit and sustain their reading for fifteen minutes as Mrs. Wright conferenced with the Thursday children.

The meeting was running a few minutes over, and Mrs. Wright knew that many of the teachers had to rush off to pick up their own children from day care. She summed up, however, by telling the teachers what she had learned during the last two years.

"Remember in your education courses, when you were taking an essay exam, no matter what the question was, you knew you should always get the words *individual differences* in the answer somewhere if you wanted an A?" The teachers all chuckled and Mrs. Wright knew they had all had this universal experience.

"Well, what I learned is that individual differences are really true—not just something we should give lip service to. The differences in the levels are the obvious ones, but there are also differences in the way children learn and respond—personality differences, I guess you would call them. This year, I taught twins—born within minutes of each other, raised in the same environment—and the two girls are as different as night and day! Not different in their ability—they are both smart girls—but different in how they approach things, in the amount of structure or freedom they need, for example."

The nods of the teachers assured Mrs. Wright that all the teachers knew these learning style/personality differences were a reality of teaching. "The four blocks—Writing, Words, Guided Reading, and Teacher Read-Aloud/Self-Selected Reading—are like four roads, four ways to get there. The reason I think my children—particularly the children on either end—are reading and writing so much better is that regardless of how they learn best, that method is present in our classroom for some consistent part of every day. The four blocks represent different ways children learn, and within each block there are a variety of levels on which children can operate. I don't have time to discuss this now, but the multi-level concept is critical when you have the differences we always have at Merritt. The Writing and Self-Selected Reading time are naturally multilevel, but I have had to work to make the Words block and the Guided-Reading block multilevel."

Sue hurriedly brought the meeting to a close, thanking Mrs. Wright and reminding the teachers to pick up their articles and leave their questions with her. Some teachers hurried off, but many others stayed and talked until late in the afternoon. Mrs. Wright could sense their genuine interest, and she reminded herself that most teachers work hard and want the very best for their children. "It's not that we don't care enough or that we don't do enough. It's just that the differences in learning style and entering level make it so complex to get it all organized," she assured them.

As the teachers left, many of them exchanged phone numbers and agreed to meet for a few potluck lunches over the summer and make plans for next year. Sue was beaming as she walked Rita to her car. "You see," she said, "those teachers know a good thing when they see it, and next year, I will arrange for them to come and visit your class and you can be their support as they move into this. Now aren't you glad I made you do this and sent Miss Media to tape for three days in your class?" Mrs. Wright smiled and said, "I'm glad it went well, and I'm glad they are enthusiastic, but I am going to have to decide how I feel about the rest of it." Sue assured her that she would be there to help and that Rita would love her new leadership role.

References

Cunningham, P. M., & Hall, D. P. (1997). *Month-by-month phonics for first grade.* Greensboro, NC: Carson-Dellosa.

Cunningham, P. M., Hall, D. P., & Sigmon, C. M. (1999). *The teacher's guide to the four blocks.* Greensboro, NC: Carson-Dellosa.

Cunningham, P. M., Hall, D. P., & Defee, M. (1998). Nonability grouped, multilevel instruction: Eight years later. *The Reading Teacher, 51,* 652–664.

Taba, H. (1967). *Teachers' handbook for elementary social studies.* Palo Alto, CA: Addison-Wesley.

Children's Books/Materials Cited

ABC Bunny, by W. Gag, Putnam, 1978.

Alphabeasts: A Hide and Seek Alphabet Book, by Durga Bernhard, Holiday, 1992.

Are You My Mother? by P. D. Eastman, Random House, 1960.

Ashanti to Zulu: African Traditions, by M. Musgrove, Puffin Books, 1980.

The Biggest Nose, by K. Caple, Houghton Mifflin, 1985.

Caps, Hats, Socks, and Mittens, by L. Borden, Scholastic, 1989.

The Cat in the Hat, by Dr. Seuss, Random House, 1987.

Clifford books, by N. Bridwell, Scholastic, various dates.

Curious George books, by M. Rey & H. A. Rey, Houghton Mifflin, various dates.

Families Are Different, by N. Pelligrini, Scholastic, 1992.

Fly Away Home, by E. Bunting, Houghton Mifflin, 1993.

Frog and Toad books, by A. Lobel, HarperCollins, various dates.

George and Martha books, by J. Marshall, Sandpiper, various dates.

The Gingerbread Man, by K. Schmidt, Scholastic, 1986.

Goodnight Moon, by M. W. Brown, Holt, Rinehart, & Winston, 1969.

The Hand Made Alphabet, by L. Rankin, Dial, 1991.

Happy Christmas, Gemma, by S. Hayes, Morrow, 1992.

Hop on Pop, by Dr. Seuss, Random House, 1987.

The Hundred Dresses, by E. Estes, Scholastic, 1980.

I Hate English, by E. Levine, Scholastic, 1989.

If You Grew Up with Abraham Lincoln, by A. McGovern, Scholastic, 1992.

If You Grew Up with George Washington, by R. B. Gross, Scholastic, 1993.

The Magic School Bus at the Waterworks, by J. Cole & B. Degan, Scholastic, 1988.

The Mother's Day Mice, by E. Bunting, Ticknor & Fields, 1988.

Mrs. Wishy Washy, by J. Cowley, Wright, 1989.

My First Kwanzaa Book, by D. N. Chocolate, Cartwheel, 1990.

NBA Action From A–Z, by J. Preller, Scholastic, 1997.
The Ocean Alphabet Book, by J. Pallotta, Charlesbridge Publishers, 1989.
One Fish, Two Fish, Red Fish, Blue Fish, by Dr. Seuss, Random House, 1987.
Over in the Meadow, by O. A. Wadsworth, Scholastic, 1990.
A Perfect Father's Day, by E. Bunting, Houghton Mifflin, 1993.
A Picture Book of Hanukkah, by D. Adler, Holiday, 1982.
A Picture Book of Martin Luther King, by D. Adler, Holiday, 1989.
Robert the Rose Horse, by J. Heilbroner, Random House, 1962.
The Snowy Day, by E. J. Keats, Puffin Books, 1976.
Ten, Nine, Eight, by M. Bang, Morrow, 1991.
The Underwater Alphabet Book, by J. Pallotta, Charlesbridge Publishers, 1991.
The Very Hungry Caterpillar, by E. Carle, Putnam, 1986.
The Wednesday Surprise, by E. Bunting, Houghton Mifflin, 1990.
What Will the Weather Be Like Today? by P. Rogers, Scholastic, 1992.
Where the Wild Things Are, by M. Sendak, HarperCollins,1988.
Where's Spot? by E. Hill, Putnam, 1987.
White Snow, Bright Snow, by A. Tresselt, Morrow, 1988.

13

Miss Nouveau: Second Grade

• •

The Parent Meeting

Norma Nouveau arrived at the school two hours before her 7:30 P.M. parent meeting was scheduled to begin. Frankly, she was nervous and dreaded having to face all the parents in a large group. But at least, she thought, Mr. Topps would be there to help. He had generously offered to come to her meeting in case she needed help answering questions about schoolwide policies she might not even know about yet.

She was looking over her new bulletin board when Mr. Topps arrived at 7:15 P.M. He told her that it was lovely and that the fall theme she had chosen brightened the room. She didn't tell Mr. Topps that she had been working on that bulletin board for two weeks, sometimes until 2:00 A.M. She wanted him and the parents to think that she was efficient and organized.

Miss Nouveau had made name tags for all of the parents to wear. That way she could easily identify each parent, and she would know from the leftover name tags who had been unable to attend. When all of the parents were seated, Mr. Topps, as had been agreed earlier, introduced her to the group.

"As you all know," he began, "I am Mr. Topps, the principal. I especially wanted to come this evening to introduce your child's teacher to you. Miss Nouveau comes to us this year as a first-year teacher. She did exceptionally well both at the university and during her student teaching, so that when this position opened up last spring, I was delighted to have her among the applicants for the job. I know that you will be as happy with her as we are. If there is anything that you would like either of us to do, do not hesitate to call. Now, let's hear from Miss Nouveau."

"Thank you, Mr. Topps. This is an exciting moment for me. All my life I have dreamed of being an elementary school teacher. Tonight, I want to explain to you the kind of program that I have planned for this school year and how my instruction will meet these guiding principles." As Miss Nouveau said this, she pointed to a poster on which were printed the twelve guiding principles the Merritt faculty had come up with two years earlier.

At Merritt Elementary, we believe that all children can learn to read and write. We hold high expectations of every child. To make these expectations a reality, we all agree to have our instruction reflect twelve guiding principles:

1. Provide a balanced literacy program.
2. Make instruction multilevel.
3. Use language as the foundation for reading and writing.
4. Teach reading and writing as thinking.
5. Use feelings to create avid readers and writers.
6. Connect reading and writing to all subject areas.
7. Read aloud to students daily.
8. Schedule daily self-selected reading.
9. Have students write every day.
10. Teach the decoding and spelling strategies reading and writing require.
11. Use observation to assess learning and plan instruction.
12. Inform parents of expectations and progress.

"I wasn't here, of course, when the faculty decided on these, but I learned about them during our new-teacher orientation, and they look pretty basic and simple to me."

Miss Nouveau went down the list of beliefs and explained each in a way that showed she didn't think that meeting these was going to be any big deal.

"Of course, I will provide a balanced program, and I will make it multilevel by putting your children in the right reading group. I will be using the reading series adopted by the school system." Miss Nouveau held up her copy of the teacher's manual. "It explains here how the series is based on language, how the comprehension lessons help the children learn to think, and how important developing reading interests and attitudes are. Of course, we will be reading and writing in the content areas because we will use these science and social studies books." Miss Nouveau pointed to the science and social studies texts displayed on the table.

"I will read aloud to the children after lunch every day, and then they will have their Self-Selected Reading time. There are lots of writing activities in the manual for the reading series, so they will write every day, and of course I will teach the phonics lessons that go with every selection. There are assessment ideas here, too, and of course, I will be reporting to you with our report cards and in our parent conferences. All in all, I don't think it will be difficult—even for a novice like me—

to do all the things the Merritt faculty is committed to." Miss Nouveau, relieved that *that* was over, hurried on to a topic she knew more about.

"You know that physical factors are quite important in determining how well your children do in school. You can be most helpful in seeing to it that your children get to bed by 8:30 at night, that they come to school after having had a nutritious breakfast, and that they play out in the fresh air for a while every day after school. I intend to emphasize these basic health habits with the children this year. We will be studying nutrition, the value of recreation, and the importance of adequate rest. Starting on Monday, I am going to ask you to send a snack to school with your child. We will have snack time every morning in order to help keep the energy level of the children high. The school nurse will test vision and hearing in October, and if there are any problems, I will be in touch with you."

Miss Nouveau looked at her watch and saw that what she had planned to take thirty minutes had consumed only fifteen minutes of time, so she asked Mr. Topps if there was anything he would like to add. There was not. The time had come for the part of the meeting that she had been dreading. She turned back to the parents and asked, "Are there any questions?"

All over the room, hands shot up. She called on Mrs. Moore first.

"How did you determine which reading group each child should be in?"

Miss Nouveau proudly explained that she had already assessed each child's reading using the Informal Reading Inventory that accompanied the reading series.

Mrs. Penn raised her hand to ask, "Why are you using *this* particular series?"

Mr. Topps intervened. "If I may, I would like to answer that one, Miss Nouveau, since the decision was made before you were hired. You see, Mrs. Penn, the teachers in this school met together last spring and selected this series. Most of the teachers at that meeting believed that this series allowed for the most flexibility while still retaining the structure and sequential development of skills that is a strong point of the basal reader approach."

Another hand went up, and Miss Nouveau called on Mr. Tomás. "When the kids aren't with you, how will they know what to do? Won't they just waste time and not do their work?"

"I will make sure they have plenty to do to keep them busy and out of trouble. They will complete the worksheets that come with the reading book, and they will do other work in the centers I am setting up. I will make sure they all make good use of their independent working time."

Mrs. Penn glanced over at Mr. Topps for his reaction. Had he pressed his fingertips to his forehead because of a headache?

There were many more questions, but Mr. Topps told the parents that it was time for them to adjourn to the cafeteria for the schoolwide meeting. He assured them that Miss Nouveau would be an excellent teacher and that he would work closely with her, as he would with any first-year teacher.

Miss Nouveau thanked them for coming. She started to gather up some of her materials when she noticed Mrs. Penn at her elbow.

"Miss Nouveau, I just want to offer to help you in any way that I can. I used to be a teacher, so I think that I might be of some help to you. *Please* feel free to call on me. I really enjoy helping out, and I know what a difficult task you have."

"Oh, thank you, but I'm sure that won't be necessary. I think that I have things pretty much under control now. But I do appreciate your offer. I will call for help if I need it."

"Fine. Good evening. It was lovely meeting with you this evening."

Mrs. Penn and Mrs. Middleman left the room together. They were talking quietly, but Miss Nouveau heard some of what was said.

> ***Mrs. Middleman:*** She's going to find out that meeting those twelve principles is easier said than done. But she is smart, and she seems to love the children, and she will learn a lot with Mr. Topps's help. She also did a lovely bulletin board. My, she certainly is creative.

> ***Mrs. Penn:*** Yes, she is. But you know, I always like to see the children's work up on the bulletin board. It's not as pretty or tidy, but there's something wonderful about your own child's work displayed. Mrs. Wright did so much of that last year.

Miss Nouveau was crestfallen. All that work, and they would rather see things that the children had done! "Maybe I should think about having the children do something to put up. Oh, but it will be so messy!"

Monthly Logs

September

My major premise is wrong! I thought that all children loved to read or that at the very least they were eager to learn. How wrong! How wrong! I just can't understand it. Butch sits in his seat (sometimes) just waiting out the day. If I ask him to do one of the assignments, he just looks at me and asks, "Why?"

"So that when you grow up you'll be able to read. You need to be a good reader to get a job."

"Oh yeah," he replied. "Well, my dad, he don't read so good, but he makes three hundred bucks a week!" That sounds like a great deal of money to a seven-year-old, but if only he knew!

One of the most frightening aspects of this teaching business is the weight of responsibility one feels. I was so excited to have my own classroom and spent a lot of time here this summer getting my room ready for the first days of school. But the full realization of the responsibility didn't hit me until I saw the first children come into the room—my room—*our* room.

I fervently hope that I will never again live through a day like the first day of school. The children were quite well behaved (I suppose the novelty of returning to school), and I had prepared an excess of material for them, just in case. I had enough for two days—so I thought! By noon, I had used up everything I had planned for the first day. They worked so much more quickly than I had ever imagined! By lunchtime I was rattled. What to do? That afternoon I used up the next day's lessons!

Another horrible feeling of incompetence came when I realized that I had to put these children into reading groups. How many *is* a group? Grouping had been talked about in my undergraduate reading course, but I now realized I really didn't have a well-defined idea of how to go about it.

I gave all the children the IRI that accompanies the series. It wasn't easy to get it done because the other children were so noisy and interrupted me so often. I think also that it was too much to try to do it all in two days. Next year (if I am alive and teaching!), I will spread it out across a week so that the children have to work independently for only a little while.

By the time of the parent meeting, I did have my groups formed, though that had not been as easy as I felt it would be. Larry gives every indication of being an extremely bright child, yet when I was scoring his IRI, I was amazed at the number of errors he made in oral reading. Instead of "He could not get the car to start," Larry read, "He couldn't get the car started." Yet with all of those errors, his comprehension remained high! As a matter of fact, he did amazingly well, answering every question correctly and completely. I put him into the middle group anyway, because the requirements for the IRI include both oral reading and comprehension. But he is clearly the best reader in the class. I think I will move him to the top group and see how he does.

Daisy and Mike didn't really meet the 95 percent oral reading accuracy criterion for the first-grade book that I am planning to use with my low group, but I didn't think I could manage another group so I put them there. Paul wouldn't read for me! I pleaded, threatened, and bribed, but he just sat there. I put him in the lowest group, but I don't know where he belongs. He won't read aloud or do his workbook. He is not mean and behaves; he just won't do anything. I must ask Mrs. Wright about him.

Once I had the children assigned to reading groups, I let them choose a group name. For some of the groups this took a long time, but eventually all three groups were named. The top group (all girls until I move Larry in) chose to be butterflies. The middle group are astronauts, and the bottom group (all boys except for Daisy) chose monsters. I tried to get them to change the name, but Mike, the leader in the group, said I told them they could choose and they chose monsters. I just hope that no one thinks that *I* named them! (They certainly chose a descriptive name!)

I work with each group for thirty minutes. They spend the time they are not with me working on their worksheets at their desks or completing the activities I have put in the centers. At least, that is what they are supposed to do! Many of them are just not independent workers. They wander around the room and fool around. Daisy draws pictures. Paul just sits and stares, except when he is crying because Butch and Mike are picking on him. Even Roberta, who is very smart, often doesn't get her work done. I don't know what to do about this. I try to make sure they have plenty to do, and I have kept the ones who didn't have their work in the "done" box in for recess a few days. But I don't think I am supposed to do this—they need fresh air and exercise. I also don't get any break at all when I keep them here, because I can't go off and leave this crew alone! I asked them if they behaved this way for Mrs. Wright last year and was informed by Mike and Butch that Mrs. Wright didn't give them all this dumb boring work to do!

I am also having problems getting it all graded and back to them to take home on Friday. Last Thursday, I ended up throwing one set of papers away in my home trashcan because I just had to go to bed and I couldn't send them home ungraded. So far, no one seems to have missed it. Creating work to keep them busy at their desks and in centers so that I can work with groups and getting them to do it and getting it graded is the biggest problem I have and is consuming most of my time and energy. There must be a better way, but I can't figure out what it is. I will have to ask someone—but I hate to admit I am having trouble with something that should be so simple.

Except for reading-group time, the rest of the day goes relatively smoothly. When I am right there with them during math, science, and social studies, they behave pretty well, and I have even taught some pretty good lessons. They and I enjoy the reading aloud I do right after lunch every day, and they are settling down pretty well with their books for Self-Selected Reading. Even Paul seems to enjoy looking at the books, and Mike is happy if he can have books with monsters in them. I have been reading as they read—to provide a good model—but now that they are in the habit of reading, I think I might take that time to grade some of that morning's papers.

October

If only I can survive until January! I student taught during the winter last year, and if we can only get to January, I'll know what to do. Why did everything look so easy when my supervising teacher did it? Either I am doing something wrong, or else I have a really rough group of children. I always wanted to teach second grade because the children are still so cute and they already know how to read. That seemed like the perfect grade to me, but how different it really is. Some of them can hardly read, and some of them are definitely not in the "cute" category.

This class makes me wonder about the first-grade experience that they had. Whenever I walk by Mrs. Wright's classroom, it *appears* that she has good discipline, but I wonder if she does really. If she had good control of her class, how could a class like this one be giving me so much trouble? I know that Mrs. Wright is an excellent teacher—listening to the reading of Pat and Rita convinces me of that—but perhaps she is just not a disciplinarian. Well, whatever the reason, I've really had to crack down on these kids. I had to close the centers because they were just going from place to place and not getting their assignments done there. Now, I have to find twice as much to keep them busy at their seats. I have put a handwriting assignment on the board for them to copy, but some of them finish it in no time and others just "slop it out" or don't do it. I have also given them some dot-to-dot sheets to complete and color. They seem to like these, but I worry about what they are learning from this. All of them already know their numbers in order, and I know that coloring doesn't make you a better reader. The worksheets that I give them with their reader are on their level, except for Paul, Daisy, and Mike, who probably can't read them, and Larry, Pat, and Hilda, for whom they are much too easy. But the other assignments that I have to give everyone to keep them busy now that centers are closed are a real problem. I know that the seatwork should require reading and writing if it is going to move them along in reading and writing, but what can I give everyone when they range from Paul to Larry?

Even Self-Selected Reading is not going as well as it did. The children are still attentive and seem to enjoy it when I read to them. This month, I read them several informational books by Gail Gibbons, *Halloween* and *The Reasons for Seasons,* which tie into our unit on seasons and holidays. They also enjoyed *Spider Storch's Teacher Torture,* an easy but funny chapter book. Some of the children are settling in well during Self-Selected Reading, but others, particularly the struggling readers along with Roberta and Mitch, are talking, fooling around, passing notes, and generally not reading. I hope it is not because I quit modeling reading and started grading papers, but I fear it may be. I may be giving them too long to read now—fifteen minutes seems like an eternity to my children who don't like to read.

Mr. Topps came in to observe me this month for his first formal observation. He let me choose what I wanted him to observe, and of course, I chose math. We do math first thing in the morning, and I am always prepared and ready to go. The children are quite attentive then, too, and I am a good math teacher, if I do say so myself. I began my lesson with some real-world mental math problems. Next we reviewed addition facts with a fast-paced fun game, and then they worked with partners, using manipulatives to solve some regrouping problems. We then checked our work together to end the lesson.

The good news was that Mr. Topps was most impressed and wrote me a wonderful evaluation. The bad news was that he wants to observe reading—my worst subject! I think I will have him observe a lesson with the butterflies, since they read well. I just have to make the others behave. Perhaps they will if he is here.

November

So much has changed this month that I don't know quite where to begin. Mr. Topps came as scheduled and observed me during reading time. I had promised the class a special popcorn party if they were all working quietly when he was there. (I felt guilty about this, but I was desperate to have things go well!) I began my lesson with the butterflies by building prior knowledge and introducing vocabulary, and then I had them take turns reading the pages aloud. They read quite well, and after each child read, I asked the others some questions to make sure they were comprehending. It took a long time to read the story, and the children who had already read got restless at the end, but comparatively, the lesson went well and the children at their seats behaved. (I didn't know whether to feel good or bad about that, since it does prove they can sit and do their work when they want to.) At the end of the lesson, Mr. Topps said he had enjoyed being here and asked me to meet with him that afternoon to talk about the lesson.

He left and the class exploded! Mike was shouting and Daisy was running around yelling. "Popcorn, popcorn, bring out the popcorn!" I was appalled. I didn't even want to give them the popcorn, but they had done what I asked, so I knew I had to. That afternoon, while we were all eating popcorn, Mr. Topps came back! "Mr. Topps," said Roberta, "come help us eat the popcorn we earned by behaving while you were watching Miss Nouveau teach!" Mr. Topps looked surprised for just a moment and then smiled and graciously accepted the popcorn offer. I wanted to disappear! I can't ever remember having been that mortified!

When the children left, Mr. Topps consoled me. "You aren't the first teacher who has ever promised the children a reward for good behavior," he assured me. "Now, let's forget about your bribe and focus on why you felt you had to make it. Your math lesson went wonderfully. Did you bribe them for that one too?" I cringed at the word "bribe" but I knew that was what I had done.

"Oh, no," I replied, "I am a good math teacher—and pretty good at science and social studies too. It is just reading that is so awful." Now that my guard was down, I poured out my soul to him. I told him how I had closed the centers and how I had to give them things to keep them busy that I knew were not helping them be better readers and writers and how Paul, Daisy, and Mike belonged in their own group and I couldn't possibly do another group. By the time I got around to telling him about how even Self-Selected Reading was falling apart, I was in tears.

Mr. Topps handed me his handkerchief (he is such an old-fashioned man in many ways), and after I had cried it all out, I felt much better. He then explained that reading is the hardest subject to make multilevel, and that what to do with the ones you aren't working with so that you can work with groups is the hardest management problem most teachers face.

"Let's not try to solve every problem right now, but let's begin with the easy ones—your centers and Self-Selected Reading. Tomorrow, I want you to observe Mrs. Wright during her Self-Selected Reading time and center time. I will come and teach your class for you while you do this, and then we will talk again."

At 1:30 promptly the next day, Mr. Topps took over my class and I went next door to observe the "venerable" Mrs. Wright. She read aloud to the children for about fifteen minutes. After reminding them that it was the Tuesday people's day to conference with her, she dismissed them to their reading. I noticed that they had crates of books on their tables, and that they all went eagerly to read. I went around and listened in on the children reading, and although some were picture-reading and others were pretending they could read the book, most were actually reading the words and doing a remarkably good job. I also observed what Mrs. Wright did. She spent only two or three minutes with each child, but the children seemed to know just what to do, and they got a lot done in those few minutes. "This is certainly a more responsible bunch than the bunch she sent me," I thought.

At 2:00, Mrs. Wright prepared the children to go home, and then children went to the centers. She dismissed them to centers by their "days of the week." The Tuesday children picked a center first and slotted their card into that center. Next, the Wednesday people picked, Thursday people, etc. Each center had a limit on how many children could go there, so the Friday and Monday people didn't get their first choice, but I see how they wouldn't mind because they would pick first on their day. "Ingenious," I thought and vowed then and there to have my children designated by days of the week by tomorrow.

As the children were working in centers, I noticed Mrs. Wright reading some very easy books individually for ten minutes each with two of the children I had noticed were not yet reading many words during the Self-Selected Reading time. She accomplished a great deal in that ten minutes alone with each child, and I realized that was what Paul, Daisy, and Mike needed. "But where could I find the ten minutes?"

I also noticed something else about the centers. The things the children were doing there were not anything Mrs. Wright had to check or grade. Children were painting and drawing in the Art Center, listening to books on tape in the Listening Center, writing or enjoying an animated book in the Computer Center, or watching and playing with George the gerbil, Tom the turtle, and Louise the lizard in the Pet Center. The children were talking, but they were using quiet voices instead of yelling like mine do. Once, when things got a little rowdy, Mrs. Wright informed two boys that they were on warning and would have to return to their desks if she saw any more "roughhousing."

After the children left, I was so excited and had so many questions for her that I forgot all about Mr. Topps in my room and stayed talking to Mrs. Wright. He came into her room, however, and we all three had a good talk.

I stayed until almost midnight, getting ready for the next day. When the children arrived, they found "transformed" centers. No more activities in each center to complete and put in the done box, but more open-ended activities that allowed the children to explore and didn't require grading! I sat down with them, and we had a heart-to-heart talk. I told them about all the things I had seen in Mrs. Wright's room. They all joined in and told me about how they got to pick first on their day and how it was their job to prepare for their conference by picking two pages to read to Mrs. Wright and tell her why they chose the book. They talked about their favorite centers, and Daisy explained that you had to use a quiet voice and not bother other people or you lost your place in the Art Center and had to sit at your desk while someone else painted at your easel!

I then bragged on them, telling them all the good things Mrs. Wright had told me they had learned to do. "I am sorry I didn't know you were grown up enough to prepare for conferences or work independently on what you chose to do in centers," I explained. "But now I know, and there are going to be some changes here.

Next, I showed them a chart on which I had listed their days. I followed Mrs. Wright's suggestions about spreading out the rowdy ones and the strugglers so they didn't all clump up on one day. Here is the chart I worked out:

Monday	Tuesday	Wednesday	Thursday	Friday
Mike	Daisy	Paul	Butch	Alexander
Chip	Horace	Daphne	Betty	Mort
Steve	Alex	Jeff	Manuel	Mandy
Mitch	Larry	Anthony	Joyce	Pat
Rita	Hilda	Roberta	Danielle	Carl

"We are going to have our center time for thirty minutes while I am working with groups," I explained. "Astronauts will go to centers for the first thirty minutes, while butterflies do their work to prepare to meet with me and I meet with monsters." (Why did I let them choose their name? I cringe every time I say that!) I then let Daphne, Jeff, and Anthony, the Wednesday astronauts, have first pick of centers—followed by Manuel and Joyce, the Thursday astronauts, and then the others. They took their card and slotted into their desired center, and I let them go to their centers. I then took a few minutes to explain the seatwork the butterflies needed to do during this first half hour. "Your center time is next," I explained. "I will collect your work as you choose your centers. It doesn't have to be perfect, but it does have to show that you tried if you are going to get to go to centers."

With the astronauts in centers and the butterflies working at their desks, I sat down with Paul's group. ("They might call themselves monsters," I thought, "but I don't have to!") I did my lesson with them, and then I showed them what they needed to do in the next thrity minutes to earn their center time. "I will collect your work before you go to centers," I explained. "It doesn't have to be perfect, but you do have to work quietly and show that you are making a good effort."

I then dismissed Paul's group to their desks, helped the astronauts get the centers ready for the next group, and let the butterflies pick their center—by days of the week—after handing me their morning work, which I looked at just enough to see there was something there that showed some effort! Amazingly, everyone—even Roberta—had their work and it was all "acceptably" done. "This might really work," I began to think.

As the butterflies worked in the centers and Paul's group worked at their desks, I began my lesson with the astronauts. Mr. Topps had told me that there was no reason to have my middle or top group read the whole selection aloud while they were with me.

"Do your before-reading set-up just as you have been doing, next read the first two pages to them to get them into the selection, and then send them to their seats to finish reading it. Give them a short writing assignment that goes along with your purpose—just a few sentences—to complete and bring back the following day. On the second day, after they have read it silently, you can let them do some oral reading, but not the whole selection—just a few sentences or a paragraph on each page to read specific things you ask them to read for. Then assign them their workbook activities to do in preparation for group on the third day."

I dismissed the astronauts to their work, helped the butterflies put their centers back in order, and then called Paul's group for their center time. Amazingly, everyone—even Mike, Daisy, and Paul—appeared to have made an effort to do their work. I let them choose their centers and met with the astronauts. Once again, I did the prereading activities with them—introduced vocabulary, looked at all the pictures and made predictions, read the first two pages to them, and let them know the purpose for reading the selection by telling them what they would do tomorrow when they came back to talk about and reread parts of the selection orally.

So far, this is working quite well. I was afraid the children would get back into their bad behaviors after the novelty wore off, but for the most part, they really seem to want to go to the centers they choose. Daisy, especially, is putting much more effort into her work. That girl loves to paint and is quite an artist! I have had to withhold center privileges one day for Roberta, Mitch, Alexander, and Butch, and two days for Mort and Mike, but most days, they do their work with an acceptable effort and behave well enough that they earn their center time.

I am also checking their work with them when they come to group, now that I don't have to spend all that time sitting and listening to them read the whole selection aloud. I still worry that they may not be reading it all, but they do seem to, and they are able to do the comprehension and activities I have them do, so I guess I do not have to hear everyone read aloud every day. I am still reading the selection with Paul's group, but I am having them do some echo reading and choral reading so that they all get more reading practice. I have not found a time to work with Paul, Daisy, and Mike individually, but I know that is what they need, so I am going to look again at my schedule and see what I can come up with.

I moved Self-Selected Reading time back to ten minutes and began conferencing with them on their day, just as Mrs. Wright does. It is amazing how much of a difference this makes. Mike still has trouble settling in, so I have given him his own crate of books and sit him at the table with me while I conference. He spends more time listening to my conferences with the children than he does reading, but he does read some, and he is not acting up and ruining things for everyone.

December

I have tried, up to this point, to write in my journal at the end of each week so that I could keep up with what was happening, but since my chat with Mr. Topps, so many things have been happening that the weeks rushed by until the holidays gave me a chance to sit down at home and continue my journal. I am so excited by the changes that I have made and the ones I am going to make!

After my afternoon visit to Mrs. Wright helped me so much, Mr. Topps hired a sub for me so that I could spend a full day this month in Mrs. Wright's classroom and another full day with Mrs. Wise. Was that ever enlightening! I saw how Mrs. Wright made her guided-reading block multilevel by reading two selections each week and by using various partnerships to support children. Mrs. Wise makes hers multilevel by choosing books on different levels tied together by topic, author, or genre. I might try one of those ways next year, but for now I think I need to stick with my groups. The problem, of course, is that it takes ninety minutes for me to meet with all three groups, and I don't have time to do writing or a word wall. I could see in both classrooms how important the writing was and how the word wall supports that writing, so I made up my mind to look at my schedule and see how I could possibly fit them in.

After my visits, Sue Port came to visit. She is the reading supervisor for the system, and I knew her from our new-teacher orientation. She visited during reading, and was I ever glad that things were going better than they had earlier. That afternoon, we had a conference and she commented on how "organized" and efficient everything was and how all the children seemed "happily engaged." I thanked her and told her that things were better and that Mrs. Wright and Mr. Topps had been my saviors. I told her, however, about wanting to find ten minutes each day to do a word wall and thirty minutes for a daily writing time, but I still thought I had to meet my reading groups every day—particularly now that they were going more smoothly.

"Let's see your current schedule," she said. "There must be a way!" Together, we looked at my schedule and decided that if I cut math from sixty minutes to forty-five minutes and cut my unit time back to fifty minutes, I could find the forty minutes I needed.

"I think forty-five minutes for math in second grade is enough," Miss Port mused, "but you need more time for science and social studies. What if you met with your groups on four days and took Friday mornings for some intensive work on your science or social studies unit?"

"That would be all right for my butterflies," I responded. "They do the first reading at their seats now, and that is saving a lot of group time for the word and comprehension lessons they need. Maybe I could get done what I need to with the astronauts—particularly if I did word wall every day to work with the high-frequency words and I didn't have to worry about that during group time. But Paul's group needs all the teaching it can get. I am reading two selections every week with his group now—one at the level of Carl, Chip, Butch, and Alexander and a second easier one that is on level for Daisy and Mike and Paul when he is having an alert day. I can't possibly get it all done with them in four days!"

We talked some more and decided that on Friday, I would do a whole-class listening comprehension or writing lesson on something related to our unit topic.

Then I would give the butterflies and astronauts something to work on—a web or other graphic organizer to complete—something to write—or a similar follow-up activity while I met with Paul's group. I could then meet back with everyone together again and follow up what the children had worked on.

"That would give you back your ninety minutes of science or social studies time, and you could still work with Paul's group every day."

"You're a genius," I said as I practically hugged her. "I don't know why I couldn't have thought of that. I used to think of myself as a creative problem solver, but this year, I just can't see beyond my nose."

"Well, my dear," Ms. Port replied, "when we are under a lot of pressure and feeling anxious, we just don't think very well. That is often the sad dilemma of the beginning teacher. That's why you need people like Mr. Topps and Mrs. Wright—and me—to help you think through these problems. In a few years, you will be the expert helping another beginning teacher solve the inevitable first-year problems."

"Now, the biggest problem I have is finding time to read with Paul, Daisy, and Mike," I told her. "I conference with them during Self-Selected Reading, and I am including a selection for their group every week that is closer to their instructional level, but if I could sit down with them for ten minutes a day and coach them individually in material on their level, I could really move them. The year is half over, and as much as I hate to admit it, they haven't moved very far in their reading."

"You mean, we need to find another thirty minutes?" she responded. "Well, let's look again at your schedule. The children come back from specials and get ready to go home. What do you do between 2:45 and 3:00 when different children are leaving on the buses?"

"The children are finishing up work or something in one of the centers. I guess I could work with one of them then but not all three. I could take turns, but then they would get only ten minutes every third day, and I don't believe that will be enough."

As I was saying this, I was picturing Roberta and Betty leaving at 3:00 every day when the car riders were dismissed. I remembered that it was their mother, Mrs. Penn, who had told me that she was a teacher and had volunteered to help at our original parent meeting. (I also remembered my cavalier "Thanks but no thanks" response. Could I have been so naïve that I thought I wouldn't need help, or was I just afraid that she would know more than I did?)

"I have an idea," I said. I then told Ms. Port about Mrs. Penn's offer. "If she is driving over to pick the twins up anyway, maybe she would come twenty minutes early. I could work with one of them every third day, and she could work with them on the two intervening days, and they would get ten minutes of individual help every day."

"Brilliant!" responded Sue. "Let's go and call her right now."

We did, and she said she would be delighted to help, and we made plans to begin as soon as school resumed in January. Here is the schedule I will be following from the first day back in January.

Time	Monday	Tuesday	Wednesday	Thursday	Friday
8:30–8:50	Group Meeting and Planning for the Day				
8:50–9:00	Word Wall				
9:00–9:30	Writing				
9:30–10:00	Paul's Group Astronauts-Centers Butterflies-Seatwork	Same as Monday	Same as Monday	Same as Monday	Science or SS Unit Comprehension or Writing Lesson
10:00–10:30	Astronauts Butterflies-Centers Paul's Group-Seatwork	Same as Monday	Same as Monday	Same as Monday	Children work on Unit Topic while I meet with Paul's group.
10:30–10:50	Break/Recess				
10:50–11:20	Butterflies Paul's Group-Centers Astronauts-Seatwork	Same as Monday	Same as Monday	Same as Monday	Science or SS Unit Follow-up
11:20–12:05	Math				
12:05–12:40	Lunch				
12:40–1:10	Teacher Read-Aloud Self-Selected Reading				
1:10–2:00	Science or Social Studies Unit				
2:00–2:30	P. E.	Music	P.E.	Art	P. E.
2:30–2:45/3:00	Children prepare to go home, finish up work and things in centers. Mrs. Penn and I work ten minutes each with Mike, Paul, and Daisy.				

I was quite eager for the holidays to begin! Not, as originally, so that I could escape from here, but so that I could have some uninterrupted time to plan how I would begin the new year. I want to work out the specifics of my new schedule and look through the books I got at the faculty Christmas party. Each teacher was to bring an "idea" book for another teacher. Mrs. Wise drew my name, and she gave me an excellent book that explains how to do story drama to improve listening and reading comprehension and one on writing. I also got two unexpected presents. Mrs. Wright gave me a timer. She says it is her most valuable teaching resource. I can see why she says that, having watched her teach. Mr. Topps also gave me an unexpected gift—a copy of the latest best-seller. "This book is totally worthless," he announced, "and your homework over the break is to relax and not think about school long enough to read this." Never in my wildest dreams did I think I would ever have a principal like Mr. Topps! This is what he wrote in his Christmas card:

> Dear Norma,
>
> As you take a well-deserved rest, 1 just wanted to tell you how glad we are that you have joined our faculty this year. I know you are discouraged at times, but almost all new teachers have a similar experience. Teaching is at once the most challenging and most rewarding profession there is. I appreciate your willingness to take counsel and to try suggestions. You have improved so much in how you teach reading that teachers with many years' experience could benefit from watching you!
>
> Merry Christmas!
> Tip Topps

Maybe, just maybe, I'm going to be a good teacher someday after all!

January

I always thought that if I could survive until January, I could make it. This turns out to be true but not for the reasons I had thought. I student-taught last year starting in January, and I figured when I got to January, I could pull out my student-teaching lesson plans. I did pull them out, but they weren't very relevant to this class. Many of my children read much better than the children in the class in which I student-taught, and then there are always Mike, Paul, and Daisy! Besides, the children in my student-teaching classroom had had an excellent teacher prior to January, and these children have had me. I'm getting better, however. Those visits to Mrs. Wright's and Mrs. Wise's classrooms and my several long chats with Mr. Topps and Ms. Port have really helped. I now have a new schedule that I have posted, and each morning, first thing, the children and I look at the schedule and decide who is going to be where doing what when. I couldn't possibly keep on schedule, however, were it not for the timer Mrs. Wright gave me for Christmas. I carry it around with me and use it to keep my groups to twenty-five minutes, to see who can get their old places cleaned up and get to their new places in the five-minute transition time, and to time Self-Selected Reading and snack time. It is so much a part of me, I feel as if I am missing something when I leave for home and do not have it in my hand.

I have begun letting the middle and top groups work on their workbook pages in partners—two children working together to come up with their best responses. We then go over these responses together when they come to the group. During reading group, we check the pages and analyze why an answer is right or wrong. I also have them explain the reasoning behind their answers. It helps children who haven't understood something to hear the thinking of others who came up with the right answer. Usually, I let each child choose a workbook partner—or choose to work alone. I stress that I am letting them work together because "two heads are better than one." Consequently, I expect to see better—more thorough and thoughtful—responses when they put two of their brilliant heads together. When I see sloppy, "thrown together" work or when I look up and see the partners not working well or quietly, I withdraw their partner privilege. I have had to do this several times with Roberta and Hilda and with Mitch and Jeff. They do not appreciate being sent to their desks to work alone while many of the others are working together, but they do understand why they have lost the privilege. With both the centers and the partners, I have to be consistent in expecting good behavior and withdrawing privileges to make them work.

I would like the children in Paul's group to work with partners, but they are all so difficult to get along with. I guess I could try and at least give them a chance. Even if two of them could partner up and work well and quietly, they would help each other, and those two would learn more. I am going to give it a try and see what happens!

Once in a while, I have children come to the reading group who I suspect haven't read the selection. I try to encourage them to do it, and I don't let them participate in our group's activities if they indicate by their responses to comprehension questions or in oral reading that they haven't read the story silently. Last week, I had to send Roberta to her seat during group time to read a story she hadn't read. When I questioned her about it, she protested, "It was a dumb sissie story." I told her I was sorry she didn't like it but that she had a responsibility to come prepared. I then sent her to her seat to read the story while I did some story dramatization with her group. Roberta, who loves to act in stories, was furious, but she hasn't come to reading group unprepared since. I have also had some trouble with Alex's not reading the selections, and I have had him sit with me in the group area while I meet with Paul's group and read the selection there. He is very unhappy about this, especially since the rest of his group is having center time.

We have increased our Self-Selected Reading time to twelve minutes. I am continuing to conference with the children and am amazed at how much I can learn about their reading interests and strategies in just two to three minutes. The children all seem to enjoy the conference, and I enjoy the little bit of individual time I have with each of them. I now know that Rita, Pat, Larry, and Hilda can read well above the level of the book I have their group in. Mr. Topps says I shouldn't worry about this because they will get their instructional-level reading during Self-Selected Reading time and get comprehension instruction and knowledge building from my guided-reading instruction.

"One of the major reasons we insist on having daily Self-Selected Reading time in every classroom is to make sure that every child has time each day to read material they choose that is on the right level. If you look only at what you are doing during guided reading, you can't meet the needs of every child, but if you consider all the reading and writing they do, you can," Mr. Topps explained with certainty and passion.

One afternoon, when I was talking with Mrs. Wise, I ended up telling her my latest "Mike story." She said that after hearing about Mike all year, she was considering retiring a year early so that she wouldn't have to spend her last teaching year with Mike! I was horrified to think that someone like Mrs. Wise would worry about discipline and told her so. She responded, "You are going to worry about discipline for as long as you teach. I have to run out early this afternoon and haven't helped you much with your problems. Why don't you come over and have dinner with me tomorrow night. We can have a long, uninterrupted chat then." Of course I accepted. We had a lovely, relaxed dinner during which she steered me away from school topics whenever I brought them up. As we were loading the dishwasher, she told me that she knew I wanted to discuss school but that her own philosophy of life prevented her from doing so. "We live with school so much of our lives as it is that I force myself to forget it, or at least not discuss it, during dinner. There are so many disturbing things about school that they can ruin your digestion!"

I could hardly believe that this woman with all those years of teaching experience could still have troubles in school! That made me feel better.

After dinner, though, we did talk. I was getting ready to do some publishing with the children and couldn't figure out how to organize it. I had seen children publishing in her room, but they were in all different stages and I couldn't figure out how they knew what to do. She explained her system to me.

"I have a list for the children to sign up on when they have three good first drafts. Good is a relative term, but I do quickly glance at their three pieces to make sure they have made a good effort (for them) on all three. I then form a cooperative revising group of all the children ready to publish. Each child reads his or her piece to the group and calls on group members to suggest ways to make it better. I act as recorder, writing down the suggestions for each writer. Next, the children go off to make whatever revisions they think are needed. When they have done this, they pick a friend to help them edit for the things on the checklist. Then they come to me for a final edit before going off to publish the final draft. This works well for most of the children. I give more help to my struggling writers, often telling them I will be their friend to help them do the first edit, because their piece often needs more than any of my children could handle."

"I can see that this takes a lot of structure, organizing, and independence. Do you think my children are mature enough to handle that?" I asked.

"I'm not sure, but you could also try Mrs. Wright's system. I think she works with a third of the class each week to revise a piece—dividing the struggling writers and advanced writers among the thirds. Your children were used to that from last year, so perhaps that is the way for you to go. Mrs. Wright should be starting her publishing cycles about now. Ask her to tell you exactly how she does it and then pick the one that seems right for you."

We talked about discipline, too, and particularly about Mike. Mrs. Wise seems to think I am handling him about as well as he can be handled. "Make sure he knows the rules. Withdraw privileges as necessary. Keep giving him chances to be responsible and show him he will not get the best of you," she advised. "Some children are difficult, and we must continue to be firm and fair with them. No system will work for everyone, but it sounds as if what you are doing is working quite well for most of your children most of the time. You are having a good year for a first-year teacher."

As I was trying to absorb the fact that Mrs. Wise seemed to have such faith in me, the doorbell rang. Mrs. Wise went to answer it and I gathered up my things. Mrs. Wise then returned with her neighbor, a new doctoral student at the university. She introduced me to Horatio Flame, who said, "Just call me Red." We chatted for quite a while and I got home much later than I usually do on a school night. As I was driving home, I realized that we had talked for over an hour about things other than teaching. What a wonderful feeling! Red seems like a really nice guy. I wonder why he just happened to drop in like that. Surely, it was just a coincidence that he came while I was there.

February

This month, I read them *Miss Nelson Is Missing* and *Miss Nelson Is Back* by Harry Allard. After reading the books, we discussed them, and I had to admit to feeling like Miss Nelson sometimes. "I wonder if there is a Viola Swamp living anywhere in this area," I mused aloud. "Don't get any ideas, Miss Nouveau," Horace pleaded. "We're being much better than we were! Aren't we?" Carl asked. "There aren't really mean teachers like Viola Swamp," Roberta declared.

The book clearly made an impression on them, and I have been tempted to buy a black wig! Rita found another Miss Nelson book—*Miss Nelson Has a Field Day*— at the public library and brought it in to read. Many of the children are now reading the Miss Nelson books on their own during Self-Selected Reading time.

At 8:50, we do our daily words on the wall practice. I do it exactly the way I saw Mrs. Wright doing it. Each Monday, I add five new words. I choose the words by looking for the words they commonly misspell in their writing. Each day, I call out five of the words from the wall, and they chant them and then write them. I have them check the words themselves, just like Mrs. Wright, but some—Butch, Mike, Mort, Alexander, Daisy—don't check them very carefully. "It doesn't matter," I heard Mort say. "She doesn't grade them." I have told them that not everything needs a grade, but a few of them won't put forth the effort required unless there is some consequence, a grade or a withdrawal of privilege.

It was Red (who knows nothing about teaching, thank goodness) who came up with the brilliant idea. "Why not have five checkers in a box," he suggested one night as I was telling him my problem while he was, as usual, whomping me at checkers, "four red ones and one black one. When the children have finished and exchanged and checked their words, let one child close her eyes and pick a checker. If a red checker comes out, this was only for practice. If the black one comes out, however, this was 'the real thing' and you can collect them, verify that they are correctly checked, and record them in your grade book." I told Red he would be a wonderful teacher, he is so creative, but he declares he hasn't "the stomach for it."

At any rate, we now use his checkers system. It is super! All the children, including Mike, put forth their best efforts each day because they never know when it will count. They love to have the black checker come out because, if they try, they can do well and they want the perfect score. I am going to try this system during math when we practice addition and subtraction facts. Each day, we will have a five-minute timed practice, check papers, and then see if it counts or not by having a blindfolded child select a checker. This will give the children the practice they need without putting an impossible grading burden on me.

Our morning writing time is one of the best parts of our day. I asked my children about the books they published last year, and the next day, many of them proudly brought in their books to show me. Even Paul, who rarely brings anything from or says anything about home, brought three books he had published. He even read them to me, with fluency and confidence! That afternoon, I asked Mrs. Wright how children like Paul could write books, and she explained about how she divided the class into thirds for publishing purposes and put one of the three lowest children in each third. She then explained how she did the editing and publishing and how she let Paul tell her what he meant to write and she wrote it for him to copy into his book. I am beginning to understand why everyone thinks Mrs. Wright is such a savvy lady.

I have gotten all the children to bring in writing notebooks, and we are writing each day. I do a minilesson as Mrs. Wright does and try to write about varied topics. Mike was the one who asked me to write a "When I Was Your Age" tale. When I admitted that I didn't know what that was, the class was amazed. They told me all about when Mrs. Wright was in the first grade, how she liked to dress up as a fairy princess at Halloween, and about her boyfriend in first grade. I must have looked a bit incredulous because Betty quickly explained that Mrs. Wright never really told them if the tales were all true or some were made up. Harriet volunteered that if they were true, Mrs. Wright was writing part of her autobiography. The children all nodded, and I was once again amazed at how much they knew.

So I wrote my first "When I Was Your Age" tale!

When I was in the second grade, I loved school. My teacher's name was Mrs. Hope, and I thought she was the most beautiful lady in the world. I only got in trouble once, and that was when Billy Higginbopper kept teasing me because I was so tall and skinny and had so many freckles. I didn't mean to knock him down, but I was so mad. When he fell, he hurt his arm and had to go to the hospital. It was a terrible, no good, very bad day!

"Is that really true?" they all asked, when I had finished. I just smiled and sent them off to do their writing.

We have begun the Editor's Checklist again. Mrs. Wright suggested that I add the items to check for gradually and remind the children to do a quick edit each day when their writing time was up. We have the first three items that they learned last year, and I will add the final review item next month. I will try to add a few new ones before the end of the year.

We have just begun publishing, and I hope that by the end of the year, the children will all have a couple of books they wrote in second grade to add to their first-grade collection. I am so grateful to Mr. Topps for arranging for my visits to Mrs. Wright and Mrs. Wise. I can't imagine that all that "know-how" was right here in this very building and I might never have realized it!

March

We had parent–teacher conferences early in March. Everyone except Paul and Jeff had a parent or other relative come. I was so much more at ease because I knew I was doing a better job. I wasn't on the defensive waiting for them to ask me something I didn't know or expecting them to attack me for something I wasn't doing. Rather, I was relaxed (relatively!) and we had good conversations about their children. Most of the parents expressed their pleasure at what I was doing with their children. I think this may have been a reflection of how relieved they were that things have gotten much better as the year has gone on. Mike's mother is quite worried about him and says she can hardly handle him at home. I told her that he is making some progress and seems to be able to learn when he settles down long enough. I suggested that she read some easy-to-read books at home with Mike each night and let him chime in when he knows a word. She said she would try but that she practically had to "rope" him to get him settled down long enough to eat, never mind anything else. When she left, I thought, "I shall be more patient with Mike. I imagine that that woman must deal with his energy for as many waking hours as I do each day, and all day on Saturdays, Sundays, and holidays."

Many parents expressed their pleasure with the writing their children were doing. Mandy's mother declared that Mandy has decided to become a writer and keeps a writing notebook at home in which she writes faithfully. She told me that the children liked writing each day and especially like my pulling the popsicle sticks out of the hat to see which children get to read their stories. (This was Red's solution to the problem of everyone wanting to read and not enough time.) When the timer signals the end of the fifteen-minute writing time, the children who wish to read their piece put the popsicle stick with their name on it in a special container. I pull the popsicle sticks out and those children whose names come out get to read their pieces. The children love the drama of wondering whose stick will come out and are very good listeners because they know we will get to pull more sticks in the allotted time if I don't have to interrupt constantly and ask them to be good listeners.

Thanks to Ms. Port, I have now learned how to get Paul's group to read silently. When I called her a month or so ago and told her that the silent reading just wouldn't work for my six poorest readers, she told me she would get back to me. One day a few weeks later, she arrived at my room after school and taught me how to teach a comprehension strategy lesson. Students like Mike, Daisy, and Paul have to have a very particular kind of comprehension lesson if they are to learn how to read silently with understanding.

She went on to explain the steps of a comprehension strategy lesson and gave lots of examples so I could plan and teach one myself. She suggested that I try it with my top two groups first before using it with my bottom two groups. "They will like and profit from it, too," she said.

Even the first comprehension strategy lesson I taught to Paul's group went surprisingly well. The third one was truly wonderful. It went like this: I attempted to prepare them to understand the particular story I had chosen to use with them to teach them the comprehension strategy of following story sequence. The story was in the easier book that I use with Paul's group. It is a modern retelling of the Aesop's fable "The Wind and the Sun." To complete this step, I followed the teacher's manual suggestions for teaching general background knowledge and specific passage vocabulary. These suggestions helped the students to call up what they already knew, as well as to learn new background information.

I had chosen to teach them *to follow the sequence of a story.* I told them that most stories would be hard to understand and impossible to enjoy if we confused the order in which the main actions take place. Their faces revealed that my telling had failed to impress them. So I started to tell them the story of "The Three Bears." When I began with the part where the bears returned home to find their house in disarray, everyone protested. I had prepared sentence strips, each of which had a major event from the story. I laid them out in front of Paul's group on the table and let them take turns organizing the strips into the right order. Even Paul took a turn, although Daisy tried to tell him what to do at each decision point. I put a stop to that. They were all able to organize correctly the events of this simple, familiar story. I then told them again how important getting things in the right order was to understanding and enjoying a story. They were with me now. I told them that as stories get harder, it gets more difficult to figure out which things happen first, next, and last. I told them that grown-ups who are good readers follow or monitor the order in which actions happen in a story, and if they become confused about the order, they reread and think until their confusion is ended. I told them that I wanted them to learn to follow the order in which things happen in every story they read or hear.

Following that, I set the purpose for reading. Before the lesson, I had determined what I thought were the five major events of "The Wind and the Sun":

The wind blew the boy's hat off.

The wind blew the boy's balloon into a tree.

The wind gave up trying to get the boy to take off his jacket.

The sun made the boy hot.

The boy took off his jacket.

I had written these five major events on sentence strips and put them in the pocket chart in a random order. I read the five events aloud once and then had the children read them with me. Next, I explained that all events happened in the story they were about to read, but that they were not in the right order. I explained to them that when they finished reading, they would have to close their books, and then we would decide as a group how to put these events in the right order.

I set the timer for ten minutes, plenty of time for them to read the story, and then walked around the room, checking in with the butterflies at their seats and the astronauts in the centers. Paul's group sat in the group area and read the story. It wasn't exactly silent because some of these children still need to hear themselves read. But they were reading, and I could see them glancing up at the events on the chart, thinking about the sequence. Ms. Port had told me they would read to themselves if I gave them enough preparation before reading and if I gave them only one clear purpose for reading, but it still had to happen for me to believe it.

I returned to the group before the timer sounded. Carl and Mike had finished reading, and I whispered to them about which events they thought happened first, second, etc., and had them go back and find places in the story that let them know the correct order.

When the timer sounded, Paul was still reading. I asked them all to close their books, telling Paul he could finish the story when he returned to his seat but we needed his help now to get the events in the right order.

They then attempted to put the events in order as a group. We had no trouble figuring out what happened first, second, and last, but Daisy and Mike disagreed about which event was third and which was fourth. I then asked everyone to open their books and see if they could find some parts to read aloud that would tell us the correct order. When that dispute was settled, they all closed their books again. We then read together the five events, now in the correct order in the pocket chart, and decided they had done an excellent job of reading to themselves to figure out the sequence in a story. Their pride in their accomplishment was evident on the faces of every one of them! We then talked briefly about the story, how they liked it, which part they liked best, what was funny about it, etc.

I have done several other comprehension lessons with the children since that first one, and they are learning to read to themselves and think about whatever purpose I set. I usually introduce a strategy first with the easier book and then do it with the selection in the harder book. For the harder book, we usually read it together, stopping to talk about each page because Paul, Daisy, and Mike cannot yet read at this level on their own. It is clearly good for everyone to learn a new strategy while working in something easier. In fact, I am going to have the astronauts read some selections in an easier book and use these to introduce strategies, and then I'll have them read for the same purpose in their instructional-level book.

I have read many books aloud this month. I have discovered that there is a veritable treasure trove of informational books that build important science and social studies concepts. This month our science unit was on planets and our solar system. We read several wonderful books by Jeanne Bendick, including *The Planets: Neighbors in Space, The Sun: Our Very Own Star,* and *The Stars: Lights in the Night Sky.* Steve brought in a marvelous book, *The Magic School Bus Lost in the Solar System,* by Joanna Cole. As soon as the children saw it, they started chattering about

Ms. Frizzle's trip to the waterworks. When they discovered that I didn't know any of the Magic School Bus books, they insisted on going to Mrs. Wright's room right then and there and borrowing *The Magic School Bus at the Waterworks,* which we read and enjoyed again. It is amazing what a lasting effect a truly great informational book has on their retention of information!

In social studies, as part of our continuing study of communities, we are doing a unit on Native Americans. Again there are many wonderful, sensitive books that portray how different groups of Native Americans live today and lived in the past. The children especially enjoyed Ann McGovern's *If You Lived with the Sioux Indians* and Mary Perrine's *Nannabah's Friend.* I even found a book that connected up to both the science and social studies units. *They Dance in the Sky* by Jean Guard and Ray Williamson recounts the myths and stories told about the constellations by various Native American tribes.

Red, who is working to put himself through his doctoral program, has offered to come to school early next month to show the children the musical instruments that he plays. He is the leader of a band that he calls "Red and the Flamers." I know that Mike and many of the others will be enthralled with his presentation as well as his personality, which matches his gorgeous, curly auburn hair. I realize how busy he is and am delighted he is willing to talk to my class.

April

Red's appearance was enormously successful! We discussed bands, and I was amazed at how knowledgeable these young children are about music groups. Mike was fascinated with the drums. Red had brought an amplifier along as well, and we caught Butch just in time; he had plugged in the electric guitar and was ready to strum—full blast!

After Red left, I had the children tell me about his visit, and I wrote what they told me on chart paper. We read it over together, cut apart some of the sentences, and relocated them in the correct order of occurrence. Here is what they came up with.

> Mr. Flame of "Red and the Flamers" came to our class. (Alex)
>
> It was really cool, man! (Mike)
>
> He showed a variety of instruments. (Larry)
>
> Some of us danced when he played. (Rita)
>
> I almost played the electric guitar. (Butch)
>
> He asked Miss Nouveau for an aspirin before he left. (Mandy)

I have begun doing some imitative reading with Paul, Daisy, and Mike. Imitative reading is a fancy name for having the children read a story enough times so that they can read it easily and fluently, "like a good reader." One day, Ms. Port was visiting our school. That afternoon, she popped into my room with some easy-to-read books and tapes. She then explained to me how I could let Paul, Daisy, and Mike each pick one of these easy-to-read books and listen to it during part of their seatwork time. Each child was to listen to the book until he or she could read the book without the aid of the tape recording. Then that child would read the book to me, and assuming that the child could indeed read the book well, that child could choose another book-tape combination.

So far, so good! Paul has read two of the easy-to-read books. He listens to them at his signed-up time each day and then will often come in first thing in the morning or stay a little late in the afternoon to listen to them. Daisy is not happy with me, however. She listens to the book-tape one time and then comes to read it to me. Of course, she can't, and I send her back with instructions to listen to it at least two more times before she comes to read to me again. Mike's mother has bought him a tape recorder, and he takes his book-tape home every night. Even he seems pleased that he can easily read, cover-to-cover, four books and seems motivated to read more. Imitative reading is an important addition to my reading instruction for Paul, Daisy, and Mike. I think that by listening to the tape of the easy-to-read book often enough, they get to the point where they can easily identify the words and anticipate what is coming next, and they have, probably for the first time, the experience of reading like a good reader. Combined with the ten minutes of easy-reading coaching they get each afternoon with me or Mrs. Penn, all three children are starting to read more fluently and confidently.

This month the children got into mysteries. I started them off, I guess, by reading *Nate the Great* by Marjorie Weinman Sharmot, *Encyclopedia Brown Sets the Pace* by Donald Sobol, and *Two Bad Ants* by Chris Van Allsburg. The children quickly began finding mysteries, including more *Nate the Great* and *Encyclopedia Brown* mysteries and the reissued *Boxcar Mysteries* series. Now almost everyone is into the mystery craze, and several children, including Hilda and Butch, have declared their intention to be detectives or spies when they grow up.

I read them books related to our science unit on plants, including a beautifully illustrated plant alphabet book, *Allison's Zinnia* by Anita Lobel. I even found some books to integrate with math this month. We are doing a unit on counting and big numbers, and the children were fascinated by David Schwartz's *How Much Is a Million?* and Mitsumasa Anno's *Anno's Counting Book* and *Anno's Mysterious Multiplying Jar.*

We have finished our first publishing cycle, and although it did not go as smoothly as Mrs. Wright had made it sound, we did it and the children all have books they are very proud of. Mrs. Wright was so pleased when I showed her the books that she brought her first-graders over and we had an authors' party. We put the children together into mixed groups of first- and second-graders and let them read their books to each other. My children all behaved very well and seemed determined to be more "mature" than the first-graders. I was amazed to see how little the first-graders are and how well they can write. My children have not gone as far in writing this year as those first-graders have, but knowing what I know now, at the beginning of next year I should be able to pick up right where Mrs. Wright left off. The first-graders seemed delighted to be "up in second grade." As many of them left, they gave me a hug and said, "See you next year!" The true rewards of teaching!

May

I can't believe this year is coming to an end. We have had a busy last month. I wanted the children to have two published books from second grade, so we did another publishing cycle. This one was easier!

I read them some of the *Amelia Bedelia* books, which appealed greatly to their seven-year-old silliness. That got them started on lots of other word-play, joke, and riddle books. We also read books connected to our final combined science/social studies unit on the environment and what various communities can do to help clean up and maintain a healthy environment. After reading *The Empty Lot* by Dale Fife, we took a walking field trip to a nearby empty lot and discovered that our empty lot was also teeming with animal life. The children also loved *When the Woods Hum* by Joanne Ryder and *The Great Kopak Tree* by Lynne Cherry.

We are now up to sixteen minutes of Self-Selected Reading time! I never thought last fall that I would be here in May, and I probably wouldn't have been if Mr. Topps and the others hadn't helped me isolate my problems and correct them. I certainly never thought that I would see my class sitting still and reading attentively for sixteen straight minutes and liking it. In some ways it has been a long year, but in others it has been too short. How I wish I could have begun my current reading program earlier!

Anticipating next year and the first day of school (it just has to be better!), I asked the children to think back over the year and all of the things we have done. I wrote their comments on the chalkboard and we filled it in no time. I had no idea that we had done so many things or that the children could remember them.

The next instructions that I gave them were to pretend that they were their own desk. As the desk, they were to write a letter to whoever would be sitting in that seat next year. They were to give the new second-graders an idea about what to expect during the new school year. We would leave the letters in the desks and surprise the new children with them in the fall. The children seemed excited about the project and eagerly began to write. Here is a copy of the letter that Roberta wrote:

> Hi, Kid,
>   You're pretty lucky to be starting second grade already. And boy, will you have fun. Especially sitting at this desk. This is where Roberta Marie Smith sat last year, and she had fun. This year you will learn to read harder books and you'll do your workbook (if you're better than Roberta). Have a good time, kid, because it won't last long. Soon you'll have to go to the third grade where they really have hard work to do! Maybe I can ask Roberta's desk in third grade to write to you, too.
>   Love,
>   Clarence, Your Desk

We have added to the supply of books this year with children's paperbacks. The children and I receive brochures every month from two companies that publish inexpensive, high-quality children's books. The children take their individual brochures home and bring back the completed order forms with the necessary money. I mail these and add the bonus books, one of which we get for each ten books the children order. Then we all eagerly await the arrival of our new books. In this way, I have added about twenty-five new books to our classroom library.

All in all, it has turned out to be a very good year for me and, I think, for almost all my children. Most of my discipline problems lessened as I established some routines and began to give the children some limited choices. I still have some days when I wonder why I ever wanted to be a teacher. Mike is most difficult to handle, and my promises to myself to be firm and patient with him just seem to dissolve when I am faced with one of his regular disruptions. He tells me they are moving right after school is out. Some third-grade teacher somewhere will have her hands full next year. I am sorry he is moving because I am sure Mrs. Wise would be able to calm him down. Paul is another one of my failures. He seems to be perking up and making some progress, and then he goes into a somber, detached state during which he might as well not be here. I don't know what is going to happen to him. And Daisy—she has made some progress in her work and behavior—mostly because she can't stand to have her center art time taken away, but she is still not an easy child to live with. Maybe Mrs. Wise can get through to her, too. I have such faith in that lady. I would never have made it through the year without her.

I *have* made it through the year, however, and I will be ready for next year. I told Mrs. Wright the other day that if I learned as much every year as I have this first year, I would never have to fear getting stale and bored. She said that teaching was many things, some positive and some not so positive, but that she had never found it to be boring. Red says that one thing he learned this year was that in teaching, there are so many intriguing problems to be solved! I guess that if I can continue to view my crises as "intriguing problems to be solved" I will someday be a good, capable, creative teacher.

The Student-Teaching Seminar

Norma L. Nouveau, veteran of one year in the classroom, had been asked by Dr. Link to talk with her student teachers at their weekly seminar. At first, Miss Nouveau protested that she was the last person who should be asked. After all, she was still learning herself, and she didn't think she had anything of significance to contribute.

Dr. Link explained that several students in the class had asked her to find a first-year teacher who would talk to them. They wanted to know what it was *really* like when one started teaching. Although teachers like Mrs. Wise could contribute a great deal to the seminar, they had been teaching too long to focus honestly on the first year of teaching. And, she added, she had been observing Miss Nouveau's progress throughout the year and was pleased with the growth that had been taking place. Miss Nouveau finally consented to address the class. "But," she cautioned, "I'm not promising that it will be any good."

"If you just tell them what you have lived through this past year," Dr. Link replied, "they will be more than satisfied."

That, she resolved, was precisely what she would do. These students would find out the truth from her before they had to live through it themselves! She requested that they meet in her room.

The afternoon of the seminar, Miss Nouveau stood at the back of her room while Dr. Link greeted the carefree students. After Dr. Link had introduced her, she began her talk by saying, "This year I have worked harder than I ever dreamed I would have to, and even so, things have gone well only at times." She then related the inaccurate judgments, errors in placement, discipline problems, and poor assignments she had made. As she spoke, she noted looks of disbelief turning to looks of pity and fear as she related anecdote after anecdote. Not wanting to discourage them, however, Miss Nouveau then began to relate the positive things that had happened to her and the consequent changes she had made in her program, especially since Christmas. When she finished, several hands went up for questions.

"If you knew you weren't doing very well in October, how come you kept right on doing things wrong? I mean, if I were doing something I knew was wrong, I wouldn't just keep on!"

"Well," answered Miss Nouveau with a smile, "maybe you would and maybe you wouldn't. I would have thought that same way a year ago, but it's so different when you're actually there day after day with the children and you know you're totally responsible for their instruction. There's neither the opportunity nor the knowledge to do it any other way! I was fortunate, though, to be in a school with a principal who cared, other teachers who helped me, and an elementary supervisor who showed me alternatives. Though they were all as busy as I was, they gave freely of their time and advice. If it hadn't been for them, I know I would have resigned at Christmas."

"What would have helped you, though, before you got to your first year of teaching?" another student asked.

"If only I had been given more experience in classrooms prior to my student teaching, then I could have spent student-teaching time learning more about classroom management. The better prepared you are when you enter your student teaching, the better you will be at the end of it. Also, if my reading/language arts course had been more practical, I would have been better prepared to teach the children."

Another student raised his hand to ask, "Could you just summarize for us a few of the most important things that you learned this year?"

Miss Nouveau thought for a moment before replying, "I learned so much it is hard to say, but I guess I learned that there is help out there if you ask for it, and that learning to be a really good teacher is too complex to go it alone. Another thing was locating the school storeroom. It's often a gold mine of books and materials just lying there, gathering dust. Also, I learned that I must have some time for myself. One reason I wasn't thinking well last fall, I'm sure, was that I had no time to do things that I had always done and that I enjoyed doing. I regret very much some of the things I did this year, and if I could be granted one wish, it would be that I could repeat this school year knowing at the beginning what I know now!

"I also learned that Mrs. Middleman was right in our very first parent meeting when she said, 'Easier said than done.' I had gotten the guiding principles in our meeting, looked at them, and wondered,'How not? Of course I am going to have balanced instruction, and my groups will make it multilevel, and following the suggestions in the manual would take care of thinking and language and feeling.' But putting into practice our twelve guiding principles with a real class of children is a major challenge. I will be more confident next year—but hopefully not cavalier!"

"How are you going to start next year, since obviously you won't repeat what has been done?"

"I thought you might ask that," responded Miss Nouveau confidently. "As a matter of fact, I have given a lot of thought to that, and I think I am prepared to get next year off to a better start. I will begin the year right off teaching children how to use my centers and making sure they know their center privileges depend on their doing their work with a good effort. I will give an IRI to all the children, but I will interpret their oral reading and not just count errors. I probably won't get another reader as advanced as Larry—Mrs. Wright says Larry was the best reader in first grade she has ever seen. But if a child reads with fluency, has good comprehension, and makes only little errors that don't change the meaning, I will know that that reader has a more mature eye-voice span and not count those errors against her or him. I will form my reading groups according to the instructional levels I find, and I will make sure that the lowest group reads in two levels of books from the very beginning, so that everyone has instructional-level or easier reading every week. I also will begin imitative reading and the one-on-one coaching with my most struggling readers much sooner than I did. I will use my timer, stick to my schedule, and try to incorporate everything I learned this year from the first day. I know I will have new problems to solve, but I will put into practice what I learned and we will all start out ahead."

As Miss Nouveau paused to catch her breath, Dr. Link interrupted to say that she regretted having to announce that the seminar time was up. Miss Nouveau and most of the students turned in astonishment to view the clock and confirm that indeed an entire hour had fled past. "Just like teaching," observed Miss Nouveau. "When you are thinking about what you have to say and do, it seems as if there is an enormous amount of time to fill. But when you start doing it, there is never enough time." The students chuckled. A few stayed afterward to further pick Miss Nouveau's brain. Dr. Link looked on proudly.

Children's   Books / Materials   Cited

Allison's Zinnia, by A. Lobel, Greenwillow, 1990.
Amelia Bedelia books, by P. Parish, HarperCollins, various dates.
Anno's Counting Book, by M. Anno, HarperCollins, 1986.

Anno's Mysterious Multiplying Jar, by M. Anno, Philomel, 1983.
Boxcar Mysteries series, by G. Warner, Whitman, various dates.
The Empty Lot, by D. Fife, Little, Brown, 1991.
Encyclopedia Brown Sets the Pace, by D. Sobol, Scholastic, 1989.
The Great Kopak Tree, by L. Cherry, Harcourt Brace Jovanovich, 1990.
Halloween, by G. Gibbons, Holiday House, 1996.
How Much Is a Million? by D. Schwartz, Scholastic, 1986.
If You Lived with the Sioux Indians, by A. McGovern, Scholastic, 1984.
The Magic School Bus at the Waterworks, by J. Cole, Scholastic, 1988.
The Magic School Bus Lost in the Solar System, by J. Cole, Scholastic, 1992.
Miss Nelson Has a Field Day, by H. Allard, Houghton Mifflin, 1988.
Miss Nelson Is Back, by H. Allard, Houghton Mifflin, 1988.
Miss Nelson Is Missing, by H. Allard, Houghton Mifflin, 1987.
Nannabah's Friend, by M. Perrine, Houghton Mifflin, 1989.
Nate the Great, by M. W. Sharmot, Dell, 1977.
The Planets: Neighbors in Space, by J. Bendick, Millbrook, 1991.
The Reasons for Seasons, by G. Gibbons, Holiday House, 1995.
Spider Storch's Teacher Torture, by G. Willner-Pardo, Albert Whitman, 1997.
The Stars: Lights in the Night Sky, by J. Bendick, Millbrook, 1991.
The Sun: Our Very Own Star, by J. Bendick, Millbrook, 1991.
They Dance in the Sky, by J. Guard & R. Williamson, Houghton Mifflin, 1992.
Two Bad Ants, by C. Van Allsburg, Houghton Mifflin, 1988.
When the Woods Hum, by J. Ryder, Morrow Junior Books, 1991.

Mrs. Wise: Third Grade

14

The Parent Meeting

Vera Wise walked around the room, carefully placing materials for the parents to examine when they arrived for the meeting later that evening. She went about the task methodically, for she had been having parent meetings for most of her thirty-one years as a teacher, long before they became an "in" thing to do. As a matter of fact, she was the one who had suggested to Mr. Topps, some ten years before, that these meetings become a regular part of the school routine. She had also initiated the parent conferences that everyone now held twice yearly. Moreover, she had been part of the group that had drafted the schoolwide guiding principles the faculty had worked on at a retreat several years ago and were still using.

There were those who called her an innovator and those who said it was amazing that a woman of her years could be so up-to-date! Mrs. Wise chuckled over that one. She told them all that it had nothing to do with innovation or age—she simply knew what her children needed and how *she* could best teach them.

She was always exhilarated by these meetings, as she was by the parent conferences. It was astonishing how much one could learn about a child in half-hour conferences with the parents. She made the parents feel relaxed by sitting in a chair beside them rather than in the more formal position behind the desk. She had acquired a knack for knowing what to say and how to say it that helped put parents at their ease, informed them of their child's progress, and elicited from them the maximum amount of information about the child. Tonight, however, she was to meet the parents *en masse*. She enjoyed explaining what she and their children were going to be doing, for she loved teaching. She was not totally looking forward to the day in the near future when she would be retiring.

Shortly before 7:00 P.M., the parents began to arrive. Mrs. Wise directed them to sign up for the October parent conference and to volunteer on any of several volunteer sign-up sheets she had laid out. She didn't begin the meeting until 7:05, however, for long years of experience had taught her that many parents would arrive late no matter when the meeting was to begin.

"Hello. Some of you I know quite well because I have had other children of yours. Some of you are new to me as I am to you. I know that we will become well acquainted this year. I want to urge you *all* to come visit the classroom. I have only two requirements for those classroom visits: (1) that you let me know in advance when you want to come, so that I can let you know whether or not it is convenient, and (2) that you plan to stay at least an hour, so that the children will settle down and forget that you are here so that you can really see the program. I warn you! You may be put to work. Any extra hands in my class can and probably will be used. Just ask Mr. Topps! I'm sure that is why he has been avoiding my classroom for the last couple of years."

She paused for breath and to let the laughter die down. "Here is a handout of our school's literacy guiding principles. The handout is the same as the poster I have hanging in the room over there to remind everyone who walks in here what they should be seeing. We at this school decided many years ago that we felt strongly enough about the place of children's literature and children's writing in the curriculum that we would make a concerted effort to incorporate them into our classrooms. For instance, you can see that guiding principles 7 and 8, 'Read aloud to students daily' and 'Schedule self-selected reading,' address children's literature specifically. Guiding principles 6 and 9, 'Have students write every day' and 'Connect reading and writing to all subject areas,' specifically address writing. I have developed my entire reading and language arts program around books for children and children's own writings. This year I am going to work especially on those cross-curricular connections. In order to make reading and writing situations as natural as possible, I have implemented a literature-based program that focuses on ensuring that students receive a balanced literacy program—guiding principle 1. Let me explain to you how it works.

"As you look around the room, you see that I am fortunate enough to have hundreds and hundreds of books that are part of our permanent classroom collection. I have been collecting these books for years. I get them from a variety of sources. My friends know never to throw out a book without checking with me first. Across the years, parents—including some of you—have given me children's books, which I add to our collection. I haunt flea markets, yard sales, thrift shops, library discard shelves, and bookstores, and I must admit that I have bought a lot of the books in this room with my own money. Don't feel too sorry for me, though, because I love books and I enjoy reading them myself and then sharing them with the children. Some people shop for clothes; I shop for books!

"In the last few years, I haven't had to buy too many books using my own money. The school system realizes that children who love reading become good readers and that immersing children in lots of wonderful books is an investment that pays off. Every year now, I am allotted a sum of money to buy books. I also apply every year for our district's teacher grants, which allow me to purchase books for the classroom. I have used almost all my funds to buy multiple copies of books, and it is these books that I use for guided-reading lessons and that the children will be discussing in their literature circles. I also used some of my book money to get classroom subscriptions to several magazines for children. This year we will be getting *Cricket, Kids Discover, Sports Illustrated for Kids, Zillions, Ranger Rick, 3–2–1 Contact, National Geographic World,* and *Kid City.*

"In addition to all the books and magazines that reside permanently in this room, the children and I make good and frequent use of the school library, the public library, and even, when we need some hard-to-find things, the university library. I have also bookmarked several research sites on the Internet that help us to locate information and resources as well. As you might imagine, Miss Page, the school media specialist, and I work together a lot.

"The books that you see in this room are my reading program. I know that some teachers use a reading series for part of their program, and I have used them in the past, but I have so many wonderful real books—including multiple copies of lots of the best books—that I don't see any need for the children to read anything but the real thing. Be assured, however, that I will be teaching your children the strategies and skills that are required by our curriculum guide for third grade. But even more, I want to ensure that your children become independent readers. So I work on guiding principle 10, 'Teach the decoding and spelling strategies that reading and writing require.' And I do a whole lot more.

"When you have taught thirty-one years, taken as many reading courses and workshops as I have, and used many different language arts series over the years, you learn what the critical reading and writing strategies are and how to help children develop these. You also know how to meet the needs of the range of students who are in the room. I aim to make as many of my lessons as multilevel as possible in order to accommodate this range. That aim is consistent with guiding principle 2: 'Make instruction multi-level.'

"I will be doing short focused lessons with the children several times a week, and in these focused lessons I will teach them the comprehension and composition strategies they need. They will then apply these strategies to the pieces they are reading and writing. I will make sure the strategies are followed up in the literature circles, and in individual conferences.

"For most of the year, expect that your child will be reading at least two books at a time. During our Readers' Workshop each morning, the children are assigned books to read. It is these books that I use to make sure that the children are reading a wide variety of literature and applying the reading strategies I teach them, and it is these books that they are discussing in their literature study groups. Sometimes I assign the book and sometimes I let them choose among four or five titles, but what the children read during Readers' Workshop is determined by me with some input from them.

"Equally important is our afternoon self-selected reading time. Each day, when we come back from lunch, we settle down for some self-selected reading. I make no demands on them during this time except that they are quietly reading something of their own choosing. While they read, I have individual conferences with the children about their reading. The children sign up when they want to conference with me, and if I check my records and I haven't conferenced with a particular child for two weeks, I sign that child up for a conference. On Friday afternoons, we take our after-lunch time to share what we have been reading in small groups.

"I find that reading and writing workshop time and self-selected reading allow me to focus on developing guiding principles 3, 4, and 5: 'Use language as the foundation for reading and writing,' 'Teach reading and writing as thinking,' and 'Use feelings to create avid readers and writers.' We think about and react to our own and others' writings."

Mrs. Wise glanced up at the clock and frowned. "Just as happens during the day here, there is never enough time to do everything as thoroughly as you would like to. We have to be in the cafeteria in ten minutes for the schoolwide PTSA organizational meeting, so just let me explain a few other critical components of our language arts program.

"Each morning, in addition to our Readers' Workshop, we have the Writers' Workshop that I mentioned earlier. Most of you know that we do process writing here at Merritt and that your children do lots of first-draft writing and publish some pieces. This year, because most of your children have some facility with writing, we will work more on revising and editing first drafts so that their writing is more polished.

"In addition to process writing in which the children choose their own topics, as the year goes on, we will take several weeks of time during which I will teach them how to write specific things. In these focused-writing lessons, I often use what they are reading as springboards to writing. Reading and writing support one another. When children write about what they are reading, they have a wealth of information and ideas to draw from. Writing also increases their comprehension and enjoyment of reading, because as they write, they must think about and decide how they feel about various aspects of their reading.

"Finally, we will spend some time each day in activities designed to move them along in their word and spelling knowledge. Like most of the other teachers, I have a word wall on which I put the words I see commonly misspelled in their writing. We add five words each week and practice spelling these when we have a few minutes between activities. As you see, the words I have put up already—*friends, because, would, people, to/too/two, they're/their/there, don't*—are words some adults still have trouble spelling and using correctly. We will also be doing lots of word sorting, which will increase their knowledge of how to spell many words.

"Most of you have already sent the three notebooks your children need. I know three is a lot, but one is a writing journal for writing ideas and their first-draft writing, one is their literature log, and the other is their word book in which they sort words and put the words they find that fit certain patterns. All three of these notebooks are critical to our program, and we will use them all year. If you have a problem getting the notebooks right now, let me know. I do have a few squirreled away.

"I also will be assessing your children throughout the school year. The more I understand what they know and are able to do, the better I can teach them. I will work very hard to keep you informed of your child's progress through conferences, notes, phone calls, weekly newsletters, and report cards. I do both of these because they help me teach your children better, but as you can see, they also fulfill guiding principle 11, 'Use observation to assess learning and plan instruction,' and 12, 'Inform parents of expectations and progress.'

"We have to move to the cafeteria now, but I will answer any general questions about the classroom as we walk to the cafeteria or if you stay a few minutes after the meeting there. I will have a lot more specific information to tell you about each of your children when we have our conference in October. Remember that I consider this *our* classroom—mine and your children's and yours—and I hope that you will all schedule some time, once we get up and running in a few weeks, to come and see how hard we work and how much we love it."

Monthly Logs

September

Now that this busy summer is over, climaxed by Norma Nouveau's marriage to Red in August, I'm ready to begin my last year of teaching. I've been around a long time. I've seen fads come and go in education, and I have observed the cyclical nature of these fads—the whole-word approach, phonics, whole language, and others. I am, I suppose, reluctant to change, but the program that I have developed for my students is one that I am comfortable with and one that has proved itself to me. Years ago I read about individualizing instruction through children's literature, and this is the technique I have continued to use, though with modifications.

I always assess the children before I begin instruction, as well as doing ongoing assessment. So many teachers have indicated to me that they could not carry through with the literature-based curriculum plans that they had established. With further questioning, I often discover that either they have not assessed the children to see what they know and can do so that they can plan intelligently, or they have simply taken the same old material and put the children through it at different rates. Both of these are contrary to the nature and spirit of a literature-based curriculum.

There are as many systems as there are teachers who use literature. The system that I have used for years with my students is one that fades to more student independence. When children first come into my room, they have often been through a reading series program that is highly structured and sequenced. One of the most difficult tasks I face, therefore, is weaning them away from an overdependence on the teacher for instruction.

I am finding that these children have had fewer problems adapting to my program than some classes. Norma Flame did an excellent job with them in the last half of the year.

As part of my initial assessment, I administer an interest inventory That is one of the papers they find in the folders on the first day. I walk around the room while they are working on it, so that I can identify those children who are unable to read the inventory and therefore need to have someone read it to them. I soon discovered that children like Larry, Pat, Hilda, and Roberta were quite willing to be amanuenses for children such as Butch, Chip, and Paul. They were a great help. Items such as "You are going to be living all alone on the moon for one year. You can take only a few personal things with you. What three things will you take?" and "I sometimes feel . . ." produce many clues to the needs, perceptions, and values of children. With some of this information in mind, I can help the children to find reading materials that will be both interesting and informative.

I have finished administering the Informal Reading Inventory to all the children. I always wait until we are a week into the school year before giving the IRIs, because some of my children haven't cracked a book all summer. If I test them before they get back into reading, I will get levels that are lower than their actual levels.

I have used a variety of commercially published IRIs over the years. Currently, I am using the Johns *Basic Reading Inventory* (2001). One of its advantages is that it has three passages at each level. This allows me to check oral reading and silent reading as well as listening comprehension for some children. With a student like Paul, I wondered how much he understood even though he could barely read anything orally or silently. So I read aloud a series of passages to measure his listening comprehension. If students get borderline scores or huge discrepancies between their word identification score and their comprehension score, I have them read aloud a second—and sometimes a third—passage at that level to try to get the most reliable indicator of their reading level that I can. I also monitor reading levels throughout the year.

I tested two children each day during their afternoon self-selected reading time. I began with a passage I thought might be on their level, based on their records from previous years. I then moved up or down a grade level until I found the level at which their word identification dropped below 95 percent or their comprehension dropped below 75 percent. Their instructional level is the highest level at which they can read with at least 90 percent identification accuracy and 75 percent comprehension.

As happens every year, I have a wide range of reading levels in my classroom, with a few children still reading at first- or second-grade levels, and many reading well above third-grade level. Here are the September instructional levels for my children, according to the results of the *Basic Reading Inventory*.

Alex 4th	Jeff 3rd
Alexander 2nd	Joyce 3rd
Anthony 4th	Larry 8th +
Betty 5th	Mandy 6th
Butch 2nd	Manuel 3rd
Carl 3rd	Mitch 3rd
Chip 2nd	Mort 2nd
Daisy First Reader	Pat 6th
Danielle 6th	Paul Primer/First Reader?

Daphne 5th	Rita 6th
Hilda 7th	Roberta 6th
Horace 5th	Steve 4th

This is about the range I usually get, with a few more children at sixth and seventh grades and of course Larry, who read the highest passage I had—eighth grade—with no problem at all. I was pleased to have only six children reading below grade level, and four of them are only one year behind. I have lots of good, easy books, so finding things for Alexander, Chip, Mort, and Butch to read during Readers' Workshop won't be any problem. I will have to include some extra easy books from time to time to accommodate Daisy and Paul. I am not really sure how well Paul reads. I tested him on three different days on all four primer and first-reader passages, and his performance was very erratic. His word identification is pretty good for sight words, and he did use some letter–sound knowledge and context to figure out some words in one of the passages. In another passage, however, he seemed unable to do anything with words he didn't immediately recognize. His comprehension was also erratic, and I am not sure he was telling me everything he knew in answer to the questions. I am sure he can read primer level, and he can read some first-reader material—probably depending on the topic and what kind of day he is having.

I am going to steer both Paul and Daisy to some of my very easy books for their self-selected reading and conference with them for a few minutes at least twice a week. I need to partner them up with someone for some of the Readers' Workshop selections. Finding a partner for Paul won't be hard. Daphne has already let me know that she "helps Paul," and Horace is very kind to him also. Daisy, however, is so difficult to get along with that I may have to pay someone to be her partner!

While the IRI scores give me an initial picture of how well my children read, I use oral reading analyses throughout the year to help me determine if a particular book is at the appropriate difficulty level for a particular child and what reading strategies the child is using. Based on these observations, I know how each child is growing and what particular reading strategies to emphasize.

I have also gotten my first writing sample to put in each student's growth portfolio. This growth portfolio is part of what I use to determine how the children are growing and developing in their reading and writing strategies as the year goes on. I include many different samples of their process writing on their self-selected topics—both first drafts and published pieces. I do, however, think it is very informative to be able to look at each child's effort to write to the same task. To do this, I give them basically the same task to write about at the beginning, middle, and end of the school year. This year, I had them describe what they liked best about Merritt Elementary School. We talked a little about Merritt Elementary. Most of the children have been here since kindergarten, and they enjoyed reminiscing about lots of the fun things they had done here. I then asked them to imagine that someone new had moved into their neighborhood and to think about what they would tell that person about Merritt Elementary. Their writing task was to describe

Merritt Elementary and tell as much as they could about it, emphasizing the things they liked best about school. I gave them as much time as they wanted to write a first draft. I have copied and dated this first draft and put it in their growth portfolios. Next week, I am going to put them in small groups to share their Merritt Elementary pieces and then ask them to revise the pieces in whatever way they choose to—and can. Finally, I will review the items on the Editor's Checklist they began last year with Miss Nouveau, have them edit their own pieces using this checklist, and have them write a final draft. I will put this final draft in their growth portfolios along with the copy of their first draft, and I will have a very good idea of their writing abilities, including first draft, revision, and editing. By looking at what they can do now, I will know what kind of minilessons to teach during process writing, when to begin some more structured focused-writing lessons, and what to work on with individual children during writing conferences.

In January, when they have forgotten what they wrote in September, I will once again ask them to describe Merritt Elementary, particularly the things they like best about it, and go through the same first draft, small-group sharing/revision, and editing process. I will do this one more time in May. It is amazing how much growth you can see in their writing when you have them write about something they know a lot about at three different points in the year, using the same procedure to get the samples. One of the most difficult things about teaching children to write better is that, because writing is such a complex process, even when there is a lot of growth in their writing, third-graders still have a long way to go. When you look at these three writing samples along with the writing they select for their showcase portfolio, you can see and document how far they have come.

Self-selected reading is going well. This is always easy to start at Merritt, because the children expect to have part of their day devoted to "just reading." We have just gotten started with our Readers' Workshop and Writers' Workshop. Next month, we will do our first big word sort and begin hunting for words. Most of my previous classes have really enjoyed these word activities, and I think this group will too.

October

October is always one of my favorite teaching months. I have set up all the routines and done the initial assessment, and we can get down to really doing things. I also like that we have four weeks of uninterrupted teaching time. Holidays and vacations are fine, but they do interrupt the teaching flow.

Writers' Workshop is going quite well. I begin each day with a short five- to six-minute minilesson in which I write something and then do a little editing on it. I have added—one thing at a time—the conventions Miss Nouveau had on their Editor's Checklist last year and will begin next month to add some new ones. Most of the children have published one piece, and my most prolific writers—Hilda, Pat, Danielle, and Steve—have already published two.

When the children are ready to publish, they sign up with me for an initial conference. I check to see that they have three good first drafts (*good*, of course, is a relative term—good for Joyce would not be good for Daphne, and three pieces that show some effort are good for Daisy or Paul). I talk with them about which one they plan to publish and how they want to publish it. Some children love to copy their first drafts into spiral-bound books and add illustrations; others like to use the word-processing software along with the clip art; still others like to write it out, scroll-like, on long butcher paper. Once they have my okay to publish, they select two friends and read their draft to them. The friends know that they are to comment on what they like and make suggestions that will make the piece better. (Better is defined as clearer, more interesting, more exciting, more suspenseful!) Often, the friends make suggestions about illustrations or particular clip art that would enhance the writing.

The writer then revises the chosen piece for meaning, using the friends' suggestions if the writer thinks they are good ideas. I require that in their first-draft notebooks they write on every other line so that some revision can be done on the blank lines.

My Readers' Workshops are organized around three kinds of units—author units, genre units, and topic/theme units. This year I decided to start with an author unit. I like to start with something of high interest to the children and something quite easy to read, so that they can learn how to write in their literature logs and how to discuss in their literature circles. I have always found that almost all the children love Beverly Cleary books. Many of her books are quite easy to read, but even better readers enjoy and empathize with Ramona, Beezus, Henry, and the rest of the gang. I began the unit by putting out all the Beverly Cleary books I could find and talking with the children about them. Many of the children had already read some of her books, and they talked about the characters—Ribsy included—as if they were old friends. I told them that we were going to spend a few weeks reading and rereading these Beverly Cleary books, and they all seemed delighted at the prospect. I showed them that I had enough copies of *Henry Huggins* so that everyone could read this one and that when we finished this, they would get to choose the next Beverly Cleary book they wanted to read.

Next, I distributed the books and told them to read only the first chapter. I told them that they could read by themselves or with a friend, and that when everyone had finished, we would make our first entries into our literature response logs. The children grabbed their books and went off to read. Many of the children partnered up, and as I had expected, Daphne grabbed Paul and took him off with her. No one grabbed Daisy, so once they all got settled, I went over and read the chapter with her, taking turns reading the pages and helping her use word identification strategies such as pictures, context, and spelling patterns. She did quite well on her pages and clearly loved the individual attention.

When I saw that some of the children had finished, I told them to take a piece of scrap paper and write down a few of the important things that had happened, so they would be ready to help us write our response log entry. When Daisy and I finished, I went to the overhead and asked the children who were through to join me, indicating to the others that they should join us when they finished. The children and I discussed the first chapter informally as other children joined the group.

When almost everyone was there, I showed them how we would write in our response logs.

Using the overhead, I wrote at the top of the page the book title and then the chapter title and pages we had read. I then began a sentence about the main character by writing

Henry Huggins is . . .

The children told me lots of things about Henry. Then, working together, we constructed a sentence about Henry, which I wrote on the transparency. Next, I wrote this beginning of a sentence:

Henry wants to . . .

Again, the children shared ideas and came up with a sentence to describe Henry's problem, which I wrote on the transparency. Finally, I wrote

I think Henry will . . .

The children had lot of predictions about what would happen next. I listened but didn't write any of these down. When they had shared their predictions, I had them return to their desks, get out their brand-new literature response logs, and write the book and chapter title and pages to head their first page as I had. I then had them copy the *Henry Huggins is* and *Henry wants to* sentences that we had composed. Finally, I asked them to write their own ending to the *I think Henry will* sentence.

We continued these procedures through this whole first book: working together as a class to discuss the chapter read, jointly composing a sentence or two that summed up some major points from the chapter, and finishing by having the children copy our class-composed sentences and make their own predictions for the next day.

By the time the children finished the book, they all understood how our response logs would work and were getting very good at summarizing one or two important events and making a prediction. I did have to collect the books each time they finished reading and make them pledge on their honor not to read ahead. They are so eager to have their predictions be right that they will cheat if you let them!

When we had finished reading *Henry Huggins* together, I showed them six other Beverly Cleary books of which I had six to eight copies each. I read them a little bit of each book and then had them write down on a slip of paper their first, second, and third choice of which book they wanted to read. Several children complained that they wanted to read them all, but I reminded them that time and books were always limited and that they would have to choose. I told them that after we finished reading and discussing these books, they could choose to read the ones they hadn't read during Readers' Workshop, at home or during self-selected reading time.

Looking at their choices, I formed them into five groups, with four to six children in each group. I tried to put a mix of children in each group, and I assigned Chip, Butch, Mort, Daisy, and Paul to the easiest book they had chosen. Daphne put her three choices down but also wrote on her choice sheet, "I would like to read the same book Paul reads if you have enough. I like to help him."

What an angel she is!

The procedure we used for the second Beverly Cleary book was basically the same as the one we used for *Henry Huggins,* except that the children got together in their groups, discussed the story, and jointly composed two or three sentences summing up what happened. Each child then returned to his or her desk, wrote what he or she liked best about the part read that day, and made a "secret" prediction for the next day.

When we finished all the books, we had a Beverly Cleary party. I pretended to be Beverly—the guest of honor—and the children told me what they liked and asked me lots of questions. This unit was a big hit with the children. Many of them (including Daisy!) are currently reading all the Beverly Cleary books their group didn't read. I was just thinking that I would start next year off with this same author unit, and then I remembered I won't be starting next year off with any unit! I'll be retired! I have really mixed emotions about that, but I want to do so much traveling and so many other projects that I can't do just in the summers.

November

A new student has arrived—Tanana—and I am afraid that she will have some rather severe adjustment problems. Tanana is an Inuit child who is so accustomed to wilderness and freedom that she must be finding her new life here rather confining. I have asked two of the girls, Daphne and Betty, to be her special friends until she becomes acclimatized. Those two girls are very outgoing and friendly and will help Tanana feel at home here.

Whenever a new student moves in, I give him or her a few weeks to adjust to us, and then I do the same kind of assessment I did with all the children at the beginning of the year. I could tell right away that my interest inventory was not going to mean much to a child from a culture as different from ours as Tanana's, so rather than have her fill that out, I talked with her and wrote down some of the things she liked to do. I put out a variety of books and had her pick the three books she would most like to read or have read to her. I got a writing sample from her by asking her to describe the school she had gone to in Alaska. I gave her the IRI, and her word identification is much higher than her comprehension. I am sure that this is because comprehension is so dependent on prior knowledge and Tanana just doesn't know a lot of the things all children growing up here would know. She could pass the comprehension criteria on the first-reader passages but not on the second-grade passages. I think, however, that her reading level will quickly get to at least third-grade level as she learns more about our culture and language.

When Tanana arrived, I decided to focus our Readers' Workshop on the topic Other Times and Places. I had several good books set in earlier years of this country as well as books set in other countries, and with Tanana's arrival, I took advantage of the chance to help children think about how people lived in other times and places. Together, we read Cynthia Rylant's *When I Was Young in the Mountains* and Karen Ackerman's *Song and Dance Man,* and then the children chose from a variety of books that take place in other times and places. I formed groups, trying once again to give everyone their first, second, or third choices and to assign my lowest readers to the easiest book they had chosen. I put Daphne, Tanana, and Paul in the same group, and Daphne read the chapters of their books with both of them. I told her she had found her calling and asked her if she was planning to be a teacher when she grew up. She just smiled happily and nodded.

I once again modeled for them how to respond in their literature response logs. I used sentence frames that lead them to compare and contrast life then and now and make decisions about what would be better or worse. I also included a sentence frame to get them to make their own personal response to what they were learning:

The most fascinating thing I learned today was . . .

To connect reading and writing, I tied in some focused-writing lessons on descriptive paragraphs with this theme. I used the books we were reading to point out examples of some good descriptive paragraphs. We talked about the words authors used to let us see and feel what the faraway and long-ago places were like. I then wrote a paragraph describing the farthest-away place I have been—the coral reef in Australia. (The children were fascinated with the notion that it had taken eighteen hours on the airplane to get there, and with the notion that day here was night there and vice versa. I brought in some books and other literature I had picked up in Australia, and these are very popular reading materials during self-selected reading.) I then had the children talk about the farthest place they had been and write descriptive paragraphs that would make that place come alive for those of us who hadn't been there.

Having written about what they knew firsthand, I had them work in their groups collaboratively to write descriptive paragraphs about some of the settings for the books their groups were reading. We took a week off from our own writing to do these teacher-guided lessons on descriptive paragraphs. We are now back to our own writing, and I can already see the insights they gained about descriptive writing being used in the self-selected topic writing of many of my children.

We have also gotten started into our word sorts, which I use to move them forward in their knowledge of spelling/decoding patterns. I make these word sorts multilevel by including a variety of spelling patterns used in short and long vowel words. For the first sort, I used common spelling patterns for the vowel *u.* I gave the children a sort sheet, and I made a transparency from this sort sheet to use with my overhead.

Forming the tops of the columns were the major spelling patterns represented by *u,* along with an example word for each. The first day we used this sort sheet, I had the children fold their sheets so that they couldn't see the last two columns—*sure* and *ture.* (I covered those columns on my transparency also.) I then showed them fifteen to twenty words that had the vowel *u.* As I showed them each word, they pronounced it and then wrote it in the column they thought it belonged in. When they had had a chance to write it on their sheets, I let them tell me which column to write it in on my transparency. At the end of that first lesson, our sort sheets looked like this:

OTHER	u us	ue sue	u-e use	ur burn	sure insure	ture nature
menu	*run*	*true*	*mule*	*turn*		
	must	*blue*	*mute*	*urban*		
	snub	*due*	*cute*	*turtle*		
	runt		*amuse*			
	strum					
	bus					

On the second day, we used the same sheet again and kept the last two columns covered. We sorted another fifteen to twenty words into the first five columns. Some of these words had more than one syllable, and I had to remind the children that it was the syllable that had the *u* that we were focusing on. I also had to remind them that it had to have the same spelling pattern and the same pronunciation as the model word that headed each column.

On the third day, I had them open their sheets, and I uncovered my transparency so that all columns were visible. This is what the sheets looked like at the end of the third day:

OTHER	u us	ue sue	u-e use	ur burn	sure insure	ture nature
menu	*run*	*true*	*mule*	*turn*	*measure*	*creature*
tuna	*must*	*blue*	*mute*	*urban*	*assure*	*picture*
	snub	*due*	*cute*	*turtle*	*treasure*	*mixture*
	runt	*statue*	*amuse*	*return*	*pleasure*	*mature*
	strum	*value*	*reuse*	*hurt*	*pressure*	*adventure*
	bus	*rescue*	*compute*			
	minus	*continue*				
	numbers					
	sunset					
	summer					
	submarines					

The first three days of our sorting activities are usually devoted to reading sorts—that is, we pronounce the words before asking the children to decide which column they belong in. On the fourth day, I do a blind sort. The children get a new sorting sheet just like the one they used the first three days, and I use a new transparency. I use the same words we have used on the first three days, but on the fourth day, I say the word but do not show it (thus the name "blind sort"). The students put their finger on the column to show where they think it should be written. I then show them the word, and they write it and I write it. On Friday, we do a blind writing sort. I say the word, and they have to try to write it in the correct column before I show it to them. This is the hardest one of all, but having worked with these words on the previous four days, most of the children are able to write the word in the correct column.

At the end of the fifth day, I have the children use two facing pages in their word sort notebooks and set up the columns as they were on their sheets. They then pick one or two of the words we sorted and write these in the correct columns. Their sorting notebooks are now set up for the best part of word sorting—the hunt. The children have one week to find other words that fit the patterns and write them into their own sorting notebooks. They can find words anywhere—around the room, on signs, or in books they are reading for Readers' Workshop, self-selected reading, and even science, social studies, and math. They do this hunting on their own and are all eager to have lots of words—especially big words—to contribute to our final sort.

For the final sort, I put a huge piece of butcher paper all the way across the chalkboard. I set up the columns as they were set up on the original sort sheets—using a different-colored permanent marker for each. We then go around the room, letting the children have a turn coming up and writing one word in its correct column, pronouncing that word, and for obscure words, using it in a sentence. We keep going around until we run out of words or space on our sort mural. Usually, we fill up the easy columns—*u* as in *us, ur* as in *turn*—but have space left on the more difficult ones. I hang the mural along the back wall, and children can continue to write in the correct columns the words they find.

We do a sort like this about every three weeks. We spend the first week together, working through the five-day cycle (reading sort, blind sort, blind writing sort), the next week hunting, and the last week experiencing the delight of finding a few more words to fit the pattern. The children responded quite enthusiastically to this sort, and I am going to do one more before the Christmas break.

December

We have done plays this month! Children love plays, and there are many good holiday plays as well as others that children enjoy acting out, so that December is the perfect month for plays. We began by choosing some plays already written as plays and later in the month wrote our own plays based on award-winning books. Each group devised a play for one of the kindergarten, first-, or second-grade classes. The children became as excited about this as they were about the approaching holiday season, so that December became a little harried (more harried?).

All the groups selected a book they wanted to act out. Some groups chose a picture book, so that they could do the whole story. Others selected a scene or a chapter from a longer book. No matter which, they all went through the same webbing process to convert their story into a play. I modeled this using a picture book they had all loved, *Sleeping Ugly* by Jane Yolen.

I began by rereading the book aloud, webbing the characters and their traits and motivations, events, props, costuming, and setting as I went along. There was a huge web begun on the chalkboard. This was very time-consuming, and after the first several pages, a bit overwhelming to them. They could not see how I could read and look for so many things at once. I stopped that day and told them we would come back to it the next day.

Day Two: I assigned each table group to pay attention to one aspect. Hilda's table was to list characters as I read aloud, and they were to put descriptors next to those characters that told what they were like. On the chalkboard, I was also listing this information as I went along. Jeff's table was to list props that would be needed to stage this as a play. Again, I listed what I noted on the chalkboard web. Other tables had other parts of the web to pay attention to. I told them not to copy what I was writing, but rather to write what they heard in order to help find things I might miss. After reading about two pages this way, I asked groups to tell me some of the things I had missed so I could add them to the big web. For example, I had not listed Princess Miserella's horse as a character, but Hilda's table thought of him as a character because he had purposely not taken Miserella home, even though he could have. That purposefulness, they argued, made him a character. I conceded to their reasoning. There were lots of props I had not listed that Jeff's table included: dishes for the shelves, little animals to stand around, and so on. So my web grew there as well. Each table had added in more things than I had, except "events"; I had identified far more than they had. I suspect this is tied to their understanding of what is an event. Some of the research articles I have read in the past seem to have struggled with that as well!

We completed the *Sleeping Ugly* web in this way, and I put them to work applying the same strategy to their own story. But this time, members of the group were each to read their story to themselves and list the aspects of their assigned element. Butch's group, which was staging *Stellaluna*, divided up the web this way: Butch was listing props; Mandy listed characters, traits, and motivations; Manuel identified events; Alexander listed scenery ideas to show the setting; and Roberta identified costuming needs. They each put their section on the group web and then reviewed it together to clarify the parts and make sure everyone understood and agreed with the listed elements.

After each web was completed (at least in a first-draft form), I called them all back together for a minilesson on how to take those elements they had listed and turn them into a play. We reviewed the format that a play is written in, and I gave each group a template for reference.

Another helpful holiday deed was sending volunteers from my class to Helen Launch's kindergarten room to write down the children's dictated letters to their parents. Helen decided this would make a nice gift from the children. She asked them to tell their parents about an incident they remembered and to tell them what is wonderful about their family.

January

Well, my expectations about this term's student teacher seem to be supported by her deeds. Amah Yung is a most eager young woman, staying late in the afternoon to complete a bulletin board or game that she is making for the children. The children have, for the most part, become quite attached to her. She and Joyce have really bonded. They talk at great length on the playground, and I have noticed that Joyce is beginning to get really involved with her work. She doesn't need to be reminded to do it and even seeks extra things to do now. Part of the reason might be that Amah Yung discovered Joyce's interest in unusual and unexplainable happenings, and she has been bringing some of Zilpha Keatley Snyder's books for Joyce to read. She especially enjoyed *The Egypt Game* and *The Changeling*. Right now she is reading *Below the Root*, a book that I found fascinating. Joyce is really growing up!

We have had an unusually busy month. Readers' Workshop focused on folklore. I chose this genre to study partly because I have always loved fairy tales, folktales, and legends and partly because there are so many wonderful things for the children to read that cut across all the reading levels. I have versions of some of the fairy tales, as well as *Pecos Bill* and *Babe the Blue Ox*, tales that are easy enough for everyone but Paul to read independently, so I could have Chip, Daisy, Butch, and the other low readers read by themselves rather than with a partner. I am always concerned that children develop independent silent reading ability during this third-grade year, and this folktale unit provided the children with lots of easy choices.

I steered my super readers—Larry, Pat, Danielle, and others—in the direction of myths. I read *Hades and Persephone* to the whole class and talked with them about Greece and Greek mythology. The children were amazed to discover that at the time these myths were first told, most people believed that they were true. After I finished reading this tale, I showed them some of the other myth stories of which I had multiple copies, and as I had expected, my most sophisticated readers gravitated to the myths.

I included many folktales from other countries in this unit. Unfortunately, I don't have many multiple copies of the folktales from other countries, so I did most of these by reading them to the whole class. For some, I read the entire book, but for many others, I just read the first chapter or story in a collection and then made these books available during self-selected reading. The ones the children liked best were *Sedna, an Eskimo Myth*, which I hunted up in honor of Tanana; *Why the Sun and the Moon Live in the Sky*, an African tale; and *Bawshou Rescues the Sun*, a Chinese tale.

Because many of the folktales and myths have clear problem-solution structures, I decided that this was a good time to teach the children to create story maps. There are many different ways of creating story maps, but all help children to follow the story by drawing their attention to the elements that all good stories share. Stories have characters, and they happen in a particular place and time that we call the setting. In most stories, the characters have some goal they want to achieve or some problem they need to resolve. The events in the story lead to some kind of solution or resolution. Sometimes, stories have implicit morals or themes that we hope children will learn from.

There are many different kinds of story maps. I like this one I adapted from Isabel Beck (Macon, Bewell, & Vogt, 1991).

Main Characters

Setting (Time and Place)

Problem or Goal

Event 1

Event 2

Event 3

Event 4

Event 5

Event 6

Solution

Story Theme or Moral

For our first story map experience, I chose *The Three Little Pigs*. The children and I retold and acted out this familiar story, and then we worked together to fill out the story map. Here is that story map filled in for *The Three Little Pigs*.

Main Characters *Mother Pig, three little pigs, big bad wolf*

Setting (Time and Place) *Woods, make-believe time and place*

Problem/Goal *Pigs wanted to be independent and have their own houses.*

    Event 1 *Mother Pig sends three little pigs out to build their own houses.*

    Event 2 *First little pig gets some straw and builds a straw house. Big bad wolf blows the straw house down.*

    Event 3 *Second little pig gets some sticks and builds a stick house. Big bad wolf blows the stick house down.*

    Event 4 *Third little pig gets some bricks and builds a brick house. Big bad wolf cannot blow the brick house down.*

    Event 5 *Big bad wolf gets scalded coming down the chimney of the brick house.*

Solution *Pigs live happily ever after in strong brick house.*

Story Theme or Moral *Hard work pays off in the end!*

We completed three more story maps together after watching the videos of *Snow White and the Seven Dwarfs, Beauty and the Beast,* and *Aladdin.* We also read several book versions of the tales on which these movies were based and discussed how they were different and the same. The children could not believe that there were no dwarfs named Sleepy and Doc in the original *Snow White.*

Once we had done these four story maps together, the groups had no trouble completing story maps for the tales and myths they were reading. For the most part, they completed these collaboratively, and then each child wrote his or her own story map in the literature response journal.

Because the children had so enjoyed doing the plays in December, and since folktales and myths just "beg" to be performed, I ended the unit by letting each group act out one of the pieces they had read. I showed them some wonderful books I bought last summer (*Overhead Transparencies for Creative Dramatics* by

Creative Teaching Press), which had on transparency important scenery from some of the myths and tales they had been reading. When projected from the back of the room, these colored transparencies transformed our room into the dark woods through which Red Riding Hood walked or a square in ancient Greece. In addition to this instant transparency scenery, the books of transparencies contain simple headband patterns that make acting out a story a snap. Because I had planned this creative reenactment response as a culmination of the unit, I made sure that at least two of the stories that each group had read were ones for which I had scenery and headbands. I didn't require the groups to restrict their choice of which one to act out to only those, but they all chose a piece that had these accoutrements.

The reenactments were a big success, and we had a special evening performance for parents before one of our schoolwide PTA meetings. We also sent performing troupes to the younger grades. Miss Yung was a tremendous help to me this month, and she had a great time. I hope I didn't overwhelm her, however. As I was pulling out books and videos and the transparency books, she kept saying, "Where do you get all this stuff? I have never seen anyone with so many different things and ideas. How will I ever have what I need next year?"

In her notebook, she has pages and pages full of things she needs and wants. I, on the other hand, am wondering what I am going to do with it all—thirty-one years of accumulated stuff is a lot of stuff! I think I will box some of it up and send it off with Amah when she leaves at the end of March. I hate to part with it, but it won't be of any use to anyone in my attic—and, come to think of it, my attic is already full.

February

Another exciting month! This month I used the broad umbrella of animals as the organizing theme for our Readers' Workshop. We read both fiction and nonfiction books, including such favorites as *Charlotte's Web* and some of the *Winnie-the-Pooh* stories. We discussed how you could tell if a book was a story or informational, and I tried to get all the children to read some of each type. We made webs for the different animals different groups were reading about and included the factual information we found in informational books. We also decided that even in a clearly fictitious animal story, there were some things that were true. Spiders do spin webs and bears do like honey. When reading animal stories, the children sometimes argued about which characteristics were true of the animals, and I helped them look up the animal in question in various reference books to resolve the disputes. We discovered some wonderful authors of animal informational books. The children were entranced with Dorothy Hinshaw Patent's books—especially *Buffalo* and *Gray Wolf, Red Wolf*. They also enjoyed the books of Carol Carrick, who writes fiction with realistic depictions of animals as well as informational books, including Mitch's favorite, *Sand Tiger Shark*. Of course, they devoured all the Gail Bibbori animal books.

Once we got lots of animal webs made, I used these to teach some focused-writing lessons on writing reports. The children and I had read several books on whales and jointly constructed the web. I then showed them how we could take this information and write a report on whales. I modeled for them how to write an introductory paragraph about whales, then to use the information from the different spokes of the web to write descriptive paragraphs, and finally how to write a concluding paragraph. The children and I jointly constructed each paragraph—they gave me suggestions and then I put the sentences together in a cohesive way. It took us several days to turn our whale web into this report. Steve, who is our resident nature expert and quite an artist, drew the whale illustrations.

Once we had done our whale reports together, the groups picked one of the animals they had been reading about and webbing and wrote reports based on their webs. They are getting quite good at writing collaboratively, probably because we do a lot of it as a class. They pick someone "who writes real nice" to do the actual writing, but they all add their ideas. I have them use the Editor's Checklist to proofread their reports, and they are getting much better at finding and fixing those things we have been working on all year.

Realizing that "time is marching on," I decided that I needed to move them toward more independence in their writing. After the groups collaboratively wrote their reports on an animal, we constructed as a class several webs about animals commonly kept as pets—dogs, cats, gerbils. They told me all about George in first grade and wanted to go get him and bring him for a visit. Steve informed them that George had been dead for over a year, and many were devastated when they realized that their first-grade pet was no longer with us. Steve volunteered to ask Mrs. Wright if we could borrow Samantha—but they didn't want "just any old gerbil."

I had each child choose one of the animals we had discussed and then asked them to write a report, using the web and the format we had used as a whole class and in their groups. After writing their report, they shared in small groups, got suggestions for revision, picked a friend to help them edit, and finally brought their paragraph to me or Miss Yung—joint editors-in-chief. They are now typing their individual reports on the computers, and we are compiling a class book on animals. Many of them have chosen their animal reports as one of the pieces to go in their showcase portfolios, and I have noticed lots more animal reports being written now that we are back to self-selected topic-process writing for a few weeks.

Miss Yung has been invaluable to me this month. We have done a lot of team teaching, and our styles mesh wonderfully. She is, however, much more organized than I am and has come up with a very clever way of keeping anecdotal records on the children. I have a folder for each child with divisions for the major areas in which I write comments on a regular basis. I always note in this folder what the children bring to read to me from their self-selected reading, as well as some observations on what strategies they are using well and which strategies I need to help them develop. I also make some notes immediately after each writing conference. In addition, I sit down each afternoon for a few minutes and sift through my folders, remembering what I observed the children doing as they read and wrote throughout the day; then I make some notes based on these remembrances.

Miss Yung, observing me do this each afternoon, would always ask how I could remember all this. I told her that it is hard to remember when you are just starting teaching, because you have so many things to think about at one time, but that with experience, she would find that she too could sift through the folders at the end of the day and remember specific observations she had made about different children as the day progressed. Not willing to wait for experience, Miss Yung has come up with a simple system. She walks around all day with a clipboard on which she has attached one sheet of file-folder labels. As she observes children, she puts the child's initials and the date on one of the labels and then writes down what she wants to note in the folder. At the end of the day, she peels all the labels off the sheet and puts them on the right child's folder. She also notices which children she hasn't made any observations about in several days and puts their initials on a label on the sheet she will use the next day. (Some quiet children like Rita and Manuel just don't get noticed unless you decide to notice them!)

Between writing observations down immediately after each reading and writing conference and always having labels there to record observations at any time of the day, you don't have to try to remember what you saw the different children doing. In fact, I realize as I watch her with her clipboard and labels that I am probably not as good at remembering as I think I am. She will be doing almost all the teaching next month, but when I get back into it in April and May, I think I will get myself a clipboard and sheet of labels! I told both Amah and Dr. Link, her supervisor, that I intended to do this, and Amah expressed delight and amazement that she had been able to teach me something. Dr. Link said that the best teachers were also lifelong learners, and they both tried to talk me out of retirement! "It's too late," I said, "I've got travel plans made and it's time to make way for the Amah Yungs of the world."

March

Amah Yung has become invaluable to me and the students, and I told Dr. Link that I was not going to let her go! She laughed at me, of course, and said that if I felt that strongly, perhaps I would be willing to recommend her for my position, which would become vacant with my retirement this June. I assured her that I would certainly do that, for Amah has been the best student teacher I have ever had. She is so creative, willing, and sympathetic to the students! Yet she doesn't let that sympathy interfere with providing them the best possible instruction.

Amah has become a real expert at managing her time. With both of us working, team-teaching style, we can accomplish even more, so I was reluctant to give her the experience that she needed in handling the entire day by herself. But I did allow her three weeks, of course, so that she had a small taste of what it would be like to be totally responsible for a class.

During those three weeks—her last three weeks with us—she had the children making "shape books." Chip made a "hand book" in the shape of a large hand. The illustrations were photos as well as pictures cut out from magazines. All were pictures of hands doing various things. The illustrations were labeled with descriptions of the hands' actions. One picture had a man's hands playing a piano, and the sentence said, "Hands can make music." Another showed a lady cuddling a baby and was titled, "Hands can love you, too." Horace made a "foot book" using the same technique. Several other children found shape books to be a fun writing project.

Another project of hers was the long-awaited poetry unit. I knew that these children had had quite a lot of exposure to poetry. They had had much poetry read to them, and they had in turn created many poems of their own. I knew that they were ripe for the kinds of activities that Amah had in mind for them.

She began the poetry unit by reading to the children from Mary O'Neill's classic and beautiful *Hailstones and Halibut Bones,* a collection of poems about colors. After reading a couple of her favorites and one of mine ("What is Purple?"), she discussed with them that Mary O'Neill is saying that colors are not only things but also feelings, moods, smells, and sounds. Then she took a stack of colored construction paper from her table and asked the children to form groups of five or six and told them that each group would receive one colored sheet. They were then to list all the things that the color could be, feel like, smell like, sound like, or make them feel like within the five minutes allotted on the timer. They began to discuss furiously and to list all of these qualities. When the timer rang, there were groans of "Oh no! Not yet! Let us put down some more." She asked each group to choose someone who could read the completed list to the rest of the class. One that I thought was particularly good was this one by Rita, Jeff, Manuel, Mort, Pat, and Steve. Their color was white:

> puffy clouds
>
> lacy snowflakes
>
> glaring light
>
> refrigerator door
>
> frosty window pane
>
> fear
>
> apple inside
>
> crunchy ice cube
>
> fluffy whipped cream
>
> winter morning breath
>
> mashed potatoes

She told the children that poetry creates images, and that those images do not need to be done with rhymes. She said that she was sure that the children could create a poem from what they had listed. She said, "Let me see if *I* can make one." This is it:

> Lacy snowflakes
>   Against my window pane
>   Fluffy whipped cream
>   Puffy clouds above.

The children were enthralled, as was I, with this creation. Immediately, each group set to work to create a poem. Amah had explained to me that she wanted the children to have many experiences in writing group poems before they attempted to write individual ones. She told me that she had come to love poetry only within the last few years, that she had dreaded and hated it before. She was sure that that was because of the way in which her teachers had dealt with it—not as something to be loved, treasured, and enjoyed, but rather as something to be analyzed, dissected, and criticized. She had vowed that she would do her best to help her students learn to enjoy poetry at an early age. A format that she used with them involved the "diamante" form that Iris Tiedt developed. It is as follows:

noun

adjective, adjective

participle, participle, participle

noun, noun, noun, noun

participle, participle, participle

adjective, adjective

noun

The first and last words are to be opposites, and images build on the first noun through the two nouns in the middle. The transition is made here to building images for the last noun. The poem below is one written by the class.

Father

Strong, kind

Working, resting, loving

Bed, baby, boy, Mommie

Working, working, working,

Tired, busy

Mother

She also had the children complete the following phrases, and with the unifying factor of "The year" repeated at the end of the poem, she found that even the less capable children could produce a poem they were pleased with.

The year . . .

The fall . . .

The winter . . .

The spring . . .

The summer . . .

The year . . .

I knew that the poetry unit had been successful when I noticed that the previously untouched poetry books in the class library became the most demanded ones, and when poetry began to appear in their writing notebooks. The children recited poetry to one another on the playground. If only they keep this enthusiasm!

April

My, how the time is passing now. With April over, only one more full month of school remains. I always begin to panic at this time of the year, wondering if I will accomplish all that needs to be done. Oh well, done or not, the year *will* end! I've started to go through my file cabinets so that I won't be here all summer, trying to move out of this room. One accumulates a lot in thirty-one years.

While cleaning, I came upon the file folder for literature-based curriculum compiled the year that I first began to become discontented with what I had been doing and was searching for something more satisfying for myself and the children. I had read a lot of articles in my professional journals, attended workshops, and taken courses at the university. I tried, then, to put all of the information together in a way that I could deal with it. I thought that I was ready after we returned from our spring break (in March of that year). There was still enough time to work out some of the problems and to give it a fair try, realizing that if it didn't work, I wouldn't have wasted an entire year of the children's time.

For the rest of that year, I used trade books for most of my reading instruction and began doing Readers' Workshops. The children responded well, but I had very few books of which I had multiple copies and no whole-class sets of books. Using what I had here, plus what I could check out from the school, public, and university libraries, we got through the year, but I couldn't offer children very much choice, and just gathering up the books took a huge chunk of my time.

The second year, I used reading series and trade books, alternating which we would read in. I had purchased some multiple copies of trade books, and the school purchased some more that could be checked out from the library. Gradually, I got to the point where I am today. My reading program is totally literature based, and I give the children complete freedom in what they read for self-selected reading and a lot of choice in what they select to read and discuss in their literature response groups. I have some selections that we all read and a lot of pieces that I read to the whole class. I make sure to include lots of variety in topics, authors, and genres so that my children all get a fairly balanced reading diet.

Our topic this month was sports! In talking with the children and looking at their interest inventories, I realized that sports is one topic almost all my children are interested in. Many of them play sports—baseball, soccer, tennis—and with the university so close, lots of my children go to basketball and football games. There is also a lot of excitement and interest this year in the upcoming Olympics. I included stories in which children play sports, including *Thank You, Jackie Robinson* by Barbara Cohen, *Never Say Quit* by Bill Wallace, and *Scoop Snoops* by Constance Hiser. I also included biographies of sports heroes. They read about some of the old pros but seemed to enjoy most the *Sports Shots Books*, which chronicle the lives and careers of modern heroes such as Michael Jordan, Florence Griffith Joyner, Wayne Gretzky, Michelle Kwan, and Joe Montana. Of course, we used reference books such as *Amazing but True Sports Stories* and *Inside Pro Football.* Both this year's and the back issues of *Sports Illustrated for Kids* were great references.

I also used the sports theme for several guided-writing lessons. The students remembered writing their animal reports and compiling them into a class book. This month, they all became sports reporters. Together we watched a video of a championship basketball game and then worked collaboratively to write up the game for *Sports Illustrated for Kids.* I told the class that reporters were always given a limited amount of space, and so we had to limit our article but make it exciting at the same time. When we had finished our class-composed article, the children chose another sport for which I had a game or match on video—baseball, football, tennis, soccer, swimming, or gymnastics—and worked in groups to write an article describing that.

We completed two fairly sophisticated word sorts this month. For the first one, we worked with some common endings and suffixes and emphasized the spelling changes that occur when these endings are added. I gave the students their sort sheets, and on the first day, I had them fold their papers so that we were sorting only words that had no ending or words that ended in *en, er,* or *est.* We had previously sorted words with endings that needed no spelling changes. All the words I gave them for this sort required that they make some change in the root word before adding the ending. On the next two days, I included more *en, er,* and *est* words and others that ended in *ment, less,* or *ness.* Following our usual procedures, I gave them a clean sort sheet on Thursday and did a blind reading sort, followed by the hardest task of all on Friday—a blind writing sort in which they had to decide where to write the word and write it before I showed it to them. The following week, they hunted words that fit these patterns and wrote them in their word sort notebooks. These words are harder to find than the ones sorted by vowel patterns that we did earlier in the year, and they had a hard time filling up the butcher paper columns during our culminating sort. Roberta and Horace teamed up together and figured out that if you started with words ending in *y,* you could get a lot of words to add. Their list included many *nasty, nastier, nastiest, nastiness/silly, sillier, silliest, silliness* combinations. Hilda complained that this wasn't fair, because they surely had not found all those words in their reading. Roberta picked up the dictionary and claimed that she had been reading it!

No Ending	en(e)	er(y–i)	est(y–i)	ment	less	ness(y–i)
sun	sweeten	sunnier	meanest	agreement	winless	greediness

The other sort we did was also a challenge. We sorted for words that ended in *el, le,* and *al,* along with words that ended in *able* and *ible.* The children were frustrated by the fact that you couldn't tell by hearing these words which way the end would be spelled. I pointed out that with some words, you can't be sure which way it will be spelled; you just have to write it and see if it looks right and sometimes use the dictionary to check.

Other	el	le	al	able	able	ible
	label	*turtle*	*general*	*table*	*notable*	*edible*

The children have begun compiling their showcase portfolios. We are having our first show for parents in mid-May, and the children all want to put their best foot forward. I have limited them to five pieces each—and they must include at least one piece they have written in response to something they read. For each piece they select, they are writing a brief description on an index card, indicating why they chose this piece and what they were trying to do with it. Some of my most prolific writers are having a terrible time deciding which five to include, while Daisy, Mort, and Chip are complaining, "You mean we have to find five things we are proud of and want everyone to read? That's too many!" I am taking them on a field trip to the university next month, and one of the things we will go to is an artist's showing. I hope that will help them understand what our showing is all about.

May

I always have approach-avoidance conflicts at the end of the school year, but this month has been especially emotional. It is strange, but I can picture in my mind and name almost all the children in the first class I taught thirty-one years ago (egads, I am getting old—they are in their forties!), and I am sure I will always remember this class too. These last few weeks, as they have been assembling their showcase portfolios and I have been selecting samples from their growth portfolios to put in their cumulative portfolios, I kept thinking that they were the best class I ever had. I wouldn't have believed it at the beginning of the year, but I will even have fond memories of Mort and Daisy!

It was apparent from looking at their beginning-of-the-year, midyear, and end-of-the-year writing samples in which they described Merritt Elementary and told about what they liked best that they have all shown tremendous growth in both their first-draft writing ability and their ability to revise and edit a piece of writing. The growth was most striking for the students who came in furthest behind. Paul can write coherent pieces now. While these pieces are short and not terribly interesting, they do say something and hold together, and he is able to improve them a little when he edits and revises. Daisy, Butch, Chip, Joyce, and Jeff have all shown marked increases in their writing ability. Tanana is writing more and is willing to write, but her language is still quite immature, and often her sentences don't sound quite right.

I did not give end-of-the-year IRIs to all the children, because I could tell from my observations of them during Readers' Workshop and from my oral reading analyses that they were growing in both their ability to read and respond and in the breadth of their reading interests. I did give IRIs to my below-grade-level children, however, because I wanted to see how far they had come.

Paul, who entered reading at either primer or first-reader level, can read most material at second-grade level if he is having an "alert" day. Daisy is also at second-grade level, but she just missed the third-grade instructional-level criteria by a few words, so she is moving along. Butch, who was reading at second-grade level, now reads at third-grade level. Of course, that still puts him one year behind when he goes to fourth grade next year, but he did achieve a full year's growth. Chip, Alexander, and Mort, who read at second-grade level at the beginning of the year, tested fourth-grade level. I am so proud of them! Chip didn't surprise me, because he is a real worker and he really got into books this year. Mort did surprise me. His daily work and attitude didn't show much improvement. If he applied himself, he could probably be a very good student. Tanana's instructional level tested third grade, and again her word identification was much better than her comprehension. She has shown amazing growth, however, and I know that with Ms. Maverick's integrated knowledge-building curriculum in fourth grade, she will continue to grow in her knowledge of the world; consequently, her comprehension will improve.

I am delighted with the growth shown by my very best students. Larry, Hilda, Danielle, Pat, Mandy, and Roberta have become quite sophisticated readers and writers. They have all broadened greatly what they like to read about and the different types of writing they can do. They are confident in their abilities and—except for Roberta, who is still too bossy—they are very helpful to the other children in literature response groups and in revising/editing conferences. Ever since I started to organize the classroom around literature and writing and include many multilevel activities, I have noticed remarkable growth for the children on the two ends of the continuum. I am not sure that the way I teach makes much of a difference for the Mitches and Carls in the world, but I know that it makes a difference for the children who come to me reading and writing substantially below or above where you would expect third-graders to be.

We finished up the year with "Your Choice" Readers' Workshops. I put out all the multiple copies of books that we hadn't used yet and let children choose from them all; then I formed literature circles based on their choices. They decided what they would write in the literature response logs and completed these individually before going to their discussion groups. Because I modeled so many different ways of responding for them, the children had no trouble thinking of what they wanted to say. As I circulated among the groups, I saw children with their logs open and heard them reading some statements such as the following:

I think the funniest part was when the dog got into the game.

I didn't think she should have told her mother what had happened when her friends had sworn her to secrecy.

I know what is probably going to happen next. They are going to lose the game and the coach will quit.

Hearing my readers make statements like this on their own convinces me that they have learned how you think about and respond to what you are reading. Because they are so in the habit of thinking this way, I bet they will continue to do this even if no one makes them write their responses down. Literature response logs are not so much for me to know what they are thinking as they are to help them clarify for themselves what they are thinking.

The Third-Grade Meeting

Mrs. Wise smiled as Sue Port departed. Some teachers felt considerable fear of that small but dynamic Ms. Port whenever she entered their classrooms. Not Mrs. Wise! She remembered when Ms. Port had been *her* student teacher some fifteen years ago. It was on Mrs. Wise's recommendation that the school system had hired Sue and later promoted her to the position of curriculum supervisor. Now Mrs. Wise was smiling, for she had just been asked if she would present the program for the final meeting of the third-grade teachers. "My valedictory," she thought. "Oh, well. I suppose they had to ask me now, since I won't be here next year. I was hoping, though, that I could get away without even attending, let alone being the program!" After thirty-one years of these meetings, she was *ready* to retire; she had often said that the meetings were things she would never miss about school.

But now to plan what to do! She began by going through some of the materials that she had selected for this final meeting, dragging out samples of books that she had used during this past year. She had asked to have the meeting in her own room, so that she would not have to transport all of her paraphernalia across town to the room in the administration building where these meetings were usually held. She sat down to plan the meeting for the following week.

One week later, Mrs. Wise was completely organized and ready for the meeting. She greeted the teachers who entered her room and then began the meeting by expressing her pleasure at seeing all her old friends and acknowledging her sincere delight at the interest they had shown in her program. She told them that she was eager to share with them the kind of program that she had been using for many years. Some of those present had visited her classroom in the past, and she invited them to make any comments that they felt were pertinent.

"Knowing me, you can expect to see a lot of books this afternoon." As she said this, she reached down and opened two large boxes, which were indeed full of books. As she talked about her classroom, she pulled out books to illustrate what she had read to the children, which books the whole class had read, and the kind of books she had let them choose from to read and discuss in their literature response groups. She showed them Jeff's literature response log (Jeff had been in the hospital the last week of school, so Mrs. Wise was using a lot of his things to demonstrate what the children did; she would drop everything off at his house after the meeting). She showed how she structured their responses early in the year, but how they were able to independently write their own personal responses by the end of the year.

She also had Jeff's writing notebook, his word sort notebook, and the five pieces he had selected for his showcase portfolio. She showed these also as she explained how she did both process writing and guided-writing lessons to move all the students forward in their writing ability.

On transparency, she had some of the webs the groups had made, from which they wrote their animal reports, along with the transparencies she used for the word sorts they did. She also had brought along the class book they made on animals and the butcher paper sheet on which they had accumulated their words from their last word sort.

As Mrs. Wise was showing them all these things and describing what they did, she could see some agitated faces. She stopped talking once she had shown them all the main things and said, "This was what I wanted to show you. What else would you like to know?"

A lot of hands went up, and Mrs. Wise called on a young teacher she had not seen before. This teacher said, "Mrs. Wise, I am awed by what you have shown us, but I wouldn't have any idea how to do this. Where do you get all the books, and how do you decide what they should read and write, and how do you know who is doing what?" Mrs. Wise could see that a lot of the more experienced teachers were thinking this too, and they all looked relieved that it was one of the beginning teachers who had asked the question. She wasn't supposed to know everything!

Mrs. Wise smiled and told them how she had begun gradually. Only after several years of transition had she accumulated the knowledge, organization, and books to allow her to do an "All Real Books" program. She talked about buying books with her own money in the old days but bragged about Mr. Topps and Merritt Elementary's decision to put more of their funds into classroom libraries and to let the teachers decide what they needed.

She also talked about her assessment system and showed them the IRI and interest inventory she gave at the beginning of each year, along with the repeated Merritt Elementary School writing prompt. She showed them the folder she kept on each child, in which she kept her oral reading analyses and observations after each reading and writing conference. She showed them her clipboard with file-folder labels and told them how she used these to record her observations and then moved them to the appropriate folders. She could tell that everyone was impressed by this simple solution to the difficult-to-manage anecdotal record system, and then she told them that it was Amah Yung, her student teacher, who had thought of this. (At the mention of Amah, the young teacher whose question had instigated this explanation looked first amazed and then delighted. After the meeting, she explained to Mrs. Wise that Amah was her sorority sister, that she had no idea she had been Mrs. Wise's student teacher, and that she was going to call her this summer and "pick her brain.")

Mrs. Wise went on to tell them about the three kinds of portfolios she used: growth portfolios that contained samples she had chosen and in which she kept her anecdotal records, showcase portfolios that the children put together to demonstrate their literacy prowess, and cumulative portfolios that contained the samples each teacher selected to move with the child from year to year.

The teachers had other questions, mainly about what she did "with the low kids" and "how she challenged the high ones." This gave Mrs. Wise a chance to explain why she believed her approach to literacy was most beneficial to both the low and high achievers. "For an average child like Jeff," she mentioned, pointing to his samples that had been passed around for the teachers to look at, "I'm not sure my literature-focus classroom really matters, but I can tell you that for students like Daisy and Chip on one end and Larry and Hilda on the other, the multilevel instruction, the cooperative learning, and the amount of choice I give them makes a world of difference."

A hand went up and Agatha Nostic said, "Now, Vera, are you telling us this Jeff was just one of your average children?"

"As average as they come," responded Mrs. Wise. "He tested third-grade level on the beginning-of-the-year IRI, and I have his initial writing sample here, which is actually a little below average in many ways for the beginning of third grade. If I were going to pick one of my kids to have his appendix out so that I could show off his things here at this meeting, it surely wouldn't have been Jeff!"

Mrs. Wise glanced up at the clock and then summed up what she did and how it fit her philosophy of teaching. "I have probably been teaching third grade longer than anyone in this room—even you, Agatha—and I have tried about every fad that came along and jumped on a lot of the bandwagons and taught a lot of 'new and improved' reading series. After all these years, I am sure of just a few things. Children are all different, and they have different interests, attitudes, home experiences, and reading and writing abilities. Some children need more structure and instruction. Some children really thrive in situations where they can work with partners and small groups. All children profit from being immersed in a wide variety of wonderful books and being given a lot of time and support to write. The program I have developed has structure and instruction. We do things to build word knowledge—primarily our word wall and word sorting. I teach them reading and writing strategies through the minilessons I do at the beginning of Readers' and Writers' Workshops. In addition to teaching, however, I give them time to do the activities I want them to value, and I let them make lots of choices about what they will read and write."

Mrs. Wise paused to notice the nods of agreement around the room. She had had the feeling when she began that some of these teachers were not very sympathetic to what she was doing, but now there was a noticeable change. Several of the teachers wanted to know how to begin her program.

She was gathering up her materials in preparation for leaving the meeting when Sue Port, with a grin on her face, told her to sit down, for the best part of the meeting was yet to come. Through the door, borne by two of her oldest friends, came a cake of mammoth proportions. The inscription read "Good-bye, Vera. We'll miss you." She was stunned and unable to speak for a moment, but one of her friends thought she heard her mutter under her breath, "I'd rather have a martini."

R e f e r e n c e s

Johns, J. L. (2001). *Basic reading inventory,* 8th ed. Dubuque, IA: Kendall/Hunt.

Macon, J. M., Bewell, D., & Vogt, M. (1991). *Responses to literature.* Newark, DE: International Reading Association.

Tiedt,I. (1970). Exploring poetry patterns. *Elementary English, 47,* 1083–1084.

Children's Books/Materials Cited

Amazing but True Sports Stories, by Phyllis Hollander & Zander Hollander, Scholastic, 1986.

Babe the Blue Ox.

Bawshou Rescues the Sun.

Below the Root, by Z. K. Snyder, Atheneum, 1975.

Buffalo: The American Bison Today, by D. H. Patent, Ticknor & Fields, 1986.

The Changeling, by Z. K. Snyder, Atheneum, 1970.

Charlotte's Web, by E. B. White, HarperCollins, 1974.

A Convention of Delegates, by D. J. Hautly, Atheneum, 1987.

Cricket magazine.

The Egypt Game, by Z. K. Snyder, Atheneum, 1967.

Gray Wolf, Red Wolf, by D. H. Patent, Houghton Mifflin, 1990.

Hades and Persephone.

Hailstones and Halibut Bones, by M. O'Neill, Doubleday, 1961.

Henry Huggins and other books, by B. Cleary, Avon, various dates.

Inside Pro Football, Scholastic, 1992.

Kid City magazine.

Kids Discover magazine.

National Geographic World magazine.

Never Say Quit, by Bill Wallace, Scholastic, 1992.

Overhead Transparencies for Creative Dramatics, by Creative Teaching Press, 1987.

Pecos Bill.

Penny Power magazine.

Ranger Rick magazine.

Sand Tiger Shark, by C. Carrick, Houghton Mifflin, 1991.

Scoop Snoops, by C. Hiser, Scholastic, 1986.

Sedna, an Eskimo Myth, by B. Brodsky, McDermott, 1975.

Sleeping Ugly, by J. Yolen, Coward, McCann & Geoghegan, 1981.

Snow White.

Song and Dance Man, by K. Ackerman, Knopf, 1992.

Sports Illustrated for Kids magazine.

Sports Shots Books, Scholastic, 1990.

Stellaluna.

Thank You, Jackie Robinson, by B. Cohen, Scholastic, 1989.

The Three Little Pigs.

3–2–1 Contact magazine.

When I Was Young in the Mountains, by C. Rylant, Dutton Children's Books, 1982.

Why the Sun and the Moon Live in the Sky, by E. Dayrell, Houghton Mifflin, 1990.

Winnie-the-Pooh stories, by A. A. Milne, Dell, 1987.

Zillions magazine.

Ms. Maverick:
Fourth Grade

. . . .

The Parent Meeting

Yetta Maverick greeted most of the parents by name as they entered the door of her fourth-grade classroom. Six years before, she had known no one and had missed the easy familiarity she had established with the residents of the small mountain community where she had taught during her first three years as a teacher.

"Welcome," she began. "As most of you know from our annual book fairs, I am Ms. Maverick. I am pleased to see so many parents here tonight. In many schools, there is a tremendous turnout of parents for the kindergarten and first-grade meetings, but attendance decreases as the grade level of the children increases. You are to be commended for your continuing interest in the education of your children.

"I want you to know that I think fourth-graders are the very best age to teach. Nine-year-olds are just so eager to learn—about everything—and they have the basic reading and writing skills that allow me to spend more class time on reading and writing to learn, rather than on learning to read and write. It's a good thing that your children have already come such a long way in their literacy journey, because as you may know, fourth grade is also the grade in which statewide tests are given in writing, science, and social studies. Some fourth-grade teachers resent this subject-area testing, but it actually plays right into what I like to teach. I love to learn about real things—history, geography, real people, how machines work, the planets, and geology have always fascinated me. When I was in fourth grade, I was going to be an oceanographer, and I read all the science-oriented books I could get my hands on. So expect to see your children coming home excited about, talking about, and collecting information about whatever our current science or social studies unit is."

As she spoke, Ms. Maverick handed out the following schedule:

	Monday	Tuesday	Wednesday	Thursday	Friday
8:30–9:00	Group Meeting and Planning for the Day Teacher Read-Aloud				
9:00–9:25	Self-Selected Reading and Individual Conferences				
9:25–10:20	Reading Workshop	Reading Workshop	Reading Workshop	Science or SS Unit	Science or SS Unit
10:20–10:40	Break/Recess				
10:40–11:40	Math	Math	Math	Science or SS Unit	Science or SS Unit
11:40–12:10	P. E.	Music	Art	P. E.	P. E.
12:10–12:45	Lunch	Lunch	Lunch	Lunch	Lunch
12:45–1:45	Writing Workshop	Writing Workshop	Writing Workshop	Science or SS Unit	Science or SS Unit
1:45–2:15	Words/Spelling	Words/Spelling	Words/Spelling	Science or SS Unit	Science or SS Unit
2:15–2:45/3:00	Centers/Projects/Individual and Small-Group Conferences				

"I want you to look at our schedule now," she continued, "because it is a bit different from that used by other teachers your children may have had. It has taken me many years of teaching fourth grade to come up with some structure that allows me to give all the essential components adequate time, and this is what works best for me. We start our morning with a planning meeting in which we talk about what we will be doing during the various times. I lead the children in a discussion of 'what we will accomplish today.' Too many children come to fourth grade just doing what they are told but without a clear sense of how what we're doing helps them become better learners or how they are adding to their understanding of how the world works. I want your children to approach the rest of the day in a purposeful way in which they see the various tasks as 'things that get them someplace'—not just 'things she told us to do.' So we will not just talk about what we are going to do when, but how and why and how doing this will help us be smarter and better learners.

"The second thing that will happen each day is that I will read to them. It amazes me to read statistics that say most intermediate teachers don't read to their children daily because they don't have time! I don't have enough time either, but reading to children is one of the major ways of motivating children to read, increasing their language and concepts, and helping them learn how you think as you read. Most of you know that thinking, feeling, and language are the underpinnings of reading and writing, and at Merritt, we take seriously the twelve guiding principles we all agreed to several years ago. Reading to children each day is one of the most important vehicles we have for building language, developing thinking, and encouraging a love of books. I try to read a great variety of books, but I must admit I prefer informational books—books that tell about real people, places, and happenings. I also tie some of my read-aloud books into our science and social studies units, thus getting a few more minutes of content time in. So, when you ask your children what I am reading to them, don't be surprised if they tell you things like 'a book about whales' or 'a biography of Rosa Parks.'

"Next, the children have their self-selected reading time. I schedule twenty-five minutes for this every day. This is a little long for some of your children this early in the year, so I have started with fifteen minutes and will increase gradually. Fourth-grade children can all read, but some are still not in the habit of sustaining their reading for long enough really to get into the book they are reading. Getting them to the point where they can sit and quietly read for twenty-five minutes is my goal, and I am sure we can do this at some point in the year. While your children read, I hold individual conferences with them. I conference with a fifth of your children each day. We only have three to four minutes for the conference, but you can accomplish quite a lot in that time, and when you multiply that times thirty-six weeks, that is a substantial amount of individual time during which I can touch base with every child every week, assessing reading strategies and encouraging individual reading interests.

"The other things that happen every day are our morning break or recess time, specials (which fourth grade has scheduled for 11:40 to 12:10), lunch, and our end-of-the day center or projects time." At this point, Mort's mother raised her hand, and Ms. Maverick acknowledged her.

"That's what I've been wondering about. I know that there is a lot to cover in fourth grade, and while I don't object to the children playing, I don't think they need thirty-plus minutes every day to play in the fourth grade."

Ms. Maverick bristled just a bit but tried to smile as she explained, "Center and project time are not playtime in this class. The activities the children do during this time are all connected to what we are learning and the skills we are working on. Sometimes the children are working in assigned centers, and sometimes they are making choices. Often, this is when they work on individual and group projects that come out of our science and social studies units. They do research and writing and work on drama and media projects to consolidate and then share what they have been learning. I got the idea of the end-of-day center time from Mrs. Wright, and I use that time to work with small groups and individuals while children pursue their own learning goals.

"Many of you know these twelve guiding principles, which the Merritt faculty came up with five years ago." Ms. Maverick pointed to a poster on her wall, on which the following statement was displayed.

At Merritt Elementary, we believe that all children can learn to read and write. We hold high expectations of every child. To make these expectations a reality, we all agree to have our instruction reflect twelve guiding principles:

1. Provide a balanced literacy program.
2. Make instruction multilevel.
3. Use language as the foundation for reading and writing.
4. Teach reading and writing as thinking.
5. Use feelings to create avid readers and writers.
6. Connect reading and writing to all subject areas.
7. Read aloud to students daily.
8. Schedule daily self-selected reading.
9. Have students write every day.
10. Teach the decoding and spelling strategies reading and writing require.
11. Use observation to assess learning and plan instruction.
12. Inform parents of expectations and progress.

"My center time helps me to achieve the first one and the second one. To me a balanced program means lots of things—a balance of types of materials the children read and write, a balance of whole-class, small-group, and individual arrangements, a balance between teacher decisions and children choices. Having the afternoon center time and the individual and group time it provides helps us to have a more balanced literacy program. It also helps me make it more multilevel. Your children are all fourth-graders, but their reading and writing levels span about six years. I make my instruction multilevel in a variety of ways, including having children choose material on their reading level during Self-Selected Reading and having them do writing at some point every day. They can only write on their own level, you know. The afternoon Center/Project time is another time when I can individualize what different children work on and help each child move along, regardless of where he or she begins."

Ms. Maverick glanced at the clock and saw that the meeting time was almost gone. "Trust me on this one for a month or so," she said. "Ask your children each day what they accomplished during the center/project time, and then see if you think they are just playing."

Quickly, Ms. Maverick explained the rest of the schedule and how the schedule helped her carry out the guiding principles. "All teachers have to follow state guidelines in terms of the amount of time given to each subject area. My schedule conforms to those guidelines, but I don't give the subjects equal time every day. Rather, I spend longer blocks of time on some days to equal the right number of minutes across the week. As you can see, our Monday, Tuesday, Wednesday schedule is different from Thursday and Friday. On Monday, Tuesday, and Wednesday, we have almost an hour of reading workshop, an hour for math, an hour for writing workshop, and thirty minutes to work on words and spelling. On Thursday and Friday, all that time is given to our science or social studies unit. This allows long periods of uninterrupted time to really get into the topics, and yet we still have separate times to make sure the fourth-grade reading, writing, and math curriculum requirements are being met.

The other thing that may not be so obvious is that we do read and write on our unit days. In fact, I teach many comprehension and focused-writing lessons on these days to help children learn the specific strategies required for informational text. Also, don't think science and social studies are forgotten on Monday, Tuesday, and Wednesday. Some of what we read during Reading Workshop and write during Writing Workshop is related to our units. Many of the big words we study and learn how to spell during our words time are connected to our units. In fact, I take very seriously principle number 6, which reminds us that we are committed to connecting reading and writing to all subject areas."

Ms. Maverick could hear parents from other rooms moving noisily through the hall on their way to the cafeteria for refreshments and the schoolwide meeting. She finished up by telling her group that she would be getting her first newsletter out to them soon and that she would be asking them to come in for individual conferences in about a month.

"Meanwhile, if you have any concerns about your child or how we 'do fourth grade,' our classroom door is always open, and I welcome your ideas and, yes, even your concerns!"

Monthly Logs

September

What an unusual class of children this is! I thought that in my ten years of teaching I had seen every possible combination of children, but this class disproves that theory. Of course, I expect to find great differences among children by the time they get to fourth grade, but I have never before seen the range represented by the span between Paul, who reads almost nothing, and Larry, who qualitatively reads almost as well as I do and quantitatively reads more than I do. Then there are the personality differences. Roberta cannot do the right thing no matter how hard she tries, and Betty, her twin sister, can't do anything wrong. Joyce and Hilda are both very capable, intelligent, and extremely independent.

I am pleased, however, with the adjustments most of the children have made to my program. I always enjoy getting Mrs. Wise's children because they have had so much experience working together in groups. It is still a shock to me to see Amah Young teaching in her room next door.

I am especially pleased with Daisy. According to her records, she just never got anything done. She is working now, although I think she is doing it for me rather than for herself. Each time she does anything, she comes to me for approval. I pat her on the head, because I want her to establish the habit of sitting down and accomplishing something, but I am trying to help her develop some internal feedback. Yesterday she brought me a picture she had painted. I said, "Yes, it is lovely. Didn't it feel good to do it?" I have a feeling this is going to be a year-long process, however; I have seldom seen a child with so little intrinsic motivation and self-confidence. For the moment, I am thankful that she is working for whatever reason. Paul is the weakest reader in the class. I will work individually with him during the afternoon time.

Mort is a pill! If I hear that child sigh and say, "Well, it doesn't matter. I don't care," one more time, I may lose my composure and shake him! I know, however, that I would be in trouble and it wouldn't do any good. Yesterday I said to him, "Mort, what do you like to do when you go home after school?"

He replied, "Oh, mostly I just sit around and get bored. Sometimes I watch television." As far as I can tell, he has no friends, no interests, and no aspirations. I guess I should think of him as "a real challenge."

I always begin the school year by doing some assessment of how well my children read and write and how they feel about reading and writing. I began by looking at the portfolios sent to me by Mrs. Wise. It is always enlightening to look at the three writing samples she has the children do on the same topic. It encourages me when I see how Paul, Daisy, Jeff, Butch, and Tanana developed in their writing with Mrs. Wise's excellent instruction. I figure if they grew that much last year, they will certainly continue to develop with all the writing I plan for them this year. Even the writing of the best writers, Larry, Pat, and Hilda, showed remarkable growth across third grade, just proving once again that even bright, able, motivated, industrious children profit from good instruction. As I was looking through these writing samples in their portfolios, I was reminded once again of Mrs. Wright's contention that Writing is the most multilevel block.

I got a beginning-of-the-year writing sample from the children, using the same procedures Mrs. Wise uses but on the topic of "My Favorite and Least Favorite Things." I looked at these and compared them to their May third-grade sample. The writing of most children remained fairly stable across the summer, although the most struggling writers showed some regression, and Mort wrote almost nothing. It appears he has no real favorites—or "unfavorites."

Mrs. Wise also indicated their reading levels at the end of third grade. All but Paul, Daisy, Tanana, and Butch were reading at or above fourth-grade level on the IRI, with Daisy, Tanana, and Butch reading just one year below level and Paul reading two years below. This was consistent with the standardized test results from last year, which showed that all the children except these four—and Mort, who probably didn't bother to read the test—read above the 50th percentile, with Larry, Pat, Hilda, and Roberta knocking the top off the test! I had Paul, Daisy, Tanana, Butch, and Mort read to me the first two pages in the first selection of our adopted reader and took an oral reading record as they read. Then I closed the book and asked them to retell the beginning of the story. Mort read it fine and clearly understood it, although it was like pulling teeth to get him to tell me. Butch had trouble with 11 out of the approximately 200 words, and his retelling was spotty. Tanana read very slowly but only missed four words. She had trouble retelling the story, but when I probed, she knew more than she could express. Daisy read "like a house on fire," missing fifteen words and never stopping to look back. Not surprisingly, she wasn't able to tell me very much of what she had read. I had her go back, however, and forced her to read one sentence at a time, and she then did correct several of her errors and was able to tell me more. I concluded that Butch, Tanana, and Daisy, though a little under the criteria for instructional-level reading, could profit from reading in fairly easy fourth-grade-level material (the first selection is a little easier than the later ones) if they were given a lot of support from me or a partner. Who will be willing to be Daisy's partner is another question! Paul, on the other hand, is not able to approach reading at fourth-grade level. I stopped him at the end of the first page, and I read the second page to him. I don't know how well he comprehended, because he doesn't talk to me very much. I will have to have him with me or find him a very supportive partner whenever we are in Reading Workshop, and I am reading with him alone in books on his level each afternoon for ten minutes during our Center/Project time.

My attempts to assess their reading and writing interests were quite successful. I told them that we were going to read some—but not all—of the selections in our adopted reader. I also told them that we were not going to read them in the order they were in the book but were going to skip around. "I need your help," I said, "to decide which ones we will read and which ones to start with." I then gave everyone a sheet on which I had listed all the major selections in the book. We spent three days during Reading Workshop previewing and talking about the selections. We identified the author, and I asked the children if they had ever read any books by that author. They got quite excited when they recognized selections by Judy Blume, Eloise Greenfield, and Chris Van Allsburg. We identified each type of selection. Most of the children seem to prefer stories, mysteries being particularly popular. They were less enthusiastic about the informational selections, including biographies. We looked at the pictures of each major selection and predicted what it would be about. We read the shorter selections—poetry and brief magazine-type articles as we got to them. Finally, after previewing all the selections, I asked the students to rank each on a 0–3 scale, with 0 meaning, "I don't want to read it" and 3 meaning, "I really want to read it soon." We tallied up the scores; *Tales of a Fourth*

Grade Nothing by Judy Blume, *Jumanji* by Chris Van Allsburg, and all three mysteries contained in the book got the most points. All the selections got some votes, with the social studies informational pieces and biographies bringing up the rear.

Because their reading interest was so high, we began our Reading Workshop with *Tales of a Fourth Grade Nothing* one week and *Jumanji* the next week. For the third and fourth weeks, I gathered up copies of two other Blume and three other Van Allsburg books and used the procedure I learned from Mrs. Wise of reading to students the first few pages of each book and then having them indicate their first, second, and third choice for what they wanted to read. They were quite excited about this and a bit amazed I knew how to do it! "I bet she stole the book club idea from Mrs. Wise," Roberta remarked. Looking at their choices, I formed five groups, putting the children who needed help in the easiest book if that was one of their choices and the more advanced readers in the harder book if they had chosen it. I was amazed when I read Daphne's choice response. It read,

> Dear Ms. Maverick,
>   I would like to read all the books so it doesn't matter but if I could I would like to be with Paul. I have been helping him read since first grade and even though he is still not too good, he is much better than he was. If you put me in his group, I will help him and he will be able to read it.
>   Sincerely,
>   Daphne Sweet
>   P.S. Mrs. Wise always let me be in the same group as Paul.

You learn something every day when you give children choices and ask for their opinions. I have been wondering how to handle Paul during Reading Workshop, and all of a sudden, here comes Daphne, ready, willing, and able!

I learned a lot about my children's attitudes toward reading and particular reading interests through having them survey different types of texts and make choices about what they like. I am also learning through our Self-Selected Reading conferences. I have divided the children into fifths according to the days of the week, an idea I learned from Mrs. Wright, as Roberta pointed out to everyone. (I think Roberta is beginning to wonder if I have any teaching ideas of my own, but she will soon find out I do!) Each day, once they are all settled in their spots with plenty of things to read within arm's reach (we have a No Wandering rule during Self-Selected Reading time), the five children who are designated that day of the week come for a brief conference. We have the routines pretty well established now. The children come in alphabetical order (we will reverse that halfway through the year), and each child gets three to four minutes. To prepare for our weekly conference, they have learned to follow these rules:

1. Choose a book you like and can read.
2. Pick two pages from the book to read aloud to me.

3. Be ready to tell me what you like about this book and why you chose these two pages.

4. If you have not finished the book, tell me what you expect will happen or what you might learn.

5. If you have finished the book, tell me what kind of book you are thinking about sharing with me next week.

I have role-played this with the children and put these on a "Getting Ready for Your Own Special Conference" poster. During the conference, I make anecdotal records for all the children of the book they bring, how well they read and understand it, why they chose that book, and their plans for next week. We have only had two weeks of conferences, but most children are getting the idea and seem to like the fact that they are the ones in charge of their conference.

Their feelings toward writing are on the whole quite positive. We talked about writing and what they had written in one of our first morning planning meetings. I invited them to bring any published pieces they could find at home, and I was amazed at how many they brought. Most of them had all three published books from first grade and some pieces published in various ways from second and third grades. They are clearly used to writing on their own topics, and they seem eager to pick a piece to publish, which we will get up and running next month. Just as with reading, they seem more comfortable writing personal narratives about themselves and stories than with informational writing. I am letting them choose what they want to write and publish now, but as the year goes on, we will do some focused-writing activities in which they will learn to write descriptive and informational pieces.

While we have not actually begun the social studies unit on our state yet, we have done some readiness activities in preparation for this unit. One of the concepts that is very difficult for children to grasp is the notion of time and sequence. Last year I had my class construct a time line showing the important events in our state and their corresponding dates. Although the children learned from this activity, it was very difficult for them to conceptualize the differences in time. Last year's class never understood that the spaces between the depicted events were proportional to the actual time elapsed between these events.

In order to provide readiness for the state time line and to help the children apply time passage and sequence to their own lives, I had the children make a time line depicting the important events in their lives. I began by having the children put their chairs in a circle and asking them to call up the important things that had happened in their lives. The children were all eager to respond, and everyone had something to share, since the subject was one they all knew lots about. Rita recalled her first trip to the library, when the librarian told her she was too young to have a library card. Tanana remembered moving here from Alaska and how scared she was when she first came to Mrs. Wise's classroom. Larry recalled the first Hardy Boys book he had read. When all the children had contributed something to the discussion, I suggested that we might create some "life lines" to show all the important events that had already taken place in their lives. I showed them how we could use string and little slips of paper with words and illustrations to depict our individual histories.

The children were most enthusiastic, so we began right then. I gave each of the children a long sheet of paper and asked them to put their birth date in the top left corner and the current date in the bottom left corner. Although many of the children knew the month and day on which they were born, only Larry, Pat, and Hilda knew the year of their birth. I then asked the others how they thought they could figure out the year in which they were born. After some discussion, they worked out the mechanics of subtracting how old they were from the current date and filled in the year on the chart they were making. In the meantime, I modeled by making my chart on the board. Next to my birth date, I wrote "Ms. Maverick was born" and next to the current date, I wrote "Ms. Maverick is helping her class to make their own life lines." The children then followed my example and put appropriate entries next to their own names.

They then listed the important events in their lives. I told them not to worry too much at this point about the date or the order but just try to get down about eight to ten events. Most children had no trouble at all listing a dozen events. Paul, however, needed a great deal of help with this, and I fear his life line represents my thinking more than his. When the children had finished listing the events, I asked them how they thought we could find out the approximate date of each event. Several suggested their parents kept lists of everything, and that if they could take the charts home that night, they could fill in many of the dates. The others suggested they could fill in by knowing in what order things happened in relation to the events with known dates.

The next day they returned with dates and many more events filled in on their charts. We then cut the charts and organized the events into the proper order. Next began the construction of the actual life lines. Since all of the children in the class were either eight or nine years old, we decided to cut the strings either nine or ten feet long. In that way, each foot could represent a year. Any events that happened in the same year would be placed close to one another. If there were a year or two in which no events occurred, that would be represented by the unfilled space for that year. We also agreed that because we were going to hang these around the room for others to read, we should try to spell the words correctly and to use readable handwriting. Each child then measured and cut his or her string and marked it off in one-foot lengths. They also cut and measured strips of colored paper to three-by-six-inch dimensions. While the children were doing this, I acted as editor, helping children correct the spelling and punctuation on their charted events so that they could copy them correctly on their life line slips.

Somehow, it all got done! The children illustrated the events and taped the slips to the strings. Those who finished first helped the others. The life lines now hang below the windows and the chalkboards, and whenever the children have a spare moment, they can be seen reading their own or someone else's life history. This activity, which started out as readiness for our state's time line, had value in and of itself. The children helped one another and learned more about one another.

They learned that we share many common experiences and that other experiences are unique to each individual. They do seem to have a better sense of time sequence and proportion, and they have certainly practiced their math, reading, and writing skills. I will do this again next year!

The other readiness activity this month was constructing a map of the school. We will do a lot of work with maps when we begin the actual study of our state next month, and for many children this is their first exposure to maps. I wanted them to connect maps to their own life space before asking them to generalize to the less tangible world outside. After a discussion about maps and what would be involved in constructing a map of our school, we walked around the whole building to observe what we would include in our map. The children suggested, and I listed on the board, all the things we might want to include in a map of our school. I then grouped the children in pairs, and each pair took responsibility for going to a particular classroom or area of the building, measuring that area, and constructing that part of the map. When all the children reassembled with their measurements, we measured the total length and width of the building and then decided what proportion of that length and width the various rooms comprised. For a while, it looked as if we had a lot less total space in what we had measured than what there actually was in the building. Larry was the one who realized we had forgotten to consider the space taken up by the hallways. After measuring these, we were able to decide on a scale. Each pair of children cut from colored paper the model for the room or area they had measured and labeled it appropriately. We then pasted the individual rooms on a piece of appropriately sized poster board and, six days after we started, had our map of the school. Well, actually, we had it for only a day or two before it was commandeered! Mr. Topps noticed it when he came in to visit and remarked that we had done a first-rate job and that this map was just the thing he needed to hang outside the office so that visitors could find their way around. He asked if he could borrow it for a while. The children all autographed it, and it now hangs outside the office.

October

As long as I can remember, October has been my favorite month. When I was a child I loved October because my birthday came in October. In college, October meant football games and rallies. Now that I am a teacher, October is the month in which my new class "gels"; the children have learned the routines and we start to accomplish things. I love accomplishing things—checking them off my list—and this desire to accomplish things is beginning to show in most of my children.

All the students, even Mort and Butch, really seem to look forward to my morning read-alouds. This month, I read *Fourth Grade Is a Jinx* by Colleen O'Shaughnessy McKenna, and *Anastasia on Her Own* by Lois Lowry. I also read relevant parts about our state from Wilma Ross's *Fabulous Facts about the 50 States* and two books just about our state.

We are now having a full twenty minutes of Self-Selected Reading time each day. The children come on their scheduled day, and most have done their preparation for the conference. I remember that when I first taught and tried to have conferences, I tried to prepare for each conference. It was impossible to read all the books my fourth-graders were reading and to figure out what to ask them. Finally, one day, I realized that I was doing all the thinking, planning, and organizing that the children should be doing, and I began devising ways to make the conference truly their conference. My five rules for getting a conference ready are taken seriously by almost all my children, and I now look forward to my short but purposeful conference with each of them every week. I follow their lead, encourage their reading tastes, observe their reading strategies, and find out more about them as people. The only thing that worries me is, what other routines could I establish that would both make my job easier and give students more ownership and control over their own learning? I'm sure there are things I am still not doing that would help me move students toward more personal responsibility and accountability. I think I will talk with Kenny about this over the weekend. He teaches at the middle school and is constantly trying to move students along in these areas.

Both reading and writing workshops are going well. We read the three mysteries from our anthology together, and then children chose from five mysteries of which I had multiple copies. I really worked on the comprehension strategies of following sequence and drawing conclusions during this mystery unit. Each day, after reading one section, we would list the major things that had happened in the correct order, make predictions for what would happen next, and list the clues that led us to these predictions. I appointed everyone detectives, and everyone seemed to enjoy taking on this new role. Larry and Hilda especially enjoyed our mystery unit and are reading Sherlock Holmes books during Self-Selected Reading—mysteries that are much too difficult for typical fourth-graders, but not for Larry and Hilda.

We have begun our revising/editing/publishing process during our Writing Workshop. My rule is that they can sign up to publish when they have three good first drafts. Each day, as we begin the workshop, I gather the children who think they are ready to publish. The number varies each day, but the procedure is the same. They bring me their writing notebook, show me the three first drafts, and indicate the one they have chosen to publish. I look quickly to make sure they do have three "good" first drafts. Some children really want to publish everything, so they write one good first draft and then dash off two others to try to fool me. I inform them that I have been teaching fourth grade since before they were born and I know a "dashed off" piece when I see one. I tell them that I understand they want to publish quickly, but rules are rules, and they must write three good pieces and then pick one. I then send them back to their desks and tell them I look forward to seeing them again soon, when they have three good first drafts. Of course, what is "good" for Hilda differs from what is "good" for Tanana, but you can still tell when a reasonable effort has been made—and when it hasn't.

Once any "slackards" have been dispatched back to their desks, I work with the children on revising their pieces. I explain to the children that what authors write is sent out for review, and the reviewers tell what they like, ask questions about things they don't understand, and make suggestions. I use the mnemonic TAG to help the children remember what helpful reviewers do. In fact, I have a poster on which I have written:

> To be a helpful reviewer, listen carefully and then:
>   Tell what you liked.
>   Ask questions about what you didn't understand.
>   Give suggestions for making the published book terrific.

As each child reads the piece aloud, we all (I and the other soon to be published authors) listen carefully, and then I tell something I liked and invite the others to do the same.

> "I liked how you make it funny by telling how your mom tricked you."
> "I liked the part where you realized this was a surprise party for you."
> "I liked how you ended it."

Next, I ask a question and invite other children to ask questions if there is anything they were unclear about or something else they would like to know:

> "How did your mother keep this a surprise if all the stuff was set up in
>   the dining room?"
> "How many kids came to the party?"
> "What did you get for presents?"

I serve as recorder for this, writing down our questions and any answers the author provides. Next, I try to give a helpful suggestion and ask if anyone else has suggestions:

> "Perhaps you need to do more at the beginning with the setting, de-
>   scribe the dining room set for the party, and then describe you being
>   'grounded' to clean the garage."
> "Why don't you name the kids as they are quietly sneaking in the back
>   door?"
> "You could use better words to show how mad you were about being
>   grounded—like 'furious' or 'really bummed out.'"

Again, I record the suggestions and hand this record to the author. We are now ready to listen well to the next author, think of what we could say when it is our turn to tell the author what we liked, ask questions, and give suggestions.

After the children who are ready to publish have their revising suggestions, they return to their desks to make any revisions needed. I always have them write on every other line in their notebooks so that they have space to add things, cross things out, and put carets (∧) where they are going to insert longer chunks. I have shown them how to write any new parts on a separate sheet of paper ready to insert in the correct place.

Next, I turn my attention to the children whose piece is ready for me to play editor-in-chief. After revising their piece, each child picks a friend to help him or her edit for the things on the current checklist. We have been adding these gradually, and I have been modeling the process by choosing someone to "be my editing friend" and help me edit the piece I write every day in my minilesson at the beginning of writing workshop. Currently, our editing checklist looks like this:

1. Do all the sentences make sense?
2. Do all the sentences start with caps and end with punc?
3. Do all people and place names have caps?
4. Do all the sentences stay on the topic?
5. Does the piece have a beginning, middle, and end?
6. Are words I need to check the spelling of underlined?

Once the child, with the help of a friend, has done some self-editing for the things on the checklist, I give the piece a final edit. Then the child goes over to one of the computers and uses our publishing program to type and format the piece. Adding the illustrations is the final step. Some children draw by hand, but many use the computer drawing tools, and they all love finding appropriate clip art.

Currently, the children are in all different stages of writing, revising, editing, and publishing. Larry, Butch, Roberta, Hilda, and Tanana have finished their first published piece and are now back writing three good first drafts. I keep up with where they all are by having them put their cards in the appropriate slot of my writing steps chart.

Working on three good first drafts	Ready for revising conf.	Revising	Editing with a friend	Ready for editor-in-chief conf.	Publishing
Larry	Betty	Anthony	Mort	Alexander	Pat
Butch	Alex	Carl	Paul	Mandy	Mitch
Roberta	Daisy	Steve	Rita	Jeff	Manuel
Hilda	Joyce			Danielle	Horace
Tanana	Chip				Daphne

We are now off and running on our state unit. Each unit actually has three overlapping phases. At the beginning, I provide the children with a great deal of input from many different sources. During most of this first phase, we work together as a whole class, building some interest and motivation for the unit, becoming familiar with new and specialized vocabulary terms, and discovering enough information so that we can begin to raise some questions to which we can seek answers. During the second phase of the unit, while we continue many whole-class activities, the children are also doing extensive reading, listening, and viewing, either individually or in small groups. Finally, they engage in several culminating activities that help them to organize and synthesize the information gained during the unit.

Throughout the unit, we do a variety of activities designed to foster concept development and to increase the store of words for which they have rich meanings. As much as possible, I try to provide direct experience for concept and meaning-vocabulary development. We take field trips to the source of real places, objects, people, and events, and the children and I are always on the lookout for things to bring into the classroom that will make new words and unfamiliar concepts real to us. Of course, we cannot go to see everything or bring it into the classroom, so I rely on pictures, videos, websites, and other media to build concepts and help develop their language foundation. When I introduce new vocabulary to the children, I always try to put these words in topical word sets. During our state unit, I will begin topical word sets for maps, state government, and places to visit. I display these words in the room, along with appropriate pictures, and the children learn to read and spell them as well as develop rich meanings for them.

My kickoff motivator for this unit was a large white outline map of our state, which I had drawn by projecting the image of an overhead transparency map onto the bulletin board at the rear of the room. After tracing the projected image, I cut along the outline and stapled the giant white map to the red-backed bulletin board. I did this all late one night (with Kenny's help) so that the children's attention would be drawn immediately to the giant blank white map against the bright red background. They noticed it immediately and were intrigued by its size and blankness. Several correctly guessed that it was an outline map of our state. I had the children move their chairs closer to the board and began to lead them in a discussion of our state. Little by little, in response to their comments and questions, I wrote the name of a particular landmark in its proper location. I let the children help me decide where these landmarks should go by consulting several maps that I spread out on the floor as we talked. At the end of this initial motivating session, we had (1) located our town, the state capital, several other cities, lakes, and rivers, (2) talked about what went on at the capital and began to use words such as *governor, lieutenant governor, legislators, laws,* and *taxes,* (3) used directional words such as *north, south, east,* and *west* and noted these directions above, below, and on the appropriate sides of our map, and (4) begun to discuss various places that the children had lived, visited, or had some other connection with.

I told them that as we studied our state, we would use again and again many of the words we had used in our talk. They would need to be able to read the words in order to find out more about our state, and they would need to be able to spell them in order to be able to write about it. Mitch, Jeff, and Daisy didn't look too happy at the thought of additional work, so I smiled reassuringly as I picked up a black marker and several half sheets of different-colored construction paper and let them help me remember the "special" words we had used that morning. I then let them watch me print these words on the colored slips of paper. As I was doing so, I remarked about the relative length and distinct features of the words, pronounced the words carefully, and had the children pronounce each word after me. I then had Mitch climb on a chair and tape the words to the wall above the bulletin board. I noted that we had eleven words to start with, and that we would add more as we continued to study about our state. I then prepared the children for our following morning's activities by showing them a little color-headed pin and a triangular-shaped slip of paper. On the triangular slip, I printed the following in tiny letters:

Ms. Maverick
was born
here.

Then I pinned this slip to our map high in the northwestern corner.

Next to the pinned flag, I wrote the name of the community in which I was born. The children were fascinated and all wanted to make little flags. I assured them that that was tomorrow's activity and that in the meantime they should look at the maps and try to figure out places they had been to or knew of, so that we could put flags on the map for them. I also suggested that they talk with their parents and perhaps even look at a map with them to determine such family history information as their parents' birthplaces, where aunts and uncles lived, and the names and locations of places they had visited. For the rest of the day, there was always someone at the back of the room looking at our giant map and investigating the smaller ones that I had placed on a table under the bulletin board.

The next day the children came bursting into the room loaded with maps and family histories they had brought from home. We immediately gathered in the back of the room, and the children began to spread out their maps, sharing the information they had with one another and trying to locate the places they wanted to flag on our giant map. While still giant, our map was no longer blank. It was covered with place names and flags, all of which the children had some personal affiliation with. We even had a flag marking the city to which their former classmate Mike had moved. Mrs. Flame would be happy to see that. She still worries about how Mike is doing. We also added the names of several neighboring towns and a few lakes and rivers to our state vocabulary.

The interest and excitement generated by the giant map motivator has grown throughout this month, as has the number of words in our state vocabulary. We now have thirty-two words up there, and as I use these words again and again in different contexts, I try to remember to point to the words and remind the children of the other contexts in which we used them. We take ten minutes during our afternoon words/spelling time to practice these words. Each child takes out a sheet of paper and writes the numbers 1 to 10 in a column. I then call out ten of the words on the wall. As I call each word, the children are allowed, and indeed encouraged, to look up at the wall, find the word, and then write it on their papers. The trick to this technique is that they are not actually to copy the words; they must look up and then down at their papers and then up again, taking a mental image of the word and then reproducing this mental image. When all ten words have been called out, the children check their own papers by chanting the spelling of each word. Most days, all the children get nine or ten right, and because they are so successful at it, they love to do it. The other day during recess it rained, and when they were trying to decide on an indoor game, Horace suggested that we do the spelling words again! I couldn't believe it, but that's what they "played," with Horace being the teacher and calling out the words. From now on, once the children are very familiar with the words, as they are now, I shall let the children take turns "being teacher" and calling out the words. Strange—I always think I am allowing the children as much participation as possible and then discover something else I am doing that the children could benefit from doing too.

I have done several comprehension lessons this month during our Thursday/Friday unit time. Through these lessons, I help them increase their knowledge about our state and work on increasing their vocabularies and improving their comprehension skills at the same time. For some lessons, I select part of a newspaper or magazine article or a short selection from a book and type it on my computer in large print. I then run the typed sheet through the copying machine to make a transparency. Using my overhead projector for comprehension lessons has several advantages: if the passage I select is unusually difficult to read, I can change a few of the words or omit sections to make it more readable. I don't waste a lot of paper making twenty-five copies of the same thing, and I can focus the attention of the children where I want it. I do, however, always show the children the source of the original article so that they know that what they are reading is "something real."

I begin my preparation for the lesson by identifying any words or concepts I think will present difficulty for many of my children. I make a distinction between unknown words and unfamiliar concepts. In the first directed reading lesson, for example, the subject was "things to do in our state." I had taken this article from the magazine section of the Sunday newspaper. Two concepts that I thought would not be familiar to most of my children were *rapids* and *currents*. In both cases, most of my children would probably be able to identify the words but would not have a meaning for those words appropriate to the particular contexts in which they were being used. The word *current* they might associate with the term *current events*, and for *rapids*, while they might have the concept of speed, they would probably not readily associate this concept with fast-moving water.

In addition to the two relatively unfamiliar concepts, *current* and *rapids,* I also identified several words for which most of my children would have listening-meaning concepts but would not be able to identify in print. These unknown words for the "things to do in our state" selection included *reflection* and *parachute.* In both cases, I was quite sure that the children would have a concept for these words once they were able to identify them but doubted that the "big word decoding skills" of most of my children would allow them to figure out the pronunciation of these familiar concepts but unknown words.

Having identified several unfamiliar concepts and unknown words, I then decided what to do about them. Sometimes, I build meanings for unfamiliar concepts or tell them the pronunciation of unknown words before they read the story. More often, however, I alert the children to the existence of these unfamiliar concepts or unknown words and challenge them to see if they can figure out what a word is or what the concept means as they read the selection. This encourages the children to use the context to figure out the meaning or pronunciation of words. This is what I did with *current, rapids, reflection,* and *parachute.* I wrote these four words on the board and asked a volunteer to pronounce *current* and *rapids.* Betty gladly pronounced them. I then asked them if anyone could give me a meaning for *current* or *rapids.* Manuel suggested that current has something to do with electricity and Steve said that it means "like in current events." For *rapids,* Roberta said that "without the *s* it means fast." I told them that the definitions they had given were right, but that, as I hoped they knew, words have many different meanings and that the words *current* and *rapids* in the selection we were about to read had meanings different from the ones they knew. I then told them that, as they were reading the selection, I wanted them to see if they could figure out what these different meanings might be. I hinted to them that the other words and sentences near the words *current* and *rapids* would give them the clues they needed to solve the mystery.

To add another element of mystery, I pointed to *reflection* and *parachute* and told the children *not* to pronounce the words. I told them that these two words were different from *current* and *rapids* in that they knew what these second two words meant but might not recognize them in print. I suggested that as with *current* and *rapids,* the words close to *reflection* and *parachute* would allow them to solve the mystery. Once the children had read the selection, they explained what they thought *current* and *rapids* meant in this context, identified the other words that had let them figure that out, and compared these meanings for the words with the meanings they already knew. Many of the children had also figured out the unknown words, *reflection* and *parachute,* and explained which other words had led them to solve the mystery.

Having identified and decided what to do about unknown words or unfamiliar concepts, I then decided for what purpose I was going to have the children read the selection. In a comprehension strategy lesson, my goal is always that the children are better at reading for a specific purpose after reading the selection than they were prior to reading the selection. Sometimes I work on improving their literal comprehension. I may decide that after reading the selection, we will put the events of the selection in order, or that we will read in order to answer the fact questions: Who? What? When? Where? How? For other selections, I may decide that we will work on being able to state main ideas in our own words.

I teach many lessons designed to sharpen the children's inferential comprehension ability. In these lessons, I show them only a portion of the text and ask them to predict what will happen next. I write these predictions on the board and let the children vote to decide which one they consider most likely to occur. I then display enough of the text so that they can check their predictions. Finally, I ask the children who made the correct prediction to read me the words in the passage that allowed them to make the correct prediction. In this way, the children who are not very good at inferring see that inferences are based on something that is directly stated in the text.

The first year I taught, I referred to inferential comprehension as "reading between the lines." One day, I watched one boy squinting at his book and then peering over the shoulder of the boy in front of him who could "read between the lines." It suddenly occurred to me that, from a child's vantage point, it was conceivable that he believed there was something between the lines that he couldn't see or that was only between the lines of other people's books. Since then I have stopped using that particular phrase. I have begun to ask those who can make inferences to point out the words in the text on which they based their inferences. This allows the children who can't make inferences to begin to observe the way the process works in the minds of those who can.

For the "things to do in our state" lesson, I decided to focus the children's attention on the main ideas of each paragraph. I displayed only the portion of the text that mentioned a particular place and asked the children to read so that when they finished they could tell me in a sentence what the main attraction was at each place. First, I let the children read silently. When most appeared to have finished, I let a volunteer read the section aloud. In this way, Paul and others whose reading skills are still limited could get the content of the selection and participate in the comprehension activity.

After each section was read silently and then orally, I asked a child to tell me in one sentence what the main thing was that people went there to see. I then made a list on the board that gave each place name and the sentence describing its main attraction. When we had completed reading about the eight places, I read over the list I had made on the board and pointed out to the children that, in addition to stating the main attraction, these sentences were also the main ideas of each paragraph. Main ideas, like main attractions, are the most important ideas (attractions), the ideas (attractions) most people would like to remember after reading (visiting) a paragraph (place). While we will continue to work on identifying and stating main ideas all year, this lesson was a good one to begin with because it helped to make the concept of main idea a little more concrete.

As a follow-up to this comprehension lesson, I put the children in eight cooperative groups. Each group was to make a flag for one of the eight places we had read about, write the place name and the main attraction on the flag, locate the place using the ever-growing supply of maps we now have in the room, and pin the flag to our giant map, which was no longer blank.

We have taken our first field trip this month, to visit the local newspaper. I bring daily copies of both the local and capital newspapers to school each morning, and since we began the unit on our state, the children have become quite interested in them. Before we took the field trip, I had the children put their chairs in a circle, and we began to talk about the local newspaper and to formulate some questions to ask Ms. Daley, the editor. I listed these questions on a large sheet of chart paper, and on our return we checked the chart to see how many of our questions had been answered.

The receptionist took us on a tour around the buildings and then took us to Ms. Daley's office. The children behaved very well, and because they had discussed and planned before coming, asked some very good questions. I was just beginning to relax and pat myself on the back for preparing them so well when the inevitable happened. A reporter came into Ms. Daley's office with some copy. She introduced him to the children and asked them if they had any questions. Hilda asked him a question about a story she had read recently in the paper, and as he was answering her question, he turned to Ms. Daley and said, "Why don't you take them down into the morgue and show them some of the dead ones?" Roberta's head twitched with excitement; Betty screamed! The reporter quickly explained that the newspaper morgue had "dead" newspapers, not dead bodies, while Mrs. Smith and I consoled Betty. A striking example of the multiple meanings of common words!

We went into the morgue and spent a long time there. Ms. Daley showed us the newspapers that recorded such historic events as the end of the Civil War, the Lincoln and Kennedy assassinations, and the state's celebration of its one-hundredth birthday. She pointed out the difference between history books that are written long after the actual events have occurred and newspaper accounts that are written immediately. She also pointed out how newspapers are one very important source of historical data. The children were particularly impressed when she showed them a copy of a biography of a famous general and explained that the writer of that book had spent many days in this very morgue doing research about our town where this general had grown up.

Upon our return from the newspaper, we looked at our collected data, computed the mileages and times, decided that the shortest route in distance was not the quickest route, and discussed reasons why this was so. We also looked to see which of our questions had been answered and decided that six had been answered quite thoroughly, three partially, and two not at all. Finally, I did a focused-writing lesson in which, after I had modeled, each child composed a short letter to Ms. Daley thanking her for her time and telling her what he or she had found most interesting about the visit. Here is Roberta's letter:

Dear Ms. Daley,
Thank you for letting us come down to visit your newspaper. There was lots to see and I can only apologize for Betty's screaming in your office. She is always doing things like that and I can't understand why. The dead newspapers were interesting but I would have liked to have

seen some dead bodies since I never have. Being a newspaper lady I bet you have seen hundreds of them.

Sincerely
Roberta Smith

November

During Reading Workshop this month, we read a science fiction selection from our anthology, and then they chose from a variety of science fiction books of which I had multiple copies. I read to them the classic science fiction title *A Wrinkle in Time* by Madeline L'Engle. Clearly, this unit has increased their interest in science fiction. Looking over my conference sheets from last week, I see that over half the children brought a science fiction book. I am quite pleased with the balance I have established between teacher-decided reading and student choice reading. By making sure to include a wide variety of genres, authors, and topics in what I read aloud to them and what we read during Reading Workshop, I make sure they are familiar with and know how to read all different kinds of books. Letting them choose their books for our daily Self-Selected Reading time helps them develop their own particular reading interests—but those interests broaden when they have experienced everything available. Hopefully, I will even turn some of them on to social studies informational books and biography once I have read more of those to them and we have read some during Reading Workshop. I have put those off until later in the year, because they are more motivated when I begin with what they already like. But we will get to them in the new year.

I have been doing some "What Looks Right?" (Cunningham & Hall, 1998) lessons during our afternoon Words/Spelling time. Looking at their spelling in their first-draft writing, I was pleased to note that almost all my children spell by pattern, rather than "one letter, one sound," the way most younger children do. In English, however, there are often two common spelling patterns for the same rhyme. That there are two patterns is not a problem when you are reading. If you are reading and you come to the unknown words *plight* and *trite,* you can easily figure out their pronunciation by accessing the pronunciation associated with other *ight* or *ite* words you can read and spell. It is a problem, however, when you are trying to spell. If you were writing and trying to spell *trite* or *plight,* they could as easily be spelled *t-r-i-g-h-t* and *p-l-i-t-e.* The only way to know which is the correct spelling is to write it one way and see if it "looks right" or check your probable spelling in a dictionary. "What Looks Right?" lessons help students learn how to use these two important self-monitoring spelling strategies.

For the first lesson, I chose the *ite-ight* pattern. I headed two columns on the board with two words my students could all spell, but with the different patterns, *bite* and *fight.* I had students draw two columns on their papers and set them up just like mine.

bite   *fight*

Next, I had students say these words and notice that they rhyme but don't have the same spelling pattern. I explain to students that in English, using a rhyming word to read another word will work almost all the time, but that spelling is more complicated because some rhymes have two common spellings. "Good spellers use rhyming patterns but also have a visual checking strategy. After writing a little-used word, they look at it to see if it looks right. If it doesn't look right, good spellers try to think of another rhyming word with a different spelling pattern and write that one to see if it looks right. Finally, if you need to be sure of the spelling, you look it up in a dictionary by looking for it the way you think it is spelled." I explained that the activity we were going to do is called "What Looks Right?" and would help them learn to check their own spelling the way good spellers do.

"I am going to say some words that rhyme with *bite* and *fight* and write them using both spelling patterns," I told them. "Your job is to decide which one looks right to you and write only that one. As soon as you have written it the way you think it is spelled, I want you to find it in the dictionary to prove your spelling is correct. The first word I will write is *kite*. If *kite* is spelled like *bite*, it will be *k-i-t-e*, if it is spelled like *right*, it will be *k-i-g-h-t*." As I was saying this, I was writing these two possible spellings in the appropriate columns. Most of the students recognized the correct spelling immediately and wrote *kite* under *bite*. They then found *kite* in the dictionary and proved it and I crossed out *kight*.

I did a few more examples with words that most of them were familiar with—*tight, white,* and *quite*. The students clearly enjoyed getting these right and then finding the words that proved it. I let students sitting near each other look up the words together if they had chosen the same spelling. Next, I wrote a few words that were less familiar to them—*spite, fright,* and *flight*. Many of the students were less sure about these, and I pointed out that if they hadn't seen these words several times and noticed their spelling, they would just have to guess at one and see if they could find it in the dictionary. If they couldn't find it the way they had guessed, they looked for the other pattern and found it and changed the spelling on their papers. When words time was up for that day, my chart looked like this:

bite	*fight*
kite	~~kight~~
~~bite~~	tight
white	~~white~~
quite	~~quight~~
~~flite~~	flight
spite	~~spight~~
~~frite~~	fright

Because words time was up for that day and I wanted to continue the lesson tomorrow, I had the children initial their papers ("Busy people don't have time to write out full names on working papers") and clipped their papers to the chart.

The following day, after we had spent a few minutes practicing the spelling of our unit spelling words, I quickly handed out the papers, calling them by initials. RJS—Roberta June Smith—grabbed hers. BAS went to Betty Ann Smith. Some children put only two initials—Mort claims not to have a middle name and Butch "ain't telling"; but whether two or three, they all get a kick out of my calling out their initials.

We resumed the lesson as I wrote *site* and *sight* on the chart. Most of the children recognized *sight* and quickly wrote it. A few weren't sure and chose *site*. Imagine their surprise when they found both of them in the dictionary! We read the two definitions and sentence examples and then made up a few of our own:

> The newspaper office was the site of our first field trip.
>
> The blind man lost his sight in the war.
>
> Your room is a sight!

I had the children add whichever one they hadn't chosen to their sheets, and I left both *site* and *sight* on the chart. Horace remarked that this was a neat one because, "You couldn't go wrong!" I smiled as I wrote *might* and *mite* on the chart. Again, most children recognized *might* but a few picked *mite*. Once again, we found them both! Many children had not heard of the tiny animal mite—but Daphne pointed out that it must be like those nasty dust mites that her grandmother is allergic to. Again, we read both definitions and sentence examples and discussed the picture of the mite. "See how helpful the dictionary is," I sermonized. "If you write a word and it doesn't look right, you can check to see if it is there, and if not, you can find the other pattern. It can also tell you which homonym you need for what you are writing."

Then I told them, "I am going to write a word that I doubt any of you have seen, so you will probably all have to guess. The word is *blight*." Under *bite*, I wrote *blite*; and under *fight*, I wrote *blight*. "When you find the one that is the correct spelling, we will read the dictionary definition, but a blight is a bad thing, often destroying crops. A blight destroyed all the potatoes in Ireland many years ago and forced many Irish people to come to America for food. Quickly, make a guess and then see if you can find your guess."

Larry, Hilda, Pat, and Roberta, who almost always know the correct answer, were clearly stumped on this one and didn't want to guess. I chided them, however, to "trust their luck," pick one, and see if they could find it. "You can change it if you pick the wrong one," I assured them. Eventually, the correct spelling got found, we read the definition, and everyone got *blight* written under *fight*. I did the same with the unfamiliar words *trite* and *plight*. Roberta wanted to write the ones she wasn't sure about in both columns. "Only if you think you will find it both ways like *sight*, *site* and *might*, *mite*," I warned. Once more, our time was up. I collected the papers and clipped them to the chart. "We need these one more day," I announced.

The following day, after once again calling them by initials, I told them that using the dictionary to see which pattern is the correct spelling also works for two-

and three-syllable words. What if you were writing and you needed to spell *invite*. Would it be like *bite, invite* or like *fight, invight*? As I was saying this, I was writing it both ways on my chart. The children quickly made a choice—most recognized *invite*—and went hunting in the dictionary to "prove" it. I noticed that the speed with which they could find a word in the dictionary had increased greatly in just these three days. I then wrote seven more words using both spelling patterns, working from most familiar to least familiar: *headlight, eyesight, uptight, bullfight, excite, ignite, dynamite*. The children all enjoyed working with these more sophisticated words, and it increased the range of the lesson so that there were things about spelling for even Larry, Hilda, and Pat to learn—truly a multilevel activity. At the end of the third day, my chart looked like this:

bite	*fight*
kite	~~kight~~
~~ite~~	tight
white	~~whight~~
quite	~~quight~~
~~flite~~	flight
spite	~~spight~~
~~frite~~	fright
site	sight
mite	might
~~blite~~	blight
trite	~~tright~~
~~plite~~	plight
invite	~~invight~~
~~headlite~~	headlight
~~bullfite~~	bullfight
~~uptite~~	uptight
~~eyesite~~	eyesight
excite	~~excight~~
ignite	~~ignight~~
dynamite	~~dynamight~~

I had the students read and spell the words with me and then helped them to summarize what good spellers do and don't do.

"Good spellers don't spell words one letter at a time. They use the spelling patterns they know from other words. If a word you write does not look right, you should try another pattern for that sound. The dictionary will help you check your probable spelling and let you know which homonym has the meaning you want."

I did one more "What Looks Right?" lesson with them this month, using the *ane/ain* patterns. Because the children understood the procedures and have gotten much speedier at finding words in the dictionary, this lesson took only two days. I plan to do a few of these each month because I can see how it is making them more strategic and independent in their spelling. Here is the Jane/rain chart:

Jane	*rain*
~~trane~~	train
sane	~~sain~~
~~brane~~	brain
lane	~~lain~~
~~chane~~	chain
~~stane~~	stain
~~gane~~	gain
cane	cain
plane	plain
mane	main
crane	~~crain~~
~~Spane~~	Spain
~~sprane~~	sprain
~~complane~~	complain
~~explane~~	explain
hurricane	~~hurricain~~
~~entertane~~	entertain
~~contane~~	contain
~~remane~~	remain
octane	~~octain~~
cellophane	~~cellophain~~

Our field trip this month was to the county seat. This was an all-day field trip, and we packed a picnic lunch. Thank goodness it didn't rain! We prepared for this one as we had for the newspaper office, by having discussions and coming up with a list of questions we wanted answered. This time, Hilda wrote down the list to make sure that we came back with at least a partial answer to all our questions.

In the morning, we visited the county courthouse. When we got to the county clerk's office, a young couple was waiting to get a marriage license. All the boys plus

Pat and Roberta thought that was hysterical. The children were most fascinated by the sheriff. They wanted to know what happened when a person got arrested and what a sheriff and his deputies did. The sheriff showed them the county map, which was very detailed, and helped them to locate our school and some of their homes.

When we went into the court, the judge was hearing a traffic case. He revoked the license of a person arrested for driving recklessly and speeding. This impressed the children greatly. When we got to the tax assessor's office, Hilda was busily checking her list to see what we might have forgotten to ask. When her question was finally asked, it came out as "We want to know how you decide how much taxes everyone should pay, and my Dad says you must be a friend of our next door neighbor's because his house is twice as big as ours and he pays less taxes."

That afternoon we toured the county historical museum. The children were especially intrigued by the original state flag and the lists of names of all those who had died in the major wars we have fought. The restored log cabin behind the museum added much realism to our study of how people used to live in our state, and the children were fascinated by the Indian artifacts.

Upon our return to the classroom, we made a list of all the people we had visited or seen in the courthouse and what their functions were. We also referred to our question chart and, with Hilda's help, did indeed have at least a partial answer to all the questions we had raised. I then helped the children form five groups. Each group composed a letter thanking one of the people who helped us on our visit.

The field trips we take each month require a lot of effort and planning, but I know that they are worth it. The children learn so much—not just on the day of the trip but in the preceding days, as we prepare for the trip. I don't ever plan one for December, however. It is hard enough to accomplish all we need to do, especially given all the inevitable holiday-related activities in that shortened month.

December

As I was sitting down to write this month's journal, I noticed my final words from last month's journal. Famous last words! We did indeed take a field trip this month—quite unexpectedly. Normally, we don't go to the state capital. It is almost a two-hour trip, and the legislature is usually not in session during the fall when we are studying our state. Early in the month, however, the legislature was called into special session in order to consider a new water pollution bill. Everyone in the state has been debating this issue for some time now, but it took a tragedy to get the legislators moving. Four weeks ago, five people died in a small downstate industrial town. The cause of death was determined to be the high level of industrial chemical wastes in the water, way above the standard already set but never enforced. The antipollution forces were able to rally support around this emotional issue, and the governor called the legislature into special session to consider a more stringent water pollution bill with provisions for enforcement and severe penalties for lack of compliance.

The children came back to school on the Monday after the five people had died, and they were all upset. Many of them brought the various newspaper stories and related the discussions they had had about this issue at home. The children, unlike the adult population, were almost unanimous in their insistence that the water pollution standards be much stricter. Not being burdened with financial responsibilities, they could see the need for clean water much more clearly than they could understand the financial strain the new controls would put on industry and, if industry is to be believed, the entire state population.

Of course, we put our chairs in a circle immediately and discussed the problem. I tried to raise questions and interject information that would allow them to consider the issue in its broadest terms. Many of the children were unclear about words like *chemicals* and *bacteria,* and I began to make mental notes on which words we might want to explore more fully and add to our wall vocabulary. I decided that the subject was such an important one and the children were so naturally motivated that a unit on ecology and pollution would be first on our agenda after we finished our current unit.

It was Mrs. Penn who suggested that we take the children to the state capital. She came in after school that very afternoon and told me that she would be going over to meet with a citizen's action group later in the week and that she would be glad to make all the arrangements at the capital and to be one of our drivers. She added that when she had seen Mrs. Smith that morning and had mentioned the possibility to her, Mrs. Smith had agreed that it would be a great experience for the children to see the legislature in session and that she, too, would be willing to drive. I told Mrs. Penn that I would talk it over with the children but that I was all for it.

The children, of course, were most excited. In addition to the general excitement of going on a trip that long and being "at the capital" was the excitement generated by the knowledge that Ms. Maverick had never taken any of her other classes to the state capital. They were not just doing the same trips all the other fourth grades did; they were doing something very special and very grown-up. As I watched their delight in this specialness, I vowed to try to think of something special for each class of children I taught.

The preparations for the trip took most of the month, and many of the activities that I had planned for this middle part of the unit went by the board. The transportation problem was solved by Mrs. Penn, who commandeered Mandy's father and Larry's mother. She also arranged for our tour through the capitol and our visit to the gallery while the legislators were debating. In addition, she got our local representative, Buddy Stans, to agree to come up to the gallery when the session broke for lunch and talk with us and answer our questions. Our list of questions for Mr. Stans took three sheets of chart paper.

Lunch was a problem. We were going to leave at 7:00 A.M. so that we could get there, park, go on a 10 A.M. tour through the capitol building, and be in the gallery from 11 A.M. to noon. A picnic lunch was a little risky at this time of year, and I thought it would be good for all the children to have the experience of eating in a real restaurant. They had all eaten at fast-food drive-ins, but many of them had not been to a restaurant, ordered from a menu, or paid their own bill plus tax and tip.

The problem with taking them to a restaurant, of course, was that many of them could not come up with the money, and that many families who would come up with the money really couldn't afford it.

As I was thinking about the lunch problem, I was also gathering up the week's supply of newspapers to take to the recycling drop point. I then remembered that some organizations had collected money for various causes by having paper and aluminum drives. It occurred to me that if our class could collect paper and aluminum for recycling as well as deposit bottles for return to the grocery stores, we might make enough money for everyone to have lunch. We might also become more personally "pollution conscious."

In two weeks, we collected hundreds of pounds of paper and aluminum and returned $56.85 worth of bottles to the grocery stores. Several parents made voluntary donations to our lunch fund, and we ended up with another $80. The children thought this was a fortune until we divided by twenty-five and realized that each person's share of the fortune was only $5.47.

Mrs. Penn had found an inexpensive restaurant close to the capitol that was accessible to people in wheelchairs like Danielle and had arranged for the twenty-nine of us to eat there. She had also gotten several sample menus, and from these each child figured out the various combinations of food he or she could buy with $4.56 (which is what each child actually had to spend before paying the 5 percent sales tax and 15 percent tip).

In order to prepare them for their visit to the capitol and the legislature, I showed a video entitled *Your State Government,* which is put out by the state chamber of commerce and the state department of education. Just as I do a reading comprehension lesson when I am going to have the class read something, I do a viewing comprehension lesson with a video. After previewing the video, I determine which unfamiliar concepts I want to teach and whether I will help them to build these concepts before, during, or after the video. Often the video provides visual experience for words for which I cannot provide direct experience. I stop the video at the appropriate point and discuss the picture that makes the unfamiliar word or concept real.

I then determine my purposes for having them view the video and decide how much I will show at a time. Unless it is strictly for entertainment, I never show a video all the way through. Rather, I set the purpose for viewing a particular segment, stop the video and discuss the fulfillment of that purpose, set another purpose, and begin the video again. If the video is one that the children especially seem to enjoy, I will often show it again the following day in its entirety. I then try to think of an appropriate follow-up activity to the video. My purpose in this follow-up activity is to help the children organize, generalize, evaluate, and apply the new information gained from the video.

Mr. Perkins came this month before we went to the capital. He brought his routing slips and maps and talked to the children about all the reading he has to do in his job as a truck driver. The children were quite impressed. He also showed us the best route to take to the capital and told us some interesting things to watch for on the way.

The actual trip was exhausting but very exciting. We left promptly at 7:30 A.M. The parents provided some apples and crackers so that the children could have a little snack when we first got there. The woman who escorted us on our tour through the capitol was very sweet and very smart, so Betty and Daphne have decided to be tour guides when they grow up. While we were in the gallery, one of the "anti-the-more-stringent-bill" legislators was talking, and the children were quite upset. I think they began to get some notion, however, that there are always two legitimate, defensible points of view. Mr. Stans was great! He spent almost thirty minutes talking with us. He commended the children on their paper/aluminum/bottle collection and told them that another way they could make a difference was by getting in the habit of writing to their legislator and letting him or her know their opinions on current issues.

Lunch was fun! The children were well prepared, and most knew exactly what they wanted. The only person who overspent was Daisy. I didn't realize it at the time, but Mandy's father had to bail her out with 34 cents. I told him he should have left her to wash dishes!

We did do a few other things this month besides holiday things and our big trip. Our Reading Workshop focused on folktales, tall tales, and legends. As usual, we read some selections from our anthology and then had a book-choice week. We also did some focused-writing lessons in which we wrote some tall tales. We made a class book of these, bound them together, and produced copies for all the children to give to relatives for holiday gifts.

We had a whole-school party on the day before school let out for the holidays. Mr. Sweep, the custodian, was retiring after being here since the day the school opened twenty-seven years ago. While we were all sad to see him leave, that sadness, for me, was lightened by the knowledge that Mr. Moppet, Chip's father, needed the job so badly. He has been out of work for months, and he and his family are too proud to accept "charity." I have, however, been seeing to it that Chip has some breakfast when he gets here in the morning, and now that his father is the school custodian, I know they will be all right.

January

This month we finished our state unit. No small feat, I can assure you! For culminating activities on this unit, I decided to have small groups work on several different activities: a time line, a mural, a historical drama, a newsletter for parents telling about all our trips and what we had learned, and a book about our state. I described the projects to the entire class, letting them know what they would be doing on each. I then had the children write down their first and second choices for the project on which they wanted to work.

Paul, Manuel, Chip, Anthony, and Carl worked on constructing a time line for our state. The completion of this project was, indeed, much facilitated by the experience of making the life lines that they had done in September. They began by listing important events in our state's history and verifying the dates on which they occurred. Miss Page, our librarian, helped them to find some of the references they needed for this part of the project. They then decided to use a 20-foot piece of string and to let each foot represent ten years. Although Paul was not much help on the researching end, he worked diligently to copy the dates and events onto the markers that would go along the line.

Rita, Mandy, Danielle, Larry, and Horace made a lovely bound book entitled *Facts You Should Know about Our State.* They took much of the information we had gained from our discussions, reading, videos, and field trips and wrote several topical pieces. They also included maps, pictures of the state flower and bird, and representations of the several flags our state has had. They typed these on the computer and made a title page and a table of contents. They then bound it with a lovely cloth cover, as they had learned to do from Mrs. Wise, and took it to the library to show to Miss Page. You can imagine their delight when she told them it looked good enough to be a library book. The children asked if it could really be a library book, so Miss Page pasted a pocket in the back, typed up a card, gave it an appropriate number, made a card for the card file, and shelved it with the other books about our state. Needless to say, it doesn't stay on that shelf long. Every child in our room wants to check it out to read, and now they are all asking to make books to put in the library.

Betty, Mitch, Butch, Hilda, and Alexander did the newsletter for the parents. They wrote about many of the activities we had done, but most of the page space went to our field trips. Hilda appointed herself editor, and I was amazed at how tactfully she coerced all the others into doing a "professional" job. Butch and Alexander, both of whom are whizzes on the computer, did most of the computer work, including using the scanner in the computer lab to put in some of the photos we had taken on our trips. The parents were quite impressed with the newsletter, and I took the opportunity to point out to Butch's father and Alexander's mother during our conferences that there are great job possibilities for technologically savvy people.

Mort, Tanana, Daisy, Steve, and Daphne did the mural that covers the side of the room. This mural depicts the changes in the way people lived, traveled, and dressed in our state over the past two hundred years. Again, Miss Page's help was invaluable in steering this group to reference works that contained many pictures. She also arranged for this group to view several videos that helped them be accurate in their representations.

The drama group—Roberta, Alex, Pat, Jeff, and Joyce—presented several short skits representing significant events in our state's history. The funniest one was their skit of the legislators debating the new water pollution bill. Pat was the "anti" senator, and Roberta, Alex, Jeff, and Joyce sat and booed and hissed as she spoke.

Most of the work on these culminating projects occurred during our afternoon Center/Project time. This is when children can work together in groups on some days and work individually on other days, depending on what needs to be done. I have centers on the periphery of the room, and children can always be found in these areas. In addition to the computer center, the writing center, the library center, the listening center, the math center, and the art center, which are always options, I have a center related to our science topic. Next month, there will be a variety of science experiments related to pollution. Most of the time, the children are working on activities of their own choosing, but sometimes I assign them specific things to do. This is also the time when projects begun during our morning unit time are carried out and when further research is done. Miss Page has an open door policy in the library, and most afternoons, some of my children are in the library researching some part of our unit topic.

I spend most of my time during the Center/Project time working with small groups or individuals. If a child has been absent for several days, I work with that child to get caught up. If a child has had serious behavior problems that day, she or he spends some of the Center/Project time with me trying to figure out why the problems occurred and what we can do about them. Both Mort and Daisy have spent quite a bit of their Center/Project time "debriefing" their day with me and planning how tomorrow could be better. Mort doesn't seem to mind missing some of his center time, but Daisy gets quite angry because she loves the art center. Her behavior recently has been more considerate, and I think she has decided that she would rather spend time painting late in the day than having a "heart to heart" with me.

I spend ten minutes every afternoon reading and writing with Paul. Although not a good reader for fourth grade, he can read and write better than I initially thought. When he is having a good day, he can independently read material at second-grade level. I have been letting him choose what he wants us to read together. He has a special notebook, and each day after we read, he writes (with my help) a couple of sentences about the book we have read. He is now able to compose and correctly write simple sentences, and I am going to expand the writing to include more complex sentences and paragraphs. Recently, he has gotten into the "Curious George" books and is reading every one I can find. He also enjoys rereading them during Self-Selected Reading time and listening to the tapes in the listening center during the afternoon. He and Daphne are fast friends, and sometimes during Center/Project time, I see him in the reading center, reading "Curious George" books with her. I also see her reading to him other books he chooses. Paul is one of those children you never stop worrying about. He is sad and withdrawn much of the time but has times when he appears involved and happier. I am just grateful that he is here at Merritt, where just about every teacher accepts the fact that, even with the best instruction, not all children will be at grade level and that all children—especially less able ones—need TLC.

Although these culminating activities occupied much of our time and energies this month, we did accomplish some other things. I took a second writing sample by having the children write once again on the topic of their favorite and least favorite things. Once they had finished, I returned to them their beginning-of-the-year sample. They compared the two and listed what they could do better now. Most children were amazed at how much better they were writing—longer sentences, more descriptive words, better spelling and punctuation. Some couldn't believe they had really done their best on the earlier sample. I assured them that they had done their best but that they were indeed becoming better writers. "Why do you think we have been doing all this writing, revising, editing, and publishing?" I asked. "It's not just to keep you busy. It's to help you become sophisticated writers."

Mort looked skeptical! I also looked at the samples and was equally amazed. I noted some things we all needed to work on and then put both sets of samples away until it was time to do the final sample in June.

We have had lots of fun devising math word problems for one another to solve. The ground rules were that (1) each word problem had to involve our state in some way, and (2) the person who made up the problem had to be able to solve it. The children worked out the problems at odd times during the day; then five children would come just before lunch and write their problems on the board. The rest of us would then work at solving the problems. The children learned that writing clearly stated mathematical word problems that contain all the information needed to solve them is a difficult task.

February

We finally got to our Ecology/Pollution unit. It has been a lot of fun, and I found many ways to help the children become involved in the community. We discussed interviewing techniques and constructed a little questionnaire to find out what people are doing about energy conservation and pollution. The children interviewed neighbors, relatives, and business owners, and we prepared a report, which we distributed to all the people interviewed. Newspapers, magazines, and television broadcasts provided much of the input for this unit, because this information needs to be the most current available.

During one of our initial sessions, the children and I decided on some categories under the general heading of ecology and began a bulletin board for each of these subtopics. The children brought newspaper and magazine articles and pictures, shared them with the class, and put them on the appropriate board. I made videotapes of the nightly national and local newscasts and played back for the children those parts that applied to our study. I also arranged for many members of the community who are involved in specific ecological concerns to come in and talk with us about their particular involvement. As the culmination of this unit, the children and I drafted a list of recommendations for conserving energy and preventing pollution, which we sent to Ms. Daley. The letter was published with all the children's names under it. The children were pleased, but their parents were ecstatic! Copies of that paper with its fifteen suggestions for conserving energy and preventing pollution have gone to doting aunts and grandparents all around the country.

The children are very careful not to waste anything anymore and are quick to point out wasteful habits in others. Sometimes these others are not so pleased to have their faults aired in public. One day in the cafeteria, Mrs. Flame took her tray up to deposit it. She hadn't even touched her roll or her cake. Butch informed her that if she didn't want to eat something, she shouldn't take it in the first place!

I read many appealing informational books to the children in connection with our pollution unit. Two books put out by the Earthworks Group, *Kid Heroes of the Environment* and *50 Simple Things Kids Can Do to Save the Earth,* are both chock-full of tips and projects that real kids really can do. We have gotten many excellent ideas from these two sources. *Greening the City Streets: The Story of Community Gardens* by Barbara Huff was another practical resource. We also enjoyed many of Dorothy Hinshaw Patent's photo essays, including *Where the Bald Eagles Gather, The Way of the Grizzly,* and *Where the Wild Horses Roam.* I also read them a marvelous fiction book with an ecological theme, *Trouble at Marsh Harbor* by Susan Sharpe, which the children all enjoyed and which many of them chose to read to themselves later.

I organized our reading workshop this month around the ecology theme. Our anthology has a whole section on it, and we spent three weeks reading the selections contained there. The children were amazed, and very pleased, to learn how the plant and animal populations in Yellowstone have come back after the terrible fires there during the summer of 1988. They were fascinated by the information they learned in the short magazine article on "Smoke Jumpers." Butch, Mitch, and Roberta have all decided that is what they will be when they grow up! They were intrigued by the notion of a rain forest and suggested we make a field trip to the Amazon. We couldn't do that, but we did find some good videos, which helped us to imagine what it would be like.

When we are all reading the same thing in our anthology, I use a variety of formats, depending on what seems appropriate. We read most of the short magazine and poetry pieces together as a class. For the longer pieces, we usually preview them together. In addition to using this preview to help my children access and build prior knowledge, I introduce new vocabulary and relate it to the selection. I also lead them to notice all the special features of the text—especially in informational pieces. We read all the headings and talk about how they give you a clue about what to expect there. We also read all captions that go with pictures and give special attention to interpreting every map, graph, or chart. When there are respellings of words in parentheses after difficult-to-pronounce words, we take a minute to figure out the pronunciation of each word and talk about how helpful this "on the spot" respelling key is and how it works.

I always set a purpose for their reading. With an informational selection, we often begin a graphic organizer such as a web, chart, or time line based on our preview. Students know that they are to read the selection so that they can help us complete the graphic organizer. We seldom do the actual reading of the longer selections together, however. I remember from my own elementary school days sitting there while everyone took a turn reading a paragraph and wondering if it would ever end! In addition to being boring and not instilling positive feelings about reading, round-robin reading is not very efficient. I know that teachers tell the other children to "follow along," but I doubt that many actually do. In order to read well, children have to read a lot—not just their one paragraph from a ten-page selection.

I use a variety of formats to get the selections read. Sometimes, I assign the children to reading partners. Sometimes, especially when we are reading a play or rereading a story to plan how to act it out, I put the children together in small acting groups. Often, for the first reading of a selection, I give the children the choice of how they want to read it. I did this with the piece about Yellowstone. We had previewed the text and begun a web. I then told the children that I would give them twenty-five minutes to read the whole piece and plan what they would add to our web. I gave them each a small index card and told them that when they finished reading, they should pick one spoke of our web and write down whatever facts they thought should go there. I also told them that we all read at different rates, so some of them would probably finish before the time was up and have lots of time to write down facts, whereas others might not have quite long enough to finish. Nevertheless, when the timer went off, we would begin completing our web. I then told them that because they were grown-up fourth-graders and were becoming more responsible every day, I was going to let them choose how they would read the selection.

"You can read it by yourself if you like, but if you make this choice you will not get any help from your partner or me, so you must decide if you can read it on your own and have some facts to help us complete the web. Another option is to read it with a friend. The only rule here is that both of you must want to read it together, and you must read quietly so that you don't disturb the individual readers or the ones reading with me. Reading with me is the third option. I will be in my reading chair, and anyone who likes can come over here and we will read the selection together."

The children all seemed pleased that they were getting to make this choice. Some children immediately found their "best friends" and began reading. Pat and Hilda went off together. Roberta went to read with Steve. Larry and Horace went off together. Butch and Mitch partnered up. Daphne took Paul to a quiet corner and began reading and explaining it to him.

Tanana, Jeff, Chip, Betty, Manuel, and Alexander chose to read with me. I read parts of some pages to them and asked them to finish the page to themselves. I then let volunteers read aloud sentences containing facts they thought they should add to the web. As I was reading with this group, I monitored the partners and the students reading individually. I had to give Butch and Mitch a warning, because they were fooling around. After I threatened them with having to join my group, they settled down to read. Daisy was drawing instead of reading, and Mort was staring out the window, so after one warning, they were moved into my group.

At the end of twenty-five minutes, we reconvened and began completing our web, which we finished the next day. As we were completing the web, I had them read parts aloud to clarify misunderstandings or confusing parts. Once the web was done, I chose one subtopic and modeled how you could turn that information into a summary. The students each chose a subtopic—any but the one I had written about—and wrote a summary of that subtopic.

The children have all been keeping learning logs this month as we have studied about pollution. Each day as we are finishing our unit time, I give them ten to fifteen minutes to write down what they have learned and their reactions to it. This is an emotional issue for my children, who have very strong feelings about "their earth" and what is being done to it, and their journal entries are filled with concerns, fears, and anger. I am trying to let them express these emotions but also to steer them toward thinking about solutions and what they individually, we as a school community, and our governmental bodies can do about it.

We have done many activities this month in celebration of Black History Month. I read them several excellent biographies of famous African Americans, including *Jesse Jackson* by Patricia McKissack, *Frederick Douglass Fights for Freedom* by Margaret Davidson, *Freedom Train: The Story of Harriet Tubman* by Dorothy

Sterling, and *I Have a Dream: The Story of Martin Luther King* by Margaret Davidson. I also read them some fiction that had strong African American main characters, including *A Girl Called Boy* by Belinda Hurmence and *Phoebe the Spy* by Judith Berry Griffin. We talked a lot about biographies, and my children once again amazed me by informing me that autobiographies were when you wrote about yourself! When they saw how surprised I was that they knew this, they explained about the "When I Was Your Age" tales that Mrs. Wright used to write and that they convinced Miss Nouveau to write. I was amazed at how interested the children were in biographies and autobiographies, so we have launched a research/publishing project. All the children have chosen some currently living famous person, and we are going to publish a book of biographies. Their chosen people run the gamut from sports heroes to rock stars to politicians to actors and actresses. They are researching their chosen people now, using resources including *TV Guide* and *Sports Illustrated*. We have posted a list in the room of who is researching whom, and almost every day children bring in things for each other that they have found in newspapers, magazines, and other sources. This project is an exciting one, and my children have already asked Miss Page about having it be "a real book in the library."

March

Having primed their interest with my read-alouds last month and in conjunction with our biography writing project, we have read biographies this month during Reading Workshop. Once again, we divided the time up between reading in our anthology, which contains two biographies, and then choice groups in which they indicated their first, second, and third choices from five biographies of which I have multiple copies. Given that they were all simultaneously researching people to write their biographies, they were very interested in how authors knew what they knew. One of the biographies in our anthology was quite factual, but the other one, while about a real person, was called a "fictionalized" biography. It had lots of quotes in it attributed to the person as a child, and the children all wanted to know how the writer knew she said that. I tried to explain that biographers do not make up events, but they sometimes make up words to make the person they are writing about "come alive." They have to be sure that the words are consistent with the personality, but these are not the exact words.

Opinion is divided among my children about whether or not they should make up quotes in their biographies. I am leaving that decision up to them, but we have been noticing how you punctuate quotes and have added a quote example to our editing checklist, which now has ten items on it:

Fourth-Grade Editing Checklist

1. Do all the sentences make sense?
2. Do all the sentences start with caps and end with punc?
3. Do all people and place names have caps?
4. Do all the sentences stay on the topic?

5. Does the piece have a beginning, middle, and end?

6. Are words I need to check the spelling of underlined?

7. Are *were* (we, you, and they) and *was* (I, he, and she) used correctly?

8. Do words in a series have commas?

9. Do the words I used paint a vivid picture?

10. Do quotes have correct punc—Ms. Maverick says, "Check your quotes."

This month, I have added a "book board" to our reading center. I selected fifty titles from our classroom library that are at a variety of reading levels and that are generally popular with my fourth-graders. Next I wrote these titles on sheets of white paper and covered the bulletin board with them. I then cut small red, blue, and yellow rectangles and put them into pockets I made along the bottom of the bulletin board. Now that all was ready, I gathered my children together and announced a new contest. In this contest, books, not people, were going to be the winners. Together, we read the titles of the fifty books. Among these were books some of my children had already read, and they commented briefly on them. I then explained that whenever they read one of these fifty books, they were to decide what color best describes the book. If it was "super, a book everyone should read," they would put their name on a red rectangle and attach this rectangle to the appropriate white sheet. If the book was "awful, boring, a waste of time," they would put their name on a yellow rectangle and attach this rectangle. If the book was "OK, enjoyable or informative, but nothing super special," that book would get a blue rectangle with their name on it. "From time to time," I explained, "we will have discussions during which you can tell us why you think a certain book rated a red or a yellow."

The board has been there only four weeks and already there are many red, yellow, and blue autographed rectangles attached to several of the books. The children love to see their names and ratings attached to the books. When they see a book with several red rectangles, they all try to get it and read it. One book has three yellow rectangles. Now everyone is reading it to see if it is "really that bad." Pat has rounded up extra copies of several books from the public library, and Danielle's dad bought her several paperback titles at the bookstore.

The book board is a new idea I tried this year, and so far I am delighted with the results. The children are motivated to read and attach their ratings to the books. I have seen classrooms in which the number of books read by each child was kept up with and in some cases rewarded with T-shirts or other items. While I think it does encourage some children to read, I also have noticed that some children start reading only very short books or very easy books. The goal seems to become the number of books read, rather than the enjoyment and appreciation of the books. Because the book board keeps up with how many children have read and how they have rated each book, rather than how many books each child has read, children are motivated to read many books but not just to accumulate titles. We have had two book discussions so far. Both were lively interchanges in which some children tried to convince others that the book was really a "red" or really a "yellow." I was reminded of the deadly dull oral book reports I had my students do during my first year of teaching. How could I have done that! For some time now, I have been curious about why children seem to understand what they listen to so much better than what they read, even when they can read almost all the words. I discussed this with Kenny, who is taking a graduate reading course, and he suggested I try some listening-reading transfer lessons (Cunningham, 1975). To do a listening-reading transfer lesson, the teacher uses two selections (or two sections of one long selection). One of these selections is read to the children and the other is used for them to read.

I decided to do my listening-reading transfer lesson using one of the biographies from our anthology and to emphasize sequence as the comprehension strategy, since determining the correct order of events is important to understanding biographies. I divided the biography into two parts and planned two parallel lessons.

I began my lesson as I always do, by having the children preview the text with me, talking about all the pictures, graphs, maps, and charts and reading all the headings and picture captions. I told the students that I wanted to discuss some important words afterwards, so that we could figure out as much meaning as possible from the context. I wrote the words *segregation, constitution,* and *amendments* on the board and had the children pronounce them with me. "As I am reading, you will hear these words, and after we read, I want us to talk about what they mean and why they are important to Thurgood Marshall's biography." I then taped to the chalkboard five sentence strips on which I had written the major events from the part I was going to read, but not in the correct sequence. I read these events to the children and set the purpose for listening. "Listen as I read so that you can help me put these events, which are now jumbled, into the order in which they actually occurred." After listening to the first part of the biography, the children helped me rearrange the strips to put the events in their proper order and explained how they knew which should go first, second, and so on. We then discussed the words *constitution, segregation,* and *amendments,* what they meant, and why they were important in his life. I reread the portions of the text that used these words, and we concluded that even though we had heard the words before, we didn't really know much about them and we learned a lot about them from our reading.

Next, I told the children that they were going to finish reading the biography and do the exact same kind of thinking while they read what they had done while listening to me read. I wrote the words *civil rights, unequal,* and *Supreme Court* on the board and told the children that we would talk about the meanings of these after they read. I then gave a sheet on which I had written the major events of the second part of the biography and told them that their job after reading was to cut these jumbled events apart and get them in the correct order.

"I want you to do exactly the kind of thinking as you read that you did when you listened to me. Think about the words on the board and how what you read will help you bring meaning to those words. Think about the order in which things happen, and after you have read, get these important events in the right order." As usual, I gave children the choice of reading and completing the sequencing activity by themselves, with a friend, or in a group with me. I then told them that they had thirty minutes before we would reconvene and check our ordering together.

The children quickly chose a friend or curled up by themselves or joined me. Daphne was absent, so Paul, who almost always reads with Daphne, joined my group. Daisy went off by herself, and I warned her that I expected to see her reading and that she had better make a good effort at getting the events in order.

Our classroom had a busy working buzz for thirty minutes as the children (individually, with a friend, or with me) read the selection and cut and reordered the events. When we gathered together again, we agreed on the correct order. It was a bit tricky, because the biography mentioned some things later in the text that had actually happened earlier, but different children who had gotten the correct order read the parts aloud and explained how you knew what had happened before what. We then returned to the words *civil rights, unequal,* and *Supreme Court,* talking about what they meant and reading aloud parts from the text that helped us figure out this meaning. Finally, I "debriefed" with the children, helping them to think about what we had done. We talked about the commonalities between listening and reading.

"When you are listening and reading, you have the same words and ideas. In reading, you have to figure out the words while you are thinking about what it means. Reading is harder because you have to do two things at the same time. But you should always try to do the same kind of thinking. If you read and you realize you have been too busy figuring out the words to know what you are reading, you should go back and reread and 'listen to yourself' read so that you can think the same way you do when you're listening. When you read and listen, you can add lots more meaning to words you just knew a little about."

April

This month we began our final science unit on Adaptation and Change. We studied animals and plants as part of this unit. I decided to focus my Reading Workshop on animals and to contrast fiction and nonfiction. We all read *Misty of Chincoteague* by Marguerite Henry and *Old Yeller* by Fred Gipson. We talked about how these two books were fiction but how you could still learn a lot about animal behavior from stories. We made a list of facts about horses and dogs that we had learned from these books and checked in some reference sources.

The children then made their first, second, and third choices from four Gail Gibbons books—*Spiders, Wolves, Sea Turtles,* and *Cats.* We constructed webs to organize the information gained from these books and then used the webs to write reports on these animals. Currently, the children have all chosen another animal and are doing research on that animal using the web to record what they find. We will publish an animals book next month.

I have begun to do some book-sharing groups every other week at the beginning of Center/Project time on Thursday. Kenny has been taking a course on Classroom Organization and Management that has spent a lot of time looking at the research on motivation and engagement. Most of what they have learned I realize I have already incorporated into my day. I read aloud to the children every morning and at other times throughout the day. I choose my books to read aloud from all different genres, authors, and topics, because I firmly believe that a child who does not like to read is just a child who has not yet found the right book. Of course, I provide time, books, and encouragement for Self-Selected Reading. In my conferences, I "ooh and aah" about their book choices—no matter what they are—and I try to build their self-confidence by pointing out their good strategies and the clever thinking they do about books.

The piece that I was missing—if the research on engagement and motivation is correct—was interaction among children about what they are reading. They talk with me about their books, but there was no place in the schedule for them to talk to one another systematically and regularly. I decided to use the first fifteen minutes of Center/Project time on alternate Thursdays to get the children together to talk about their books. Each Thursday, I form five sharing groups by pulling their names randomly. Each member of the group then has a few minutes to share what she or he is reading and why she or he likes it, and to answer questions from group members about the book.

Our social studies unit this month has been on Alaska. We always study other cultures after we finish our state unit, and I have been concerned about helping Tanana adapt to our culture. It occurred to me last month that one way to help her feel more comfortable would be for us to learn more about her and her home. Tanana was a great resource during this unit and helped us empathize with native Alaskans who see their traditional ways threatened by the advance of civilization.

We have gathered and used many books about Alaska, and as a member of the American Automobile Association, I was able to get many free maps and brochures. I read the class two informational books, *In Two Worlds: A Yup'ik Eskimo Family* by Aylette Jenness and Alice Rivers and *The Igloo* by Charlotte and David Yue. I have also read them some contemporary fiction with Aleutians as main characters, including *Julie of the Wolves* by Jean Craighead George.

The children and I are on an imaginary journey, and we have a time machine that allows us to move back and forth in time as we move through the vast and diverse state of Alaska. The children are all keeping logs of our trip, and each day they record the date, place, temperature, and so forth, and their thoughts and feelings about all that we are seeing. At first I was afraid that the children might consider the time machine and log idea kind of "hokey," but they have wonderful imaginations, delight in using them, and are clearly engaged in our Alaska adventure.

After talking with Mrs. Wright, I decided to try a "List, Group, and Label" lesson as a kickoff to our unit. I asked the children to tell me all the words they thought of when they heard the word *Alaska,* and I listed them on the board. When the children had exhausted their Alaska vocabulary, I read the entire list to them and asked them to listen as I was reading for any that seemed to go together in some way. Mrs. Wright had suggested that the next step was to let individual children list the things they thought went together, tell why they put them together, and give a label to that group. I did this, but in order to get greater participation, I let each child write on a slip of paper the items he or she wanted to put together. Individuals then read their lists and responded to my questions on why they had put those words together and what they would call that group. When each child who desired to had read his or her group to us, explained the reason for grouping, and labeled the group, I suggested that each one of them make another group that was different from any they had already made. We then repeated the explaining and labeling process with these second groups.

This has been a very effective technique to kick off a unit. I learned what kind of prior knowledge and preconceptions the children had about Alaska, and they began thinking about Alaska and using the specialized vocabulary: *caribou, Aleuts, pipeline.* I also think it helps their classification skills and thus their thinking skills. I plan to begin many units with a "List, Group, and Label" lesson.

We are constantly discussing things in this class, but I have done some more structured discussions as part of this Alaska unit. I have formed discussion groups that stay together for the entire unit. I have tried to divide my children so that each group has some leaders and some quiet ones, and I have spread out my "rowdies." Here are the groups I formed:

Daisy	Paul	Butch	Mitch	Mort
Alex	*Betty	Carl	Chip	Daphne
*Rita	Hilda	*Joyce	Pat	*Horace
Larry	Alexander	Roberta	Tanana	Mandy
Manuel	Anthony	Steve	*Danielle	Jeff

In order to keep the discussion focused, I give them concrete tasks to do that will require discussion and that also will result in their drawing some conclusions. Once they were in their groups, I gave each child a card with his or her name on it and explained that the person whose name had a star next to it would be the recorder for that group for the day and would do all the writing for the group. (I picked the recorders according to their fluency with spelling and writing.)

For the first discussion, I gave each group index cards and a felt marker and told them they had five minutes to list the resources of Alaska. They were asked to write only one resource on each index card, because they would use the cards later. Since they had all seen a video a few days before on Alaska's resources, and many had read about Alaska's resources in various source books, they had no difficulty thinking of resources. When the timer rang to signal the end of the five minutes, each group had a stack of cards and was still talking!

Next, I gave them two large sheets of construction paper and some tape. On the top of one sheet of construction paper, I had the recorders write, "Resources that will be used up" and on the other, "Resources that will last forever." I explained the concept of renewable and nonrenewable resources to them, and gave them a few examples from our local resources. I then gave them ten minutes to tape each of their index cards to one of the construction paper sheets. The discussion that ensued was lively and on task. When the ten minutes were up, we displayed the charts from each group and compared the results. When two groups had put the same resource in two different categories, the groups explained their reasoning, and if we could come to any resolution, the resource was changed to the appropriate chart. In several cases, we decided we would have to do some research to resolve a controversy, and several children volunteered to see what they could find out during our afternoon Center/Project time.

I have always believed that language was the foundation for reading and writing and that thinking was at the essence of all reading and writing. As I watched all my students talking and listening during our discussions and our List, Group, and Label lesson, it was obvious that they were using and building their language and thinking processes. I am going to have to do more of this earlier in the year next year.

May

Well, once again the year is ending, and although we did a lot, we didn't get it all done. I wonder if I will ever have a year in which I accomplish everything! I ran into Vera Wise in the library last weekend and told her about our trip to the capital, my book-sharing groups, and how I was using much more discussion; but I also lamented that there were things I had planned that I didn't do. She replied, "As long as you are a great teacher, you never will do all you planned. You have to start out with goals and plans," she chided, "but then you have to look at your children and be open to opportunities. 'The teachable moment' is more than just a phrase we all learned in our education courses, you know." I felt somewhat better after talking with her—I always do—but I still would like to have one year that goes according to plan!

This last month has been frantic. Our class did the annual book fair, and although I put all the children to work and have learned some shortcuts to all the paperwork, it still took a lot of time. We did historical fiction and plays for our Reading Workshop. After reading the play in our anthology together, the children chose from five plays that they read in small groups. Each group acted out their play for the other four groups and for Mrs. Flame's second-graders.

We assembled the portfolios that will be going to Mr. Dunn. There are some things which everyone had in the portfolio and other things that the children got to choose. Of course, we did the final "Favorite and Unfavorite Things" writing sample. This time, when I asked the children to do it, they knew that I had their beginning-of-year and January samples and wanted to see these before they wrote. "No fair," I responded. "I want you to write your best, and then you can assess how much growth you have made since January." They all—including Mort and Daisy—put their best effort into this final sample, and the results showed it. I and they were equally impressed with their growth. These three samples, along with their self-evaluation of their writing growth and my evaluation, are all going to the middle school.

The other things that are in every portfolio are each child's written summary of an informational piece we read, a story map related to some of the historical fiction, and an audiotape made during one of our final Self-Selected Reading conferences. On this tape, each child is reading two pages from a chosen book and then carrying on a discussion with me about it. They also talk on the tape about what they like to read, some of the best books they have read this year, and how their reading interests have broadened. Several children mentioned the book board and book-sharing groups as providing the impetus for them to read certain books they heard their friends talking about. More proof I need to include these next year—probably earlier in the year.

In addition, the children chose one piece of published writing, one example of a response from their reading log, and one other "something" to represent them.

"Think carefully about what you want to send forward," I instructed. "It should be something you are proud of and have worked hard on, and something that shows what kind of person you are—what really matters to you." Daisy, of course, chose a painting she had done. She has become quite an artist. Steve took a photo of his prize-winning science fair project. Paul, with some help from Daphne, wrote a "Curious George" book and wanted that sent to Mr. Dunn. Mitch constructed a map showing lots of truck routes he wanted to drive when he got his "big rig." Roberta, who has persevered in her desire to be a "smoke jumper," researched some of the major fires of this century and wrote and illustrated a report on this. Picking or creating one "thing" that represented them was clearly an intriguing task for the children. They took it quite seriously, and I realized that they have moved along toward my goal of taking responsibility for and pride in what they are learning and accomplishing.

Once the portfolios were assembled, the children made a table of contents and wrote an explanation of each piece and what that piece demonstrated about them and their reading and writing growth and interests. I shared each of these with the parents in our final parent–teacher conference. During my conference with Mort's mother, we talked about his apathy and lack of enthusiasm. We both agreed that while he still had a ways to go, he was better about doing what he needed to and even got a little bit excited about some of the things we did—particularly when he had chosen to do them. "I have been meaning to tell you all year, Ms. Maverick, that I was very wrong in thinking that the Center/Project time was a waste of time for fourth-graders. Usually the only thing I could get any feedback about from Mort was related to what he was doing during that time." I had forgotten that she was the one who voiced that concern way back in the fall parent meeting, but I was glad to hear she had changed her mind.

I am taking all the portfolios with me when I go to talk to Kenny's graduate class next month. I don't know how he roped me into this, but somehow he got me to agree to come talk to his class about my "strange but effective" schedule and about how I try to engage and motivate my students. He has promised to take me to our favorite restaurant for a spectacular meal afterwards. I don't particularly want to do this, but he has been a big help to me this year, and as Norma Flame keeps reminding me, "A good man is hard to find."

Kenny's Graduate Class

After the break, Kenny went to the front of the class to introduce Yetta Maverick. "You have been hearing about Yetta's great ideas all semester from me," he began, "but now you are going to hear them 'from the horse's mouth'—no offense, Yetta." Kenny went on to tell a little more about Yetta Maverick, and then Yetta got up and began to talk. She was a little nervous at the beginning—"much easier to talk in front of children," she reminded herself. But once she got into talking about her class and her schedule, she forgot to be nervous.

"Getting it all done in the intermediate grades is a major challenge," she began. "I have tried all kinds of schedules, and the one I am going to show you now is one

I have used for the past two years and works better than anything else." Yetta put her schedule transparency on the overhead and quickly explained how she spent large blocks of time on Thursday and Friday with her science and social studies units and had separate times for reading, writing, words, and math on the other days. She showed them examples of the kinds of things they had read during Reading Workshop and explained how she used both the adopted reader and multiple copies of books. She also talked with them about her Writing Workshop and how some weeks students were writing on self-selected topics and other weeks everyone worked on focused-writing lessons, learning to write a particular form. She then showed them some examples of things her students had read and written connected to science and social studies units and explained how integrating reading and writing with the content areas helped the children learn more content, gave them real purposes for reading and writing, and allowed her to accomplish more by "killing two birds with one stone."

Besides her schedule, the other main topic Kenny had asked her to talk about was motivation and engagement, a topic that loomed large in the minds of almost all teachers. She began by telling them how she and Kenny had discussed the components that seemed to play a major role in engagement: success, self-confidence, interest, choice, and interaction. "As I looked across my day," she explained, "I determined that I was providing for the first four but not for interaction. I added some biweekly book-sharing sessions on Thursday afternoons during our Center/ Project time to provide all my students with regular opportunities to share their reading and their opinions with their friends."

Success is related to what you ask children to do as well as making sure that they can succeed at it. It also matters that they see their success as related to their efforts. I spend a lot of time with my children helping them see what they are accomplishing, not just what they are doing."

She could tell by the looks on some of their faces that they didn't understand the distinction. "For example," she said, "during Reading Workshop, I include a wide variety of genres, authors, and topics. I want students to learn how you read different kinds of texts, and I want them to know about the whole universe of literature that is available to them. When we finish working with a particular kind of text, I ask the children to tell me what they have learned about mysteries and how to read them, or biographies and how you read them. I don't want my students just to think, 'We read mysteries,' but rather, 'We learned a lot about how mysteries are written and how to read them.' In writing, we worked a lot with summary writing— not an easy task for most fourth-graders. I wanted my students to see that we weren't just writing summaries; we were learning to summarize. Children are more motivated and engaged when they see that they are growing and accomplishing things they couldn't do before. I provide as much success as I can, but I try to tie that success to the things they are accomplishing and to let them see the link between their effort and the accomplishment. When they don't do something correctly, I try to help them find another way to go about it so that they can succeed. I want them to think, 'I don't know how to go about this,' rather than 'I can't do this.'

"Success and understanding what you did to be successful is what I think leads directly to self-confidence. Self-confidence is not just thinking that you can do anything but knowing that you can learn to do the things you haven't learned yet to do. Interest and choice are also critical. All of us are more motivated when the topic is one we are interested in and when we have some choice in what we do." She then explained how she tried to balance the things children must do if she was going to accomplish the curriculum goals against the need to allow children choices to pursue their own interests. She pointed to Self-Selected Reading time and her afternoon Center/Project time as two points in every day when student interest and choice played paramount roles in what they did. "But these are not the only times children make choices; there are also lots of opportunities to give students what I call 'limited choice.'"

As she said this, she pointed to copies of the five plays she had brought with her. "After everyone read the play in our anthology—to learn how plays are written and the special ways we have to read plays—they made a first, second, and third choice of which play they would like to read and put on for the rest of us. I formed the play-acting groups based on their choices, but also considering the reading ability of my students," she explained. "This play is written at a late second-grade level and is a lot easier than all the others. This one is much harder than the others. If the children who were struggling picked the easier play as any of their choices, I put them in that group. Likewise, if my advanced readers chose this hard one, I slotted them to that group. I then divided the other children to include some grade-level readers in the easier play group."

At this point, Ms. Maverick looked up at the clock and realized that although she could go "on and on," she needed to stop to let them ask questions. There were lots of questions.

A young teacher asked, "Don't the low readers resent being put in the easy book every time?" Ms. Maverick quickly explained that the groups changed every time a new type of book was being read, and that the low children were not always in the easier book group. "If they didn't choose the easy book as any of their choices, I slot them into one of the other groups and let the group support their reading," she explained. "I also don't think the children realized that one of the books was easier and one harder," she mused. "They were all reading plays, and they all had gotten one of their choices, and the composition of the group changed each time we did choice groups."

"What about when you read in the anthology," an older man asked. "Did you group them by ability then, or did the whole class read it together?"

"Neither," answered Ms. Maverick. She then explained how the before- and after-reading activities were done as a whole class but the actual reading of the selection was done in a variety of ways, including some children reading with partners and some with her. She told them about Daphne's wish to be Paul's partner and how she sometimes let the children choose whether they wanted to read a selection by themselves, with a friend, or to join her in a group to read it.

"But what about children who choose to read it with a friend and then just fool around and don't get it read?" a teacher interjected.

"I give them one warning and then they join my group," Ms. Maverick responded, in the same no-nonsense tone her children had learned to pay attention to in her classroom.

The questions went on until the instructor finally had to call a halt to it. Ms. Maverick quickly showed them all the portfolios she had lugged to the meeting and invited them to look through these if they had a few minutes. Many teachers lingered to ask more questions and look at the children's work. Finally, they all left and a beaming Kenny took an exhausted but relieved Yetta off for a truly scrumptious late dinner.

References

Cunningham, P. M. (1975). Transferring comprehension from listening to reading. *The Reading Teacher, 29*,169–172.

Cunningham, P. M., & Hall, D. P. (1998). *Month-by-month phonics for upper grades.* Greensboro, NC: Carson-Dellosa.

Children's Books/Materials Cited

Anastasia on Her Own, by L. Lowry, Yearling, 1986.

Cats, by G. Gibbons, Holiday House, 1998.

Curious George books, by M. Rey & A. Shalleck, Houghton Mifflin, various dates.

Fabulous Facts about the 50 States, by W. Ross, Scholastic, 1989.

50 Simple Things Kids Can Do to Save the Earth, by the Earthworks Group, Scholastic, 1974.

Fourth Grade Is a Jinx, by C. O. McKenna, Scholastic, 1989.

Frederick Douglass Fights for Freedom, by M. Davidson, Scholastic, 1989.

Freedom Train: The Story of Harriet Tubman, by D. Sterling, Scholastic, 1987.

A Girl Called Boy, by B. Hurmence, Houghton Mifflin, 1990.

Greening the City Streets: The Story of Community Gardens, by B. Huff, Clarion, 1992.

The Igloo, by C. & D. Yue, Houghton Mifflin, 1992.

I Have a Dream: The Story of Martin Luther King, by M. Davidson, Scholastic, 1986.

In Two Worlds: A Yup'ik Eskimo Family, by A. Jenness & A. Rivers, Scholastic, 1992.

Jesse Jackson, by P. McKissack, Scholastic, 1992.

Julie of the Wolves, by J. C. George, HarperCollins, 1974.

Jumanji, by C. Van Allsburg, Houghton Mifflin, 1995.

Kid Heroes of the Environment, by the Earthworks Group, Earthworks, 1991.

Misty of Chincoteague, by M. Henry, Houghton Mifflin, 1990.

Old Yeller, by F. Gipson, HarperCollins, 1989.

Phoebe the Spy, by J. B. Griffin, Scholastic, 1989.

Sea Turtles, by G. Gibbons, Holiday House, 1998.

Spiders, by G. Gibbons, Holiday House, 1993.

Sports Illustrated magazine.

Tales of a Fourth Grade Nothing, by J. Blume, Dell, 1976.

Trouble at Marsh Harbor, by S. Sharpe, Puffin Books, 1991.

TV Guide magazine.

The Way of the Grizzly, by D. H. Patent, Houghton Mifflin, 1987.

Where the Bald Eagles Gather, by D. H. Patent, Houghton Mifflin, 1990.

Where the Wild Horses Roam, by D. H. Patent, Clarion, 1990.

Wolves, by G. Gibbons, Holiday House, 1995.

A Wrinkle in Time, by M. L'Engle.

Index